Readings for
Teaching English in
Secondary Schools

READINGS *for*
Teaching English in
Secondary Schools

THEODORE W. HIPPLE

University of Florida

THE MACMILLAN COMPANY *New York*

COLLIER-MACMILLAN LIMITED *London*

THE MACMILLAN COMPANY
866 Third Avenue, New York, New York 10022
COLLIER-MACMILLAN CANADA, LTD., Toronto, Ontario

Library of Congress catalog card number: 72–75871

Printing: 1 2 3 4 5 6 7 8   Year: 3 4 5 6 7 8 9

PREFACE

RAPID change in virtually all areas of civilized living is today the rule, not the exception. Moreover, both the pace of this change and the communications about it are themselves speeding up. That activity known as the teaching of English provides numerous examples to support this thesis. English teachers are presently facing their own future shock, to borrow Alvin Toffler's useful phrase, their own collision with new purposes, new methods, and new materials. This book is designed to help them meet the awesome challenges these innovations inevitably bring about.

Many of the selections included in this volume offer practical advice to teachers, strategies and tactics that can be implemented in classrooms almost immediately. There are also numerous theoretical articles intended to provide the novice and experienced teacher alike with the requisite philosophical foundations that lead to successful classroom teaching. This blending of theory and practice is intentional. Neither sound philosophy nor good pedagogy is itself sufficient; the truly able teacher must have solid grounding in both.

Section 1 begins this grounding with general articles about English teaching. These include statements that attempt to answer the traditional but still immediate question, "What is English?" Also contained in this section are articles dealing with specific problem areas in English: accountability, behavioral objectives, ability grouping, and teaching nonmotivated, barely literate students. There are also practical selections that cut across the component parts of English; these parts are given separate and more detailed treatment in the later sections.

The focus of Section 2 is on the teaching of literature. As Squire and Applebee note,[1] literature study is the dominant activity in the English classroom. Because of this dominance, the section on literature is the largest of the specialty sections. The forms that the study of literature takes—its goals, directions, and teaching methods, its relevance in an age of student demands, its recent inclusion of works by black authors —are the chief concerns of this section.

Had this collection been compiled a decade or more ago, Section 3 might not have been a part of it. Media study is hardly new in English classrooms, but its exciting and widespread applications are recent. The days are gone when media served only in an adjunct capacity, as frills

---

[1] James R. Squire and Roger K. Applebee, *High School English Instruction Today* (New York: Appleton-Century-Crofts, 1968), p. 93.

[v]

when the more important work was completed. Today students everywhere are making their own films, examining with a newly developed critical eye the outpourings of television, cinema, newspapers, and magazines and concentrating on all aspects of media with a fervor that would have seemed almost unimaginable a few years ago. McLuhanism has arrived in the secondary school.

The articles in Section 4 discuss written composition with, again, an emphasis on both the theoretical and the practical. New trends in composition reveal a long-overdue student participation in their own learning of writing skills and in the evaluation of that writing. Methods of helping students become active learners are outlined in this section.

The area of concentration of Section 5 is language, but not the traditional grammar of yesteryear. Today's English teacher must be knowledgeable about other kinds of language study—the "new" grammars, semantics, the relationships between language and thought, and the emergence in the schools of greater numbers of students who use nonstandard English. Each of these important areas is discussed in this section.

The final section of the book explores oral work. Frequently "oracy," to use Andrew Wilkinson's felicitous term, is as neglected in the English classroom as it is in books on the teaching of English. The articles in this section suggest specific ways through which oral activities may attain their deservedly important place in the total English program.

One additional purpose of the book may go unnoticed unless specifically mentioned: I have consciously tried to include articles from a variety of sources. Given the prodigious output of the National Council of Teachers of English, I could simply have gone to the many NCTE journals and pamphlets and compiled a book several times the size of this one with excellent articles. I chose not to do so, not out of any lack of confidence in the work of the NCTE publications departments—overall, their products are superb—but, instead, from a desire to alert teachers of English that other journals contain much that is valuable. In large part, this decision stemmed from some research conducted by Thomas R. Giblin and me. Our findings suggested that numerous teachers of English were not even aware of many of the journals in education. The following table, taken from the much longer lists in the research report,[2] reveals this lack of familiarity. (The total number of respondents was 386, all of whom were fully certificated teachers of English. All possessed at least a bachelor's degree, and 125 had earned advanced degrees.)

[2] Theodore W. Hipple and Thomas R. Giblin, "The Professional Reading of English Teachers in Florida," *Research in the Teaching of English*, Vol. 5 (Fall 1971), pp. 153–164. Reprinted by permission of the National Council of Teachers of English.

TABLE 1
READERSHIP IN PROFESSIONAL JOURNALS

Meanings of Response Code Numbers
1. I have never heard of this journal.
2. I am slightly familiar with this journal, but do not recall reading it.
3. I once used this journal some, but no longer read it.
4. I do not subscribe to this journal, but do read it occasionally.
5. I do not subscribe to this journal, but do read it regularly.
6. I subscribe to this journal, but seldom read much of it.
7. I subscribe to this journal and read it regularly.

Name of Journal	1	2	3	4	5	6	7	Degree
Elementary English	92	107	28	27	3	0	4	B.A.
	40	45	16	20	1	2	1	M.A.
The English Journal	7	12	16	67	53	13	93	B.A.
	0	6	4	27	20	3	65	M.A.
Media and Methods	78	49	25	52	27	3	27	B.A.
	25	23	7	30	22	1	17	M.A.
Clearing House	144	62	20	29	3	2	1	B.A.
	45	25	16	18	8	2	1	M.A.
Journal of Secondary	112	76	17	49	4	0	3	B.A.
Education	48	33	19	22	3	0	0	M.A.
Phi Delta Kappan	143	71	13	28	4	1	1	B.A.
	44	37	9	17	8	3	7	M.A.
School and Society	172	52	8	27	2	0	0	B.A.
	62	21	17	22	3	0	0	M.A.
Today's Education	28	32	26	54	18	11	82	B.A.
(formerly NEA Journal)	8	11	17	16	11	8	54	M.A.

This table happily makes plain the English teachers' knowledge of the *English Journal,* but, sadly, also reveals their unfamiliarity with such extraordinarily valuable resources as *Phi Delta Kappan* and *Media and Methods,* to name but two with a distressingly small readership. It seemed advisable to include articles from such journals in this volume.

Moreover, I have tried to include articles from the journals of some of the state English associations. Such journals comprise another excellent source of ideas for teachers of secondary school English.

All told, then, the following journals are represented in this volume:
Adolescence
American Secondary Education
Audiovisual Instruction
Bulletin of the National Association of Secondary School Principals
Clearing House

Connecticut English Journal
Education
The Educational Forum
Educational Leadership
English in Education
English Journal
The English Record
The High School Journal
Holt's Dialog
The Independent School Bulletin
The Leaflet
Media and Methods
Minnesota English Journal
Phi Delta Kappan
The Record
School and Society
The Speech Teacher
Teachers' Guide to Television
Today's Education: NEA Journal
Wisconsin English Journal

Selections were also taken from books and original contributions. It is hoped that this broad range of sources will suggest to readers that much worthwhile material is available for people willing to dig it out.

There are numerous people whom I would like to thank for help with this volume. Without the gracious consent of editors and authors I could not have reprinted most of the pieces included in this volume. My undergraduate and graduate students in English Education at the University of Florida helped immeasurably with the selection of articles, approving some I recommended, rejecting others, and suggesting still others they had run across in their reading. My wife, Marjorie, deserves a special vote of thanks for taking time from her doctoral studies to assist in the selection of materials and in the proofreading of copy. Finally, but certainly not least, my able secretary, Mrs. Pam Malone, should be recognized for her contribution. It was she who typed the voluminous correspondence to the editors and authors whose works are represented herein. It was an arduous task, she performed it well, and I thank her.

                                                          T. W. H.

CONTENTS

WRITTEN COMPOSITION   289

LANGUAGE STUDY IN THE SCHOOLS   349

This Subject Called English

AMONG the many issues that confront prospective and practicing teachers of English, few have had so long and an exciting a history as that which is embodied in the apparently simple question: "What is English?" There have always been answers provided by this scholar or that commission, but seldom have these either gained universal acceptance or lasted beyond a couple of decades. In the early part of this century English in the secondary schools was almost exclusively a college-preparatory subject, the contents of which were often dictated by the colleges and universities. The emphases in this preparation were on Latinate grammar, classical rhetoric, and accepted literature that had won the stamp of approval of the leading literary scholars.

But then, in 1917, a joint commission of the National Education Association and the National Council of Teachers of English, both organizations at that time less than a decade old, issued a report entitled Reorganization of English in Secondary Schools. This document had far-reaching and powerful effects, perhaps the most pronounced of which was its persuasive appeal for an English for all students, not simply for the college-bound, intellectually elite. Grammar study was to be "functional." Composition was to focus on "the expressional powers of the individual pupil." The literature taught in the schools was to contain "a natural appeal" for students. Speech activities gained a legitimate foothold in the English program.

In 1935, to this more liberal attitude about the scope of English was added another dimension, the experience of students. The NCTE released a new document, An Experience Curriculum in English, that concentrated on "strands of experiences" for students. These experiences were to be designed to help them become productive, communicating adults. Creative writing was stressed in this curriculum. Also emphasized were such less formal speaking activities as simple conversation (including telephone conversation), inter-

*views, and speeches for special circumstances—poetry reading, intro-
ducing a speaker, and the like. Literature units were presented in the
report under such headings as "Informational Reading," "Reflective
Reading," "Reference Reading," and so on. Grammar study received
a minor emphasis.*

*Another major trend in English assumed center stage in the post-
Sputnik era of the late 1950s and early 1960s. English teaching in
the secondary schools became discipline oriented, harking back, in
the minds of some, to the kind of English taught in the earliest
years of this century. A triad or tripod approach divided English into
grammar, composition, and literature and the study of these components was intended to illuminate their structures, no matter how
many conflicting and competing structures were proffered by scholars
in each discipline.*

*Today, not many years since Sputnik, the sands seem to be shift-
ing again. Media study, for example, has attained a prominence in
English hardly dreamed of in 1960. Grammar study is a curious
blend of the traditional, the structural, and the transformational in
some schools, but is ignored entirely in others. Dialect studies and
semantics are ever increasing in popularity. Literary works now include last week's best sellers and the novels written especially for
adolescents. Speech activities abound.*

*In sum, "What is English?" is today no more easily answered than
in earlier years. The importance of the question, however, lies in the
attempts to answer it, in the provocative suggestions for curricular
improvement such attempts lead to. New ideas both philosophical
and pedagogical emerge from discussions about English as a secondary school subject. It is in keeping with this spirit of provocative
discussion that the initial articles in this section have been chosen.
Kitzhaber, Bennett, Gill, DeBoer, Wingler, Hogan, and Goldstein
all discuss issues and ideas that may be subsumed under the heading
"What is English?" But there their similarity ends. For each of these
men has quite properly slanted his presentation to accord with what
he believes English should be and the resultant mix, when the
articles are brought together, is both stimulating and challenging.
The prospective or inservice teacher who reads these seven pieces
will be well equipped with data for generalization and synthesis, out
of which may come his own answer to the question "What is
English?"*

These articles are followed by several that deal with specific prob-

lem areas in English: behavioral objectives (*Ulin* and *Maxwell*), accountability (*Hembree*), ability grouping (*Kelly*), and flexible scheduling (*Bakken*). These articles are really position papers, either advocating a particular posture or discussing the issues that arise from the problems. In both instances the reader should discover answers to his own questions about the problems, in addition to discovering the existence of new questions he had previously not considered.

The remaining five articles offer practical advice to teachers. Fagan suggests a kind of English program that will enable teachers to "salvage the disaffected" students. Lederer recounts his experiences in "Ghettoburg" and, in so doing, provides some useful insights into what works and what does not work with inner-city students. Orick's "multi-unit approach" works well with his slow learners and could be duplicated in other classrooms. Hipple advocates the elimination of certain assignments and practices common to most English programs. Finally, Sherwin discusses an area too often ignored in English teacher preparation—research—and provides summaries of investigations into the pedagogical usefulness of diagramming, Latin study, traditional grammar, and spelling.

WHAT IS ENGLISH?

Albert R. Kitzhaber

THE subject usually called "English" is required of virtually every
child in English-speaking countries, from the beginning of school
instruction until graduation from secondary school or until school-leav-
ing age. The same cannot be said of any other subject taught in the
schools, neither arithmetic nor history, geography nor science. So universal a requirement suggests a widespread faith in the value and efficacy of this study, not only among educators but among the general
population, for the requirement could scarcely be enforced without
strong popular support. The average citizen's sense of the importance of
English accounts, in fact, for the keen if not always informed and helpful interest that he takes in such matters as methods of teaching reading
and spelling, the presence or absence of grammar lessons, and the
choice of literature to be studied.

The reasons for the popular conviction that English is central in education are not hard to find. It is self-evident that training in the use
of language is essential to any child. Until the child has learned to
utter his thoughts with reasonable clarity and fluency, to listen and understand, to read and write, he cannot be a fully effective member of
the society he finds himself in. This is especially true when the society
is democratically based. Moreover, since vertical mobility is characteristic of a democratic social order, it is important to try to give every
child a command of the standard dialect. Although it is obvious that
not every child will become a banker or a physician or a government
official and therefore need to speak the prestige dialect, one cannot be
absolutely certain that he won't. Therefore the schools have to assume
that nearly every child is potentially able to rise in the social scale to
the point where he will find it important to shun "ain't" and to prefer
"he doesn't" to "he don't." To the average citizen this is clear enough
so that, even though he himself may not be a habitual speaker of the
standard dialect, he will usually want his children to master it for
purely practical advantage.

As for the teaching of literature—an invariable part of the English
course—literary scholars and English teachers in the schools would
defend it as the chief bulwark of the humanities, that segment of the
curriculum in which a major effort is made to transmit to young people
the cultural heritage due them as speakers of English. The average

FROM *Holt's Dialog* (Winter 1967), pp. 1–17. Reprinted by permission of Holt,
Rinehart and Winston, Inc. and the author.

citizen, on the other hand, is more likely to tolerate literature in the English course than to support it wholeheartedly; or, if he does support it, he may often do so for what the teacher and scholar think are the wrong reasons. Literature—especially poetry—is often suspect to the common man. He regards it as effete, if not effeminate. But if he is willing to put up with the presence of literature in the curriculum studied by his children, it is often because he sees it as a convenient way of inculcating attitudes and values that he approves of—a belief in orthodox social philosophy and moral standards, or merely the stock responses to flag, home, and mother.

As the object of so much attention and interest, and the occasion for so vast an expenditure of effort by thousands of teachers and millions of pupils in each generation, it would not be unreasonable to hope that English as a school subject was reasonably well defined, clearly organized, and rigorously taught. But we all know that it is not. Barring only perhaps the conglomerate school subject known as "social studies," English is the most confused, and the least well defined, of any subject in the school curriculum.

It is true that, at a minimum, the English course does include some characteristic content—literature (but of widely varying kinds and quality), and grammar or usage, or an indiscriminate mixture of the two. At a minimum, the English course tries to foster certain skills—reading (though explicitly only in the early years) and writing (though often more by precept than practice). But English also may include a fantastic variety of other subject matter—journalism, play production, study of the mass media, forensics, advice on dating, public speaking, career counseling, orientation to school life. And it may accept responsibility for developing such other skills as library use, elementary research technique, proper study habits, use of the telephone, procedures for filling out forms and taking standardized examinations, choral reading, group discussion, and parliamentary practice. It is noteworthy that, although "English" is the most generally taught of all school subjects, it is always possible to get a warm argument started, even among English teachers, by asking what exactly "English" is. And since the question has by no means been answered so far to everyone's satisfaction, it deserves the attention that I propose to give it here.

The Causes of the Chaos

As background, it will be useful to take note of the circumstances that have led to the chaotic state of this basic school subject. At least four main causes may be listed.

First is the vagueness of "English" as a term. Since English is the language of everyday life, it is subject to many social pressures and has an enormously wide range of purposes. "English" as the native tongue is, in one sense, a part of all other subjects that the child studies in school. As the general medium of communication, it touches every aspect of existence and so must inevitably appear blurred when regarded as a special school subject compared with geography, arithmetic, biology—disciplines whose outlines are sharply defined in comparison to "English."

A second reason why the English curriculum is confused is that, since it is taken by almost all children, it is an easy way to reach all children with any item of instruction that someone or other—an organized pressure group, a school administrator, an educational theorist—thinks all children should be exposed to. Since English teachers and English textbooks have not shown a strong sense of identity, the resistance point of the English course has usually been negligible. As a result, all sorts of odds and ends, from suggestions on how to achieve social success, to the importance of reforestation and of preventing cruelty to animals, get dumped into the English course, often through the subterfuge of improving the students' writing ability by assigning essays on such topics. When the teacher of biology or geography ceases to teach biology or geography, the shift is not hard to detect; but an English teacher can teach almost anything without anyone, including the teacher, realizing that it is no longer English that is being taught. English, as someone has said, is not so much a curriculum as a receptacle.

English teachers themselves are a third cause of the confusion. Their training in their own subject is likely to be extraordinarily uneven. Less than half the people teaching English in American secondary schools have an academic major in English; others have specialized in home economics, Spanish, physical education, social science, or almost anything else, and have been assigned to teach one or more English classes on the simple-minded theory, still held by some administrators, that anyone who can speak English can teach it as a school subject—literature, grammar, writing, and all. Even when a teacher does have an academic major in English, there is no certainty that the pattern of preparation has been either thorough or wholly relevant. Courses in literature have likely been emphasized, to the virtual exclusion of courses in writing or language; and those teachers who have had a course in language may still be ill prepared to teach any of the new systems of grammar, since the grammar they studied may have been as much as half a century behind the present state of linguistic knowledge.

Because of widespread deficiencies in professional background, English teachers often reflect in their attitudes and their teaching the confusion that exists in the English curriculum, and in turn help to perpetuate it. They hold varying theories, of varying degrees of validity, about the purposes and content of the course, and they are likely to cling to these theories with a grim and uncritical tenacity. Unlike most teachers of such subjects as, say, biology or economics, English teachers sometimes give the impression that they "learned" their subject once and for all when they were in college, and they have been teaching it without change ever since. They developed, early in their careers, the private conviction that the only way to teach writing was through workbook exercises, or the research paper, or sentence diagraming, or précis-writing, and they are impervious to suggestions for other approaches. They may have worked up a set of lesson plans on *Julius Caesar* or *A Tale of Two Cities* twenty years ago, and though schools of criticism have come and gone, they teach from the same notes year after year and are unnerved at the thought of change.

This basic conservatism might lead, one would think, to a degree of uniformity, but unfortunately it does not, since one teacher's orthodoxy may be another's heresy. One gets the impression that many teachers want things this way. Secondary school teachers in a recent NDEA English Institute were frank to say that they did not especially want to have a cumulative, sequential, purposeful curriculum in English, for it would oblige them to take account of the year's course on either side of their own and restrict their field to skills and knowledge mutually agreed upon. As one of them said, with disarming candor, "Actually, we like chaos."

A fourth cause of the lack of clarity in the English curriculum is the influence of educational theorists. This influence, exerted mainly through administrative planning, teacher indoctrination, and textbooks, can be traced, for better or worse, back to Schools and Departments of Education in the colleges and universities. It is only fair to admit at the outset that, although some college English professors do not wholly approve of the results of this influence, the self-imposed isolation of the professor from the teaching of his subject in the schools is principally to blame. The aloofness, until recently, of college and university English teachers created a vacuum which professors of Education, to their credit, tried to fill. They have worked hard and closely with the schools to improve the quality of teaching and of the curriculum. But, in the nature of things, a professor of Education usually does not have quite the same view of English as a person whose entire professional interest lies within this subject. The main loyalty of the professor of Education may rest with an educational theory or philosophy applicable to a wide range of subjects—not merely to English. The Education professor, therefore, may sometimes reveal a lack of suitable regard, from the English teacher's standpoint, for the claims of the subject we call English and for its integrity as a body of knowledge worth studying for its own sake.[1]

English as "Language Arts"

This difference in viewpoint can nowhere be seen more clearly than in conflicting attitudes toward the "language arts" rubric, under which a great deal of English instruction in the United States is commonly included. Originally, this term, which can be traced back almost three-quarters of a century, was used with some precision. For example, B. A. Hinsdale, the first professor of pedagogy at the University of Michigan, published a book in 1896 called *Teaching the English Language Arts*, in which he restricted the phrase to specific skills—"speaking, reading, composition." He drew the familiar nineteenth-century distinction between *arts* and *sciences*, ranging the "language arts" alongside arithmetic, drawing, manual training, etc., which had as their object the development of a specific skill. Sciences, on the other hand, included not just the natural sciences but also "geography, history, grammar, literature, mathematics," all of which aimed at an intellectual grasp of a body of knowledge.[2]

Hinsdale's view is in sharp contrast with that of later theorists who were affected by the progressive education movement. By the 1940's and 1950's, "language arts" had come to embrace the entire province of English as taught in the schools.[3] "The work of the English teacher," according to a popular "English methods" textbook of the 1950's,

> is to improve both phases of the process of communication. The English teacher assists his students in *sending* by teaching them the skills of writing and speaking, and he assists them in *receiving* by improving their ability to read and to listen. He knows that his students, to get along well in this complex world, must be able to make their meanings clear to others and understand what others are saying to them. . . . "Where does literature come in?" may well be asked. The answer, of course, is that literature is included under reading.[4]

Behind this attitude lies the assumption that the main purpose of the

[1] An exception should certainly be made here for the professor of English education —a growing specialization, and a needed one.

[2] B. A. Hinsdale, *Teaching the English Language Arts* (New York, 1896), p. 70.

[3] Sometimes, probably through administrative expediency, it included Latin and modern foreign languages as well. It was not uncommon a few years ago to encounter in American high schools or in the administrative offices of school systems a "Chairman of Language Arts" or a "Director of Language Arts," who was responsible for overseeing courses in Spanish, French, German, and Latin, even though the person often knew only his native English.

[4] J. N. Hook, *The Teaching of High School English* (New York, 1950), p. 29.

school curriculum is to "socialize" the child, to teach him things that will enable him to "adjust" to life and get along well with others, both in school and outside it. Whether or not one agrees that this should be the primary aim of education, there can be no question that the skills of language are central in accomplishing it. But, as can be seen from the above quotation, subject matter is made subservient to the development of the skills. Literature is studied as a means of improving skill in reading, grammar supposedly as a way of improving writing.

More than this, since the overall purpose was to socialize the "whole child," there was no real need to use only grammar and literature to develop the necessary communication skills in the English class. "Content [for the English course]," said the *1956 Yearbook* of the Association for Supervision and Curriculum Development, "is selected on the basis of the 'activity-experience' approach. Since many kinds of activities-experiences may presumably contribute to pupil growth in reading-writing-listening-speaking, no particular activity-experience can necessarily be assigned as best for any one class or grade."[5] Another theorist at about the same time wrote that curriculum decisions in English should be based not on considerations of subject matter but on "the nature and needs of society . . . and the needs, problems, interests, and growth patterns of youth as determined by expert opinion and research."[6]

Where all this led can be seen in another quotation from the same ASCD *Yearbook* quoted from above:

> The many courses of study being produced reflect the confusion in the field of English as teaching has moved from organized content to activity-experience. . . . The variety and range of topics are so great that no clear answer can be given to the question, "What is English?" . . . In some respects, therefore, English is "what English teachers teach."[7]

A parallel development, also serving to confuse the identity of the English course, was the so-called "core" program that, though no longer so common as it was a dozen years ago, still flourishes in many parts

5 Kenneth Hovet, "What Are the High Schools Teaching?" *What Shall the High Schools Teach?* (Washington, D.C., 1956), p. 86.

6 Arno Jewett, *English Language Arts in American High Schools* (1958), p. 54.

7 Op. cit., p. 86. A striking example of the influence of this trend on popular thinking was revealed during the hearings in the U.S. House of Representatives on the amended National Defense Education Act in 1964. When federally supported institutes for English teachers were being debated as a part of the Act, one Congressman proposed an amendment that would have substituted the phrase "language arts" for "English." Under questioning, he admitted that by doing so he meant specifically to exclude instruction in literature from the institutes and confine the teaching solely to communication skills. This is, of course, also another instance of the national view of literature as a mere "frill."

of the United States. In its characteristic form, it combined "English" with "social studies" under a single teacher in one or more grades of the junior high school. The class met for either two or three consecutive hours, rather than for the usual one. This arrangement was commonly justified by two arguments: the child would get to know this teacher two or three times as well as he would any of his other teachers (being in this class that much longer each day) and so would regard the teacher *in loco parentis* and feel more "secure"; and the combination of English and social studies would create a significant integration of subject matter, thus enriching the child's education. Regardless of whether or not the former argument was well founded, it was evident from the beginning that the latter was not. Teachers rarely were competent in both of these fields; instead, they were specialists in English or in social studies—or in neither—and found themselves unable to do justice to the diverse content they were confronted with. More serious for the study of English, however, was the invariable tendency to regard the social studies content as primary (since socialization of the child was the aim) and to select the English content to fit the social studies content. What this meant in practice was that when, as in one large city school system, the class studied the people and cultures of Asia and Africa, the literature read was selected because of its relevance, real or imagined, to Asia and Africa. The consequences of such a policy on the kind and quality of literature studied may be conjectured. English was made the handmaiden of social studies, which in turn served the ends of "life adjustment."

Subject: English

Widespread dissatisfaction with the educational results of the "core' courses and the heavy emphasis on "language arts" skills at the expense of well-defined subject matter have been largely responsible for the current efforts to reform the English curriculum in the United States and Canada. Typical of these undertakings is the conviction that intellectual goals must come first and must not be subordinated to socializing aims. As Northrop Frye says in the introduction to *Design for Learning*, ". . . the aim of whatever is introduced into the school curriculum, at any level, should be educational in the strict and specific sense of that word. It was the confusion of educational and social functions, implicit in the motto, 'The whole child goes to school,' that made 'progressive' theories so fatuous."[8]

Along with this intellectual emphasis goes a greater respect for the

---

[8] (Toronto, 1962), p. 7.

claims of the subject itself, considered as an organized body of knowledge with an integrity of its own that should not lightly be violated. No one denies, to be sure, that an important part of the concern of an English curriculum must be to develop language skills; but there is a strong feeling that English has a specific subject matter that deserves to be taught in its own right, not merely as a means of improving communication skills, much less as a way of "enriching" the social sciences.

The new emphasis may be seen in typical statements made by individuals and groups interested in bringing forward a "New English" to take its place alongside the "New Mathematics" and the "New Science" now being taught in many schools. As long ago as 1959, the report of the Portland (Oregon) High School Curriculum Study declared:

> It is a basic premise of this study that the English course must resist both the pressure and the temptation to be all-inclusive. It must, rather, have two basic purposes: (1) to help the student read with understanding and appreciation some of the significant works in the world's literature; (2) to give the student some understanding of the nature and working of language, particularly his own, and to help him use his language in thinking, writing, and speaking.[9]

George Winchester Stone, Jr., then Executive Secretary of the Modern Language Association of America, wrote in 1961 that

> English, the humanistic course required of all students in our schools from the grades to college, has, as a subject and a discipline, long been drifting toward chaos in our schools. The values of reading the *literature* which forms the magnificent English and American heritage, of achieving precision and effectiveness of style in *writing*, and of knowing the grammatical *structure of English* (the three staples of an English course) would seem to be self-evident.[10]

And in *Freedom and Discipline*, the final report of the Commission on English of the College Entrance Examination Board, Recommendation 12, is "That the scope of the English program be defined as the study of language, literature, and composition, written and oral, and that matters not clearly related to such study be excluded from it."[11]

It is, of course, one thing to issue statements and definitions, and quite another to carry them into practice. Many projects and agencies are now at work in the United States to reform the English curriculum, but even

9 Robert M. Gorrell and Paul Roberts, *English Language and Composition*, vol. 3 of the complete reports (Portland, Oregon), p. 5.

10 *Issues, Problems, and Approaches in the Teaching of English*, ed. George Winchester Stone, Jr. (New York, 1961), p. v.

11 *Freedom and Discipline in English* (New York, 1965), p. 13.

with the somewhat clarified view of English that is beginning to emerge, much remains to do. One can, for instance, agree with the Commission on English that the English course should be restricted to "the study of language, literature, and composition, written and oral"; but this still leaves unresolved such specific questions as whether the English curriculum should include journalism, public speaking, "yearbook," dramatic production, library research, remedial reading, and literature in English translation. "English" still looks like a hodgepodge, even after telephone technique and career counseling have been eliminated.

Because of this dilemma, a number of arguments have been advanced in favor of a particular subject-matter "center" for the English curriculum around which could be ranged the legitimate content and activities of English in a way that would indicate their relative importance and their interrelationships. "English," says H. L. Gleason, the American linguist, "must have a center about which it can integrate—a center of such significance that it can overcome the centrifugal forces clearly at work to dismember the field of English."[12]

It is still an open question whether such a center can be agreed upon —whether, that is, English is basically a single subject at all, or whether it is merely a group of related subjects that are more conveniently taught in one classroom than in several. Gleason argues persuasively that *language* (not just the English language) should be regarded as the organizing center.[13] The Commission on English seems to agree: ". . . language, primarily the English language, constitutes the core of the subject. . . . The study and use of the English language is the proper content of the English curriculum."[14] D. F. Theall, in an "Appendix: on Rhetoric" in *Design for Learning*, appears to argue that, as rhetoric was once the center of all education, it might now be made the center of at least the English curriculum, where it would make possible a spiral structuring of the course of study.[15] J. N. Hook says that the English teacher should think "of his task not as the teaching of unrelated fragments but as the teaching of the whole art of communication. . . ."[16] George Winchester Stone, Jr., says that English does have its own characteristic subject matter, and "That subject matter is the cultural heritage, in literary form, of the English-speaking people."[17]

All of these statements are plausible, and there is no question that they are made in good faith. But, as Hans Guth has observed, "Often, what at first seems to be a comprehensive interpretation of our task as

12 "What Is English?" *College Composition and Communication,* October 1962, p. 2.
13 Ibid., p. 7.
14 *Freedom and Discipline,* p. 2.
15 Pp. 71–72.
16 *The Teaching of High School English,* p. 44.
17 *Issues, Problems, and Approaches,* p. 2.

teachers of English turns out to be but the lengthened shadow of a specialist's personal interest and commitment."[18]

Aside from this problem, it seems evident that nearly everyone would agree that "English" as a school subject must include literature, of whatever kind and for whatever purpose, and must attempt to teach skill in the use of language—reading and writing certainly, speaking and listening probably. And many people, though by no means all, would argue that language itself, chiefly English, should be taught as a kind of subject matter, whether for its own sake or for some hoped-for bearing it may have on the development of language skill. I should like now to draw attention to some of the specific problems touching on literature, language skills, and language itself that must be dealt with if the question "What is English?" is to be answered authoritatively.

Literature

To begin with literature, the first question one might ask is whether literature comprises the *only* legitimate subject matter for the English course. Some people forthrightly believe so, and many teachers conduct their classes as if they believe so. Instruction in the skills of communication seldom is ruled out in the thinking of these people, but such instruction, even when it makes use of specific rhetorical and logical principles, does not constitute a subject matter in the sense that literature does. Though rhetoric and logic are disciplines with a long pedagogical history, they have, as Aristotle said, no proper subject matter of their own. What *is* ruled out usually is language, particularly grammar, on the grounds that it is irrelevant or futile or stupefying, or all three.

Another question which bears on the nature of the literature curriculum is whether or not we can accurately identify the central or organizing principles of literature, for these will affect not only sequence but also content and approach. ". . . The ability to explain the elementary principles of a subject to children," says Northrop Frye, "is the only real guarantee that the subject itself is theoretically coherent. The physical sciences are theoretically coherent by this test at present; literature and the social sciences much less so."[19] Nevertheless, several English curriculum projects are using Frye's "pregeneric forms"—Comedy, Romance, Tragedy, Irony—to organize a curriculum in literature, usually emphasizing the first two in the earlier years and the last two as the child grows older. Another project has settled on the concepts of Subject, Form, and Point of View as organizing principles, recognizing that these

[18] *English Today and Tomorrow: A Guide for Teachers of English* (Englewood Cliffs, N.J., 1964), p. 4.
[19] *Design for Learning*, p. 5.

are not all-inclusive (setting, for example, or character cannot easily be fitted under any of the three heads), but arguing that these principles (unlike setting and character) are exhibited in any literary composition, regardless of genre. These schemes, whether one subscribes to them or not, have the advantage of rising from the literature itself, rather than being imposed upon it from the outside, as are schemes based on chronology or national origin or quasisociological themes.

The reasons for teaching literature in the schools must also be considered, since these will affect the nature of the literature curriculum. One consequence of the "literature-as-preparation-for-life" theory, for example, has been the organization of anthologies according to various themes embodying attitudes that the anthologist wants the literature to inculcate in the child—"The Significance of Freedom," "Understanding Our Neighbors," and the like. The effect on the literature curriculum has been to water it down with selections that have been chosen because they say the right things about freedom and neighbors, rather than because they have any significant claim to literary merit. Teaching literature as cultural heritage will markedly improve the quality of the literature taught, but it will raise other questions of choice: English literature alone? Or good literature originally written in English, whether in England, the United States, Canada, or elsewhere? Foreign literatures in English translation? If so, representative masterpieces from certain literatures? Or only those works which, like classical myths, the fables of Aesop, the Homeric epics, the Bible, have become reservoirs of theme and allusion for literature composed in English? Again, if an understanding and appreciation of literature is a major purpose of the curriculum, how much technical information about literature—devices of structure and style, literary theory and criticism—should be taught and at what age levels should it be introduced? Or should such information be avoided and reliance placed instead on wide and relatively undirected reading? Are historical background and biographical details relevant to understanding and appreciation? If so, how can they be made to enhance the reading of the work rather than substitute for it?

There is a whole range of other questions. What weight should be given to the student's own preferences in selecting works to be studied in a literature curriculum? Should it be assumed that the student cannot be interested in anything that he does not already find interesting? Some educational theorists have so argued in the past. Or is Robert B. Heilman right when he says that "The idea that knowledge follows interest is a scandalous half-truth," and that "it is a better-than-half-truth that *interest follows knowledge*"?[20] Should the average student's difficulties with older forms of the language be a reason for weighting

[20] "Literature and Growing Up," *English Journal*, September 1956, p. 310.

the curriculum with works from the last half-century? Or should an effort be made to teach Shakespeare and Milton (if not Spenser and Chaucer) to most children before they graduate? Should all major genres, including epic and tragedy, novel and lyric, be taught? Or are some less important than others for the purposes of popular education? Should the literature curriculum be confined to belles lettres? Or should it include both discursive prose and a selection of great speeches from the literature of rhetoric—Burke on conciliation with America, Lincoln's Second Inaugural, Churchill on Dunkirk? If stage drama is a proper concern of the literature curriculum, what about television and the film, since these provide the overwhelming part of most children's experience with drama? Finally, is it realistic to regard "reading" as a subject separate from literature (or indeed from English)? Obviously, reading cannot be taught without something being read. Should what is read have a measure of literary merit? Is it the business of the literature curriculum to teach reading throughout the school years? Or is this the concern of "reading specialists"?

The Skills of Communication

Whereas one can argue over whether literature has or ought to have a direct practical value for the students asked to study it, no one doubts the value of mastering the skills of communication—reading, writing, speaking, listening. It is the popular conviction of this value that makes English a required subject throughout the school years. Yet this part of the English curriculum, which everyone agrees is of the utmost importance, is clearly the least effective. Perhaps it could hardly be otherwise. Language, the tool which is to be sharpened by instruction in the English classroom, is employed not only there but everywhere else, in school and outside it; and whenever it is used, for whatever purposes and under whatever circumstances, the act of using it may perpetuate errors and reinforce habits that the English teacher futilely tries, in a few hours a week, to eliminate or change. More than that, because of the inseparable relation between language and thought, any attempt to render the use of language more precise, more meaningful, is really an effort to change habits of thinking—which again cannot be isolated and worked on exclusively in the English classroom.

This part of the curriculum is also the most confused, mainly because of conflicting theories—often supported by no more than hunch and prejudice, but passionately held—as to how language skills can best be taught. The theories are free to flourish since, in the first place, not many English teachers have had any significant professional preparation for teaching writing, speaking, or listening. (Only the elementary school teacher will usually have had adequate preparation for teaching reading.) And in the second place, when training in the teaching of these skills has been available, it has generally suffered from the lack of a coherent modern theory of rhetoric. The textbooks teachers must use in teaching language skills reflect the same limitations, purveying injunctions about topic sentences and emphasis and outlines, the barrenness of which has been apparent for the last fifty years. Above all, both teachers and textbooks have been oppressed by what Donald Lloyd a few years ago called a "national mania for correctness." The tremendous popular pressure for a narrow and rigid standard of conformity in spelling, punctuation, and usage has sometimes squeezed nearly everything else out of the English course. Certainly "good writing" and "good speaking" mean little more than "correct writing" and "correct speaking" to the general population—and, it is to be feared, to many English teachers. This fact has led to unrealistic expectations for the English course and mistaken notions of its content, scope, and purposes.

With these general considerations in mind, let us now consider a number of specific questions about the several language skills, their place in the English curriculum, and the means of fostering them. To begin with writing, we might ask whether this skill is as important for a great many of the slower students as speaking, reading, and the ability to listen and comprehend. Does the low-ability student actually do enough writing after his schooling has ended to warrant the heavy emphasis placed on it throughout his school life? Or is writing perhaps the best way to make his thinking more precise, and is it therefore to be justified for its general educational value? Is it possible to establish at least a plausible, if not a rigorously logical, sequence in writing instruction?

When the student writes, he needs punctuation, spelling, usage, vocabulary, sentence structure, transitions, paragraphs, substance—and he needs them all at once. Are there central principles of rhetoric or logic that could be identified and taught early with simple applications, then, in a Brunerian spiral, repeatedly in later years with increasingly sophisticated applications? If not, how can the deadly repetition and aimless eddying so apparent today in the teaching of writing from one year to another be avoided? Should rhetoric be explicitly taught, or should instruction in writing be entirely through supervised practice with no mention of a systematic theory of discourse? Should both "creative" and expository (or discursive) writing be taught? If so, what should be the relative emphasis, and in what years? What specific forms, if any, should be singled out for practice? Should logic, formal or informal, be taught as part of the English curriculum for its bearing on language use?[21] If so, should it be the traditional classical logic of Aristotle, which few English teachers know well; or modern systems of logic, which they do not know at all and probably have so far not even heard of? Should class instruction be given in general semantics? In propaganda analysis as an aid to clear thinking and hence clear writing and speaking and discriminating reading? Can a meaningful relationship be established between exercises in writing and the study of literature, so that the one reinforces the other? The present practice of merely assigning three hundred words on a character from a play or a scene from a short story can hardly be said to exemplify such a relationship. Finally how can adequate instruction be given in spelling, punctuation, and usage, making clear the great social importance attached to these things but not allowing them to pre-empt the course as they now so often do? And how can it be made clear to students that the use of "ain't," though not to be condoned in educated circles, is neither a moral nor a theological issue?

Now consider speaking. Speech instruction is nearly always neglected in the English classroom, although speech is as much a part of the English teacher's responsibility as writing. The separation of speech from English, as a distinct subject, is perhaps more a political than an educational matter; but it is nonetheless a fact that has helped to downgrade speech in the English class. Other factors are also involved. If English teachers are often not well prepared to teach literature and writing, they have even less claim to a professionally adequate background in speech. The speech lessons in English textbooks are, as a rule, little better than pitiful—hindering adequate instruction rather than helping it. And finally, since learning to speak well requires that one practice speaking under supervision, the English teacher is faced with the problem of how time can be found to have each child speak often enough to afford significant practice. A single three-minute talk by each of thirty or thirty-five children, with some discussion of each presentation, can take up the better part of a week of class time.

In view of all these difficulties, is it possible to teach speech adequately as a part of the English curriculum—not just hints on voice and gesture? Can the teacher provide thorough and rounded instruction in the principles and practice of oral presentation, with attention to finding and selecting subject matter, organizing it, and presenting it in suitable language, with due regard to purpose and audience? Or should the English teacher resign such instruction, once and for all, to a speech teacher, along with such specialized activities as choral reading, forensics,

21 "As part of their language study, all high school students should be given some formal training in logic and the application of logic to the study of language." "Report of the English Study Committee" in *Design for Learning*, ed. Frye, p. 50.

speech therapy, and the like, which, though often regarded as a part of the language arts curriculum, are usually taught by a specialist?

Like speech, reading has recently assumed a kind of autonomy. There are now, for example, federally supported institutes in reading under the National Defense Education Act. The International Reading Association, a large and effective professional organization, is distinct from the National Council of Teachers of English and enrolls more elementary school teachers than the Council does. These teachers, by the way, sometimes do not think of themselves as "English" teachers at all, though on the average they spend about forty percent of their time teaching language skills, and literature or language content. Is this separation natural and inevitable, or illogical and undesirable? To what extent is the teaching of reading, after the elementary instruction in the first years of school, a separate mystique outside the English teacher's ordinary competence? Remedial reading, "speed" reading, and the like are clearly special techniques. But to what extent is every teacher of literature— indeed, every teacher—a teacher of reading? Should the English curriculum do more, especially in the later years of school, to teach reading overtly? If so, by what means? Or should reading improvement be left to a reading specialist, as speech might be left to a speech specialist?

Finally, a word on listening, an activity which is always included under the language arts designation and which everyone agrees is important, but which no one appears to know how to teach. Can it be taught at all in a direct way? Or is it something that we should assume develops naturally with the other language skills and therefore needs no special attention other than what it normally gets in the course of classroom activity? Current practice suggests the latter, but one suspects that this situation is due more to default than to logic.

Language

For as long as English has been a recognizable school subject, English grammar has been a part of the course of study. Throughout the first half of the nineteenth century, grammar was taught (mainly out of Lindley Murray) as an effective means of enforcing "mental discipline," in accordance with the psychology of the day. Rules were memorized, and sentences were parsed—etymologically, orthographically, syntactically. Generations of students testified to the deadliness and futility of the study. Later in the century, though grammar was still heavily emphasized, the justification changed from mental discipline to the improvement of writing, which meant, simply, making it more "correct." Students still found the work deadly, and it was apparent from the first that the alleged connection between the study of grammar and improvement in language use was negligible, possibly nonexistent. Grammar study declined after the turn of the century, disappearing entirely from some classrooms but usually surviving in a vestigial form—definitions of the parts of speech and exercises in sentence diagraming. This is about where the study of grammar is today in most classrooms.

Linguistic research, however, has gone forward with great rapidity, and at the present time we have a number of new scientific grammars to choose from—structural, transformational, tagmemic, stratificational, to name the best known. An invariable feature of the curriculum-reform projects undertaken in the last ten years is a renewed emphasis on grammar and language as proper English subject matter, equal in importance to literature. The grammar introduced is invariably one of the new systems, usually either structural or transformational. Several textbooks have already been published for use in schools, and many others are now being written.

In the new curriculum projects the justification of language study is primarily on humane grounds: Language, the most important and complex of all human inventions, is deserving of study for its own sake, just as literature, history, and "pure science" are. Advocates of this point of view usually do not expressly deny any relation between the study of language and greater skill in its use; they simply say that, in the present state of knowledge, such claims cannot be satisfactorily substantiated. Many of them *hope* that a detailed study of an accurate grammar of English will make children more aware of the patterns and resources of the language and will eventually give them better control over it; but they carefully avoid saying so at present.

The question of whether or not linguistic material, especially one or another of the new grammars, is a legitimate part of the English curriculum is still a debatable issue. Argument tends to focus on such problems and questions as these: Is the scientific study of language, as exemplified in the new systems of grammar, appropriate content in a course of study that has traditionally been ranged with the humanities? Is it true that this kind of language study is itself humane, as its advocates argue, leading children to a genuine understanding and appreciation of language? Or do the premises and methods of science, which underlie this study, make it inappropriate matter for the English course and incompatible with the experience and perhaps the natural bent of most of those who teach English?

Assuming for the moment that a scientific grammar would not be unacceptable on philosophical grounds, can it be taught successfully to children? Certainly most of the new textbooks in transformational grammar look as forbidding and incomprehensible to one who knows only the old grammar, as the textbooks of the New Mathematics look to someone who learned his school mathematics a generation ago. Yet we must take into account numerous curriculum projects which have taught, with apparent success, structural and transformational grammar to both elementary and junior high school children.

If grammar is to be studied, does it matter which of the several competing systems is presented? Is it true, as transformationalists argue, that their kind of grammar achieves "explanatory adequacy" and develops a general theory of language, whereas structural grammar achieves only "observational adequacy" and does not shed much light on language itself? Does tagmemic grammar have a better claim to attention in an English course because of its concern with prose units larger than the sentence? Or should an attempt be made to develop an eclectic grammar program?

One of the most pressing questions is whether, if linguistic material is judged appropriate for the English course, time can be found to teach it adequately without slighting other necessary instruction. Assuming that room can be found within the English curriculum for the study of language—not just grammar—what other kinds of linguistic knowledge should be included: American dialects? linguistic geography? lexicography? history of writing systems? phonology? All of these and others have been introduced in experimental programs in the United States. How well have they succeeded? What criteria should be used in selecting such material for study? And—a central question—how can teachers be equipped to teach linguistic subject matter when their professional backgrounds almost certainly include little if any work in this area?

Finally, there is the question of whether or not *language* furnishes the only reasonable basis for the unity of English. A number of writers have so stated—Edwin H. Sauer[22] and Hans Guth,[23] to name two. The most extended case for this point of view has been made by H. L. Gleason in his article "What Is English?" "I am asserting," he says,

> . . . that language must be the integrating center about which a new English curriculum is to be built. It must be that center for several reasons: First, language underlies both composition and literature and is the only fundamental point of contact between the two. Second, it is with language that school education begins, and it is out of the reading and writing instruction of the elementary grades that the English program of higher education must come. Third, language is one of the most important characteristics of human existence, and it most emphatically deserves close and scholarly study. Fourth, it is here in the close study of language that the English curriculum can best advance the integration of the humanities and the sciences.
>
> Do not miss the point here. I am proposing a shift in the basis of integration. It has traditionally been in English as *a* language. I am proposing language. You must move your focus from the specific language

[22] *English in the Secondary School* (New York, 1961), pp. 1–2.
[23] *English Today and Tomorrow*, p. 5.

to the language in general. English must become not the defined center of attention, but the central exemplification of a far broader interest.

Along with this shift of the focus, there must come a reforming of the internal structure. I would foresee emphasis on three points: the understanding of language, the manipulation of language, and the appreciation of language.[24]

Gleason is to be commended for trying to provide a philosophical basis for unity in the English curriculum. But it might be asked whether his notion of a language-centered curriculum would really unify English. Or would it merely underline the obvious and superficial fact that grammar, literature, and linguistic skills all employ language? If language is not the "integrating center" of the English curriculum, what is? Is one needed at all? Would it be possible to introduce language subject matter into the curriculum without subordinating all other subject matter and skills to it? Would we all agree with Gleason's argument that, since the sciences are becoming more humane, the humanities "at peril of death" must "become more scientific"; and that a language-centered curriculum would at once insure the survival of English as a school subject and go far toward closing the breach between Snow's Two Cultures?

We are living at present in the middle of an educational revolution, of the kind that comes no oftener than once in a generation. This activity has now reached past mathematics and the sciences to the other academic subjects. As reassessment and revision of the English curriculum go forward, it will be well for the reformers to pause first and try to ascertain just what it is they are reforming. For unless satisfactory—or at least defensible—answers can be reached to the kind of questions that have been raised here, we are likely, in our anxiety to produce a New English, to do little more than substitute one kind of muddle for another.

[24] Op. cit., p. 7.

THE ENGLISH CURRICULUM:
OUT OF THE PAST, INTO THE FUTURE

Robert A. Bennett

THE English curriculum in any high school is a product of the past. It reflects the prior training and experience of the English teachers on the staff. The content of the curriculum is concerned with study of a language that has been evolving for hundreds of years. Effective use of language in speaking and writing dates back to the beginning of civilization. Through literature the student comes into contact with the great ideas that form the heritage of our Western culture. Textbooks and other instructional materials were written or prepared at least several years before the student comes into contact with them. And when these materials are based on research, it is research usually conducted with students widely separated by time and space from those sitting in the classroom today.

The goal of the English curriculum, on the other hand, is to prepare students to communicate more effectively and to respond more perceptively to language and literary experiences in the future. The past is significant, but the future is vital. To reach this goal, curriculum designs must be continually evolving and flexible. They must be built on accumulated knowledge which sets the most recent innovations and studies into perspective. But the thrust of the curriculum must be into the future, where it will find its meaning in the lives of people entering the twenty-first century.

Not only this time factor, but also traditional fragmentation of the subject of English into its component parts, may prevent the curriculum designer from gaining a holistic view of his task. A view of the "one world" of English is essential. To gain this view, we will shun the now outdated Gemini capsule and climb aboard a yet untried, but soon to be superseded, Apollo craft. Three, two, one . . . . .

As Viewed From Afar

Above the day-to-day complexities of teaching, we might see the world of English as a sphere complete with the grid marks of longitude and latitude. Marked out on the lines of longitude (beginning not at Greenwich, England, but further east in a land where the language and literature of

➤➤➤➤➤➤➤➤➤➤➤➤➤➤➤➤➤➤➤➤➤➤➤➤➤➤➤➤➤➤➤

FROM *Bulletin of the National Association of Secondary School Principals,* Vol. 51 (April 1967), pp. 7–16. Reprinted by permission of the publisher and the author.

Western civilization first appeared) is the study of English as a humanity. Here we see the great creations of man: his language and his literature.

Language is, after all, the greatest of the humanities. It is the invention of man that sets him apart from all other forms of life. Every major advance in the history of civilization has been made possible only because man has created a reliable system of communication. But because language was invented by man to represent phenomena he observes in his universe and because his universe is so infinitely intricate, the language man created to represent this universe is equally complex. The mastery of language is not the task of the primary grades, nor of the elementary school, nor of the secondary school or college. Mastery of language is, rather, a lifelong pursuit.

Based on his language is man's second great creation, the literature he has written. No study of the humanities is complete without a close reading of the great ideas of Western civilization and the imaginative reflections of experience that come to us through our literary heritage. It is the power of literature to capture experience and hold it in suspension for examination from many viewpoints that provides its meaning in the lives of readers of all ages.

So far we have circled the globe once, examining English as a humanity marked out on the lines of longitude. Now let us go into a polar orbit as we view the parallel lines of latitude, English as a tool subject.

North of the equator we see all the skills needed in *receiving* ideas effectively: reading, listening, and perhaps even viewing. The skill of perceiving graphemic distinctions and translating them into meaningful phonemic combinations is certainly a task of the primary grades. But reading, we all know, is much more than the grapheme-to-phoneme translation process; it is the process of discovering and reacting to significant elements of meaning in what is read. This is a developmental task that must be achieved not once and for all, but at every stage of sophistication from first grade through graduate school and beyond. As we get near the Pole, the climate gets frigid and so do many teachers when they discuss listening and viewing. We have left, they claim, the world of English. But we are still dealing with an aspect of language learning, be it the oral language interpreted through listening or the visual or "silent language" of gestures and images which frequently accompany the spoken word. The relevance of the art of viewing to the world of English has never been more clearly or more forcefully presented than in the new NCTE volume, *The Motion Picture and the Teaching of English.*[1]

South of the equator the parallel lines of latitude reveal the skills of *expressing* ideas through speaking and writing. Again the development of these skills is extremely important in the early years of school and continues its importance, but in a different relationship to the content lines of

1 Marion C. Sheridan, et al., *The Motion Picture and the Teaching of English.* New York: Appleton-Century-Crofts, 1965.

longitude, as we progress through the grades to the college level. The development of fluency in oral language appears first, followed by early attempts at writing. Later the student learns to modify both his oral and written language through accepted principles of correctness and rhetorical principles of effectiveness to achieve his self-determined communication purpose or objective. Thus he learns to speak and write so that he gets what he wants. The teacher maintains the role of the guide, suggesting to the student ways of more effectively achieving his goal, and more importantly, leading him to set more challenging goals for himself that will enable him to achieve greater self-realization through mastery of the power of language.

The world of English maintains its rhythm in its universe. Each day there is a complete rotation as each part of the world comes in for a share of attention. As it revolves and the relative position of its axis changes, the lines of longitude and latitude are viewed from different points and receive different emphases. Once a year the world of English completes a revolution of its orbit, and, as in a spiral curriculum, the varying emphases are revisited each year on higher levels of sophistication.

A Unifying Principle

To forge out of the past a curriculum for the future is no easy task. One attempt, *Freedom and Discipline in English* by the Commission on English of the College Entrance Examination Board, provides many valuable insights.[2] This commission viewed English as composed of three major areas of study—language, literature, and composition. The California Association of Teachers of English, in developing guidelines for an English curriculum framework for California, searched for a principle to unify these three divisions of the subject. The following statement is quoted from these guidelines:

The divisions of the discipline—language, composition, and literature—are interrelated in a way that sustains the unity. Language includes the essential structures and varieties of English. Composition concerns the disciplined and patterned creation of forms of thought in language. Literature emphasizes the most memorable forms of composition, the imaginative ordering of values in the medium of language.

In school, the study of language, of grammar, spelling and punctuation, and word usage, leads to the study of composition. Composition in turn is the effective use of language in its written and spoken forms for both utilitarian and imaginative purposes. Literature includes the memorable forms of composition. From the simplest unit of sound through word,

2 Commission on English. *Freedom and Discipline in English.* New York: College Entrance Examination Board, 1965.

sentence, paragraph, to whole composition or complete work, meaning finds form and significance in language. It may be conveyed directly or indirectly, by rational argument or by visionary embodiment. Recognition of its recurrent forms and significances extends and deepens the range of human understanding.

Recognizing that it is the teacher's perception of the discipline that will determine the content of the curriculum, several individuals have also dedicated themselves to the task of defining English. In his analysis, Archibald MacLeish states that "teachers of English have better things to do than instruct the young in the composition of simple declarative sentences."[3] He then postulates that "if 'English' isn't the teaching of the writing of the language, it may well be the teaching of the reading of the language—the reading of what has already been written that deserves to be read again."

In defining reading, MacLeish proceeds from recognition of words and structure and explication of the text to reading "what the words in their combination and their structure, their sounds and their significance, are *about*." Here this definition is in difficulty for, as MacLeish puts it, "The substance of the literature of our tongue is the whole substance of human experience as that experience has presented itself to the mind, the imagination, and the most sensitive of the users of that tongue. Nothing is foreign to it. Nothing is excluded." His final conclusion is, therefore, that English "is something more than the teaching of the reading of words as words but something less also, surely less, than the teaching of the private life the words come out of, or the public life toward which they look. 'English' always stands with a foot in the text and a foot in the world, and what it undertakes to teach is neither the one nor the other but the relation between them."

Structural Reform

H. A. Gleason, in his seminal article, "What Is English?" predicted a reforming of the internal structure of English around three headings: the understanding of language, the manipulation of language, and the appreciation of language.[4]

In his view, "the understanding of language" is much broader than the study of grammar in most present curricula. For example, he believes that English teaching "must take cognizance of the similarities and differences and the continual interplay between the spoken and

3 Archibald MacLeish. "What Is English?" *Saturday Review* 44:12–14; December 9, 1961.

4 H. A. Gleason, Jr. "What Is English?" *College Composition and Communication* 13:1–10; October 1962.

written language. Students must understand the difference in purpose and functioning between the two. This contrast must be a central theme in the new language curriculum."

He goes on to emphasize the interrelationships among the three sections he has proposed as he decribes the first emphasis, the use of language. "We should teach composition and literature so that people are helped through them to understand language and its operation. Language is used to communicate. We can only understand its function by examining it at work communicating and by experimenting with communicating through it ourselves. Language provides a framework within which meaning, both denotative and connotative, can be conveyed. We understand this function thoroughly only as we try seriously to extract that meaning from passages, or to express fully and succinctly such meaning in language."

In his second emphasis, the manipulation of language, Gleason points out that to the child the process of learning a new medium of language, writing, is very similar to the learning of a new language. Here English teachers can learn from the experience of teachers of foreign languages that "productive and receptive control must go hand in hand." This special relationship must be preserved not only in the teaching of reading and writing in the elementary grades but also in the literature and composition programs of the secondary school.

In his third emphasis, the appreciation of language, Gleason goes beyond the teaching of literature. He also includes the appreciation of language as structure. Thus he comes full circle, and although the three divisions he proposed at first sounded similar to the language, literature, and composition of the tripartite curriculum, he has provided us with a key for a closer drawing together of the components of the curriculum with language as its integrating center.

Relating New Work to Actuality

The task of the Commission on the English Curriculum of the National Council of Teachers of English is to relate emerging concepts of curriculum theory, recent discoveries about the language learning of students, new packages of curriculum programs developed by universities and colleges under U.S. Office of Education sponsorship, and the latest scholarship in the field of English to the present background and experiences of classroom teachers of English and to the needs of students living in the society of tomorrow. This is a humbling assignment. It can only be achieved through a maximum of effort and a variety of approaches. The agenda of the Commission's meetings last November included such diverse items as the review of new English curriculum guides submitted by schools throughout the country, plans for an inservice education series to be video taped, discussion of high school courses in the humanities, study of high school reading instruction, programs for the disadvantaged, liaison with English curriculum committees from other national organizations, and the influence of testing on the curriculum.

Two bulletins were published by the Commission in 1966. One is a summary of the work of 25 curriculum study centers funded by the Program in English of USOE.[5] It is the first in a series of guides designed to help local school districts in using effectively the mass of new materials being prepared by college and university departments of English for high school programs. A workshop on this topic for local school district English curriculum leaders is already being planned for November 1968 in Milwaukee, prior to the 58th annual convention of the National Council of Teachers of English.

In the second publication, *Ends and Issues,* the Commission attempts to identify key unresolved disputes about purpose and program in the English curriculum.[6] As it does so, it also delineates what it believes are generally agreed upon principles which should serve as a professional base for intelligent participation among curriculum planners in resolving these issues at the local district level. Most of the issues are grouped around five of the content areas: the study of language, composition, literature, speaking and writing, and the popular culture. Other concerns include differentiation in general education, new developments in instructional materials, and innovations in instructional organization. The following quotations and paraphrases from this report reflect its point of view:

> *Language.* The Commission supports a broad view of language instruction including study of its nature, structure, history, and power. To some advocates of language study, the utilitarian argument is too narrow and may lead to too much attention to such lesser concerns as telephone manners, the form of thank-you notes, and advice on how to run a club meeting. Language study that is useful only for serving the marketplace, or even for serving social and aesthetic ends, will differ substantially from language study which focuses on man's curiosities about that which makes him human.
>
> *Composition.* The writing of letters, of reports, of explanations, or of opinions on topics drawn largely from the social studies and more recently the sciences, and the recording of personal experience have formed a large part of the composition program. Such writing gives students an opportu-

5 Robert A. Bennett (editor). *Summary Progress Report of English Curriculum Study and Demonstration Centers.* Champaign, Ill.: National Council of Teachers of English, 1966.

6 Commission on the English Curriculum. *Ends and Issues.* Champaign, Ill.: National Council of Teachers of English, 1966.

nity to test their powers of clarity, organization, and self-expression. Such writing gives teachers an opportunity to discover the effectiveness of their teaching of many subjects and many skills. And it furnishes insights into the students themselves. However, thoughtful observers have recently begun to question this approach, arguing that a program in composition ought to be firmly rooted in the unity of the discipline of English. Language, composition, and literature, taken in combination, should and can be used to illuminate and strengthen one another. Literature, conceived as the most artistic form of composition, should surely aid the composing process, heightening powers of observation, displaying for the young writer patterns of organization and structure, and strengthening his sensory perceptions. Taken with the study of language, literary analysis reveals the many resources of the language—imagery, vocabulary, and syntax.

Literature. While larger and larger numbers of graduates do leave high school as avid readers of literature, too many still do not. In fact, some adult Americans who presumably could pass as educated rarely, if ever, read a book of any kind after they escape our tutelage. Why this should be is what concerns the profession today. Although teachers are assuming new and vigorous responsibility for helping learners at every level engage in rewarding literary experiences, many issues still exist. Their refinement and resolution will require the best efforts of all.

Speaking and Listening. Some aspects of the present scene would seem to support renewed concern for the role of speaking and listening in the English curriculum. Increased understanding of the impact of the popular culture upon the student, for example, is accompanied by new insights into oral language development. Furthermore, the pedagogical inferences being drawn from a speech-based linguistic science are only now beginning to be formalized for school testing and promise to alter most profoundly our teaching of language in general. New insights into the role of rhetoric promise to illuminate and possibly integrate the teaching of written and oral composition.

The Popular Culture. The Commission recognizes that appreciation of the literary experience is much broader than understanding what is read. Too often unrecognized is the aim of helping students develop an understanding of the techniques and artistry of the newer media, so that they will not only appreciate the best product of these media but will develop finer critical judgment in all the arts. Despite the growth of a literature of criticism and the development of an ever-widening public appreciation for the film as an art form, few teachers will have had any opportunity to study the best of its products. In consequence, many teachers may feel inhibited, not knowing how to teach what they may truly feel they ought to teach.

General Education. In differentiation of the curriculum to meet the objectives of general education for all students, the Commission recognizes that students can work toward the same goals without necessarily utilizing the same content. Understandings, values, and skills toward which all students can make some degree of progress may be reached through the use of different subject matter for different students. For example, not every student in general education English classes must read the same literary pieces. Not only subject matter but classroom experiences may differ. Taking notes on a lecture may be an experience appropriate to some students but not to others. Enacting scenes from a play may be an invigorating experience in one class, a catastrophe in another. Nor can all students attain specified objectives to the same degree of proficiency. It is clear, for example, that all students will not attain the same level of reading ability during twelve years of schooling. A reading standard attainable by all would have to be set too low to challenge most students, but improving everyone's ability to read can be a common goal.

Instructional Materials and Innovations. No local choice has more influence on instruction in English than has the selection of instructional materials. Probably at no other time in the history of education has more ingenuity been exercised in developing instructional materials than is being shown today. Variety in kind is matched by an abundance coming in part from improvements in the mass media—television, transparency projection, and copying machines, to name a few. Both variety and abundance can lead to confusion. Faced with myriad choices for organizing the instructional program in English, those concerned with the teaching of English must continually inform themselves of curriculum innovations. To become informed requires a willingness to study and to try out new ideas, an ability to distinguish between change that produces progress and change merely for its own sake, and a knowledge of old and new procedures for evaluating innovations.

The English curriculum is more than a set of skills necessary for success in other areas of endeavor. It is also more than a humanistic study. The discipline of English is both skills and humanistic study. Together they provide the student with the competence and the awareness without which he cannot achieve his potential. While keeping clearly in mind the unity of English, teachers in planning the curriculum must analyze each phase of the program for its contribution to the whole. The goals of the curriculum will only be achieved if each of the parts is taught individually in a developmental sequence meaningful to the student and at the same time is taught in such a way that all the parts reinforce and support each other.

To develop this curriculum, teachers must build on their preparation in the discipline of English and their teaching experiences. By sharing their present knowledge and relating it to their continuing inquiry into new content and methods in English and recent research in curriculum and learning theory, teachers in each local district will be able to build an effective program for the students in their classrooms. From the heritage of the past and the scholarship of today, the English curriculum must be developed to meet the requirements of the citizens of tomorrow.

WHITHER AN ENGLISH CURRICULUM FOR THE SEVENTIES?

Kent Gill

I N these times when institutions are being criticized for a host of inadequacies, when public education particularly is being evaluated and found lacking by critics of diverse orientation, the English teacher for the new decade must expect powerful pressures for change. As he views the contemporary scene, as he responds to the criticisms and moves to the crucial decisions, he must ponder a basis for determining how far and in what direction he'll go. What should school English for today be? What should it do for students?

Both thinking about English curriculum and the practice in English classrooms are displaying some intriguing new trends. English teachers are much interested in improvised drama. But what about improvisation and English brought the two together at this point in time? There is the marked contrast between the easy, natural modes of language acquisition by which the child learns to talk and the formal, analytic ways by which we expect him to learn to read by phonics drill or to control syntax by structural and transformational analysis. But what leads us English teachers to select one mode over the other, or to use one even when we don't really prefer it? Film study and filmmaking are booming as English class activities. But what about film (except that technology and affluence make the medium available and that students like the gadgetry) justifies its inclusion in the English program?

Convincing answers to these questions can certainly be framed. But we still must ask what principles really guide us in the curriculum decisions we each make as we design overall programs or as we plan the day-by-day classroom activity? The circumstances of the times and the special conditions facing education demand that all teachers come to terms with a broad set of values and beliefs, a philosophical platform within which short and long range decisions make sense.

Three major curriculum movements currently appear to be in competition on the American educational scene, each movement striving for the attention and support of teachers, for the minds and the spirits of the young, for the research and development funds of government and foundations. Each movement projects a different model for the English

F R O M *English Journal* (April 1971), pp. 447–454. Copyright © 1971 by the National Council of Teachers of English. Reprinted by permission of the publisher and Kent Gill.

curriculum; the differences arise from basically variant views of human nature, of learning, and of the purpose for education. Here we will examine the choices these models offer, to see what kinds of English programs result and to seek guidance for our own decisions.

A still-vital curriculum model is the familiar knowledge-centered academic plan. For English it was patterned in the Commission on English publication, *Freedom and Discipline,* and developed in the NDEA Summer Institute series and Project English centers. This model, extensively used in recent years for state and local curriculum development, was based on a tripartite definition of English which specified that content be drawn only from the areas of language, literature, and composition. It assumed that the appropriate disciplines of English were the principal significant contributors to the curriculum; it promised that curricular unity resulted as content from each area supported and interacted with the others.

This knowledge-centered curriculum was part of the post-Sputnik movement which resulted in the New Math, BSCS biology, PSSC physics, and a whole set of national, federally-supported, university-directed curriculum projects for most academic disciplines which have K-12 counterparts. The implementation of the content curriculum in English is well known; we've all observed or participated in such school English programs. It might be worthwhile, though, to review some of the premises underlying this kind of curriculum:

1. It sets as the primary educational goal the cognitive development of a learner whose significant qualities are intellectual ones.

2. Knowledge is seen as the way to make sense out of the chaos of life. Knowledge can be created and it does exist; it not only explains, but it also predicts and controls.

3. Knowledge becomes the real stuff of education—not knowledge narrowly construed as fact and information, but more broadly defined as the concepts, the structures, and the methods of discovery peculiar to each of the scholarly disciplines. Knowledge in any discipline is accessible in some respectable form to learners at all stages of development.

4. The teacher, who is seen as a special kind of scholar, acts as a mediator between the structures of the field and the learning processes of the student. In so doing, the teacher is likely to use academic modes —lectures, books, laboratory, inquiry, and maybe even media and activity.

5. The student who is most successful is the one who has academic talent, who goes on to contribute to the creation of knowledge; he is particularly successful if the contribution relates to national purposes. The student tends to be seen as an object with certain useful learning characteristics—memory, ability to organize, linguistic versatility.

6. Language, literature, and, to a lesser degree, composition represent the legitimate academic areas for disciplined inquiry; hence they are the legitimate sources for content in English.

7. Sequence for instruction derives first from the inherent logic of the subject.

This academic approach to curriculum, dominant in the '60s, did add valuable content to English programs; it placed some limits on a school subject submerged in minutiae and it spurred some students to extraordinary achievement. But this view of curriculum is being vigorously challenged as we move into the '70s for its irrelevance, insufficiency, and pettiness. A major challenger is the functional curriculum, a model which is built upon skills and behaviors which the student is expected to learn—and henceforth to display.

For the English classroom, this model emphasizes the four language skills as the basic blocks of the curriculum. In activating this functional English curriculum, a three-part plan is typically applied. First, a careful analysis of language activity in the adult world reveals the essential and desirable behaviors which are to be taught. Just such a process resulted in the letter-writing units of yesterday's textbooks. An analysis of the letter-writing habits of girls' school alumnae revealed that they wrote invitations, thank-you letters, bread-and-butter notes, condolences; so generations of all kinds of students were asked to accurately produce these social epistles.

Second, a set of strategies is developed to teach the desirable behaviors, be these strategies ITA or Gattegno color codes, grammatical analysis to correct word usage errors or memory for learning to spell, checklist approaches to the analysis of a short story or programmed texts for transformational grammar. Increasingly these days, the strategies reflect the availability of electronic technology and the techniques for programming and packaging skills.

In a final step, testing and evaluation reveal whether or not the sought-after language behavior is indeed displayed—hence the weekly spelling test, the diagnostic and evaluative reading test, the correctness of expression achievement test.

Much about this curriculum model is old stuff. The early days of the Saber Tooth Curriculum were indeed functional as the students learned arrow head making and woolly mammoth stalking. The three R's of the little red schoolhouse and the progressive education emphasis on learning by doing reflect aspects of a functional curriculum. Most classroom programs in English display functional elements. But the recent influence of neo-behaviorism in psychology and the application of McNamara-Pentagon program budgeting to education have given a new impetus to this curriculum model. With only a little imagination, we can envision the programming of speech training through sophisticated audio devices to eradicate dialectal variations; we might expect visual training via TV consoles to usher in the day of total McLuhan; we can certainly speculate about the time when the only language objectives which are valued are those involving overt behavior, verifiable in the short run.

Such a skill-oriented curriculum seems to be based on certain principles which are worth noting and checking on a personal scale of values. They include the following:

1. The primary goal of education is the development of certain demonstrable behaviors and skills by a learner whose significant quality is his ability to learn to respond in predictable and desirable ways (desirable, that is, in terms of an exterior judgment).

2. Knowledge must be defined in terms of operations, in terms of behaviors the mastery of which is desired, in terms so that mastery can be proved. Matters not easily defined in these terms become less valuable or not important at all.

3. Teaching is the selection of efficient, effective means to induce the desired behavioral changes which have been selected by reference to an existing or extrapolated world.

4. Learning involves the exploitation of the subtleties of stimulus-response principles; motivation becomes a reward for the desired behavior or, at least figuratively, "hunger."

5. Technology looms large in carrying out strategies, in assessing behavior modification, virtually in doing the teaching.

6. The content of English involves the four language skills—listening, speaking, writing, and reading.

7. Sequence in curriculum derives from the most efficient learning order.

Although certain language skill areas—reading, spelling, and mechanics of writing—have long been developed in the functional mode, a total English curriculum according to this plan had not been seriously proposed until recently. But with the advent of the behavioral objectives movement and the projection of systems approaches to management into school operations, powerful political forces at state and national levels are calling upon educators for performance accountability. The lure of USOE funding seems heavily dependent upon adoption of this curriculum view. California faces a statewide application of program budgeting, complete to behavioral objectives, so some English teachers face the demand that they write their own functional English curriculum or have it imposed upon them. The skills-centered English curriculum, with the added machinery of evaluation to prove to a skeptical public that the job has indeed been accomplished, seems like a very real possibility for curriculum direction in the years just ahead.

Then there is today a curriculum concept which I refer to as the individual fulfillment model. This view of curriculum might become most accessible by examining an English program which illustrates its specifications. The Dartmouth Conference alerted us to the existence of such a program when we discovered that some British educators were describing a very different kind of school English, basing their programs of instruction on ₄very different premises, expecting rather different responses, reaching quite different goals. Although the individual fulfillment curriculum has diverse and numerous adherents in this country, our trans-Atlantic colleagues do present the best picture of English in this mode.

In the forward-looking British secondary school, the English program is a remarkably relaxed and unregimented series of activities which use language. They write—and write—and write, they talk, they dramatize, they enjoy literature. Analytical or mechanical approaches to language study seem to be largely and purposely neglected; genre or chronological study of literature is similarly absent. Authors, except for Shakespeare, are modern, at least D. H. Lawrence and since. English is at once barren of content, with no apologies by the British teachers to their Oxford mentors, and yet as full of content as life itself and the whole range of life experiences, English being everything one does with and through language. The goals of English are directed toward personal development, valuing personality over mind, purporting to prepare the individual for life instead of for college. The order of English class experiences seems to be improvised in terms of the students' maturity level and expressions of interest. English serves to examine, to clarify, to communicate, and to exalt one's experience, they say. And their program would support their assertions.

In the British school, writing of a free-flowing, creative kind is a dominant classroom activity. The teacher typically plans an experience to stimulate the writing, often with an extensive warmup period. The experience of writing is valued over the product, honesty is valued over correctness. The writing assignment is open; its development involves personal choices. The writing exhibits fidelity to the experience, directness, freshness, and a mechanical proficiency at least comparable to that of the student in the U.S. One educator describes the writing program as helping students to "use fully what they have within themselves—ideas, impressions, fears, hopes, their imagination—and such language as they can command." Through writing, one may reach conclusions about self, about others, about life.

Talk is viewed as a central concern of English education in Britain, the quality (not to be confused with correctness) of people's speech determining the level of companionship and the level at which their lives will be lived. The British classroom prizes the informal atmosphere, the small group, the vigorous discussion, the reading aloud. There seems to be little, if any, formal instruction, just a faith that much casual talk surrounding all classroom activities will produce dividends. Obviously there is no planned assessment to measure those dividends.

Drama, especially but not exclusively the improvised type, is widely acclaimed in these schools. It is particularly essential in the primary school and in the lower forms of the secondary school. British students shift from movement and mime to role playing to enactment of complex situations and stories from literature. Sequences in drama include going from the immediate to remote, from first hand to vicarious, from individual to small group to whole class, from spontaneous to deliberate, from improvised to scripted. The British teacher sees expressive, organizational, and therapeutic values resulting. Drama becomes a way to trying out possible life styles.

Literature is important, not as content nor as a means to skillful reading, but as a commentary upon experience. The experience of the book is to go deep, affecting values and understanding, permitting the reader to work out difficulties through the vicarious experience. (Bibliotherapy is back.) Both intensive and extensive reading are part of the English program. Poetry and student-written material are widely used as texts for literature.

Some of the conclusions drawn by an American study team which visited many highly-reputed British secondary schools (from *A Study of English*, NCTE) are particularly important as an insight into basic curriculum principles. They include:

1. A deemphasis on content in favor of individual programs of experience and growth.

2. A heavy emphasis on creative uses of language.

3. Formal, direct instruction replaced by informal activity sessions.

4. Speech and oral language dominant in the lower forms.

All of this is done in the British school in a practical, pragmatic way. British teachers of English do not see themselves as curricular crusaders nor as revolutionaries for a new kind of school. Rather they value this kind of English program simply as being the one that works best.

The example of this divergent English program, coinciding with a series of strong attacks on American school programs for their irrelevance, inhumanity, and wrong-headedness—and specific recommendations of program and method to correct these faults—is sufficient evidence to demonstrate existence of a third curriculum model, one stressing individual fulfillment. Its psychological and philosophical underpinnings, its implicit values, make for some challenging speculation. Some of these basic characteristics can be summarized as follows:

1. The basic goal of education is not knowledge nor skill development but rather is the maximum personal development of the individual

according to the idiosyncratic pattern which he discovers in and for himself.

2. Knowledge is defined in terms of the meaning which experience has for each person. One person's experience is as good, as valuable, as another's.

3. Teachers provide a rich, appropriate learning environment and stimulate a variety of experiences; they are helpful, companionable, and supportive, not talkative or demanding.

4. Learners, in the final analysis, determine what they will learn— as well as the pace and the sequence of their learning. They are seen to be capable of directing their own learning. Motivation arises from innate curiosity and a native desire to learn that which is meaningful and interesting.

5. The full realization of the human potential requires an emphasis on the affective side of human development. Human beings are seen as being by nature positive-tending and self-actualizing, if their emotional development is not blighted.

6. The content of English is experience as gained and filtered through language. Language is a strongly-deterministic factor in the quality and direction of the life experience. It is not only a means of communication and a vehicle for thought, but it is also personally creative in that it is a productive element in experience. "Mastery of language is prerequisite to a mastery of lives," says an official British paper on education. Indeed language control is the ticket for admission into full humanity. Maximizing one's control of language is the means for maximizing him as a person.

7. This general curriculum model is particularly applicable to English since the humane qualities in the traditional disciplines of English are readily applicable to the individual fulfillment model.

So the curriculum planner in English in the '70s faces an apparent dilemma. The proponents of each of the three distinct curriculum models tend to be exclusive, urging us to their position alone. James Moffett sees his K-13 curriculum as "replacing rather than fitting into the conventional curriculum." The academician is understandably protective of that which is his life work. Romantic critics, such as John Holt, Jonathan Kozol, and Edgar Friedenberg, leave little room for compromise as they condemn the present curriculum and offer new patterns for the schools of tomorrow. The advocates of media, programming, cybernetics, and program budgeting aim at 1984 with a resolution that would suggest the machines had already mastered their masters.

The question for us all, then, is the proper response to the fact of divergent curriculum theories which display contradictory premises, which demand widely-different practices, which promise outcomes which we hadn't always known we'd wanted. The dilemma really exists at a very fundamental level, dealing with values and with views of the nature of man. These differences are not reduced by reference to research nor to history; they challenge us where we live.

Two obvious responses to the fact of competing models occur. One might enlist as a partisan in defense of language, literature, and composition or in fear of cybernation or in enthusiastic support of a child-centered curriculum. On the other hand, one might explore these models to collect recipes, to glean ideas and practices which could be randomly inserted into an existing program largely built on tradition, availability, and chance, evaluating each practice only by intuition or its presumed acceptability to students.

Yet English teachers need not be too anxious to cast their lot with one or the other of these grand curriculum movements. Nor need they be just gleaners. The exhortation that "if you're not fer us, you're agin us" reveals the kind of disjunctive thinking which is behind those wild pendulum swings which have so characterized educational thought. It is not that easy to know for sure where the truth lies; with Benét, we know "truth is a hard deer to hunt." The tendency for one extreme position to engender an equal and opposite reaction is all too familiar, being an unhappy part of our very professional experience. What educational practitioners need is not necessarily a chance to be partisans; rather each may need the opportunity to engage in a mediation of extremes. In viewing the curriculum conflict in English,

—I wonder why I must choose between intellect and emotion as the focus for an English program. I know that man is a creature of both his mind and his feelings and that knowledge of English relates to both in important ways.

—I question that I must forego my active role as an English teacher so that the student may experience entirely through self-discovery. Surely it is not necessary for each new human to go down all the *cul de sacs* of human history on his way to selfhood.

—I doubt that I must depend entirely upon intrinsic motivation; however, the reinforced S-R chain is not the only way students will learn, either. Young people can learn in many modes, and I must help them to exploit each appropriately.

—I inquire if all valid experience really must be direct and firsthand, but I must also ask if that remote, vicarious, analytical experience commonly purveyed in the English classroom has any value at all.

—I rejoice when my students display a natural enthusiasm for self-directed learning, but I would not be surprised should lethargy and reluctance seem like natural responses, too.

—I welcome more efficient ways for people to master basic language skills, including ways that are programmed, computerized, and packaged, if those ways are indeed demonstrated effective; however, I insist that English also include unhurried personal exploration through language into the primary stuff of human experience.

The contradictions in these three curriculum models are probably no greater than those basic to human nature, which contradictions we manage to live with. Instead of buying one package and rejecting the others, English teachers might better seek to move the argument from the present thesis-antithesis stage to a synthesis stage, to find a new theory for curriculum in English that will encompass the knowledge of the discipline as well as the direct experience of the learner, the skills with language as well as the search for identity through experience with language.

If the search is at all successful, what appeared to be contradictions may reflect opposite but equally-important facets of that incredibly diverse creature, man, and his incredibly complex use of language. A comprehensive program in English would then necessarily range across a wide but not unlimited span of cognitive and affective development as experienced through language. Just as biological and physical scientists find new theories explaining away inconsistencies in the old, the best English curriculum might rationally be supported by a new superordinate structure that combines what currently seem to be irreconcilably different approaches.

To illustrate a potential, if oversimplified, conceptualization for this effort, I'll use a geometric symbol, an extension of the now-familiar triangular scheme which visualized a unity to the knowledge-centered English by drawing on and interrelating the disciplines of language, literature, and composition. For our superordinate scheme of English in the '70s, I suggest that we visualize a three-sided pyramid which is enclosed by a plane of knowledge drawn from the disciplines of English, a plane of language skills developed in the most efficient way we can devise, and a plane of individual development and discovery through language as defined in humanistic and existential terms, all three surfaces to cover a·base which is the language-using animal himself. English, insofar as it survives in the curriculum at all, would be limited to the space encompassed by that pyramidal structure.

Then the task for English educators would be to investigate the potential interrelationships, invent appropriate classroom strategies and activities, define teaching and learning roles, mark out content in terms of skills, knowledge, and experiences—in a word, build within those pyramidal limits a curriculum which reflects significant aspects of earlier programs in the light of a broader view of the human possibility. Then education in English could certainly contribute to the rise of a new kind of Renaissance man, so badly needed in these badly-bruised times. He would glory in his humanity in the face of the electronic revolution, his language competence functioning fully in his thinking, his feeling, his communicating, his remembering, and in his inner search for personal meaning and understanding.

THE "NEW" ENGLISH

John J. DeBoer

FEW terms in the contemporary lexicon of education are so misleading as the expression, "The New English." "New" may be applied to school mathematics and to school science. The enlistment of scholars in mathematics and science for the updating of the content of elementary and high school science and mathematics is new and welcome. As for English, there is little that is new except as changes in emphasis, which have occurred for hundreds of years in American schools, may be dubbed "new." The pendulum keeps swinging, but seldom outside a fairly restricted path.

To be sure, we read about the "new linguistics," the "new rhetoric," the "new criticism." The "new criticism," a formalistic approach to literature, can hardly be called new. It is associated with well-known authors like John Crowe Ransom, Allen Tate, Robert Penn Warren, Cleanth Brooks, and others in the post-World War I period. The French school which employed *explication de texte* is even older. These writers have not had and probably could not have much influence on the way literature is taught in American secondary schools. The "new" rhetoric is really the neoclassical rhetoric, as old as Aristotle. It is not therefore wrong or untimely, but it is not *new*. Of these three, only the new linguistics has significantly affected school practices in English, thanks largely to federally supported institutes in linguistics and a growing interest in the subject on the part of teacher-education institutions. A few pioneer language textbooks are including materials from structural and transformational grammar. A few professional articles have claimed superior results for the new grammars in the improvement of student writing. But grammar (as distinguished from reading, speaking, writing, and listening) constitutes a relatively small part of the school subject called English. What is really new in English is the increased support being given to in-service education of teachers of English and the

FROM *The Educational Forum* (May 1968), pp. 393–402. Reprinted by permission of Kappa Delta Pi.

extraordinary attention that English is receiving in curriculum centers and school systems throughout the country. For this greater emphasis on research and writing on the teaching of English, we are indebted to the Modern Language Association, the College Entrance Examination Board, and most especially the National Council of Teachers of English.

Linguistics and educational scholarship relating to language is getting a better hearing today than at any time in the past. Sterling A. Leonard, Albert Marckwardt and Fred Walcott, C. C. Fries, Robert Pooley, Bergen Evans, and others vainly pleaded in the late twenties and the thirties for a more realistic and objective treatment of usage standards in the classroom. Webster's Third International Dictionary, which is based on descriptive rather than normative standards, was looked upon with suspicion by many teachers of English and denounced by sophisticated but nonlinguistic critics. Educators who summarized the negative findings of fifty years of research on the effects of formal grammar study on students' growth in language power made little impact on classroom English.

Today the linguistic scholars are being heard, but new difficulties have arisen. First the linguists have moved from a preoccupation with the practical problems of English usage to the study of syntax. Here they find themselves in disagreement on nomenclature, and indeed on the basic philosophy governing the understanding of sentence patterns. The disagreements are too technical for nearly all but professional linguists to understand. Teachers brought up on traditional concepts of sentence structure are baffled by the new science and confused as to what course they should now follow in grammar. A few have grasped some principles from one or another school of linguistics and have reported successes with them in the classroom. But most of the linguists have found it impossible to deal equally with their subject matter and the pedagogical implications of their generalizations, except in a few instances when certain of them have sought to apply linguistic principles to beginning reading.

There is at present scant evidence that the teaching of any kind of linguistics in high school will be much more effective in improving students' English expression than the Latinate grammar proved to be. If it is to be taught in high school at all, it will probably have to be an eclectic grammar, one which would not fully please any of the scholars and which would be elective for verbally minded students who have a keen interest in language. In any case, theorists engaged in planning the English curriculum will have to address themselves to the question, "Should all pupils be required to study the structure of English in order to know more about this fascinating manifestation of human behavior, or should our major effort be directed to the refinement of the skills by means of which English-speaking people communicate?" The two objectives are by no means the same. Social pressure for the development of "language power" would predispose the curriculum-maker toward the second.

The present tendency in publications and reports on the high school English curriculum is to advocate a return to what one might call the "pre-progressive" days. This trend is not necessarily to be deplored, but it would be inaccurate to refer to it as the "new" English. It is new only because it refers to a change of emphasis from that of pre-depression days. Reading the report of the Commission on English on the College Entrance Examination Board, *Freedom and Discipline in English*,[1] one is impressed with the value of the long tradition of instruction in English, and to some extent, American literature. The names of the authors who are part of our great inheritance—Chaucer, Shakespeare, Milton, Pope, Shaw, Dickens, and so many dozens of others who are cherished in the world of the literate of the earth—abound in the report on *Freedom and Discipline*. It is not necessary for English to be the "new" English in order to be the *right* English for millions of high school students.

But those who are appealing for a return to the "old" and for deliverance from an alleged educational wasteland are often unfamiliar with the vast diversity of the American high school population. We do not know how many high school dropouts were driven to the streets by Shakespeare, Chaucer, and Milton. Many of the dropouts could possibly have been saved by teachers who did not hold them in contempt, and who knew how to discover and interpret the universal elements in the literature. The attitude of the advocates of the old English is suggested by the following passage from *Freedom and Discipline:*

> Claims are frequently advanced for the use of so-called "junior books," a "literature of adolescence," on the ground that they ease the young reader into a frame of mind in which he will be ready to tackle something stronger, harder, more adult. The Commission has serious doubts that it does anything of the sort. For classes in remedial reading a resort to such books may be necessary, but to make them a considerable part of the curriculum for most students is to subvert the purposes for which literature is included in the first place. In the high school years, the aim should be not to find the students' level so much as to raise it, and such books rarely elevate. For college bound students, particularly, no such concessions as they imply are justified. Maturity of thought, vocabulary, syntax, and construction is the criterion of excellence in literature, and that criterion must

[1] Harold C. Martin, Chairman (New York: College Entrance Examination Board, 1965).

not be abandoned for apparent expediency. The competent teacher can bridge the distances between good books and the immaturity of his students; that is, in fact his primary duty as a teacher of literature.[2]

Notwithstanding the brilliance and charm of this report, as it discusses the literature program for high school students who are able to find pleasure in it and to make it a part of their lives, it fails to recognize the needs of a vast number of young people to whom its recommendations do not apply. One can quarrel with the statement that the "aim should be not to find the students' level so much as to raise it, and such books [literature for adolescents] rarely elevate." The experience of many high school teachers of English contradicts the statement, which on its face is unconvincing. The only defense for it is that the authors' own experience is largely with "college-prep" students, and the report is primarily concerned with them.

A similar confusion appears in the excellent report of a survey entitled *A Study of English Programs in Selected High Schools Which Consistently Educate Outstanding Students in English,* by James R. Squire and Roger K. Applebee.[3] This report is probably the most comprehensive and detailed survey of English instruction in American high schools since the New York Regents Survey by Dora V. Smith and Robert C. Pooley's later survey of Wisconsin schools. But here again we are faced with the term "excellence," which places the study on the plane of the superior student and necessarily omits the schools which achieve superior results with students in the whole range of abilities, interests, and socioeconomic levels. Quite possibly these selected schools do well with the deprived and the retarded, but the basis for selection of the schools would not assure us of this.

A third, earlier report further describes the trend, and in my judgment demonstrates that we are dealing with the old English rather than a "new" English today. This is the report on *The Basic Issues in the Teaching of English,* produced by representatives of the American Studies Association, the College English Association, the Modern Language Association, and the National Council of Teachers of English. The report may be found in *Issues, Problems, and Approaches in the Teaching of English,* edited by George Winchester Stone, Jr.[4] Two quotations will suffice. (1) "We agree generally that English composition, language, and literature are within our province, but we are uncertain whether our boundaries should include world literature in translation, journalism, listening, remedial reading, and general aca-

2 Op. cit., pp. 49–58.
3 (Urbana: University of Illinois, 1966). (Available from the National Council of Teachers of English, Champaign, Illinois.)
4 (New York: Holt, Rinehart and Winston, 1963).

demic orientation. . . ." (2) "Can agreement be reached upon a body of knowledge and set of skills as standard at certain points in the curriculum making due allowances for flexibility of planning, individual differences, and patterns of growth?" The second question is not only the basis of the old curriculum, but it is naive. How does one agree on a body of knowledge and set of skills as standard at certain points in the curriculum, and at the same time make allowance for individual differences, which may be twelve years in one high school grade?

What is lacking in many of the statements referred to is an examination of the part that literature and language plays in the life of youth. English is considered an independent discipline, the content of which has self-evident value. Thus in one report the flat statement is made that teachers of English should know the language which Chaucer used. Now, reading Chaucer in his own idiom can be a delightful experience, but reading Tolstoy in the original or in translation could be as rewarding. Why insist on Chaucer?

There is a kind of sophisticated chauvinism in the demands of college people that teachers of English should confine themselves to English literature and to a lesser extent, American. This preference for the writings of British literary men and women is quite natural, especially for two reasons: (1) Our students can understand them; and (2) English literature ranks with the best of European literature. The American writers who have been accepted generally as great artists are necessarily few in comparison. Yet is it not time for us to cultivate in our youth a feeling for the life and culture of people in other parts of the world? Graduates of our high schools who are serving in Viet Nam would perhaps be less likely to refer to the natives as "gooks."

How contemporaneous should a curriculum (high school or college) be? At the moment, many young people are concerned about sex, LSD, the revolt of youth, "Black Power," and, overwhelmingly, our invasion of Viet Nam. These concerns are likely to be with us for some time.

There are similarities and differences between the present concerns of youth and those of earlier generations. Professors in large colleges and universities have difficulty in perceiving the differences because the students are polite in their classes. Many of them are quiet and attentive and ready to absorb the knowledge and perhaps the wisdom of their academic elders. Others are smoldering but retain their self-control. (In earlier times the domination of the teacher was accepted by all, at least until the class bell rang.) The docile ones are the hopeless ones; those who are in overt or inward revolt can be either the saviors or the destroyers of our society.

But Professor Jerome Bruner tells us that every subject has a structure that must be mastered and that the procedure must be spiral from the first grade up. I will not dispute his thesis, as far as other subjects are concerned, but for school English the idea simply will not work. In the first place, English embraces many different kinds of learning. Moreover, much of the learning in English occurs when a child gradually develops language and reading skills. He does not see the outline, at any level of the spiral, of the great skeleton of language. How could he, when the linguists themselves perceive the outlines and the language behaviors differently?

Henry C. Morrison knew this back in 1926, when he categorized the language arts as something distinct from the science-type or appreciation-type subjects. To him language, in its various uses—speaking, writing, reading, and listening—was a combination of cognitive and noncognitive factors.

What kind of "structure" evolves from a reading of Frost, Wordsworth, Milton, or Norman Mailer? This is not a question of finding a "structure," but of making a response to oneself and the world. The language stimuli may gain meaning from the larger context of a person's outlook on the world of things, living beings, and the ends of human life, but individual passages or selections do not necessarily add up to a "structure."

And has anyone raised a question about the term "structure" as applied to a school subject? The word is a metaphor suggesting a building. The builders in each generation, like those who created the great cathedrals, added to their fathers' achievements until the Great Design was complete. Even a musical creation can be called a structure. Robert Browning quotes Abt Vogler saying after he extemporized on a musical instrument of his invention, "Would that the structure brave, the manifold music I build. . . ." But when is a school subject complete? Does it not constantly change and grow? A school subject is a living thing, with complex interrelations with other "subjects."

Whatever the case may be in science or mathematics, we cannot think of English as a static "structure." In the first place, the responsibility for teaching English is shared by the entire school, when English is the medium of communication. There are generalizations about language and literature which can be learned, but these do not add up to a "structure." Since language is in continuing flux, and since the language of American high school youth can be described only as a collection of geographic and class dialects, we must deal with it not as a finished product, but as a varying, ongoing behavior which can change as a result of conditioning.

If English is to be considered a separate subject, as nearly everyone believes, it must have a content of its own. It is fashionable today to assert that school English consists of three independent parts—language, composition, and literature. Many of the English language institutes are organized according to these three divisions. The influential report of the Commission on English of the College Entrance Examination Board, *Freedom and Discipline in English*,[5] consists of four chapters, one on English in general, and the other three on language, literature, and composition, respectively. Certainly all three belong to English. But composition is not unique to the subject of English, and it is an art or skill rather than content. Literature belongs pre-eminently to English, but does not the content of literature embrace all aspects of human experience and deal with the content of many other school subjects? And what about speech, dramatics, journalism, the mass media of communication, remedial reading, and listening? All of these have been questioned by those who deplore the diversity of activities characteristic of modern high school English. Even foreign literature in translation and letter writing, an art which should need no defense, have been considered of dubious value for the high school student.[6]

For many years we have tried to develop strategies for reducing the extreme fragmentation of the high school curriculum. We have tried to emphasize, through various modifications in curriculum organization, the interrelations between literature and history, mathematics and science, music and art, the practical and fine arts. At the higher levels of scholarship, we are witnessing the growing trend toward interdisciplinary studies, and the development of courses in biophysics, biochemistry, physical chemistry, radiochemistry, geolinguistics, astrophysics, bioclimatology, historical geography, and psycholinguistics—and one could go on. Now the currently popular conception of English as an independent field, and the triad, or tripod, theory of English as a group of separate disciplines, would encourage a return to an even greater degree of specialization at the high school level than we have known before, just when the scholars are emphasizing the need for greater integration.

From a practical point of view, the triad theory has only limited applicability. The study of language, it is true, is fairly self-contained, although it is encountered constantly in composition and literature, and it could be included incidentally in fields other than English, if teachers have some familiarity with the subject. But composition? When we write, we need a content, which we must borrow from every subject in the curriculum. Literature? It is art, language, history, economics, psychology, ethics, religion—the whole spectrum of human concerns. Thus while language, composition, and literature are obviously

5 Op. cit.
6 From *The Basic Issues in the Teaching of English*. Reprinted in *Issues, Problems and Approaches in the Teaching of English*, p. 7. Edited by George Sylvester Stone, Jr. (New York: Holt, Rinehart and Winston, 1961).

central to the English program, the tripartite design is not especially helpful to the curriculum planner.

Still the search for a "core," a central organizing principle, continues. In one promising curriculum project, language has been made the center, with composition and literature revolving around it. The plan is logical and will no doubt arouse the enthusiasm of creative teachers.

Many of the efforts to find an essential "structure" for English reflect the current preoccupation with form and genre, in the spirit of Marshall McLuhan's "The Medium is the Massage," instead of significant content. Thus we are often more concerned with syntactic structures than with what a sentence says; with the organization of a paragraph or questions of mechanics than with the indignation or enthusiasm or insight which the student writer reveals; with close analysis of literary passages, often outside of social or verbal context, than with the total meaning or impact of a book.

I propose in this article that teachers of English proceed on the following three principles: (1) That English shares in the task of the high school as a whole; (2) that a certain amount of integration of English, within its own field and with other subject fields, is necessary; and (3) that English encompasses many activities which are not necessarily connected with a central organizing theme.

The first of these principles implies that we are teachers first and teachers of English second. It means that nothing human in our students is alien to us. We are "concerned," in the Quaker sense, about students' problems, attitudes, and outlook upon the world of men and events. We desire, along with our colleagues in all other departments, that students make good school citizens, consider carefully their occupational goals or their plans for college, find constructive uses for their leisure time, seek to improve the present society rather than drop out of it.

We may despair of enlisting teachers of mathematics, social studies, or science in the task of accurate communication in language, but until we secure their help in the improvement of verbal communication we will operate under a great handicap. Thus, unless English instruction becomes an all-school function, utilizing all the specialized knowledge in a high school faculty, we teachers of English fight a losing battle, and will feel isolated except in the faculty lounge and near the coffee urn.

The fact that we are teachers of English second in no way suggests that we regard English as a task of secondary importance. We bear a very special responsibility for the improvement of students' language communication. But it is a shared responsibility, one which necessarily involves in some degree all teachers who recognize communication in English as central to their teaching success.

The second principle sets forth the necessity of supplying in the English curriculum a cohesive factor which enables the students to see details in relation to a larger pattern. The question in dispute among English education professionals is what the unifying principle ought to be. For some the "core" should be language. This viewpoint has the unquestionable advantage of providing the teacher with a reliable base from which to operate, but it deprives English of the flesh and blood which the reader finds in the assassination of Julius Caesar, the spiritual struggle of Hester Prynne, the long journey of Clyde Griffith to the electric chair, or the hegira of the Joads of California. It provides a unity, but the unity is in the package, not in the contents.

To me, a more satisfactory organizing principle is the body of human anxieties and aspirations. The issues about which students in English classes should communicate are psychological, social, political, ethical, moral, aesthetic, international. These are issues with which young people are struggling, often at the cost of derision by their middle-class parents.

Such an "idea-centered" curriculum as has been described deals with both the personal concerns of youth and the broader problems of society. It may consider love, sex, romance, and marriage; adventure, exploration, sports, humor, problems of relations with the older generation, problems of growing up, problems of personal decisions, problems of values. It should also deal with the values of nations and social classes. It should study the dilemma of moral man in an immoral society. It should honestly face the hypocrisies which repel the youth, and at the same time sternly challenge the youth to produce their own brand of honesty and rationality. Inserting blossoms into the rifle barrels of military police may be a dramatic act of faith, but a more constructive *credo* is needed. And it should not be too humiliating to consult the thousands of intellectuals, including the Nobel laureates of many countries, to discover what mature thought has to say about the means of survival.

The illustrations thus far given may seem like admonitions for social studies teachers. On the contrary, they are intended for teachers, period. If teachers of English may without feelings of guilt teach the chronicle plays of Shakespeare, Southey's "Battle of Blenheim," Hugo's *Les Miserables,* Milton's sonnet on the massacre in the Piedmont, and Whittier's denunciation of the Southern pro-slavery ministers ("Clerical Oppressors"), we can confidently refute those who say that only those issues which are dead today are fit for the English class. The *Grapes of Wrath* is recent, but it is literature, and belongs to all teachers.

Who will deny the parallel between Aristophanes' *Lysistrata* and today's Women Strike for Peace? Is the Negro marcher who is at the wrong end of a southern sheriff's electric cattle prod different from

Spartacus? The eloquence and the art which ancient struggles evoked from the singers and dramatists of a Golden Age long gone can come again, probably after the obscenities of politicians have been filed in their proper places in the metropolitan newspapers' morgues.

The sharp distinction between English and the social studies cannot possibly be defended. And if the subject fields are no longer realms unto themselves, they cannot be divided into such separate subjects as language, composition, and literature. The effort made no sense in the beginning.

The question whether English should constitute a structure or a group of three substructures is less appropriate than a similar question applied to such subjects as mathematics or science. To be sure, English should have a central organizing strategy which binds its parts together, even if loosely. But this subject is unique in that it inevitably invites extemporaneous and impromptu activities of communication—reading, writing, speaking, and listening.

Two developments in the field of English teaching offer great hope. One is the Dartmouth Seminar of 1966, attended by teachers of English from the United States, England, and Canada. The proceedings of this remarkable series of meetings are reported in two volumes, one for the profession and one for the general reader.[7]

The second is the International Conference on English Education held at Vancouver, British Columbia, in August, 1967, where hundreds of teachers of English from several English-speaking countries conferred on their common problems. At this meeting Dr. James Squire, Executive Secretary of the (American) National Council of Teachers of English, told of his visits to schools in the United Kingdom. The story he tells illustrates the value of such conferences as this one, in that it corrects what must be a widespread misunderstanding of what is occurring in education in other countries. The following is a brief excerpt from his report:

> Those individuals who have a mental stereotype of British schools derived from the reading of *David Copperfield* and *Nicholas Nickelby* are in for a shock as they meet the British schoolmaster of today. Sweeping forces of reform, initiated during World War II, but reaching a crescendo during the expansion of educational opportunity of the past decade, have transformed many infant and primary schools and are now working their magic at the secondary level as well. Concern with authoritarianism, with selectivity and education of the elite, with the great literary tradition, with 'the Queen's language' that so many Americans regard as character-

---

[7] John Dixon, *Growth Through English*, 1967. Herbert J. Muller, *The Uses of English*, 1967. Both available from the National Council of Teachers of English, 508 South Sixth Street, Champaign, Illinois 61820. Muller's is for the general reader, Dixon's for the profession.

istic of British education, seem very difficult to discover. Rather one is struck—perhaps too struck—with the freedom, the informality, the emotional, unstructured approaches to instruction, approaches which to disciplined Americans seem determined to turn each classroom event into a spontaneous 'happening.' When the 'happening' actually happens, it is wonderfully exciting to see. But when it doesn't—! But then should any program in education be judged by its conspicuous failures?

Through such developments as the Dartmouth Conference and the visits to British schools, we may hope to find a corrective to the current trend toward formalism in American high school classes in English. They may not bring us a "new" English, but they can restore some of the flexibility, irreverence, and wonder that characterized earlier periods in our educational history, and—who knows—may relax some of the tensions we are creating in so many of our high school students.

THERE AIN'T NO ENGLISH ANY MORE

Edward F. Wingler

I HOPE it does not come as too profound a shock, but English died some years back—as a subject, that is. The language itself, in spite of the best efforts of some of us English teachers, is still alive and flourishing. But English as a subject is dead; and as an English teacher I must admit some feeling of guilt at not lamenting its passing. In fact I might as well admit also that, in recent years, I have been an active advocate of its demise.

Lest we get ourselves into a discussion of motives for violence and assassination, perhaps I should say that it is more accurate to say English as a subject probably never really existed. Many years ago when the world was a much simpler place to live in, people were quite certain that schooling consisted of readin', writin', and 'rithmetic; no doubt there about the proper province of the English teacher. Even later, when secondary schools really began to grow in this country and the high school diploma became more and more common among the populace, we were still very comfortable with *Silas Marner,* "My Summer Vacation," and objective complements. Many of us *are* still comfortable with these —very comfortable. After all, once you've been through the literature anthology and the grammar book a few times and "corrected" summer

R E P R I N T E D by permission of Edward F. Wingler.

vacation themes for a few years, it does become a fairly comfortable "life." If only those radical-liberal publishers would quit confusing everyone by changing the color of the covers on those anthologies and grammar books, we'd have it made.

Fortunately, the foregoing is something of an exaggeration, but unfortunately not so much of an exaggeration as I would wish. One of my graduate students recently reported attending a P-TA open-house at a middle- to upper-middle class, suburban, college-prep high school where the English teacher, after stating that she was a traditionalist, said, "There are a few supposedly new things around. They call them linguistics, but they're just new names for the same old stuff." And one must admire that woman's pertinacity. It must be *incredibly* difficult to remain that ignorant in this day and age.

The point is that too many English teachers still believe nothing has changed since the nineteenth century, that there were no English writers after Dickens (or maybe Hardy) and no American writers after Twain (although I understand *Huckleberry Finn* is still considered pretty risky in some quarters), that composition instruction still consists of marking sufficient mechanical errors in student papers to give the papers the appearance of having been the floor covering at an axe murder, and that English can still be fit into the same slots as *amo, amas, amat*. Nor is youth any guarantee of liberality or even of up-to-date knowledge. The unfortunate fact is that many undergraduates, because of the major in English, simply do not have the opportunity to read contemporary authors, do not take courses that study the language systematically, and do not learn anything about composition save how to write a paper that will please cranky old Professor Whosits. This sorry state of affairs, this institutionalization of ignorance known as the requirements for the English major is, of course, defended by English professors on the nobly humanistic grounds that the courses required are in areas that have "stood the test of time" and proven to be the concern of mankind down through the ages, since time immemorial, and so on. What they neglect to tell you is that English professors are trained by other English professors who were trained by other English professors and so on, whose only concerns were the past. These are the concerns of professorkind; *mankind* had nothing to do with it. So it is entirely possible in the process of gaining a thorough knowledge of your subject matter that can be used successfully with secondary school children, that you may have acquired the backward-looking orientation of your scholarly, much-respected professors and, thus, the seeds of conservative teacher behavior. Even so, there would be nothing *wrong* with this and nothing really wrong with trying to make your secondary classes into miniature college classes if everyone were planning to be an English professor. But so far as I know, the world is not currently experiencing a dramatic realization of the indispensability of English professors to its survival and happiness.

Yet, to return to the anecdote, things may not be entirely hopeless; for it illustrates, to some extent at least, that even in the minds of the willfully benighted there is a growing uneasiness, a sneaking, creeping awareness that all is not well in what has for so long been the "tight little island" of English. This is not to imply that linguistics—or, more accurately, the *discoveries* of linguistics—is the hope and salvation of English, although some prominent linguists, who ought to know better, are making a great deal of money on textbooks where such a claim is implied. No, linguistics is not going to "save" English any more than diagramming sentences did. (And now that I think about it how different are the "trees" of transformational grammar from regular sentence diagramming? Maybe that teacher had something *after* all!) But that isn't the point anyway.

The point is that the suspicion is spreading that there may be more— or perhaps *less* would be more accurate—to English than we have heretofore assumed. At least there is something to it other than what you have been doing in English courses most of the time. Of course, some students have known this for eons. Ask any of the legions of students who never take an English course after their freshman year in college or never read another "good" book so long as they live. Most of us would rather not think about the latter; and I suggest it is because we know perfectly well that all those nonreaders are living *perfectly happy lives.* In other words, we English teachers have failed; and we don't like to face the fact that it *doesn't make a bit of difference.* But the students know it—those, at least, who don't go on to become English teachers themselves. The students you will be teaching know it.

They know that English class has nothing whatever to do with reality. And the tragedy of it is that because literature, language, and composition are taught in English class, students assume these things have nothing to do with reality either. "This is school, man; my life is what starts at 3:30."

But I don't propose to discuss the current "in" thing, *relevance.* As it has been used, it is a concept already bankrupt of meaning (and relevance) and one which it is presumptuous—if not absurd—for people to use who are as different in age and education from their students as you (soon) will be. But, obviously, I am not going to come on like the poor man's Robert Maynard Hutchins and say that something, to be an eternal verity, and thus suitable for the English class, must be four years older than God.

No. Neither of these positions—or more accurately, poses—serves a very useful purpose in the training of future English teachers. What I want to present for your consideration is the concept implied in the title of this article, "There Ain't No English Anymore." And what I mean is that we must be about the business of replacing "No English" with "Yes English."

What we have had up to now is a kind of English that contained at least two major flaws; it was, especially in literature, unapproachable for most students; and it was at the same time, *required* for all students. I shall not argue that *A Tale of Two Cities* is a bad book—although its author thought it was—and should be thrown out. But I do suggest that to require it for every student in every freshman or sophomore class because somehow students must have the experience of "reading good literature," is what has produced a population of nonreaders, particularly nonreaders of fiction. It is the English of "No": regressive, repressive, nonhuman, and ultimately counterproductive, and self-defeating.

Would it be so terrible, so unthinkable, so blasphemous, would it, after all, be so unforgivable to have students read something they would like to read more of? Most of the time those of us who are labeled liberal, radical, or progressive in the profession talk about this kind of thing in terms of "allowing" students to read what they like. Let that phrase roll around in your mind a moment and see if you don't begin to see its incredible arrogance! Perhaps even worse than its arrogance in a democracy where the right to read is guaranteed, is the mockery it makes of our claims of wanting to educate people to enjoy literature and reap the rewards literature can bring. When we say we "allow" students to read what they like, we simply imply two things: that this practice is the exception, not the rule, and that what they would like to read is still inherently inferior, like-to vs. should.

Even though it is a considerable cut above other forms, this is still "No English." "Yes English" would encourage—maybe even demand that a student read what he likes. It would also, through the use of creative dramatics, help students to discover dimensions of enjoyment they were unaware of. And if we are sensitive enough, if we keep our "third ears" open to what students say to us and ask us, we will be able to suggest books they might be able to tackle when they signal they are ready to pass from one stage of growth to another. Now, this may not be teaching—in the Old English meaning to show or betoken—but it is educating—in its Latinate meaning of leading out.

In the area of language instruction, as I've said, it seems silly to me to move in the direction of merely replacing traditional grammar with transformational grammar. It really seems like replacing a system that's of no use, with one that can't be understood, at least by secondary students. Besides, grammar has come to mean—among linguists anyway —the scientific study of what a language *does,* regardless of any applicability the results of such a study might have. In terms of the English class, then, the "No English" has concentrated and—even with the aid of the "new grammars"—will continue to concentrate on what *not* to say. The "Yes English," insofar as it would deal with language study formally at all, would emphasize such things as dialect study and attempt to induce students to take a bit more liberal attitude toward dialect and usage. In the area of language, the main concern of "Yes English" is to encourage the student to say and record what he sees, feels, thinks, believes, wants, does, and so on. It is premised on the assumption that each individual must learn to use his language in a way he finds useful, *not* because he needs to get a job (I have never known personnel directors, for example, to be particular paragons of "linguistic virtue"), but because ultimately he must order and make sense out of and come to terms with his experience. Language, as the human races' fundamental symbolizing medium, is *ipso facto* the primary means to that end.

Thus the important thing in this area is for the student to develop *toward* (note the preposition) gaining control over his language. Also note "his language." I should think the classroom implications of this idea are fairly obvious, but just in case they are not, let me sketch some of them briefly.

First of all, something shall have to be done to do away with the concept of theme grading. In fact, it seems clear we should very likely do away with the concept of the theme itself if for no other reason than that nobody writes that kind of thing *except* in the English class. Doing away with The Paper might also be the first step toward obliterating the problems students have with the difference between spoken language—where fluency is seldom a problem for young people—and written language—where it is. Everyone is familiar with the difference between the vitality and directness of students' talk in the halls and the arid wastes of the five-hundred word theme. Because of its directness, clarity, and gutsy vitality, adults even use their slang: hung up, up tight, like it is, where it's at, and that whole scene, man.

Now we always say that we are trying to teach clarity and communication in student writing. Yet far too often we expect a completely different kind of prose in student writing from what the student normally (and successfully) uses in his regular speech. What we expect is, of course, what was expected of us—particularly in all those marvelously lively, vitally interesting papers we wrote in our college literature classes. (And if you think those papers were something, wait till you get to graduate school!) We would in most instances react at least suspiciously to a high school or junior high paper that used phrases like "where it's at" and the like, innocuous as they are. Heaven knows what most English teachers would do faced with a paper using words like *shit* and *fuck* which, of course, kids use all the time—and very effectively too. No, I'm afraid the concern of most teachers of "No English" is not clarity or effective, forceful communication; rather it is linguistic propriety and maximum artificiality.

But this is straying somewhat from my point about classroom implications, though not really when you think about it. In any event, one of the implications of the use of language I am advocating is that the English classroom will be a place where a great deal of talk takes place —a great deal more talk than writing and student talk, not teacher-centered *recitation*. As things stand now, students probably learn more —at least through practice—about using and controlling their own language in gym class than they do in English class! The purpose of this talk is to work toward what Andrew Wilkinson calls "oracy," the speaking and listening equivalent of "literacy." As before with reading, this not only involves allowing students to "do their thing," it involves encouraging them to. "Yes English" would encourage them to explore through talking (and writing) about their experiences, hopes, fears, desires, and, in short, their universe. Much of what we recognize as reality is catelogued through the medium of language, and most of us use oral language about 900 times more than we do written language.

Nowhere is the importance of "Yes English," as we've just been discussing it, more apparent than when we do get into the area of writing. First of all, writing should be thought of as an extension of talking, rather than something altogether different. If we can get them to write enough, students will discover the important differences on their own. One elementary fact about writing, of course, is that it is meant to be read and in this case, I would suggest it be read aloud to other students in order both to facilitate the "transition" from talking to writing and to give the writer a more realistic audience than he has when writing to a college graduate English major who is a minimum of four years older than he. But most important here, the "Yes English" involves saying "yes" a lot! In other words, if you don't do anything else, *reinforce* them. And at first at least, give them only reinforcement; not indiscriminate reinforcement (they can spot insincerity fast enough) but find something in every paper you can praise, and comment only on that. Correction and rigorous criticism, *if* they are necessary, can come later when the student has a degree of confidence about writing or, at least, no longer hates it or is afraid of it, terms which are probably synonymous anyway. Believe it or not, if you reinforce that which is good or even sort of good and ignore the bad, the bad will eventually begin to drop out. Try it.

Finally, it should be obvious that the "Yes English" classroom physically and atmospherically is going to have to be a rather different place from the "No English" one. Physically, it should be a bright, warm place that anyone would like to enter. There should be, as the NCTE national study recommended, a classroom library of *at least* 500 titles.

The teacher's inevitable desk, chair, and filing cabinet should be as inconspicuous as possible, if there at all. Those asinine desks that seem to have been built for dwarfs with a perfect sense of balance ought to be replaced with lounge-type furniture. It would be nice if the lights could be controlled rheostatically and if there were also a small stage, a motion picture, slide, and overhead projector, a tape recorder, and a record player in each room. It is, however, very unlikely that the public would be willing to spend this kind of serious money on education. But there are a few things you can do without lavish expenditure. First you can bring a lot of your books from home, and you can ask your friends and neighbors to save those paperbacks and magazines they normally throw out. Some book distributers will—if asked pitifully enough—donate paperbacks or loan them. If you have each student buy one paperback (each a different one), you will quickly amass a collection of several hundred books. My own students decided at one point to bring old pieces of furniture and carpet from their attics and basements to furnish the classroom. The school, remarkably enough, had no objections so we were actually comfortable. The very least a teacher can do, though, is to arrange those silly little desks in some way less formal than on the grid system, so that each student sees something other than the back of the head in front of him. The teacher can also let the students sit where they like—and change seats daily if they want—rather than insist they sit in alphabetical order.

Truth is, we can do without the machines. But the two things we *cannot* do without are freedom and imagination. No array of machines, no matter *how* sparkling and breathtakingly expensive, can do what one imaginative teacher can do. And no teacher, no matter how knowledgeable, professional, or *beautiful*, can succeed without imagination. Use your head. *Make* yourself think of new, interesting ways to do things. Go on: be somebody!

And freedom. The freedom for the teacher to free his students. But freedom for the students as well. If "as the twig is bent, so the tree inclines," we must realize we are not in the business of producing bonsai or topiary trees. And we must mean it, *be* it—not do the sort of thing Geoffrey Summerfield reports hearing when some eight-year-olds were playing school:

Sit down!
Shut up!
Now we'll have some free activity!

No. That just won't do, and we all know it, because it *is* No. And we also know that we shall have to educate citizens for a free society if there is to be one or continue to be one. Freedom and imagination are Yes. And that's why, *"There Ain't No English Anymore."*

"YOU'LL LIKE IT—
IT'S CANNELLONI!"

Robert F. Hogan

I BEGIN this writing securely strapped into seat 25D on American
Airlines flight 630 from Phoenix to Chicago. The plane left on or
nearly on schedule—10:10 A.M. (MST)—and is expected to reach Chicago on time—2:04 P.M. (CST)—two hours and 54 minutes, and one
time zone, from now. And I'm struck with the similarity between this
and school. Here we are, 99 of us, in six parallel rows. We are attended
to and watched over and occasionally instructed by two young women.
They look a little harried, but still that's not an unusual pupil count for
two teachers in a large-group setting. Up front in another room is the
"honors" section, with two young ladies and a class of only 24, but I'm
in the "regular" program. There's a P.A. system which occasionally interrupts our thoughts. It is used mainly by a chief administrator whom
we never see.

At 10:45 A.M. (MST) it's lunchtime. I debate with myself and frown
at the thought. One stewardess sees the frown and says perhaps the
only thing she could say: "You'll like it—it's cannelloni." And that's it.
It's not the right time for lunch, surely. But it is time. There's only one
menu. And there will be no other chance for food for the next two
hours.

Down come the desk tops and the two young women go to the
galley. It's just across the aisle from seat 25D; I watch curriculum
building in action. They prepare the materials for all 99 of us, young and
old, sleepy and alert, hungry and fed, omnivorous and picky. But for
everyone it's the same curriculum in the same amount in the same length
of time. (I wonder if students feel very different when they sit through
a well-structured, team-taught, large-group humanities program.) Out
of cupboards and drawers they assemble 99 identical kits, all built
around identical servings of cannelloni.

It's a long period today and several of us get up to go for drinks of
water, not because we're thirsty, but because it is a long time to sit, and
drinking water is, after all, doing something. Others get up to go to the
bathroom. They don't have passes, but it's an orderly, self-disciplined
group. Besides, the two bathrooms open right off the main classroom.
Where else could they go? And since it's only one at a time in a bath-

FROM *Phi Delta Kappan* (April 1971), pp. 469–470. Reprinted by permission of the
publisher and the author.

room, what devilment could they try? The unseen administrator interrupts with another geography lesson.

American Airlines is in the transportation business. In consideration of its customers, it is, like most airlines, in the nutrition business as well. But the economics of coach travel, the limited galley facilities on most aircraft, the duration of most flights—all of these argue against anything but a one-choice menu, usually including green beans with no character.

Coincidentally, the schools share both interests with the airlines—nutrition and transportation. (Probably the less said here about school lunches, the better.) A few schools transport children not just geographically, but intellectually, emotionally, aesthetically, imaginatively. Not often enough, though, and not nearly enough children. Yet that kind of transportation is central to the mission of the schools.

Of course, there is a parallel mission, one commanding more headlines now, more column inches, one embracing the skills of literacy. But if we were to concentrate on that mission alone, as some would have us do, we would produce even more of what we turn out in too great a supply now—adults who know how to read, but who have forgotten why they should read. While it's true that one of the great scandals of the school program is measurable in the number of adult illiterates, another can be counted in the far greater number of presumably literate adults who found that as their skills in reading were being strengthened, their interest in reading was being dulled.

The most widespread criticism of classroom programs now is that they are in fact emotionally and educationally destructive. Actually, we never really kill creativity, curiosity, imagination, and emotional and aesthetic growth. Despite all our soul-searching and breast thumping at the moment, we do not kill them. We are powerful, but not omnipotent. We just kill them in the classroom setting. Imagine, if you can, the typical atypical stream in the ninth grade. In the room students are unresponsive, uninterested, unambitious, unmotivated—*un-* almost everything we prize and praise. But stay with them and see them in the nooks and crannies of their day, in the breaks between classes and at lunchtime. Look at them. Listen to them. They're articulate, energetic, communicative, emotional, boisterous, humorous—everything they are not in the classroom.

We are not even powerful—just influential. Their creativity, as (or especially) in their devilment, is whole, intact, thriving. We don't kill it; for six periods a day (or 24 modules, if your school is up to date and has a computer), we send it underground. The difference is that in those nooks and crannies, without even a committee meeting or the publication of a syllabus, they choose, revise, adopt, innovate, reject, and recreate their own curriculum. Then they set out to teach it to one another. It may not be the curriculum we would choose for them, but it's one that helps many of the economically deprived children survive in and even endure a hostile environment that would destroy most of the rest of us. It's a curriculum that ranges from games one can actually play on ghetto streets to the ground rules of welfare to the grammatical rules for a ghetto dialect.

The poor child isn't the only one to worry about. There are enough of a different kind of student that we even have a cliché to designate him: the "golden ghetto dropout." The suburban child, often advantaged, almost always white, shares with the slum child at least one trait: his determination to come to functional grips with his own world, not a world that we conjure up for him and tell him he'll enter later, when he'll be most grateful for the very things he most dislikes about school now.

It was easier once when it was the kids against the grown-ups. Then we could argue that the problem was rooted in the natural resistance of some children to organized schooling. Today, however, more and more adults share with the children their rejection of the traditional curriculum and have become their advocates for reform. Not just Holt, Kozol, Silberman, Featherstone, and the other romantic critics of education, either. On this flight and between these paragraphs I skim an article in this week's *Life*. Not angry and hostile children but concerned parents set up that free school in Decatur, Illinois, and others like it across the country, with their unstructured schedules and flexible curriculums that take into complete account the roving nature of children's interests and the spontaneous processes in learning. As long as the chief response of the public schools to such institutions is to ignore them and to resist any voucher system in the reasonable hope that they will soon go bankrupt, we'll continue to have the free-school spirit in the community, even if that actual school in the Baptist church closes up this year.

Articles and speeches, when the composer really cares about them, have a way of developing their own life, their own spirit, their own muscle. They refuse to bend entirely or even much to the composer's will. So it is with this one. I set out to compose a piece on the right of the student to help choose the materials and the experiences that make up the curriculum. The thing that strikes home now is that he is going to exercise that right whether we recognize it or not. If the curriculum is prepared the way the meal was on flight 630, a fair number of children will take the option that the passenger in 25F did. They will nibble away at the edges and consume only what we let them choose freely (the whiskey sour in 25F's case). They'll do that even if we make it a moral issue and scold them.

They will nibble away at the edges of some Victorian novel that no one has taken the time to show is about *them,* and they will read voraciously in the curriculum they devise for themselves: *Brave New World, The Catcher in the Rye, The Stranger, Catch 22, 1984.* They will reject "Thanatopsis" in our classes and buy books by Rod McKuen on their own, and they will copy down and memorize and trade back and forth the lyrics to songs by Jim Webb. They will doze through *The Land of Liberty Part I* and spend their own money to see *Easy Rider.* And the farther our curriculum gets from their world, the more they will exercise their right and their power to reject it.

It may be that the direction of this argument is too romantic to be useful. It may even be that the natural working relationship between children and schools must be one of open and admitted hostility. Although the image is out of scale, it may be that the school curriculum will always function as that abrasive piece of sand around which the organism will build its own unique pearl. Or that the function of the curriculum is the same as that of the wall in handball. Without it, the game that takes place mostly on the open court would not be possible.

But if that is the case, then all talk about curriculum reform and improvement, about selecting the materials and pacing the drills, is foolish. The trick is as simple as making certain that there are some hard things in the program (because they will be "good" for the children) and plenty of things they don't like. Yet children try to learn and often succeed in learning many of the things we teach them. The contrary argument that the children will always devise a counter-curriculum for anything we include in the program is not necessarily so. Including driver education in the secondary schools does not send the youngsters back to horses and bicycles. They learn to drive. Including a reasonable program in sex education will not make adolescents celibate. That contrary argument is too simple.

Children learn what we teach them when we teach it in a way that makes them believe they can learn it, when they see its connection to their own life—either it makes that life more enjoyable or it helps them to cope with parts of life that may not be enjoyable—and when the likelihood of failure is slight. Some children also learn things that don't seem to have any connection to life and that have a higher risk of failure—conjugating Latin verbs, solving quadratic equations, diagramming sentences. But either they are convinced that these matters will someday be useful (whether that is true or not) even if the connection to life now is not apparent, or they find them inherently interesting and fun. Traditional grammar teachers took heart because some children actually liked to diagram sentences. It's not those children I'm concerned about here. It's the other 97%

We don't spoil interest in things simply because we teach those things. We spoil them—when we do—because of the ways in which we teach them: by drilling children in skills whose significance they've never been led to see, by offering them subject matter whose meaning as well as significance we have never made clear. Giving them a voice in what they read will not only insure greater interest in what is read; if the teachers read it, too, they may come to feel, if not wholly understand, what it's like to be, say, 16 in 1971. It helps to understand not only what one is teaching, but whom.

Enough. . . .

We are landing in Chicago now, and the two young ladies have tidied the place up. They've stored away all the permanent equipment and gotten rid of all the remaining consumable supplies. They're getting ready now to help us with our winter coats. School is over for the day.

IS "ENGLISH" STILL TEACHABLE?

William Goldstein

> "I couldn't afford to learn it," said the Mock Turtle with a sigh. "I only took the regular course."
> "What was that?" inquired Alice.
> "Reeling and Writhing, of course, to begin with," the Mock Turtle replied, "and then the different branches of Arithmetic—Ambition, Distraction, Uglification, and Derision."
>
> LEWIS CARROLL

To many students, especially those former students who are now adults, the teaching of English seems just about what Alice's amphibian friend describes. Traditionally, the parade of academic agonies was led by English; and, generally, the teacher of English was blamed for this state of affairs. There has been a tacit but widespread acceptance of the idea that discontent with the teaching of English in secondary schools is simply a fact of life about which nothing can be done; but this bleak point of view is not really warranted, nor is it justifiable to blame the teacher for what is wrong. English is commonly called "dull" or "boring," while other courses, especially those with apparatus to manipulate, are called "interesting." But surely there

F R O M *Teachers College Record*, Vol. 71 (September 1969), pp. 70–73. Reprinted by permission of the publisher and the author.

is nothing intrinsically superior about the science teacher. What, then, causes the difference in students' perceptions of English and science? More than likely, the differences can be explained by the nature of the *content* taught in each class and the *process* by which it is taught.

Unreal Expectations

What is conceived as "English" is no more English than political science is history; yet English continues to be treated as a discrete body of content. The teacher, of necessity, becomes a kind of factotum—a Pooh-Bah, a Lord High Everything Else. Specialization, sophistication, and "micro-scholarship" are increasingly used to measure competence. The teacher of English is expected to remain omniscient in an academic specialty which has become a composite of many scholarly disciplines. Unless the field of "English" is to be given over to well-programmed androids, steps must be taken to ameliorate a situation which is deteriorating almost as rapidly as the megatonnage of the knowledge explosion increases.

In the fall-out, "English" has taken on instructional responsibility for areas of learning which, in and of themselves, are so esoteric and so complicated that years of scholarly study are needed for mastery of even one of them. Yet the English teacher is expected to teach all these subjects and to teach them well. Even a casual glance at the complexity of the task reveals the illusory nature of such expectations.

Massive Pluralism

The English program is still simplistically and naively perceived as a combination of composition, grammar, and literature. There is much that is accurate in such a perception; but the sweep of each area now demands far more attention, organization, and mastery than any single teacher—no matter how well-intentioned—can give.

COMPOSITION. The peculiar failure of students to master the elements of English composition continues to haunt English teachers and to remain one of the most troubling questions with which they and their students have to contend. The inability to deal with written communication obviously blocks success in other academic activities, causes continual embarrassment, occasions all sorts of frustration. Some English teachers do not write well themselves, and yet they are expected to teach others how to communicate effectively. When one adds to this the complexity of the scholarship required to teach adequately, one soon sees that effective composition teaching is not possible under our traditional schemes of organization.

"Composition" is being linked today to respect for and understanding of the nature of language—something not taken into account in the traditional scheme of things. There is a renewed interest in logic today as well, a concern which presumably permits a student to learn a *process* which leaves a residue usable in the confrontation of new problems related to what has been previously learned. An acquaintance with syllogistic reasoning and the nature of logical fallacies gives the student the joy of a *thought process* in contrast to the experience of mechanical memorization. Semantics, formerly an exotic intellectual commodity, is also getting increasing attention. This, too, can play a part in communicating a pungent and intriguing message on the nature and use of language.

An intellectual and practical *entente* of logic, semantics, and the elements of mechanics, style, and construction is, therefore, being established. But it is so complex that it is naive to expect the traditionally moored English teacher to perform successfully in all the areas included.

GRAMMAR. The study of syntactical relationships within the English sentence has absorbed numbers of scholars throughout their lives; yet secondary school English teachers are expected to distill the essence of the study, package and wrap it, and deliver it palatably to all students —even while they are teaching a modern course in English composition. The difficulty of the teaching task is compounded by the prevalence of scholarly controversy on the value of teaching grammar altogether, as well as confusion as to what brand of grammar ought to be taught. Does the teacher, for example, deal in the traditional, "classical" approach, or does he work with transformational grammar, one of the syntactical approaches in linguistics? Whatever approach is chosen, there remains the problem arising from the lack of definitive research on how and to what extent grammar and written composition combine to make students "write better." And even that is not all.

LITERATURE. The study of literature also is in a state of flux. Even the casual observer of American literature knows that contemporary letters may be in a "golden age"; but a proper perspective on the literary scene must be grounded in knowledge of literary history, an acquaintance with literary form and genre, a grasp of comparative literature, some familiarity with aesthetics, and a working knowledge of literary criticism. The student is expected to move from Aristotle to Ruskin to Kazin, from Virgil to Dante to Eliot, from Homer to Dickens to Malamud . . . to move easily, resourcefully, and at length deal (in a sophisticated manner) with what I. B. Singer calls "the eternal questions."

Because of its internal vigor and the way in which it embodies human values, literature is inherently interesting; and students should find the study and analysis of literary works intrinsically rewarding and compelling. But the English teacher, more often than not, is unable to deal intensively enough with the literature because of the need to divide instructional time among the other areas of "English." The result is, too frequently, a superficial and hasty treatment which actually destroys student interest. Deprived of opportunities for delight in literature, the student feels progressively disengaged from the "global" considerations which are so much a function of literary involvement.

Towards Solutions

If one accepts the premises that 1) the field of "English" has grown too complicated to be taught as it has been in the past; that 2) "English" as an eclectic discipline, composed of other scholarly disciplines, is inherently interesting when appropriately taught; and that 3) a reexamination of the process and the organization of English content is desirable, it follows that the discipline may be taught more effectively by "combinations" or teams of teachers.

English is first and foremost a language; but, ironically, this aspect of the field is given the least attention. If one grants the crucial need for a "feel" for and sensitivity to language, it might seem reasonable to create two kinds of teachers of English—one, a teacher of the language and its complementary sub-disciplines (grammar, composition, logic, semantics, etc.); the other, a teacher of literature, dealing in literary form, aesthetics, criticism, and the rest.

If this is to be done, of course, schedules must be reorganized in the secondary schools, and a new perspective developed on the recruitment of teachers. As much as double the currently committed time sequence would be required, although initially the time allotments might be variously shifted so as to avoid the need for doubling the English staff immediately. For instance, the time block committed to English might be increased arbitrarily by 40% (from five periods a week to seven) and students' exposure to teachers might be subsequently rearranged. They might, for example, at first receive four periods of instruction in language and three in literature, with the system being reversed for the following term.

Needless to say, new instructional configurations demand teachers with somewhat different areas of concentration and interest. Would-be high school English teachers today are mainly committed, by interest and training, to the teaching of literature. Local school systems, concerned with renovating their English programs, might well be the places best equipped to initiate changes in orientation and preparation. In-service courses, new college training programs, and the experiences made possible by team teaching are all means for attaining such ends.

Teaching teams, with highly specialized personnel within each team, can be created; and these certainly would alter the existing state of things. If a four-man team in English were established and given responsibility for teaching the reconstructed program proposed above, the teachers in the team might proceed to develop both the all-over program and the individual specialties required by the new arrangement. Individual teachers might develop and refine particular aspects of the new program and associate themselves with them. This would ultimately yield a better instructional flow and make possible a far more advantageous use of teachers' specialized talents. And, as each new program gained in stature, so would the teacher responsible for it. Individual contributions would, for the first time, become visible.

Paraphrasing George Orwell, we are suggesting that some methods make the English program more "teachable" than others. As knowledge burgeons in these changing times, the English teacher may be faced with a double paradox: through division (between language and literature) a new kind of unification may emerge; and through unification (team teaching), a productive division. In any event, one would hope that the field of English does not find itself some day in the position described by Lewis Carroll's Tweedledee:

> "If seven maids with seven mops
>   Swept it for half a year,
> Do you suppose," the Walrus said,
>   "That they could get it clear?"
> "I doubt it," said the Carpenter,
>   And shed a bitter tear.

BEHAVIORAL OBJECTIVES: VIETNAM FOR THE ENGLISH CURRICULUM?

Richard O. Ulin

"Look, you can argue all you want about behavioral objectives—whether they're the answer to all our problems or whether they're just another fad. But make no mistake about it. They're here. I'm in this room for only one reason. I'm here to find out where I get a set of them—and fast! At our last faculty meeting last Wednesday my superintendent told me to

➤➤➤➤➤➤➤➤➤➤➤➤➤➤➤➤➤➤➤➤➤➤➤➤➤➤➤➤➤

F R O M *The Leaflet,* Vol. 70 (February 1971), pp. 3–10. Reprinted by permission of the publisher and the author.

show up at a meeting next Tuesday with a full set of behavioral objectives for English, K-12. Just what do you suggest I do?"

"Make him happy. Dress up your old objectives in behavioral terms."

"Make a few phone calls and get a set from some system that has already done it."

"Just write to the Instructional Objectives Exchange in Los Angeles for their package."

"Simply refuse."

THE above interchange, practically verbatim, I heard at one section meeting of the NCTE annual conference in Atlanta this past November. With variations, I heard it repeated in countless other meetings and corridor conversations. Teachers who arrived in Atlanta already opposed to the Movement acquired a sense that across the land the behavioral objectivists, like a plague of locusts, were already devouring our green fields. In fact, by their presence on our platforms some had obviously made inroads into the prestigious professional associations themselves. Other teachers who came hoping that the convention would recognize behavioral objectives as a means of clarifying the muddle we have called English and also as an effective tool for rallying public support for our ends left appalled at what they saw as a groundswell of unthinking reaction. Those who came either without bias or blissfully unaware of the issue were struck by both the pervasiveness of the problem and the passionate rhetoric it aroused. The usual kind of oratory and breast-beating the conventioneer expected on questions of censorship, pornography, electronic media, Black Literature and linguistics, he was surprised to find shifted to the hitherto academic and innocuous process of phrasing objectives.

Although it is not the most agile of organizations, the NCTE had nevertheless scented the rising storm well in advance of the Atlanta meetings. Its Commission on the English Curriculum had studied the question and had reported cautiously that while it "by no means condemns the writing of behavioral objectives," it felt "compelled to warn the profession against premature and unsophisticated attempts."[1] Was the Commission taking the position of a medical board and suggesting that until the profession reached a higher level of technical expertise, practitioners should not attempt heart transplants? Or was it suggesting that possibilities do exist now for highly skilled practitioners to perform the operation, but only when particular conditions are present and understood? Whatever the inference to be drawn, still without condemning the

1 John Maxwell and Anthony Tovatt, eds., *On Writing Behavioral Objectives for English* (Champaign, Illinois: National Council of Teachers of English, 1970), p. ix.

movement, the NCTE then picked up and amplified the storm signal by passing a resolution at its fall 1969 convention which still refrained from condemning the practice:

> Resolved, That those who propose to employ behavioral objectives be urged to engage in a careful appraisal of the possible benefits and the present limitation of behavioral definitions of English with reference to the humanistic aims which have traditionally been valued in this discipline.[2]

In the spring the NCTE announced that John Maxwell, Director of the Commission on the English Curriculum, and Anthony Tovatt had edited a monograph titled *On Writing Behavioral Objectives for English*. Requests for the publication poured in from teachers, some looking for information on where the NCTE really stood on behavioral objectives, others wanting a Baedecker on how to get on with the business of writing them. The chances are that few in either group had their expectations met. As provocative, engrossing, and comprehensive as the little volume is, it did not take or claim to take a stand, nor did it provide a set of easy-to-follow instructions. What it succeeded in doing, both in Maxwell's opening narrative as well as in the ten individually authored papers that follow, was to pose the problem sharply, put it in perspective, point to concomitant issues and raise the general anxiety level of the profession to the point where it exploded at the 1970 convention. Out of that convention one might have expected some Jovian thunderbolt. What emerged was yet another resolution, more shrill than the 1969 original, but still somewhat equivocating. The resolution insists "That when members of the NCTE are put in the position to use or develop behavioral objectives, they secure satisfactory answers supported by adequate evidence to the following questions among others." What follow are seven basically rhetorical questions e.g. "Who has the professional and moral right to predetermine and control what shall or shall not be the limits of acceptable behavior of young people? In short, do we help students grow or shape them to a mold?" In a convention setting political conditions are generally conducive to the emergence of bloodless party platforms, and perhaps one should rather be surprised at the transparent quality of the hostility contained in the resolution's language.

One may ask what there is about behavioral objectives, other than their unwise imposition or premature installation, which rouses such hostility at these gatherings of the faithful? Most educators, including English teachers, would, I think, agree with W. James Popham that "The quality of any instructional sequence must be evaluated primarily in

2 Ibid., pp. ix–x.

terms of its ability to promote desirable changes in the intended learner."[3] Most of us would also probably agree with Robert F. Mager, founding father of the movement, that "When *clearly defined* goals are lacking, it is impossible to evaluate a course or program *efficiently,* and there is no sound basis for selecting appropriate materials, content, or instructional methods."[4] No one can dispute the fact that until he knows what he intends to accomplish with it, a machinist cannot select a tool. These are statements to which we can readily pledge allegiance. However, such a pledge in no way obligates us to subscribe to a definition of our goals or an evaluation of our English programs in the terms demanded by Popham, Mager and the behavioral objectivists.

In one Massachusetts town I know, call it Greenville, an enlightened and in many ways an advantaged community, the staff took the job of writing behavioral objectives as seriously and worked as long and as hard as Mager and Popham warn us is necessary. Religiously they obeyed Mager's injunction against using "words open to many interpretations" e.g. *to know, to understand, to appreciate, to enjoy, to believe* and phrased their terminal objectives in "words open to fewer interpretations" e.g. *to write, to recite, to identify, to list.*[5] The latter, we are advised, are words to use if we wish to force ourselves to identify and define the terminal pupil-behaviors our instruction is designed to produce. In this way, we are told, we can avoid taking the traditional humanist dodge i.e. hiding behind goals so stated that they defy objective measurement.

Now let's take a sampling of the behavioral objectives the Greenville staff produced for seventh grade English classes. First those for Poetry:

1. Given a poem to read, the student will demonstrate a knowledge of rhyme scheme by writing the rhyme scheme of the poem. This must be done correctly at least 90% of the time.

2. Given a poem to read and 4 themes, the student will demonstrate a knowledge of the underlying theme (controlling idea) by choosing the appropriate theme for the poem. This must be done correctly at least 80% of the time.

3. Given a poem to read and 4 moods, the student will demonstrate a knowledge of mood (created atmosphere) by choosing the correct mood for the poem. This must be done correctly at least 80% of the time.

No one is likely to quarrel with instruction designed to help children respond more fully to rhyme or to sensing poetic moods and controlling

---

3 James W. Popham, "The Instructional Objectives Exchange: New Support for Criterion-Referenced Instruction," *Phi Delta Kappan,* 52 (November 1970), pp. 174.

4 Robert F. Mager, *Preparing Instructional Objectives.* (Palo Alto, California: Fearon Publishers, 1962), p. 174.

5 Ibid., p. 11.

ideas. But large questions may be asked about the propriety of judging the success or failure of a month's immersion in poetry on the basis of whether youngsters measure up either to these or any other three "objective" criteria. How much pride should we take in a student's choosing 80% of the time that option *we* decide is "correct" among the four *we* decide to give him? Who is to pick the poems? On what grounds are they to be chosen? Who is to phrase the options and determine the optimal choice? On what grounds does one decide arbitrarily that 80% or 90% of "correct" responses defines "successful performance" i.e. the attainment of our objectives?

Do we really agree with Mager that "the best statement [of an objective] is the one that excludes the greatest number of possible alternatives to your goal?"[6] In drama we find a single all-embracing objective:

> Given a short play to read and five sentences explaining elements within the play, the student will demonstrate a knowledge of the elements (plot, tone, setting, theme, the character) by matching the description with the appropriate element. This must be done correctly at least 80% of the time.

What does this statement of "performance" actually mean? Once the student has read a play, are the testers to hand him five sentences, each purporting to explain the significance of one of the five elements in the play assigned? or in any play? What kind of "descriptions" of what is he then supposed to label *plot, tone,* etc.? Incidentally I should be rather uneasy at this point if the writers of this "objective" were to take Mager at his word and relax when he says, "If you give each learner a copy of your objectives you may not have much else to do."[7]

In composition we find the writers struggling valiantly to use the new terminology and in so doing oscillating between global statements which defy definition, let alone measurement, and statements which provide illusory possibilities of concrete measurement. Announced vaguely as the Overall Objective is the admonition: "The student will communicate his experience effectively in writing." With equal fuzziness, the general objective for a particular unit on Descriptive Paragraphs declares: "The student will write paragraphs that effectively describe the items he intends." Terminal objectives call for the student to write paragraphs "90% free" of such errors as run-on sentences, fragments, dangling modifiers, etc., on such topics as "a single object of your choice," and "a scene of your choice." Are terminal objectives, even such pedestrian ones as these, actually measurable in percentage figures? Do we now have, or should we even try to develop, instruments that will tell us when paragraphs are 90% fat-free? Certainly we are dissatisfied with the re-

6 Ibid., p. 53.
7 Maxwell, op. cit., p. 43.

sults of our current modes of instruction. But in order to demonstrate results in concrete terms, are we really ready to abandon the larger, often non-cognitive aims of English instruction: developing in our students aesthetic sensibility, creativity, empathy and imagination, helping them make sense of themselves and their world?

If I have been harsh with the particular performance criteria I have described, it is not because they are bad—they are probably better than most. At least they have the virtue of having been developed by the teachers who plan to try them; they were not picked up hurriedly like TV dinners at the frozen-food counter to make do in an emergency. In the process of formulating them, I would agree with Mager, teachers may have reached a new level of awareness of what they have been about, of how much of their time has been devoted to trivia. Ironic and distressing, however, is the fact that with tools as unsophisticated as those we now have for measuring affective and humanistic gains, when we subscribe to goals in strictly behavioral terms and count our successes only in observable, measureable phenomena, we enthrone the very trivia we deplore.

Those who would dismiss the whole behavioral objectives movement as just another passing fad are, I believe, underestimating its strength. As Sue Brett of the USOE's Center for Research and Development says, "At this moment the Office of Education is up to its ears in behavioral objectives."[8] When she also says, as she did at the NCTE convention in Atlanta, that in order to satisfy the taxpaper we must have some way statistically to measure what the schools—and English classes —accomplish and therefore we must have behavioral objectives to measure against, the reasons behind the groundswell begin to come through. Money for education we know is tight and obviously getting tighter. Since Sputnik federal, state and local agencies have expended gigantic sums on projects like compensatory education. Disappointed in observable results, legislative bodies and the public are insisting on "accountability." One attempt to meet this demand is the National Assessment of Educational Achievement, a massive project, finally airborne after a rough take-off. Another is the statewide student achievement appraisal announced by Massachusetts Commissioner of Education, Neil Sullivan.

It is not hard to account for the pressures which lead educators to apply what look like hard-headed cost accounting procedures to the instructional program. In a business-dominated society the techniques of the systems analyst, the old efficiency expert now armed with a computer, look particularly appealing. Though he was referring to an earlier period in American education, Raymond Callahan might well have been describing the current situation in *Education and the Cult of Efficiency:*

8 Ibid., p. 50.

"What was unexpected was the extent, not only of the power of the business-industrial groups, but of the strength of the business ideology in the American culture on the one hand and the extreme weakness and vulnerability of schoolmen, especially school administrators, on the other."[9] In his scholarly but impassioned work Callahan insists that education is not a business, that the school is not a factory, that students are not products. Some thirty years ago one of Franklin Bobbitt's disciples drew up a list of 1581 social objectives for English, and today we see ascendant once again what James Hoetker calls "specificationism."[10] Lo, the wheel has been reinvented—this time on a behavioralist axle. Once more the danger is that, however efficient the wheel, schools and children may suffer.

Pressured by tax-conscious Congressmen and school committeemen to show tangible results, it is not surprising that educators borrow the human engineering tools industry and the military find useful. Hence the technocratic talk of "pipelines," "flow charts," "inputs and outputs," "feedback" and "performance criteria." Hence the Rube Goldberg schematics and the Donald Barthelme parodies they have produced. Hence the insistence on objectives only in terms of conveniently observable behaviors. The fact that such an approach may prove fruitful in the field of vocational education, with its primary emphasis on salable skills, provides no assurance that it will enhance a well conceived program in the humanities. As John Dixon has pointed out, we have moved in stages from a model of English which once centered on skills at a time when literacy was our essential need; to a model which focused on the cultural heritage, when we were most in need of the cohesive and civilizing effects of content; to our current model (hopefully) which stresses self expression and personal growth. While the behavioralists' tools might have applied with some efficiency to the two earlier models, they can, as I see them at their present level of sophistication, only retard the development of the third, the personal growth model enunciated at the Dartmouth Seminar in the summer of 1966.

What saddens me is the distinct possibility that this highly promising development, now showing real signs of revitalizing English programs across the country, will be swept away in the rising tide of behavioralism. USOE dollars which flow only to projects and systems subscribing to the behavioral format will be hard to resist. If students are to be judged on the "concrete" evidence provided by their attainment of specific behavioral objectives, it will not be long before teachers, knowing

9 Raymond E. Callahan, *Education and the Cult of Efficiency* (Chicago: University of Chicago Press, 1962), pp. vii–viii.

10 Maxwell, op. cit., p. 50.

their fate rests on their students' meeting these circumscribed criteria, will focus their teaching on measurable, albeit insignificant, learning.

Perhaps we can take hope in the fact that English teachers have always proved stubbornly resilient and resourceful in the face of external pressure. Under the present circumstances perhaps their agility with language will enable them to have their cake and eat it too, to pursue the personal growth model in their instructional programs and still satisfy the clamor of the times by couching their activities in behavioral terms. This is a dangerous but, so some think, a necessary expedient. It reminds me of the veteran actor who confided to his apprentice the secret of his own success. "I have found," he said, "that the most important thing in acting is *honesty*. And once you've learned to fake that, you have it made."

At least one scholar committed to the Dartmouth Seminar recommendations, however, refuses to "fake it." James Moffett, author of the highly influential *A Student-Centered Language Arts Curriculum, Grades K-13* agreed in 1969 to serve as a consultant on the Tri-University BOE Project, a carefully conceived, well directed, and bountifully funded USOE attack on the knotty problem of writing behavioral objectives for English. However skeptical he may have been about the possibilities of designing behavioral objectives to fit a humanistic curriculum, he must have accepted the plausible argument that the English profession, whatever its misgivings, had better tackle the job itself. A year later, still respecting the integrity of the project directors but convinced of the inadequacy of *any* formulation of behavioral objectives for English concerns and appalled by the potential damage to be done English instruction by the application of principles of operant-conditioning, he left the project.

Bitter about what he considers unwarranted government pressure, he wrote in resigning:

> In short, we are being MacNamara-ed, and we should fight it. But, I am told, if we don't write these behavioral objectives, "they" will. If this is true, then let's recognize this for just what it is—extortion. Lend your name and support to this project or else you-know-who will write these objectives instead of you. I simply cannot accept these conditions. I respect the directors of BOE, appreciate their good intentions, and sympathize with their own conflicts about possibly contradictory commitments, but with the submission of this position paper I must withdraw from the project.[11]

However one interprets it, Moffett's personal action should serve as a warning. It should make us think long and carefully before we commit

11 Ibid., p. 116.

ourselves and our schools to a course of action which clamors for total involvement, which will resist deescalation, and from which we may later find it impossible to make any "honorable" withdrawal.

BEHAVIORAL OBJECTIVES FOR ENGLISH: SOME PRO'S AND CON'S

John Maxwell

LIKE it or not, the writing of behavioral objectives is one of the largest inservice sports current in American education today. From coast to coast, and especially *on* the coasts, (spectacularly, Florida and California), writing behavioral objectives has become a major activity and for some, a major worry.

At the moment, the worriers seem to be concentrated in departments of English. As one of the "humanistic" studies, English seems least amenable to reducing learning to observable events—the *sine qua non* of a good behavioral objective. The Commission on English Curriculum of NCTE has gone on record, not *against* behavioral objectives, but against a less than rigorous approach to writing them for English.

In the words of a resolution offered by the Commission and adopted and passed by the Board of Directors at the Washington convention in November 1969:

> While the Commission advocates that all teachers be open-minded about possible alternatives for defining and structuring the English curriculum— including the use of behavioral objectives—at the same time it urges caution.

Both within the Commission and within the Board of Directors, there were substantial numbers who would have taken a stronger negative stance on the writing of behavioral objectives for the English language arts. In the words of one widely-known scholar in English education, "Once you begin to play the game of writing behavioral objectives, you have lost the game to the systems people and the educational-industrial juggernaut." This statement implies that consequent on a behavioral definition of the subject would be a highly mechanistic approach to education, an overwhelming focus on skills, a denigration of the "men-

FROM *Minnesota English Journal*, Vol. 6 (Fall 1970), pp. 3–11. Reprinted by permission of the publisher and the author.

talistic" emphasis on attitudes and feelings which has been near the core of English teaching for decades, and, ultimately a sharp shift in curriculum.

What's a Behavioral Objective?

To draw such a response from an eminent man, a behavioral objective must be pretty insidious. What, after all, is a behavioral objective? Seen in the usual examples, a behavioral objective looks pretty innocuous. A behavioral objective merely states that, upon completion of a certain set of curriculum materials and activities, a student will be able to do something he could not do before such work.

To be more explicit, an example might help.

1
Given a play by Shakespeare, the student will be able

2　　　　　　　　　　3
to state the locale of the play accurately.

Note that the objective has three parts: a *condition* which more or less describes "the test," an *action* by the learner relevant to the subject-matter at hand, and a *quality criterion,* or a statement of how well the student will be able to do on the test.

The objective (and we admit it's a trivial one) does not require that the student read the play (nor does it prohibit him), but merely requires that he do something observable (i.e. state the locale). The great emphasis in behavioral objectives writing is stating an action that can be observed so that one can tell whether or not the student has indeed learned something.

The word *accurately* in the objective (which could be interpreted as *correctly* in this case) tells how the student should be expected to perform. In some objectives, a percentage might be stated, such as "95% of the time." This is to allow for reasonable inaccuracy.

It should be noted, however, that the quality criterion in behavioral objectives is usually quite high (85% to 95% being the ordinary range). This is done on the grounds that if an objective is worth going after, then it ought to be one that the student does attain. The ordinary passing grade of 70% would be thought much too low to be tolerable.

It is also consequent in the logic of behavioral definitions of a subject that the student is to succeed. It is implied that one ought not set forth objectives unless students are going to attain them, and it is incumbent on planners and teachers to grant that failure is in the teaching, not the learning. The student must be able to do something new and do it well. If he doesn't, then some recycling and/or retooling must take place until he does.

Another aspect of behavioral objectives is that, when correctly written, they ought not be tied to specific teaching materials, such as "The student is able to spell all the words in the X Speller 90% of the time." This openness of statement permits a multi-materials approach to mastery of a concept or skill, though, in operation, a local district might indeed tie instruction to a specific material, with alternative materials used when the student fails to attain criterion after using the basic material.

So What's a Behavioral Objective For?

Behavioral objectives are essentially a new way of stating the curriculum of a subject. English teachers have for many years tended to state curriculum objectives as descriptions of what the teacher would be doing (e.g. teach the Spenserian sonnet), for certain purposes (enlarge student understanding of prosodic forms), in hope of affecting attitudes (help students appreciate the genius of our poetic heritage). Perhaps the illustration is a bad one, but an examination of most curricula reveals this essential focus on the teacher's actions and objectives.

In behavioral objectives writing, on the other hand, the focus of attention is completely on the student. The objective states what the student will be able to do, not what he will experience (the activities) nor what the teacher will do.

The behavioral objective breaks broad objectives into smaller concrete objectives. It also demands that the teacher demonstrate that the student has mastered the objectives. Furthermore, it tells the learner specifically what he will be able to do, and the argument goes that he will perform better if he knows what the teacher will be expecting of him.

The behavioral objective also represents a shift away from "norm" evaluation (how well can he read compared with his age mates) and toward "criterion" evaluation (Can he read a newspaper with 90% comprehension of news stories?) Reading "at grade level" is no longer enough.

In advanced conditions, the behavioral objective is a critical element in the use of individualized instruction. In operation of such instruction, the teacher would first find out whether the student already possesses the skill. If he doesn't, then he pursues the subject matter; if he already possesses control over the objective, he goes on to work on other objectives.[1]

The virtue of behavioral objectives in such instances is that the teacher and the student can know quite precisely whether the student

[1] John C. Flanagan, "Visions of the Future Schoolroom," in *On Writing Behavioral Objectives for English,* edited by John Maxwell and Anthony Tovatt (Champaign: National Council of Teachers of English, 1970), pp. 61–69.

has succeeded. The skill of detecting the major metaphors in Antony's speech is much more readily checkable than "appreciating" Elizabethan drama. One you can measure, and the other is almost impossible to assess. (We almost always assume the student doesn't appreciate Elizabethan drama when we start the Shakespeare unit, don't we?)

Behavioral objectives are fundamentally important to the development of programmed instruction, to systematic analysis of the learning process in a classroom, and to the development of computer-assisted and computer-managed instruction. The entire advance of the so-called technology of education is predicated on precise statements of the behavioral objectives of the educational process.

Some of those who see spectres in the behavioral objectives movement frequently cite the growth in recent years of a desire for "accountability" in schooling. A giant fortune goes into local schools each year, and, for better or worse, it is almost impossible to tell who is responsible for success or failure and even whether the process succeeds. We're all familiar with the chain of responsibility which goes back to the parents and to the society in general when failure in learning occurs, but buck passing is no longer acceptable.

It is given that specificity of objectives will permit "accountability." The superintendent will know who is responsible for the fact that a youngster has failed to acquire a certain skill because he knows where that skill was taught and by whom. It doesn't follow, of course, that finding a locus of failure means that someone will be fired. More probably (we are assured) it means that steps can be taken to boost support to that aspect of curriculum or method to assure that future failure rate can be lessened on that particular skill. The administrator and the teacher will have a better idea what needs to be done if the specificity of objectives is high.

It seems fair to say that those who advocate behavioral objectives and "accountability" are after the same goals that teachers espouse: better education for the kids.

Administrators generally favor objectives written in the behavioral mode because they are capable of ready translation to the public. If the superintendent can tell the public rather precisely what is being accomplished at the school, it follows that people will be more likely to support the school, usually with money.

But, beyond administration, numbers of department chairmen and teachers find value in writing and using of objectives that state clearly what is to be accomplished. In one Indiana high school, the faculty has enthusiastically cited the clarity of behavioral objectives as the means by which the department has found agreement on what each member is supposed to do.

Indeed, many observers have noted that the advantage of using behavioral objectives is their capacity to increase clarity and thereby communicability of curriculum objectives not only among professionals but also to students and the public. A few feel that this alone is enough to justify the use of behavioral objectives in curriculum planning, that improvement of instruction is bound to follow this clarity even if no further steps are taken.

But most of the advocates of behavioral objectives would not stop at clarity of statement. The overriding objective is individualized instruction, the use of "learning packs" (or contracts) and a rather radically altered function of the teacher. In its more advanced form, the vision is one in which students are largely (but not exclusively) working on their own, in accord with their own progress sheets, under the guidance of the teacher who is not (was he ever?) a dispenser of information. The teacher, through this "technology," is the manager of a learning situation; he is aided in the less intricate aspects of his work by sub-professionals, prompted and guided by data from a computer or its near-equivalent, and spends the bulk of his time in individual contact with students. In the vision, mass teaching disappears.

Who's Against Behavioral Objectives?

A few people can be counted as instinctively against anything that they have not seen before. Stasis and comfort and a show-me attitude prevent this group from responding to any innovation. (Perhaps because they've been burned too many times by the latest enthusiasm which is, usually, built on a research base of sand.)

But a great many teachers are responsive to the notion of individualized instruction. The idea (if not the fact) of bringing each student to his maximum potential has a long history in pedagogy and seems in accord with the democratic ideal. Any plan which promises a step toward individualized instruction within reasonable expenditure of time and effort will be received with interest. Team teaching, for example, was thought such a step because large-group instruction offered opportunities to work with students in small groups while the large classes met. (That it didn't always work that way is beside the point.)

The link between individualized instruction and behavioral objectives allows the latter to come center stage for consideration because the former is attractive. And here the trouble begins.

James Moffett is perhaps the most outspoken of those who are dismayed at the national trend toward "systems" approaches to education, including behavioral objectives, computer assisted and managed instruction, and undergirding notions of stimulus-response psychology. He gives behavioral objectives short shrift: "As an exercise in clear thinking, it might be a helpful thing for English teachers to write behavioral objectives—and then throw them away."[2] The action of writing objectives in this manner, he believes, might do something to ameliorate our tendency to be more "fuzzy-headed" than teachers of science or mathematics, but we should stop far short of actually using behaviorally stated objectives.

Moffett and others argue that the insistence of measurability in behavioral objectives leads to the loss of intangible but important goals. Most critics grant that some parts of the discipline do lend themselves to objective observation (e.g. spelling, punctuation, capitalization, and, possibly, handwriting). But major problems arise in even the relatively overt objectives of written composition. Defining "good" writing has ever been a plaguy matter, and a behavioral assertion that the student after instruction will write "good" prose becomes accordingly slippery.

While it may be attractive to avoid the question "what is good writing" by specifying that the learner will demonstrate those behaviors which are possessed by admittedly excellent writers (e.g. adapts style to audience, states a purpose, puts forth a logical scheme for development of the idea, etc.), we know that writers consistently violate the rules that they and the rule books establish—yet do so with effectiveness. And further, we know that recognized writers with the full quiver of such behaviors can also write "bad" writing on occasion.

There are probably ways out of this problem, for in composition there is a visible product and the behaviors of the fledgling water can be observed and improved. But in the matter of literature, the hardest of the objections to behavioral objectives are voiced.

To a degree, literature does lend itself to behavioral specificity. Recognizing metaphors, writing a precis which corresponds with the original, stating the plot outline, listing the various metrical schemes used in the 17th century, and other factual matters can be handled in the behavioral mode. The New Criticism was itself, in part, an attempt to be specific about literature.

James Hoetker[3] has observed that learning can be characterized as can-do, may-do, and will-do behaviors. The can-do behaviors would cover the items in the preceding paragraph—skills and knowledge. The may-do behaviors are those lying at the higher levels of the so-called cognitive domain—the application of abstractions in novel situations, analysis, synthesis and evaluation—behaviors which occur of course, but for which there are few reliable gauges for determining quality of work. Teachers constantly evaluate the performance of

2 James Moffett, "Misbehaviorist English: A Position Paper," ibid., p. 111.
3 "Limitations and Advantages of Behavioral Objectives in the Humanities," ibid., pp. 49–50.

students in these higher cognitive skills, but the reliability of their yardsticks could hardly be called constant, and only constant measures will do.

The will-do behaviors that Hoetker classifies are those which manifest themselves "down the line." Does the student continue to read after he leaves school, does he read quality literature, does he find pleasure in language, does he act responsibly toward others, does he participate in his society in a positive way? These questions are first of all fuzzy and very dependent on the values of the observer, and, second, they occur in the "real world" of the students' lives long after they have left the school. All that can be known of will-do behaviors are certain signs and hints that the behaviors exist in the repertoire of the student while at school. Whether he *will*, indeed, manifest those behaviors simply cannot be known, at least not within the present schemes for evaluating the attainment of behavioral objectives.

Measurement and evaluation are the chief stumbling block, even for those who urge that the profession use the behavioral mode for stating outcomes of instruction. Indeed, the Tri-University Project, under the direction of J. N. Hook, which is attempting to write a sample of responsible behavioral objectives for English, has begun its work with an assertion that "objectives must not be derived from, or be centered on, evaluation—especially as evaluation is traditionally and narrowly conceived.[4]

One of the most treasured of the objectives of English instruction is response to literature, what J. N. Hook has characterized as the "gleam in the student's eye."[5] This is the "turn on" which results when a student has had a strong personal interaction with a work of literature, when he is excited, when he feels deeply about himself and his condition and the condition of others. Clearly, this is the affective domain, beyond, in complexity and mystery, those skills and knowledges of higher order in the cognitive domain.

Teachers of English are especially incensed when the suggestion is made that if you cannot state in behavioral terms what the "gleam" or the response means, then it does not exist. Each of them (we hope) has experienced the same response, and each has seen it occur in others. But it is difficult to characterize with precision, if at all.

It is at this point that communication between English teachers and systems people breaks down. The realm of skill is relatively easy to describe behaviorally. Both sides admit that the realms of affection pose problems. While the systems person might prefer to avoid the problem, the English teacher cannot ignore it, for the production of

4 Donald A. Seybold, "A Response to 'Misbehaviorist English,'" ibid., p. 118.
5 J. N. Hook, "The Tri-University BOE Project: A Progress Report," ibid., p. 77.

response to literature may be what brought him into English teaching in the first place and continues to be a major object of his work.

The Commission on the English Curriculum of NCTE worried, among other aspects of the problem, particularly about events which might occur when the English teacher and the systems advocate would cease to talk about the affect of literary experience. The danger, in such an instance, of abandoning or de-emphasizing classroom activity aiming toward response to literature is a real one. If both sides abandon thought about the objective, then much is lost from the curriculum and a distorted curriculum will result. The Commission advised the profession that when faced with the obligation (or the task) of writing behavioral objectives, that the writers: "(a) make specific plans to account for the total English curriculum; (b) make an intention to preserve . . . [the] important humanistic goals of education; and (c) insist on these goals regardless of whether or not there exist instruments . . . for measuring the desired changes in pupil behavior."[6]

The position of the Commission, though urging caution on the topic of behavioral objectives, did not proscribe this mode of curriculum planning; but neither did it grant, by any means, that it is "the" answer to improved instruction as most of its proponents (and apparently the U.S. Office of Education) believe.[7]

The Commission has left the door open for responsible development of behavioral objectives but has warned that it is not a task to be undertaken lightly nor by lightweights. Writing behavioral objectives for English is a demanding intellectual task because of the complexity of the subject and its concern with the affective domain. Isabel Beck[8] has argued that there is no inherent conflict between systems people and the humanistic aims of English teaching. She grants only that there are sizable problems in stating what it is that we mean, in such a way that a systems person can get hold of the objective so that planning can take place. Moffett and others, on the other hand, argue that there is no way to "win" the behavioral objectives game, and we'd better stay out of it.

Such a course, in most school districts, will become increasingly impossible, for behavioral objectives are "in" and promise to be "in" for some time to come. At the least, a cautious attitude is necessary, for much of value in the curriculum can be lost by giving away the hard-to-measure, the intangible, and, yet, withal the important goal.

6 Commission on the English Curriculum, NCTE. Resolution to the Board of Directors, ibid., pp. ix–x.

7 Sue M. Brett, "The Federal View of Behavioral Objectives," ibid., pp. 43–47.

8 "Towards Humanistic Goals through Behavioral Objectives," ibid., pp. 97–105.

On the other hand, a head-in-the-sand approach is bound to be disastrous. The ubiquitous "others" will write our goal statements for us if we don't, and we may cry "extortion" if they do, but the task will have been done, and more's the harm. But there is hope if the English teacher gets himself informed, learns the information needed to create the forms of behavioral objectives, tries his hand at them, earnestly writes them as far as he can go, and then says, "Stop, this can go no further."

If these things happen, I think there's nothing to fear from behavioral objectives. There may, in fact, be much to learn about ourselves, about our subject, and about our teaching.

ACCOUNTABILITY IN SECONDARY ENGLISH

C. W. Hembree

C AN the demand for accountability and the use of behavioral objectives be applied in the field of English? Proponents of the behaviorist movement somehow leave us with the relatively unqualified assurance that they can, and this has been the case since the movement's inception.

Nicholson's article[1] in *American Secondary Education* is typical of the advocacy of performance objectives that leaves the reader basking in the overly optimistic assurance that education's problems are now all but solved. Let me hasten to say that I have no quarrel with what Nicholson has written; his enumeration and explanation of the three domains of learning, though brief, are accurate as is his discussion of behavioral objectives. Rather, what he has failed to elaborate upon is at issue here. His failure, as with so many others writing in the area of performance and accountability, may be attributed to the general nature of his exposition. That is, when discussed in general terms, the inherent difficulties in application are easy to underestimate, and hence those who have the responsibility for implementing accountability theories—administrators, department heads, and teach-

[1] Everett Nicholson, "Secondary School Leadership Thrusts into Performance Accountability," *American Secondary Education,* I (December 1970), 25–28.

➤➤➤➤➤➤➤➤➤➤➤➤➤➤➤➤➤➤➤➤➤➤➤➤➤➤➤➤➤➤➤➤➤➤

F R O M *American Secondary Education* (March 1971), pp. 11–14. Reprinted by permission of the publisher and the author.

ers—are frequently left with a false sense of their universal and un-
complicated applicability. This can yield unfortunate results.

Perhaps it is appropriate, then, to attempt to cut through the cloud
of generalities to some of the problems and implications of using behavioral objectives in English. For English, as with the humanities
in general, does not fit the stereotype of the round peg that fits into
the square hole of accountability. To shave the peg to fit would be
to alter, *i.e.* eliminate, some or all of the worthmaking characteristics
of the content of English. This is patently undesirable. The alternative is to make the hole less square. To appreciate why the latter is
the preferable course for English, we need briefly to examine the
background of the problem and some of the specifics affecting the
use of performance objectives in English.

Although behavioral and performance objectives have been a subject
of discussion and debate for at least the last ten years, only recently has
the field of English felt, in any comprehensive way, the demand to
couch learning outcomes in terms of expected student behavior. This
increased pressure led Hogan,[2] Executive Secretary, National Council of
Teachers of English, to point out that the most disturbing problem in
English today is proving that English does make a difference in the lives
of people. Thus the point at which the discipline of English finds itself
now is roughly analogous to the emotional and fearful response teaching machines elicited a few years ago and to the more current but
similar problems of computer assisted instruction.

Several factors in combination are working to sustain the reticence and
suspicion which characterize the English educator's attitude toward performance objectives. One group of factors is common to teachers as a
class and is largely attitudinal—fear, pride, etc. Another group is unique
to teachers of English because of the nature of the material with which
they deal. Without any real attempt to differentiate between the classes,
let me list some of the inhibiting factors which face those who would
implement instructional objectives in English.

First, if I may make a diagnosis, the threat of behavioral objectives
puts English teachers on the defensive because they have not been able
to prove empirically that they are achieving meaningful results. Given
that the use of behavioral objectives yields demonstrable results, and
even accepting the premise that some pupils are inherently, genetically
ill-equipped to gain mastery over the many skills and states of mind
subsumed under the title "English," acceptance of behavioral objectives
in English would be an admission of failure. That charges of failure are
as old as Methuselah and are a matter of public record makes it no

---

[2] Robert F. Hogan, "Toward New Priorities in the Teaching of English," Presented
at the Fourth General Session, *The Thirteenth Annual Conference on the English
Language Arts in the Secondary School,* Indiana University, July 11, 1969.

easier to accept responsibility for the Johnny's who cannot read; rather, teachers seem to have accepted the "Mad" magazine mentality, and in some sense at least, have indorsed it, saying in effect, "Well, at least they are reading something." This, it seems, is a kind of sublimation of guilt which the demand for accountability forces to painful consciousness.

Popham[3] has isolated eleven of the plethora of objections to behavioral objectives. Five of these seem to be major objections or are particularly applicable to English. First the objection is made that trivial behaviors are the easiest for which to write objectives. These, primarily cognitive, will be the ones attention will focus upon at the expense of the real ends of English education. Next is the objection that insisting upon measurability leads to standard behavior and this is mechanistic and dehumanizing and thereby in direct opposition to the aims of English. Third, in the fine arts and the humanities, it is difficult to identify measurable pupil behavior. Fourth, teachers can be evaluated in terms of how well their pupils have learned; but as Popham points out, this kind of evaluation reduces the effects of personality on the evaluation.[4] McNeil[5] lends credence to the foregoing. In an experiment with student teachers of English and their supervisors, he hypothesized that by using behavioral objectives, mutually arrived at, supervisors would perceive their student teachers as more effective in the classroom than would the supervisors whose student teachers did not use behavioral objectives. Results not only supported the hypothesis but revealed that pupils in the experimental group made greater gains in punctuation than did the control group. While evaluation as an objection might thus be laid to rest, the others do not fall so easily. Performance objectives in this study once again demonstrated their effectiveness in the cognitive domain, but certainly not in the affective.

The final objection to be mentioned claims that peripheral learning outcomes, possibly more important than the specified ones, may be overlooked. Popham[6] claims that alertness negates this possibility. Atkins,[7] however, convincingly argues that there is some doubt that we either know or can identify all the objectives toward which teaching aims. For every specified objective, in other words, there are numerous other out-

3 James W. Popham, "Probing the Validity of Arguments Against Behavioral Goals," *Current Research on Instruction*, ed. Richard C. Anderson, et al., (Englewood Cliffs, N.J.: Prentice Hall, Inc., 1969), pp. 66–67.

4 Ibid., p. 69.

5 John D. McNeil, "Concomitants of Using Behavioral Objectives in the Assessment of Teacher Effectiveness," *The Journal of Experimental Education*, (1967), pp. 36, 69–74.

6 Popham, op. cit., p. 71.

7 Myron J. Atkins, "Behavioral Objectives in Curriculum Design: A Cautionary Note," *The Science Teacher* (May, 1968), pp. 27–30.

comes of which we are either unaware or only dimly aware. By focusing on a given objective, then, we may overlook other beneficial outcomes. Suppose a teacher assigns a composition, the behavioral objective of which is to write a 250-word composition addressed to the pupils' peers on a free subject, within a 30-minute time limit and containing no grammatical errors.

Assuming that prior instruction has concentrated on appropriate grammar usage and that some prior practice has been given in writing within a time limit, it becomes clear that the teacher's goal is to have pupils produce an error-free composition. Evaluation necessarily is restricted to the paper's grammar. But what of content? Have the pupils demonstrated originality, freshness and clearness of diction? Is the teacher to ignore these areas and award a grade on the basis of grammar alone? What of other learning outcomes that may ride in the same saddle: the intense dislike of writing that may result, or, conversely, the intense self-satisfaction in a job well done? Will these peripheral outcomes, as Atkins fears, atrophy or remain uncorrected from lack of attention? To these and similar questions, Popham does not seem to have addressed himself convincingly.

These and other objections voiced over the years, plus the fact that the important desired outcomes in English, especially literature, are affective in nature, resulted in the National Council of Teachers of English taking a position.[8] While that position is not overtly anti-accountability, it does voice a strong note of caution by urging that those who would implement behavioral objectives plan to account for the whole English curriculum, fight to retain the humanistic goals of education, and insist on these goals despite the lack of evaluative instruments to measure them.

The Council's position, of course, will not halt the movement of accountability and behavioral objectives into the field of English. Lazarus and Knudson,[9] for example, have published a set of objectives for use in grades 7–12. While these objectives are not, in any strict sense of the word, behavioral, they do represent a major attempt to catagorize those areas that traditionally have been the concern of English. Furthermore, the federally funded Tri-University Project (Indiana, Purdue, and Illinois) is currently developing a catalog of representative behavioral objectives for grades 9–12 which will probably be published this year. In addition, individual school systems over the past few years have begun curriculum revisions using behavioral objectives as the base. These efforts plus the numerous general books dealing with writing objectives that are

[8] Resolution "On the Need for Caution in the Use of Behavioral Objectives in the Teaching of English," *Convention Concerns*—1969, Fifty-Ninth Annual Meeting of the NCTE, (November 27–29, 1969), p. 5.

[9] Arnold Lazarus and Rozanne Knudson, *Selected Objectives for the English Language Arts, Grades 7–12* (New York: Houghton Mifflin Co., 1967).

gradually finding their way into the hands of English teachers, plus the instruction new teachers are receiving from their methods classes, all point to a growing effect on English.

And perhaps this is as it should be, for there can be no doubting that very real results are being achieved in other disciplines through the use of behavioral tools. But there are some conclusions that ought to be considered by teachers of English and curriculum planners. First, the charge is fact that very real limitations obtain in terms of the blanket application of behavioral objectives to English. Second, not only are the problems of identifying peripheral outcomes real, but overcoming the inherent tendency to operationalize trivial behavior will require extreme caution. In addition, English teachers and curriculum writers must recognize that even though not all outcomes are measurable, they nevertheless may be worthwhile. In this connection, the affective domain with which English teachers are concerned has not been defined sufficiently to guarantee measurable achievement. The worthwhile task of teaching for the aesthetic appreciation of literature, for example, is often a trackless wilderness in which teachers must follow intuition and the few vague signs left by those who have gone before. Until the terrain is mapped each teacher must be his own cartographer, carefully and intelligently mapping his way. Nevertheless, despite the unanswered questions regarding the use of behavioral objectives, their obvious successful use in other disciplines cannot be ignored.

Three levels or modes of operation offer themselves to those who may be thinking of writing objectives in English. The first mode consists of identifying a specific, low-level learning outcome the planner believes desirable. Then he must write an objective that identifies the behavior act, defines the important conditions (the givens, restrictions, and limitations), and clearly states the criterion of acceptable performance.[10] For example, assume a teacher believes it important for a pupil to be able to identify the metaphor in literature. An appropriate statement of such an objective might read: "Given an unfamiliar poem (paragraph, short story, etc.) containing ten metaphors, pupils will be able to identify and write a minimum of eight within a fifteen minute period."

Obviously this is a low-level outcome, but one that is prerequisite to literary analysis and perhaps even to a greater appreciation of literature as a whole. The point here is that any given cognitive skill can, in isolation, be couched in behavioral terms.[11] More appropriate and realistically, however, such behavior ought to be considered as en route behavior —some skill or knowledge that is prerequisite to a later, terminal be-

10 Robert F. Mager, *Preparing Instructional Objectives,* Fundamental Research Laboratory, Xerox Corp., Fearon Publishing, Palo Alto, Calif., 1962.

11 James Popham and Eva L. Baker, *Planning an Instructional Sequence* (Englewood Cliffs, N.J.: Prentice Hall, Inc., 1970), p. 10.

havior. Used out of the context of some broader goal, such isolated objectives become ends in themselves and hence are of limited and even of doubtful value.

The second level is for teachers to approach the problem from the overall English curriculum. In other words, start from the top. This approach would be in keeping with the NCTE resolution. But the approach is simply not feasible for individual classroom teachers for it requires an analysis of all the general goals of the total English program and a systematic, cause-and-effect relationship to be determined. From such an analysis and determination, appropriate equivalent and analogous practice and en route behaviors can be decided upon which will lead to the ultimate terminal behaviors the curriculum planners have decided to be worthwhile. This method of using behavioral objectives is by far superior, for within a curriculum so devised, specific, low-level objectives would not be arbitrarily decided upon but rather would be an integral and necessary part of the whole. To be thoroughly and adequately done, such a program, assuming the necessary resources and free time for workers were available, would require from one to two years to write. To expect even this detailed and thoughtful treatment to eliminate the problems of non-quantifiable objectives, however, is expecting too much. They will not disappear and they are too important to ignore for the sake of the empirical verification of achievement.

In the absence of the necessary time and resources, department heads and individual classroom teachers may successfully employ the third option in short learning sequences of from two to four weeks. Such short units are manageable enough that, given patience and expertise in what is required, teachers can determine reasonable, overall performance goals. Once these have been formulated, a sequence of learning activities leading to the teacher's overall goals can be established. The question, "What does the learner need to be able to do before he can successfully meet the overall goals of the unit?" will yield the specific performance objectives that will comprise the sequential development of the unit.

Necessarily the step-by-step procedure and the inevitable difficulties associated with specificity in the affective domain have been glossed over. Similarly, the seriousness of the threat to relegate the affective domain to a trivial role because of the difficulty of measuring has been treated only lightly. However, it is this very point that raises the most serious doubts among English educators. Yet with this limitation in mind, curriculum planners may still approach the discipline of English with productive results as long as they do so with the necessary concern for the humanistic goals of English.

Evidence is abundant that the use of behavioral objectives can bring significant results. The limitations in their applicability to the whole discipline of English exists is no excuse for a collective burying of heads in the sand. Such action, in the idiom of the day, would be "a cop out" and would be less than fair to the thousands of pupils to whom English instruction is something to be borne but not absorbed.

In English, unlike the cognitive fields of math and the sciences, it will be no easy matter.

ABILITY GROUPING IN ENGLISH

Robert L. Kelly

I CONTINUE to be shocked by the way educators challenge, belittle, and condemn ability grouping. The clever person can puncture any system, but nobody has convincingly proved that ability grouping is unfair, undemocratic, or unsuccessful.

In this paper I will avoid references to other articles and selfishly explore my observations, beliefs, questions, and deep convictions about ability grouping in English. I suspect that grouping would be successful in other subjects, but tenth, eleventh, and twelfth grade English classes are my main focus here.

The English teacher's job is to become involved with students, react to their needs, interests, and abilities, and stimulate an exciting and healthy classroom experience. In a heterogeneous situation the teacher is forced to teach reluctant learners and the gifted together, plus numerous students with average skill. Can this be done well? A degree of success arises only when the teacher establishes his own rail system within the room. Then there is a partial instructor for each group.

Low-ability and high-sensitivity are strong co-partners. The slow learner can sense that he represents a deterrent to steady class progress. Often the teacher gives everybody the same test; here the ultimate D or F is the brand of failure which remains. Soon the lad rebels by skipping assignments or shooting a spitball. The teacher pounces upon this development and takes prompt disciplinary action. Now two strikes are blazing on the scoreboard. This boy has failed academically and socially. Desperate is his craving for attention, and the teacher finds himself in a real plight. The instructor either nags or ignores; either approach is harmful. The student is labeled as a person who "doesn't try, is impolite, and a general problem." And the mental block toward English grows stronger.

REPRINTED by permission from the May 1969 issue of *The Clearing House*.

Many teachers honestly admit that they can do little for the slow learner, but vow to pass him if he tries. In fact they even enlighten the student with this benevolence. But these kids abhor charity. Let the people who claim that grouping is artificial to true-life experiences (a statement which I will attack later) defend the realism of a system where 20 F's average a D—.

There are other teachers who pride themselves in possessing a deep knowledge of grammar, composition, and literature. These lofty scholars refuse to prostitute their standards for any laggard. Every test is graded on a strict, rigid percentage. Often these teachers will say they are sympathetic to the slow learner, but will actually refuse to extend even a grain of honest pity. And their favorite remark, which they might even believe, is, "Johnny could do better if he worked harder." There may be a spot for these teachers on a large college campus, but most assuredly not in a high school.

Low-Rail Classes

Many teachers complain about the difficulty of accurate placement in low-rail classes. Frankly, I have never recognized this as a major problem. True, there are borderline cases, but then the problem is simply this: Should the student excel somewhat in a low-rail class or struggle in an average class? The advanced low-rail candidate probably profits most from this class, for here he has an opportunity to forge into a leadership role and give a reasonable stimulus to the other members.

The claim is sometimes made that the low-rail class becomes a dumping ground for discipline cases. And let's be honest. A large number of students who are weak in language ability do rebel in numerous ways. A true teacher will want to reach them. However, with our repetitious English programs stamped with grammar and vocabulary drills, the recurrent theme on "My Favorite Hobby," and the book report every five weeks, the English teacher has not exactly discouraged the potential dropout. Mental blocks are not easily smashed. The answer is definitely not to pass the student "if he makes a reasonable effort." He needs a complete change—different materials, a highly informal, personal approach, and a chance to earn a B.

Skillful teaching of a low-rail class is an art. The teacher must be extremely sympathetic and imaginative and one who truly knows that the real joy in the classroom is giving the student joy. Traditionally, the vast majority of strugglers in English classes have been boys. Since stimulated discussion sessions should be a major educational goal, I would favor the male with a background in hunting, fishing, football, car repairing, and radio tinkering. I am not saying that a woman cannot do a sparkling job in an all-male class; however, the instructor must be a colorful, dynamic soul who can dive deeply into and outside of a story's meaning.

Each year I hear the comment, "Why don't we take turns and pass the low-rail classes around?" I deplore this suggestion and for two obvious reasons. First, it implies quite strongly that this is a wretched class and second, it implies that anyone can handle the assignment well. A low-rail class incorrectly taught becomes an intensified experience in frustration; taught correctly, it becomes a pleasant revelation of limited success.

In reaching the low-ability performers, the teacher must dare to be different. Under no circumstances should he use textbooks suitable for higher-level groups. Furthermore, he should scrap the ponderous literature anthology, shelve any grammar books, and stop using any drill sheets, prepared examinations, or workbooks. Scholastic goals should be limited to oral and written proficiency and reading progress. Certainly an S. R. A. Reading Laboratory is a must. Although numerous sets of paperbacks designed for reluctant readers should be purchased, discretion of choice must be exercised. These students are very sensitive to childish or patterned stories. Poe, London, Saki, and Bradbury stories should have widespread appeal for four main reasons: The stories are short, display a rapid movement, are highly imaginative, and have an explosive ending.

The selection of novels is also a tricky challenge. Don't use an adapted classic unless you can forget your deep acquaintance with the unabridged version. For example, one of my favorite novels is *Moby Dick,* and I found minor frustration in handling the adapted version as an exciting whaling yarn. Like short stories, the novels should be short and ripple with movement. Three distinct possibilities are *The Red Pony, Shane,* and *The Call of the Wild.* Records, filmstrips, and movies should be interspersed skillfully throughout the semester. Scholastic's *Scope Magazine* is a masterpiece for this group. Each copy has pertinent and diversified articles by people who write in a refreshing, simple, and direct manner.

The Three-Track System Defended

Before I discuss the high-rail classes, I would like to address the critics who label grouping as undemocratic, stereotyped, and artificial.

At no time should a student be forced into a special section. Teachers and counselors, however, do have a professional obligation to guide selected students into special classes. The counselor and teacher must support one another harmoniously. Occasionally, educators use students as ammunition to prove personal or professional convictions; and this is a tragedy. The curriculum of each section should be available to teachers, counselors, students, and parents. Ultimately the decision for change must be the student's. Most strugglers welcome an opportunity to enter a section more compatible to their skills; however, around 20 per cent of the high-ability students will decide to by-pass the challenges of an honors group. Common reasons are too much work, an otherwise difficult schedule, a lack of interest, and honor roll pressure. These reasons must be accepted.

Upon hearing people classify grouped students as one intellectually stereotyped clump, I quiver with annoyance. Even in a multiple-track system the wide ability range demands special treatment for the individual. There are slower students who prefer the average class, and gifted students who also prefer the average class. Never will a teacher have all the "slow" students in low-rail classes; neither will he have all the "fast" students in high-rail classes. The middle-rail classes are not settings of intellectual mediocrity. I would keenly challenge this statement: "The real loser in the three-track system is the 68 per cent of the youngsters in the middle rail. They dearly need the high-rail people to push them along." High-average students will shortly be waving hands, and a few brighter ones will in turn be challenging them. I am amazed at the perceptive comments of my low-rail students. Here I could easily find another three rails. These students, however, now have a healthier atmosphere for mental exploration.

The grouping program suffers from a cluster of poor words. *Rail system* connotes rigidity; *easy English,* a childish game of word toss; and *slow learner,* a plodder who will eventually reach the finish line. Rigidity has no place in any grouping system. Teachers should willingly exchange students throughout the entire semester. This class will not be an easy course because that stamp indicates comparison with other classes. The slow learner can be the fast learner in an atmosphere that challenges his ability. Let's obliterate all these words and give the three sections different numbers. English 101 is far preferable to any descriptive word.

Are these special classes artificial situations in the cold eyes of realistic society? For several years this question has precipitated considerable personal observation. I am now convinced that the striking single criterion for social grouping is academic ability. Grouping is a social phenomenon that floods our country. Frankly, the ungrouped classes are, I believe, the artificial situations.

High-Rail Groups

My next specific concern is the high-rail group. These groups are neither less important nor easier to teach than the low-rail groups. Expert and challenging guidance is a major function of the instructor of this class. He must be an academic master and know his material perceptively, imaginatively, and questioningly. He himself must thoroughly enjoy the stimulation of vigorous and prolonged research. He must allow ample room for intellectual expansion, but set definite standards for scholastic excellence. Above all, the teacher must not parallel this class with an average section. Here is a pressing temptation. The instructor will give similar assignments with the rationalization of "probing more deeply into the lesson."

Unless the teacher presents these students with a full opportunity to expand intellectually, he is shirking a professional obligation. By using courageous individualism to tackle complex assignments, the instructor will be amazed at the accurate responses. The ability range of many of these students is unlimited. Don't become upset by the passing thought that some exceed you in intellectual potential. Most assuredly they probably do, but you can still be instrumental in sharpening, refining, and channelling this relatively raw brilliance. When you cannot answer a question, don't try to lose the pupil in a mass of verbal spaghetti. Confess your ignorance and promise to ferret forth the information for the next day. These kids are experts at spotting a phony.

Critics have stated that average sections suffer because of the absent intellects, but I have seen other students burst into prominence and become more effective leaders. In a cross-country race the lad ten yards ahead presents a better stimulus to the pack than the far-distant runner.

Identification for Grouping

Many teachers complain that students are not chosen accurately for special English classes. Apparently they feel that any mistake is irreparable. However, to err in placement is possible. If a student flounders in an average section, he should be quickly switched to a low-rail group. This is not an upsetting procedure, unless the teachers choose to make it so.

But now to specifics of identification. A low-rail candidate in English will usually exhibit these signs: I. Q. of 90 or less; test scores below the 26th percentile in language areas; a rather steady diet of D's in English and history classes; a poor reading rate. A high-rail candidate will often show these signs: I. Q. of 118 or more; test scores above the 70th percentile in language areas; a steady diet of A's or B's (some teachers absolutely refuse to be generous with A's) in English and history classes; a high reading rate.

There are exceptional cases and no criteria should be binding. Perhaps the best single basis for selections, however, is the composition. Of course, this is unreliable if the school system does not have a sequential program for language learning. An incredible number of sophomores have never written a theme.

Grading Clarified

An English department should formulate a careful philosophy of grading. I once heard an instructor say that even though a lad might do "perfect" work in low-rail, he would assign no grade higher than C since this level of work was still academically deficient. Occasionally a high-rail instructor will "challenge" the youngsters by instituting an incredibly hard grading system. A real problem does develop when students receive 98 in average English, while others do better work and receive 90 in the honors group. The assignment of a grade must be fair. To penalize a student gradewise because of his membership in a special section is to surround that class with a dismal stigma.

I advocate composition work in low-rail classes; therefore, a final grade of A would be a surprise here. This student should be considered for advancement, but not arbitrarily forced ahead. If he is responding well, to tamper with success might be to invite renewed frustration. I am assuming, of course, that the initial placement was accurate. If a low-rail class is functioning well, C's and B's should be the predominant grades. A D should never represent more than minimum achievement.

Teachers of honors classes should set high standards; yet every student who does acceptable work should receive an A. B's should be assigned to students whose work is somewhat deficient. C students should be returned to the average group. Unless a teacher gives 75 per cent A's and 25 per cent B's, his system is too rigid.

To refuse to assign an A to a student in average English would be to commit an indirect comparison with honor students. The grading system of each section must be independent. The teacher who refuses to give an A in an average section has no more business instructing this class than does the honors teacher who must never exceed 20 per cent A's.

On all report cards the specific rail should be indicated. I am told that most colleges readily acknowledge the superiority of the A in honors English over the A in average English.

"Switching" Students

Some teachers are reluctant to transfer students to special groups. Often in honors classes the struggler will be permitted to stay "because he tries very hard and appears to be learning in spite of his low grades." Although this may be a noble and sincere gesture and an illustration of flexibility, I do question the decision. Is a continued struggle to match the group's level a procedure channelled to promote healthy attitudes toward the language? Perhaps the teacher is simply unwilling to "inconvenience" a few people with a schedule change. Is a possessiveness present here? Occasionally a teacher will remark, "These students were poorly selected. I could easily name seven who should be in average English." My snappy reply is always, "Then why don't you move them?" And the comeback: "Oh I have plenty of room and they are improving, so I think I'll wait awhile."

In an average section some teachers dread the thought of switching the gifted. Often they openly say, "Mary and Judy are discussion leaders and my only joy in the entire day. If I lose them the group will collapse." Are teachers entitled to such selfish thoughts? Mary and Judy are not on salary and probably don't enjoy being intellectual misfits. The two should at least receive a warm invitation to consider a schedule change. But their teachers are usually too busy pounding at the counselor's door to switch little Johnny, "who can't even write a sentence."

Truly exceptional cases arise that do merit exceptional attention. For example, if an eleventh grade student rebels against work, a switch to a low-rail class might arouse some response. Forget the previous placement criteria. Ability level is not the main focus here; an attitude problem must be met. Never will teachers crack severe mental blocks without severe changes. A new teacher, new class, new philosophy, new material, and a new hope. Yet this answer reechoes: "I won't reward Joe with a switch to an easier section. He can do the work, but simply refuses to try." I cannot guarantee success by this switch, but I can guarantee two points: (1) Joe's problem is not simple and (2) the teacher who says, "I've done everything possible for this boy," is not engaging in true confession.

Communication and Critics

Truly the major problem of ability grouping is that it lacks the full support of all English teachers. This attitude largely affects the other problem, lack of clear communication with parents. Without exception, I have discovered that parents who oppose grouping are the victims of misinformation. We must communicate our philosophy to the public via radio, newspaper, meetings, and letters. Seldom does the student give his parents accurate school information. One reason is that instructors rarely discuss the philosophy of the rail system with their classes. Also they are unwilling to justify assignments and state long-range and short-range goals to the students. Often parents believe that their children are being forced into special groups. They must be told that placement into a special class is a privilege, not a punishment. They must be convinced that the purpose of this program is to help their children learn the joy of true accomplishment. Then the foe often becomes a willing advocate, and the price may only be a 5-minute phone call.

Ability grouping is absolutely necessary in an English program. Certainly most low-rail youngsters will never learn to love English, but they will develop better oral and written skills. The high-rail student will have continued challenges to stretch his academic potential. And a skillful adjustment to individual differences in all the groups must continue.

In this program no one will suffer and the vast majority will gain. The people who criticize grouping have seldom been involved with the students in the classroom. These critics are unaware of the specialized teaching materials available for all ability levels. They refuse to acknowledge that when a principal says his teachers use "enrichment" to reach the extreme students, this simply means that the teachers do virtually nothing that is outlined, sustained, or evaluated. They have been swayed by the emotional remarks of the mediocre instructor. They have also demanded the results of special classes to be startlingly superior in academic achievement. Student satisfaction has never been a foremost concern. And they have not encouraged teachers to communicate with parents and clearly define the outline of this program.

Despite these loopholes, the critics have still failed to find clear proof that ability grouping is either useless or harmful. In fact, in some studies the experimenters hint that the system might be advantageous.

If the critics of ability grouping can construct a better program, I will happily study it. I would like to hear the advantages of heterogeneous grouping over homogeneous grouping. In ability grouping the students gain academically, socially, and emotionally. The set-up is now ideal for individualized instruction and specialized texts. Flexibility is still desirable and necessary, but now it is much easier.

And the students will be happier. Shouldn't that really be our main concern?

FLEXIBLE SCHEDULING: FACTS, FANTASIES, AND FADS

James J. Backen

W E live and teach in a deeply troubled society—a society perhaps on the brink of revolution. In the light of what is happening to people and to institutions in this country, that is neither a very profound nor a very enlightened statement. Yet, with riots and bombings and divisive rhetoric pervading the social scene, does it not seem rather

FROM *English Journal* (March 1971), pp. 363–372. Copyright © 1971 by the National Council of Teachers of English. Reprinted by permission of the publisher and James J. Backen.

mundane to gather in convention to discuss the topic of flexible scheduling? Or behavioral objectives? Or the structure of literature? Or the anatomy of composition?

What exotic language we educators have created to banter about in good company! What great fun to debate the veracity of this theory or that innovation! What delight we feel in the ancient tribal ritual of saluting the latest bit of euphemistic jargon! Does it really matter if the very people we serve understand our ritual language—or, for that matter, believe in it?

It also seems just a little anachronistic that we have come together here, on the threshold of the seventies, addressing ourselves to flexible scheduling, one of the great fads of the sixties. Of course, it is true that great fad has not yet wound itself down. Its growth, while hardly spectacular, has been persistent, and if we are not too soon overwhelmed with the latest exotics—behavior objectives, learning packages, and accountability—then the flexible scheduling fad may yet have some relevance.

I use the term "fad" not facetiously, but with both sincerity and sadness. There was a time in the early sixties when it seemed that flexible scheduling might help lead us out of our enslavement to narrow tradition in the teaching of language arts. It seemed that we owed a great deal to those geniuses who dared challenge the Carnegie Unit more than a decade ago, for they slew a Goliath that had long impeded genuine progress in coping with the individual differences among children. Certainly we have been talking about those differences and doing little about them for too long.

Unfortunately, somewhere along the line of progress too many people have forgotten that most important original premise of flexible scheduling—that *its primary purpose is to individualize and personalize learning for students.* In too many schools, in too many *minds,* flexible scheduling has become an end rather than a means, a master rather than a servant. Such misdirection would have accomplished damage enough without the glorifications we give to every new idea in education, a glorification which in this case has created in the eyes of the beholder either a savior or a monster. Of course, it is neither. Flexible scheduling is a mere tool, a system of arranging times and spaces and numbers, which can be used advantageously or abusively in a school program.

Recently, in the flexibly scheduled school in which I teach, a mother came to school with a list of complaints about her son's bad behavior at home—all of which could be traced, in her thinking, to our flexible schedule. The lady's inventory included all the following: a belligerent attitude, a penchant for lying, hyperactivity, smoking, and excessive masturbation. The lady, I think, gives far too much credit to flexible scheduling.

That's not surprising. Almost everyone overrates flexible scheduling. Because of our excessive claims for what a flexible schedule can do, it is natural for many parents to assume that it is also responsible for our failures and for the failures of their children. It is fundamental, I believe, to begin to examine with care some of the fantasies which the dream of flexible scheduling has generated, along with some of the facts which have been discovered by those who have experimented with it. There are nine rather common fantasies which seem to have grown out of the mystique that flexible scheduling has engendered. It is time that we explode some of these myths before they build any more expectations that cannot possibly be fulfilled by any scheduling scheme.

How do we love thee, flexible scheduling? Let me count the ways, beginning with *Fantasy Number One* which characterizes perhaps the most basic misunderstanding about flexible scheduling—that naive belief that all flexible schedules are flexible.

The fact is that computer generated schedules (and that is the nature of most so-called "flexible" schedules in this country) can be terribly inflexible. Although such schedules rearrange the traditional time segments and group sizes, ordinarily spacing them out over a weekly cycle, teachers and students and content are then frozen into that repetitive cycle throughout the year, regardless of day-to-day needs or desires. Flexible? Hardly! This is patent rigidity, wrapped in new window dressing. In such cases, the schedule ultimately dictates much of what can happen in the classroom. Perhaps it should not be surprising in a technologically oriented society that a system which has been designed to serve people may ultimately become the master of those people. In education particularly, human safeguards must be offered against the creeping encroachment of an impersonal technology.

A worthwhile flexible allotment of time and space to students and teachers must be designed by human beings to serve human beings. If a computer can serve as a helpful intermediary in this process, then let us be served by computers. But if a computer hinders our search for the means to administer individually to children's needs, then let us discard the computer and search for other means. Ultimately it is the people involved in a schedule who make it flexible or inflexible. If administrators and teachers and students are inclined to be adaptable, then a new kind of schedule can serve them flexibly. Otherwise we may as well retain or return to the traditional teaching/learning environment.

Fantasy Number Two promises that students will be so inspired by the adoption of a flexible schedule that they will universally love the pursuit of learning. As teachers we should know better than that. It usually takes people to inspire other people, and, while a *truly* flexible schedule may provide teachers with a better opportunity to inspire (or motivate) students, inspiration doesn't ever occur automatically or universally. We place a great deal of stock in the premise that children have a natural curiosity to learn, and although that may be generally true by itself, we are rarely willing to admit that schools, as we know them, are an unnaturally confining environment for children, and often unfriendly to genuine and natural curiosity. The school is, at best, an artificial context for facilitating the child's desire to learn. We can make it a better place, and flexible scheduling can help us make it a better place, but not automatically, not by itself, not without dramatically creative changes in adult assumptions about education.

That brings us to *Fantasy Number Three*, which is that a school can, with a flexible schedule, operate under the same set of assumptions about education and about human beings that conventional schools use. On the surface, conventional schools can appear successful even when they are not, simply on the basis of commonly used evaluative criteria that have no real validity. There has always been a tacit assumption in the secondary schools, for example, that silence and immobility are the earmarks of a good class and, therefore, a good teacher. More movement and more noise are inherent in a flexible schedule, immediately forcing a conflict of values on most teachers.

Furthermore, given the relative freedom to make choices, some students will at times reject certain classes and also certain teachers, who may find that they no longer have quite the same kind of captive audience. After all, we have rarely demonstrated that we trust students to be self-directed. Do we have the courage, then, to teach in a situation which cannot guarantee that our students will always show up for class?

Finally, by virtue of changing time blocks and group sizes, it becomes immediately apparent in a flexible schedule that many of our assumptions about how to approach the task of instruction simply do not hold up, and that some of our content itself must change.

Fantasy Number Four, then, implies that a flexible schedule allows teachers to teach the same content more effectively. And sadly enough that is precisely what happens in many schools which adopt flexible schedules. It would seem axiomatic that when we implement a flexible schedule to individualize instruction better, then we cannot teach the same content in the same way, simply because that content and those modes of instruction may be inappropriate and irrelevant for some students.

Even our marvelous newly discovered content cannot be taught indiscriminately to the large mass of students. Perhaps it was an unfortunate accident of fate that the growth of flexible scheduling during the sixties paralleled the great era of content rebuilding in the various disciplines. Thus, new schedules became a framework into which new content could be poured, and out of that unholy alliance have been conceived educational programs designed to serve content, rather than the needs of children. If we see flexible scheduling as merely a device to fit any content that we happen to be using into a more convenient time capsule, then it is not worth the effort and expense necessary to generate a new schedule and to train students and staff to its peculiarities.

Fantasy Number Five assumes that flexible scheduling automatically provides appropriate groupings of students. All of the failures of ability grouping over the years should have alerted teachers to the pitfalls of any educational group larger than one. How individualized is the large group lecture, that most damnable of all the many creatures spawned by flexible schedules? How much personal satisfaction does a student feel in a lab section which merely teaches a new grammar in an old way? Or, for that matter, how personalized is a small group discussion if it is dominated by a teacher, as many are?

The most important feature of a flexible schedule is the independent study time which it may build in to each student's schedule. It is during this time that we can catch the student at his leisure and work with him as an individual human being. But, groups by any other name are still groups, offering only a limited amount of educational advantage.

Fantasy Number Six is related to Fantasy Number Five. It dictates that the small groups made possible by flexible scheduling will magically result in student-centered discussions. Mere observation will often prove the contrary, a demonstration that many teachers do not know how to create a small group climate conducive to genuine student involvement. What results in many cases is the same teacher-centered lecture/question-answer sessions which dominate the traditional classroom. Thus, students are pawns again in the ancient game of deductive information-giving.

Fantasy Number Seven takes two forms. Stated one way, it says that students *are* mature enough to be responsible for their own learning. Stated another way, it says that students are *not* mature enough to be responsible for their own learning. Teachers and laymen alike use both of these forms of the fantasy, and both are false, simply by virtue of the fact that they are such gross generalizations.

It would be relatively simple to adjust to the needs of students in a flexible schedule if they fell into two groups—one group equally capable of being responsible and one group equally incapable of being responsible. The fact is that students, by virtue of their individual learning styles, fall along a wide scale of responsibility. This phenomenon demands a corresponding scale of systems within the flexible schedule to cope with these varying capacities to function effectively in an open school situation. Without systems which have the capability to control in various degrees the less responsible students and to free in various degrees the more responsible students, a flexible schedule can never fulfill its promise.

In addition, the first form of Fantasy Number Seven—that children *are* mature enough to be responsible for their own learning—has an underlying assumption that flexible schedules always provide youngsters with the freedom to be responsible. Unfortunately, in many flexibly scheduled schools the insulation of the educational womb prevails, so that young people are not allowed to make mistakes. In these schools opportunities for genuine student freedom are limited, and without freedom there can be little incentive for demonstrations of responsibility.

Fantasy Number Eight involves the feeling that a flexible schedule somehow makes the teacher's job easier. There is no way this can be true, unless the flexible schedule is not functioning effectively. The teacher's task may be more *appropriate* in a flexible schedule, but never easier. Team teaching, a requisite to flexible scheduling, is agonizingly more difficult. The onslaught of students, freed by an open schedule to seek out teachers for individual help, can be mentally, emotionally, and physically exhausting for the staff. The planning necessary to create new and more appropriate curriculums and teaching approaches demands even more of a dwindling supply of teacher time and energy. Routine record keeping is infinitely more difficult. More supervision is necessary.

Somewhere along the line, then, administrators and school boards must recognize that any real attempt to personalize instruction, to deal with students as individuals, will result in an increased pressure on the teaching staff, and, ultimately, a need for more staff.

Fantasy Number Nine states that "A flexible schedule is geared to the bright, the dull, the interested, and the disinterested." That direct quote from a book on flexible scheduling is flatly misleading. No kind of schedule, by itself, is geared to anything or anyone. Only creative academic programs, sensitive approaches to instruction, and the human desire to see children as individuals will turn our students on or turn them off. A schedule merely serves this larger interest in a minimal way.

These nine fantasies seem to represent much of the false ambition and loose thinking which are too often used to sell flexible scheduling. They cause untold damage to the concept itself, and unbelievable human frustrations in schools which adopt flexible schedules.

All of this must sound terribly anti-flexible schedule. Nothing could be less true. I am a firm advocate of flexible scheduling if it has been planned and implemented in a thoughtful and reasonable manner. However, it is true that I am tired of the popular view that flexible scheduling is some sort of saint or devil, set apart from the people in the school—indeed, *above* those people, dominating the entire school situation and dictating all the good or bad that happens there. It is also true that I am frightened by the condition of our country, and even more frightened by the ineffectual response that education has made to that condition. We teachers of language arts should be especially sensitive to the fact that a root cause of the social disorder in this country is the inability of people to communicate with each other. Communication, after all, is our bag. How have we responded to this most vital of human and social needs? Well, we have invented new grammars; we have fiddled with schedules; we have devised new ways to pursue our literary witch hunts; we have created a rhetoric of the sentence; we have apparently taught our people well how to toy with the language, to distort meaning, to enlarge misunderstanding, and to use the language as an instrument of gain and a weapon of deceit rather than as a tool of understanding and reconciliation. Certainly we have accomplished one thing—everybody knows what the term "rhetoric" means. And when some of our most distinguished Americans refer cynically to "keeping the rhetoric hot," we cannot help knowing that we have failed to teach many of our students over the years how to cope with the abuse of language.

Of course, blame cannot be laid entirely on those of us who teach language arts. But perhaps you can understand my impatience with the excessive expectations we attach to innovations in education. We cannot continue to grasp desperately at each gimmick-straw that emerges on the educational scene. We cannot continue to treat mechanical systems and abstract theories as panaceas for our difficulties. We can no longer afford to worship *things*.

Each tool that we use in our struggle to improve teaching performance, whether it be flexible scheduling or a new novel, learning packages or the latest composition transparencies—each of these *things* must be touched with human warmth, must be regarded as an extension of the human mind and the human heart. We must return to people as our primary point of focus, rather than centering on content and the mechanical apparatus we use to exploit content.

In that context, then, what can flexible scheduling do for the teacher of language arts? It can do many things, because basically it is a design to help us accomplish that most humane of all endeavors: to recognize people as individual human beings and to add a dimension to their lives. A flexible schedule can open up the teacher's day and the student's day, giving both time for the personal relationship that is essential to good education. What more can we ask in a world gripped by fear and suspicion and misunderstanding than to elevate education to a person-to-person level?

Flexible scheduling can also generate more active learning situations for students, freeing them from the appalling routine of passive knowledge intake—but only if we as language arts teachers are willing to spend less time telling students *about* language and more time *involving* them in the actual use of language. The transition from teaching language as content to teaching language as a natural, human activity is fraught with problems. But if we choose to believe in a perceptual approach rather than a conceptual one, then instruction will normally begin not by "telling how," but rather by thrusting students into actual experiences in language and building from that point with appropriate response and information.

A flexible schedule can promote self-learning, self-discipline, and self-confidence in individual students. If we are willing to allow those students capable of self-learning to teach themselves and to teach each other wherever it is feasible, then we will have more time and better opportunities to work with those students who are dependent learners.

Flexible scheduling can create opportunities for varied and creative in-school supplementary learning activities related to the language arts. A flexibly scheduled school should provide many special interest opportunities in creative drama, in speech, in literary pursuits, in writing, in filmmaking, in stagecraft—in every phase of language arts where the imagination of a teacher and the interests of students might coincide.

Flexible scheduling can aid us in eliminating some of the deadly repetition and irrelevance that has plagued students in language arts over the years. A good flexible schedule will allow us to bring together the *right* students at the *right* time in the *right* space with the *right* teacher. In the areas of reading and writing and thinking skills a student should be able to proceed at his own ungraded pace. In the area of coordinated group learning activities, the student should often be able to select from a number of options which are appropriate to his needs, to his tastes, and to his learning style. All of this can be possible through team teaching and a flexible schedule.

Finally, it seems possible that a flexible schedule can foster a climate of mutual trust and respect among teachers and students by making them partners rather than adversaries in the process of learning. Flexible scheduling is capable of helping break down many of the traditional barriers that separate students and teachers. When young people recognize that their teachers view them as individuals rather than as masses of humanity on an intellectual production line, they will take more pride in achieving the goals we have helped them establish. When we are able to refrain from the mass teaching of *Julius Caesar* and the petty pursuit of grammatical games, substituting instead a variety of literature appropriate to individual tastes and a genuine interest in the immediate problem of communication, then students will begin to believe that we are interested in their real world. And when we begin to allow students the dignity of learning independently whenever it is possible, then they will be more likely to seek us out when they have a genuine need for our guidance and our knowledge.

These are the things that flexible scheduling can help us accomplish.

These are *facts*—facts which more than balance the fantasies outlined earlier. The point is that a flexible schedule, by itself, is neither good nor bad. It should be viewed as a single element in the total school design, merely one tool in a whole set, which can be used to facilitate individualized learning. By itself, the flexible schedule is only a mechanical system, requiring as a supplement the rigorous inspection of the other paraphernalia of our trade.

We must look to our curriculums in language arts, not to determine if they will fit into a flexible schedule, but rather to determine if they are real and alive in today's world, or merely nostalgic fossils of an older and simpler world. We must carefully examine the very assumptions upon which we base our instruction in language arts, for unless these assumptions are inspired by an enlightened view of the needs of a future generation, then a flexible schedule is merely another superficial scarecrow in a garden of poor judgments. Finally, and most importantly, the positive potential of flexible scheduling which I have outlined can be fulfilled only by a superior staff of teachers. A flexible schedule demands a remarkably sensitive and creative staff, teachers who are enlightened, courageous, aggressive, and themselves flexible. These teachers must be human beings who respect young people, who like young people, who trust young people.

With these essential ingredients, it seems likely that our grand fad of the sixties has the potential to become a respected fashion of the seventies—and, what is more important, an effective response to the miseries of a society which seems dangerously close to self-destruction.

UNIFIED ENGLISH:
SALVAGING THE DISAFFECTED

Edward R. Fagan

Background

ENGLISH as used in this paper is defined more as process than as content. A process definition of English implies that instructional strategies, learning principles, and classroom climates are prime directives for students' interaction with English. Processed English deals with content where content is defined as language experiences—verbal

->>>

REPRINTED by permission from the January 1971 issue of *The Clearing House*.

and nonverbal, visual, auditory, esthetic, dialectical, and graphic. Defined in this way, English provides a vital potential for a unified curriculum.

A unified curriculum is one where sharp, territorial demarcations among subjects are blurred so as to encourage students to put together common principles related to a particular phenomenon. Gestaltists have obliquely espoused this cause by their recommendation that whole patterns be studied as opposed to atomistic pieces of those patterns;[1] sociologists, too, with their concept of "holism" fully supported the gestaltists; more recently McLuhan renewed the plea for organic curricula when he wrote:

> All forms of mathematics and science, as much as the changing modes of historiography and literature, offer instruments and models of perception. It follows that any existing "subject" in our curricula can now be taught as a more or less minor group of models of perception favored in some past or at present. Taught in this way any "subject" becomes an organic portion of almost any other "subject." Moreover, it also follows that "subject" taught structurally in this way offers innumerable opportunities for new perception and new insight even at elementary levels. The idea of the "content" of education as something to be lodged in the mind as a container thus belongs to the preelectronic phase and to the era of Euclidean space and Newtonian mechanics. A structure cannot be contained. Any conceivable container is at once part of the structure, modifying the whole. The idea of "content" at once reveals a structure of perception and assumptions from which the artist and the poet have been trying to free us for a full century. But now the nuclear physicist has intervened on the side of the artists, and the pressure to heed the message of the artists has become more urgent.[2]

Moving from McLuhan's pleas for a unified curriculum to similar recommendations for English, Moffett recently noted in the Introduction to his curricular guide:

> The program thus outlined is meant to be integrated both in the sense that continuity is sustained from one general stage of growth to another and in the sense that reading, speech, literature, drama, composition, and language are learned by means of each other and inter-related to the point of effacing some conventional categories of the field.
>
> I would like to propose a way of teaching the native language that requires almost no textbooks or materials except reading selections and that, indeed, offers an alternative to the installation of a prepackaged curricu-

[1] Kurt Koffka, *Principles of Gestalt Psychology* (New York: Harcourt Brace, and Co., 1955).

[2] Marshall McLuhan, "We Need a New Picture of Knowledge," *New Insights and the Curriculum* (Washington, D.C.: NEA, ASCD Yearbook, 1963).

lum. Featuring the learner's own production of language, and not incarnated in textbooks, the curriculum adjusts automatically to the students at hand. It is therefore meant for use in any kind of school, public or private, and with any kind of student population, advantaged or disadvantaged, or low or high ability. But what I am presenting is not a definitive, thoroughly tried-and-proven course of learning; it is, rather, a chart for further exploration and a kind of rallying call.[3]

One last example to support the value of language experiences as the basis for a unified curriculum. Postman and Weingartner reported in their chapter on Languaging the following aphorism:

> To begin with, we are in a position to understand that almost all of what we customarily call "knowledge" is language. Which means that the key to understanding a "subject" is to understand its language. In fact, that is a rather awkward way of saying it, since it implies that there is such a thing as a "subject" which contains "language." It is more accurate to say that what we call a subject is its language. A "discipline" is a way of knowing, and whatever is known is inseparable from the symbols (mostly words) in which the knowing is codified. What is biology (for example) other than words? If all the words that biologists use were subtracted from the language, there would be no "biology," unless and until new words were invented. Then, we would have a "new" biology. What is "history" other than words? Or astronomy? Or physics? If you do not know the meanings of "history words" or "astronomy words," you do not know history or astronomy.[4]

Postman and Weingartner, Moffett, McLuhan and others who hold similar views are contributors to the process-content definition of English described in the opening paragraph of this proposal.

Credo and Rationale

Language experiences as the foundation for all English programs can supply teachers with a dynamic, self-regenerating system for engaging disaffected students with today's world. "Disaffected" in this context is not a pejorative; it crosses economic, educational, ethnic, and religious lines; it describes students who are engulfed by traditions of English teaching which are unnecessary, unneeded, and ritualistic. To make clear the onerous nature of these rituals consider the following:

> Grammar taught as the identification of the parts of speech, phrases and clauses; sentences taught by types and diagrammed; usage taught as shib-

[3] James Moffett, *A Student-Centered Language Arts Curriculum, Grades K–13* (New York: Houghton, Mifflin, 1969).

[4] Neil Postman and Charles Weingartner, *Teaching as a Subversive Activity* (New York: Delacourt, 1969), p. 102.

boleths, for example, correct uses of *who* and *whom*. Textbooks dominate the teaching selections and recitation-drill is the method used in the grammar ritual.

Composition taught as the display of rhetorical principles drawn from expository essays by professional writers which become models for students' vapid writing assignments on packaged topics to provide teachers with scrap to score with their red pencils.[5]

As to the literature ritual, Squire described it well when he reported practices of English teaching in superior high school classrooms in *College English:*

> Our real quarrel is with the incessant superficiality of much classroom study of literature—with, if you will, the evasion of literature represented in too many classrooms. Despite a decade of recommendations to the contrary, many teachers continue to teach the dates and places as if these and not the literary works were the essence of our subject: an overreliance on history and geography, a preoccupation with the lives of the poets, a fascination with the Elizabethan stage, a concern with definition and memory work (the Petrarchian sonnet, the heroic couplet, the accepted definitions of figures of speech)—these clutter the minds of too many teachers and students alike.[6]

Faced with such grammar, composition, and literature rituals, it is not surprising that high school and college students are protesting, striking, and withdrawing from the archaic ceremony called English. The "here" and "now" in a world some ecologists predict may end by 1985 are the urgent concerns of today's students—all students.

Recently McLuhan pinpointed this malaise in an interview:

> *Question:* Why do you think they [the students] aren't finding it [personal identity] within the educational system?
> *McLuhan:* Because education, which should be helping youth to understand and adapt to their revolutionary new environments, is instead being used merely as an instrument of cultural aggression, imposing upon retribalized youth the obsolescent visual values of the dying literate age. Our entire education system is reactionary, oriented to past values and past technologies and will likely continue so until the old generation relinquishes power. The generation gap is actually a chasm, separating not two age groups but two vastly divergent cultures. I can understand the ferment in our schools, because our educational system is totally rearview mirror. It's a dying and outdated system founded on literate values and fragmented and classified data totally unsuited to the needs of the first television generation. . . . The challenge of the new era is simply the

5 Robert W. Blake, "The New English: Hot Stuff or Cool, Man, Cool?" Brockport, N.Y.: State University College at Brockport, 1970. (Mimeographed.)

6 James R. Squire, "The National Study of High School English Programs," *College English*, Vol. 27 (May 1966), p. 619.

total process of *growing up*—and mere teaching and repetition of facts
are as irrelevant to this process as a dowser to a nuclear power plant.[7]

McLuhan's reference to a nuclear power plant reminds us that the
subtle tensions of a potential nuclear war have been embedded in students' nervous systems since their birth. It is not surprising then, that
they prefer to explore language strategies for survival in preference to
the rhyming scheme of the Elizabethan sonnet or how to diagram a
complex sentence.

Many English teachers feel that the kinds of openness described by
Moffett, McLuhan et al. will destroy English as a subject. Their fears
are unfounded if the experiences of English teachers in the United
Kingdom can be used as a precedent. There, English teachers' major
concern is to provide a learning climate which allows students to increase their sensitivity to life processes. Squire and Appleby reported
this difference between British and American teachers of English as
follows:

> Writing, speaking, interpreting, and reacting are thus seen as similar
> and central to a process in which the ultimate end is a fuller, more sensi-
> tive response to life itself. While engaged in this evolving experience of
> learning how to live and how to respond to living, the child will acquire
> some skills, some knowledge, some perception of form, but such acquisi-
> tion is peripheral and incidental to the totality of the experience itself.
> "We do not think that anyone can instruct children in how to 'realize'
> their experiences in words, how to shape them, how to 'choose' words or
> to use varied sentence structures before they write their compositions. In-
> deed, even markers should not approach a composition armed with stylistic
> criteria: they should set out to be as receptive as they can, to be 'good
> listeners'!" writes a committee of the London Association for the Teaching
> of English in arguing against the direct teaching of language skills. This
> is why many British teachers see no need to plan a curriculum to teach
> discrete skills, and this, in essence, is why so many cannot share the Amer-
> ican concern with the literary heritage, grammar, or rhetoric. It is not
> that they fail to recognize that such subject matter exists; it is rather that
> they focus on different goals.[8]

The increasing popularity of the British position on this matter seems
apparent in the following excerpt from Klein's February 1970 *English
Journal* article:

> Continuing to teach "subject matter," with its typical disregard of the
> student's deepest concerns, is educational suicide. It is the teacher and his

7 Marshall McLuhan, "Playboy Interview," *Playboy*, Vol. 16 (March 1969), p. 62.
8 James R. Squire and Roger K. Appleby, *Teaching English in the United Kingdom*
(Champaign, Ill.: National Council of Teachers of English, 1969), pp. 245–246.

relationship with the child (or adult) that is far more important today than any technique, method, curriculum, or technological innovation.[9]

It should be clear from the foregoing material that the teaching of English must be changed, can be changed, and is changing in ways that promise to increase students' interest, ignite their imaginations and, ideally, improve their sensitivities to life itself. Focused on process, supplied with adaptable materials, English teachers can use their discipline to provide fundamental contributions to the education of every student. Specifics of such contributions will now be examined.

English Contributions to the Disaffected

English with a process-content definition can enliven the education of disaffected students by combining students' interest through language, the humanities, and elective programs in English. Each of these areas is discussed in the material which follows.

Language procedures in too many English classrooms today are based upon contents which utilize the English-as-a-second-language rubric, that is, cloture, drills, pattern practices, and slot filling as used by foreign language teachers to "teach" language skills. Supposedly, these procedures used to teach a foreign language will be effective in changing dialects, just as it is assumed that some dialects must be changed.

Justification for such language experiences for disaffected students is based upon findings from research studies which have a built-in flaw: the controlled variable. Where language experiences are involved, for example, variables are narrowed to discrete phenomena such as "vocalization," "verbal responsiveness," "comprehension," and the like.[10] Theoretically, these little pieces of information can one day be put together in such a way that grand insights about language acquisition will be possible. Yet as the gestaltists, McLuhan, O. K. Moore, and others point out repeatedly, language is acquired within organic contexts or (to use McLuhan's description) by "involving the individual's total sensorium," that is, all the senses. Moore's studies with youngsters who learned to read at the age of two and one-half or three showed that these youngsters were simultaneously subjected to sight, sound, feeling, and hearing stimuli; that they proceeded at their own pace, discovered language phenomena, and were positively rewarded for their efforts. Such an environment for students' language experiences is more realistic and

9 Thomas D. Klein, "Personal Growth in the Classroom: Dartmouth, Dixon, and Humanistic Psychology," *English Journal,* Vol. 59 (February 1970), p. 235.

10 Cf. Jane Beasley Raph, "Language Development in Socially Disadvantaged Children," and Doxey A. Wilkerson, "Programs and Practices in Compensatory Education for Disadvantaged Children," *Review of Educational Research,* Vol. 35 (December 1965), pp. 389–400; 426–440.

efficient than the drill-oriented classroom—a fact which the television program *Sesame Street* dramatically demonstrated.

Another alternative to fragmented language study is described by Bostain, a linguist with the United States Government's Foreign Service Institute.

> So a good English class, I think, is one where the teacher writes something on the blackboard, and then says, "How else can we say this?" And the kids can tell her every way they can think of, slangy, neat, grammatically wrong, whatever they want to do. She writes them on the board, and when she gets about ten or twelve of them, she says, "Now what do we know about a guy who says it this way? What social information is transmitted to us by the man who makes this choice? What image is projected by the man who says it this way?" And the kids get the idea there are 1,620 ways to say everything, and it makes a real difference what choices you make. It makes a social difference, and that means that you won't use the same choice on all occasions, you see, for the social circumstances that accompany the occasions change. When that happens, you have to switch your language. If you talk the same way to everybody, see your local psychiatrist; you need help; you've got a rigid personality.[11]

Bostain's point is that with a stable message (grammatical) students should explore the varied images (usage) and their meanings. Examples: "There aren't any more trains until four o'clock this afternoon." Stable message: standard informal image. Example II: "1600 hours, next train, Mister." Same message, colloquial image, professional jargon. Language experiences, Bostain continues, should provide students with the opportunity to explore and develop alternate habits which may compete with students' established usage habits. This alternative would give students some sensitivity to the social circumstances which require one or another of the language habits for best social results. Bostain concludes, "If a kid were taught that, if that's the way the classes were run, then I think the teachers of English could justly claim that their subject is one of the humanities. Right now, I don't think it is."[12]

Humanities teachers might regard Bostain's judgment as too narrow. They feel that the humanities are broader clusters of usually discrete disciplines such as art, music, and literature. But in the humanities (which are process oriented) the blurring of subjects (as previously recommended by Moffett and McLuhan) tends to provide more flexibility for the exploration of competencies usually associated with English. This broader base Maxine Green describes as an "organization of

11 James C. Bostain, "A Stable Message, A Varied Image," *The PCTE Bulletin* (Bethlehem, Pa.: Pennsylvania Council of Teachers of English, May 1970), p. 18.
12 Ibid., p. 19.

possibilities" in Schwartz's *Teaching the Humanities;* Green details these possibilities as follows:

> The humanities for the existing individual—in many senses free to create what he will be—may then become an organization of possibilities. Not only can he discover a range of potential fulfillments in the literature he reads; he can explore the linguistic behaviors of man, as he learns to put his thoughts in words, and how to make himself clear. He can formulate the kinds of philosophic questions which will permit him to relate himself to what is known—and what is not. Clarifying, criticizing, find his own particular way, he can create a perspective instead of find one, as the rational humanists used to do. He can fashion his own life order as he seeks out meanings—an order reaching as deeply into the past as T. S. Eliot's, but consciously defined through thoughtful exploration of the history of his kind.
>
> The point is that he must be considered as in some sense unique, in some sense "open," undetermined—free.[13]

The "openness" and "freedom" Green refers to are outcomes of a humanities stratagem for developing language competencies for the disaffected, and the impact of such an approach can be inferred from Cleaver's description of his study of the humanities during his imprisonment in San Quentin. Cleaver noted that "Under Lovdjieff [his teacher] I studied world history, Oriental philosophy, Occidental philosophy, comparative religion, and economics. I could not tell one class from another—neither could the other students and neither, I believe, could Lovdjieff. It was all Lovdjieff."[14] Cleaver recognized the teacher as key to the success of the courses and later on, in the same article, noted that exposure to Lovdjieff had helped him (Cleaver) to free his mind though his body was confined.

If the humanities can help prisoners to feel free (assuming a teacher with Lovdjieff's dedication and skill), then a humanities focus for disaffected students needs to be used more often as a substitute for, or the basis of, English programs.

One way of getting humanities courses into English programs is to make them available as "elective" or "mini" courses, or sometimes both. Elective courses are usually based on a six-week focus such as: speech, semantics, contemporary novels, research, writing, humanities, and the like. During an academic year about 60 elective courses are available, but not all courses are taught. Those courses most frequently elected by students at the beginning of the regular semester are the ones offered.

13 Maxine Green, "The Humanities and the Public School: 'You Must Change Your Life,' " *Teaching the Humanities,* ed. Sheila Schwartz (New York: Macmillan, 1969), p. 118.

14 Eldridge Cleaver, "The Guru of San Quentin: 'The Christ' and His Teaching," *Teaching the Humanities,* ed. Sheila Schwartz (New York: Macmillan, 1969), p. 313.

Students must take at least one reading, one writing, and one speaking course. All students must take at least three English courses per semester (18 weeks). If a student fails one six-week course (which he must make up), he can still get a passing grade for the semester by doing well in the other two required courses.

Mini courses are of shorter duration—about two weeks—and pick up segments of applied English such as newspapers, magazines, television, job applications, interviews, and letter writing. Again, students elect which of the mini-courses they will take. The mini-course is particularly useful for English programs which operate with vocational-technical high schools where four weeks of the students' time are spent in the vocational program and two weeks in the "academic" program.

That elective and mini courses show signs of cracking ritualized English can be inferred from Denton's report about the three-year impact of an elective English program at the Bellefonte (Pennsylvania) Senior High School. Denton reported:

> Pupils exposed to the program have scored considerably higher in their college boards than students under the old program. Wolford [the principal] rightfully boasts of significant improvement in verbal scores—the direct benefit from English courses that have greatly strengthened the average student's ability and skill in comprehension.
>
> In the past school year, library attendance and book circulation has risen 20 per cent; circulation of magazines has soared nearly 100 per cent. There has been a marked increase in the demand for nonfiction books.[15]

Elective English programs embody the principle of structural openness; they provide for individualization, use humanistic principles for the organization of content, and are evaluated according to criteria for the judgment of students' competencies. With language as the center of increasingly flexible explorations of all aspects of the subject, and with broader instruments for the evaluation of students' competencies in languaging, there are strong indications that students' engagement with this "new" English will provide them with tools to shape their survival and with sensitivities to respect the preciousness of life.

15 Clifford Denton, "How a High School Cured Its English Hang-up," *Pennsylvania Education*, Vol. 2 (January–February 1970), p. 7.

TEACHING ENGLISH IN GHETTOBURG: THOUGHTS AT THE HALFWAY POINT

Richard Lederer

> *The Ghettoburg Address*
> Nine score and fourteen years ago our white fathers
> brought forth upon this continent a black race of
> slaves, deceived in liberty and dedicated to the sup-
> position that all men are created equal and treated
> equal except black men. . . .
> —tenth grader; Simon Gratz High School;
> Phila., Pa.

Thursday, February 12. In commemoration of Abraham Lincoln's birthday we have a school holiday in Philadelphia. And the schools will stay closed tomorrow, our fourth "heat holiday"; by keeping the furnaces idle and making up the days in warmer, less costly weather, the system will save about $160,000. So I have a four day weekend to sort out impressions of my first sabbatical leave from St. Paul's School —a church, boarding, college-preparatory school in Concord, N. H.

During the year I've been teaching English in a North Philadelphia inner-city high school. I'm not sure that my busman's holiday will be as "refreshing" as a year of travel or academic study, but I can't think of another experience that could have shown me as much about myself. Teaching at Simon Gratz High School has been the best course I've ever had.

Gratz sits on the corner of its boundaries. In other words, if you happen to live across the street (in which case you might be white or middle class), you don't go to Gratz. So, whether or not gerrymandering aforethought is at work, the results are the same: our student body is 100% black (we have three Oriental students and one Caucasian on our rolls) and 95% poor, and the kind of social mix that raises achievement levels is taken out.

One begins to feel the political facts of life at Gratz; one begins to see that the way things are hooked up produces a lot of built-in failure. While two sexually segregated schools sit underutilized just outside our boundaries, we bulge with 4700 students who are processed in two sequential shifts—7:50 a.m.-12:05 p.m., then 12:15-4:30 p.m. (I, like

FROM *The Leaflet*, Vol. 69 (September 1970), pp. 34–45. Reprinted by permission of the publisher and the author.

most of the rookies, work the afternoon, tenth grade shift.) Our kids are with us at least an hour less than most youngsters in other schools, and they spend their shifts going straight through classes, without any breaks for lunch, study hall, or just plain rapping. When two of my "slow" classes come to me each day for sixth and seventh periods (3:10-4:30), many are numbed, hungry, and anxious to get out of the place.

And it is apathy that is the most formidable opponent to education at Gratz, not, despite the extravagant rumors that buzz through Philadelphia ("Gee, you teachers are like soldiers in Viet Nam!"), danger to the teacher's physical person or disruption in the classroom. Those rounded metal handles sticking out of back pockets are attached to combs, not knives. True, there were close to fifty gang-related homicides in Philadelphia in 1969; true, one of my young men is currently charged with murder and conspiracy for passing a knife to four girls who punched and stabbed to death a Gratz girl. But the school turf is very seldom the scene of such tragedies.

According to their collective reading and math scores, our tenth graders come to us with sixth grade academic heads; they grow at seven-twelfths rate and leave us with more than a year's additional retardation, a total of four-and-a-half years behind:

> Books
> Not Nice.
> I don't like them.
> Help

Only one-third of these tenth graders will graduate from Gratz—a distressingly low figure, but what bread and butter reasons can the school offer its students to complete their senior year? We at Gratz affect our students' social mobility hardly at all. When we tell our kids that studying and staying in school will help them get a better job and a higher salary, we are saying something that is *barely* true, as the table below illustrates:

MEDIAN INCOME OF MEN 25 TO 54 YEARS OLD,
BY EDUCATIONAL ATTAINMENT, 1968

		Black	White
Elementary:	Less than 8 years	$3,558	$5,131
	8 years	4,499	6,452
High School:	1 to 3 years	5,255	7,229
	4 years	5,801	8,154

(*The Social and Economic Status of Negroes in the United States,* Bureau of Labor Statistics Report No. 375, p. 21)

Perhaps the most striking comparison in the chart is that the median income of Negro men, 25 to 54 years old, who have completed four years of high school is lower than that for white men in this age group who have completed only eight years of elementary school.

The hurly-burly of the double shift hook-up also has its effects on the teachers, most of whom have but one forty minute "prep period" break which is generally taken up with drudgerous but necessary paperwork. Since there is virtually no time to reach out to other teachers for warmth, comfort, and stimulation, our satisfactions must come almost entirely from contacts and relationships with the students. For me, and I think for many others, this is a perilous dependency, especially if your ego is inextricably bound to your job, as mine most certainly is. At St. Paul's I had come to the point where my self-concept floated along with relative serenity. At Gratz the kids quickly unlock your deepest weaknesses and needs, and your ego soars and dips like a mad kite. A student can give you the biggest hello in the halls and skip your class later in the day.

> Mr. Lederer isn't bad, just the teacher for Gratz. He has a very nice appearance. Sometimes he tells the kids to behave, but it just don't seem to come out right. Some kids say he's funny, while others say he's dumb, while still others say he's a fool.

When you work with youngsters many of whom have never learned in school, you really find out if you can teach. At a place like St. Paul's you know that there has been and will be relatively continuous progress in academic skills. Seldom do you worry about such movement and your relation to it. But in the Gratz situation it really matters whether or not learning has happened in a given period of time, and you are haunted by your failures. It's a lot easier to be relevant than it is to be instructional.

To a boarding school master the attendance patterns at Gratz are appalling. In December, for example, our average daily attendance figure for the tenth grade was 64% (69% schoolwide). And once inside the building the student body collectively cuts thousands of classes a week. Tracking down the cutters by searching through the endless daily lists of homeroom absentees is one of the omnipresent paper labors I mentioned earlier. Chronic absence and cutting are related to a number of complex causes, and illness is not a primary factor. When a compulsory school program is imposed on the life of the ghetto, weird things happen.

So you telephone the homes, and almost inevitably you talk to the mother, who tells you she is unaware that her child has been hookying or cutting for the past three months. These strong, beautiful mothers go off to work early each day, leave streetcar tokens, and seldom call the school about their children's attendance, in part because the school seems like such a frighteningly large institution. A typical Home and School Association evening meeting draws an average of twenty parents out of 8,000.

Sometimes the parent is aware of the attendance problem and explains that her child has been home taking care of younger brothers and sisters, or has been running with a gang, or has not been home for a month, or is a foster child who has been spending school hours with his natural mother, or has reached seventeen and has dropped out, or is under legal age and has dropped out anyway.

The telephone calls confirm what you have already suspected in class—that school is a very small part of so many of the kids' lives, an enormous contrast to my seven years of community living at St. Paul's School. Compared with the student's family, race, social class, and the kids he hangs out with, the socializing effect of the school is minimal indeed. For so many, Gratz is a building that hardly exists except as a place to go to stay out of trouble, to keep warm, and to look over 3,000 girls. Until the black family becomes more stable, until there are more fathers at home as role models (the BSL Report indicates that the trend is in the opposite direction), until a high school degree makes a real economic difference for black people, and until the gang structure ceases to be the chief purveyor of masculinity for ghetto men, the system of compulsory public education that we know is not going to make much difference to the very economic class of people for whom it was originally set up.

> My father is nice.
> My mother is better.
> What do you expect?

One of the reasons there is a hold back of constant progress of Black Men in the White Man's world is gang war affairs. Really I think this is a very senseless thing, black brothers shooting and killing each other for no specific reason. One reason for such a senseless thing is a lot of them fellows want to have a reputation. I cannot see why a brother who wants a rep can't do something to help the black man instead of hurting us just to get a little rep.

I must mention one last component of the system at Simon Gratz High School. Our black student body comes to school to be taught by a 72% white faculty. Our 28% representation of black teachers is the highest for senior high school in a city whose student population is 60% black, but we cannot increase our black staff until other schools get up to the official "integration" figure of 10%.

At West Philadelphia High School, from which I was graduated in 1955, the issue of the white teacher in the black classroom flared up last October. A number of black students began boycotting a history class taught by a white teacher, charging that his methods and materials were "irrelevant" to them. When the West Philly principal acceded to the students' demands that the teacher be transferred, an imminent city-wide teachers' strike was threatened and tension ran through all the black schools. Ultimately the Board of Education reversed the principal's decision and a strike was averted.

It would be presumptuous for me to make any pronouncements about this prominent and fiery issue, but I will offer a few scattered observations. Again and again in their writing my students questioned their place in and control over the universe, as in these haiku:

Why have I risen	The birds sing with beauty
from the bosom of life	Blood stains the soil of the turning earth.
Into this world of hatred?	What does it all mean?
I am lost in a river—	Where is the key to education?
The river of prejudice.	What will I find
What am I doing here?	When the door is opened?

According to the Coleman Report (*Equality of Educational Opportunity*, 1966, based on 600,000 school-age children), this sense of relationship to environment, what our principal calls the student's sense of "fate control," is crucial to his ability to learn. One of the conclusions of the Report is that "Negroes and other minority children show a much lower sense of control of their environment than do whites." [p. 289] We can only ask ourselves what happens to a black student's sense of life's promises when he comes to school and sees white teachers in the obvious majority.

But as I recollect in the tranquility of this long weekend, the dominant vibrations I feel are good and joyous ones. I don't often feel like shouting, "wow, teaching is so rewarding!" but the joy does come in subtle ways. If education means change, then I *know* that some of my students have had at least a day of education in my classroom. I *know* I have touched some of them and they have touched each other. Years from now it will be the faces that I'll remember best, faces often vacant, hostile, and weary of the ritual. But almost every day something beautiful happens in some of those faces, and then the heavens open.

Every day it seems that I can't help damaging at least one student. Each time I can't believe that it is I who let leak the peevish innuendoes, that it is I who put kids down who are already way down. It's one of the things you learn about yourself in this job.

As best and as truly as I can I try to support the personhood of all my students. I physically touch them and embrace them whenever it seems right, and as an English teacher whose living is made with words I try hard to avoid subjecting my kids to a damaging linguistic ethnocentrism. In *Black Skin, White Masks* (1952) Franz Fanon states that

Every colonized people—in other words, every people in whose soul an inferiority complex has been created by the death and burial of its local cultural originality—finds itself face to face with the language of the civilizing nation (p. 18, Grove Press).

I want my students to know that language is not a set of thou shalts *out there,* but an instinct *in here,* as natural as digesting and sexing—a part of people, not apart from them, a making of meanings in the brain, a gathering of meanings from the universe, an offering of meanings to the universe. In the service of such a philosophy, the core of my writing program in all classes is a weekly journal, ungraded and risk free, in which each student begins, not with an exterior assignment, but with himself. I stress that bold and sincere thinking, and even sheer quantity, will take precedence over mechanics. In response has poured forth talent so rich and so vast that it makes the blood quicken.

Still, at this juncture in our history, it seems only fair to warn the students that in certain contexts someone, perhaps a prospective employer, might make a damaging judgment about a double negative or an "a" before a noun beginning with a vowel. Those who may want to get a job outside their community will have to think about learning to tune in on the mother tongue and play the game of second dialect. At the same time, I ask the students to pray with me for the most rapid withering of that so very comforting, so uniquely human myth: *We* talk right; *they* don't. Would anyone want to snuff out such "non-standard" expressions as: "I offed (killed) him." "I just snapped out" (went wild). "She runs her mouth too much." (May we never kill that metaphor.) "The boys in our neighborhood throw their eyes up the girls' dresses."

Such sentences suggest an integral part of my students' writing that constantly delights me. In the academic life of St. Paul's we take for granted a convention called a writing voice that differs in varying degrees from one's speaking voice, depending on the writer and the task of writing. At Gratz, few of our students employ such an aesthetic distance in their writing.

It is unfortunate that the beautiful oral language of so many of our Gratz youngsters gets clogged up in their pencils. But when the style and content are able to traverse that tricky route from spirit to paper, the results are often as Fanon describes: "a vigorous style, alive with rhythms, struck through with bursting life; . . . full of color too, bronzed, sunbaked." (*The Wretched of the Earth,* p. 220, Grove Press)

> "I'm all alone in this world," she said.
> "Ain't got nobody to share my bed.
> "Ain't got nobody to hold my hand.
> "The truth of the matter's I ain't got no man."

Big boy opened his mouth and said,
"Trouble with you is you ain't got no head!
If you had a head and used your mind,
You could have me with you all the time."

She answered, "Babs, what must I do?"
He said, "Share your bed and your money too."

I remember once when I was stopped by a fuzz for suspicion of snatch-
ing some lady's pocket book. So he took me down to the thirty-ninth police
station, and it seemed like it was two hours while I was down there, and
you talk about somebody being hungry, man, I was ready to eat the cigarettes in my pocket. But as I was saying, the fuzz threw me in the sweat
box and I was hollering my lungs out, trying to tell some of those so-called
cops that they had the wrong person, and they told me to shut my d–
trap. . . .

Although I am an apolitical person, it is in the writings of ideolo-
gists Franz Fanon (*Black Skin, White Masks; The Wretched of the
Earth*) and Stokely Carmichael and Charles V. Hamilton (*Black Power*)
that I have found the most useful construct into which to fit the varied
writings of my students at Gratz. Briefly, Fanon contends that "the juxtaposition of the white and black races has created a massive psycho-
existential complex." From the French-Algerian colonial context Fanon
attempts to generalize for all colonial situations, and his lead is taken up
by Carmichael and Hamilton, who assert that black people in the United
States form a colony and stand as colonial subjects of their white "fellow
citizens."

In *The Wretched of the Earth* Fanon traces three stages in the writing of the colonized "native." In the first phase the writing reflects and
copies the values and styles of the literature of the colonizer, the mother
country. In the second phase the native writer tries to recapture the
bygone days of his history. He searches the depths of his memory "in
the light of a borrowed estheticism and of a conception of the world
which was discovered under other skies." Finally, as the process of de-
colonization quickens, there is a third phase, that of a fighting literature
which attempts to express "a new reality in action."

In their increasing affirmation of their negritude, in their exploration of aspects of their consciousness which are in the process of being
liberated, and in the combative tone of much of their writing, my students are acting out the history of black literature in America and the re-
arrangement of political relationship during their lifetimes. Here are
a number of examples:

Black is beautiful   Black is colorful.
Beautiful is black.   Black is cool.

Let's shout together.
That's where it's at.

We're no nigger children.
We're no fools.

Black is powerful.
Black is sharp.
Everybody's learning
To be proud of their dark.

Black is being proud.
Black is black
Let's stick together
Cause that's where it's at.

I've got a name.
Don't call me boy.
I've got a name.
I'm not a walkin' toy.

Try "Mister" or "Sir"
To suit your taste.
But don't call me boy
Cause you're out of place.

When the freedom or should I say "bush" came out, the pink man did not like this one bit. And he was really mad when our females started wearing it. Want to know why? Well, I will tell you why he is so mad. He is angry because some of our women are not spending their money on all that possum fat. VO-5 pinkys are mad. Every company that sells all of that greasy mess are angry because they can't go home and tell their families about "that dumb nigger lady," as they would say it, who has bought $10 worth of hair lard.

MOTHER AFRICA'S PAST

This is my land.
I've made it so;
With the sweat of my brow
I've helped it grow.

By the laws of man
I should be free.
But the white man's laws
Are as chains to me.

Back off Whitey
Cause Nigger is no longer my name.
Back off Whitey
Cause your dog and I are no longer the same.
Back off Whitey
Cause I'm hip to your dehumanizing game.

More than parenthetically, I should mention that, along with the passion and muscular tension of the passages above, a rich counterpoint pervades the works of my students; there is a repeated cry for peace:

Why must I hold this gun?
Why must I kill my brother?
Is God alive?

Boy in Vietnam—
Life is so very precious.
Will he ever return?

Brother against brother
Sister against sister
What has made us turn?

In the Ghettoburg classroom, one must also avoid an ethnocentric approach to one's literature program. At the ABC (A Better Chance) Conference on Afro-American Studies this past June I asked Professor Finley Campbell of Morehouse College if he agreed with the standard criticism that Richard Wright's *Native Son* is shot through with excessive didacticism, that is, that Wright is too pushy with his messages. Campbell's reply went something like this: "The book certainly is didactic, but surely not too didactic for today. Now the didactic is on top. Since Wordsworth, we have been worshiping the white man's aesthetic, a set of disembodied aesthetic constructs. But no literature can be divorced from the community and political realities from which it springs."

My students at Gratz will not let me get hung up on aesthetic abstracts *out there*. Either the material overlaps their needs and desires or they turn off with unsophisticated visibility. They allow me a few castles in the air, but early in each building program they demand foundations underneath. Thus, in preparing to study the techniques of *Animal Farm,* we spent a couple of weeks with a number of short Ethiopian and Greek fables. The students wrote their own fables, taking care to use appropriate animals and to supply a moral that followed from the story. Then we discussed this question: "If you were a modern writer of fables, what aspects of contemporary society would you choose to make a comment on?" From the discussion to the blackboard went such social problems as gangs, violence, racial prejudice, cars, cigarettes, and pollution. Finally the students fashioned their own fables for our time:

THE ALLIGATOR AND THE FROG

Once upon a time there lived an alligator and a frog. Each lived on the opposite side of each other. One day they were sitting on a rock and the alligator said, "we the alligators are better than you green and all colored frogs." And the frog said, "we the frogs are better than you scaly punks." And they just kept it up until they challenged one another.

"All right, you little short sissy, we'll see you and your puny gang tomorrow," said Alligator. "Your challenge is accepted," said Frog hatefully.

The day arrived and the fight was about to begin. After a five minute prayer they all began to fight. The frogs were hopping all over the alligators with knives and clubs in their feet, while the alligators were biting and snapping at the frogs with their mouths.

And finally the fight ended and the alligators and frogs realized that their leaders had been killed along with others. So from that day on everyone took heed of the killing.

MORAL: Gangwar—it just don't make no sense.

THE GORILLA AND THE DINOSAUR

Once upon a time there was a Gorilla named Igor who was always in trouble. One day Igor decided to go around and find a new way to get into trouble, so he found out how to use drugs.

He got so caught up in drugs that he went around raping animals. First it was a duck; then a snake; then a bear. One day the Gorilla said, "I'm tired of raping little things, so I'm going big." While he was walking he spotted a dinosaur, and the dinosaur turned around and raped him. The Gorilla was under the state of shock until he died.

MORAL: Never be greedy. OR Stay with the little stuff.

In experiencing *Animal Farm* itself, our emphasis was on the uses and abuses of power and the malignant growth of discrimination among the animals. During one lesson we compared the goals and command-ments of the Animal Revolution with those of the Black Panther Party: for example, "Any party member found shooting narcotics will be ex-pelled from the party." "No party member will use, point, or fire a wea-pon of any kind unnecessarily or accidentally at anyone."

A week ago, two of my classes finished reading some Greek myths. The first story we looked at was the Black Muslim myth of the creation of white people by Mr. Yacub, a malevolent, "big-headed" scientist who, on the Island of Patmos, masterminds the gradual bleaching of a white devil race (as told in the *Autobiography of Malcolm X*, pp. 164 ff., Grove Press). We saw that whether or not a myth is scientifically true is not important. What counts is that it furnishes a transcendent set of explanations for a particular group of people, that it fills their lives with sufficient meaning to make their living and striving worthwhile. The stu-dents have been creating their own gods and fashioning their own myths, and some have caught and crystallized a sense of their own existence.

My god is the God of Drugs. He doesn't come in one form, but in many shapes and sizes. He at times may look like a sugar cube or even a needle or a pill.

Jason, god of Drugs, is a descendant of Linus, god of Laziness. Jason and his followers are very dangerous people. They steal and kill just for money to keep their habit going, and they call to their god Jason to bring them Speed, Monster, and Skag.

Jason is an evil god. After his followers have taken the dope, Jason makes them sick and they need another shot. Many of the followers die from O.D.'s for many don't know how to take it.

Finally Zeus promised to overthrow Jason by Fire. One day Zeus conjured up one of his biggest fireballs. It struck Jason and that's where we get Sunday.

When Zeus created the heaven and the earth, there was black man and there was white man. It was in the afternoon and Zeus said, "*you* will be as light as the universe, and *you* will be as black as the night." Then he said, "since it is light, the light man will go first." And he took from behind him a shovel and some chains and money and a key that read "Good Life." The light man took the money and the good life, and the dark man took what was left.

Last year, as part of their Independent Study, several of our St. Paul's students worked in the New York and Washington ghettos. They told me that when you go into the ghetto, you go to learn all you can and you musn't delude yourself into thinking you are going to do good. I have tried to follow this wise injunction. Still, it doesn't seem fair that most of the time I am the one who has been doing all the learning.

I am indebted to Dr. Frederick Holliday, Gratz High School principal, for many of the facts and statistics that support my discussion and a great deal of the philosophy that shapes it. My statements on the language of the ghetto are significantly influenced by Dr. Charles Calitri's speech at the 1969 School and College Conference and Dr. James Sledd's article, "Bi-Dialectalism: the Linguistics of White Supremacy," in the *English Journal*, Dec. 1969.

Unless otherwise indicated, the quoted passages are products of my tenth graders at Gratz. I have corrected spelling and punctuation.

TEACHING ENGLISH: A MULTI-UNIT APPROACH

Roger E. Onick

THE idea of using the multi-unit approach came to me after I read a newspaper article about a grade school teacher who got the idea after visiting the homes of his students in which he saw different activities taking place simultaneously.

Comprising my three ninth grade English Language Arts classes are Mexican Americans, Puerto Ricans, Polish students and American whites.

≫≫-≫≫

F R O M *Wisconsin English Journal,* Vol. 13 (October 1970), pp. 28–31. Reprinted by permission of the publisher and the author.

Most of these students are below average, many who have received D's and U's in English and whose attitude toward school is that it is the most irrelevant place to be in. Quite frankly, they hate it. They are called potential dropouts. Many boys in my classes have been in a detention home and have returned to society bitter. I knew from the outset that unless I would come up with something motivating to all and different from what they had ever received in an English class, my students would tune me out for the semester.

My first concern was to make the classroom the most attractive place to be in, to create a setting that would sustain my students' interest. I bought ten packages of bright, solid-colored yellow and orange crepe paper, cut them into 1½-inch strips and began making five smaller class-rooms within the classroom by hanging the strips of crepe paper, alternating colors, from ceiling to floor. The crepe paper not only created the five rooms I wanted but also strikingly illuminated the room. Within each room I put students' desk chairs, book cases, and in two rooms, a table for each. In addition to this physical setting, the room was equipped with encyclopedias, dictionaries, two almanacs, supplementary readers, magazines and daily issues of newspapers.

First reactions of the students were "Is this a jail?" or "Oh, what are these—cages?" or "Oh, boy, I like this," or "Say, Mr. Onick, this is a real neat room!" The setting really turned students on and showed them, I think, that their English class was going to be a bit different from what they had experienced.

I asked students to select persons they would like to work with for the entire semester. Enthusiastically, they did. Segregation prevailed, but I made no attempts to integrate the males with the females. They next quickly selected a room, each group arguing with the other about their preference. In less than five minutes, however, everybody was settled but were still marveling at the physical setting.

Realizing the importance of offering a variety of things to try to interest the slow learner, I divided the course into six aspects of the language arts. I provided students with a description of each aspect on a mimeographed sheet. Their job was to reach a consensus about which aspect they would study first and so forth in order of preference. They were told that by the end of the semester they would have completed all six.

1. *Mass Media Study: Magazine, Newspaper, Motion Picture and Television* (6 weeks).

Tentatively, each medium will be studied according to its function in American society. Students will learn how to distinguish propaganda from facts in newspaper reporting, will learn what makes a "good" film, will see how television influences what they say and do and will be involved in activities requiring of them dramatizations, special projects, reports, etc.

2. *Reading Readiness* (3 weeks).

Students studying this aspect will have all opportunities to improve their reading. Techniques will vary to the needs of each group member as he dictates needs. Reading anthologies including exciting stories for boys and girls will used. Also, students will be given freedom to read materials of interest to them. Students will be involved in many activities: panels, reports, research, writing skits, dramatizations, using the tape recorder, making book jackets, seeing films relevant to group focus, word and dictionary study, etc.

3. *Perceptive Writing* (3 weeks).

Based on the principle that all effective writing depends primarily on accurate, insightful observation, this unit will teach students how to see life with the perceptive eye of a photographer. The student will learn how to write from studying pictures. He will create his own poems and short stories and will learn how to express himself and what he observes in an entirely fresh and original way.

4. *Experiencing Grammar* (3 weeks).

The objective here is not to teach grammar, for it is fact that you already know grammar. Students will primarily be working on "sentence embedding." Usage will also be touched on if time allows. Students will prepare language bulletin boards, play games, be involved in projects, write reports, dramatize sentences, use audio visuals, pantomime sentences, etc.

5. *Literature Experiences* (3 weeks).

Students in this area will study works of a literary nature, interpreting, evaluating, expressing themselves, writing. Students will be involved in a "sensory experience." Many exciting things are in store for students who study this unit.

6. *Linguistics* (3 weeks).

Students will study morphology, phonology, semantics, meaning as they all relate to the above facets of the English program. The ninth grade language text will be required for this unit study.

These students were so excited about seeing such a variety of things offered, about being able to decide what they would like to study first, second, third and so forth (No more than two groups chose the same aspect and the names of the last three did not turn them off.), and about working in groups. English had become a new thing for them, their thing! As Randall commented, one of my students whose dream is to become an actor, "This room is the most exciting room I've been in. All my other English classes were boring. They were just regular English classes." The physical setting and the introduction to the multiunit had unquestionably motivated the students.

I asked each group to select a person who would each day pick up the assignment for his room. This is the procedure used to begin class. I do not lecture to students about what they are to do; the sheets communicate for me. The directions on the sheet for each daily lesson usually initiate a discussion between my students and me. Included here is an example from my unit on "Perceptive Writing" of how directions for a lesson are structured.

PERCEPTIVE WRITING: WORD PICTURE

There is another version of thinking by comparison: seeing in simile and metaphor.

Most people look at one thing, and see it as just that one thing: they do not instinctively notice resemblances. As they watch an athlete, or a snowstorm, or a girl's face, or a sunset, they are not reminded of anything else. Or, if they are, the comparison rarely appears in their writing or their conversation.

Such "double vision" is usually the result of long training in the use of the eye and the mind and the other senses, a training I intend to start you on. It does not come quickly or nonchalantly, except in genius.

Today your focus will be on the ability to see what things "are like," and to express that likeness in simile and metaphor. Emphasis, also, will be placed on appropriate comparison. The word "appropriate" is important, for students, when asked to find similarities, generally make bizarre comparisons; and they are not usually conscious of their grotesque images.

Try to perceive the spirit of your analogies, so that there is no wild conflict between what you see and what you are reminded of. A superficially clever, but very bad metaphor will illustrate this clash of feeling: *The leaves were lipsticked with autumn.*

There may be some similarity of color here, but everything else is wrong, especially the clanking sound of "lipsticked." Nature is honest; lipstick is commercial—nature is natural; lipstick is artificial. In this instance, nature is not funny, but the comparison is almost a joke.

A good metaphor will always be visually sharp and mysteriously imaginative. It will, almost always, be something of a surprise, too. One of the best tests to apply is the statement: "Why, I never thought of that before." If you can say this, and at the same time be impressed with the appropriateness of the similarity, then the metaphor is good. Finally, a metaphor should suggest more than it actually states, unlike the directions on a medicine bottle.

What you are to do is write a dozen or so sentences identifying things which you know are unfamiliar to your classmates: actions, buildings, accidents, clothes, noises, shapes, people, etc.

The word "identify" has been used here, instead of "describe," to focus your attention more sharply on the idea of conveying the essence of what you see; that is, the most important part of anything that tells what it really is.

Also, this time, in contrast to writing directly, which is what you do most of the time, write each sentence with a metaphor that suggests what a thing is—its identification—by showing what it is like.

Complete your assignment by the hour's end and submit it to the teacher.

Students are always told by teachers to behave well but are never or seldom told *how* to behave well. Each week I hand my students three forms, a self-evaluation form, a group-member and group evaluation form. They are given time to discuss the evaluations openly with each other. How they evaluate themselves, other members in their group and their group is not my business, but I have had some students come to me and say, "This is how I came out," in pride of themselves. Below is one of the three forms.

OUR EFFECTIVENESS AS A GROUP

SCALE 1 2 3 4 5 6 7 8 9 SCALE
(low)   (high)

. . . How free have the members felt to state their real opinions?

. . . What has been the ability of the group to define what it chose to discuss?

. . . How free have I felt to state my real opinions?

. . . To what extent have members accepted the responsibility for the outcome of the meeting?

. . . How productive have members thought the group was?

. . . How positive do members feel toward the work of this group this day?

. . . How well do I know myself?

. . . How well do others really know me?

. . . How free do I feel in having other members of the group express their feelings toward me?

. . . How well has this learning experience been going?

From the cooperation of students with each other, the effort of each group to be successful in their endeavors, to stick to the job until it is finished, to define their goals and procedures in light of mine for them, to complete a given task, the evaluation forms are to date successful.

I keep track of all the activities going on according to lessons outlined thoroughly in all the units. Below is an example of unit objectives with a lesson used in a ninth grade class.

A PSYCHEDELIC POETRY UNIT

Objectives: To help students see the artistry used in poetry
To make students aware of words as the poet's medium
To help students see that poetry can be their medium of making someone else aware

And from all the above, one major objective should result, an appreciation of poetry, emitted from an opportunity to understand it . . .

Lesson One

Announce to group that they are going to have a happening. Have them select an un-man-made object. Then tell them that for a period of twenty minutes, they are to stare at their object, feel, smell, and even taste it. In other words, the students are to become aware of their object in greater depth. Why use this technique?

Think of the artistic mind. Isn't an artist one who is aware in-depth? "He perceives more about select forms of existence than the average man. He spends time observing, appreciating, and, if he has talent, rendering his sensitivity through one of the art mediums." If a person spends twenty minutes staring at a simple object, the laws of visual perception demand that "more about that object is seen as time passes." In other words, a person becomes more aware of the makeup of the object.

After the twenty minute happening, have students begin talking about things they never had observed before. Summarize by telling students they had experienced in a small way what an artist experiences all the time. And, further, their own experience of awareness should contribute to their appreciation of the artistic mind.

Within the structure of this multi-unit approach are taking place many different activities: dramatizations of exciting scenes from a book read or based on a skit written originally by a group; dramatizations of phonemes-graphemes by the group studying the linguistic unit; commercials originally written by some groups studying television; special reports on a book read through a book jacket or student-made newspaper or television set; making dictionaries from names and types of racing cars; writing creative poems, short stories; and many other projects initiated by students and assigned as part of the daily lessons.

I contend that tests are subjective; and I knew that my students had been drowned in all kinds: essay, multiple choice, true and false and many more fact-centered ones. One of the worst things I could do would be to give my students such tests. Instead I evaluate by assessing the quality of students' contributions through panels, special reports, dramatizations, projects, compositions, group discussions, extra credit, student-teacher conference about their academic performance, their ability to be initiative, their willingness to stick to a job until it is finished, the quality of their work.

The multi-unit approach requires the teacher to take on a new role. I have defined mine as a resource person. I also have defined myself as a member of the group until a time of crisis. It requires the student to take on a new role too. He must learn to be self-directive, initiative. He must learn to explore on his own. I've found with many of my students that they are so used to being told the answers that when they are given merely leads to explore for themselves, they become frustrated because the answer is not right there for them.

This approach is releasing, however, a lot of the human potential in the students. David, a boy who came to my class fearful of the traditional dosage of noun, verb, adjective, adverb drills comments, "I always made D's and U's in English. I could never learn that stuff. In here I can do a lot of things that help me learn. . . ." Another boy, just released from a detention home, with an unbelievable truancy record and a low academic record, suggested a science fiction project idea to his group after they had read *Land of the Giants* (in three days). It was accepted: the group wrote a story about the population explosion, copies of which were given to their classmates; they made a project; they discussed their project in the auditorium before their own and another class. The boy has developed pride in himself and is now the most active member in his group besides leading his peers.

Whatever the multi-unit approach is doing for students, one thing is happening: students are now seeing that English is relevant by their involvement in activities which are allowing room for the release of human potential. To date the multi-unit approach has met the needs of my students. If it is meeting their needs, it is usable. After all, isn't meeting the needs of students our concern, our main concern?

ELIMINATING THE NEGATIVE IN ENGLISH TEACHING

Theodore W. Hipple

A COUPLE of decades ago a popular song attempted to solve many of the problems of romance by suggesting to young lovers that they "accentuate the positive and eliminate the negative." Half of this advice seems to have been followed in English teaching, where we have constantly tried to accentuate the positive in such matters as assigning more compositions, providing individualized instruction, offering work in reading improvement, and experimenting with the findings of the new grammars. But rarely have we tried seriously to follow the second half of the sage wisdom in the song; we have not tried to identify the negative and then to eliminate it. In the paragraphs which follow I hope to make a

➤➤➤-➤➤➤

FROM *English Journal* (March 1971), pp. 373–378. Reprinted by permission of the National Council of Teachers of English.

small beginning by identifying some practices in the teaching of English which I think are negative and which I believe could and should be eliminated. I include seven such practices in all.

1. *Pop quizzes.* About the only thing the teacher of English who uses pop quizzes reveals is the unfortunate paucity of his motivational skills; rarely, do such insults to students provide much other information. They may tell us who has studied the night before and who hasn't, but the damage they do far outweighs this meager information which we could discover anyway with a few well-chosen discussion questions. That teacher who suggests to students that they had better read the short story for tomorrow "because I just might give you a little surprise quiz on it" is doing more disservice to the short story in particular and to English study in general than he could do if he deliberately set about the task of ruining both. In truth, I must confess that such quizzes sometimes get students to read the lesson assigned to them, but so also would threatening them with death and destruction if they didn't read it. Though this line of argument smacks of *reductio ad absurdum,* it does categorize the pop quiz where I think it properly belongs: with a group of threats which have little place in good teaching.

There are times when a student ought not to read the assignment, when he ought instead to study for his chemistry test, or dream Walter Mitty-type dreams, or telephone his girl friend. What we English teachers must do is to make the reading we assign as intriguing or as desirable as these other activities. We hardly make reading pleasurable by holding a pop quiz over the student's head like some sword of Damocles which will be dropped, posthaste, upon his entering the class and hearing the fateful sentence (Pun on the last word intended): "Take out a sheet of paper and a pencil."

We can get the student to read the literary selections we assign and even to put them ahead of chemistry or dreams (but perhaps not of girl friends) by making our assignments more exciting. Let's let the student read the first few paragraphs in class or even read them ourselves. If it is a good short story, these first few lines will hook the student and he will finish the story. With longer assignments let's give him more class time to begin the reading; we can still rely on the gripping effect most literature, if wisely chosen, has on adolescents. Let's ask the student questions about this preliminary reading, get him to commit himself, and let him read on to learn if he is right. If we can do these things, then we can forget about pop quizzes.

2. *Book reports, oral and written.* When our daughter entered seventh grade this year, her first day in English, a subject in which she has, I hope, more than a passing interest, was ruined by the teacher's handout, a ditto of the year's great expectations. Among other things this sheet included the requirement of eight book reports, seven written, one oral.

Gad! What a thought to begin the year with. She'll survive, though, because she likes to read and has a father who can, if necessary, help her with the plot and characters and tell her to recommend the book to other seventh-graders who like horses. I shudder to think of her younger brother, now in sixth grade, who hasn't read a book since second grade. Perhaps he'll learn earlier than most about the usefulness of *Cliff's Notes* or the *Reader's Digest Book Condensations*. He may even try to fudge a report or two out of his sister's rough drafts. What I am certain of is that his interest in reading will not be heightened.

Book reports, and by that term I mean those written or oral responses a student must make to a book he alone has read (and no one else will read after they have studied or heard his report), seldom produce the results we have in mind when we assign them. They don't make the good reader read more or make the reluctant reader read at all. Instead, they produce a hatred for the report which very soon carries over to the book itself. When that happens, literature is the loser. Instead of having our students prepare oral or written book reports, let's give them class time to read, say one day a week. In that time the student can get hooked enough on the book (same principle as in #1 above) that he will finish it. If he wants to write or talk about the book, we'll be all eyes or ears, but let's not insist that he do so when he could instead be reading another book.

One final comment needs to be made about oral book reports. One wonders how many Mays of each school year are devoted to oral book reports. By that time teachers of English have about had it; their enervation is showing through. And, then, like a cooling summer breeze, inspiration hits: "Oral book reports! I'll have my students do oral book reports for the rest of the year. Me? I'll just sit in the back of the room and fight sleep with the rest of the audience who, like me, really don't give a damn about whether Penny Farmer, girl nurse, marries the rich old doctor or the struggling young intern."

3. *Spelling drills and tests.* Next on my list of negative practices to be eliminated is our present method of teaching (?) spelling. It usually goes something like this: On Monday the teacher reads the new words for this week, generally about twenty of them, and uses them in a sentence. Often the students have to create sentences of their own employing the new words and we get some dandies here ("The fireman came out of the burning building pregnant." *Pregnant* means "carrying a child."), but usually the students simply write the words as the teacher pronounces and spells them. If skillful, the teacher can kill half the period with this dictation exercise. Then on Wednesday the students take, and grade themselves, a practice test. The score they earn doesn't count. Again, half the period can be eaten up with this activity. Finally, Friday, the big day, comes and, amid a flourish of trumpets and the sound of a lot

of last minute cramming, the test is given; another half period shot. And then Saturday arrives and the students forget this week's words, clearing their minds for the twenty new words to be "given" on Monday.

This attention to spelling in the secondary schools far outweighs its importance. Spelling is the guest who has long overstayed his welcome, the man who came to dinner and now consumes 30 per cent (three half periods a week) of the English repast. We know we really don't teach much spelling in this manner. What we do is to provide an easy way to get top grades for those of our students who enter our classes knowing how to spell already and condemn the rest to a kind of weekly punishment similar in psychology and duration to the Chinese water treatment.

A far better method would be to discover early in the year which of our students do not spell well or who, in the words of an English teacher I know, exhibit their most heightened creativity during the spelling test. With these students we try to provide remedial work in the form of a dictionary and, ideally, a friend, preferably of the opposite sex, whom they can ask the spelling of a word they are uncertain about. In this way we would avoid the many spelling errors that now fill our students' papers and still have some time remaining to teach and to learn some really important parts of this stuff called English.

4. *Literature tests on the details.* Quick, now. Who in *Julius Caesar* said, "Let me have men about me that are fat"? About whom was it said? To whom was it said? In what act was it said? What scene? What line? Ah, yes, it's test time again and the teacher is poring over the literature text, searching for the smallest detail he can find. "There's a good one," he shouts sadistically and pounds it into the perpetuity of the ditto master. "That'll teach them to horse around in my class."

But I am being uncharitable. Surely the thousands of English teachers, both in secondary schools and in that citadel of intellect, the university, can't all be wrong and they're all, or most of them, giving literature tests that their colleagues couldn't pass; in fact, neither could they had they not made out the test. The obscure quote from a footnote, the multiple-choice item on how many pennies Della had when she left to have her hair cut, the tricky true-false question, should all go the way of the dodo bird. Literature is too rich, has too much to offer, to permit our sacrilege by reducing it to the irreducible and then testing on that. Let's focus our evaluative efforts on broad ideas and, by so doing, allow students to make differing responses to literature which we selected, after all, because we wanted the literature to affect our students. Please: no more questions that not even the author could answer.

5. *Usage.* "Cheers, students, it's time for our yearly excursion into the happy realm of usage. Pay careful attention these next two weeks and then you won't have to worry about these matters for a whole year. Take *who* and *whom,* for example. What do you mean—you don't want to

take them? You've got to. They're required as part of the curriculum. Just whom do you think you are? From *who* and *whom,* we'll move to 'six troublesome verbs': *lie, lay; rise, raise;* and *sit, set.* These verbs ought to take us about three or four days. And, next, we'll tackle the section on 'words often confused' like *imply/infer* and *affect/effect.* Now I know that some of you are disinterested in this material, but we have to cover it for the six weeks' test. So, open your books to page 63."

Surely a pep talk like that one will stimulate undreamed of amounts of student apathy. Yet it occurs all too often in our schools and in a form not too much different from that one (or is it *different than?*). Isn't it about time we began focusing our teaching of usage on that which the students use? The word *lain* doesn't appear in their vocabularies except after *lovers* and no amount of *lie/lay* drill is going to put it there. Rather, let's work on basic elements that, unless put in appropriate form, will cast the students in a bad light with reasonably well educated adults. We have to warn him that his use of *ain't,* if continued, may cost him some status and that there will be those who disapprove of his saying "between you and I," but please let's not confront him with these problems until we know for certain that, for him, they exist. To spend an entire hour for drill on subject-verb agreement in a suburban high school which sends three-fourths of its graduates to college is to waste time on a scale which, had it been duplicated by the founding fathers, would have them still trying to figure out which truths are self-evident. Even the non-college-bound ought not to have to suffer through period after period of meaningless, irrelevant drill. When one of them exhibits a usage pattern that may someday get him into trouble, let's get him aside, explain his problem, and help him try to overcome it. But we surely don't want to spread his disease to the entire class by making them study the problem whether they have it or not.

6. *In-class themes.* The in-class theme continues in full force in most secondary school English classes, presumably required to assist students in gaining the skills needed to write essay exams. But where are the essay exams? (See item #4 above.) In all honesty, of course, the in-class theme is assigned to assure that the teachers get what the student wrote, not what his parents or older sister produced for him.

Whatever its motivation, its stupidity as a teaching practice remains. To demand of adolescents that they produce something literate or profound (surely no teacher is so dull-witted as to expect both) in the space of forty or fifty minutes is to give them a task too difficult for even the *Mission Impossible* team. Writers don't write that way. They take their time in selecting content and directing it to audiences they have thought about and choosing voices for themselves compatible with their material and audience. They ponder over diction and style and, above all, they revise, revise, and revise. Why do English teachers expect fledgling writers to behave differently, to write something they are proud of (and their teachers can read) in one period?

Wouldn't it make more sense if the teacher assigned the paper several days in advance of the due date and, on the day after the assignment, gave the students the entire period to begin their rough drafts? The teacher could then collect these drafts, read through them quickly, making comments about improvements, and then return them to the students for completion and polishing out of class. Even if Dad or a sister did help out on the final product, most of the writing would still be that which the student did himself. Too, he might even learn something from Dad or a sister. Of course, this system means that the teacher must read the themes twice, once initially to suggest improvements and then again for final evaluation, but the better writing would be worth the extra effort.

7. *The blood-red theme.* No, constant reader, the "blood-red theme" is not from *Macbeth,* but from our common practice in composition grading. The themes we return look as though we cut our fingers while reading them. These red-filled adventures into sado-masochism (both student and teacher suffer in the process) get back to the student resembling some MacDonald's farm of abbreviations: Here an "awk," there a "sp," everywhere a "frag, frag." The research evidence indicates abundantly that this kind of never-miss-an error marking benefits no one, save possibly the manufacturer of red pencils. Seldom studied has been its devastating effects on the self-concept of the student who was really proud of the paper he turned in, only to have it returned looking like his dog's breakfast.

Why couldn't we devise a more humane and productive means of marking compositions? Perhaps if we graded only one or two aspects of writing per set of themes, we could return papers that had room for positive, flattering comments, as well as for the symbols necessary to indicate lapses on the one or two items stressed. Especially could this system work if the one or two key items were thoroughly taught in preparation for the writing assignment.

These, then, are seven practices that I would recommend for proscription in the English classroom; I am sure each teacher can think of as many more. With such proscription we *can* accentuate the positive by eliminating the negative.

RESEARCH AND THE TEACHING OF ENGLISH

J. Stephen Sherwin

IT seems to me that on almost any subject there is likely to be more opinion than information. I should like to offer some information today, but, of course, I cannot avoid including interpretive opinions. What I am offering is not THE word but A word, and I can only trust that what I say springs directly from a diligent and largely successful quest for genuine information.

For a period of eight years I devoted spare moments and some moments not easily spared to doing a critical survey of research in several selected areas which I considered important. I sought to discover what, if anything, research had to say about how spelling should be taught, about whether traditional sentence diagraming is a worthwhile instructional technique, about whether Latin provides a road to English mastery, about whether a knowledge of formal grammar or linguistics helps people in their writing, and, finally, about whether practice in writing helps people to improve their skill in writing. Although I cannot give a full report on all these investigations at this time, I should like to review some of the findings and comment about some implications which I think are worthy of the attention of anyone who is serious about teaching English and who considers himself a member of a learned profession. For analyses of the many studies I have inspected, I must refer you to *Four Problems in Teaching English: A Critique of Research,* which NCTE and the International Textbook Company published recently.

Before I became involved in the details of what I found, I must stress that my purpose was to find out what-we-know or whether-we-know-anything about these subjects. Experiments usually claim results; but are the results reliable and verifiable? Do they tell what they purport to tell? In short, to what extent can the research studies be believed when examined in the light of the research techniques used to obtain the results?

These are obvious questions. But they are also hard questions. Perhaps that is why they have not been asked as often as they should. The typical summary of research in a professional journal hardly tells more than what a number of people during a given period of time found or claim to have found. Different studies may have contradictory findings.

FROM *The English Record* (December 1970), pp. 35–43. Reprinted by permission of the publisher and the author.

Such information does not help people to decide what to do. All it does is provide excuses for those who want to justify what they have been doing all along.

Do not think for a moment that research can always be counted upon to provide neat answers. Sometimes answers elude even the best efforts to pin them down. Later on, by way of conclusion, I shall speak of the things which I think prevent research findings from influencing teaching. But for the moment it is enough to bear in mind that facts—even when they truly are facts—are not easy to recognize and that research needs to be interpreted. What I have done is interpret the research in the hope of pinning down a few bits of information which appear to me to be well-substantiated and therefore qualify as facts until, perhaps, better information comes along.

This tentativeness on the subject of "fact" is essential to what is called pompously the "scientific attitude." The study of science in high school or college should demonstrate (if it demonstrates anything) that knowledge is not final. To my generation H_2O was a fact about water. But now we know that there is more to the story—that there is something called heavy water which the formula H_2O does not reveal. Furthermore, recent findings suggest that there are arrangements to the molecules which can cause water to resemble heavy oil, so that ice and liquid and vapor are not the only forms that water can take. Again, there is more to the story of water than the formula H_2O tells. Facts are elusive. In science, nothing is final. All we know is what seems to work under given conditions and what seems to explain why something works under those conditions. In this respect educational research is no different from research in, say, chemistry. What I am now going to report to you is true or factual so far as I know at the present time. It may also be true next year, but I am making no guarantees.

First about traditional diagraming. Fundamentally, there are two kinds of sentence diagrams which have been in use in schools for a long time. These are the formal and the informal diagrams. The informal diagram is merely a series of impromptu arrows, circles, or underlinings which involves no special learning by students. It is used as the occasion arises by the teacher to illustrate rapidly some grammatical relationship, and it retains the linear form in which the language ordinarily occurs. The effectiveness of the *informal* diagram is not so much a question of its being a diagram as it is a question of its being a grammatical approach to language problems. But the *formal* diagram is both a grammatical approach and a definite schematic device intended to achieve a modification of students' use of language. It is the formal diagram which is ordinarily at the eye of controversy and is the subject of a few comparatively recent investigations.

Without exception, the studies find against either the efficiency or the effectiveness of diagramming as a method of teaching students how to write good, straightforward sentences. Experimental investigation began in 1940 with a master's thesis by Kenneth Barghahn which was methodologically weak. Walter Barnett's thesis, in 1942, repeated Barghahn's study with important improvements in method. In 1941, James Stewart completed his methodologically sophisticated dissertation on diagraming. All three studies agree that diagraming is no more effective in teaching language skills than are other methods of instruction. In 1945, Clair Butterfield examined direct and indirect methods of teaching punctuation and found that direct methods are more effective, thereby raising doubts about the effectiveness of other indirect methods such as diagraming. Anthony Tovatt, in 1952, found that diagraming is not used by the overwhelming majority of people when they write and that 38% of his participants who could not diagram claimed nevertheless that when they wrote they visualized their sentences as they would diagram them.

It is better not to teach traditional diagraming. I believe that the studies rightly conclude that diagraming is not a superior method of instruction. The reason for the opposition to diagraming is not that it fails utterly but rather that it imposes unnecessary, time-consuming tasks without conferring any special advantage. Recommending diagraming is like advising someone to count the cows in a field by totaling the legs and dividing by four. Almost anything else would do as well—and in less time.

Just as there continue to be hardy advocates of sentence diagraming, so there are hardy advocates of Latin as a means for improving skills in English. The question is—Is there really a Latin road to English mastery?

The history of the English language provides no reason to suppose that a knowledge of Latin grammar will help one to understand the structure of English and use it more deftly. English relies primarily upon word order to convey meaning, Latin upon inflection.

But does a knowledge of Latin increase a person's English vocabulary? There are many English words which come from Latin. But the most commonly used words are of Anglo-Saxon stock. This fact immediately restricts the significance of the Latin component in English. Studies comparing groups of Latin students with groups of English students show a small difference in favor of the Latin students, but not one of these studies allows for the fact that Latin students had a double exposure to language. The Latin students studied Latin and English in school, but the students to whom they were compared studied only English. After one allows for the built-in advantage for the Latin students, then their slight additional mastery of the English vocabulary is remarkable only because it is so slight. Intelligence seems to be a more reliable predictor of students' vocabulary achievement.

Does translating Latin improve students' ability to write English? Apparently not, according to the studies.

Does study of Latin improve students' ability to grasp another foreign language? No consistent experimental evidence in support of this contention was found. Among any group of related languages, the study of one is likely to be of some help in learning another. But no one language has been shown to be of such help that it should be studied *because* it paves the way for another.

Apparently Latin study did help students a little in mastering English spelling. But the advantage was too slight to serve as a justification for undertaking the study of Latin.

In short, there is no Latin road to English mastery, but, then, neither is there a royal road to geometry, as Euclid is reported to have said to Ptolemy I. The way to master English is the same as the way to master Latin—attend to it diligently, and, if possible, with the help of a good teacher. Any benefit transferrable from the study of one to the other is likely to be a meager reward for one's efforts. Latin should not be regarded as a means to an English end.

It may well be that the most widespread pedagogical theory among laymen and teachers alike is that a knowledge of traditional grammar will help one to use the language, especially in writing. Yet this widespread idea has almost no research support. Among 22 studies conducted between 1906 and 1963, all but one cast doubt upon the efficacy of traditional grammar to improve writing. Among the remaining 21, 2 are superior studies (by Frogner, Kraus) and one other (by Harris) has been listed by Professor Richard Braddock as being among the 5 best studies ever completed in its field.

Rarely does one find studies pointing so consistently in one direction. But of course consistency alone is meaningless, and as Emerson observed long ago, consistency can be foolish. The path of error, no matter how often trod, leads to error. The really germane issue is whether the methods by which consistent conclusions are reached are defensible. Only then is one justified in attaching importance to the conclusions.

What makes the experiments referred to here worthy of consideration is that they are generally well-controlled, their variables are isolated, and their measuring instruments are designed with care. When a good study, like Frogner's, achieves an objective measurement by using a test, it is possible to complain that a test is a less direct measurement than might be obtained by using the act of writing itself. But such a substitution would increase the chances of a subjective evaluation—which illustrates another Emersonian dictum, namely, that for everything which is given something is taken.

To overlook the valid in a quest for the definitive is also foolish. These experiments, by various means and with such safeguards as were devised, came to similar conclusions. This is not the sort of consistency which is the result of a compounding or repetition of errors. The research techniques do not appear to influence results in any one direction. Nor are the techniques so crude that any result would be suspect. The research is of sufficient quality to warrant the conclusion that instruction in formal grammar is an ineffective and inefficient way to help students achieve proficiency in writing.

As I said earlier, I cannot give a report on all the findings. I shall add two more points before undertaking to comment upon some implications I see. There is a theory which maintains that the way to teach writing is to give students repeated writing jobs to do. Writing teaches writing, it is said. The experimental evidence collected between 1932 and 1965 shows clearly that mere frequency of writing does not produce the desired result. One study, by McColly, in 1963, suggested ways in which writing can be taught without multiplying assignments. According to McColly, teachers should give a weekly writing task and spend 2 or 2½ days upon practical explanations, student practice, discussion, revising, rewriting, etc.

Last of all, I should like to review for you some of the findings about spelling. I spent more time exploring the research on spelling than I spent on any other two subjects combined. There is a certain irony in this because I am not convinced that spelling is the most consequential subject in the world or, for that matter, in the more restricted world of English teaching. On the other hand, the vast professional literature on spelling suggests that other people attach importance to spelling. Privately I may lament their concern for it and playfully court the idea that the educated man is the one who knows more than one way to spell a word. But ability to spell is a point of pride to some, a sign of culture to others, and a necessary point of conformity to still others (some of whom may be secretaries to people who cannot spell). It does seem that society is going to continue to expect conformity to its spelling conventions and that English and language arts teachers are going to continue to be charged with the job of teaching spelling.

How badly do we spell, really? One study (by Thomas Clark Pollock) presents convincing evidence that—however good or bad we may be at spelling these days—the situation is made to seem worse than it really is because linguistic conservatives decline to accept the legitimacy of alternative or variant spellings. Another study by Donald Emery reveals that even good dictionaries do not agree on the spelling of some words, on what is the usual spelling, and on what is the acceptable variant. Certainly English teachers should remember that the spelling lesson is not the place to indulge their language prejudices.

Still, the question remains—how well do we spell after allowance is made for confusion over alternate or variant forms? Several studies comparing the spelling performance of students around mid-century with the performance of students much earlier in the century show that the students closer to our time consistently misspell more often. This distressing finding may be softened by noting that the studies do not allow for the existence of a more select student population years ago. Nevertheless, students do not, as a group, spell as well as did their predecessors.

A great many studies seek to identify effective methods of teaching spelling. Here are a few major findings.

Rules. After examining the studies and weighing their methodological virtues and defects, it appears that rules offer only limited help in the teaching of spelling. To be at all effective, the rules must apply to many useful words and have few exceptions. Therefore, rules must be carefully selected. Instruction should probably be inductive and follow the test-study plan. Teaching by rule will probably be more effective with the brighter students. Because rules help in only a limited way, it follows that spelling instruction should not rely principally upon the use of rules.

Hard Spots. Two kinds of studies deal with hard spots in spelling words. The first seeks to identify the hard spots; the second seeks to determine whether marking hard spots or drawing attention to them in some way is an effective teaching method. The principal study of the first kind is by Gates, and the principal study of the second kind is by Tireman. The conclusion, after assessing the findings and how they were reached, is that teaching the hard spots is a waste of time.

Syllabication. Does dividing words into syllables help students to improve their spelling? The problem is complicated by the fact that the system of syllabication in present use was established by eighteenth century English printers who did not, unfortunately, identify unerringly the sound segments of the language. At present, there are no investigations of the value to spelling instruction of a linguistically accurate system of syllabication. The studies we have compare spelling instruction without syllabication to spelling instruction utilizing conventional syllabication. Although the findings of these studies are contradictory, the better ones suggest that syllabicating spelling words is a doubtful practice.

Test-Study or Study-Test. The evidence here is that the test-study method is superior.

Now I wish to turn away from summarizing in order to comment briefly upon the status of instructional research.

It has become a matter of increasing concern that classroom teachers are very little influenced by instructional research. I would say, for example, that the studies dealing with diagraming and formal grammar and other subjects are unknown to the overwhelming majority of English teachers. Those who do *not* (for example) diagram do *not* know about the studies. Those who *do* diagram do *not* know about the studies. Some who do indeed know about the studies seem to have no difficulty rationalizing a continuation of the practice.

Where does the trouble lie? Physicians do not, as a group, blithely disregard the results of research in their laboratories and clinics. Physicists do not write articles about what-works-for me. Of course, research in the physical sciences has certain built-in advantages over research in the social sciences or in education. I must also admit that a certain degree of skepticism *is* justified when one considers *any* research dealing with human behavior. However, a degree of skepticism is different from cultivated hostility to research findings—or apathetic unconcern for research findings.

It seems to me that we are barely beginning to emerge from our Phlogiston Period. When Lavoisier in the 1770's discovered the process now known as combustion, he overthrew the almost universally accepted phlogiston theory which held that when a substance burns phlogiston escapes. Today, of course, we recognize burning as a process in which oxygen *combines* with a substance, and this is a process which is directly opposite to what the phlogiston theory claimed to happen during burning. Yet Joseph Priestley (d. 1804), the discoverer of oxygen, went to his grave believing in the phlogiston theory which his colleague Lavoisier had disproved.

There is a clue in this situation which may help us to understand our own problem in gaining acceptance for research findings and methods. When concepts, practices, or theories seem to be useful or have a surface appeal to common sense, they become barriers to the acceptance of new and better concepts, practices, or theories. When long familiarity with an idea generates emotional ties to the idea, it becomes exceedingly difficult to displace it with another idea which actually has more to recommend it. Abstract devotion to truth is as uncommon among teachers, I fear, as it is among other people. Change comes hard.

Some educational research is not worth the ink to print it. Some of it is worthwhile and should command attention and exert influence. Certainly the principle that research is a means for revealing reliable information deserves the respect and adherence of every person who teaches. What is the alternative? To follow the wandering fires of mere opinion? I hope not! Yet how hard it is to breach the walls of dearly held opinion. Recently I received a letter from the head of a department of foreign languages in a high school. She wrote to object to my position on the Latin-English question. Her first point was that her students did not know any Latin or English grammar at the start but quickly learned such things as tense, person, voice, number, case, and subject-verb agreement. Her second point was that her Latin students obtained satisfaction by being able to answer grammatical questions in their English classes. Her third point was that all the English teachers in her school with whom she had spoken agreed that Latin had helped them to master English. Aside from the question of which of us is correct, I think I am justified in saying that we speak from quite different frames of reference. We do not agree on the basic issue of what constitutes evidence.

Fortunately, there are many people whose minds are not yet made up and who are willing to consider the kinds of evidence that scholarship can provide. The future is in their hands. No doubt some will cop out. I am thinking of a very good student I had some years ago who had been carefully educated, who knew the research, who knew what every young teacher should know. Two years after he graduated he returned to campus for a visit. I asked him how he taught the language. I confess to surprise when I heard him say that he used workbook drills, diagramed sentences, organized his instruction around the parts of speech, gave tests which called for the labeling of words and phrases, and so forth. Where was inductive teaching? Where was most of what supposedly he had learned at college? And why was he teaching this way? Because, as he explained, that was the way it was done in the school where he was employed. And had he done anything to change the way it was done? Well, no, he had not.

To be sure, programs in teacher preparation have also been remiss in not cultivating a concern among future teachers for research. It has been remiss in not encouraging a high valuation of research as a method of discovering truth. I can only hope that this state of affairs will not be with us much longer. There are small signs of improvement. If progress is ever to be made, it will be applied intelligence that makes it.

The Study of Literature

OF *all the "subareas" of English, it is literature that dominates class-room activity. The 1968 NCT study,* High School English Instruc-tion Today *by James R. Squire and Roger K. Applebee, revealed the extent of this domination when it reported that literature study consumed over 50 per cent of classroom time. Doubtless, even in the few years since that report, the trend has shifted somewhat—today the study of media, for example, is probably given some class time formerly devoted to literature—but it is still safe to say that litera-ture is the mainstay of the secondary school English program.*

Both the content of the literature being studied and the methods in which it is studied, however, have undergone and are undergoing significant changes. Silas Marner, *the "grand old man" of English, is on the decline and is being replaced in many schools by literature written especially for adolescent audiences. No longer are the works of such authors as Rosamund du Jardin, Betty Cavanna, Mary Stolz, Henry Gregor Felsen, and Paul Annixter, to name a few whose novels appeal to adolescents, relegated to book report days; they now often comprise the readings-in-common of entire classes. Shifts in the content of poetry lessons demonstrate a similar trend, with the poems of the Beatles, Simon and Garfunkel, or Ferlinghetti as common in today's classrooms as the more honored lyrics of Keats and Wordsworth. In drama Shakespeare competes for time with Tennessee Williams, Arthur Miller, and Edward Albee. Literature by and about members of minority groups, especially blacks, is at long last earning its overdue place in the English program.*

Methods, too, have changed. Today's teacher of English is less concerned with questions of the old sort ("Who did what to whom and in what act?") and more interested in questions that cause the students to probe their own responses ("How do you feel about what happened?"). Approaches that focus on values, responses, and, to use James Miller's phrase, "the development of the imagination," are now assuming major roles in literature classes.

The articles in this section reflect these changes. The first three selections (Turner, Miller, and Foster) discuss in broad terms the goals of literature study in the modern English classroom. Burton

[141]

and Fillion offer a valuable specific approach—"guided independent reading"—to be used in middle schools; with only minor modifications, it could be used in secondary schools as well. Christensen questions the common assumption that many students cannot or will not read and provides his own data to serve as refutation. The next three selections (Finn, Kaplan, and Mangione) offer numerous examples of literature which meets the demands for relevance of today's youth and then Mollenkott follows these with a perceptive statement demonstrating that traditional literature is also relevant to modern times. The two final selections confront issues that most teachers of literature face sometime during their careers: Small questions some of the reasons justifying the inclusion of black literature and appends a substantial bibliography that should prove beneficial to all teachers of English. Fransecky argues for a loosening of the restraints of censorship; literature, he believes, cannot flourish if it is "for adults only."

LITERATURE AND SOCIETY'S VALUES

Darwin T. Turner

I suppose that I have sinned no more than most teachers in my professorial generalizations about the uses of literature. Yet, during these days of anxious scrutinizing of the schoolroom shibboleths, I am haunted by one generalization in particular: that a study of literature helps one to understand people of different cultures, different social groups, and different classes. That dangerous demi-truth glistens enticingly today, its submerged nine-tenths in the path through which a humanitarian teacher hopes to sail his students from provincial ignorance to cosmopolitan awareness. Unless a teacher is alert to possible problems, he may fail in his efforts to inculcate understanding, for a brief and superficial study of literature more readily reinforces prejudices and fosters myths than it provides new vision. The problem is intensified today when many teachers and students have determined to use more literature from different cultures in an effort to create understanding across a continent if not throughout the world. Because the problem is acute, because the crash is imminent and dangerous, I wish to look both at the enticing surface of the generalization and at the deadly depth. If I seem to raise questions more than I offer answers, I wish to emphasize that my greatest concern is that the individual teacher should begin to think through these issues for himself.

Let me begin by confessing some of my own crashes as a careless captain. I have taught a short story, "Mateo Falcone," about a father who kills his son after the boy has betrayed a fugitive to the police. While attempting to help the students to understand and believe in the father, I have emphasized his ancestry among a people who value honor above all else. Certainly, that is what the story suggests; in fact, that is what the author states explicitly. But have I helped students remember the people of the story only as mountain criminals possessed of a disturbing code of ethics?

I also recall a French story about a mother who avenged her soldier son by killing the enemy youths billeted at her house. The question arises again: have I helped delude students into stereotyping the French as brave but treacherous and vengeful people? I trouble myself less about the second story, for I can rationalize that at some time during the years

FROM *English Journal* (May 1971), pp. 577–586. Copyright © 1971 by the National Council of Teachers of English. Reprinted by permission of the publisher and Darwin T. Turner.

[143]

before he finishes college, the student has learned or will learn other characteristics which will flesh the flat stereotype into a three-dimensional concept of French life and character.

I am subject to dangers even in the apparently simple matter of selecting materials from English and American literature. If I teach only William Congreve's *The Way of the World* as an example of the literature of the eighteenth century, do I persuade my students to believe that most Englishmen of the time were cold, witty, and wealthy Mirabels and Millamants? Or, in American literature, may I carelessly create the impression that the East is populated by Fitzgerald's millionaires, the South by Faulkner's frustrates, and the Midwest by Lewis' Babbitts? "Of course not," comes the response. In any classroom in America, there will be one or more readers capable of knowing, without my explanation, that other types populate at least one of these regions. In the same classroom, however, how positive can I be that students will not generalize about American minorities from whom they have been separated? How do I know that students will not presume that Mark Twain's Jim or Richard Wright's Bigger Thomas is a faithful likeness of the majority of black Americans?

In short, whenever a reader cannot use his personal experience or his previous study to expand the portraiture of a single work, he may believe that the values represented are faithful and full representations of the values of that unfamiliar group. Moreover, if he has already formed judgments about the characters, attitudes, and experiences of groups whom he does not know intimately, his prejudices may be fortified by the reading of a single work which seems to conform to those prejudices; in contrast, his prejudices probably will withstand the onslaught of a single work which refutes them.

I believe that the implications of my statements are significant. If we are truly concerned with using literature for the humanitarian purposes of helping students analyze the values of their own groups and helping students understand the values of others, we must be cautious about the quantity and the dimensions of the samples selected. This caution must not only govern a choice of materials from cultures about which students know nothing; it must also regulate the selectivity for cultures about which the students have false information.

The general dimensions of the problem should be obvious. But let me explore them further in a more specific context. As we seek to define the values of particular groups, we may be guilty of describing only the values approved by scholars and editors, by publishers, or by the mass of the reading public—that is, the individuals sufficiently educated in a particular tradition to seek recreation in reading and sufficiently affluent to purchase reading materials. In each of these instances, we may unsuspectingly accept values which falsely reflect the group described in the work: the values may be unimportant to the group or even contrary to the sentiment of the group.

To provide a useful angle for considering the problem, let me ask you to imagine that you have never lived in America. As a teacher of literature in another country, you wish to help your students discern America's values. Except for what you have read in local newspapers, your only knowledge of America has been derived from a chapter in a history book and a memory of *Porgy and Bess,* a musical which the American government exported to your country as an example of American culture. Although white Americans played only minor roles in that show, you feel that you have gained insight into the lives of black Americans.

Let me remind you of the plot. Porgy, a crippled street vendor, falls in love with Bess, an attractive woman who has been the mistress of a killer, who is a fugitive. When the criminal returns to reclaim Bess, Porgy kills him. The police arrest and imprison Porgy. When he is released after a week in jail, he discovers that Bess, resuming her habit of taking drugs, has run off with another man.

The musical has taught you that black Americans casually accept and approve sexual relationships not sanctioned by marriage laws, kill each other, take drugs, and lie to police. With such a view of the standards of the Afro-American community, you have sympathized with white Americans when newspaper reports have informed you that these blacks are demanding opportunity to attend schools with Euro-Americans, to work on jobs with them, and to live among them.

Now that you are beginning a more intensive study of American group and class values, however, you look for examples in anthologies of American literature. You find one anthology which seems useful. Published as recently as 1965, it is a four-volume work, which includes one volume entitled *The Realistic Movement in American Writing.* The title suggests that the volume is ideal for your purposes. Perusing the volume you learn a little more about Afro-Americans through introductions by the editor, works by Joel Chandler Harris and Thomas Nelson Page, and even works by two black authors—Paul Laurence Dunbar and Booker T. Washington. In the introduction to the stories by Harris and Page, the editor explains, "If their pictures of the old South are nostalgic and idealized, they preserve a truth no less real than the slave driver's lash. The fact that during the War no slave revolt developed is proof enough that within the institution of slavery there frequently developed a bond of affection between slave and master."[1]

Although the stories by Harris and Page show nothing about the lash alluded to by the editor, they certainly illustrate his picture of affection. In the two Uncle Remus tales from Harris, a kindly slave affectionately

[1] Bruce R. McElderry, Jr., ed., *The Realistic Movement in American Writing* (New York: Odyssey Press, 1965), p. 235.

tells animal stories to his master's young son. In the story by Page, the adventures of "Marse Chan," an heroic, gentlemanly Virginian, are narrated by the slave who loved him. Since you have found these stories presented by an American editor as examples of the realistic movement in American literature, you have reason to believe that you are viewing a representative picture, not only of the blacks, but also of the well-mannered, aristocratic Virginians who never mistreated slaves, never sold them, but treated them almost as indigent relatives.

The works by Afro-Americans do not alter your picture. In Paul Laurence Dunbar's poems you learn that a "picanniny's" weariness, gloom, or anger can be dispelled by his "mammy's" cabbage, bacon, chitlins, and corn pone and that a black coquette can be won by bringing her possum meat. In the introduction to a chapter from Booker T. Washington's autobiography *Up from Slavery,* included in a section entitled "Representative Ideas," the editor praises the perception of "the unofficial spokesman of his race" that "the Negro must first learn to be useful in society, must accept a gradual extension of opportunity as he earns a right to it" (p. 611). In the chapter itself, which the editor has referred to as a description of Washington's boyhood presented "without melodrama or exaggeration" (p. 611), Washington states, "The most trying ordeal that I was forced to endure as a slave boy, however, was the wearing of a flax shirt" (p. 616. According to his recollection, he was only six or seven when the Civil War ended). Washington follows this mild remonstrance almost immediately by denying most slaves nurtured bitterness towards their masters and by affirming the mutual love of slaves and masters.

As a foreigner, you do not know that Washington, Dunbar, and many other black intellectuals and writers of that period, trying to oppose the violence of the Ku Klux Klan and other terrorist groups and trying to secure the Constitutional rights supposedly granted to all Americans, sought to elicit the help of the "silent majority" in the South and North by agreeing to forget the past, by reminding them of the fidelity with which blacks had served through the centuries, and by appealing to them to use mutual love and respect as a guide for the future.

Directed only by the anthology, you do not know about a pamphlet published in 1829 in which David Walker urged slaves to unite and overthrow the slave system. You do not know about such slave rebellions as those of Gabriel, Denmark Vesey, or Nat Turner. You do not know about the increasing numbers of laws passed in the South during the 1830s and 1840s to prevent flight or rebellion by the slaves who, here, are reported only to love their masters and their conditions. You do not know the harsh appraisal of slavery in the 1845 autobiography of Frederick Douglass, who, unlike Washington, matured to manhood as a slave and fled from his master. You do not know that Paul Laurence Dunbar, among other blacks, vigorously opposed Booker T. Washington's conciliatory proposal to trade voting rights for the right to work or that Washington himself later repudiated the very appeasement for which the editor praises him. Perhaps you do not even perceive the editor's unintentional irony in commending Washington's calculated admonition that blacks must *earn* the right to those opportunities which white Americans and immigrants *expected* as a natural result of living in a country which promised equal opportunity to all.

Guided only by the editor's selections, you do not even know that he might have chosen a poem by Dunbar in which a plantation preacher, using the Moses story as a pretext, attacks slavery[2] or that he might have selected a short story in which Dunbar describes the atrocious lynching of two black men for a crime committed by a white girl.[3] You do not know that the editor might have selected folktales or stories from Charles Chesnutt, a black contemporary of Dunbar. Even though he admitted that some slaves loved their masters, Chesnutt preferred to write about Afro-Americans who respected their own dignity. Chesnutt's Uncle Julius tells folktales to a white audience but always with expectations of a profit for himself.[4] Chesnutt's novels dispel any illusion that love bound white and black in the South. You do not know that the editor might have used an essay from DuBois' *The Souls of Black Folk,* a collection of essays published only two years later than Washington's autobiography (McClurg, 1903). In that collection DuBois perceptively appraises the personalities of Southern blacks and, without bitterness, examines the barriers between the sons of masters and men. These facts, however, you do not know. Trusting the anthology, you might conclude that blacks of the pre-Civil War period were gay, irresponsible individuals, easily appeased by good food and kind treatment from the masters whom they loved. You might be somewhat perplexed that there was any reason for waging the Civil War; and, comparing Uncle Remus with Porgy, you might even agree with Page's propagandizing protagonists that black people would have been happier and worthier if the North had not forced them to leave the confines of slavery.

If your curiosity prompted you to look back to an earlier volume of that anthology of American literature to learn how Americans generally reacted to the issue of slavery, you would not have learned more. In that volume of pre-Civil War literature, which includes work from such anti-slavery authors as Emerson, Thoreau, Whittier, and Melville, there seems to be nothing about slavery, except Melville's "Benito Cereno,"

[2] "An Ante-Bellum Sermon," in *The Complete Poems of Paul Laurence Dunbar* (New York: Dodd, Mead, 1913).

[3] "The Tragedy at Three Forks," in *The Strength of Gideon and Other Stories* (New York: Dodd, Mead, 1900).

[4] *The Conjure Woman and Other Tales* (Boston: Houghton Mifflin, 1899).

an ambiguous story which affords a reading hostile to blacks. You might conclude, therefore, that slavery was so casually accepted among the standards and approved values of America that no one bothered to write about it.

Perhaps, however, you, a foreigner, have chosen to educate your students by avoiding scholarly anthologies in favor of novels which are currently popular among Americans. Here again, you might enforce belief in values which are questionable.

Almost a decade ago, I made a study to determine which values could be inferred from an examination of some best sellers of 1959–60.[5] I chose best sellers because purchases by large numbers of Americans implied general approval by the reading public. I excluded romantic fantasies and scrutinized only those best sellers in which American authors professed to interpret American society.

If I were to summarize the results for a foreigner interested in American culture, I would be forced to state that Americans superficially affirm traditional values—love, the Golden Rule, ethical principles, tradition itself, and service to humanity. In contrast, however, they admire and seem to envy the ruthlessness which tramples all codes to seize its desires, and they fear loneliness. Furthermore, they believe that love, courage, decency stabilize childhood but must surrender later to the realization that the highest pleasure results from the adult's abnegating childhood virtues, an action which will corrupt and destroy the adult but which will furnish the intensity essential to meaningful existence. If it seems to you that this does not effectively picture the values of America at the beginning of the last decade, remember that the conclusion is derived from a study of fifteen best sellers. If I had limited myself to one or two, the picture might have been even more distorted.

For instance, one of the authors included was John O'Hara, who wrote in *Sermons and Soda Water* (Random House, 1960),

> The United States in this century is what I know; and it is my business to write about it to the best of my ability. . . . The Twenties, the Thirties, and the Forties are already history, but I cannot be content to leave their story in the hands of the historians and the editors of picture books. I want to record the way people talked and thought and felt, and to do it with complete honesty and variety (p. x).

Surely, in the work of such a concerned social historian, one would expect to find a perceptive presentation of American values. Judge for yourselves.

O'Hara's best seller during 1959 was *From the Terrace* (Random House, 1958), the story of Alfred Eaton, who, as a child of a wealthy

5 "Ambivalent Values in Recent Best Sellers," in *Journal of Human Relations,* X (Winter–Spring 1962) 163–180.

Eastern family, became estranged from other members of the family. Rejected by a father blinded by love for a dead son and isolated from a mother who compensates for her loneliness by escaping into a world of alcoholism, he derives understanding and sympathy only from one sister. The absence of love in childhood compels a search for love, a search unfulfilled by sexual conquests which end invariably in his seeking to transmute the physical act into a spiritual union. Although he can rationalize his enjoying the embraces of more than one woman, he suffers disillusionment when each woman whom he selects can enjoy the embrace of more than one man.

As a young adult, he meets a beautiful girl, Mary, restrains his desire to possess her (to her regret), convinces himself that he loves her, and marries her. With a suddenness, however, which causes the actions to seem simultaneous to the honeymoon's end, the lovers quarrel, Mary Eaton consoles herself with her former fiancé, and Alfred swears eternal love for Natalie, the most physically beautiful woman he has ever known. Through the remainder of the novel, Alfred demonstrates his fidelity— first to his mistress, then to his wife, and finally to his mistress, whom he marries. Thus, O'Hara implies, Alfred Eaton has proved that significant and permanent relationships between the sexes must be based on love.

Of course, a careful reader might be somewhat puzzled about the contradictions between the hero's protestations and his actions. Although he has castigated his wife's assumptions that physical satisfaction produces happiness, it is difficult to determine what other satisfaction he finds in Natalie, for whom he swears undying love less than seven hours after they have met and at a time at which they have exchanged scarcely more than the banalities of introduction. When he believes that Natalie has abandoned him, he forgives his wife's indiscretions, permits her to seduce him, and certainly seems happy enough beneath the bedcovers of a wife whom he does not love. This is America's standard—for the wealthy at least, O'Hara seems to say.

Possibly Americans would deny that O'Hara has appraised America's standards and values accurately. Then perhaps they would also deny a thesis which Irving Wallace advances in *The Chapman Report* (Simon and Schuster, 1960), another best seller. Among a motley collection of women depicted in the book—most of them neurotic and lascivious, only one seems happy. Because she loves her husband, she experiences orgasm when they engage in sexual intercourse. The heroine of the novel endorses the value implied by Wallace. Having been divorced by a war hero who has denounced her frigid responses, the heroine, attracted to a new man, insists upon a premarital relationship in order to determine whether their love can thaw her former restraint. For the sake of romance, a reader rejoices that the lover is sufficiently adroit to help her succeed in their first attempt. Otherwise, Wallace implies, the heroine would have rejected him because of her belief, as an average American, that true love produces orgasm every time, from the first to the last. Nonsense? Ridiculous as a value to be presumed for all American women? I think so, because I know many Americans who perceive the fallacious reasoning which underlies this belief. But how do we American teachers know that the values which Jane Austen posits in her "realistic" novels actually characterized the English society which she delineated? What were Tennyson's actual values—those found in *Idylls of the King,* or those in the salacious stories which he told privately?

In O'Hara's novel, Alfred Eaton never forgives his father for having sent him to a school which was not adjudged the most exclusive prep school in the country. Since I do not know Eastern millionaires personally, I cannot dispute O'Hara's contention that children of these people may nurse lifelong hatred because they have been required to attend schools which are reputed to be only second or third best in the country. I cannot dispute the contention even though I may judge it absurd. But if I reject O'Hara's depictions of Americans whom I do not know, how can I justify my discussions of realism in the portrayals of foreigners whom I do not know—the English in Galsworthy's novels, the Germans in Thomas Mann's *Buddenbrooks,* the Russians in Tolstoy's *Anna Karenina?*

Am I judging realistic and commendable those values which my education and background have taught me to approve while rejecting those disapproved by my education? If so, what can I do with stories in which the approved values seem to conflict with mine? For instance, in *The Lion and the Jewel,*[6] African Wole Soyinka presents as a protagonist an African chief who makes a fool of another black African who, educated in European schools, tries to end tribal dependence upon tradition. Do I refuse to believe the values implied because they conflict with those which I have been taught to approve? Do I argue that the play is therefore a farce, or do I ridicule the characters and the author as exponents of inferior values? Turning closer to home, when I read Erskine Caldwell's *Tobacco Road,* do I refuse to teach it because, loving the culture of the South, I judge it a melodramatically false picture? Or do I, contemptuous of the South, choose to teach the play as a perceptive presentation of the mores of a backward people? In short, while I condemn the arbitrariness and deceptive persuasions of editors and authors, am I as a teacher guiding students' vision by my own prejudices and provincialities?

This final question constitutes a critical issue at this present time, when many teachers conscientiously wish to use literature to help students

---

[6] Wole Soyinka, *Five Plays* (London: Oxford University Press, 1964).

understand, and perhaps sympathize with, the values of people with whom they are unfamiliar. The question of concern is, with so many opportunities to be misled by the preferences of editors, by the tendency of writers to present ideas which will be approved by the public, by the publishers' tendencies to base decisions on their perceptions of what will or will not sell, and by a teacher's personal ignorance or prejudices as a middle-class American, how does one ever determine the value of the unfamiliar group? How does one ever determine which literary works to teach?

Jean Toomer's *Cane* (Boni and Liveright, 1923), a beautifully-written collection of stories about the South, is commended as a realistic presentation of Southern blacks. Toomer, a Northerner, spent fewer than six weeks in the South. In his sketches about the South, only one black male is a central character; that one is a conventional character in the familiar triangle of black female-white male-black male. A female friend of Toomer insisted that he never saw women as they actually were. Toomer's intense intellectual and moral biases regulate all of the ideas in his writing. What makes it possible to assume that Jean Toomer depicts the values of black society competently? Let me hasten to add parenthetically that I am not attacking Toomer, whose writing I admire and recommend. But I must continue to ask, "What makes us assume that Toomer's work reveals actual values of rural Southern blacks?"

Toomer was identified as Negro. His non-Negro friend Waldo Frank, like Toomer, briefly visited the South before writing a book about Southern blacks. Does awareness of this fact affect our evaluation of the authenticity of Frank's picture? Despite the justified protests from black critics and readers, many Americans accept the values of William Styron's Nat Turner as the values of the actual Nat and of slaves (*The Confessions of Nat Turner*, Random House, 1966). How then should we judge the values revealed in Daniel Panger's *Ol' Prophet Nat* (Blair Publishers, Winston-Salem, N.C., 1967), which, published at approximately the same time, is almost a point by point refutation of the standards and values which Styron invents?

As a speaker charged only with the responsibility of stimulating discussion this afternoon, I should stop now so that you and the commentator may talk. But as a teacher fearful that my remarks may be misconstrued as an argument for teaching literature solely as an art form with as little reference as possible to the social ideas of a work, let me quickly suggest a few ways to solve the dilemma or minimize the deleterious effects.

One, I believe that, rather than generalizing wildly, a teacher must help students to perceive the social, class, or group limits indicated by the author. For example, in *Native Son*, Richard Wright did not attempt to describe the values of all blacks living in Chicago's ghetto.

His awareness of different values is made clear by his presentation of some of those other values in such novels as *Lawd Today* and *The Outsider*. Nor did Lorraine Hansberry depict the values of all ghetto-housed Chicago Afro-Americans in *A Raisin in the Sun*. Nevertheless, each author in his own way reveals values which are significant to black people in Chicago and which, added to still other pictures, might reveal the people clearly. (Incidentally, this illustration is itself an evidence of some of the errors of the past. Although I have seen *Native Son* and *A Raisin in the Sun* evaluated separately as reflections of Afro-Americans, I have never seen the two works compared, despite their obvious focus on the same socioeconomic classes of Afro-Americans in the same city. The two works were created only nineteen years apart. Both the Thomases of *Native Son* and the Youngers of *A Raisin in the Sun* migrated from the South to the North. And Walter Lee Younger is only three years younger than Bigger Thomas would have been if he had lived until 1959.) When talking about the literature of any people with whom the class is not intimately acquainted, the teacher should help the students to understand that a single work reflects the values of a part of a group or class, no matter what the class or group may be.

Two, rather than presuming that all literary works are art objects which can be studied without reference to their creators, each teacher discussing a work which implies social value—and most works do imply such—should try to learn as much as possible about the author—his background, the particular group for which he might speak, and his biases.

Third, when treating materials from a culture unfamiliar to most of the students, a teacher must not limit the sampling unfairly. All introductions to propaganda and logic, taught in freshman courses in college and often in senior courses in high school, examine the fallacy of drawing inferences from a sampling which is too limited. Yet, guided by anthologies, many of us, in the name of liberal education, infer conclusions from only one sample or two. I remind you of the Merimée story which I mentioned at the beginning of this paper. Was there any other story about those people in the anthology from which I taught? I doubt it. Do Dunbar, Booker T. Washington, and James Baldwin constitute a satisfactory panel to describe the values of all black Americans during the past one hundred years? Of course not. A few weeks ago, when I attended a meeting of Afro-Americans in one small town of 75,000 people, I could have identified at least five groups of blacks who would have diverged sharply from the positions of Dunbar, Washington, and Baldwin, who diverge sharply from each other. Nevertheless, these five groups coexisted in the same community, which also included Afro-Americans who would have echoed the values of those three writers.

Ultimately, the classroom teacher must be the individual to introduce reason to discussions by proceeding cautiously and by burning the study lights into the hours which madden mates. But, because I sympathize with those teachers whose time is limited by preparations for four or five classes and by committee work, I wish that assistance would be provided by editors of anthologies and by literary critics.

Editors cannot be expected to rid themselves of the biases which they have developed in thirty or more years of life; nevertheless, they should attempt, as objectively as possible, to explain the criteria which they have used as a basis for their selection. Moreover, when their selections conflict ideologically with other works by the same author, they should call attention to the fact.

Literary critics—especially the academic critics, the scholar-critics— have just as grave a responsibility. They should search into the authors' lives, personalities, and prejudices, and use this information as part of their discussion of an author's specific works. Please do not misunderstand. I am not merely proposing that more biographies be written. I am not suggesting that all critics abandon their fun-filled hunts for and explications of symbols, myths, archetypes, allusions, and sources. And I am certainly not suggesting that literary scholarship be further burdened with searches for Oedipal complexes and father fixations. I am merely suggesting that more literary critics should conscientiously inform their readers about the author's familiarity with and attitudes toward the values of a group or class which he is purporting to describe in a particular work. More work in this direction would provide teachers with the information which they must use to determine the reliability of those particular works as a basis for a discussion of the values of a group.

Until editors and critics assume these responsibilities, however, the burden, as usual, falls upon the classroom teachers. These individuals will determine whether the next generation sees the values of an unfamiliar group—the Afro-Americans—merely through the eyes of Dunbar, Harris, Page, Baldwin, or Malcolm X, or becomes sufficiently perceptive to understand that no group, no region, no class, no nation is ever defined fully by the actions or the words of a single human being.

LITERATURE IN
THE REVITALIZED CURRICULUM

James E. Miller, Jr.

THE place and role of literature in contemporary education is best understood in the context of a simplified view of the recent history of American education. By taking a sweeping and somewhat arbitrary view of the last 100 years or so, we can discern four stages in American educational history. These four stages may be loosely labelled the Authoritarian, the Progressive, the Academic, and the Humanitarian.

The first of these stages, the Authoritarian, we identify with the arid classicism and rote learning of the nineteenth century; the second, the Progressive, with John Deweyism (something different from the real Dewey), indiscriminate permissiveness, and social adjustment, all running deep into the twentieth century. In more recent times, we have been witness to a revolution in our schools which we may, for convenience, date from Russia's Sputnik launching in 1957, and which I have arbitrarily designated Academic. In this stage we have seen the introduction of the new math, the new physics, and the new English in our schools, together with emphasis on intellectual grouping or tracking to identify and challenge the intellectually gifted—all rather much under the supervision of the academic rather than the education establishment, and all somewhat a reaction to the academically thin curricula of the schools awash in the back eddies of extremist progressivism.

We are now, in my view, on the threshold of the fourth stage, which I call the Humanitarian. If we pause for a moment and glance backward, we note that the stages I have described are not clearly defined historical periods but merely the slow swinging of a pendulum between two poles of emphasis which may be variously described as substance and psychology, subject matter and student, or intellectuality and society. The recent emphasis on the academic disciplines was, as I have suggested, brought to a focus and accelerated by Russia's Sputnik in 1957. Even before this date, the Supreme Court (in 1954) handed down its decision on racial integration of the schools. In some ways this launching of a social revolution, though slower felt, had more profound consequences than the Sputnik launching. And as this social revolution has gained momentum in the 1960's, it has definitely affected—and will certainly affect more deeply in the future—the trend of the 1950's to-

→>>

FROM *Bulletin of the National Association of Secondary School Principals*, Vol. 51 (April 1967), pp. 25–37. Reprinted by permission of the publisher and the author.

ward academic emphasis (or, as some would charge, academic over-emphasis) in the schools.

If we talk about trends or "new developments" in English, it is important to keep this historical context in mind. And though I have introduced the metaphor of the pendulum, I do not want to suggest that the schools have been simply moving back and forth between two extremes of educational theory. On the contrary, I think that there has been change and advance in educational theory, that the Academic stage of the 1950's is fundamentally different from the Authoritarian stage of the earlier time, and the new stage we confront now—the Humanitarian—is and will continue to be radically different from the Progressive stage before it. Perhaps it would be best to substitute the metaphor of the spiral in place of the pendulum, to suggest that successive stages veer away and return—but the return is never back but forward.

To talk about literature in the contemporary curriculum is to talk about a subject and a program both of which are in a state of flux. As I have indicated, there are at this moment revolutions and counter-revolutions in progress in the curricula and there are basic reconsiderations under way of the nature of language and literature and the ways they relate to learning. Before turning specifically to the new look of literature in the curriculum, I need to describe briefly a new way of looking at language and literature.

A New Way of Looking

The old way of looking at language was to consider it as a logical system originated and elaborated primarily by man's rational faculty and learned by him basically for the purpose of communicating thought. It followed from this conception that literature was fundamentally embellishment and decoration, a nice refinement of the use of language, but not central to the pragmatic purpose of communication of thought. Many consequences have flowed from this bundle of misconceptions of language and literature, but I shall now only point an accusing finger at such English courses in the curriculum as Business Letter Writing or Grammar for Composition, "practical" courses frequently preferred over the "impractical" literature courses. We have known for a long time that such courses as these never achieved their aims, but we have been a long time finding out why. The reasons lie deep in the heart of our misconceptions.

How may we free ourselves from the constricting terms of such a narrow view of language? The way to such freedom is not long and not hard. If we would simply look honestly at our own experience with

language, how we learned (and still learn) it and how we use it—
how we are involved with it or entangled in it—we would discover
quickly that language is filled with more mystery than sense, more ca-
price than logic, more surprise and defiance than compliance and capit-
ulation. Language is not something we take or leave, learn or not learn;
it is as inescapable and engulfing as the air which surrounds us, and
like the air it is the substance by which we live our lives, by which
we create and understand our nature and world. It is as vital to our
nonphysical being as blood is to our body. In short, language is the
most compelling manifestation we have of our humanness.

Another way to liberate ourselves from the utilitarian, reductive view
of language is to listen to philosopher-scholars who have devoted their
lives to speculative study and investigation of language. Take, for example, the great linguist and philologist Otto Jespersen, in *Language:
Its Nature, Development and Origin:*

> The genesis of language is not to be sought in the prosaic, but in the poetic
> side of life; the source of speech is not gloomy seriousness, but merry play
> and youthful hilarity.[1]

Or note Edward Sapir's observation in *Language:*

> The autistic speech of children seems to show that the purely communica-
> tive aspect of language has been exaggerated. It is best to admit that
> language is primarily a vocal actualization of the tendency to see realities
> symbolically. . . .[2]

Or consider the philosopher Ernst Cassirer's statement from *Language
and Myth:*

> It is language . . . that really reveals to man that world which is closer to
> him than any world of natural objects and touches his weal and woe more
> directly than physical nature. For it is language that makes his existence in
> a *community* possible; and only in society, in relation to a 'Thee,' can his
> subjectivity assert itself as a 'Me.'[3]

Or, finally, observe Susanne K. Langer's statement from *Philosophy in
a New Key:*

> The fact is that our primary world of reality *is* a verbal one. Without words
> our imagination cannot retain distinct objects and their relations, but out of
> sight is out of mind. . . . The transformation of experience into concepts,

[1] Otto Jespersen. *Language: Its Nature, Development and Origin.* New York: Macmillan Co., 1949; also New York: W. W. Norton & Company, 1964 (paperback).

[2] Edward Sapir. *Language: An Introduction to the Study of Speech.* New York:
Harcourt, Brace & World, 1921.

[3] Ernst Cassirer. *Language and Myth.* New York: Dover Publications, 1946.

not the elaboration of signals and symptoms, is the motive of language. Speech is through and through symbolic; and only sometimes signific. Any attempt to trace it back entirely to the need of communication, neglecting the formulative, abstractive experience at the root of it, must land us in the sort of enigma that the problem of linguistic origins has long presented. . . . One might say that, if ritual is the cradle of language, metaphor is the law of its life.[4]

Imagination Central

If we accept this new (but really very ancient) view of language, certain consequences for education are immediately evident. This view places language at the center of human existence and experience, and it places the imaginative (creative or symbolizing) rather than the logical (signifying or communicating) faculty at the center of linguistic life and growth. It follows from this concept that language should be at the center of any defensible curriculum, and that imaginative verbal experience (especially literature) should be at the heart of the language sequence. Reduced to its barest terms, the English curriculum from beginning to end should have as its primary aim the education, development, and fullest possible extension of the linguistic imagination. The construction of the curriculum should emphasize the primacy of creativity and imagination in learning to live as a full participant in the vital world of language.

If there is a "new English," it is English that has placed literature, defined in the broadest terms, at the center of the curriculum, and that has taken the development of the imagination, conceived in the most liberating sense, as its ultimate aim. In a skeptical world of logical positivists, the very existence of a faculty labelled Imagination may be called into doubt. But we must insist on its existence because we know that we cannot live lives as human beings without it. Like the dream or the unconscious or even mind itself, we know the imagination exists because we have experienced it within us and have witnessed it in others. That is sufficient proof for all but the most material-minded and unimaginative. Most thoughtful people and many speculative writers have paid tribute, at one time or another, to the imagination as vital to human life. Wallace Stevens, in *The Necessary Angel*, has put the matter this way: [Imagination is] "an aspect of the conflict between man and organized society. It is part of our security. It enables us to live our own lives. We have it because we do not have enough without it . . . the imagination is the power that enables us to perceive the normal in the abnormal, the opposite of chaos in chaos."

[4] Susanne K. Langer. *Philosophy in a New Key: A Study in the Symbolism of Reason, Rite, and Art.* Cambridge, Mass.: Harvard University Press, 1957.

In this new conception of English, focusing on the faculty of the Imagination, there is a new realization that imaginative growth involves both receptivity and creativity, both witnessing and making, both intake and output. In short, there is realization that the creative impulse is an inherent part of the imagination, and that deep engagement with literature will naturally involve the creative act. Every English teacher has long known that the world is full of secret poets. It is the shame of our profession that we have not before now nourished rather than suppressed this natural—and, indeed, even *vital*—impulse to imaginative creation. Every English course should be a course in the imagination in its dual capacity as receptacle and creator. Put another way, every English course should become a course in imaginative reading and creative composition.

Literature's Moral Dimension

Before turning to some practical aspects of English in the contemporary curriculum, we should for a moment contemplate the complexity of the job of educating the imagination of our students. The imagination is no narrow faculty, but filters through and colors every part, every corner of our lives. Let us take, for example, the matter of morality, or character, or ethical values. In order to provide dramatic contrast between the old and the new, consider the following quotation from a 1917 volume called *The Teaching of English in the Secondary School,* by Charles Swain Thomas: "The literary selection [to be taught] must breathe the right ethical and social message. . . . Our most important task in teaching is the building of character, and our most effective agency is the literary selection."[5] Noble as these sentiments ring, we as English teachers must forego them—first, because they represent a superficial view of literature as containing "message"; second, because they are presumptuous in assuming that English teachers know what ethical and social messages are "right" not only for themselves but for everybody; and, third, because English teachers are (or should be) committed to the higher aim of educating the imagination.

Now, in the "new English" the teacher will need to come to terms with something we may call the "moral imagination." Although it is reductive to conceive literature as sending ethical messages to readers, it is blindness not to see that there is a moral dimension (among many other dimensions) in literature. This dimension is more frequently implicit than explicit, more often pervasive than concentrated in single

5 Charles Swain Thomas. *The Teaching of English in the Secondary School.* Boston: Houghton Mifflin Co., 1917.

lines or sentences. However we may conceive of this dimension—whether as a system of values, a vision of the nature of things, a truth—we must somehow come to terms with it in the classroom. How we might come to terms with it honestly and with any measure of success requires careful consideration, along the following lines.

There are two ways to achieve a major failure: first, to treat the moral dimension as though it were the sole end of literature, to extract it, to encapsulate it, to divorce it from its material or dramatic embodiment and offer it to students as abstract truth; or, second, to avoid the difficulties and dangers of discussing the moral dimension by ignoring it and concentrating on formal, aesthetic, structural, or other elements. Both of these methods are reductive and lead to apathy and imaginative sterility in the English classroom. Nor can the teacher avoid these failures by selecting solely works of literature to teach that do not disturb, that are not "subversive" or upsetting—works that appear, in short, to be ethically or morally neutral (or neutered).

The curriculum should be open to books of a great variety of values and visions, including those that rub against the grain of society, that counter prevailing values as they are either preached or practiced. As the teacher is concerned with developing and expanding the student's total imaginative capacity, so he must be concerned with all aspects of the imagination, including the moral imagination. He should not become didactic and attempt to inculcate beliefs; rather he should question, discuss, and explore with his students. Such exploration will lead more frequently to complexity than to simplicity, to ambiguity than to precision, to paradox than to resolution. Literature so explored should open to the student a variety of possibilities of values and visions, confront him—like life itself—with a multiplicity of ethical systems or moral perspectives. This expansion and deepening of the student's moral awareness constitutes the education of his moral imagination.

It is perhaps useful to emphasize that the moral imagination is but one facet of the total imagination, which in some sense involves the whole person, the total personality. Other facets of the imagination will demand other strategies, other emphases, other approaches by the teacher. Although the concept of the education of the imagination as the aim of literary study is meant to be liberating for both student and teacher—liberating from narrowing notions of technical literary knowledge—it is in no sense meant to suggest that there will be fewer demands on the teacher's ingenuity. On the contrary, the teacher will confront greater and more intricate challenges than ever.

With these basic principles of a new approach to literature before us, let us turn to a few more specific questions about literature in the English curriculum.

Methods in the Classroom

The terms most useful in describing the contemporary literature teacher in the classroom are *informality, flexibility, improvisation.* There is general recognition that a student's real or lasting education in language and literature goes on outside rather than inside the classroom; that is, the shaping linguistic and literary experiences are those provided by the general culture—at home, by trusted or admired companions, by the generally uncontrollable encounters in a sometimes rich, sometimes brutishly deprived life. It is in recognition of this overriding fact that today's alert English classroom is more likely to look like a classroom moving beyond (but not out of) the Academic phase and into the Humanitarian (but not sentimental) phase of recent American educational history, as outlined in an oversimplified way at the beginning of this essay.

The modern literature teacher will concentrate on two major goals that will be approached so obliquely as perhaps to appear hidden. He will try to meet each student wherever he is, to honestly engage his understanding, his interest, his imagination, his emotional energies. This may mean that we will have to connect with or build on some unapproved or even disapproved story-teller secretly indulged and admired. And after he has reached the student, the modern teacher will try every means at his disposal to provide the experience that will grow into the lasting commitment—whether with *Huckleberry Finn, Sons and Lovers, Catcher in the Rye,* or *Catch-22;* whether with Edgar Allan Poe or A. Conan Doyle, Ernest Hemingway, Flannery O'Connor, or James Baldwin. No genuine literary education was ever the sole or even the major work of the schools; it has always been primarily the work of the individual fired with curiosity, drawn to the world of books by a great or even terrible hunger.

In the Academic phase of our educational revolution, much emphasis was placed on saving our intellectual resources by bringing together the brightest students into a single class and providing them with the most challenging and advanced academic program. In the current Humanitarian phase, there has come a recognition that such isolation and such accelerated programs can be damaging—damaging psychically in artificially separating students into status groups, depriving them of the stimulus of a wide range of associations; and damaging in encouraging phoney or sterile literary experiences in which complex books are intellectually analyzed but never emotionally felt or experienced. The modern literature teacher will welcome to his class students of a wide range of abilities, and he will encourage common experiences in language and literature—experiences to which all can contribute from their varied lives and from which all can benefit by a widening of linguistic and imaginative awareness. The teacher will see not one track but thirty individual tracks before him, all of them capable of sharing and contributing something to classroom experiences in the imagination, and each one following his own bent, interest, or enthusiasm outside the class.

Vitality an Imperative

In the modern literature classroom, three elements will be stressed more and more: vitality, drama, and creativity. It is imperative that the literature offered to students connect somehow, in meaningful and vital ways, with their lives. In some classes, this may mean throwing out *Julius Caesar* and *Silas Marner* and introducing in their place James Baldwin's *Go Tell It on the Mountain,* Ralph Ellison's *Invisible Man,* or Edward Albee's *American Dream.* It will mean bringing the literature to life by involving the students emotionally as well as intellectually —that is, dramatically—in it.

A dramatic teacher, engaging his students immediately in the dramatic spectacle of literature, including direct participation in the living drama of it, will find his students involved in spite of themselves. And as their appetites for the imaginative life of literature mount, the creative teacher will encourage the production and sharing of the student's own works—poems, stories, or plays. Stultifying criteria of correctness or form or convention will be banned from the classroom; students will be emboldened to follow the lead of their liberated imaginations, to write honestly out of the depths of inner experience and out of the perplexities of outer entanglements. By moving easily and naturally between their own lively imaginative productions and the literary experiences of classroom, library, and paperback bookstore, students should reduce that formidable distance between their everyday lives and the printed page, rendering the literary encounter as natural and necessary as other staples of life such as food and drink. In such a free and fluid environment, the imagination of each student will ideally develop to its full potential.

Close Reading and Critical Analysis

Connecting with, involving, awakening, and inspiring the student— these are the beginnings. But there are distances to go and the student must be transported as far as his abilities allow. Whereas the reading of a poem or story without emotional involvement is no experience at all, in any genuine sense, still the experience cannot honestly remain *only* a matter of the emotions. If the student is to carry out of the classroom into his other life a developing imagination that will lead to a

continuation of vital literary encounter, his critical and analytical facul-
ties must be developed through meaningful experience.

There is an intellectual as well as affective content to the literary experience, and to deny the one is as harmful as to deny the other. While
an overemphasis of the intellectual response results in a tendency to
glibness, abstraction, and sterility, an overemphasis of the emotional
response may result in superficiality, muddlement, and gush. As in so
many areas of life, a sensible balance needs to be struck. At this point
we should remind ourselves that the Academic phase of the contemporary educational revolution significantly endures. Once our students are
literarily "hooked," once they are imaginatively committed, it is our
responsibility to lead or lure them to ever-deeper understanding of literature of ever-greater complexity and variety.

At some point, then, in the upper level of the literature curriculum,
experiences in the close, detailed, line-by-line reading of texts, whether
of a Sir Francis Bacon essay or a Gerard Manley Hopkins poem, are
likely to appear. And this kind of experience will tend to merge with
later experiences in the analysis and criticism of a variety of kinds of
literary texts. In these more deliberately intellectualized approaches, the
teacher must proceed delicately and with caution in order not to inhibit
the uninvolved student and to avoid eliciting phoney responses and
glib explanations. As in all teaching, the best methods are the inductive,
and the student is most likely to be moved by a poem or story that he
has discovered on his own, perhaps for an exercise in critical analysis.

When the student leaves school, it is hoped that he has developed a
lifetime habit of reading books. But it is hoped further that he has
developed the habit of reading with understanding books of real merit.
For selection of books to read he needs a critical sense, an ability to see
through the dustjacket blurb or the puff-review to the honest value of
a book.

In developing a critical awareness in his students, today's literature
teacher may turn his class into a lively session of critical controversy,
arousing interest as well as passion in questions of value and how they
might best be approached. As interest and curiosity grow, the teacher
might introduce some of the more famous or notorious professional critical controversies over value or meaning—for example, the dispute over
John Keats' "Ode on a Grecian Urn;" or he might encourage individual
students to investigate the various critical treatments of a work in which
the student finds an attractive but puzzling enigma. Teacher and students will discover in these joint explorations that there is, of course,
genuine critical disagreement. But they will also discover that what
frequently looks like disagreement in criticism is really a difference of
approach, the several approaches not in conflict but actually comple-
menting one another. In developing a critical sense, the student will

come to know that there are many ways of seeing, many ways of entering, and many ways of understanding any piece of literature.

Organizing Sequences

English teachers are in some degree the custodians of our cultural heritage, and in this role they are constantly in search of the key that will unlock the door for their students. Although it may be necessary in the beginning to select a contemporary book of minor merit in order to reach a student, ultimately the teacher will want to move the student, or provide opportunity for the student to move himself, into the great works of the literary tradition. It is vital that the teacher be aware of the richness and abundance of that tradition in order to select from its infinite variety the works that will lure students in. Any view that reduces the tradition to *Silas Marner* and *Julius Caesar* is niggardly and unworthy of the profession. Too often the literary tradition is presented in our classrooms in such a way as to alienate the students permanently from it.

The literary tradition must be presented as a living and vital thing, not there to be swallowed whole, but at hand to answer the wide range of interests or fill the astonishingly various needs of readers of all ages and kinds. When this tradition becomes embalmed in an unwieldy, blockbuster textbook (it may be titled *American Literature from Jonathan Edwards to Edward Albee,* or *English Literature from Beowulf to Virginia Woolf*), it is most likely to remain dead in the classroom and unread outside it. This is not to say that vital and exciting units of study cannot be constructed with a historical-geographical emphasis, but such units are more likely to emerge from and connect with teacher-student interests if they are free of the rigidity imposed by a curriculum-dictating anthology.

Today's advanced English class is likely to be cut loose from the single omnibus text, and will move from a unit on tragedy to a unit on "man's aspirations and dilemmas," to a unit on lyric poetry, to a unit on composition, to a unit on the novel, and so on through the year. And the literature will be American, English, and (in translation) Continental European, Asian, African, and South American. Emphasis will be removed from coverage—galloping through 40 authors in 15 weeks—and placed on understanding and responding in depth, and on the arousing of curiosity and interest that will lead each student to deeper and wider explorations. The teacher will be constantly experimenting, trying new works, discarding those that refuse to come to life, retaining the new or old that really connect with students. In short, the curriculum will be in constant flux and change, but revitalized throughout with the rich heritage of English, American, and world literature.

If we glance once again at the historical survey of education with which I began, we may see the weaknesses of each period. In the Authoritarian stage, we were trying to preserve an elitist culture for an elitist group. In the Progressive stage, emphasis shifted to democracy —but unfortunately also to mediocrity. In the Academic stage, we have reintroduced the idea of an elite—an intellectual elite—but have, perhaps, lost ground socially. In the current Humanitarian stage, the challenge will be to preserve our schools as microcosms of genuine democracy, but at the same time to educate for excellence. The problem of balancing equality and individuality is an old, old one in America. Whitman summed it up thus:

> One's-self I sing, a simple separate person,
> Yet utter the word Democratic, the word En-Masse.

Perhaps the most important aspect of literature teaching today is the teacher's new view of the significance to the individual of language and imagination. It is through the linguistic imagination that the human being creates, orders, or comes to terms with his world, both inner and outer. In a fundamental sense, an individual's identity is achieved through the linguistic imagination. His all-important relations with other individuals are shaped by his lingustic imagination, and his role in the world is to a large extent created and determined by his linguistic imagination. Language shapes or symbolizes experience; imagination shapes or extends language; and literature shapes or liberates the imagination. Language, imagination, and literature are inseparably intertwined and are central to the human being and the educational process, from the earliest stages to the last. It is this enlarged view of the crucial significance of his subject that identifies the new or contemporary English teacher. And he will not be completely unfettered in his vital tasks until the public generally gives up its narrow notions that an English teacher is a policeman of propriety and correctness in language and accepts the view that an English teacher, in dealing with language and literature, is dealing with the precious stuff of life itself.

ADOLESCENT SUBJECTIVISM
AND THE TEACHING
OF LITERATURE

Benjamin G. Foster

WE are discussing "The Red Wheelbarrow" by William Carlos Williams in Fifth Form English. One boy sees the wheelbarrow as insignificant or, as he calls it, "stupid." "A wheelbarrow is a trivial, ordinary thing," he tells the class. "It shows how life is filled with unimportant objects. That's all there is to it—just some stupid wheelbarrow and those white chickens. It's all so meaningless." The boy speaks with conviction, as if he believes he has found the meaning of the poem.

To open up alternatives to this boy's interpretation, I propose a contrary view: perhaps the poet has seen in ordinary things like chickens and a wheelbarrow objects of beauty and significance. "That may be your opinion," the boy answers, "but that's not the way I see it. In my opinion, wheelbarrows are just plain stupid. There's nothing beautiful about a wheelbarrow." "But what about the poet's view?" I ask the boy. "Shouldn't we forget our own opinions for the moment so that we can understand the poet's attitude toward the wheelbarrow and the chickens?" Not at all, the boy thinks. "Sure, the poet has a right to his own opinion about the wheelbarrow and the chickens, but then so do I. And he can't say my opinion is wrong. We look at wheelbarrows differently, that's all." "But isn't the purpose of reading the poem to get us to see the wheelbarrow with the poet's eyes?" I ask the boy. He hesitates over this but he concludes by voicing an attitude common to many of his classmates. "I thought the point of reading poetry was to stimulate our own ideas." His earlier conviction, then, which I understood to be his belief that he had found the meaning of the poem, was in fact a conviction that he had discovered his own ideas about it. And having discovered his own ideas about the poem, he felt his work was done—the purpose of English class was fulfilled.

Many of my attempts to teach literature to secondary school students reach a similar impasse. Again and again, my students reveal an inability or an unwillingness to go beyond themselves in their discussions of literature. What begins as literary analysis ends as self-exploration, with students talking about their own opinions and attitudes.

⋙⋙⋙⋙⋙⋙⋙⋙⋙⋙⋙⋙⋙⋙⋙⋙⋙⋙⋙⋙⋙⋙⋙⋙⋙⋙⋙⋙⋙

FROM *The Independent School Bulletin* (December 1970), pp. 47–50. Reprinted by permission of the publisher and the author.

While not all of my students feel that the meaning of a literary work can be reduced simply to personal opinion, few of them see any alternative to this subjectivism. They are tolerant of great differences in interpretations of literature and suspicious of anyone who sets himself up as an authority on matters which to them cannot be settled with finality by objective standards. For such students, a teacher's opinion may represent the most informed view in the classroom, but it remains one opinion among many. Student subjectivism thus restricts the teacher's role in class discussions of literature. If the teacher dictates values or speaks *ex cathedra* about meaning, he suggests to the students that he is arbitrary, old-fashioned, narrowly dogmatic and authoritarian. Once seen in that light, he has undermined much of his credibility. The surest way for a teacher of literature to close the minds of his students is for him to show them his own is shut. A lively discussion can be fatally short-circuited when the teacher flips the switch marked "The Answer." Not that the answer convinces the students; it may persuade one or two of the more intellectually passive, but it merely shuts up and turns off the inquiring minds. And at that moment many of them are apt to find something outside the classroom window more interesting than the proceedings inside.

The alternative extreme to the teacher's dogmatism and authoritarianism lies in an intellectual permissiveness. It provides different but equally dangerous pitfalls. Some students, it is true, respond with enthusiasm to an intellectual free-for-all; they grow expansive in the untrammeled class where anything goes and every comment enjoys equal acceptance. Such permissiveness removes the need to prune ideas or structure thinking. Inevitably, the gain in spontaneity is paid for in a loss of discipline. Such classes soon resemble a therapy session in which the doctor encourages free-association in his patients. Confession rather than discussion flourishes in such an atmosphere. Fortunately, most students do not carry their subjectivism to this degree of anarchy. In the long run, this kind of free-for-all stultifies rather than stimulates discussion, and even the least perceptive student soon recognizes that some opinions about a poem or a novel or a play are obviously better than others. Limits to their subjectivism appear when students recognize that outside of themselves there exist at least rough standards for judging the meaning and value of a literary work. This is the small end of the wedge, but it is enough to drive home a recognition that if any discussion of literature is to move beyond a mere airing of personal prejudices to something deserving the name of communication it must be based on irreducible and discoverable meanings.

Students sink into an uncritical subjectivism most easily when examining poetry, especially the poetry of our own age. In fairness to our students, we must admit that many of our poets invite such a response.

In our age, we must puzzle over poets who use language with personal and often private references to reveal their inner moods. Many contemporary poets offer us their work without carefully controlling the language, in an attempt to suggest that their poems are a kind of welling-up of the deep, illogical part of themselves—their instincts and gut responses. This by no means describes all of our poetry today, but this attitude is very much in the air and carries obvious attractions for the young. Whenever I allow a class complete freedom of form and content in a composition, about a third of the students rush to write material scarcely distinguishable from the intimate revelations women once reserved for their diaries. Their feelings of loneliness, their fear of failure, their relationships with parents or girl friends, their sexual longings and experiences come tumbling out in a style some of them think of as stream of consciousness. Though the words are not always structured as lines of verse, the students call this writing poetry, because for them poetry is the medium for soul-searching. If the work is short, introspective, and confessional, it is a poem.

Surprisingly, these most subjective of outpourings can open up a way out of the slough of solipsism in the students' understanding of poetry. For example, a Fifth Form boy who had submitted for class discussion a poem he entitled "The Wall," began his explanation of its references with the usual tolerance of any view. The poem's symbols, he told the class, could be understood any way we wished. As will be seen, the poem insists on a fairly limited range of interpretations despite the author's assertion. It reads as follows:

> "Climb that wall!
> Dig your nails into it!
> Throw yourself against it!
> So what if you end up bloody and in pain?
> Get back there!
> Attack it!"
>
> "But what if we just can't make it?"

In the boy's private view, the wall stood for society—the rigid, demanding, over-critical society of adults. If other readers found something else in the poem, well, they were entitled to their discovery. Any reading was valid. "Can the wall represent freedom?" I asked the boy. "Can it represent joy and love and happiness?" He showed his annoyance with the questions—they weren't fair. "No, the wall can't represent those things," he conceded. He and the rest of the class agreed that the wall must represent some resisting and psychologically destroying barrier. The poem demands a negative response to the wall and to the drill-sergeant's voice that commands us to climb it. From this the students moved to a recognition that any consciously created structure of words must of necessity exclude certain interpretations and invite others. And how do we arrive at the best interpretation? By accepting the invitation the words offer us, not by examining the contents of our own minds or indulging in private responses. An obvious conclusion, perhaps, but it is not one my students take for granted.

Adolescent subjectivism imposes an especially distorting medium when students turn to the literature of earlier periods. To present *Antigone* or *Hamlet* or *Moby Dick,* a teacher must often spend much of his time clearing away not only the perennial obsessions of the young but the prejudices of the mid-Twentieth Century. To the student trapped within himself, all ages are one—his own. Not surprisingly, he labels Hamlet's problem "alienation" and calls the melancholy Dane an existentialist in a meaningless universe, or he finds in *Antigone* a study in the generation gap, with the young rebel doing her own thing. The violence done to a text by students obsessed with their own problems was dramatized for me in a class discussion of Amy Lowell's "Patterns." One boy offered the view that the speaker of the poem was a repressed nudist. She wants to throw off her clothes and be free to make love. For this boy, the poem discredits an artificial society that forces the girl to wear absurdly ornate and restricting clothing. She should be allowed to run naked if she wants. A second boy agreed that the poem attacks a false society, but he found its thrust aimed at war. The lover has been killed "in a pattern called a war," and it is this pattern which dominates the world she lives in as the poet's attack on it dominates the poem. In these interpretations, contemporary culture provides the lens through which the boys viewed the poem's references. They looked at the poem with the distortions of someone suffering from astigmatic vision; they saw what was there, but they saw it out of focus. A more pronounced astigmatism in a third boy caused him to see figures moving between the lines—the figures of the poor girl's parents. They are responsible for the girl's misery, the boy asserted. They have tricked her out in foolish clothes, and they have brought her up according to an old-fashioned and joyless morality. When I asked the boy if the poem anywhere mentions her parents, he conceded that there was nothing specific for him to go on. "But you can sort of feel their presence," he informed the class. "In fact, I can almost picture what they look like. The mother has bleached hair and lots of jewels. She likes to gossip with her rich friends over tea. The father is a rich banker or businessman, plays golf at an important country club, and stuff like that." He went on to point out how these two monsters of etiquette had, out of social and business considerations, forced their daughter to be a debutante and had imposed their choice of Lord Hartwell on the girl. Such an interpretation shows how a student in the grip of his own preoccupations needs very little external evidence to find those preoccupations mirrored in the literature he reads. Where specific references are lacking, mood and atmosphere will carry him along the path he wants to take, and it is often difficult to convince the student that the mood and atmosphere have been supplied by himself.

So far, I have found no simple formula for exorcising the demons of first-person reference from my students' reading habits, and I recognize that there probably is none—there is only the difficult way of concentration and self-discipline. When their self-absorption causes students to read into a poem or a story, my technique has been to rub their noses in the work and force them to read and re-read the exact words. Close scrutiny of a text is often new to them; many of my students are more adept at reading between the lines than at following the words on the page. Again and again I find I must pull a student up short with a question pointing back to the text: "Is there anything in the poem to support your opinion?" Often students show surprise that no specific evidence for their conclusion can be dug from the work, and they see (or so I hope) that careful attention to the text provides the only reliable base on which to erect an interpretation.

I have been writing as if this subjectivism poses a problem in the teaching of literature, but I recognize that many English teachers will disagree. Indeed, this subjectivism in our students reflects a similar subjectivism in their parents, teachers, and the culture generally. They hear in their schools that self-expression and the cultivation of personal opinions are among the major aims of education, and in classrooms they are invited to explore their own attitudes and responses. Many English classes are taught with self-expression as the goal and literature as the stimulant. The teacher then conceives his role as based on the model of the psychologist; he tries to draw the student out and get him talking about himself. In this process, a poem or short story is introduced much as an inkblot is presented to the patient in an exploration of personality—it is looked at to reveal the contents of the viewer's mind. As English teachers, we encourage this subjectivism in our students whenever we use their limited tastes and sympathies as the limits of our course. Many of us are guilty of selecting literature that caters to the students' love of self-analysis and gets discussion going, and we are apt to label a class of students aroused to talk about themselves "exciting" and consider it a success.

Excitement, like relevance, has become one of the shibboleths of modern education, and it is clear from the uncritical use of the term (we want to exchange exciting ideas about exciting books, and we want to teach exciting material to exciting students) that few educators have stopped to ask whether a student in a state of excitement is genuinely receptive to knowledge. How many of the important lessons of life can be termed exciting? Is it exciting to learn patience or concentration or self-discipline? Is excitement the quality to expect in learning calculus or the rudiments of a foreign language? In any case, the desire for excitement leads the English teacher (who is especially susceptible to student demands for it) to works that share the adolescents' ideals and anxieties and interests and give students situations and characters which they can identify with. It leads to exciting issues: sexual promiscuity, the new morality, confrontations on the campus, integration, revolution, drugs, and so on. It leads to exciting media: tapes, television, film, light shows, electronic gadgetry, mind-blowing combinations of sight and sound.

The printed page appears to many adolescents as one of the least exciting of media, and if English teachers teach that excitement provides a good test of worth, they must stand confounded when the young give notice that much of English literature fails to make the grade. The most signal failures are obviously those works in which the thought is deep and thus difficult, difficulty making up the antithesis of excitement for many adolescents. Consequently, literature which fulfills the classical ideal of seeing life steadily and seeing it whole is slighted in the search for stimulants. To woo students back to the printed page, many secondary school departments of English build their curriculum more and more around the writing of the present. *Portnoy's Complaint, To Kill a Mockingbird,* the novels of Bradbury, the poetry of Ginsberg, and the lyrics from the latest album of The Beatles and The Grateful Dead often take a prominent place in today's English courses, and why not? If sheer excitement is the test, Bob Dylan performs better in class than Robert Frost.

The question of what literature to read in secondary school is a perplexing one, and I do not want to suggest that there are easy answers to it. Certainly, I would not like to see departments of English go back to the force-feeding of *Paradise Lost, The Faerie Queen,* and *Ivanhoe* on the grounds that these are the classics. As the Latin root reminds us, to educate is to lead, and we can lead students only when we start where they are, and most of them are not in a position to find meaning in the travels of the Red Cross Knight or the fall of Lucifer. But the alternate extreme of using relevance and excitement as the test results in English courses that resemble seminars in contemporary problems, with students using their favorite issues as launching pads for explorations of their own glorious identities. This is heady stuff, of course, and nothing turns on students like feeding them the latest froth from the best-seller lists or the latest pornography and pretension from the underground. Any teacher can run an exciting course with such material, but the excitement comes at a heavy price—a price that includes ignorance, not only of works that would be permanently valuable to the students, but of the way that good literature can take us out of our-selves and allow us a few hours of grace from our habits of self-ab-sorption. While it is true that much good literature can be said to illuminate our own condition or to serve as a mirror in which we find ourselves, it can also serve as a bridge for finding others. If we concen-trate exclusively on the way in which writing gives shape to our own experience, we lose sight of the way it can point to experiences of which we are ignorant, to pleasures we have not enjoyed, and pain we have not endured. Better than anything else, literature can present the "otherness" of life to us, so that like the Ancient Mariner we travel through seas unknown. Only in this way can we see the world around us in its true colors. Like the Ancient Mariner we must first rid our-selves of our own preconceptions and prejudices, exciting and relevant as we may find them at the moment. Only then can we bless life and find that it blesses us in return.

Too often, the cry for relevance, like the demand for excitement, leads only to the familiar and the fashionable. When relevance signifies no more than what is contemporary, it functions as the new disguise for the Philistine's ages-old resistance to hard thinking and serious art. Furthermore, relevance as a yardstick determining what to teach leads us nowhere; the question remains, relevant to what? If you are content to stay home all your life you will find a passport an irrelevant docu-ment, and if you propose no more than merely to be hip and stay abreast of the times you will need nothing but the mass media. Why bother with Melville or Emerson or Thoreau when you can tune in on modern America with Ginsberg and Mailer and Bob Dylan? The easy answer is inescapable if we limit the aims of our teaching to explora-tions of self, the quest for personal identity, and finding our niche in the electronic age. Because it *is* a bother to read *Walden* or *Moby Dick;* we must pay close attention, pen in hand, a dictionary and a history text at our elbow.

But surely this is where our teaching should begin. We can make works like *Walden* and *Moby Dick* relevant by revealing what is of perennial value in them, and we can show students that by their very nature the highest values are best expressed in works of literature which at first reading may seem not only irrelevant but positively re-pellent, works that dash cold water in the face of our fond longings and easy answers and pat formulas, works such as *Oedipus Rex, Eccle-siastes,* the parables of Jesus, *Macbeth, Pilgrim's Progress, Gulliver's Travels,* the poetry of T. S. Eliot. No one has ever arrived at the first stages of his literary education finding these works relevant. We come to realize that they speak to us and for us only through struggle and self-denial and painful experience. The process can be called growing up. It can also be called education.

A LITERATURE PROGRAM
FOR THE MIDDLE SCHOOL

Dwight L. Burton and Bryant P. Fillion

A GUIDED INDEPENDENT READING PROGRAM is not merely a list of "suggested books" which is given to the students; it is not a "free reading period" once a week, while the teacher catches up on paper grading; and—above all—it is not a dreary "book report day." Such "programs" accomplish little. A good program requires the teacher's active guidance in helping students to select books and in encouraging their reactions to books that they read. It requires the teacher's willingness to devote class time to insure the program's success. And it requires a belief in the benefits of such a program.

An organized program to supplement total class work in literature encourages more extensive reading than possibly can be done in ordinary class study; it helps to develop a recognition of the worth of reading as an individual activity; and it allows students to satisfy their own interests and read at their own level as a part of the literature program. Guided independent reading implies a faith in students' interests which helps to break down the "real world-school world" differences and can extend the teacher's influence on students' reading much farther than is possible with total class study alone. Also, with such a program as is suggested here, teachers often find their communication with and understanding of students much improved. English teachers should never forget Lou LaBrant's anecdote in *We Teach English* about the boy who failed high school literature because he was too busy reading the Harvard book shelf on his own. Too many teachers, like the one in the anecdote, never discuss students' individual reading with them.

Managing the Program

If a guided independent reading program is to be successful, students must see it as an important part of their English work. They must know that the teacher takes it seriously and is willing to devote time and effort to it. The program outlined here may be adopted by one teacher, or it may be used by an entire English department. With several teachers participating, helpful materials and ideas are accumulated more rapidly and there is less work required of any one teacher.

GRADES. There are advantages and disadvantages in tying students'

REPRINTED by permission from the May 1971 issue of *The Clearing House*.

independent reading to a grade for English class. If students are to be graded for their guided independent reading, they should know how these grades are to be earned and how much influence they will have on their English grade. Also, if grades are given, they should be based, as much as possible, on the reading itself, and on the student's reaction to the reading, and not on a subsequent writing assignment. One great difficulty with conventional "book reports" is that grades are too frequently determined by the writing rather than by the reading.

USE OF CLASS TIME. A proportion of class time should be devoted to the program. At least half the class time given to literature should be allocated to the individualized programs so that students may go to the library, order books, discuss their reading with the teacher or other students, or work and report on reading-related assignments. Unless specific class time is set aside for the program, neither the teacher nor students will "find" time for it, and unless the teacher feels that individualized reading is worth some of his classroom time, students are unlikely to feel that it is worth much of theirs.

BOOK DISCUSSIONS. When a student finishes a book, usually he should discuss it briefly with the teacher. During these discussions the teacher (a) asks questions to determine that the book has been read—a policing function that is always necessary for some students if the reading is to be graded; (b) attempts to clear up misunderstandings about the book; (c) asks questions to stimulate the student's further consideration of the book; (d) possibly suggests an activity or assignment based on the reading; (e) suggests other books the student might enjoy reading.

To facilitate these discussions, a file of discussion topics and questions on books read frequently is a big help for the teacher. No teacher will have read all of the books students will choose to read, and even for books the teacher is familiar with, good discussion topics are sometimes difficult to devise on the spur of the moment, especially if several different books are to be discussed during one class period. Topics and questions may be kept on file cards, and, for books the teacher is unfamiliar with, may be obtained from other teachers or a librarian who has read the book, from good students who have read the book, and from commercial publishers. At least two kinds of questions should be included: fact questions, to determine if the book has been read and understood, and interpretive or evaluative questions to stimulate discussion or response or perhaps to serve as follow-up assignments. As the program progresses and the teacher becomes more familiar with students' tastes and with popular selections, the file of topics, questions, and possible assignments should grow and become increasingly useful.

In most cases, book discussions may be quite brief, though most teachers find themselves spending more time with them than is "necessary" because they are rewarding. For some students, book discussion sessions will be the only opportunity they have to talk individually with a teacher.

Book discussions should not be limited to student-teacher conferences, however. Students who are enthusiastic about selections should be encouraged to tell the class about them. If several students are reading the same book, they might discuss it jointly with the teacher, perhaps as a panel to which the class can listen. Students reading the same books might be encouraged to compare notes during and after their reading. Through oral presentations, informal book discussion sessions, and perhaps through a file of student comments on particular books read, students should receive feedback on what they and others are reading. Such feedback provides encouragement, helps in book selection, and is a constant reminder that independent reading is an important part of the literature program.

READING LISTS. When initiating a guided independent reading program, it is advisable to begin with a reading list. Such a list provides guidance to students and permits the teacher to keep some control. At least until they get to know their students' reading interests, problems, and strengths, teachers should be familiar with the books they discuss with students, and this is almost impossible unless the selection is limited in some way. As the program progresses, perhaps in the second marking period, students should be asked to recommend additional books for the list and they may be permitted to read works not on the list.

The reading list for a program should not be "comprehensive," but it should include a fair number of selections (75 to 150) covering a wide range of interests and types of books. It should *not* be merely a list of literary classics, but it should include recent works, adolescent fiction, and easy materials for light reading. The list might also include specific groups of five or six short stories as well as novels, and collections of plays and even of particular records might be included as well.

A book list can be compiled in any number of ways, but student interest should be a primary consideration. In addition to book selection guides available from the National Council of Teachers of English, the American Library Association, and commercial publishers, teachers might consult with other teachers, librarians, reading specialists, and the students themselves for suggested titles. Local paperback book dealers can often offer valuable advice about what students actually are reading.

A lengthy reading list should be subdivided in some way to facilitate student selection, and the list should be revised occasionally to include popular new material and remove selections which are never read. One method of subdividing the list might be by broad topics—Romance and Adventure; Mystery; Science Fiction and Fantasy; War and History; True Adventure; Biography; Family and Animals; Sports and Hobbies; etc.

INDIVIDUAL READING DESIGNS. An alternative to the general reading list as a means of controlling and guiding students' reading is Stephen Dunning's suggestion of working out individual reading designs with each student.[1] Dunning advocates helping students set their own independent reading goals for a semester or some given period, perhaps using some general theme or category or subject matter chosen by the student. The student writes out a statement of purpose for his reading, telling what he wants to accomplish and citing a sample bibliography. The teacher discusses the proposal with the student, guiding him to set challenging, interesting, and realistic goals for himself. The student's final outline of his independent reading proposal is a form of "contract" with himself and with the teacher, indicating his intention and bibliography, and serves as the basis for subsequent discussions of the outside reading.

Although such a proposal permits more freedom than a general list, it should probably be used cautiously in middle school or junior high school where any student's reading interests and attitudes are subject to extreme changes at any moment. Students should be encouraged to follow new tangents which interest them, even if such shifts involve radical changes from proposed plans, and students unable to choose a particular theme which interests them probably should not be forced to follow a bibliography which they find uninteresting.

Encouraging Independent Reading

Students will need considerable help in selecting books to read independently. As the teacher's experience with book discussions increases, however, a growing awareness of students' tastes and of high-interest selections should enable him to be of greater help in recommending books. It is helpful (for this purpose) to keep a record of the most frequently read books.

Without encouragement and prodding, many students will procrastinate, especially when the program is first introduced. This can result in, among other things, a big rush to discuss books at the end of a marking period. Use of reading periods to encourage laggards, and the use of several devices discussed below can help to keep students moving.

Some students inevitably try to read books which are beyond their ability, especially when a program is first begun. When students "bog down" in a book, they should be advised to drop it for the time being and to try an easier or different selection.

[1] "Sequence and Literature: Some Teaching Facts," in Dwight L. Burton and John S. Simmons (eds.) *Teaching English in Today's High Schools* (Holt, Rinehart and Winston, 1966), 86–98.

Parental help. It is helpful when launching an independent reading program to send a note to parents explaining the program and its purpose. Parents might also be advised of the student's progress through an informal "reading report card" about two-thirds of the way through the marking period, listing the books read up to that time.

Most parents are very helpful in encouraging their children to read for an organized program, but teachers should be aware of the danger of over-enthusiastic parents who insist, for example, that their children read their own old favorites.

Wall charts listing students' names and selections read may be a helpful motivational device if they do not produce anxious competition. A recommendations chart on which students "recommend" or "advise against" books they have read is helpful to students who are having problems choosing books to read.

Classroom libraries of books from the school library or of donated paperbacks are often helpful in encouraging interest and in aiding in book selection.

Student panels, debates, or sales talks on books can help generate enthusiasm for a reading program. For instance, students who have read different war stories might present a panel discussion on "What is a hero?" or "What is courage?" using incidents from their books as raw material. A student who is enthusiastic about a particular book might be asked to "sell it to the class" rather than to write a report on it.

A *reading record* should be kept for each student, indicating the books he has read, any follow-up assignments completed, and other information helpful in providing reading guidance.

The Slow Reader. In establishing book lists or other "controls" for an independent reading program, the teacher must allow for the full range of reading interests and abilities in his class. It should be *possible* for slow readers to succeed, especially if the program is to be graded. High-interest easy books should be included on any list which will be given to slow readers, and selections for these readers should not be singled out in any way as low-status reading. Special arrangements might be made for students in remedial reading classes, on the advice of the reading specialist, such as permitting them to read books which are not on the general list.

THEY'LL READ IF YOU'LL LET 'EM

J. A. Christensen

A S REGULARLY as the falling of the leaves, each autumn the same old recriminations fall upon the schools. "My kid can't read." "The schools are wasting the taxpayer's money on all these gadgets and so-called experiments, but they're not teaching the kids how to read."

For some unexplainable reason, parents, administrators, the public at large expect every student to graduate from the public schools with the ability to read "intelligently, coherently, and with comprehension" as though this were a talent native to every individual granted some supreme power from the moment of birth. Place forty lukewarm little bodies in a classroom, stir with enough motivation from a frustrated teacher admonished to "individualize your instruction" and every student WILL READ. Like hell! It has never been so; and unless some modern miracle occurs, it will never be so.

Quoting the September 1970 NCTE *Council-grams:*

> In an article in May 1970 issue of *Harvard Educational Review* David Harman asserts that approximately 50 percent of the people over 25 in this country "probably lack the literacy required to read such basic items as newspapers, job applications, driving manuals, or the simplest exposition." These figures are much higher than those which have been reported by the U.S. Census Bureau, which has indicated only a 10 percent functional illiteracy rate among adults. According to Greg de Giere of the College Press Service, several prominent authorities believe that adults are too dependent on television for information and do not find it necessary to read newspapers and magazines to obtain the minimum amount of information they consider vital for their lives. Much of the blame, as usual, is placed on the schools.
>
> Not only is it charged that the rate of illiteracy is rising, but also that many people who could read and write effectively are not using their skills to become well informed and effective citizens.
>
> Mr. de Giere reports that Walter Cronkite of CBS believes that "lack of reading ability is the most severe problem in communications today." Cronkite wrote in the May issue of *Signature Magazine:* "Of the television audience, a number we cannot begin to estimate—tens, or hundreds of thousands, millions perhaps—seldom read a newspaper or a news magazine,

➤➤
F R O M *Media and Methods*, Vol. 7 (December 1970), pp. 34–39. Reprinted by permission of the publisher and the author.

and never read a journal of opinion." And, de Giere adds, ". . . the amount of information broadcast in an hour TV news program could be printed on a single page of a standard-sized newspaper.

Mr. de Giere also quotes Richard L. Tobin, communications editor of the *Saturday Review*, on implications of the widening literacy gap: "It may be that we are drifting into two classes of adults, not divided by social position, income, color, religion, or background, but by those who can read and write and do so habitually, and those who, for all practical purposes, cannot." (reported in *The Summer Illini*, University of Illinois, July 23, 1970)

Several points in this report require further consideration. "Much of the blame, as usual, is placed on the schools." Happily, not *all* the blame. Even though society, year after year, forces the public schools into a greater role as parent-surrogate, insisting that the schools assume more and more of the functions traditionally held by parents, the amount of time the student spends in the classroom is not sufficient to overcome home environment. If Mom and Dad are spending the evening watching TV, who can expect Junior to spend the evening curled up with a book —good, bad, or otherwise. If the only reading matter in the home is the daily newspaper, and if the bookcases are filled with trinkets and knick-knacks, there is little motivation for Junior to spend his leisure hours with a paperback murder mystery, much less a best-selling novel or a Shakespeare play.

Although we pay lip-service to intellectual attainment in our society, such attainment is, in actuality, more often regarded with suspicion than with praise. Parents have been known to insist that a teacher not give their child an A grade because "his friends will make fun of him." And if I can earn more money from my ability to kick a ball across a field, or to knock a ball around a 20-acre pasture than I can by earning my Ph.D., what motivation do I have to become a good reader?

"Many people who could read and write effectively are not using their skills to become well informed and effective citizens." Reading and writing effectively involve effort. With a society oriented toward labor-saving devices, and the pursuit of easy and momentary pleasures, who is going to expend the energy required to read a book? Besides, reading is not a matter of skill and effort alone. And again, neither is reading a God-given gift granted to every individual. True, the *skills* of reading may be taught, but more is required than mere skill to become a good reader.

In their introduction to *The College Survey of English Literature* (Harcourt-Brace, 1947), the editors state:

> The question whether one is to be a good reader may depend on the sheer physical, mental, and emotional energy that one can bring to bear on the reading process. Much may depend upon the strength, the precision,

and the delicacy of one's physical senses. Sight, hearing, touch, taste, and smell are the pathmakers of literature and the scouts of those who follow the trail. Much depends upon the reader's power of visual and auditory imagination. One who cannot make and revive clear mental pictures will of course find many of the finest passages in literature "as a landscape to a blind man's eye."

One key to the problem may be in the statement: "much depends upon the reader's power of visual and auditory imagination." Traditionally, we have not been an imaginative society. In a society historically oriented to practicality and technology, we have placed little value upon the imagination. The wide acceptance of movies, of TV, certainly bears this out inasmuch as little imagination is required for the enjoyment of these two media. The viewer merely relaxes, sopping up the sights and sounds like some damp kitchen sponge. A minimal quantity of imagination is supposedly required for the production of film and TV, however, as yet the American public has not taken to the whole-hearted production of home movies and TV shows to fill their leisure hours.

In a society based upon the Puritan ethic that "the Plow-man that raiseth Grain is more serviceable to Mankind than the Painter who draws only to please the Eye," we have not expected every child to become an artist or a musician; but we have insisted that every child become a good reader. And yet, beyond the level of reading "such basic items as newspapers, job applications, driving manuals, or the simplest exposition," reading well is an art, as much so as the ability to paint a picture or play a musical instrument. Even when it comes to reading the classics, the public demands that such learning have practical application as can be seen, for example, in the tendency we have had for years to emphasize the moral value of a literary work, or as using the work as nothing more than the basis for critical analysis and *expository* writing. Another example: recently in a social gathering, I found myself in discussion with several business people concerning just this problem of reading. I said I felt that perhaps too much emphasis was being placed upon the study of the classics in the schools, and that that may be one of the reasons why many people never developed a great love for reading —that the mere study, often deeply analytical, of a work killed the sheer joy of reading for reading's sake, and that perhaps we should focus on more contemporary material. The response was both interesting and revealing. "But the classics are so important," one of the group insisted. "It's always so helpful to be able to quote from the classics in your conversation." Having never considered this highly useful aspect of the classics, I asked if she might give me an example of the type of quote she was referring to. "Why, yes, Shakespeare's 'A little learning is a dangerous thing'." With proof such as that, one could only bow to "Shakespeare's" superior wisdom, and realize how deeply some people drink from "the Pierian spring."

It must be admitted in all honesty, however, that part of the problem in developing reading as an art, beyond the stage of a mere skill, does lie with the schools. Too much emphasis *is* placed upon the analytical study of the classics; too much emphasis is still placed upon literature as a source of moral values or as the transmitter of our cultural heritage; too few teachers concern themselves with contemporary literature as a source of relevant ideas in a changing society; and, too few teachers are, themselves, practiced in reading as an art. In fact, and we might as well face it, many of them are just damned dull. Confining themselves to materials they studied in college, or to materials contained in the textbooks, too few keep themselves current in their reading, many of them not reading as much as their students. The last teacher I personally observed reading, was deeply involved in a Nora Lofts' romance. Another confessed a weakness for Emilie Loring—yet both confessed a difficulty in getting their students to read "good" books. If neither parents nor teachers function as models for good reading, how can this generation, or any other generation feel that so-called "good" reading is important? As my classics quoting friend might say, "After all, it was Shakespeare who said, 'The child is father to the man'."

In an article entitled "Visions of the Future Schoolroom", (*On Writing Behavioral Objectives for English,* NCTE, 1970) John C. Flanagan writes:

> To enable the student to acquire the detailed knowledge of contemporary life and its opportunities, it may be necessary for the curriculum makers in such subject areas as language arts, social studies, science, and mathematics to draw only sparingly from the great literature of the past. Contemporary models and problems may have to play a greater role in the novels, biographies, and other written materials used in achieving the primary objectives of the language arts curriculum. There is so much to learn about how to live in the twentieth century that we may not be able to afford the luxury of a detailed knowledge of life in the Roman Empire.

In their review of the Geoffrey Summerfield *Man* (McDougal, Littell) series, Blount and Searles (*English Journal,* Sept., 1970) state:

> We are all aware that part of the "gentleman's agreement" of teachers has been the avoidance of honest and contemporary social issues. To teach the evils of censorship teachers have used "Areopagitica" and to teach freedom they have used the myth of "Prometheus". Quite a juggling feat—to be teaching important social concepts in a way to turn students off.

Luckily, we haven't, neither parents nor teachers, succeeded in turning them off completely. The prophets of intellectual doom notwithstanding, there is still a glimmer of hope in this miasma of literary illiteracy.

Lois Caffyn in "Behavioral Objectives: English Style" (*On Writing Behavioral Objectives for English*, NCTE, 1970), says: "It has been said of reading that the important thing is not whether one can read but whether he does read." And on a positive note, I submit that our young people *are* reading. Certainly not all of them, nor is the major portion of their reading matter that good stuff that Miss Grundy and her analytical brain dotes upon, but it is, without doubt, several degrees better than the Loft and Loring literature.

Concerned with all those reports that students can't read, won't read, I decided to play Mr. Gallup, and conduct my own survey of student reading habits. There was nothing overly scientific about it; not one control group, not one behavioral scientist to observe and record this empirical phenomena. I merely asked some four hundred students what they had read during the past summer months. The students surveyed were from several different schools, from various social backgrounds, and from both urban and rural areas, so that at least to my satisfaction, I gained a fair sampling of what students are reading. (But that isn't scientific at all, you say? Several state narcotics divisions have found out how many kids are smoking pot by the same methods. If it's scientific enough for them, it's certainly scientific enough for me.) Anyway, only five of the students surveyed had read nothing on their own during the months they were not in school.

The average number of books read during the three month's vacation period was three with some students having read as high as ten. One-hundred-twenty-three different titles appeared on the list, twelve of these in the category considered as "teen-age" novels and twenty-three considered as the type of "serious" works studied in school.

Joseph Heller's *Catch 22* and Mario Puzo's *The Godfather* were tied as the most widely read books in the group, with Arthur Hailey's *Airport* next in line. Now, critics might point out that the only reason students are reading these books is because of the movie, because of super-charged advertising, or because of such labels as "sexy," "violent," etc. To which my only comment is, "So what?" Adults are reading them for the very same reasons, so why condemn the kids? However, with *Catch 22* at least, the reason is not so superficial. The book is strongly anti-establishment, anti-rational, and anti-war, pointing out the meaningless stupidity, the lack of organization, the meaningless waste in any war. Most of the students disliked the movie, but loved the book. The teachers condemn it (such nasty words), to which one can only answer, "Stick to your Lofts and Loring, and leave the kids alone."

WHAT THEY'LL READ IF YOU'LL LET 'EM
(*In order of popularity*)

Joseph Heller, *Catch 22*
Mario Puzo, *The Godfather*
Arthur Hailey, *Airport*
Ray Bradbury, *Martian Chronicle*
Boris Pasternak, *Dr. Zhivago*
J. D. Salinger, *Catcher in the Rye*
Ayn Rand, *Atlas Shrugged*
Jacqueline Susann, *Valley of the Dolls*
Margaret Mitchell, *Gone With the Wind*
Catherine Marshall, *Christy*
Ayn Rand, *Fountain Head*
Ernest Hemingway, *A Farewell to Arms*
Ernest Hemingway, *Old Man and the Sea*
Isaac Asimov, *Foundation Trilogy*
F. Scott Fitzgerald, *This Side of Paradise*

Hermann Hesse, *Beneath the Wheel*
Hermann Hesse, *Siddhartha*
Ray Bradbury, *October Country*
Ray Bradbury, *Dandelion Wine*
Ray Bradbury, *The Illustrated Man*
Robert A. Heinlein, *Stranger in a Strange Land*
Truman Capote, *In Cold Blood*
Harper Lee, *To Kill a Mockingbird*
William Golding, *Lord of the Flies*
John Griffin, *Black Like Me*
Charles Dickens, *Oliver Twist*
Leon Uris, *Exodus*
Ray Bradbury, *Fahrenheit 451*
Michel Crichton, *Andromeda Strain*
Philip Wylie, *Triumph*
Daphne Du Maurier, *Rebecca*
J. R. R. Tolkien, *The Hobbit*

The most widely read author in the survey was Ray Bradbury, followed by Hermann Hesse and F. Scott Fitzgerald. The interest in Bradbury is not difficult to explain. Although his works are usually categorized as science fiction, they are highly imaginative, beautiful fantasy. I stated before, "Traditionally we have not been an imaginative society"; however, the young are breaking that tradition as well as many others. To them, the world of imagination is becoming far more important than our technological, materials-oriented society. Theodore Roszak in *The Making of a Counter Culture* (Anchor Books, 1969) indicates that much of the present youth movement is based upon imagination, fantasy, the search for the mystic and the non-rational. He says:

> They see, and many who follow them find the vision attractive, that building a good society is not primarily a social, but a psychic task. What makes the youthful disaffiliation of our time a cultural phenomenon, rather than merely a political movement, is the fact that it strikes beyond ideology to the level of consciousness, seeking to transform our deepest sense of the self, the other, the environment.

And again:

> This, so I have argued, is the primary project of our counter culture: to proclaim a new heaven and a new earth so vast, so marvelous that the inordinate claims of technical expertise must of necessity withdraw in the presence of such splendor to a subordinate and marginal status in the lives

of men. To create and broadcast such a consciousness of life entails nothing less than the willingness to open ourselves to the visionary imagination on its own demanding terms. We must be prepared to entertain the astonishing claim men like Blake lay before us: that here are eyes which see the world not as commonplace sight or scientific scrutiny sees it, but see it transformed, made lustrous beyond measure, and in seeing the world so, see it as it really is. Instead of rushing to downgrade the rhapsodic reports of our enchanted seers, to interpret them at the lowest and most conventional level, we must be prepared to consider the scandalous possibility that wherever the visionary imagination grows bright, magic, that old antagonist of science renews itself, transmuting our workaday reality into something bigger, perhaps more frightening, certainly more adventurous than the lesser rationality of objective consciousness can ever countenance.

To the young reader, the visionary imagination is well present in Bradbury's works as well as in those of Robert A. Heinlein and Isaac Asimov whose *Stranger in a Strange Land* and *Foundation Trilogy* are among the most widely read books on the list. In fact, science fiction was the most widely read category. "So you disprove yourself," some will say. "They're reading science fiction which proves they're fact-minded and technically oriented." Come off it, Miss Maud! They're not reading "Buck Rogers in the 25th Century." Look at them. In *Stranger in a Strange Land,* an earthling marooned on Mars as a baby is returned to earth. Because water was such a rare thing on Mars, it becomes a ritual symbol with him; and the people who drink water with him become "Water Brothers." He overcomes his enemies, those who don't care for his love, peace, and brotherhood ideas and try to destroy him, with completely non-violent, non-technical methods. There are also some nude "bathe-ins" which should immediately remove it from Miss Grundy's approved reading list. *Foundation Trilogy* could almost be considered as the *Decline and Fall of the Roman Empire* on a galactic scale. And what about Michael Crichton's *Andromeda Strain?* If that isn't a perfect satire on the inefficiency of government technology, then I certainly don't read my books right. And Arthur Clarke's *2001: A Space Odyssey?* The hero achieves a psychic goal, far greater than a physical one, only after the break down of his rocket ship. Fact-minded and technically oriented, indeed. It is also this irrational world of magic and fantasy which explains the long popularity of *The Hobbit* and the "Ring Trilogy."

The struggle for individuality, also very important to the young, accounts for the popularity of the works of Ayn Rand; and the disillusion with society accounts for the inclusion of F. Scott Fitzgerald and Hermann Hesse.

An immediate response to this list by the guardians of public literacy will certainly be: "But why don't they read *good* books?" Well, the list does have a smattering of those good things—some Aristophanes,

Shakespeare, Eugene O'Neill, and a smattering of James Joyce, Mark Twain, and Charles Dickens. Hopefully, the students read these books because they wanted to, and not because they felt it was the proper thing to do or was expected of them (the same reason some of our adult pseudo-intellectuals have read them—because of the "impression" value or the quantity of appropriate quotes).

The students who answered my questions have indicated a love for reading, and have also indicated that without the Damoclesian sword of "literary analysis" hanging over their heads they will read.

It is entirely possible that if we taught students the skills of reading, then moved literature out of the attic cobwebs of antiquity into the light of the twentieth-century sun, our students just might read. If we could consider literature as a source of pleasure, as a tool for intellectual *and* imaginative growth through reflective thinking, rather than as a practical tool for critical analysis, semantic dissection, and the development of social and moral values, our students just might read. In fact, perhaps if we taught them the skills of reading, and then got out of the way, our students just might read. Reading is difficult enough without having to push that rock of Sisyphus labelled "teacher" out of the road every time you wish to proceed.

Looking at the matter realistically, of course, no matter what we do, not every student is going to become a good reader, because "the strength, the precision, and the delicacy of one's physical senses" differ from individual to individual, but at least if we can remove our traditional obstacles from their paths, point out that it isn't un-American to enjoy something for its sheer pleasure, that everything doesn't have to have a "practical" price tag attached, and it doesn't have to be analyzed to an agonizing death, we might move a step forward toward literary freedom for many. And it just might move them a step closer to the development of full adult competencies in English. These competencies, according to Lois Caffyn are:

1. Listening (eagerly, courteously).
2. Attending (community meetings, clubs, concerts, lectures).
3. Participating (in discussion, conversation, government).
4. Discussing (issues, beliefs, new knowledge).
5. Conversing (with poise, imagination).
6. Explaining (with clarity, patience).
7. Seeking (unassigned knowledge, interesting side issues).
8. Choosing (some challenging reading, stimulating dialog, some drama and poetry).
9. Reading (variety, for various satisfactions).
10. Sharing (experiences, humor).
11. Habitually using (preferred language forms, appropriate degrees for formality).

12. Employing (colorful language, interesting vocal and bodily expression).

13. Relating (new knowledge to old, different areas of learning).

14. Showing (language courtesy, curiosity, emotional control).

15. Demonstrating (thought through considered language rather than through violence or profanity).

16. Responding (to sensitivity, beauty, fine distinctions).

We are still left, of course, with Richard L. Tobin's problem that: "It may be that we are drifting into two classes of adults, not divided by social position, income, color, religion or background, but by those who can read and write and do so habitually and those who, for all practical purposes, cannot." However, one must question his position that "we are drifting" in this direction. There has never been a time in history, never been a society where these two classes did not exist (at least since man began to write). It is unfortunate that many people cannot, nor do not read; but in spite of this historical division, the society of mankind has continued to exist. It is naturally agreed that we should not give up in our desire to make every person a good reader; but looking at the matter realistically, neither should we cry havoc, and become prophets of doom if our dream of a verbal Utopia does not come true. And certainly we should not give up in our desire to develop the superficial skills of reading, but our greatest emphasis should and must be upon the *art* of reading wherein lies the greatest value and pleasure to humanity. After all, as the Bard of Avon said so aptly: "Those move easiest who have learned to dance."

(You say that's Pope? Which Pope?)

THE NOW YOUNG ADULT NOVEL: HOW WILL THE SCHOOLS HANDLE IT?

Tom Finn

ABORTION, premarital sex, homosexuality, draft resistance, "ripping off," use of drugs, and all sorts of anti-establishment behavior are taking place between the covers of, would you believe it, the young adult novel. Yes, the young adult novel, a name generally associated with pets,

⋙-⋙

FROM *Phi Delta Kappan* (April 1971), pp. 470–472. Reprinted by permission of the publisher and the author.

apple pie, kindly parents, the first kiss, *no* sex, and *no* four-letter words. But "the times, they are a'changin'," and authors, publishers, students, public librarians, and a few school people are aware that the change has come to novels expressly written for the 12- to 16-year-old.

"But," you ask, "*Silas Marner, The Red Badge of Courage, Great Expectations, The Scarlet Letter, Moby Dick,* and the one we had all the fuss with back in the late '50's and '60's, *The Catcher in the Rye*—certainly these are strong enough fare for the schools to make available to young readers?" Almost every school librarian or teacher of English will argue that the themes of these classics are universal and "relevant" for today's American youth. Why then consider such queer titles as *I Never Loved Your Mind; I'll Get There, It Better Be Worth the Trip; Dave's Song; My Darling, My Hamburger; I'm Really Dragged But Nothing Gets Me Down;* and *The Pigman?* Why indeed? Perhaps these particular works speak directly to some of the *now* considerations of white, mostly middle-class, American youth. True, their themes may not uniformly qualify as universal, their form and style as unforgettable, and their place in American letters as unassailable, but their importance does not lie in those directions. Well, then, what is a *now* young adult novel?

First of all, the author and publisher of the *now* young adult novel have expressly directed the book to that audience whose parameters are loosely defined as between the ages of 12 and 16, junior high through about the sophomore year of high school. The main characters of the novel are generally a bit older, 17 or 18, than the intended reader; the characters are urban, white, middle-class youth and are involved in problems and concerns of *live* youngsters—sex, drugs, the environment, parents, school, and all the other elements of youth searching for self-identity. The authors depict these youngsters in a realistic way, which means they speak and act as believable youth, living in the late 1960's and early 1970's. The characters seriously consider the society in which they live, their bodies (sexually), and their emotions; and they speak the actual language of youth—even using four-letter words, the long-time taboo in young adult novels. Most of the authors choose to write in the first person, which gives the books the air of a personal diary, although this is not always true. The books are uniformly short, a little over 100 pages and at times reaching 200 pages; therefore, they are easily read in one or two sittings. All of the authors of the mentioned *now* young adult novels are male, which may or may not be significant. The authors attempt not to moralize overtly, but few successfully accomplish this feat. The novels are first published in hard cover by major publishers and take at least a year or more to surface as paperbacks; their impact on young readers is not felt until they appear in soft cover. The paperback edition is presented and marketed like any adult paperback, although, as yet, none has had a particularly lurid cover, and the prices have been a bit lower ($.50 to $.75) than those of standard paperbacks. Not many are found in school libraries or bookrooms, and not all would be appropriate to purchase as class sets, for they are probably enjoyed most when read independently and shared with close friends or under-standing adults who will listen to a youngster's comments on them.

"Well," you say, "what's the problem? Why aren't these books in school libraries and classrooms? We've fought the censors; *The Catcher in the Rye* is available in schools. And now *Soul on Ice, Manchild in the Prom-ised Land, The Learning Tree,* and most of James Baldwin are in our urban schools. Why not *these* novels?" It seems to me the censorship fighters and all who helped bring about the use in urban and suburban schools of so many important books dealing with the black experience are not really interested in Johnny's "right-to-read" novels concerned with white youngsters involved in dope, stealing, sex, and general dis-satisfaction with American society. It was acceptable to those who ap-proved school books that youngsters read a novel, biography, or auto-biography in which a young black character, given the conditions in which he lived, smoked pot, took an overdose of "H," had an illegitimate child, indulged in various types of sexual activity, and generally behaved like a real human being. Black literature, both fiction and nonfiction, has broken barriers in school libraries and bookrooms. Can books dealing honestly with white, middle-class students' concerns do the same?

Why is there a reluctance to accept the current novels treating young whites in a realistic manner? Could it be because the main characters are *white* and their behavior is not what teachers, administrators, and parents wish to admit is taking place among our "advantaged" youth?

In 1968, Nat Hentoff's *I'm Really Dragged But Nothing Gets Me Down* was reviewed by school librarians and English teachers, and com-ments about the problem of "improper speech of the characters" and "swearing" were made; but since the book is almost puritanical in vocabulary, I believe what really bothered the school reviewers was the fact that at the end of the novel the main character, Jeremy, a high school senior, decides to refuse to be drafted and plans to establish a draft counseling service for other young men. Now, in 1971, with a greater anti-Vietnam War sentiment, the book is found in junior and senior high schools and even in some two-year college freshman classes. It is my belief that today Hentoff's anti-war stand is more acceptable to many in the schools who are responsible for introducing books to stu-dents. This was not true when the book was first published, and therefore it did not find its way into schools at that time.

It is important to distinguish school personnel responsible for making books available to youngsters from people in other areas, such as public librarians, publishers, and commercial book outlets. The young adult public librarians I come in contact with are well aware of these *now* novels through their journals and reviews and readily make these novels available in adequate quantities for their younger clientele. As for the publishers, they are printing them. The time lag between the book's first publication in hard cover and its appearance in soft cover seems unfortunate, since we know how much more attractive pocketbooks are to young readers, but the pattern does not seem to differ from that of "adult" books. Finding the original hardback book in most bookstores has been a problem for me. Book dealers don't seem to know where to place a young adult novel, for few distinguish between children's, "juvenile," and young adult fare, and most of them carry few young adult titles. Once the paperback has been published, most bookstores and bookstands place these books side by side with other fiction, and many adults browse through and choose to read these novels along with *The Godfather, Love Story,* or whatever else is the current best seller among paperbacks.

If these books are available at public libraries and in bookstores, why is it important for school people to make them available to students? The most important reason may simply be that when the novels are available to young readers they read and enjoy them and ask for more. In a local school, a student teacher purchased and took two paperback copies of Paul Zindel's *The Pigman* into a junior class of "nonreaders," and overnight two students read the novel. Returning the next day, they commented that this was the first book they had ever read and asked where they could find more like it. *The Pigman* quickly circulated the room as the teacher scurried to obtain Zindel's other novels, *My Darling, My Hamburger* and *I Never Loved Your Mind* (as yet available only in hardback). The student teacher also had other titles to suggest, but none was available in the school library and most had to be purchased by him at local bookstores. When he talked to his master teacher and the chairman of the English department about ordering these books for class use, lengthy descriptions of the process of ordering books and placing them on the "approved" list were the reply. The school library had no way of getting his suggested titles on the shelves for at least six months, so here he was with a group of 20 excited "nonreaders" asking for books, and he was told to choose from English department approved books and a library collection which his students had rejected for the past several years. With a little personal financial sacrifice, he obtained other titles, and some students bought and contributed others. Luckily, the master teacher and administrators did not object to his use of nonapproved titles, and his students read and discussed these novels during the semester. Not all students read the same novels, some students chose nonfiction, and the books were not "taught"; but every student was engrossed in the reading process because it was meaningful to him. Their reading began with a few of the *now* young adult novels but led away and for a few, eventually, included some of the Steinbeck, Hemingway and Stephen Crane found within the approved school sources.

In addition to these eleventh graders, there are seventh, eighth, ninth, and tenth graders who are enjoying and reading the teacher-assigned novels but who also find enjoyment and relaxation in these *now* novels. Often they bring a more critical literary eye to the books, but most of them agree that the incidents and characters are believable and that the novels provide possibilities for discussing and writing about their vital concerns. I recently visited an honors English class in which the quality of the environment was being discussed and found students citing examples from Thoreau's *Walden,* the local newspaper, and *Dave's Song,* by Robert McKay. These "able" students had been directed to this *now* novel by an aware teacher, and it fitted nicely with Thoreau's "classic" work, but added a current and sympathetic element important to their consideration of possible solutions to a problem they face. True, the *now* novel may be ephemeral and have little meaning in a year or two, but *Dave's Song* did have meaning for these students at this time which is reason enough to have it available in the school.

The possibility exists that teachers may "institutionalize" some of these novels and make elaborate lesson plans and units in which the books then take on the pallor of school materials. I am afraid, if this happens, the students' joy of reading these novels will vanish. Nat Hentoff's *Jazz Country,* an early *now* young adult novel without sex and four-letter words which takes a sensitive look at growing up in the multi-racial world of jazz, has already suffered the fate of having journal articles explicate it and lesson plans written on it. But knowing the reluctance and built-in delaying processes of schools, I don't consider this to be a problem for many young readers or the fate of many *now* novels.

All agree that we wish to promote reading among all students, but *what* the schools are willing to support and encourage as reading material still remains a problem. I encourage school administrators, school librarians, and teachers to read at least one or two of the books listed below and then examine purchasing practices so that these and the yet-to-be-published *now* young adult novels can find their way into the hands of our students.

RECOMMENDED BOOKS

Donovan, John. *I'll Get There, It Better Be Worth the Trip.* New York: Harper and Row, 1969 (hardback).

Hentoff, Nat. *Jazz Country.* New York: Dell (4197), 1967 (paperback).

Hentoff, Nat. *I'm Really Dragged But Nothing Gets Me Down.* New York: Dell (3988), 1969 (paperback).

McKay, Robert. *Dave's Song.* New York: Bantam (SP5733), 1970 (paperback).

Zindel, Paul. *The Pigman.* New York: Dell (6970), 1970 (paperback).

Zindel, Paul. *My Darling, My Hamburger.* New York: Harper and Row, 1969 (hardback).

Zindel, Paul. *I Never Loved Your Mind.* New York: Harper and Row, 1970 (hardback).

OUTSIDE READING BELONGS INSIDE

Milton A. Kaplan

ENGLISH teachers have long known that time spent in analyzing and discussing a book in the classroom would be paltry service indeed if it did not encourage students to go off to do reading on their own. If students read but the prescribed work in an anthology or the few books scheduled for the semester, then they are subsisting on very thin intellectual fare. It is, therefore, a common occurrence in the secondary school to find teachers assigning what has been termed "outside" reading, and usually that means at least three books a term to be read outside of class. The usual way to check on outside reading is to require the writing of book reports in the hope that students writing about a book will first have to read it. A more fundamental hope is that perhaps a student compelled to read a book will somehow develop the habit of reading on his own.

Much has been written in criticism of book reports because they often represent an artificial device that, in the opinion of many educators, defeats the very purpose for which they were intended, for the emphasis is on the report rather than on the reading, and many students, unfortunately, are guilty of concentrating on reading the book for the sake of the report or writing a book report without even reading the book.

This procedure, furthermore, generally compels students to select their books from a prescribed list that often turns yellow with age as it flaps on the classroom bulletin board. Some progressive teachers remove all restrictions and permit students to read "anything you want." Their purpose is laudable, and if the plan works, it certainly takes care of individual differences in interest and ability and stimulates intellectual curiosity. The trouble is that in many cases, as any teacher who has observed students outside class can testify, the library is *terra incognita* to many of our boys and girls, and to these "anything you want" merely

→≫→≫

FROM *The Educational Forum* (March 1971), pp. 375–380. Reprinted by permission of Kappa Delta Pi and the author.

means reaching out blindly and coming up with a book with a red cover or a blue one.

It therefore becomes obvious that students need guidance in the selection of books, some preparation, and a great deal of stimulation and encouragement. One teacher reports that his most successful venture into encouraging outside reading came as a result of a little book talk he gave in which he tried to demonstrate that biography can be interesting reading. He brought Charles Courtney's *Unlocking Adventure* into class and told the students that the author, a locksmith by trade, had been commissioned to go underwater in a diver's suit to open the strongroom of a wrecked British freighter. When he succeeded in opening the door, the water, flowing in, caused the two officers, who had died sitting at the table in the water-tight room, to rise and float out. Courtney, aghast, reached out to intercept one of them, and as he tugged at the officer's arm, it came off in his grasp. The book talk ended there, but the startled school librarian discovered a run on the book "where the guy's arm is pulled off." A brief talk on various books can thus direct the students' attention to those they would enjoy reading and even stimulate them to read.

The responsibility of directing and encouraging outside reading is obviously an important one for the English teacher, but if he is to be responsible for the multifarious other tasks that are important, too, he is simply torn apart, and it is small wonder that sometimes he throws up his hands and proclaims, "Read anything you want."

It becomes clear that a more focused and expedient procedure must be devised. If outside reading is an important part of English instruction— and one could argue that perhaps it is the most important part—then it would seem that it should become part of the English curriculum. After all, if the English curriculum is to be perceived as a unit in which each element reinforces every other element, then all aspects of English should be fused into a functional unit of instruction. Therefore, if a class studies a major work in intensive fashion, it would seem natural and functional that the outside reading cluster around this work and that the significance of this outside reading be brought *into* the classroom instead of being shunted into book reports.

Let us take, for the sake of illustration, a novel that is being taught with increasing frequency in the high school, Margaret Rawlings' *The Yearling*. The novel deals with the conflict between Jody as a child, who thinks only of his own gratification, and the needs of a society that demand that he think of others, too. The fawn that he adopts becomes a symbol of that childhood. It gives him love, companionship, and pleasure. But the fawn heedlessly threatens the crops the family grows, and no matter how high Jody builds the fences to keep him out, Flag manages to leap over them and nibble at the plants. It is Ma, therefore, who has to shoot the fawn, for she must protect the welfare of her family, but it is Jody who actually kills the fawn, for he must kill his own childhood to grow into the responsibilities of maturity. With the realization and acceptance of responsibility, Jody gains insight, but he loses childish joy.

This is a theme that is close to the lives of the students in the class. Every adolescent, no matter how acquiescent, comes in conflict with his parents, for he is concerned with himself and he is trying to establish his own identity. His parents—and his teachers—prod him constantly into undertaking responsibility. They try to direct him, to control him. Conflict thus becomes inevitable.

In this conflict is the opportunity for discussion, for writing, and for functional outside reading. Here is where the teacher can suggest and direct the reading and then bring the results of that reading right into the classroom study of *The Yearling*.

Let us now list a number of books that would fit into the theme we have been discussing:

Carson McCuller's *Member of the Wedding*, both as novel and play, makes the reader realize how much a child needs to belong and needs to cling to the events around her.

Anne Frank's *The Diary of a Young Girl* sees a girl growing up under the most unnatural circumstances, sees her in a garret concealed from the Nazi occupiers of her country, but also sees her in conflict with her elders, who do not understand her. The reader begins to understand her needs, her problems, and her maturation.

Mark Twain's *The Adventures of Tom Sawyer* reads like a simple book on the adventures of a boy who lives in a time far removed from ours, but it concerns every boy and girl in the class because it marks the revolt of the child against established authority, in Tom's case, against parental authority in the person of his aunt and against society and its institutions as represented by the school and the church. Written lightly and satirically, it reveals the adolescent at odds with his world.

Mark Twain's *Adventures of Huckleberry Finn* looks at adult perfidy through the innocent eyes of childhood. Huck on his raft is on an island of innocence. Every time the raft touches the shore, however, it touches the infamy and the evil of adult society.

J. D. Salinger's *Catcher in the Rye* is, in a sense, a contemporary *Huckleberry Finn*. Holden Caulfield cannot understand the hypocrisy and artificiality of adult society. Failing to come to terms with the world around him, he breaks.

Booth Tarkington's *Seventeen* is suggested because it looks at the adolescent through the eyes of the typically blind adult. To this adult the agonies of adolescence are amusing. There is no realization that children suffer torment and that puppy love can be powerful and real.

Just as in some novels we find the adolescent incapable of understanding the adult, here we have the adult, in the person of the author, insensitive to the adolescent and his problems.

Rudyard Kipling's *Captains Courageous* pictures the child who has to learn, like Jody in *The Yearling*, to grow up to think of others as well as of himself.

John Knowles's *A Separate Peace* reveals the conflicts adolescents have with each other as well as with the outside world, conflicts that result, all too often, in cruelty and violence.

William Golding's *Lord of the Flies* finds that in the very nature of children we have the roots of adult evil. In the novel we see the rise of violence, of repression, and of cruelty. For a complementary view we can bring in a discussion of the motion picture *The Wild Bunch*, for here the director tried to indicate, not with complete success, that the incredible violence of the adults could be found in the children themselves, who enjoyed torturing and burning insects.

Richard Hughes's *The Innocent Voyage* (*A High Wind in Jamaica*) outlines a similar theme, for in the story of children kidnapped by pirates, the children prove more savage than their captors.

James Joyce's *A Portrait of the Artist as a Young Man* would be an excellent novel for the mature reader in the class. He could see the young man trying to find his identity by tearing himself away from his parents and his teachers, and in the process renouncing their values and even their religion.

This list can easily be extended, but perhaps the value of the list is that it is short. A brief talk can introduce but not "give away" each book. Then the student is asked to select the book that seems to interest him. He does not have to write a book report; he brings his experience with the novel to his class and slips it into the discussion of the general theme raised by *The Yearling*. A panel discussion is one good way to introduce each book and show its relevance to the subject under review. Incidentally, since we are concentrating on the conflict between child and adult, it may be a good idea at this juncture to invite parents to join the panel discussion and give their viewpoint, and, it is hoped, to consider their children's viewpoint.

In this way we combine outside and inside reading, and we show how the books play variations on the theme. At the same time, students begin to see the complexity of the subject and thus gain insight into literature, themselves, and the problems they face. In doing so, they may be induced to read the other books discussed in class and thus become better and wider readers.

Another example can be adduced here to illustrate the process of using outside reading as an integral part of the classroom study of literature. O. E. Rölvaag's *Giants in the Earth* is being used in the high school today as a focus of study, for it touches on an important aspect of American history and life and thus correlates literature and history. It is the story of a Norwegian family in the United States that transforms the wilderness of the prairie into a productive farm but pays the price for the transformation, death in the case of Per Hansa, the settler, and insanity in the case of Beret, his wife. This novel easily becomes the core for the outside reading of the class.

The joys, the rewards, and the hardships of building a home and earning a livelihood in the wilderness constitute a universal theme, as we find in Pearl Buck's *The Good Earth*, which, of course, is set in China, and Knut Hamsun's *The Growth of the Soil*, which takes place in Norway. Both catch the gratification a man feels in turning the soil into productivity and the tragedy that nature can exact in exchange. Willa Cather's *My Antonia* presents a different picture of the pioneer woman, one who is more resilient than Beret and thus able to survive physical and psychological hardships. For the able student who likes to read how a man creates a world out of chaos, Daniel Defoe's *Robinson Crusoe* can be very satisfying fare. For the less able student, Rose Wilder Lane's *Let the Hurricane Roar* presents a somewhat melodramatic but exciting chronicle of a family fairly similar to the one in *Giants in the Earth*. Rölvaag's two other novels that form a trilogy with *Giants in the Earth*, *Peder Victorious* and *Their Father's God*, show how pioneer communities eventually grew into towns and how the children of the pioneers had to break away from the traditions and the prejudices of their parents. Hamlin Garland's *Son of the Middle Border* and *Daughter of the Middle Border* give us an account of actual events in the life of a boy and girl in the rigorous environment of the prairie. These two biographies also give the class an opportunity to contrast the way novels and biographies handle what is basically the same material. Poetry can be brought in, too, for Edgar Lee Masters' *Spoon River Anthology* can be read and discussed for its commentary on the lives of the people who grew up in prairie communities that gradually became towns. As a final commentary, a print of Grant Wood's oil painting, "American Gothic," can stir students to associate the grotesque and desiccated couple in the picture with the physical and psychological rigors of prairie life.

A third and final example uses Sinclair Lewis's *Arrowsmith*, a satirical account of a doctor's education, aspirations, and experiences. The study of this novel directs the students along several paths to seek their outside reading. A. J. Cronin's *Citadel* is a complementary novel to *Arrowsmith*, for it, too, dissects the hypocrisy and the materialism in the supposedly idealistic motivation of a physician. As an antidote, we can turn to Robert Payne's biography, *The Three Worlds of Albert Schweitzer*, for it gives us a picture of altruism and sacrifice in the life of a doctor.

For other examples of Sinclair Lewis's satirical thrust, we have two of his other novels, *Main Street* and *Babbitt,* in each case the author using his scalpel to lay bare some of the diseased tissue of society. For an example of satire in earlier literature, we have Jonathan Swift's *Gulliver's Travels.* His essay, "A Modest Proposal," is particularly apposite for its corrosive use of satire. A contemporary example of satire would be, of course, George Orwell's *Animal Farm.* When these and other similar books are brought into the classroom discussion, it would be instructive to find how doctors are depicted in television and motion picture drama and to speculate on why satire is strangely missing in television programs.

These examples can be multiplied many times, but the principle remains the same. Outside reading is important, so important that it should be at the core of English instruction rather than on the periphery. Obviously a Shakespeare play studied in class should lead to another Shakespeare play read outside. Just as obviously, the study of a Shakespeare play can be enhanced if the students read a background work like Marchette Chute's *Shakespeare of London.* Stephen Crane's *The Red Badge of Courage* in class suggests at once Erich Remarque's *All Quiet on the Western Front* outside of class. All these titles are by no means sacred, and undoubtedly others can be substituted or added. The point remains that the books for outside reading should relate to the books and the themes studied in class, that the teacher introduce the books and motivate the reading, and that the reading be *used* in the classroom.

LITERATURE FOR TODAY'S CLASSROOM

Anthony Roy Mangione

ROBERT HOGAN, in the April, 1967 issue of *The Bulletin,* comments on the gap that exists between the literature curriculum and the modern adolescent: "For the bright, the slow, and the disadvantaged— and in all likelihood for the average, too—the gap between the curriculum and the student widens almost beyond bridging."[1] Failing to bridge the gap serves only to antagonize pupils and to whet their appetite for stronger, less literary fare. Moreover, efforts to limit their reading experiences to innocuous offerings shortchange pupils and are, at best, educa-

[1] Robert F. Hogan, "Book Selection and Censorship," *The Bulletin,* LI, April, 1967, p. 73.

->>>

F R O M *The High School Journal* (February 1971), pp. 357–361. Reprinted by permission of the publisher and the author.

tionally dishonest. Pupils must cope effectively with the society in which they now live, and must be prepared to meet successfully the many worlds of adulthood—social, political, ethnic, and sexual. For the English teachers to involve their pupils in all of these worlds, they must select the most effective materials to do the job, and must treat these materials fully and honestly. Stephen Davenport, writing in the October 19, 1968 issue of *The Saturday Review*, re-enforces this need for candor:

> A literature class studying an author like Faulkner whose works deal with such subjects as miscegenation, and in whose diction the word "nigger" appears on almost every page, can be a real test of everybody's cool. Some teachers, simply because they are embarrassed, or because they do not want to embarrass their Negro students, avoid the issue altogether, and thus serve up a watered-down view which intelligent students greet with contempt. But more and more teachers are taking the issues head on and calling on their Negro students to provide their classes with their own first-hand experiences. The result is very often a better understanding of the complexity of our racial problems, and frequently among the white students a keener dissatisfaction with the way things are.[2]

Instead of despairing of the fact that neither *Silas Marner* (the story of a good woman who reforms a miser) nor "The Devil and Daniel Webster" (the tale of a fast-talking lawyer who outtalks the devil), for example, seems to interest today's hardbitten adolescents, English teachers should look for alternatives;[3] they can no longer expose pupils to one set of values in the classroom and allow them, simultaneously, to be abandoned to another set—many sets—in the outside world. Until the hypocrisy of this contradiction is unmasked, and remedied, pupils will

[2] Stephen Davenport, "Farewell to the Old School Tie," *The Saturday Review*, October 19, 1968, p. 69.

[3] To help teachers decide on substitute selections for up-to-date literature programs, consider the following questions posed by Alfred DeGrazia and David A. Sohn (editors). *Revolution in Teaching: New Theory, Technology, and Curricula* (McGraw-Hill, 1964), New York, pp. 246–248.

What should be the common ingredients in our culture other than current television shows?

What literature suitable for young people is so timeless and yet so contemporary that it speaks to today and will speak to tomorrow as it spoke to yesterday?

What literature from nonEnglish-speaking lands should we know to reduce our provincialism?

How can we avoid the present overemphasis on literature that depicts only the middle and upper classes?

What great fiction, drama, poetry, biography, and satire should everybody know, regardless of his probable future occupation?

How can pride in our American heritage be combined with informed respect for the cultures of other people?

The implications for improving pupils' self-image are obvious.

continue to despair and their contempt for the literature curriculum will flourish unabated.

One alternative—equally applicable to drama, fiction, and biography—is to ferret out appropriate folk-rock lyrics, teaching these together with traditional but pertinent poems. These songs and poems (samplings of which follow) complement each other and help pupils to verbalize their feelings about life (e.g., about war or alienation).

SOME SONGS AND POEMS ABOUT WAR

Songs: Buffy Sainte-Marie's "The Universal Soldier"
Bob Dylan's "Blowing in the Wind"
Lennon/McCartney's (The Beatles) "Revolution 1"
"Masters of War" (as sung by Judy Collins)
"Handsome Johnny" (as sung by Richie Havens)
Pete Seeger's "Where Have All the Flowers Gone?" adapted from a Russian folksong as quoted in Sholokhov's *And Quiet Flows the Don*)
Benjamin's *War Requiem* (excerpts)

Poems: Siegfried Sassoon's "Does It Matter?"; "Dreamers"
Thomas Hardy's "The Man He Killed"
Lovelace's "To Lucasta"
Rupert Brooke's "The Soldier"
Carl Sandburg's "Buttons"

SOME SONGS AND POEMS ABOUT ALIENATION

Songs: Paul Simon's "I Am a Rock;" "The Sounds of Silence"
Phil Ochs' "Outside a Small Circle of Friends"; "William Moore"
Simon and Garfunkel's "Richard Cory"

Poems: W. H. Auden's "Musee des Beaux Arts"
Edwin Arlington Robinson's "Richard Cory" (cf. sung version)
James Stephens' "The Road"

A second alternative, already implemented in some schools, is to abandon chronological and generic approaches to literature. Freed from the lockstep, and paralysis, of conventional anthologies, teachers have adopted a diversified literature program that appeals to pupils of wide ability and many backgrounds; they have interested some pupils in *Romeo and Juliet* by way of *West Side Story,* used *Huckleberry Finn* with everyone except nonreaders, and encouraged still others to enjoy such works as *The Caine Mutiny, The Ox-Bow Incident,* and *To Kill a Mockingbird,* which, traditionally, have hardly been *belles-lettres.* In short, teachers have experimented; they must continue to do so, if the gulf between the literature curriculum and the pupils' experiences is to narrow.

A further alternative, unacceptable to many teachers, is to do away with grade levels, substituting material that cuts across the superficial concerns of survey-oriented courses and the narrow purview of genre-based literature programs. Instead of straitjacketing pupils with literature, and holding it so sacred, as to be worshipped like an icon, or so lightly, as to be skimmed hurriedly rather than savored, teachers should help to link material with their pupils' past experiences and present emotional levels. As Abraham Bernstein suggests, in "Confrontation with English," literature presented as "something you reach out for, handle, manipulate, and chew, which you interact with . . . on the basis of *your* life and experiences"[4] is bound to generate interest among pupils. A sampling of courses offered at the new John Dewey High School, Brooklyn, New York, underscores the educational implications of a flexible, nongraded literature program.

LITERATURE OF PROTEST

An examination of poems and essays of the past and present which reflect the theme of protest against certain aspects of society (social injustice, war, technology, materialism). Discussions and written work will center on the implications of these ideas for today's youth.

THE GENERATION GAP IN AMERICAN LITERATURE

An examination of a variety of works of American writers which reflect alienation and the generation gap in American society. Attention will be specially given to works whose themes examine the conflicts which rise between young people and adults.

MASS MEDIA STUDY

A survey course examining the mass media as persuasive forces in shaping the minds of men. Students will explore selected examples of mass media to determine its (sic) effect (sic) and the manner used to obtain the effect.

THE BIBLE AS LITERATURE

An examination of various passages in the Old Testament and New Testament as to variety of prose and poetic style, and to theme.

A sine qua non of such an innovative program is literature saturated with meaningful, experiential attitudes, values, concepts, and conflicts rather than with piddling details, little pertinent substance, or both; for example, Jackson's "The Lottery," not Lewis' "Ring around a Rosy;"

4 Abraham Bernstein, "Confrontation with English," Kent State Lecture, October 11, 1969.

White's *The Once and Future King,* not Tennyson's *Idylls of the King;* Sackler's *The Great White Hope,* not Rattigan's *The Winslow Boy.* After all, while Bob Dylan's "Blowing in the Wind," for example, provides experiences that are germane to pupils, Kipling's "Recessional" glorifies England's past achievements. Replete with symbols, poetry, and situations posed as questions, the Dylan song generates ideas about war, peace, and patriotism, and sharpens the interest of pupils in ways that the hymn in celebration of Queen Victoria's Diamond Jubilee cannot hope to do.

To bridge the gap between the literature curriculum and today's pupils teachers must, as a final alternative, function as catalysts, inquirers, discoverers, and probers. When they teach literature, they should ask questions that produce understanding, rather than convey only information or answers. They should also use role playing, group discussions, and multisided debates, generated by questions, to involve their pupils affectively, minimizing simple recall assignments that direct pupils only to read, listen (if they do), and answer questions about literature at the end of chapters. In developing a capacity for open-endedness, teachers should continue to beget new questions about literature and give high priority to the queries posed by pupils, valuing these as more important than the answers given. As with their own inquiries, pupils' questions must be real, felt ones that point to the pulsating world in which they live, not to the rose-colored anemic world that so often typifies the average classroom.

After experimenting with these alternatives for today's classrooms, teachers of English may decide after all to keep a weaver named Marner, an assassin named Brutus, or a one-legged man named Silver; but they will not do without first considering the far-reaching interpersonal implications to be drawn from teaching literature affectively rather than chronologically or generically: teachers' heightened literary awareness and a concomitant better understanding of themselves and their pupils. Their pupils, in turn, will respond more sincerely; and if they also become more keenly sensitized to literature, the gap between the curriculum and pupils' experiences will indeed have been narrowed. It may then be said, "The Times They Are A'Changin' "5—for better.

---

5 Compliments and due acknowledgement to Bob Dylan.

LITERATURE
AND THE NOW GENERATION

Virginia R. Mollenkott

IN the October 1969 *MLA Newsletter,* Professor Paul D. McGlynn of Eastern Michigan University made an honest confession:

> I know from experience the painful realization that one is talking earnestly to oneself in front of forty uncomprehending, though not necessarily hostile, faces. At thirty-one I have been made to feel more than once like an eccentric old codger. But it is neither relevant nor practical to assume that my students' abilities are inferior to my own and then hurry on to Blake so that at least they can jot down officially that the tiger 'stands for' one thing and the lamb another.

Dr. McGlynn couldn't be more right. It is never relevant or practical to assume that generational differences imply the inferiority of the younger, and it is neither relevant nor practical to ignore the glassy eyes and go on talking into the multiplying void. If one approach is not working, then it is surely time to try another.

If, as Professor McGlynn claims, literature teachers are the last ambassadors from Western civilization, trying to communicate with people for whom Ché Guevara and Malcolm X have totally eclipsed Odysseus as portrayed by Homer, then we urgently need to make meaningful contact for reasons far deeper than our own professional success. McGlynn suggests an emphasis on metaphor: "I suspect our students might be less likely to confer codgerdom on us if we could display a convincing awareness of the analogy between young life in America in 1969 and the metaphoric process: both trying, as man and especially his poets have always tried, to bridge a gap . . . or impose order on chaos."

McGlynn should have added that while we are stressing the metaphoric process, we might evade codgerdom by the honest admission that the youthful counterculture is in many ways as necessary a revolution as was the revolution of the early Christian church against Roman decadence. The young are alienated from many aspects of our culture that call for the alienation of decent men and that have *always* alienated some poets.

To point out Blake's alienation from hyperrationalism and to demon-

FROM *Today's Education* (October 1970), pp. 64–67. Reprinted by permission of the publisher and the author.

strate its parallel to contemporary alienation from noncommittal indifference, for instance, might make the lamb and the tiger take on new dimensions for the now generation.

Sidney Simon and Merrill Harmin, in the October 1968 issue of *Educational Leadership*, offered another excellent suggestion for relevant teaching. Like McGlynn, Simon and Harmin begin with an honest confession:

> How increasingly irrelevant the schools seem. . . . Almost all of us feel tremendous ambivalence as we wrestle with that question of just how much of the standard subject matter of the school is to be set aside to make room for dealing with current concerns of our society.

In answer, Simon and Harmin propose that teachers must go beyond the level of factual information, must also go beyond Bruner's higher level of concepts, and must include vigorous discussion of values. It is not enough to teach *Hamlet* on the level of Hamlet's tragic flaw (fact-for-fact's sake), say Simon and Harmin. Nor is it enough to teach *Hamlet* on the level of Aristotelian tragedy vs. Shakespearean tragedy (the conceptual level). They say that *Hamlet* urgently needs to be taught so that the play will help students clarify their values and evaluate their lives. Discussion must be pointed toward such issues as Hamlet's cruelty to Ophelia: What does this imply about relations between the sexes? Has the student ever been cruel in that way or been the victim of such cruelty? What does the student think about such cruelty?

Unlike McGlynn, who generalizes but does not illustrate, Simon and Harmin amply demonstrate how to carry out their proposal. They fail to emphasize, however, that their three levels of discussion must not become isolated units. I am convinced that discussing facts-for-facts' sake one day, concepts another day, and values a third day will surely defeat the quest for relevance. Truly relevant teaching on *any educational level* will constantly move back and forth from one plane to another, relating this fact to that concept, that fact to this question of value, this concept to that value.

Never for even five minutes will discussion be permitted to sink to mere factuality or even to mere conceptualizing. Always, always, the focus must be on what the literature says about you, about me, about our culture, about the way we live our lives. Facts and concepts are necessary to keep such discussion from becoming amorphous, but facts and concepts exist for man, not the other way around.

One way to preserve the focus and heighten the sense of relevance is to approach literary classics by grouping them around contemporary themes and by relating them to contemporary art forms. Because of the constantly shifting levels of discourse, I think providing two detailed illustrations will be more valuable than making myriad unsubstantiated suggestions.

Certainly a vital concern in today's America is that of the generation gap. The modern student may not be turned on by the thought of studying medieval ballads or a difficult Shakespearean play like *King Lear*, but he probably *does* go for the Beatles and Bobbie Gentry, and the effects of the generation gap are of personal concern to him. He will not be likely to turn off his hearing aid if the great medieval ballad "Edward, Edward" is compared technically with "Ode to Billie Joe" and conceptually to a song from the Beatles' 1967 album, *Sgt. Pepper's Lonely Hearts Club Band*.

What better way to study the techniques of the ballad than by trying to decide why Gentry was wrong to call her song an ode? "Ode to Billie Joe" is a perfect minstrel ballad—narrative rather than lyrical verse, operating by hints and implications, making effective use of parallel repetition. By contrast, "Edward, Edward" is a folk ballad, using less of the subjective element but likewise operating through hints and implications, utilizing both parallel and incremental repetition. Both concern family relationships; to varying degrees both concern human callousness toward the suffering of another.

But where concepts and values are concerned, "Edward, Edward" works far better with the Beatles' song. "She's Leaving Home," in which the Beatles twice repeat that the girl described in the song is leaving home and family "after living alone"—emphasizing the fact that without meaningful communication, a person is *especially* alone in the home of his parents. The song makes clear what sort of communication the girl *has* received from her parents, who have impressed on her that they had given up much themselves in order to give her every material advantage. Naturally the girl feels alienated; she wanted the things money *can't* buy, and she has been made to feel desperately lonely and guilty.

These are emotions our students will recognize. Vaguely, they know that there is no sacrifice involved in a relationship of mutual love, respect, and concern and that if one person chooses to do something for another (especially for a child), it is the foulest kind of betrayal to ask at a later date for subservience in return for the "sacrifice." Vaguely, students are aware that something unjust is going on in many homes and possibly in their own, and they are relieved and certainly interested when class discussion helps them to verbalize it all, bringing it to the conscious level. Of course, at an appropriate point in such discussion, a teacher must be sure to indicate that students—like mature people of all ages— must accept responsibility for their own behavior regardless of mistakes that may have been made in their upbringing.

What has this to do with "Edward, Edward"? Plenty. The ballad (here translated into modern English) consists of a conversation between a mother and her son across a frightening gap. "Why does your brand so drop with blood, Edward?" and "Why are you so sad, Edward?" asks the mother. After several evasive replies, the son admits the truth: "O I have killed my father dear,/Alas, and woe is me, O!"

The mother's immediate reaction is significant in the light of further revelations: "And what penance will you do for that, Edward?" He replies that he will banish himself. "And what will you do with your towers and your hall?" He will let them stand until they fall down, for he must never return. "And what will you leave to your children and wife, Edward?" He will let them beg through life, for he will never see them again.

It is the final stanza that makes the crushing revelation:

> "And what will you leave to your own mother dear,
>   Edward, Edward?
> And what will you leave to your own mother dear?
>   My dear son, now tell me, O."
> "The curse of hell from me shall you bear,
>   Mother, mother,
> The curse of hell from me shall you bear,
> Such counsels you gave to me, O."

What counsels? As is customary in the ballad, a great deal is left to the imagination of the audience, but here it is not difficult to discern that the mother's remarks throughout her son's life have poisoned him against his father. Only after Edward has shed his father's blood does he realize that his father is dear to him. In his shock, he repudiates his own wife and children—running a good home is hard for the person who did not grow up in one—and curses his mother for her baleful influence upon him.

Students are often unsure of whether to pronounce Edward's mother a hypocrite or merely a victim of acute psychological naïveté: "What penance will *you* do for that, Edward?" Her first reaction is thus to place the blame for her husband's death solely on her son's shoulders, leaving herself above reproach and free from guilt. Is she consciously hypocritical, or is she really naïve enough to miss the fact that, although she did not use the sword, she provided the impetus for its use? Students are not sure that it matters; but either way, in dealing with their own adult contemporaries, their name for it is *hypocrisy*.

How many parents have conditioned their children toward drug addiction (with a medicine cabinet full of tranquilizers and pep pills), and then have judged them for being addicts? ("What penance will you do for that, Edward?") How many parents have, by lack of loving attention, driven their children to promiscuity, and then have judged them for being promiscuous?

Students understand that parents do not *mean* to send their children astray, and they can feel pity for the anguished mothers in "She's Leaving Home" and "Edward." But from their point of view, adult ignorance is no excuse. It is Edward who will suffer the stigma of murder, not his mother; it is the young girl who will bear the illegitimate child or wind up deserted in a big lonely city, not her parents. To young people, psychological naïveté is in the same bag with conscious hypocrisy because the results are the same. They will hardly be listless or glassy-eyed when such issues are being aired, but at the same time they are getting practice in the art of literary interpretation.

And what about *King Lear?* Perhaps because teachers tend to be parents and representatives of the Establishment, they usually approach *Lear* as a play about filial ingratitude: the ingratitude of Goneril and Regan toward their father, the king, and the ingratitude of Edmund toward his father, Gloucester. But when Lear cries out concerning his daughters, "Is there any cause in nature that makes these hard hearts?" modern students are apt to answer, "Yes, certainly. A primary cause of hardhearted children is hardhearted parents!"

And I believe the play bears them out. When Goneril and Regan are alone after Lear has repudiated Cordelia, Goneril comments that Lear has "always loved our sister most" and that "the best and soundest of his time hath been but rash"; and Regan accurately observes that "he hath ever but slenderly known himself." Not knowing himself, he has not known the effect of his willfulness on others. Only after his purification through suffering does he begin to recognize the former hardness of his heart:

> Take physic, pomp;
> Expose thyself to feel what wretches feel,
> That thou mayst shake the superflux to them
> And show the heavens more just.

I have always been amazed that Goneril and Regan are regularly played as inhuman vixens from the very start. They are, instead, two girls who have grown up with a self-centered and impulsive father who adores and openly favors their sister Cordelia. They have, of course, toughened under Lear's selfishness and favoritism, so that when he proposes to divide his kingdom according to their professions of love for him (thinking that surely thus he will be able to give Cordelia the most), they are willing to make hypocritically overstated professions of love. But is this not understandable, all things considered?

Later, when Goneril tries to reduce Lear's 100 retainers to 50 because they are "disorder'd, so debosh'd, and bold," Lear storms out of her palace in a fury. When Regan further reduces the number to 25, he grows angrier yet, and finally the two girls decide to accept Lear alone into their homes, "but not one follower." Strictly speaking, they do *not* evict him personally, as he claims; but they *do* refuse to go along with his childish scheme of retaining the privileges and retinue of kingship while shedding the responsibilities of a king. As the play progresses, of course, they become hellishly corrupt, but their corruption is gradual, and Lear, in my opinion, deserves a large share of the blame.

The same kind of filial ingratitude appears in the subplot. In the opening scene, Shakespeare makes plain the reason for Edmund's "ingratitude" to Gloucester: His father twits him in public about being a bastard, speaks slightingly of his mother, and promises to send him out of the country very soon. "He hath been out nine years, and away he shall again." Who can blame Edmund for being fiercely jealous of the legitimate and favored son Edgar? Is Edmund's tough selfishness and villainy really very surprising in the light of his background?

Both Gloucester and Lear are totally blind to what I consider to be their responsibility in the corruption of their respective son and daughters. They see only that the children have failed in their filial responsibility. Generation gap, indeed!

Had Gloucester ever paused to think how his son Edmund might feel about his own bastardy and his mother's status, the twitting might have ceased. (Ask the black students about the effect of constant vilification!) This is what twentieth-century young people plead for—to be considered as people, as equals-because-human, as fellowmen rather than as objects. Do they ask too much?

Gloucester has neatly categorized Edmund. He is a bastard, and therefore does not merit full consideration. Similarly, students of the now generation resent being neatly packaged, categorized, and discriminated against. They want to be judged on their individual, personal characteristics, not on their age group. On the job, they want candidates for promotion to be judged on the basis of intellect and capability rather than on chronological seniority. In a discussion they want to be listened to and judged not by age but by the worth of what they contribute; they do not want people to use age differences to avoid arguments and involvement. They need to articulate these longings, and under the stimulus of great literature and a sympathetic teacher they will do exactly that.

At the end of *King Lear,* Albany utters some platitudinous promises to administer just rewards and punishments to everyone in the kingdom that has now become his. But his words are refuted by the sight of Cordelia lying dead in Lear's arms—no poetic justice here! Sobered by reality, he becomes less flamboyant: "The weight of this sad time we must obey,/Speak what we feel, not what we ought to say." Here again is a major burden of twentieth-century youth: They want everyone to tell it like it is. And they ask the older generation to be realistic in its requirements, to be honest with them, not to preach ideals that are impossible for both young and old. They are able to empathize with Albany, and they are relieved to discover that Shakespeare "understood."

Is it dangerous to listen sympathetically to youthful concerns in classroom discussions of literature? Is it likely to foment greater misunderstanding and more violent rebellion? Hardly. Psychotherapy allows people to talk freely about their grievances, and the result is not greater fury but greater ability to accept one's own personality and hence to forgive the violations against that selfhood by those who know no better. I am convinced that the growing gap is not caused by honest discussion but by the *refusal* of the older generation to listen to the concerns of the young (as witness the recent movie entitled *If*). Because the discussion of literature can simultaneously attract the now generation to accurate interpretation, help them grasp subject matter, and assist them in coping with very real current problems, literature classes need not be guilty of an increasing irrelevance. If they are, the fault is ours.

Literature deals meaningfully with all manner of contemporary concerns in addition to the generation gap. One might therefore group literary classics around such themes as the essential aloneness of each human being when he suffers, the difficulty of moral choice in a complex world, the uncertainty of tomorrow, and the extent of one's personal responsibility to society. Contemporary art (especially folk music) is so full of social concern that it will not be difficult to find popular art which will lead into meaningful discussion of the classics.

Certain members of the now generation are cutting themselves off from traditional values. They see no reason why recreational sex should not be substituted for responsible love, or why anybody should regard kindness as good and gross selfishness as evil. Many of their less extreme contemporaries retain some of the tried-and-true values but cannot for the life of them see how reading the literature of several centuries ago can possibly have meaning for today.

To both of these groups it is imperative that we communicate one fact: *If we cut ourselves off from the accumulated experience of mankind and refuse to learn from the wisdom of the past, we are condemning ourselves to a costly trial-and-error type of living.* Without any precedent and without vicarious experience, we are condemned to base our values upon the whim of the moment. And God help us when we fall prey to strong politicians who force us to submit to *their* whims. Hitler's whim that Jews should be exterminated cost millions of lives in addition to the casualties of the European phase of World War II!

As a matter of fact, the personalistic and communal counterculture of American youth has been compared to the energy and power of the German youth movement of the 1930's. Obviously, any revolution, no matter how good at its inception, can turn demonic unless its power is responsibly channeled. Through courageously creative teaching, we still might possibly combine the best of traditional education—analytical and detached—with the best insights of the youthful counterculture—integrative and committed. The alternative is hardly pleasant.

It should by now be obvious that we need not set aside the standard subject matter of literature in order to "make room for dealing with the current concerns of society." We need only to see that literature has always dealt with mankind's perennial concerns and to encourage discussion of facts, concepts, and values with a constant focus on the needs of the now generation.

NEGRO LITERATURE IN HIGH SCHOOL ENGLISH: THREE REASONS FOR ITS USE

Robert Coleman Small, Jr.

IN recent years, an interest has developed among English teachers in the use of what is frequently termed "black literature" as a part of the school program. Although this interest has been most noticeable during the last few years, it was apparent at least as early as 1932 when the White House Conference on Child Health and Protection discussed in its report on children's reading the need for imaginative and inspiring books for Negro children. In that same year, writing in the *Children's Library Yearbook*, the poet and novelist Langston Hughes, in a comment which prefigures much of the more recent commentary on the subject, stated,

> Faced too often by the segregation and scorn of the surrounding white world, America's Negro children are in pressing need of books that will give them back their own souls. They do not know the beauty they possess. (p. 110)

Despite such early signs of interest, however, the real development of concern with the reading by students of books about black Americans has come since the end of the Second World War as a result of what Charlemae Rollins has called "a growing consciousness that the Negro must be fully integrated into American life and that the surest way to such integration was to understand him and to accept him as a fellow

→→→-→→→

FROM *The High School Journal*, Vol. 54 (May 1971), pp. 475–483. Reprinted by permission of the publisher and the author.

human being with all the privileges and responsibilities that such acceptance entails" (*We Build Together,* 1967, p. x).

If one examines the flood of articles, bibliographies, and books devoted at least in part to the subject of black literature in high school English, there are, it becomes apparent, three main, student-connected arguments given to support this use of this material. Perhaps the most frequently encountered of these arguments are those which relate to Negro students. English teachers always have placed great emphasis on their students' attitudes toward literature; that is, they wish to achieve student interest in and identification with the books, their characters and events, which the students read and study. Thus, it has frequently been suggested that black students, who, as a group, have seemed to show little interest in the traditional literary content of the English class (often called "white literature"), will be more interested in books by and about Negroes and also better able to identify with the black characters in such books.

Although little work has been done to determine the reading interests of black students, many educators have concluded that black students would indeed be more interested in and identify more fully with books about members of their own race. Of course, an occasional writer has rejected the idea that black children will enjoy reading about members of their own race, agreeing with the statement that "it is not natural . . . for Negro children to want to read only of children of their own race, and those who guide children's reading . . . should not single out a Negro boy or girl to whom she may recommend a book about a Negro child."[1] Only a very small percentage of recent books and articles agree with this position; teachers who have used works of black literature with black students all seem to agree that their students showed and openly expressed far greater interest in and ability to identify with such books than with the generally all-white material found in the textbooks which they had previously used. Barbara Dodds, for example, in her book *Negro Literature for High School Students,* writes about her own experiences, "The students definitely appreciated the Negro literature we had studied," and lists the following comments which her students made:

> I've really found out that we were somebody.
> All the Negro literature we've studied, I've enjoyed it.
> It makes you feel pretty good that we've contributed something too.
> (pp. 5–6)

Attempting to express the reason behind this increased interest in and identification with literature, she remarks,

[1] B. B. Preer, "Guidance in Democratic Living Through Juvenile Fiction," *Wilson Library Bulletin,* May, 1948, p. 680.

It is frequently asserted that one reason many Negro children have difficulty learning to read is that they cannot identify with and are not interested in the white children in their textbooks. By the time they reach high school, Negro students have become accustomed to reading about white people, but they have not become interested. My students seemed to be much more interested in reading about Negroes than whites, though it is difficult to measure reading interest accurately. (p. 6)

Dodds is not alone, however, in this belief. Another writer, in an article entitled "Literature for the Negro," supports the same idea, writing,

One thing I do know . . . is that Negro children do like to read books about Negro teen-agers. These are the books they carry around, discuss, and pass along from one to another. Until I began to read these books myself, I felt very much like an outsider. I taught "literature" and became annoyed at students who, ignoring me, would sit engrossed in their favorite works of "Negro fiction." I now feel that their fierce interest in these books should be "harnessed" and used to stimulate an interest in reading.[2]

Despite these strongly expressed opinions, few attempts to support through research the idea of black interest in black literature have been made. In fact, only a very few instances of research into black students' reading interests exist. W. E. Anderson and S. L. Crawley, as a result of their study entitled "The Reading Interests of Negro High School Pupils," conducted over twenty years ago, stated that "Negro high-school boys and girls involved in this study have a keen interest in books and periodicals whether fiction or non-fiction written by or about Negroes" (p. 10). On the other hand, Elinor McClosky found in her study of reading interests that few of the black sixth-grade boys she tested mentioned books by or about members of their race as read, enjoyed, or desired for reading. She explained this anomaly as a result of "an uneasiness in thinking about matters of race" and of the fact that the interviewer in the study was white. She concluded, however,

The slim mention [of such books] may demonstrate a lack of awareness of any of the books currently being written about minority cultures. The mention by even a small number of these children may indicate a new acceptance and interest in racial identification in the light of increased action by the Negro population. . . . It would seem that the interest evinced by these children, together with the stress they laid upon achievement and accomplishment, would prepare a fertile field for an increased number of books about the achievements of leading Negro figures.[3]

2 Linda Smith, "Literature for the Negro Student," *High Points*, October, 1965, p. 22.
3 E. F. McClosky, *A Study of the Free Reading Interests of Sixth-Grade Negro Boys Living in Disadvantaged Areas in the City of New York*, p. 378.

A second widely expressed reason for the use of black literature with black students is a result of a concern with the problems of black students, who have low self-concepts, a lack of self-respect and pride. Indeed, many authors have suggested that an important part of the black student's interest in and identification with black authors and with black characters in literature, if, in fact, such interest and identification does exist, is the feeling of self-respect and racial pride which such authors and characters give him. In his 1932 article, Langston Hughes expressed the relationship of books and a black student's self-concept, pointing out that

> overcoming this racial inferiority complex is, undoubtedly, one of the greatest tasks of the teachers of Negro children. To make their little charges feel that they will be men and women, not "just niggers," is a none too easy problem when textbooks are all written from a white standpoint. (p. 108)

Repeatedly, in more recent books and articles, one encounters the idea that black students often have poor opinions of themselves and their race. From these low opinions, it is claimed, results an acceptance of a blighted and hopeless future on a limited social and economic level. Thus many authors have argued, in agreement with Langston Hughes, that an important mission of the school, and especially of the English class, is to help the black student to a better opinion of himself and his race. Frequently, literature is a primary means suggested to achieve this goal. For example, a teacher who developed a unit in black literature gave as the reason for teaching it the opinion that

> by teaching about the people of a minority group we give that group status and erase some of the inequities felt by members of that group and proclaimed by others. A Negro student familiar with intelligent and creative members of his own race may feel that his efforts and aspirations will not be wasted.[4]

For similar reasons, Barbara Dodds, in the book previously mentioned, concludes that "the Negro student is injured . . . by a false idea of his inferiority. Everything in his heritage of which he can be proud is carefully hidden from him"; and she maintains that "for many years English teachers and textbooks in American schools have lost many of their bright Negro students because they have not introduced them to their own literature; they have not aroused their interest in education" (pp. 5–6).

Such experts as Dwight Burton and Robert Carlsen in the field of literature for adolescent readers have recognized and emphasized for many years the idea that works of literature used in school with teen-age readers should have a sufficient number of elements such as char-

[4] Smith, op. cit., pp. 15–16.

acter, event, and problem in common with the interests and experiences of young readers if those materials are to influence the lives of those readers. In other words, because reading of literature, especially by a student, is not merely a simple, mechanical response to words on a page but rather is a process of bringing one's own experiences, interests, and problems to it, the content of that literature should resemble in important ways the life of the student reader. The logic and evidence of adolescent reading in general, therefore, suggests that, in order to have reading produce a positive effect among black students, appealing books about members of their race should be added to the English curriculum and to school libraries. In addition to this logical argument, however, the experiences of those teachers who have tried such literature with black students—and who have reported the results—support the belief that black students are more inspired by reading black literature than by reading white literature. On the other hand, there seems to exist nothing in the way of direct, object research into the effects of reading black literature on black students. The few studies of black reading interests are either very dated or, as in the case of the McClosky study, disappointing and, at best, inconclusive.

A third commonly encountered argument for the use with secondary school students of literature by black authors and/or about black characters relates to the white student only. Many educators have suggested that such literature will serve as a means either of avoiding the creation of prejudice in white students or of counteracting already existing prejudice. Thus, Nancy Larrick, writing in the September 11, 1965 *Saturday Review* says,

> The impact of all-white books upon the 39,600,000 white children is probably even worse [than on Negro students]. Although his light skin makes him one of the world's minorities, the white child learns from his books that he is kingfish. There seems little chance of developing the humility so urgently needed for world cooperation, instead of world conflict, as long as our children are brought up on gentle doses of racism through their books. (p. 63)

In another example of this idea, Ted Hipple argues in the *English Journal* that many students, even the most intelligent, are prejudiced in matters of race. It is his opinion that, if this prejudice is to be overcome, the schools and especially the English teachers must take the lead. A bit more tentatively, other teachers have claimed that white students who have experience with intelligent and creative black characters in literature will probably be less susceptible to prejudice.

The belief that reading black literature will reduce or eliminate racial prejudice in students is, of course, merely an aspect of the more general idea that literature can accomplish what no other part of the school can do so well—the development of attitudes. Libraries and schools both proclaim this idea; indeed, it is the most generally accepted excuse for or justification of the teaching of literature. Parents and teachers alike believe that literature influences opinions and attitudes and helps to develop goals and values. In other words, the belief that literature can cause changes in both attitudes and actions is generally accepted. The reading of black literature, it is therefore believed, can change white students' attitudes by giving those students a chance vicariously to live the life of a black American, to identify with black characters and problems. An author who has skillfully depicted what it is like to be a black person in America gives the reader a chance to move inside black existence. Thus, it is believed, prejudice will be destroyed by vicarious but strong feelings and experiences.

Little has, however, been done to test these contentions, possibly because they concern matters of personality change and the effects of reading on individuals. It is, of course, a great deal more difficult to test the effects of reading than to speculate about them. A few books read by a few students during a few weeks are not likely to have a great and lasting effect on them, although they might, of course. In order to be able to test for the effects of such reading, some means of measuring the state of a student's mind on matters of race would have to be developed. Such a device would not only have to discover prejudice (which present tests claim to be able to do) but also would have to measure it in exact degrees. It would have to differentiate between kinds of prejudice and assign them weights of seriousness. In short, to measure the effect of reading on the prejudiced attitudes of students, the researcher faces a complex and long-range task. Probably for this reason, there have been few efforts to test the contention that reading books by and about black Americans will give the white student insight and thus make him more understanding and less prejudiced.

Robert Carlsen, in his study of this question in 1948, found that the attitudes toward race of a group of eleventh grade students did not change significantly after the students read several books about black characters. He did feel, however, that the students were influenced by what they read. In an earlier study, E. P. Jackson found that prejudice as measured by a standardized scale did decrease among a group of elementary school students in the deep South when they read books favorable to blacks. However, he also found that, when the students were tested sometime later, their levels of prejudice had returned to the pre-test levels. These two studies suggest that prejudiced attitudes are more difficult to influence in older than in younger students and that a brief exposure to materials about blacks can have at best only temporary effects. In fact, however, too little research has been done in this important area to draw any firm conclusions. Therefore, as in the case of the arguments for the use of black literature with black students, the teacher of English can find a plentiful supply of opinions and logical arguments to support teaching black literature to white students as an antidote to prejudice. Unfortunately, the evidence of research is both scanty and inconclusive.

Among all of the arguments, suggestions, lessons, and anecdotes proposing the use of black literature in the high school, three reasons are, then, the most commonly encountered. Two, interest in and identification with literature and increased self-respect, relate to black students; and one, elimination of prejudice, relates to the white student. All three are manifestations of a belief in the effects of literature on student readers, the latter two reasons being more a matter of therapy than literary appreciation. Although many of the educators who present these reasons argue strongly and sincerely and give vivid personal evidence to support their claims, research evidence is largely non-existent. The few pieces of research which have tried to examine the claims for black literature have yielded largely negative or inconclusive results. Much of the evidence is old. Consequently, the teacher of English considering the use of black literature in his classes must, unfortunately, make his decision without the help of definite evidence or must look for other reasons not connected with the effect of the literature on his students.

SELECTED BIBLIOGRAPHY

Anderson, W. E., and S. L. Crawley. "The Reading Interests of Negro High School Pupils," *Quarterly Review of Higher Education Among Negroes*, January 1945, pp. 5–11.

Arnez, Nancy L. "Racial Understanding Through Literature," *English Journal*, January 1969, pp. 56–61.

Bone, Robert. "Negro Literature in the Secondary School: Problems and Perspectives," *English Journal*, April 1969, pp. 510–515.

Carlsen, G. Robert. *A Study of the Effects of Reading Books About the Negro on the Racial Attitudes of a Group of Eleventh Grade Students.* Minneapolis: 1948.

Corbin, Richard, and Muriel Crosby, *Language Programs for the Disadvantaged.* Champaign: 1965.

Daigon, Arthur. "The Strange Case of Nancy Drew," *English Journal*, December 1964, pp. 666–669.

Deane, Paul C. "The Persistence of Uncle Tom," *The Journal of Negro Education*, Spring 1968, pp. 140–145.

Dodds, Barbara. *Negro Literature for High School Students.* Champaign: 1968.

Groff, Patrick J. "New Books for the Slum Child," *Wilson Library Bulletin*, December 1963, pp. 345–348.

Hipple, Ted. "Through Literature to Freedom," *English Journal*, February 1966, pp. 189–191.

Hughes, Langston. "Books and the Negro Child," *Children's Library Yearbook.* Chicago: 1932, pp. 108–110.

Jackson, E. P. "Effects of Reading upon the Negro Race," *Library Quarterly,* January 1944, pp. 47–54.

Joki, Virginia. "Let My People Go"—A Unit on the Negro for High School English Classes," *Journal of Education,* December 1964, pp. 96–109.

Karl, Jean. "An Editor's Point of View: Enough for All," *Interracial Books for Children,* Summer 1966, pp. 1, 7.

Klineberg, Otto. "Life Is Fun in a Smiling, Fair-Skinned World," *Saturday Review,* February 16, 1963, pp. 75–77; 87.

Korey, Ruth. "Children's Literature for Integrated Classes," *Elementary Education,* January 1966, pp. 39–42.

Larrick, Nancy. "The All-White World of Children's Books," *Saturday Review,* September 11, 1965, pp. 63–85.

McClosky, Elinor R. *A Study of the Free Reading Interests of Sixth-Grade Negro Boys Living in Disadvantaged Areas in the City of New York.* Colorado: 1966.

Marcus, Fred H. "Cry, the Beloved Country and Strange Fruit: Exploring Man's Inhumanity to Man," *English Journal,* December 1962, pp. 609–616.

Millam, Carl H., Chairman. *Children's Reading: A Study of Voluntary Reading of Boys and Girls in the United States.* New York: 1932.

Preer, B. B. "Guidance in Democratic Living Through Juvenile Fiction," *Wilson Library Bulletin,* May 1948, pp. 679–708.

Rollins, Charlemae. "Books About Negroes for Children," *ALA Bulletin,* April 1959, pp. 306–308.

———. "Promoting Racial Understanding Through Books," *Negro American Literature Forum,* Winter 1968, pp. 71–76.

———. "The Role of the Book in Combating Prejudice," *Wilson Library Bulletin,* October 1967.

———. *We Build Together.* Champaign: 1967.

Smith, Linda. "Literature for the Negro Student," *High Points,* October 1965, pp. 15–26.

Sterling, Dorothy. "The Soul of Learning," *English Journal,* February 1968, pp. 166–180.

Witty, Paul, and S. D. Scruggs. "Reading Interests of Negro Children," *Bulletin of Education, University of Kansas,* December 1926, pp. 7–11.

THE RIGHT TO READ: ADULTS ONLY?

Roger B. Fransecky

VIEWPOINTS on censorship and the teaching of English cover quite a spectrum these days. There are the pietists like Billy Graham who denounce the law courts' anti-censorship decisions as "contributing to the moral decadence of the nation." There are the self-appointed censors who manage to get their kicks and engage in tongue-cluching at the same time (e.g. for 25 cents you can obtain from Californians for Morality, in San Diego, three copies of a pamphlet telling "exactly what was said in a vulgar and filthy speech made at the Berkeley Student Union"). And there are the legislators who have introduced nearly 20 procensorship bills in recent sessions of the Massachusetts House of Representatives. At the opposite extreme are the permissivists like social critic Paul Goodman who defend even hard-core pornography, the hip hedonists who regard *Playboy* as a bit square, the "new morality" theologians who define "obscene" by the slanderous vocabulary of the racist. And in the agonizing middle are the many who sincerely value freedom of expression but who just as sincerely doubt that their children would benefit appreciably from viewing a film biography of the Marquis de Sade. Now, the figure of the English teacher has entered the nightmare landscape of literary censorship, probing for assistance with an ugly problem which neither his training nor experience have left him ready to cope with.

In a number of small faculty rooms in grey-bricked high schools, hitherto uninterrupted except for the rustling of waxed paper around slightly stale bologna sandwiches, voices are heard asking questions about that "dirty book" *Catcher in the Rye* currently being taught by the new Mrs. Pedagog to her 11th graders. The book may vary, the questions rarely do.

The same questions have been asked by school board members, principals, left (or right) wing leaders of pressure groups, and of course, by parents. Too often, however, the question is left unanswered, the book is silently dropped from the curriculum (and so, too often, is the "offending" teacher), and that's that. Teachers stare into their empty Tab bottles, parents select appropriate books for the consumption of their young, and the great antiseptic literature program grinds ineffectually on.

➤➤➤➤➤➤➤➤➤➤➤➤➤➤➤➤➤➤➤➤➤➤➤➤➤➤➤➤➤➤➤➤➤

FROM *The English Record* (October 1970), pp. 88–96. Reprinted by permission of the publisher and the author.

Is this an accurate picture? Does the ugly voice of the uninformed censor (or the thoughtful voice of the informed censor?) reach into the English classrooms of our land?

The Professional Organizations Speak Out

Many concerned professionals within the structure of the National Council of Teachers of English, the American Library Association, and the ALA-affiliated Office on Intellectual Freedom, have directed considerable professional energies toward a national assessment of problems in book selection and incidents with literary censorship, in libraries and in schools. The American Library Association has led the professions in its efforts to open the literary marketplace—its "Library Bill of Rights" and *Newsletter on Intellectual Freedom* are important anti-censorship publications.

The National Council of Teachers of English has provided considerable national support to regional affiliate censorship committees, and NCTE has sponsored several useful monographs on censorship for professional English teachers. Perhaps the most important step taken within our profession was the 1962 publication of *The Student's Right to Read* by NCTE, for this pamphlet features responsible and responsive commentary on the vital task of the English teacher, and of the professional responsibility of the teacher and administrator to meet objections to literary sections with fairness and vision. *The Student's Right to Read* contains a form for handling complaints about a book, and while some have complained that it puts the objector on the defensive to an inappropriate degree, the form represents a useful model for handling many of the incidents of informed and uninformed censorship that reach a principal's desk.

In 1967, the National Council of Teachers of English's Committee on Case Studies in Censorship produced a helpful monograph, *Meeting Censorship in the Schools,* edited by Dr. John Hove of North Dakota State University, the Chairman of the NCTE Committee. Hove's monograph examines nine case studies of actual censorship incidents in high school situations. There is a particularly useful chapter on Lee's *To Kill a Mockingbird* with a model defense given of the book by a teacher-under-attack to her school board. The Appendix contains Dennis Hannan's Book Selection Procedure from the Wappingers, New York, Central School. The procedure is most complete in detailing the professional responsibilities inherent in any book selection problem, from first-year teacher to school board president. Mr. Hannan's thoughtful procedure has provided valuable assistance to teachers looking for help *before* the censor comes. Most NCTE members are familiar with Wayne C. Booth's strong and reasonable arguments against censorship in his March, 1964 article in *English Journal*. This is the express statement of the NCTE's Commission on Literature:

> No literary work is in itself proper or improper for the schools. Its suitability must be judged in terms of its development of the student's intelligence and critical sensibility; and the effect on the student of the book taken as a whole. The responsibility for making judgement in any given case must rest with those best qualified by training and experience to do so, the members of the teaching profession in English.[1]

There is little question that the urgent need for more teacher-centered decisions affecting what students have the right to read is the thrust of this collection of essays, for many of our authors (i.e. Kenneth Donelson and Ronald LaConte) go to some lengths to remind us all, as teachers of English, of our important responsibilities in cases of literary censorship.

Our "New" Students

Of central concern in any discussion of literary censorship is the student—for he is properly central in any professional discussion about intellectual freedom. There seems little question to many English teachers that today's pupil is remarkably aware of himself as part of what Henry James called "our booming, buzzing environment."

Today's junior and senior high school students view larger-than-life sex from screens and stages, posters and pages, and from what *Time* magazine calls, "the words and rhythms of pop-music erotica." The word is out that sex will save you and your libido will set you free—and the new disciples fill our classrooms.

Our sex-affirming culture's newest sport is Spectator Sex—what may be seen or read. Freud's clinical prose is now translated into a lyrical prosody by Calder Willingham and John Updike and is readily available at the friendly neighborhood drug store or supermarket, along with *Lust Queen, Lust Girls,* and *Lust Team.* Spectator Sex becomes more pleasant with the new freedom in American clothing fashions—spirits are up, girdles are out, and the "un-cola" new figures are better than ever. So who can object?

As professional English teachers we must be able to react to this new culture and its unique in-school manifestations with many skills, and responsive attitudes, some not taught in English methods classes. We must be aware that we are confronting a student who is terribly *present* tense—some call him "The Now Generation." The urgent statement this kid makes to the world is reflected on cinema and disc, and only occasionally in print. The generation gap becomes very important to the

[1] The Commission on Literature, NCTE Council—Grams, November, 1967. No. 8.

English teacher who is discussing, Gawd forbid, *Silas Marner* with a senior group who have been bombarded with Benjamin and the Beetles who lured them to Abbey Road with a tune far more inciting than any that we can play.

In a recent interview in that now-almost-respectable "journal" *Playboy*, communications expert Marshall McLuhan responded to an inquiry about the present state of our educational system and the reason why the young aren't finding a sense of personal identity within that system with these words:

> Because education, which should be helping youth to understand and adapt to their revolutionary new environments, is instead being used merely as an instrument of cultural aggression, imposing upon retribalized youth the obsolescent visual values of the dying literate age, our entire educational system is reactionary, oriented to past values and past technologies and will likely continue so until the old generation relinquishes power. The generation gap is actually a chasm, separating not two age groups but two vastly different cultures. I can understand the ferment in our schools, because our educational system is totally rear view mirror. It's a dying and outdated system founded on literary values and fragmented and classified data totally unsuited to the needs of the first television generation. . . . The challenge of the new era is simply the total creative process of *growing up* —and mere teaching and repetition of facts are as irrelevant to this process as a dowser to a nuclear power plant.[2]

Some teachers would react negatively to McLuhan's rhetoric, but we cannot deny the reality of the "generation gap," or McLuhan's suggestion that it is, in reality, a "chasm." Nor can we hide from his accurate suggestion that much of our educational system is "rear view mirror." The challenge of change to the English teacher is to provide both the rear view mirror, for there is a special urgency to make the experiences of past cultures relevant to NOW, and the microscope to the present— through a mixed media "package" of print, disc, and cinema. The problems of censorship and the difficulties in making appropriate professional decisions of what is relevant and what is inappropriate in this media-age makes the censorship question more real and alive than ever before.

To those of us who spend most of our professional time in English education and media, we express our concern that teachers must be *aware* of media and its potential to speak to today's students with power and precision. Father John Culkin and others have reminded us of the terrific media exposure (mostly passive) kids have had by the time they graduate from high school. Culkin suggests that the average pupil has watched 15,000 hours of commercial television, seen more

2 Marshall McLuhan, Playboy Interview, *Playboy*, (March 1969). Vol. 16, No. 3, p. 61.

than 4,000 hours of feature films, while he has spent only 10,000 hours in the classroom from K-12! In other words, he's had twice the media exposure as he's had classroom exposure, and yet rarely do we consider those rich and sophisticated media experiences when we make choices of textual materials for reading and analysis, or rarely does our English classroom—that "room with a view" of something larger than itself—become the open marketplace it might become. Perhaps we need a new publication, *The Student's Right to See,* (*or Listen?*) to counter the inevitable internal and external objections that the teacher will encounter when teaching English in a multi-media culture. Perhaps "Hud" or "The Pawnbroker" is more "censorable" than *Catcher in the Rye?*

Today we must confront a student who needs to be both media-literate and verbally literate. Today's culture demands a student whose concept of literacy is both visual and verbal, and he needs to understand the modes and styles of both literacies if he expects to be totally responsive to his new culture. The literary, and new media, censor will be just behind the door (or screen) in the new English classroom, but the "new pupil" demands "new teachers"—responsible and responsive professionals who can teach and learn using *all* the media at his command. The future is dim unless we can become *new teachers,* for then our pupils will find Holden Caulfield's private vision behind the rows of Jujubes and Necco Wafers at the corner drugstore, or over coke-stained counters at the local teenage watering holes, instead of within the English classroom where the right to read—visually and verbally—is not denied him.

The "New" Teachers

> "At 16 our convictions are hills from which we look;
> at forty they are caves in which we hide."
> F. SCOTT FITZGERALD

One of the obvious discoveries emerging from the several censorship surveys and studies done since 1960 is that English teachers are not trained in their pre-service or in-service experiences to deal with incidents of literary censorship. This lack of training in selecting and defending literary selections for use in the English classroom had manifested itself in some ugly tales told by teachers of disgraceful mistreatment by communities and school boards. Richard Kennan, Executive Secretary of the NEA Commission on Professional Rights and Responsibilities cited a case which should make any teacher cringe:

"He (the teacher) was awakened in the middle of the night, arrested, and put in jail as a result of a warrant sworn out by the board of education resulting from a protest by a parent.

The man's personal library was seized by the police and some of the books destroyed. As soon as he recovered from the shock of this experience and began to move logically, he notified his state professional association.

The association went to bat for him, got him out of jail, and supported him in the courts. His crime was that he allowed some of the students in his high school class to read *The Stranger*, by Camus."[3]

The fact that this case occurred in one of the more educationally "enlightened" sections of the country makes the story doubly disconcerting, and the fact that in a review of censorship incidents one will find dozens of similar cases is frankly shocking.

This teacher was attempting to open that "room with a view" to include some of the dark perspectives of modern literature in a course in the humanities, while many of his peers would have chosen Norman Vincent Peale, *Reader's Digest* and other solidly antiseptic prose for study. This teacher was simply exercising his professional right to select the best and most challenging literature for his pupils! *The Student's Right to Read* states this professional right (*distinctly*)!

> The right of any individual to read is basic to a democratic society. The right is based on the only tenable assumption for democratic living: that the educated free man possesses the powers of discrimination and is to be entrusted with the determination of his own actions.[4]

English teachers need to be aware of the book selection procedures and policies for in-class and library materials in their own school district. If the school district does not have a book selection policy (and studies indicate that most do not) then models of such policies should be obtained from NCTE, ALA and AASL.

The whole question of paperbacks in the classroom has mushroomed in the past six years, and English chairmen are finding that with the paperback explosion the return to the "classics" may simply be a safer move. But teachers are finding that with careful selection many exciting titles are now available to their classes in attractive, readable, and inexpensive editions, and the resulting flexibility and range in the English curriculum has made the paperback an exciting addition for the pupil, and a potentially troublesome situation for the English chairman or administrator. The need for clearly defined curriculum boundaries and book selection procedures is made even more apparent with the addition of paperbacks in the classroom.

Here this writer joins with Kenneth Donelson and Ronald LaConte in stressing the major professional responsibility the English Depart-

[3] Richard Kennan, "Censorship and the Schools," *N.J.E.A. Review* (April 1965), p. 453.

[4] Committee on the Right to Read of the National Council of Teachers of English, *The Student's Right to Read*, 1962, p. 8.

ment Chairman has to report to the administration his professional judgement about books added to the English curriculum, particularly those that potentially could stimulate external objections.

After the English chairman has discussed the appropriateness of the selection with his department colleagues (is it readable? will it evoke fruitful discussion? does it relate to other *genre* study? etc.) he then *must* inform his administrator (one is tempted to say, "educate" his administrator) about the rationale for selecting the title, citing appropriate critical judgements of the book and the probable objections one might anticipate from a potential objector. In this way the Chairman is exercising his professional responsibility to inform and articulate decisions and rationale to his colleagues and his administrators.

The Librarian and the Right to Read

It is interesting (a safe word here) to note that several censorship studies indicate that the most invisible censor is internal—the school librarian. The irony is that she is operating within a professional organization that has led the professions in attacking censorship, yet the school librarian is frequently seen with her gleaming scissors, nipping off *Life* covers or underwear ads from the latest copies of *Teen* and *Seventeen*.

Lee Burress has reported in the recently completed NCTE-AASL study of book selection and censorship practices that schools without high degrees of censorship did not have many books in their school libraries. Instead the significant fact emerges that the more books in a library, the greater the incidents of censorship; the better the library, the better the possibility of upsetting established notions and the more objectors are certain to appear.

In the recently completed NCTE National Study of High School English Programs, the high school library ranged behind the home library as the source of interesting voluntary reading, according to Robert F. Hogan, NCTE Executive Secretary. Drawing on the findings of an earlier study by Robert S. Whitman, the study team selected thirty-five titles most often cited by graduates in the selected high schools as providing their most moving, significant reading experience in high school. Hogan reports, "of these, the book most frequently cited by students, *Catcher in the Rye*, was found in only half of the high school libraries; the sixth ranking book, *Atlas Shrugged*, in only twelve percent of the libraries."[5]

In the list of specific recommendations arising from the National Studies of High School English Programs the authors summarized the problem of school librarians in this way:

5 Robert F. Hogan, "Book Selection and Censorship." *Statement: Colorado Language Arts Association Journal* (October 1968, Vol. 4, No. 1, p. 29.)

Like literature programs in general, librarians have not been responsive in their selections to the tastes and interests of the students whom they hope to serve. Although the students report obtaining an amazing average of almost eight books a month, they prefer to go to the public library for their selections. . . . When asked to give reasons for their preference for the public library, the majority of students point to larger collections which include the major twentieth-century fiction which they prefer but which most school libraries, like most literature programs, avoid.[6]

In a recent speech before a conference group at the 1968 Milwaukee NCTE Convention, Mrs. Judith F. Krug, Director of the ALA's Office for Intellectual Freedom, reviewed some of the basic policy of the American Library Association in the area of censorship. The ALA's "Library Bill of Rights" briefly states that—

"it is the responsibility of library service to provide books and other library materials that are chosen for values of interest, information and enlightenment of all people of the community. Materials should not be excluded from a library because of the race or nationality, or social or political views of the author. It is likewise the responsibility of libraries to provide books and materials representing all points of view concerning the problems and issues of our times. No library materials should be prescribed or removed because of a partisan or doctrinal disapproval."[7]

The high school librarian is a vital link in the English Chairman-Administrator "network" suggested earlier, for she must be sensitive to the English department's needs for supplementary textual and non-print materials to support instruction, and she will need support from her colleagues in the English department and from her administrator to make decisions and selections.

There is, I think, a close correlation between Albert Einstein's comparison of reality to a closed watch and the teaching of "controversial" literature in schools. Einstein said, "in our endeavor to understand reality, we are somewhat like a man trying to understand the mechanism of a closed watch. He sees the face and the moving hands, even hears its ticking, but he has no way of opening the case. If he is ingenious, he may form some picture of the mechanism which could be responsible for all the things he observes, but he may never quite be sure his picture is the only one which could explain his observations."

The reality of sex, evolution, control of atomic power, and a wide range of subjects that fall under the heading of "controversial topics"

---

6 Roger K. Applebee and James R. Squire. *High School English Instruction Today: The National Study of High School English Programs.* (New York, Appleton-Century-Crofts, Inc. 1968), p. 260.

7 Judith F. Krug, from an unpublished paper. *National Council of Teachers of English Annual Convention,* November 1968.

are basic facts of life that should be discussed in a controlled situation. To say that we have educated a child is to imply that we have given him something that will help him lead a useful life in today's society. To leave out the very things in his humanistic education that will challenge him most when he leaves the warm womb of his classroom, is to do him great injustice. Much like the man studying the closed watch, students observe life and are caught up in the rumblings of issues that too often they know very little about.

The Freedom to Read is a freedom that is shared by all—by teacher and pupil—and it can never be a right we label "For Adults Only."

Literature as man's illumination of man by artificial light, can do much to add depth, breadth, color, and life to the young reader, but the light of truth can only flame in the open marketplace. The censored teacher breathes foul air and gets only intellectual claustrophobia in a marketplace that is closed and boarded up by those unwilling to listen to his cries and his curses.

Media Study
in the Schools

FOR most of the years in this century what went on in the English classroom was largely a determination of the English teacher in that classroom or of a larger group of English teachers in the school English department who devised the curriculum guide for each year and subject. In such a setting study of the mass media fared poorly. On the one hand were those teachers who regarded the media as arch-enemies: Students went to movies, read comics, or watched television when they should have been studying English. At the other extreme were the teachers who used the instruments of the media, but only as adjuncts to the more important printed materials: Students watched filmstrips on "How to Outline" or saw a movie of Julius Caesar as a reward if the important matters—the reading of the play, the writing of a composition on it, the taking of the objective test— were completed satisfactorily.

But in the mid-1960s English teachers began to see in the media the means for achieving objectives not always attainable through printed materials. Students who could not or would not read the poems in the anthology would both listen to and respond to poems the Beatles or Simon and Garfunkel had recorded. Film study became a legitimate classroom activity, as did film making. Television offerings were studied with some of the same techniques teachers had formerly employed with short stories or drama and with some new ones particularly suited to this medium.

The reasons for the emerging popularity of media study in secondary school English classrooms do not lie solely in the success teachers had with media in attaining traditional objectives. New forces also had an impact. For one, the tools of media—magazine subscriptions, television sets, super-8 cameras, aural- and video-tape recorders— became sufficiently inexpensive to enable schools to purchase and use them. Then, too, there existed a growing belief that media deserved study, in and of themselves; they were, after all, important elements of communication. Finally, the students' demands for "relevance," whether they could articulate what they meant or not, were *often responded to with greater study of the media in their English classes.*

In sum, the decade of the 1960s ushered into the schools the instruments and artifacts of the mass media and the movement shows every sign of continuing and increasing during the decades ahead. The articles in this section support the trend. Deer, McCullough, Fillion, and Giblin write about the teaching of the media in a broad sense, providing both philosophical and pedagogical foundations. Kilpatrick offers a perceptive discussion of the relationships between adolescence and McLuhanism. Smith narrows the focus somewhat in his advocacy and explanation of the uses of television commercials as learning aids. The final three articles (McGlynn, Sheratsky, and Powell) discuss film study and film making.

MASS MEDIA AND THE ENGLISH TEACHER

Irving Deer

I THINK you will all agree with Denys Thompson that as teachers we would like "to help our students nourish their imagination, train their emotions and strengthen their ability to choose." Unfortunately, there are a great many conditions in modern life which work against these aims. One of the most persistent of these is the profit motive behind the mass production processes which supply our daily needs for goods and services. Mass producers are heavily committed to making profits. In order to build and maintain the huge physical plants necessary in their business, they must invest heavily and keep their machines operating as much as possible. Since fundamental changes of design require substantial new outlays of capital, they try to keep variety and change to a minimum. To promote the maximum distribution and sale of their products, they employ every means of influencing taste at their disposal. They sponsor extravagant advertising campaigns. They make minor changes in design and promote them as if they were major innovations. They appeal to the most widely accepted and often the simplest tastes. Most important of all, by providing little opportunity for individual choice, they promote mass conformity to the oversimplified values implicit in the choices they offer. Given no opportunity to extend its experience and choice of a product, the public soon comes to accept what it gets.

As mass produced services, mass media fare and the popular arts are "manufactured," distributed and publicized in accordance with the profit-seeking goals which to a great extent determine what is produced on a mass scale in our society. Since most people (including high school and college students) get a great many of their ideas, facts, values, and opinions from the mass media and the popular arts, it seems reasonable to expect that high school students (and perhaps college Freshmen) should receive some instruction in how to approach the mass media and the popular arts critically. It is not only reasonable to expect that they get such training; it is necessary that they get it. If students are to learn to make imaginative, mature choices, and if the mass media and the popular arts promote uniform, immature acquiescence, the schools and colleges not only have the responsibility of training students to re-

FROM *Reflections on High School English*, ed. by Gary Tate (Tulsa, Oklahoma: University of Tulsa, 1966), pp. 38–45. Reprinted by permission of Gary Tate and Irving Deer.

sist those influences which would deprive them of the ability to choose;
they have the responsibility of training students to evaluate the choices
offered them and to promote the production of more mature and imaginative offerings.

This is a formidable task, but it can be an enjoyable one as well.
Students like to examine the mass media and the popular arts critically.
They can and do talk about movies, popular fiction and newspaper reports at great length. They gain a great many of their ideas and attitudes about art, literature and life from the mass media and the popular
arts. It is in fact startling to discover just how much, for example, a
film hero, like, say, Marlon Brando in *The Wild One*, can actually create
new values and attitudes or at least crystallize latent ones. The book on
which the film was based, Frank Rooney's *The Cyclist's Raid*, went
practically unnoticed. On the other hand, the film created and promoted
a national, even an international fad for the tough manners, uniform
(black leather jacket) and motorcycle gang ideal. If the new mass
media can create such ideals, they must certainly be reckoned with.
With the proper guidance, young people can learn to analyze and evaluate the ideas and attitudes offered them from such sources. Moreover,
from what they learn by mature, critical reflection about this "literature
and art" that is meaningful to them, they can become prepared to gain
a critical appreciation of the literature and art valued by their high
school and college instructors. For the English teacher, especially, the
mass media and the popular arts are a marvellous find. Not only do
they provide interesting sources for the examination of stylistic and
logical problems, they provide ample materials for the study of every
other type of composition and literary problem students must eventually
face in learning how to read and write critically. How better can an
English teacher take his students from where they are to where he
would like them to be? Where can he tap a fund of experience they
all share that is more meaningful and interesting to them?

Most intelligent people would like to see great improvements in the
mass media. Yet very few of the people who would like these improvements are willing or able to do anything to bring them about. Ironically,
those best able to do something, the teachers dedicated to showing
others what languages can and should do, are often the least willing to
work for these improvements. There are many reasons for this. One of
the most important is the general disregard, if not contempt, most critically trained people have for the mass media. Seeing everywhere in
them the tawdry, mechanical and spectacular, they assume either that
such stuff is intrinsic to the mass media, or that the producers and consumers of drivel have absolute control of the mass media and are beyond saving. In either case, those who are the best possible mass media
critics often prefer to spend their time in the book-culture where per-

fection, if rare, at least seems attainable. Moreover, the excesses practiced in the name of "communication" both inside and outside of the
classroom have been enough to harden many a good heart against the
idea of taking the study of the mass media seriously. And if we add
to these excesses the semi-scientific (rather than critical or aesthetic)
slant that has in the past often dominated communication courses, we
can get some idea of why English departments often have resisted including in their offerings anything which smacked of such concerns.

Only the strongest sense of the (harsh, if you like) reality of two
facts can overcome such resistance: one, that the mass media are here
to stay, and two, that it is from them that most people get much of
their information, ideas, attitudes and values. The media are more
and more taking over the functions until recently assumed exclusively
by book-culture. That is why book-culture men must assume some responsibility for them. They are substitute literatures. To assume no responsibility is to leave the field to those less prepared to command it.

We can best understand this if we adopt a new attitude toward the
mass media, an attitude which should be most congenial to those given
to critical thinking about the arts of language. We must in fact think
about the mass media, in Edmund Carpenter's phrase, as "new languages." Briefly, the main idea is this: films, television, radio, magazines and newspapers all have "subjects" which they can communicate
best, and unique ways of communicating those subjects. Both the subjects and the ways of communicating them contribute, sometimes unintentionally, to the thoughts, feelings, attitudes and values promoted by
the mass media. Both must therefore be closely studied in the effort to
determine what they communicate and how they communicate it.

In the abstract, the program may not sound very startling. But anyone who has ever noticed any important differences between the way
in which a story is presented in a novel and the way in which it is
presented in a film will surely see the significance of this approach to
the mass media. As a film the book is translated, perhaps "transmuted"
is more accurate, into the new language of a new medium of communication. It is not simply a matter of taking a story and transferring it
from one carrier to another. The film story is very different from the
novel. Obviously, the film is not merely a motion picture recording of
the black marks found on the pages of a book. Nor is it merely an acted
out version of the novel. The camera is a performer too; it moves up
and down, in and out, to one side or the other. Only the naive can
assume that in a good film these movements are arbitrary. There are
other movements, too, which must be coordinated with the camera; for
the film is after all a medium of motion pictures. There are the movements created by the editor in his laboratory. He cuts and patches the
filmed sequences, arranging them for dramatic interest. When we watch

a film, we see what has been selected for us, a series of large moving images which are often greatly magnified even if they are composed of a wiggling toe or a frowning eye-brow. When we watch a stage performance, although the director may try, by composition, lighting or other devices, to direct our attention, we are our own editors. We see the whole stage at once and choose to see whatever we like.

The playwright and play director must use the languages of their media to suggest important dramatic relationships. Speeches, objects, space, even silence must be charged with dramatic significance. Everything must be created and arranged to express the meaning a scene should have. The same thing is true for the camera artist, whether he is a motion picture photographer or a still photographer. People who feel that a film is intrinsically more true or real than a play should remember this. The real buildings, actual locations or even the real people used in an imaginative work, whether it is created for the stage or the film, have only an imaginative reality. This should be especially evident, perhaps shockingly so to the naive movie enthusiast, when he sees a late film on television which stars an actor who in real life is dead. On a three dimensional stage or a two dimensional screen, people, objects, and even space are real only insofar as they express the imaginative relationship essential to the presentation. These relationships and the means of expressing them are different in each medium, even in two such apparently related media as the motion picture and the photograph. All we need do to understand this is to look at the still photographs which are used outside a movie theater to advertise the film showing inside. After we see the film we often notice that these stills are different from any actual scene in the film. This is because the stills are especially composed to express within their single frame compass relationships similar to those expressed through a sequence of visual action in the motion picture.

We will be in a good position to understand this "language" approach to the mass media only if we think of media subjects as experiences capable of being best transmitted by one medium or another because of that medium's unique capacities and materials. We will remain confused if we think of the subjects of the various media as narrative or informational content which a medium contains and carries in the way vacuum tube containers carry messages from one busy desk in a large office building to another. Just as the sound, rhythm, and rhyme of a good poem contribute to and become part of its sense, so do the means and manner of presentation of a story, play or dance become part of its sense. We have all seen Hollywood spectaculars which glorified war in blazing technicolor while the heroes mouthed bland platitudes about the horrors of war. Students can easily recognize such discrepancies. They enjoy recognizing them, and the practice they get in doing it can prepare them to recognize discrepancies between form and content in poetry. Once a student learns how to see that a film which pretends to be against war actually glorifies it, he can much more easily see that a trivial, artificial rhyme scheme in a poem actually destroys any pretense the poem makes at a serious, specific interpretation of life.

He can also see that a book, play and film all based on the same story, have, in a very real sense, very different meanings. The means and manner of presenting a subject through one of the mass media become part of its sense even when the subjects transmitted are essentially narrative or informational. The *pot-pourri* of information parcels presented for our daily choice in newspapers or magazines, for example, communicates something in itself, apart from the specific information reported. For one thing, despite the certainty we would like to associate with the facts reported, this disorder communicates a sense of arbitrariness, uncertainty and confusion. As Edmund Carpenter says: "The front page is a cosmic *Finnegan's Wake.*" Except for the sometimes uncertain advantage given them by placement or headline size, items are presented to equal advantage—or disadvantage. We must make sense out of the hash by selecting the items we wish to read.

As literary critics know, similar principles apply to books. A condensed book is not the same book as the original any more than a comic book version of *War and Peace* is Tolstoy's masterpiece. The condensation tends to oversimplify and make a spectacle of what in a good book is treated in the length proper treatment demands. Where the condensation is as good as or better than the original, the original was padded and perhaps arbitrarily arranged. Well-written books have as part of their meaning not only all (or at least nearly all) of the words written in them, but the order in which the words are written. The linear and chronological development of a good novel is part of its conception. Deletions or rearrangements change its meaning.

The meaning contained in a story, report, article or film comes, then, not merely from its informational content, but from the amalgam this makes with all the qualities of experience communicated by the medium used. The meaning of a play, for example, comes in part even from the play-presentation situation, the large theater with a large audience all actively sharing a common experience. And the meaning of an article in a popular digest does not come simply from the information it conveys—for example, that a new cure for some dread disease is on the verge of being discovered. The meaning comes as much from what is not said as from what is. The tone of the article, its simplicity, and its presentation in a magazine whose articles generally signify good tidings may all contribute to its meaning. It is what we are to make of the information in human terms that counts. Perhaps what this information about a new cure really means is that simple, homey, undifferentiating sincerity will surmount all obstacles. More sophisticated magazines, too, are not exempt from such considerations. If for example, we accept Robert Washow's interpretation of the *New Yorker,* we can believe that the magazine communicates two strong attitudes between its lines: one, that although the world is a complex and dangerous mess, we can remain aloof from its tension and confusions by maintaining objectivity and good humor; and, two, that really serious problems can be solved merely by treating them seriously.

Think of this approach to the mass media in this way: what is the meaning of a film sequence which shows railroad tracks or telephone wires flashing by the sun glinting on them? Of a turning piece of polished brass which captures the sun's rays in its movement? These "meanings" are no more purely informational than that of a good painting which shows a quiet cabin against a green hill at sunset, or that of a lively contrapuntal passage in a Corelli concerto. Everything in the film sequence is part of its meaning, the camera movement, any movement by the object filmed, the angles from which we see the objects and movement, and the changing movement of light, shadow or color. The painter conveys not merely a picture of a house in a particular location at a particular time of day; he may be interested in the sense of warmth or security the scene expresses, or perhaps in the senses of loneliness he sees in it. The kinds of strokes, the texture of his paint, the contrast of light and shade—all these and more are part of his meaning. And as for the Corelli concerto, it has no representational content to confuse us. If we pay attention to it at all, we must pay attention to its true meaning, the sounds in all of the rich variety, force, repetition and contrast which their order, manner and means of presentation offer us.

To think about the meanings of films, TV programs, reports or magazine articles in such ways is to think about them as human communication rendered by potentially artistic means. Extensive use of jargon or cliches, for example, by reporters or sob sister story writers shows that they are reducing communication to a mechanical, quick response affair. Continual bombardment by reductions of this sort can eventually blunt our ability to make mature responses or judgments. This is what happens if we begin responding like robots to advertising appeals, stereotyped descriptions in pulp or slick fiction, or to the highly charged but unsupported conclusions of facile persuaders. Formula thinking, as Benjamin De Mott has said, can soon lead to "flaccidity of mind, moral limpness and silliness." And as David Reisman has pointed out, the continual immersion in the mass media culture which sustains flaccidity, amorality, and silliness can lose for us any possibility of genuine literacy or of a maturely adventurous individual life.

But the mass media need not have these horrendous effects. If they provide an essentially soft-minded, soft soap orientation, it may be, as David Reisman and Marshall McLuhan argue, because we relegate most of our tough-minded views to book culture. If so, it is time that we learn something from that culture to help us bring the others up to its level. To do this we must take the mass media seriously. But we, too, must be tough-minded about the way we do this. We must see clearly what book culture can do at its best. We must also see clearly what the mass media are doing, what possibilities they have for improvement, and what help they can get from book culture.

Before any great changes can take place, however, we must understand and take into account the ways in which mass media producers respond to the real or imagined mandates of the public. If the society which the media reflect and serve is itself a mess, how much can the media themselves be blamed for what they do? If the media producers feel compelled to meet the public demand for sensationalism and indifferentism, what can ever be done to turn them into tough-minded purveyors of the truth and nothing but the truth? These are knotty questions, not given to simple answers.

Perhaps the answers lie in a recognition of the fact that the relationship between the mass media and the public is a two way affair. The media cannot only affect public taste, they can be affected by it. After all, no audience today would accept a new film made with the crude film conventions of the early silent film experiments. If in no other way, film producers have changed public taste by leading the public to expect technical sophistication. They must now fulfill that expectation, no matter how easy it would be for them to lapse into occasional technical crudities. However the public came to demand technical sophistication, it now demands it, and the producers must come across with it or fail in their search for profits. If its demands are of the kind which promotes freedom, and it asserts those demands strongly enough, the producers will have no choice but to supply what meets the demand. Perhaps, then, as Gilbert Seldes believes, the mass media may be a way of freeing the mass rather than enslaving it. This is a point worth considering. One of the men best qualified to consider it is the English teacher. He owes it to himself and his students to try.

MASS MEDIA CURRICULUM: FANTASY OR REALITY?

Martin A. McCullough

YOUNG people are major consumers of the mass media fare. Their appetites for commercial television, magazines, movies, and even newspapers appear to be without limits. The typical youngster spends an average of one-sixth of his waking hours watching television, and by the age of 16 has spent more time in front of a television set than he has in the classrooms of his schools.[1]

The movie industry sees young people as the major audience for their products today, either as a member of a family group or with their peers. Recent mergers in the publishing industry give all of the major publishers of monthly periodicals at least one magazine for the "younger set."

However, the bulk of time devoted to the mass media is spent on commercial television. In many ways television is typical of, and reflects the posture of, the other media. All are commercial enterprises and in the final analysis look to the profit sheet for determining success or failure. Their offerings, whether printed or filmed, are similar, and television manages to program much of what is available from the other media. Therefore, many of the following remarks which refer to commercial television are also applicable to other components of the mass media.

The Planned Mass Media Curriculum: Less Than Reality

The mass media offerings can be conceptualized as a curriculum. Using commercial television as a model, there are generally accepted objectives, a body of research knowledge, carefully defined content, scope and sequence charts, program dissemination strategies based on age groupings, and thorough evaluation procedures.

The mass media curriculum, as planned, produced, edited, and offered

[1] Wilbur Schramm, Jack Lyle, and Edwin B. Parker. *Television in the Lives of Our Children.* Stanford, California: Stanford University Press, © 1961. p. 30.

FROM *Educational Leadership*, Vol. 26, No. 5 (February 1969), pp. 447–450. Reprinted with permission of the Association for Supervision and Curriculum Development and Martin A. McCullough. Copyright © 1969 by the Association for Supervision and Curriculum Development.

to young consumers, is surprisingly simple and direct. On the basis of research and audience reaction, the mass media, and especially the television industry, have a major commitment to fulfilling the fantasy needs of young people. Schramm identified the purposes for watching television in the past decade, and the 1960's have seen the mass media orient their offerings on the basis of his and other research. Schramm states the need of young people for fantasy experiences as the primary reason for watching television, with the need for programs concerning real events a poor second.[2] These needs, along with some social usage, determine the current strategies behind the offering of the mass media.

The overwhelming capability to produce fantasy experiences vicariously for all ages and types of children accounts for the majority of time they spend in front of a television set, in a movie theater, or between the covers of a paperback book or magazine. Within their own set of objectives, the curriculum developers of the mass media are successful. It is not possible to overlook the omnipresence of commercial television and the rest of the mass media. A basic fact is obvious that they have identified a low but generally acceptable level of young people's fantasy needs and taste.

The Consumed Mass Media Curriculum: Little More Than Fantasy

The basic commitment tends to influence materials about real events. The curriculum makers of the mass media realize correctly that youngsters carry over their criteria for fantasy consumption to other types of reading and viewing. The young reader or viewer wants reality presented in a fast-paced, exciting, and action-packed manner. Since youngsters get what they want from the mass media, reality-oriented material, even when committed to "telling it like it is," ends up "giving them what they want." The difference does not necessarily subordinate the truth but does allow the young consumer to sit back and be entertained again.

It is obvious that youngsters do change as a result of watching commercial television and utilizing the other mass media. The depth of these changes it largely unexplored and there is a need to seek answers to many basic questions. How have the mass media affected the values of young people? Do the young look more favorably on direct, even authoritarian action and control? Are they so exposed to violence and crime that they are more prone to accept this behavior? Or even to copy it?

In the absence of substantial research data, the position can be taken that the mass media do not influence greatly the basic values of the vast

2 Ibid., p. 170.

majority of young people. The introduction to books and television early in life on a fantasy-fulfillment basis and the continued expectation to be entertained in this way have, in effect, cut off the mass media from the real developmental process of growing up. There are major exceptions to this generalization, but it appears that value determination continues to center around the core of home, school, peer group and church. The influence of the mass media revolves on the periphery and fills in gaps where there is no prior influencing or is selected when leverage is needed to pry loose from imposed restrictions.

Youngsters' reactions to the recent assassinations of three national leaders can serve as an example. Young people were shocked and sickened as were adults with the tragedies. It is interesting to note that the mass media which had brought so much violence and death as fantasy in no way prepared them for the shock of seeing death come to real people. This violence and the subsequent sadness of the families and the entire world did more to show youngsters the true nature of violence than the thousands of hours of fantasy consumption prior to these events.

The real curriculum of the mass media is determined by the individual. The mass media do not command a captive audience of young people. In the case of commercial television, research concludes that:

> It seems clear that in order to understand television's impact and effect on children we have first to get away from the unrealistic concept of what television "does to children" and substitute the concept of *what children do with television.*[3]

Most youngsters use the mass media for relaxation and recreation, but for others it becomes more than fantasy. Aside from matters of taste and style, the impact of the mass media and especially commercial television could be relegated to an unimportant position except that some young people do not use the mass media in ways anticipated by producers and editors. Consumption in these instances is a symptom of deeper problems that should be recognized by school personnel. In some instances too much dependence and too much time are committed to the mass media for vicarious experiences that are unrelated to life.

In other instances the dependence on visual "inputs," whether photographs, films, or video tapes, creates an unrealistic desire for new or different experiences at a faster pace than that at which they are provided in real life. A third pattern is typified by the popularity among lower socioeconomic youngsters of situation comedies that take place in middle-class families. Here the planned curriculum of comedy is used as fantasy to compensate for deprived environments.

3 Ibid., p. 169.

Fantasy and Reality: Implications
and Strategies

The roots for developing strategies for coping with an influencing mass media usage are found in a realistic approach to the whole business. Basic to this is the acceptance of the mass media as a normal, healthy outlet for young people. They do place a wealth of information literally at the fingertips of young people. On the negative side, the mass media are basically anti-intellectual, though this is of their own choosing. They focus on crime, violence, and other baser human acts but usually couch these acts within the womb of fanstasy fulfillment. If these facets can be accepted, then the job at hand is to influence the manner in which individuals relate to the mass media.

If the assumption is accepted that a certain amount of mass media usage is normal, then one strategy is to "contain" the quantity of consumption. This can be done by involving young people in learning or recreational activities that include satisfying interaction with others and opportunities for use of one's own personality in task-oriented situations. This task will not be easy since many youngsters use television to compensate for their reluctance to become involved. These are the shy ones who seldom speak or make contributions to classroom discussions and who are the social and personality "dropouts" in our schools. Teachers and other professionals too often look without concern on this type of behavior and see this docility and compliance as a welcome balance for other more aggressive children. These young people are not receiving the satisfactions of being involved so they "escape" to the fantasy involvement of television and the other media.

It is not feasible to compete for the hours of the day that are spent watching television. But it is possible to enhance the process of being involved through sensitive and consistent structuring of school activities, so that involvement will be able to compete with the projective, vicarious experiences found through mass media consumption.

To achieve meaningful, satisfying involvement for the over-consumers of the mass media who occupy the inconspicuous middle sections of our classrooms, it will be necessary to make basic changes in many typical classroom procedures. Student involvement will result when teachers release their hold on instructional planning and classroom time and let students do some of the important things that go on in any learning situation. Student involvement can occur when the risk-level of the classroom is reduced so that students can share feelings and ideas without fear of embarrassment or condescension.

Obviously, the second strategy would deal with making the young user more sophisticated in his use of the mass media. Young people need the opportunity to experience the mass media as technical, business, social, and artistic entities. The first steps would involve the study of units devoted to developing a body of knowledge about the realities of corporate business and the use of technology in the communications and publishing sectors of the economy. A second step would be the study of the characteristics of the various media and how they are used within our society. A final step would be the development of the concepts of style and taste based on an appreciation of the artistic functions of directing, writing, acting, etc.

In conclusion, the mass media and especially commercial television have largely replaced the comic books of yesteryear. They fulfill a function by providing fantasy experiences for young people and, to a much lesser degree, serve as a window to the world around them. Young people, as a whole, use the mass media as expected with no real adverse effects. Those who do not so use the mass media need the help and concern of school people because misuse of mass media fare is not a discrete phenomenon but is symptomatic of deeper problems. The curriculum of the schools should acknowledge the existence of the mass media by encouraging greater understanding and appreciation of the mass media as a complex and essential enterprise. Perhaps then a start can be made toward changing the "locked-in" habits of the young consumers of the mass media.

TURNING ON: THE SELLING OF THE PRESENT, 1970

Bryant P. Fillion

IN the rising tide of social unrest, change, conflict, and violence, we teachers may get to feel like the devoted maid in a burning hotel: determinedly polishing the woodwark for a tomorrow that will never come. Her actions may be irrelevant, but she is not prepared to put out the fire, so she does what she knows how to do in the blind faith that somehow, in some way, it will make a difference.

Today, we English teachers are often advised to abandon our traditional methods and concerns and be relevant by being contemporary. For the novel, substitute feature films; for composition, filmmaking; for

FROM *English Journal* (March 1971), pp. 333–338. Copyright © 1971 by the National Council of Teachers of English. Reprinted by permission of the publisher and Bryant Fillion.

poetry, pop-rock, and so forth. And then, we are told, simply get out of the way and let the kids experience and do their own thing; by turning on the machines we will turn on the kids, and unless we blow a fuse all will be well. The activities inside the classroom will reflect the world outside the classroom, and by selling the present we will sell our subject and ourselves. I contend that merely capturing our students' interest and attention is not nearly enough, even if media could do it. And if all we are doing with media is selling the present—bringing the outside world into the classroom—we and our students had better stay home. If the hotel is on fire, and there is certainly enough smoke around these days to suggest that *something* is burning, merely showing pictures of the flames is little better than polishing the woodwork.

Just turning on and selling the present are not enough, and neither is the use of electronic media as "audiovisual aids," as gimmicks to introduce or cover traditional fare. The use of media as AV aids does indeed change the pattern of the English curriculum, but it does so in unintended and misunderstood ways, by significantly altering the classroom environment and consequently altering what is learned in it.

If we assume that the function of media is merely to do more efficiently what we were doing before, we will probably be disappointed. The use of media is no panacea. Electronic media will not, by themselves, make traditional English more relevant, effective, or even necessarily more interesting; the gap between students and eighteenth century poetry is not automatically bridged by first listening to Simon and Garfunkel. The use of media will not necessarily humanize English teaching, a point which should be self-evident in the notion that we can turn on people as we turn on machines. Electronic media do not automatically bring us closer to the truth of things than do traditional approaches; the media are new and different messages, but they are not the only messages. And, despite some confusion on this point, although the impact of the electronic medium itself on students is IMmediate, because it is directly experienced, the communicated "content" is no more IMmediate, by definition, than is the content of a book. That is, the experience of the media environment (the lighted screen, darkened room, silence except for the projector speaker) is IMmediate, not mediated, but the content being conveyed *through* the medium is as processed as the same content told in printed form. Consequently, we should not be surprised if students do no better on exams testing the content of, say, films (Who said what? What are the characters' names? What happened first?) than they do on exams testing their reading.

Both of the approaches just mentioned, media as self-sufficient experience and media as AV aids, suffer from underlying assumptions about teaching English. In one case we simply plug in a new aspect of or replacement for the literature program, teaching technologically-dependent art forms in place of printed literature. In the other case, we spruce up our methods by switching on a lecture rather than giving one ourselves. We are locked in by our preconceptions of what English teaching is all about; we know too well what it means to "teach English." In our routines and activities, most of us are playing out roles put together in and basically unchanged from the past. English teaching is what we saw in our own school and college days. It is what the methods text said it would be. One difficulty with such fixed perceptions of our job is that when we are confronted with new imperatives or with new things to teach, such as media, we are likely either to ignore them as of no concern to us or to include them for the wrong reasons: because they are "interesting" or have to do with language in some vague way, or because they "work," but without any real sense of what they work for. And we will probably feel vaguely guilty about abandoning standards, or about taking time from the "real thing."

In the teaching of media, I believe these preconceptions are particularly limiting, primarily because we fail to see our students' genuine need for mediacy, which is perhaps as significant in the 1970s as the need for literacy. And, second, because we are often tempted to take an either-or approach, electronic media *or* printed media, rather than to emphasize the complementary role they play in the life of contemporary man in a technological society. When we teach a film study course to nonreaders as a substitute for teaching them to read, or when we ignore media study with bright college-bound students because they can "do better," we fail to recognize our potential value to the children of a society in transition. There is a double challenge here. On the one hand, we must recognize the significance of media to all of our students. On the other hand, we should not capitulate to technologically-dependent art forms simply because they seem easy. We must resist the temptation to arm ourselves with the latest in short and feature films, stereo cartridges, and records and go into the business of selling images to children instead of stimulating their intellectual and creative energies.

Electronic media demand a place in the schools simply because they already have a commanding place in today's world. As recent elections have made clear, a significant index of political power in our society is one's access to television time. For those who were upset about the revelations in Joe McGinness' *The Selling of the President, 1968,* from which I took the title for this paper, I suggest that you consider further that myth-making in modern America is in the hands of the filmmakers, rock musicians, and television producers. Consider, for instance, that contemporary rock music, so uniquely dependent upon electronic instruments, amplification, and recording effects, has been inextricably bound up with the new youth culture, and remember, too, the key role of electronic media in such negative utopias as *1984* and *Fahrenheit 451.* To recognize the part media study can play in improving our students' situation and its relevance to our present social turmoil, we must first recognize how deeply involved the media are in today's world, and particularly in our students' view of that world.

The media are more than just conveyors of information, and they are even more than "messages" and "massages." They have a profound influence on what we take to be reality and consequently they affect the whole web of human motivations and relationships. Where the myth-makers of the past built their worlds from the common stuff of language, today's myth-makers build their worlds of visual and sound images. In earlier media, heavily dependent on verbal symbolicity, there was always the possibility of an exchange in kind: we could answer a writer or speaker. But there is no answer in kind to the sounds of electronic rock or to the images of the television and screen. We can only *talk about* it, or turn it off. We have all been learning for a long time how to discount the written and spoken word. We have not yet learned to do the same thing with the visual and sound images of the electronic media. There is no phrase for the visual equivalent of "mere rhetoric," and we are often as not trapped by the old notion that "seeing is believing." Particularly with visual media, since it can so closely approximate direct experience of events, we often do not even see the need to discount. After all, we saw it with our own eyes, didn't we? But Walter Cronkite notwithstanding, tonight's news will not be "the way it is, Friday, November 27th," even if we have seen it. Televised news, like printed news, is a selection of reality filtered through the perceptions of others. By selecting, editing, juxtaposing, and proportioning, the electronic media, as the print media before them, are involved in naming situations in such a way that they shape our attitudes toward them. Just as we discount such naming when it is done verbally, so we must learn to discount the visual and sound naming of the media. More and more children are growing up with perceptions of the world shaped through film, tapes, stereo, and video, and we are perhaps in danger of becoming a society of media-somnambulists, moved unthinkingly to attitudes and behaviors by the images we have learned neither to answer nor to analyze.

What has this to do with English teachers? I believe electronic media should be a significant part of the English curriculum for at least two reasons. First, because English is the only humanistic subject which has any real clout in the contemporary high school setting. If the study of media and its impact on us is to be given an adequate place in the schools, it will most likely be through English. Second, and perhaps most important, media study is a natural and necessary outgrowth of a key concern of English: human symbolicity. Symbolicity is a term coined by Kenneth Burke in *The Rhetoric of Religion* (Beacon Press, 1961) to refer to those aspects of human experience and behavior not reducible to our animality. We are, in Burke's terms, the symbol-using animal, and we build our cultures, as he says at the end of *Permanence and Change*, 2nd Revised Edition (Bobbs-Merrill, 1965), "by huddling together, nervously loquacious, at the edge of an abyss." With the advent of electronic media, and particularly of film and television, we have learned to be visually loquacious, and we are still very much on the edge of an abyss. With our symbol systems in a state of upheaval, as they always are in times of cultural transition, we can scarcely avoid attending to those forces which are so dramatically shaping and conditioning our language, our perceptions, our relationships, and our selves.

The study of media needed in schools today is a humanistic study which will both enlighten and liberate. We must recognize the need to be mediate as well as literate. We must learn to "read" the technologically-dependent art and communications forms as we learn to read print, and to acknowledge with fearful appreciation the subtle and perhaps subconscious impact of media upon us. And we must, if possible, allow ourselves an escape, developing an independence capable of pulling the plug. Lewis Mumford, noting disaffected youth's rock festivals and television and radio "happenings," observes that "despite their gestures of revolt against the established goods of civilization, the young are in fact addicted to its most decadent mass products" (*Horizon*, Autumn 1970). The August 1970 cover of *Esquire* pictures a cathedral with a movie marquee featuring *Easy Rider;* the caption for the picture: "The New Movies: Faith of Our Children." In that issue, Craig Karpel notes that the young American is the only mythic role which can sell tickets today:

> Today, only the young American is plausibly a wanderer, external and/or internal. . . . And only he, unlike the genre heroes before him, is capable of being a spectator at, of *financing* his own cinematic apotheosis. . . . Hollywood has suddenly discovered the mother lode of narcissism, and the rush is on to hold a smash-cut push-processed rock-scored hand-held mirror up to the kids (p. 59).

Combine an addiction to such narcissistic content with new film techniques that make our minds into the theater and the world into a light show, and there is a genuine cause for concern, a concern which goes beyond a mere desire to improve students' taste in selecting movies. I am disturbed by college audiences viewing today's films such as *M*A*S*H*, *Easy Rider*, *Z*, and *Joe*, and I have the recurring fear that I am somehow reliving Hitler's Nuremberg rallies. The cues, causes, and code words have changed, but the mindless responses are still there: flash an image and see Johnny jump. The film viewer must be liberated from such manipulation, and he should understand that he is not experiencing something necessarily "truer than life," but a very powerful expression of another man's view of life.

It is perhaps unfortunate that serious media study is appearing on the scene while we are still so involved in the spirit of Dartmouth. We are attending—and rightly so—to students' involvement, personal responses, and self-expression, and a call to rigorous analysis and criticism sounds somewhat anachronistic. But, unlike the print media, electronic media have no appreciable history of serious analysis or critical theory. In view of this, and of the dramatic media-impact on individuals and society, I believe we cannot afford the luxury of a *laissez faire* approach to media. I believe that students' responses to media can be analyzed by the semantic and rhetorical criticism developed in the study of fiction, drama, and speech, and that if we fail to engage students in such analysis, we leave them open to an increasingly ominous manipulation by media. The experience of media is and should be recognized as important to the individual, but so is the understanding we come to have of that experience. The viewer of a film or documentary responds to the experience as a participant, not as an evaluator. We must assert the need for evaluation.

What does all of this mean in terms of English classes? First, we must give a prominent place to media study. We must be willing to work with an expanded notion of human symbolicity and acknowledge the importance of visual and sound symbols which may seem more properly the concerns of art or music. Second, we must develop a critical method for examining the content of and responses to media. Although we must not make of media study the overly-cognitive dull pedantry we have made of literary criticism in the schools, neither can we simply show movies or conduct multi-media happenings. We should encourage students to examine such matters as image intensity, juxtaposition, sequence, and proportion, to ask what goes with what to create a rhetorical impact. The objective here is an attitude of "fearful appreciation" embodied in a method of inquiry: the ability to experience and to question and offset the experience at the same time. I do not expect that we can become immune to media, but I do believe that we can methodically guard against unthinking actions and attitude changes in response to the experience. At the very least, we must impress students with the need for media dialectics, a willingness to hear all sides and experience various media: electronic and print, visual and verbal.

Third, it is advisable for students to use and to express themselves through various media: preparing tapes, films, and video documentaries as well as writing themes and poetry. I believe the value of such activities is at least as much in teaching about the media as in promoting self-expression. Fourth, students should investigate the role of media in contemporary society, particularly as it relates to an individual's view of the world and contemporary issues. Although such concerns may seem more properly the province of social studies, it is in media's involvement in human relations that we can see most clearly the role of "languaging" and its relevance to "real life": naming, valuing, expressing, abstracting, and identifying. With media as with literature and language, we cannot be satisfied with the study of lifeless artifacts; we must go beyond them to the individual and social realities of human interaction.

Finally, students should investigate the strengths and limitations of various media, including print. Especially with the media of communications, students should consider the fact that, as Herbert Brucker says,

> even though we get substantially identical news from radio, newspaper, newsmagazine, and Walter Cronkite, the various journalistic instruments through which we get the news have startlingly different effects upon us, without our even being aware of it ("Can Printed News Save a Free Society?" *Saturday Review,* October 10, 1970, p. 53).

And before we or our students give up the newspaper as a subject of study, we might consider such questions as Brucker poses:

> Can television tell enough about enough issues—their origins, details, values, and meanings—to make an informed citizenry possible? Painstaking analysts have questioned whether what seems like (and often is) the immediate, overwhelming reality of an event on television cannot also be, and sometimes necessarily is, distorted. What appears to be the visible, self-evident truth is not necessarily the truth (p. 55).

I maintain that it is the very illusion of truth which makes television so potentially dangerous. We must learn to allow for the fact that the eyes of the cameras are not our eyes, and that their very presence to report on a scene can change the scene dramatically in the process.

We must recognize at the outset that just as media study is no panacea for the schools, so it may be very unpredictable and even threatening. We cannot significantly alter the environment without changing people's reactions to it. By cutting into talk and reading time, media alter the established, expected patterns of classrooms and may alter behavior as well. Students may resent a teacher's demand for analysis of experiences they consider none of the school's business. Class schedules will depend on such unpredictables as machine maintenance, suppliers' schedules, and budgets. Class activities such as filmmaking or other creative uses of media will require greater noise tolerance and more confidence in our students than do conventional teacher-dominated class activities. In serious film study, community censorship is always a potential threat. And finally, for better or worse, there is our own lack of hard knowledge about the subject. Few teachers can depend on college notebooks crammed with facts about media, or even about mass communication.

To most, McLuhan is still on their "must read someday" list. However, it might help to realize at the outset that despite a daily increase in media bibliographies there is still relatively little which is known "for certain" except for historical information and technical terminology. Our lack of knowledge might even prove advantageous, reducing the temptation for teacher-talk and forcing us to join our students in important inquiry and exploration.

In summing up, I retreat to the relative security of precedent and the prestige of a great poet. In the involvement with electronic media which the preparation of this paper required, I was reminded of Wordsworth's "Preface to the Second Edition of *Lyrical Ballads*":

> . . . the human mind is capable of being excited without the application of gross and violent stimulants; and he must have a very faint perception of its beauty and dignity who does not know this. . . . It has therefore appeared to me, that to endeavor to produce or enlarge this capability is one of the best services in which, at any period, a Writer can be engaged; but this service, excellent at all times, is especially so at the present day. For a multitude of causes, unknown to former times, are now acting with a combined force to blunt the discriminating powers of the mind, and, unfitting it for all voluntary exertion, to reduce it to a state of almost savage torpor.

Times are again bad; they may get worse. But we can help to improve matters. We can recognize that turning on the electronic media is a powerful fact of modern life, and that the media are seriously implicated in our shifting symbol systems. We can work with our students toward a better understanding of media's personal and social effects, and toward freedom from media addiction and somnambulism. Our task is not the selling of the present, but neither can we sell it short if we hope to make a difference. We must be involved in helping students to cope with the present if we are to have a part in the future.

THE POPULAR MEDIA:
AN ENGLISH TEACHER'S CHALLENGE

Thomas R. Giblin

RECENTLY I was about ten minutes late for my English Education seminar. My tardiness was not a problem that day because a group of my students was scheduled to report on contemporary trends in popular media—film, television, records, magazines, newspapers, and paperbacks—and the teaching of English. As I approached the classroom I could hear unusually loud sounds coming from within. I entered the darkened room very slowly and with some trepidation.

Mind-blowing sights and sounds permeated the room. It was a case of total immersion in a sea of media. Slide projectors shot colorful pictures to every wall, competing for space with the images coming from four 16mm projectors and several strobe lights. Two stereos set my eardrums into motion and obliterated the sounds of the TV set that was, for the moment, only a visual medium. Paperbacks, magazines, and newspapers offered an obstacle course for anyone seeking to move toward a seat. Multimaterialed art projects, collages, and posters covered the windows, acting as draperies to darken the room. Adjustment was gradual, but quicker than one might expect. And then, as quickly as I had gotten involved, I was cut off: The machinery stopped, the "drapes" were removed, the traditional lights came on, and we were ready for "class."

The contrast was the message. Those responsible for the media presentation had ably demonstrated that there is a significant difference between the outside world and the classroom environment.

Outside the classroom today's high school students are frequently totally immersed in the media; inside, use of the media constitutes a rare and seemingly special occasion. In fact, the media should appear in the classroom far more often, not as a special event, but as an integral part of this subject called English.

My future teachers are not alone in their concern about the direction of the English curriculum. For the past decade or so English teachers have been discussing the role of the new media in the English program. At one extreme, the POTs (print-oriented teachers) have put down the FILMNUTS for selling out and trying to be too present tense, yet they consistently refuse to modify their print emphasis. Those at the other extreme have virtually ignored print materials in their effort to explore

REPRINTED by permission of Thomas R. Giblin.

[246]

the visual media. As a result, very little progress has been made toward reconciling these divergent positions. Somewhere between the extremes are those who believe there is room for study and use of the popular media in the conventional English program. These teachers are willing to set aside time for a two or three week unit on the mass media every year, and they regularly show films or play records. But even this use may not be enough.

The popular media contribute significantly to our rapidly changing world and English teachers, as specialists in the language arts, have a responsibility to guide people to an understanding of the media and their many influences. We can no longer afford to label TV as a "boob tube," to reject loud music as a passing fad, to assume everyone understands the propaganda power of all media, or to dismiss McLuhan as if he were a crank. We must begin to learn and to teach about the media in the hope that our students will be better able to use the media wisely, rather than to be used by the media.

What can the prospective or inservice English teacher do to learn and to teach about the media? He can read, write, speak and listen, and do it.

Read

A natural starting point for the print-oriented teacher is to read about the contemporary media. There are few comprehensive bibliographies at hand, but once one becomes familiar with the many resources available, his major problem will be to find time required to scan all the material. He might well start with *Media and Methods* or *English Journal* articles that suggest practical ideas for media study and use in the classroom. He can look at some of the newer "textbooks" such as Mahoney and Schmittroth's *The Insistent Present* or Weber's *Prose of Relevance;* investigate specific topics through books such as Schillaci and Culkin's *Films Deliver: Teaching Creatively With Film* or Moyes and White's *Journalism in the Mass Media;* read on all topics through general collections such as Giblin's *Popular Media and the Teaching of English;* and then get into McLuhan's *Understanding Media* and Carpenter and Heyman's *They Became What They Beheld*. Eventually the teacher should try to read everything written by McLuhan, Carpenter, and Culkin, whose works about the modern media of communication continue to have a profound impact on what goes on in the schools. Soon he will have ideas for use in the classroom tomorrow and thoughts on the direction of tomorrow's classroom.

Write

The English teacher can help himself and others to learn more about the media through writing, which can include everything from writing for information about the media to making statements of personal beliefs and experiences. For example, there is no reason that every teacher of English should not receive information almost weekly regarding the new media—no reason except that most teachers of English seldom take time to write to publishers, media-oriented companies, or professional organizations to indicate their interest in receiving relevant information and materials. A simple written request such as "Please add my name to your mailing list" will keep a teacher in touch with a great deal of current information. Such a request to every advertiser in an issue of *Media and Methods* is an excellent starting place. Naturally, some materials will cost money but a little-at-a-time approach will soon create a sizeable library. A second example of writing is for the English teacher to share his daily media experiences and beliefs with his peers. Whether he is writing for the *English Journal* or for a local curriculum council bulletin, the English teacher should begin to record his experiences and beliefs in writing for exchange with others. As he learns to "write" with music, poetry, pictures, slides, tapes, or film, it seems inevitable that he will begin sharing both the process and the product with his peers, and they with him.

Speak and Listen

Learning and teaching about the media demands a *cooperative* approach that is very dependent on frequent communication. One can learn more about the media by voicing questions and listening to replies from other English teachers—especially those who attend workshops or take university courses pertinent to media study; from teachers in other fields—it is not surprising to find a social studies teacher who has been a newspaper reporter or an industrial arts teacher who is active in photography; from students—they use the media more than most teachers, they own the hardware (cameras, records, magazines, and so on), and they are usually interested in exploring new activities related to media; from parents and administrators—they can often lend unexpected expertise and, even more important, they will usually support a changing curriculum when they understand the need and direction of the change; from the local community—TV, radio, and newspaper personnel are generally cooperative and interested in visiting a school to talk about media or in having a school group visit them to learn firsthand about media production. These resource people need to be involved, but they seldom initiate the communication. The English teacher must talk with them and listen to their perceptions of the new media.

Do It

The English teacher should get involved with the media in his own classes. The frequently quoted proverb,

> I hear and I forget,
> I see and I remember,
> I do and I understand.

seems very appropriate for the English teacher. He should try to listen to and discuss current music and lyrics, to compose with a variety of media such as slides or film, to read and analyze contemporary paperbacks, underground newspapers, and adolescent-oriented magazines, to view television, movies, and drama at every opportunity. But his own knowledge and practice is insufficient if he never brings his ever-increasing expertise into his classroom. Initially he may fail, but his attempt is the grand thing. And, sooner than he thinks, he will begin experiencing success and reap the dividends of his reading, writing, speaking and listening, and doing.

McLUHAN: IMPLICATIONS FOR ADOLESCENCE

W. Kirk Kilpatrick

Proposition

EDGAR FRIEDENBERG (1959, 1963) has suggested that adolescence is vanishing from our culture and the theories of Marshall McLuhan (1964) if valid, would tend to confirm this suggestion. Friedenberg feels that the essence of adolescence is self definition and individuation. Adolescence is the process of finding an identity as an individual apart from the mass. In his more recent writings (1965) he expresses the fear that adolescence so conceived may no longer be possible in McLuhan's "global village."

-›››

F R O M *Adolescence*, Vol. 6 (Summer 1971), pp. 235–258. Reprinted by permission of Libra Publishers, Inc. and the author.

McLuhan has proposed in effect that we are entering into a totally new Age—the age of the retribalization of man created by electronic interdependence. If his hypothesis is true then those theories of adolescence and education based on the previous Age, i.e. based on observations of "linear man" may be in danger of losing their relevance. In any event the McLuhan hypothesis calls for a reappraisal of traditional theories of adolescence. If there exists the possibility that "they don't make 'em like that anymore" (i.e. print oriented, individualized man) then it seems in order to investigate McLuhan's thesis and its implications for adolescent theory.

Understanding McLuhan

Marshall McLuhan is a 58 year old professor and head of the University of Toronto's Center for Culture and Technology. His *Understanding Media* (1964) is listed by *Time* as one of "the decade's most notable books." Some consider it to be one of the most important works of the century. "Compared to Mr. McLuhan, Spengler is cautious and Toynbee positively pedantic," writes literary critic Dwight MacDonald.

What has McLuhan done to merit such plaudits? According to his admirers and by his own account, he is the first to have recognized and heralded the advent of a new age of mankind—the post-literate, electronic age. If true, this is quite significant since ages of mankind come at intervals less regular even than the trains on the Long Island Railroad. In fact, the last Age (which we are just now leaving) made its debut with the invention of the printing press in the Fifteenth Century. *The Gutenberg Galaxy* (1962) is McLuhan's analysis of that Age.

If we substitute the word "environment" for "galaxy" in the title we can begin to grasp McLuhan's underlying thesis: Media create environments. The media of print ushered in by Gutenberg's invention of the printing press created a whole new environment for man. Media are so pervasive in their cultural and social consequences that they leave no part of us untouched or unaffected (McLuhan and Fiore, 1967). The impact of any media, according to McLuhan, lies in its power to alter the ratio among the senses. The extension of any one sense alters the way we perceive the world and therefore the way we think and act. A change in the sense ratio produces a change in man (McLuhan, 1962).

Print, according to McLuhan, emphasizes and extends the visual sense and deemphasizes the other senses. It also tends to separate and fragment the senses from one another (1964). Exactly how this occurs is never made entirely clear in McLuhan's writings since he prefers to argue by analogy rather than by logic or cause-and-effect approaches. Culkin (1966) explains it this way:

To communicate [an] experience through print means that it must first be broken down into parts and then mediated, eye-dropper fashion, one-thing-at-a-time, in an abstract, linear fragmented, sequential way. That is the essential structure of print. And once a culture uses such a medium for a few centuries, it begins to perceive the world in a one-thing-at-a-time, abstract, linear, fragmented, sequential way. And it shapes its organizations and schools according to the same premises. The form of print has become the form of thought. The medium has become the message (p. 8).

As an example of the way print media shapes our technologies and culture, McLuhan (1962) offers the assembly-line, mass production system. Like print, the assembly line is linear, fragmented and sequential. And like print it has had profound effects on our culture. The main effect of the Gutenberg environment has been the making of typographic man: literate, print-oriented, individualized man (1962). The section following this one will attempt to describe print-oriented man in more detail, but first let us look at the post-Gutenberg era, the electronic age.

The electronic media (television, telephone, computers, phonograph, etc.) have broken the monopoly of print and its extension of the visual sense, says McLuhan (1964). Electric media extend all the senses but especially the tactile and auditory senses, which according to McLuhan (1967) has the effect of returning us to a pre-literate mode of perceiving. The shift from the visual mode of perceiving to a unified sensorium somehow (again McLuhan is not entirely clear) recreates the world in the image of a global village (1967). Perhaps a few quotations will give the flavor of McLuhan's thought:

Phonetic writing alone has the power of separating and fragmenting the senses and of sloughing off the semantic complexities. The TV image reverses this literate process of analytic fragmentation of sensory life. (1964, p. 333).

The tactual mode of perceiving is sudden but not specialist. It is total, synesthetic, involving all the senses. Pervaded by the mosaic TV image, the TV child encounters the world in a spirit antithetic to literacy (1964, p. 334).

It helps to know that civilization is entirely the product of phonetic literacy, and as it dissolves with the electronic revolution, we discover a tribal, integral awareness that manifests itself in a complete shift in our sensory lives. (1968, pp. 24–25).

And

After three thousand years of specialist explosion and of increasing specialism and alienation .in the technological extensions of our bodies, our world has become compressional by dramatic reversal. As electrically contracted, the globe is no more than a village. Electric speed in bringing all social and political functions together in a sudden implosion has heightened human awareness of responsibility to an intense degree. (1964, p. 5).

And finally

The new electronic interdependence recreates the world in the image of a global village. (1962, p. 43).

Primitive and tribal man were (and in parts of the world still are) bound together by their dependency on oral communication. Everyone was involved in the life of everyone else because everyone was dependent on everyone else. Because the primary means of communication was speech, no man knew very much more than any other man. With the coming of literacy and the book it became possible for man to learn and gain knowledge apart from the community and the concepts of the "individual" and "individualism" were born. Tribal man took part in a collective existence; literate or visual man has created an individualistic environment (1964). With the coming of the electric age and its instantaneous communication, modern man is being cast into another web of interdependence, this time on a global scale (1962). Because of electronic interdependence man is once again becoming involved in the life of every other man. As one proof of the new age, McLuhan (1962) points to the decline of the linear, sequential assembly line in industry and its rapid replacement by the non-linear, non-sequential, all-at-once system of computer automation. Like its predecessor, the assembly line, automation promises to have (and already has had) profound effect on our lives. The chief result of the electric revolution is what McLuhan (1964) calls "post-literate" or "neo tribal" man.

Print Oriented Man and Neo-Tribal Man

We are now, writes McLuhan, as far into the electric age as the Elizabethans were advanced into the typographical and mechanical age (1962). We are experiencing, he says,

The same confusions and indecisions which they had felt when living simultaneously in two contrasted forms of society and experience. Whereas the Elizabethans were poised between medieval corporate experience and modern individualism, we reverse their pattern by confronting an electric technology which would seem to render individualism obsolete and the corporate interdependence mandatory. (1962, p. 9).

The main source of confusion in our society is that some of us (the older ones) were brought up in a print-oriented environment and the rest of us (the younger ones) were raised in a primarily electric environment:

The generation gap is actually a chasm, separating not two age groups but two vastly divergent cultures. I can understand the ferment in our schools, because our educational system is totally rearview mirror. It's a dying and outdated system founded on literate values and fragmented and classified data totally unsuited to the needs of the first television generation. (Norden, 1969).

First let us look at print-oriented man. What are his characteristics? As said before, literacy and print permitted man to find an identity apart from the group and thereby spurred the advent of individualism in Western society. The characteristics of print became the characteristics of man and his thought. Whereas tribal cultures cannot entertain the possibility of the individual or the separate citizen (1964), the fragmented nature of print made it possible for an individual to separate himself from the mass. The literate man's mode of thought is itself modeled on print. "Rational" to him means linear and sequential; thinking to Western literate man means a step by step process along a straight logical path (1964). In addition the literate man is "convinced that all real values are private, personal, individual." (1962, p. 191). Print has the power "to install the reader in a subjective universe of limitless freedom and spontaneity—But by the same token print induces the reader to order his external life and actions with visual propriety and rigor—" (1962, pp. 190–191). Print carries the individuating power of the phonetic alphabet to its extreme; "Print is the technology of individualism." (1962). A print culture inevitably confers on its members what Riesman has called "inner direction." Inner direction depends on a private point of view and a high development of individuality of character (1962).

But in the new electric age, says McLuhan, the virtues of print-oriented man are falling into disrepute (1964). As a result of electric implosion, neo-tribal man is in the ascendancy. The characteristics of neo-tribal or post-literate man are similar in many respects to pre-literate, tribal man, McLuhan quotes with approval J. C. Carothers' (1959) description of tribal man:

a (tribal) man comes to regard himself as a rather insignificant part of a much larger organism—the family and the clan—and not as an independent, self-reliant unit; personal initiative and ambition are permitted little outlet; and a meaningful integration of a man's experience on individual, personal lines is not achieved. By contrast to the constriction at the intellectual level, great freedom is allowed for at the temperamental level, and a man is expected to live very much in the "here and now," to be highly extroverted, and to give very free expression to his feelings. (Carothers, p. 308).

Pre-literate man is concerned with corporate and collective, not individual values (1962). The tribal man is bound into a seamless web of kinship and interdependence (1964). By McLuhan's account, the opening of the electronic age has the effect of sealing the entire human family into a single world tribe (1962).

> The immediate prospect for literate, fragmented Western man encountering the electric implosion within his own culture is his steady and rapid transformation into a complex and depth structured person emotionally aware of his total interdependence with the rest of human society. . . . Fragmented, literate and visual individualism is not possible in an electrically patterned and imploded society. (1964, pp. 50–51).

Just as specialist technologies like print and assembly line detribalize, the nonspecialist electric technology retribalizes (1964). In great part this fusion results from the instantaneous speed of electric media:

> The alphabet (and its extension into typography) made possible the spread of the power that is knowledge, and shattered the bonds of tribal man, thus exploding him into agglomeration of individuals. Electric writing and speed pour upon him, instantaneously and continuously, the concerns of all other men. He becomes tribal once more. The human family becomes one tribe again. (1964, pp. 171–172).

Unlike print which extends only the visual sense, electric media extend all the senses. McLuhan goes so far as to say that electric technology is really an extension of our central nervous system and eventually will become an extension of our consciousness as well. The end result may make of the entire human family a single consciousness (1964).

Although such mental musings may seem rather far out and far fetched, McLuhan is not alone in his vision. Pierre Teilhard de Chardin, widely acclaimed as one of the great intellects of this century, has set forth a similar hypothesis in *The Phenomenon of Man* (1959). Chardin proposed that the earth's biosphere is being supplanted by what he called the noosphere—literally a web of thought and consciousness covering the globe (1959).

Or take a recent *Newsweek* article about youthful folk singer and symbol of the Woodstock generation, Arlo Guthrie:

> Arlo and his friends talk very little. Often a cheerful exchange of 'How ya doin' will be followed by long silences leading to nothing. . . . 'We don't talk about the weather, if that's what you mean,' Arlo says by way of explanation. 'We just look outside. We communicate by a kind of osmosis. It has to do with shared experience. The kids who are growing up now, I don't see why they have to talk at all . . .'. (*Newsweek*, Sept. 29, 1969, p. 102).

McLuhan might well point to the Arlo phenomenon as one sign of our return to a tribal existence of shared experience or even as a partaking in the global consciousness.

If McLuhan is correct in his assertion that print-oriented man is being replaced by neo-tribal man, then what are the implications for theories of adolescence, which for the most part seem to be based on observation of print oriented man? Let us look at some of the salient features of current adolescent theory.

The Process of Adolescence in Theory

At the outset it seems safe to say that most theorists recognize that adolescence is in part a cultural invention (Muuss, 1962). The studies by Mead (1950), Benedict (1959) and other anthropologists have shown that adolescence as we know it in the West does not exist in many primitive societies. But since most theorists write about and for their own culture (e.g. Havighurst and Gesell writing mostly for American audiences) it didn't seem to make much difference that what held true in Kansas City might not be applicable in Samoa. The point of the present paper, however, is that what held true twenty years ago in print-oriented Kansas City may no longer hold true in electric age Kansas City. And a survey of adolescent texts and theories will show that their authors are obviously concerned with what McLuhan would call print-oriented, individualized man.

According to Erikson, adolescence is the period during which a positive ego identity is to be established (Muuss, 1962). Ego identity ". . . is the creation of a sense of sameness, a unity of personality now felt by the individual and recognized by others as having consistency in time . . ." (Erikson, 1963, p. 13). Ego identity also involves a conscious effort to make the future a part of one's personal life plan (Muuss, 1962). It means establishing a personal separate and individual identity (Erikson, 1950). "Maturity begins when identity has been established and an integrated, independent individual has emerged who now can stand on his own feet . . ." (Muuss, 1962). The danger in adolescence is that youth may fail to actively integrate their own identity; they may assume a ready made or synthetic identity supplied to them by society or by some ideological group. For Erikson a mature identity is a self-made, democratic identity (1950).

It is obvious that Erikson's concept of positive ego identity assumes a social environment which allows an individual to assert his individuality and his independence from the tribe. This state of affairs, says McLuhan, is only possible in a "book culture." For tribal man identity is ascribed rather than achieved and it is a group rather than an individual identity.

The central theme of adolescence, according to Church and Stone (1957), is to find one's self:

The adolescent's search for himself appears, then, to be more than merely an attempt to find something that is already there. More basically, it is also an active attempt to create a personality. As he tries on various roles and manners, his interior experience crystallizes and becomes his own, to change, to conceptualize, and to act upon. (Stone and Church, p. 306).

Such a statement seems to take for granted the private point of view, the inner direction which Riesman speaks of, and the print culture without which, McLuhan says, such things are not possible.

A further excerpt from Stone and Church seems instructive, since it mirrors the type of adolescence which is often celebrated in film and literature and which is probably typical only of a self-reflective and literate society:

The young adolescent, viewing himself largely from the inside, experiences himself (when he is not embarrassed, despondent, or self-accusing) as pure spirit, and the only worthy external counterparts of this experience are to be found in the majesties and austerities of religion, in the beauties of nature, in certain idealized public or fictional personalities, in poetry or music, in political abstractions . . . (p. 316).

When the adolescents' idealism is thwarted by the "slings and arrows of outrageous fortune" he is prone to that type of depression called *Weltschmerz* by the Germans.

It is in a state of *Weltschmerz* that the adolescent likes to take long, solitary, nocturnal walks, or write long, melancholy poems, or toy with the idea of suicide—a special kind of suicide following which the adolescent can stand by disembodied and contemplate the remorse that other people will feel 'after I'm gone.' (p. 317).

These authors are quoted because their descriptions of adolescence seems to reflect the concern with private, subjective, personal and individual values which McLuhan (1962) sees as the hallmark of literate, print-oriented man.

In Central Europe, Eduard Spranger has become one of the most widely read authors on adolescence. Although he limits his investigation to Germany, his theories are consistent with the American writers mentioned above. Once again there is the stress on inwardness, individuality and self-discovery. The following is a comment by Muuss (1962):

In referring to the discovery of the ego, Spranger does not say that the child has no ego experiences. Rather, his ego and the world appear to be united. During pubescence this unity is divided, and the juvenile begins to reflect upon himself by directing his attention internally and analyzing himself. The discovery of the internal ego, experienced now as separated from the external world, results not only in loneliness but also in a need to experiment with one's own undifferentiated ego, in order to establish ego unity. (Muuss, p. 49).

In Spranger's view, then, adolescence is a time for reflective discovery of the self. Identity is not conferred upon the individual in a ceremonial rite. He must acheive identity by looking inward; the central question for the adolescent is "Who am I?" Other writers on adolescence echo the same theme. Thus for Gesell the central task of adolescence is to find one's self (Muuss, 1692). Nixon also stresses the centrality of self-discovery. Unless there is self-discovery, Nixon maintains, then emotional and psychological maturity cannot be obtained (Muuss,1962).

Perhaps one of the most perceptive people writing about adolescence today is Edgar Z. Friedenberg. He is particularly relevent to the current discussion because he deals directly (though briefly) with McLuhan's theories (Friedenberg, 1965). Friedenberg is cognizant of far reaching changes taking place among American youth and he parallels the present paper in his contention that traditional concepts of adolescence are losing their relevance. In fact, he says, the adolescent is vanishing from our society (1959). The process of adolescence is self-definition according to Friedenberg. Self-definition means becoming a person in one's own right; learning who one is and what one feels. It involves differentiating oneself from one's culture. It means finding a unique identity as an individual apart from the mass. And it inevitably brings the individual in conflict with society (1959, 1963). "Inwardness" or "subjectivity" is what makes self-definition possible. Inwardness is "the capacity to attend to and respond to one's inner life and feelings, to the uniquely personal in experience, to personal relationships." (1963, p. 211).

What is happening in our schools, Friedenberg (1963) claims, is a process of Darwinian selection by which the inward values become extinguished in favor of the social techniques necessary to get ahead in an organization man society. In this light the curious title of his best known book, *Coming of Age in America* makes sense. It is of course a paraphrase of Margaret Mead's classic study, *Coming of Age in Samoa*. In primitive cultures such as Samoa there is no extended period of adolescence. Instead there is an abrupt passage from childhood to adult status usually marked by rites of puberty. This sudden passage into adult society leaves little time for self-definition or for differentiating oneself from one's culture. The conflict between individual and society which Friedenberg (1959) considers essential to mature development does not occur. While not suggesting that there is an abrupt transition in our culture, Friendenberg suggests (1963) that protracted exposure to our institutions, especially the high school, is bringing about a similar absence of adolescence as occurs in primitive societies.

Since reading McLuhan, Friedenberg seems to have changed his mind somewhat about what it is that is making the adolescent vanish. Friedenberg (1965) considers McLuhan to be accurate in his assessment of our changing society and since he perceives the deterministic nature of McLuhan's history, his own writings about the adolescent process tend to take on a nostalgic air. In *The Dignity of Youth and Other Atavisims,* Friedenberg so much as says that he was glad he grew up when he did when adolescence was still possible. If they don't make 'em like that any more, says he, then so much the worse for America (1965). Friedenberg reminisces about Salinger's Holden Caufield and the youthful heroes of A *Separate Peace* as though that type of adolescence is forever gone. In fact that type of adolescence is a definite handicap in a neotribal society:

> What I have been calling integrity is really the integrity of a print-oriented individualized people; and the very self-awareness that I have conceived as the source of their nobility is also, it seems, the instrument of estrangement which saps their vitality. (1965, p. 5).

Conclusions

A consideration of the foregoing authors from the point of view of McLuhan's theory seems to lead to the conclusion that they are all speaking of what McLuhan has called print-oriented man—the product of the typographic age. The next logical conclusion (if I may take the liberty of being linear and sequential) is this: If print-oriented, private, individualized man is on the wane then many of our ideas about the process of adolescence, which seem to be based largely on such a model of man, are becoming less and less applicable to modern youth and more and more irrelevant. The next question then, has to do with the accuracy of Mr. McLuhan's vision. Is he right?

The question, I think, can best be answered by breaking it into two questions. Question One: Is McLuhan correct in his assessment of what is actually happening to Western society i.e. a kind of retribalization? Question Two: Assuming he is correct about what is happening, are the explanations he offers for it's happening, the right ones? Let's look at Question Two first.

For support of his electronic era thesis, McLuhan draws upon the whole history of mankind as well as numerous literary sources; his thesis is also based on his claim to understanding the inner workings of television and other electronic media and their physiological and psychological effect on man.

It is genuinely difficult to follow his line of argument since there is no line. He has abandoned the outmoded "linear" or logical presentation of events in favor of an historical mosaic which supposedly creates reader participation in the same way that the electronic mosaic of the TV demands viewer involvement. Finkelstein, a critic of McLuhan, has this to say:

He presents this history in a fantastically jumbled form, with widely separated ages and subjects jostling each other, as if produced by a time machine that had gone haywire. (Finkelstein, 1968, p. 8).

Even to the non-expert, McLuhan's history seems highly selective. He deals for the most part with certain significant inventions and their social implications but the historical connections he draws seem vague and tenuous. He has also been criticized for writing history backwards to prove the point he starts off with (Finkelstein, 1968).

He has a tendency to quote freely from a wide variety of classic literary sources for confirmation of his theories and he has a particular affinity for the more obtuse writings of James Joyce. The best that can be said about these sources is that they simply do not confirm his theories in any way.

Finally, unless one is extremely knowledgable in electronic physics and physiological psychology, one simply takes on faith McLuhan's proclamations about the effects of electronic media on the human psyche.

Others (Stearn, Finkelstein) have taken McLuhan to account on these issues in far more detail, but for the purposes of his paper I see no reason to go further because these criticisms are not directed toward what I consider to be the main issue. That issue concerns the first question: Is McLuhan describing a phenomenon that is actually occurring—whatever explanations he may offer for its occurrence? Whether McLuhan's explanations are right or wrong is of secondary importance to the phenomenon he tries to explain. This is the phenomenon of the global village or the retribalization of Western man; the replacement of private individualized man by neo-tribal man. It is not within the purview of this paper to deal with the historical and scientific arguments McLuhan offers. They may be valid or far-fetched. But if his prediction of the shift from literate to neo-tribal man is correct, then the central thesis of his paper still holds true, and our adolescent theories are in need of revision.

McLuhan can be criticized on several counts but he does seem to describe a phenomenon which other observers of the current scene have also noticed. Here are some excerpts from a recent *Newsweek* article reviewing the 60's:

Drugs enhanced the flight away from reason and into other regions of the mind. And if grass was scarce and you weren't into acid, rock music alone could also help in opening up the path. Its soaring flights of electronic sound, quick-changing rhythms and sheer loudness enveloped the listener, banning ordinary thought and sensation, and its words sometimes preached a message of transcendental union among all mankind. . . . For a few, escape from technological society was a literal thing: the '60's spawned the hippie movement and its scattered encampments of drop-outs. They evolved their own culture of brightly colored beads and flowers, macrobiotic foods, mind-expanding drugs and universal love (which the Beatles said was "all you need"), and for a while they flourished in San Francisco's Haight-Ashbury and other city settlements. Then the urban "vibrations" turned bad, and the hippies followed the natural paths of all questers after a simpler life: either to disillusionment or to the countryside, where they clustered in rural communes. (*Newsweek,* Dec. 29, 1969, p. 19).

Newsweek goes on to elaborate on the communal trend:

It seemed significant that the hippie phenomenon, like so many other signs of the '60's, was essentially a communal thing. Negroes thought of themselves as members of the black "community." Radicals and peace marchers discovered a sense of purpose by plunging into "the movement." Young people found happiness and self-definition in the gigantic Woodstock gathering of the clans. (p. 19).

And

With all this community-mindedness going round, detachments became very difficult for Americans during the '60's. (p. 19).

Obviously the *Newsweek* writer has a very different conception of self-definition from the one Friedenberg uses. For Friedenberg, self-definition is the result of inwardness, not participation in the masses. But by *Newsweek*'s account, self-definition is now found in the "gathering of the clans." Detachment and non-involvement which McLuhan sees as characteristic of the literate man became, according to *Newsweek,* "very difficult for Americans during the '60's," and modern music "sometimes preached a message of transcendental union among all mankind." With the new emphasis on communal involvement it was beginning to be possible to speak once more of a seamless web of kinship and the terms "brother" and "soul-brother" came to designate anyone who felt the same vibrations as you.

Time had its own review of the '60's. Here are some excerpts:

In the long run, this decade and the next may well constitute an historical era of transition, like that which followed the Middle Ages and preceded the Renaissance.

The veneration of rationality was the special myth of modern man. The world view created by the enthronement of reason included a universal belief in individualism and competition; now that myth is dying. (Dec. 19, 1969, p. 22).

And,

Individualism may continue to wane as men seek personal identity in group identity. (p. 22).

All this is very similar to what McLuhan had written back in 1962. There is the waning of individualism, the distrust of rationality (and among some sectors a new faith in magic and astrology) and the trend toward group and communal experience. *Time* goes on to cite Margaret Mead's feeling that "today's generation gap is wider and deeper than any other recorded in history." (p. 23).

Further corroboration of McLuhan's theories can be found in the nationwide interest in T-groups, sensory awareness groups, hippie communes, and even the gradual dropping of denominational barriers between the churches. In fact it is not unlikely that McLuhan (a devout Catholic) may have taken some of his cues from recent trends in the religious sphere. In his own church there has been a curious resurgence of the doctrine of the mystical Body of Christ—a mystical union of all Christians—which had been neglected since the Middle Ages (the last age of community before the Gutenburg Galaxy set in, according to McLuhan). Concomitantly the churches have placed renewed stress on communal involvement and participation in their liturgical rites. And of course there is Chardin's vision, already referred to, of a world evolving toward global unity.

Another trend which seems to comfirm McLuhan's view is the changing perception of time among adolescents. Traditional theories hold that the process of adolescence involves a future orientation. Unlike the child, who lives for the present, the adolescent becomes conscious of past and future time and begins to plan his own future (Douvan and Adelson, 1966). This future orientation has been characteristic of print-oriented man in general. Older Americans were brought up in an environment which emphasized postponing today's pleasure for tomorrow's reward and stressed the importance of building and saving for the future. Now things seem to be changing. In fact the current breed of youngsters is referred to as the "now" generation. Kenneth Keniston has addressed himself to the issue in his usual perceptive fashion:

> Tomorrow tends to disappear as a center of relevance in our lives, for building toward the future means building toward the unknown.
> What is left of course, is the present, and all that can be enjoyed therein: "today" becomes the one rock of constancy in a shifting sea of change. (Keniston, 1969, p. 75).

He continues:

> The traditional American postponement of present enjoyment for the sake of greater future reward is disappearing as well.
> We have seen some of the varieties of this outlook among alienated students—the emphasis on sensation, sentience and experience; the reluctance to make future commitments, the sense of temporal confusion; the

extreme emphasis on the present; the choice of 'realistic' and present-oriented values. (p. 75).

McLuhan might comment that youth's concern with the present is merely a reflection of media's ability to shape man in their image. Just as print fostered its linear, sequential style on man, so the instantaneous TV image (along with other electric media) creates the all-at-once-person (McLuhan, 1964). It is also instructive to note that the tendency to live for the present rather than the future is quite often a characteristic of illiterate tribes and societies. In fact the language of some primitive people has no future tense.

The current emphasis on the present is of course no proof that we are retribalizing ourselves, but it does seem consistent with McLuhan's thesis. The study of adolescent society by James Coleman (1961) also seems to corroborate McLuhan's thought. Coleman advances the hypothesis that the adolescent subculture is becoming more sharply differentiated from adult society. Increasingly the young look to each other for social rewards and recognition:

> He (the adolescent) is 'cut off' from the rest of society, forced inward toward his own age group, made to carry out his whole social life with others his own age. With his fellows, he comes to constitute a small society, one that has most of its important interactions *within* itself, and maintains only a few threads of connection with the outside adult society. (Coleman, p. 3).

Coleman's thesis seems to augment McLuhan's contention that what we have been calling the "generation gap" is really a chasm between two divergent cultures.

It has been argued (Muuss, 1962) that Coleman's postulate actually contradicts Friedenberg's prediction that adolescence is vanishing. If adolescents are becoming a more clearly differentiated subculture then how can they be disappearing? (Muuss, 1962). This argument fails to make the important distinction between "teenager" and "adolescent." Friedenberg argued that the process of adolescence was disappearing, not the "teenager." It could be further argued that Friedenberg's criteria of "differentiation from the culture" is being met by the adolescent society—and, if they are differentiating themselves so successfully then they must be adolescents as well as teenagers. This argument would be valid if the teenager's culture was adult society, but it is precisely Coleman's point that it is not. Teenagers have their own culture, their own society, according to Coleman (McLuhan would say that they are the first generation of the electric culture). While they may be differentiating themselves from the adult culture, the question to ask is whether they are differentiating from each other.

I think Riesman (1969) is correct when he says that the young have become captives of each other. In order to achieve self-definition, the contemporary adolescent must not only differentiate himself from adult culture but also from the teen-age sub-culture. The latter may turn out to be the more difficult task. If McLuhan is correct, the adolescent sub-culture has more and more of a tribe-like quality. And anthropologists never stop reminding us that primitive man is practically incapable of differentiating himself from his tribe. The tribal man, as Carothers points out, ". . . comes to regard himself as an insignificant part of a much larger organism. . . ." (McLuhan, 1962, p. 27). What I am suggesting is that the process of adolescence is being aborted. Many youth seem to get to the point of separating themselves from adult society and the schools. But they stop short of differentiating themselves from their own society of peers and as a result their adolescence never comes to full term. That youth are able to achieve the initial differentiation and definition may of course be attributed to the sharp divergence between the two cultures. With the passage of time, if McLuhan is correct, there will be only one culture: the post literate, retribalized culture and differentiation and self-definition will be all the less likely. Then, in fact, the process of adolescence as we have known it will have completely vanished.

Throughout this paper there has been an implied comparison between modern youth and tribal man. There are also, of course, differences, some of them striking. Unlike most primitive societies there is in America no opportunity for youth to really participate in the social process in a meaningful way. The adolescent is largely irrelevant to adult society. The opposite is true in primitive societies where the youth quickly takes his place as a vital member of the community; and it is perhaps for this reason that the passage into adulthood is so smooth and swift. Whether the passage of time will bring about a similar situation in American society is a question for another paper.

It is also important to realize that in McLuhan's thought, post-literate does not mean illiterate. Print is probably here to stay but it will no longer hold the predominant position (Culkin, 1966). Since every culture has its own preferred sense-ratios, it follows that new media will affect different culture in different ways. Thus the effect of electric technology will be different for a print-oriented culture than for a culture which had never detribalized itself to begin with (it should be made clear at this point that the present paper has been concerned almost exclusively with the implications of McLuhan for Western societies and primarily the North American Continent). (McLuhan, 1964). For this reason it would be foolish to try to draw too close a parallel between pre-literate tribal man and post-literate, neo-tribal man.

Summary

To summarize: Marshall McLuhan believes that we are in a transition period between two ages. The Gutenberg Age is dying, to be supplanted by the electric age. The typographical or Gutenberg age created a certain type of man which is also dying. This was print-oriented, individualistic, private and future-time oriented man. The new man is post-literate, neo-tribal, present-time oriented, involved with all others in a globe electronically shrunk to the size of a village.

It should be obvious at this point that there is no way of proving McLuhan right or wrong. Only time will tell, and it may be a long time since the ability to fully comprehend an era usually falls to the succeeding era. Nevertheless, there is sufficient confirmation of McLuhan's theories to warrant his being taken seriously and to warrant a serious reexamination of our traditional theories of adolescence.

REFERENCES

Benedict, Ruth. *Patterns of Culture.* Boston: Houghton Mifflin, 1959.

Carothers, J. C. "Culture, Psychiatry and the Written Word." *Psychiatry,* Nov. 1959.

Chardin, Pierre Teilhard de. *Phenomenon of Man.* Trans. Bernard Wall, New York, Harper: 1959.

Coleman, James S. *The Adolescent Society.* Glencoe: The Free Press, 1961.

Culkin, John, S. J. "Education in a Post-Literate World." *Media and Methods,* Nov. 1966, pp. 6–9.

Douvan, Elizabeth and Adelson, Joseph. *The Adolescent Experience.* New York: John Wiley, 1966.

Erikson, Erik H. *Childhood and Society.* New York: W. W. Norton, 1950.

Erikson, Erik H. (ed.). *The Challenge of Youth.* Garden City, N.Y.: Anchor Books, 1963.

Finkelstein, Sidney. *Sense and Nonsense of McLuhan.* New York: International Publishers, 1968.

Friedenberg, Edgar Z. *The Vanishing Adolescent.* New York: Delta, 1959.

Friedenberg, E. Z. *Coming of Age in America.* New York: Random House, 1963.

Friedenberg, E. Z. *The Dignity of Youth and Other Atavisms.* Boston: Beacon Press, 1965.

Keniston, Kenneth. "Stranded in the Present." (c. 1963) in *Adolescence for Adults,* Indiana Blue Cross and Blue Shield, pub. 1969.

McLuhan, H. M. *The Gutenberg Galaxy.* New York: Signet Books, 1962.

McLuhan, H. M. *Understanding Media.* New York: McGraw-Hill, 1964.

McLuhan, H. M. and Fiore, Q. *The Medium is the Massage.* New York: Bantam Books, 1967.

McLuhan, H. M. and Fiore, Q. *War and Peace in the Global Village.* New York: Bantam Books, 1968.

Mead, Margaret. *Coming of Age in Samoa.* New York: New American Library, 1950.

Muuss, Rolf. *Theories of Adolescence.* New York: Random House, 1962.

Newsweek, Sept. 29, 1969, pp. 101–106.

Newsweek, Dec. 29, 1969, pp. 12–19.

Norden E. "Playboy Interview: Marshall McLuhan." *Playboy,* March 1969, 53–74, 158.

Riesman, David. "The Young Are Captives of Each Other: A Conversation with David Riesman" by T. George Harris in *Psychology Today,* Oct. 1969.

Stearn, Gerald. (ed.). *McLuhan: Hot and Cool.* New York: Signet Books.

Stone, L. Joseph and Church, Joseph. *Childhood and Adolescence.* New York: Random House, 1957.

Time, Dec. 19, 1969, pp. 22–26.

LEARNING WITH TELEVISION COMMERCIALS

Rodney Smith

THE history of the development of advertising is a fascinating tale. It is a story of man's attempt to influence his own fellow man. The telling reaches back into the beginnings of recorded time where some of the earliest records were themselves advertisements.

The Rosetta stone, for example, was a type of early public relations release declaring that Ptolemy was the "Son-of-the-Sun . . . Father of the Moon . . . and Keeper of the Happiness of Men." The "copy" was aimed at audiences in three different languages—Greek, Egyptian hieroglyphics, and Coptic—a commercial of 136 B.C.

Other public-relations notices carved in stone were the inscriptions on the face of Mt. Behistun in Iran carved by workers of Darius the Great around 500 B.C., or even earlier, the battle scenes of "scare propaganda" ordered into stone by the Assyrian kings around 4000 B.C.

One of the earliest original source advertisements is a papyrus notice offering a reward for a runaway slave. Found in the ruins of Thebes, and now in the British Museum, this notice (over 3000 years old) is a remote ancestor of our classified advertisement page in today's newspaper.

In old Babylon of 3000 B.C. barkers and criers shouted notice of

F R O M *Teachers Guides to Television,* Vol. 3 (Fall 1970), pp. 11–12. Reprinted by permission of the publisher and the author.

excellent wares in the shops, and in the ruins of old Pompeii may still be seen emblems and symbols picturing the trade of this or that shopkeeper.

The printing revolution of the Fifteenth Century enabled eager printers to spew forth handbills, and broadsides (larger sheets containing advertising) and even commercial announcements bound into book form.

The first daily newspaper of the English speaking world was established December 1, 1702. This featured the famous Joseph Addison, but also advertised Dr. Chamberlen's Anodyne Necklace which played on testimonials. It was the newspaper which brought commercial advertising close to its present state. Magazines, radio, and more recently TV, have developed this commercial form even further.

Those wishing to explore the economic consequences of advertising need only note that though as early as 1867 only $50,000,000 was spent for advertising, by 1969 the United States was spending 19.6 billion—an apparently tremendous increase. Of course during this time the national income had risen from $5,770 million to over $932 billion—advertising had increased to a little more than 2% of the gross national product. The story is worthy of tracing in your encyclopedias, for this is a part of the American success story, all the way from George Eastman's Kodak newspaper ad: "You Press the Button—We Do the Rest," of the late 19th century, to tomorrow's television commercials.

Such titles as "Kitten Taste Test" (advertising a canned cat food), "Bumps of Life" (advertising an instant breakfast), and "Birthday Party, Backup" (an evaporated milk), are titles of little works of art known to our contemporary world as television commercials. No one will ever see these real titles, for they are code names known only to 'Madison Avenue' writers and to company advertising liaison personnel who pay millions and millions of dollars every year so that their company's product can be sold to the American populace.

Young people today cannot turn in any direction without running into a message, some form of communication, of one sort or another. Sign boards, magazines in full color spread, car radios in the family automobile, transistors the youngster sometimes carries in his own pocket, store window displays. There are some who believe that young people are told what to eat, what to wear and, through magazine and signboard, storewindow, newspaper, and television, even told what to say and think.

A few years ago, Vance Packard in his book *The Status Seekers* reported that young people are sometimes subjected to 1500 sales messages alone in a single day. Note, for example, what happens to a youngster who leafs through one magazine. How many messages a young person receives!

The McLuhan Message

Actually, our students are being bombarded with messages from all sides: colorful printed magazines, the wide range of parent and peer talk, the transistor radios, and popular phonograph records, not to mention television. This is what McLuhan means when he writes in The *Medium is the Massage* (sic):

> It is a matter of the greatest urgency that our educational institutions realize that we now have civil war among these environments created by media other than the printed word. The classroom is now in a vital struggle for survival with the immensely persuasive 'outside' world created by new informational media. Education must shift from instruction, from imposing of stencils, to discovery—to probing and exploration and to the recognition of the language of forms.

To emphasize further what McLuhan has called "the civil war among these environments created by media other than the printed word," let me quote from an article by John Culkin of Fordham University. You may have heard him speak at one of his many conferences about the country. Culkin is talking about the media revolution, particularly about film television.

> The simple cultural fact (is) that we live in a world which is being increasingly dominated by the projected image. By the time a typical American student graduates from high school today, he has watched more than 15,000 hours of television and has seen more than 500 films (another thousand or so hours). The TV figure is the result of an average of twenty hours of weekly viewing for fifteen years, adding up to two full years of twenty-four-hour-a-day televiewing. During the same period of time, this average student has attended school five hours a day, 180 days a year, for twelve years, to produce a total of 10,800 hours of school time. Only sleeping time surpasses television as the top time consumer.

How Teachers Can Use Television Commercials

Given that the pervading media is a powerful force, how can teachers use this for learning activities? There are many ways. Some of these will be outlined below.

Sensory Imagery

One way teachers may capitalize on television commercials is by working with children to recognize the types of imagery used in television commercials. The five senses: taste, smell, touch, sight, and sound are being played upon in every commercial. Allowing students to discover and note that in a given coffee commercial smell is predominant, for example, is a good way to start. Outcome of this could be that students devise their own "commercials" based on sensory imagery.

Form and Structure

Structure and form are also evident in television commercials. In every television commercial there is a distinct beginning, middle, and end. Letting students determine how the commercial gets started, what the middle part does, and how the "little masterpiece" ends can go a long way toward helping a youngster to understand form and structure. Naturally, by imitating this structure the student begins to get his own speech and writing under conscious control.

In the upper grades, and the middle and senior high school, a teacher might even go so far as to use a rather sophisticated structure such as that mentioned in Dr. Alan H. Monroe's *Principles and Types of Speech* (Scott, Foresman, and Company, Chicago, Atlanta, Dallas, Palo Alto, and Fair Lawn, N.J.: 1962). In this book, actually a speech book designed for college level students, there is much to learn for students and teachers in the elementary and secondary schools. One item of particular interest would be Monroe's "motivated sequence."

The motivated sequence is a formal structure, a formula, which was designed to be used to make speeches. However, an adaptation of this formula can allow even seventh graders to analyze TV commercials.

Monroe's sequence goes like this: attention, need, satisfaction, visualization, and action. In essence, when observing television commercials students should be asked:

1. How does the commercial command your attention? (attention)
2. How does the commercial establish in you a need to have or use their product? (need)
3. If you have a need for the product, how will the product satisfy your need? (satisfaction)
4. How does the visualization step work? (visualization—actually, this step is often a before and after situation, although it can often be just an "after" picture.)
5. The action step is usually a suggestion that one buy the product.

These steps are not always mutually exclusive, nor are they always in this order. However, using this structure provides an advanced way of analyzing structure.

Training Students as Critical Observers

One role which we as teachers might have in mind is to train clear thinkers, critical observers for a better society, a more observant world.

In teaching, we want the student to develop critical reading skills so that he can clearly comprehend what the author says . . . so that he can learn to distinguish between fact and opinion. If young people can come to understand that they are daily exposed to 1500 messages or more and that they must learn to survive in this kind of message world, then their learning role should become clear. Today's civilization is no longer one of the food gathering tribes of pre-history but one of information gathering and discovery.

Basic Appeal

Many writers in discussing rhetoric have written that young people should be taught to recognize and understand the major devices in media, in messages which are found not only in advertising but in the world of politics and in every facet of life today.

Commercial advertisements are most successful when they are based on *basic appeal*. Simple devices are bright splashy color or fast action, quaintness or cuteness, sex appeal, or appeals to savings (for example use of the word "free"), travel and adventure, courage and patriotism, belonging, keeping up with the new—the modern world, companionship, personal enjoyment (creature comfort), pride, independence, competition.

Sometimes "positive" appeals are used, like creating, love, pleasantness; but at times one's destructive nature is appealed to or one's anger or the thrill of horror and revulsion. Many of these techniques are centuries old. They would have been as familiar to Cicero of ancient Rome as to the practitioners of Madison Avenue.

Students might wish to explore the strategies for holding attention and influencing opinion that they find in TV commercials. Which has *Sesame Street* adopted for teaching young children? Why have they proved effective? Have the same techniques that sold cigarettes convinced people to stop smoking? How? Each student might choose a commercial and analyze his own psychological response to it. Is he responding to information about price? performance of the product? an appeal to his emotions? brand name? (Play around with brand names. Would you be more likely to buy a car called "Dragon" or "Snail"?) Students might try creating their own commercials or public service messages—preventing forest fires, supporting education, staying in school, etc., and testing their effectiveness on their classmates. Explore how ancient civilizations developed around the market place. What influence has modern man's ability to bring the market place into 96% of the nation's homes had on the development of his civilization? on the revolution in aspirations on the American scene today?

Conclusion

Teachers and students can utilize television commercials on elementary levels by exploring the use of the senses of touch, taste, smell, sight, and sound and on the simple structure of beginning, middle, and end. Advanced lessons may be explored in rhetoric using any good speech book such as Monroe's *Principles and Types of Speech*. Finally, psychological motivation may be explored by noting use of persuasive devices.

Television commercials are a part of the real world, one you can join, and which can improve classroom learning. In fact, the whole history of advertising as well as the economics of this commercial aspect can lead to a great deal of understanding and learning.

RHETORIC IN FICTION AND FILM: NOTES TOWARD A CULTURAL SYMBIOSIS

Paul D. McGlynn

FEW people would dispute that our age is dominated by the visual (or more accurately, visible) narrative. It is a commonplace of the faculty lounge that students are increasingly reluctant to make the active intellectual effort required to "appreciate" a novel; the passivity fostered by television and movies supposedly carries over to the bookshelf where students expect stories to read themselves to them in some form of learn-while-you-sleep. What insights teachers of literature are prepared to give about beginnings, middles, and ends, themes, major and minor characters, points of view, and the like, are filed as arcana in the same drawer with the old composition categories of argumentation, comparison/contrast, and the rest. There is a strong temptation for the literary man to despair and to imagine himself defending lonely outposts, surrounded in the night by movie stars, disk jockeys, television announcers, and other dangerous philistines.

The danger, it seems to me, lies more in the demoralization and consequent paranoia than in the actual situation. Faulkner's Hightower learns of "the voluptuous ego of the martyr," and we might do well to examine

⇢⇢⇢⇢⇢⇢⇢⇢⇢⇢⇢⇢⇢⇢⇢⇢⇢⇢⇢⇢⇢⇢⇢⇢⇢⇢⇢⇢⇢⇢

FROM *The English Record* (December 1970), pp. 15–22. Reprinted by permission of the publisher and the author.

our feelings of persecution a little more closely. The emotional bubble-bath is a species of quicksand we'd all be better off to avoid. There is no doubt, of course, that the movie has had a tremendous impact on our culture. And there is no doubt too that in one respect it *is* an easy form to experience: just pay your money and keep your eyes open for two hours. But our impulse to arrange a hierarchy of the arts with literature on some higher plane than the film, the distance more rigidly fixed than Ptolemy himself could have arranged, not only betrays an archaic cast of mind, but it leads to unnecessary quarrels with our culture and classroom frustrations such as I mention at the outset.[1]

A movie of any quality at all cannot, of course, be perceived passively any more than a painting, a symphony, or a novel can. It takes no specialized training to realize that a motion picture is an art form of intricate complexity, the execution of which demands the integrated skills of hundreds of professionally trained people. If a novelist reviews his every word and comma, a conscientious director considers each of the tens of thousands of frames that a feature-length film comprises. These are truisms that I suspect even the most linear-minded academicians accept in at least some dim way. We don't have to know the jargon about lenses and filters and sound synchronization to understand that an intelligent viewer must be very active indeed.

These general truths are not usually taught us through customary academic channels, however. Unless we have taken a course in film appreciation,[2] we infer them from our own experience, mostly from our college years on. And while the streets are said to be filled with youthful amateur directors, and while cinematography is supposed to be one of the current undergraduate religions, no more than .001 per cent of my own students seem to have been affected at all, let alone converted. The fact is that at an early age the American child's rattle is removed and the Saturday matinee put in its place. From his earliest years, in other words, the film is merely a diversion, and it continues to be such, perhaps for life, unless someone trains him otherwise. Popcorn and John Wayne are today's bread and circuses.

This leads to my basic point. Our purpose is, as critics and professors of literature, to heighten our students' critical understanding of literature. Few of us are inclined or technically equipped to say many expert things

1 This is not another McLuhanite argument. While I have no essential quarrel with McLuhan, I feel that his general lack of acceptance in the literary profession—I mean at the college classroom level—is due at least in part to his own intractability. He might start with his prose style. The simple declarative sentence is a medium that is also a message.

2 R. J. Monaco, in an article in *Saturday Review*, "You're Only As Young As They Think You Are," December 27, 1969, p. 15, says that only 168 American colleges or universities have one or more courses in film, and only 51 grant degrees in film production or criticism.

about film. But to respect one art is of necessity to respect all arts, which via their several media lead to the implosive and exciting experience of aesthetic pleasure, that point when we commune with the *claritas* of the art object—if McLuhan and Aquinas will forgive my saying it that way. Since we are teaching literature in the age of the film, it is eminently practical that we learn how both arts operate, how each achieves its artistic ends, how the experience of one can elucidate the experience of the other. (Two things seem to impress my own students: one is that a professor talks about movies with respect and enthusiasm, and the other is that he discusses them as critically and analytically as he does literature. I mention film in my lectures at all, of course, to illustrate aspects of literature; what I think impresses them is that when I view a film I do something with my mind while I am there. If there is any pedagogical accomplishment in this, it is that habits of intellectual analysis can be made demonstrably relevant to contemporary experience. I don't know how well I do it, but I have a hunch that to my classes I am like Dr. Johnson's dog who walks on his hind legs; they are surprised that I do it at all.) I would, however, make my point in terms of principle rather than practical classroom strategy. If we ignore this major cultural and technological phenomenon, with its indisputable influence on modern letters and the modern imagination, as members of a profession we may very soon become functionally illiterate.

The point is really quite simple. Literature and the film each employ a rhetoric analogous to the other. By "rhetoric" I mean methods of achieving effects. A directed camera is no more neutral than a directed typewriter; what Wayne Booth has said about the rhetoric of fiction applies to that of the film. The director of a movie (in effect its author) makes innumerable conscious decisions and value judgments whose sum total provides the film's unity, coherence, and emphasis, if I may borrow more antediluvian terms. Themes, characterization, ambience, and the rhythms of narrative are all affected, as they are in a novel by the author's decisions.

The film employs visual rhetoric. The world may be charged with the grandeur of God, but the visible, secular world is charged with the values we attach to it. Dickens and Shakespeare give us a pretty clear picture of what Scrooge and Falstaff look like. But why is Katharine Ross the perfect coed for *The Graduate?* Language, as far as I know, does not exist to express this particular kind of visible aptness. Is it her innocence, her youth? When she and Benjamin share their eucharistic hamburger, what is it about the way she chews that is so entirely right? Why is Billy's nervous laugh in *Easy Rider* so appropriate for this species of shady hippie? When the small boy in *Medium Cool* asks "What's so good about those shitty cars?" why do we feel that some small corner of mimetic truth has been nailed down? Realism, as any reader of Auerbach must agree, is no simple quality in fiction, but it is equally complex in the film. One difficulty is that the proper terminology has never been invented; to talk of actors projecting "inner reality" is not, after all, to say much. What *really* is the inner reality of the way Elaine Robinson chews a hamburger? Mike Nichols, presumably, knew what he wanted, elicited it, filmed it as an existential moment, and threw away the false tries.

The literary "director" does the same thing. After all, what *does* depend upon a red wheelbarrow, glazed with rainwater, beside the white chickens? Imagism is very much a photographic genre. One thinks too of Joyce's epiphanies, or of Nabokov's statement, in the afterword to *Lolita,* of his relish for certain memorable scenes in that book, or of his quick, dazzling photo-flashes in various short stories—"the awful smile of the bald man with the glasses, who had been told that his passport could not be found."[3] A movie director would call this a fast shot in a montage, and a closeup at that. The camera, through all of this, is not a neutral recorder insofar as it is aimed. Red wheelbarrows or bald men with awful smiles may be unconscious connoters of certain values, but filming such value-transmitters and arranging the footage is to be rhetorical as we have defined it. A closeup in film does what a literary closeup does, both positively and negatively: with Mrs. Robinson we see the sickness, with Benjamin the drift and despair. With Nabokov's bald man we feel terrible empathy; in Sir Plume's "earnest eyes and round, unthinking face" we see all the fatuousness of eighteenth-century London social life.

Closeup, then, we have intimate scrutiny. At a distance, we see extrinsic values of time or space brought to bear. The subject, like the questing mother in *Medium Cool,* is dominated by superior forces and movements. The cowboy is lost in the desert or among towering mountains. Nick, in *The Great Gatsby,* observes "on the green sound, stagnant in the heat, one small sail crawled slowly toward the fresher sea."[4] and Lena Grove first appears in *Light in August* against the mythic enormity of southern geography and human history. The novel of *Dr. Zhivago* gives us a greater sense of the immensity of Russia than the movie does, despite the latter's spectacle. The enormous office, with its thousands of desks and dwarfed clerks, in Orson Welles's version of *The Trial,* manages to capture what I imagine Kafka saw in a sprawling bureaucracy. Cameras also shoot from above or below. Barring simply the novelty or grotesque effect—note Anthony Perkins as desk clerk as Janet Leigh checks into the motel in *Psycho;* no Adam's apple ever looked so gothic —these shots can convey general values or impressions too, basically

3 "That in Aleppo Once," from *Spring in Fialta* (New York, 1959), p. 109.
4 New York, 1925, p. 118.

Lilliputian and Brobdingnagian. Seen from below, the human figure becomes overpowering or menacing. We think of Gulliver, or of Joseph K. being dominated by bureaucrats. Seen from above, a person is diminished, ironic; children on an archway toss pebbles on the wild bunch as they pass below.

The moving camera, or the sense of rapidity in montage, gives a sense of physical or temporal progression, like the literary effect of Odysseus's tale to the Phaeacians or Holden Caulfield's description of getting out of the "perverty" Mr. Antolini's apartment. In film, we may note Joe Buck, of *Midnight Cowboy*, getting from Texas to New York; the entire journey is not filmed any more than Odysseus gives a daily account of his seven years with Calypso, or Smollett details every inch or moment of the Brambles' journey in *Humphry Clinker*. It is the *sense* of progression that is crucial in each instance: movie sequences shot from moving cars, for example, are often filmed in slow motion so that the end result does not show too *much* speed. On the other hand, the slow-motion sequence is a device that has proved so effective that it is being made trite by overuse. One effect of slowing motion is to slow time, approximating for the viewer's imagination the apocalyptic world of the dream or wish-fulfillment, or the Grecian Urn world of static memory and nostalgia. We may recall the schoolgirl idylls in *The World of Henry Orient*, the bad trip in *Easy Rider*, or the pre-Hitler memories in *The Pawnbroker*, the movie, as far as I know, that made this technique faddish enough eventually to appear in shampoo commercials. It is used in the movie of *The Reivers* in the horserace to capture what Faulkner in the novel calls the "dreamlike indolence" of the straining horses as they change positions. Humbert remembers Lolita in slow motion, approaching to look at gifts. Slow motion in film expands our examination of *zeitgeist* the way Joyce expands Bloomsday to 768 pages: by slow painstaking awareness of detail. (Slow motion, of course, is achieved by taking *more* frames of film per second than for normal speed.) The effect is often one of nostalgia, say in *The Shop on Main Street* or *The Pawnbroker*, but not always. The final bloodbath in *Bonnie and Clyde* partakes of the dream, like some demonic ballet, but like the dream it isolates and magnifies *angst* almost to physical pain on the viewer's part. Few theatre audiences have much to say when the movie ends after this sequence. The deaths in *The Wild Bunch* become almost isolated case studies; here is how a real human being dies. We seem to see the quintessence of violence. It can be lyrical in effect or as analytical as, say, the catechism chapter in *Ulysses*. The telephoto lens can produce much the same effect, as when Benjamin is shown running straight at the camera as he rushes to "rescue" Elaine; the lens compresses distances and the effect is running without progress. All of Benjamin's frustration is captured in the one shot, just as Tod is imprisoned by a mad, suffocating society in the mob scene at the end of *The Day of the Locust*. Perhaps a more lyrical use of the telephoto lens is in *A Man and a Woman*, where racing cars and strolling couples, even ragged dogs, take on a romantic unreality. Rather than being diminished by the distance (the camera does not shoot from above) they become almost allegorical characters: Every Man and Every Woman.

Color, another aspect of film rhetoric, has its counterpart in literature, though it is difficult to define in either form, partially because, once again, the lexicon of critical terms is so inadequate. Certainly we acknowledge that color and black-and-white films are different somehow, just as novels of proletarian realism are different from western thrillers. Oddly enough, however, we are likely to associate the film western with color rendition, and the "realistic" proletarian story with black-and-white, e.g., *Sons and Lovers* or *Look Back in Anger*. Yet "real" life is in color, and absence of color perceptivity—colorblindness—is a pathological condition, cause enough to classify a man 4-F. So the counterpart of color in fiction is something like "tone" that results from an author's "vision." These terms seem inadequate, and perhaps a favorite word in freshman lit papers is better: "atmosphere."

The social ladder paralleled by Frye's scale running from romance to irony is apparently what determines the general appropriateness of color treatment. The *Odyssey* should be a color film; Joyce's *Ulysses* should not (and isn't). *Gone with the Wind* should be, and *Paths of Glory* should not. Color, in other words, suits romance. Black-and-white suits irony, a world whose reality is so harsh that it is drained of color. *Bonnie and Clyde* is developed as a ballad and ends grimly, like many ballads; it begins with the motif of the lady in the tower—Bonnie at the second-story window—and ends with dreamy death in a sylvan glade. *Elvira Madigan* is *Bonnie and Clyde* in Swedish. The Pawnbroker becomes a symbolic Christ, and thus mythical, but the black-and-white treatment entirely suits the grim setting. I am speaking in general, of course, and there are many exceptions. Color heightens the realistic irony of the forgotten individual in *Medium Cool*, like seeing the Late News in living color, and the Manhattan lyrical joy of *A Thousand Clowns* seems best without it.

Specific colors are as important in film as in literature for their symbolic or connotative values. Green is as important in *Bonnie and Clyde* as in *Portrait of the Artist as a Young Man* or *The Great Gatsby*. I would even argue that color *per se* is a central metaphor in *Blow-Up*, and I regret I do not know the South American story upon which the movie is based. The metaphor is from Newtonian optics: pure light (God? Absolute Truth? The white house on the hill over the park? The cryptic neon sign?) breaks up into spectrum colors, just as pure Truth is always perceived as particular "truths." The photographer knows his colors, but finite "truths"—photography, sex, marijuana—keep him from *the* Truth. Too bad he ignores the pictures on his walls of the sun's corona and the spectrum. *Midnight Cowboy* needs its dark neon-at-night tints, suggesting hell, just as *Elvira Madigan* needs its dappled greens and golds, suggesting youth, innocence, and blooming love.

Musical background in film works toward the same goals that color does, that is, establishing a general ambience. It seems, and in one way is, a more mechanistic device than a literary artist has at his disposal, but its integral employment is never achieved merely mechanically. Simon and Garfunkel suit the motifs of bubbling water and blooming flowers in *The Graduate*, just as "Try a Little Tenderness" is the perfect accompaniment for the copulating airplanes in *Dr. Strangelove*. Novelists cannot provide music, though they have the rhythms and sounds of language to suggest it. At his first Gatsby party, Nick observes that "The moon had risen higher, and floating in the Sound was a triangle of silver scales, trembling a little to the stiff, tinny drip of the banjoes on the lawn."[5] This, I would suggest, is simply a 1920's version of "The Sounds of Silence."

Naturally, the greatest danger in film rhetoric is the bigness and dominance of the image, just as in fiction the danger is an overwhelming interest in "what it's about." The visual impact of a broad scene or a small detail may give the viewer an exaggerated sense of its importance; this must be something that conscientious directors worry about. Subtlety on a forty-foot screen is indeed possible but easily lost. Sometimes it is lost on purpose. Consider, for example, the bombardment of visual "facts" we get in the James Bond movies. These are fun, mind you, but no one should be fooled about anything other than some kind of technical significance, such as the authenticity of sets and locations. (A few years ago, a survey of high school students indicated that *Goldfinger* was the best movie they'd ever seen.) The Bond books do the same thing:

> His two battered suitcases came and he unpacked leisurely and then ordered from Room Service a bottle of the Taittinger Blanc de Blancs that he had made his traditional drink at Royale. When the bottle, in its frosted silver bucket, came, he drank a quarter of it rather fast and then went into the bathroom and had an ice-cold shower and washed his hair with Pinaud Elixir, that prince among shampoos. . . . Then he slipped on his dark-blue tropical worsted trousers, white sea-island cotton shirt, socks and black casual shoes (he abhorred shoelaces), etc., etc.[6]

Compare this use of detail with Joyce's in *Portrait*, where every tiny gesture seems to have its organic function. Or compare the spectacular Alpine scenery in the movie of *On Her Majesty's Secret Service* with the

5 Ibid., p. 47.
6 *On Her Majesty's Secret Service* (New York, 1963), p. 19.

spectacular aerial shot of Benjamin crossing the Golden Gate bridge in *The Graduate*. One is gratuitous travelog, the other an archetypal moment in a young man's life—crossing a bridge is thematically logical, and so is showing his diminutive size from above as he moves into vast new landscapes.

This is a very general, tentative, and non-technical analysis of rhetoric in film and fiction. It is non-technical for the simple reason that I have no formal competence in the film. My profession is literature; in film I am a layman. But professors of literature can scarcely ignore this important and popular medium. For it speaks essentially the same language that we do and addresses a public that includes professors and their students. It is thus a common ground and therefore of crucial importance in a world where means of human communication sometimes seem in very short supply.

FREAKING AROUND WITH FILMS

Rodney E. Sheratsky

FILM, we have been assured by four writers under 30, is The Art That Matters.[1] Educators impressed with the truth of this and desperate to turn their students on, bought it. They announced curricula made relevant through film.

Film study and filmmaking are becoming endemic. The American Film Institute, which in part exists to foster screen education and filmmaking, lists more than 1000 teachers on its current roster.[2] Presumably, these are the Film Teachers. There are thousands more who are only film teachers. Moreover, 73 members listed in the directory advised AFI that their institutions are sponsoring filmmaking activities. . . . The question, obviously, is not how many, but how effectively, how intelligently and skillfully are these teachers using film and making film? One way of finding out is to examine the views of students themselves.

Why do students want to make films? Stefan Kanfer, film critic of *Time*, has reported some of the reasons: "Everybody's making a movie

[1] "The Art That Matters—A Look at Today's Film Scene by the Under-Thirties," *Saturday Review*, December 27, 1969, p. 7.

[2] The American Film Institute, *Educational Membership Directory 69*, Introduction.

→))
FROM *Media and Methods*, Vol. 7 (November 1970), pp. 40–42. Reprinted by permission of the publisher and the author.

. . . ,"3 "[It's] a form of artistic expression . . . ,"4 ". . . film is the most vital modern art form."5 Where will all this burst of creativity lead? "In the long run . . . the contemporary enthusiasm for student films is likely to turn out a far greater number of enlightened appreciators than new creators. That in itself could be a boon to movies; whether cinema grows as an art form depends largely upon whether film-educated audiences demand better things of it."6

Fortunately, Mr. Kanfer's article acknowledges that, because of the limitations of certain equipment and the talents of some students, not all films are excellent, imaginative, or worthy of an audience. If one doubts the notion that film "is the medium of youth"—and it is a notion that could be challenged—he should ask students why teenagers should *not* make films. After studying Film Production for four months, two high school seniors expressed it this way:

"Too many students want to major in filmmaking after their initial exposure to the medium. Although these students' first films might be excellent, only a handful of people in the world will ever become renowned for their films. Film making is a terribly expensive interest; as such, it is a fine diversion for the rich."7

"Isn't it more important for students to become involved with techniques and ideas which are absolutely essential? Frankly, making films is not essential. The majority of students could spend their time much more profitably reading about the history of man and thinking about what he has done to cause the horrible dilemmas we face. The 'film freaks' I know are 'freaks' because they know nothing about the history of ideas; all they know is the method necessary to achieve certain effects with their cameras."8

Who can reject either statement, particularly the last in which one student has implied why so many student films are failures? Without respect for the tradition of ideas, a filmmaker can think only of technique.

But, no matter how many argue against teaching students to make films, some are still going to insist that students have a right to "use" *their* medium to foster their "creative expression," even if they have nothing worth expressing. There are at least eleven types of students who should not make films. The types, by the way, were compiled by

3 Stefan Kanfer, "The Student Movie-Makers," *Film 68/69* (New York: Simon and Schuster, 1969), p. 247.

4 Ibid., p. 248.

5 Op. cit.

6 Ibid., p. 252.

7 A survey, "Why High School Students Should Not Study Film Making," conducted at the Center for Film Production, Northern Valley Regional High School at Demarest, Demarest, New Jersey.

8 Ibid.

high school seniors who completed the first half of a two semester course, Film Production. Who should not study film making? Students . . .

1. Who are not willing to admit their films do not have even adequate photography and lighting.

2. Who habitually announce projects they are not intellectually capable of fulfilling.

3. Who cannot work alone. ("Much of what is good in a student's film is the result of working alone, during those periods in a project when the work is tedious," cautioned one senior.)

4. Who insist that a good film can be made only after a committee of seven, eight, or more designs and approves every phase of the project.

5. Who are irresponsible, lazy, and undisciplined.

6. Who do not respect the equipment (cameras, editor-viewers, lights, and exposure meters) and budgets they have been permitted to use.

7. Who want to make films because they cannot read or write.

8. Who think they have become "expert" filmmakers just because they have learned the elementary techniques of filmmaking.

9. Who cannot realize that their films are hopelessly inept, boring, and banal.

10. Who want to make films because filmmaking is "in."

11. Who do not have an appreciation and a feeling for life.[9]

There is a very practical reason to discourage students from making films. The reason was suggested by a poet, working on a screenplay for Warner Brothers:

> The question remains: how many will get a chance? A person can become a great poet in the privacy of his home, accumulate twenty or thirty years' worth of manuscripts and bitterness, and, perhaps, finally have his day. A filmmaker without the machinery for making films can accumulate only twenty or thirty years of bitterness. It is a conceit of the successful that talent will out. However, as there are always so many incompetents among the successful, it seems clear that there are no doubt many gifted people among the failures. "You have to sell yourself," says Steven Gaines. "In the end, it's luck," says Jeff Young.[10]

The writer, of course, referred to those who hope to work in The Film Industry. What about those who want to work independently? Or those who insist on making their films their way, The Establishment be damned? Or those independents, members of the American underground whose work has the look of Home Movies rather than "real" movies?

There are still other practical questions to answer before a high school encourages students to make films. Who will teach filmmaking—the En-

9 Ibid.

10 R. J. Monaco, "You're Only As Young As They Think You Are," *Saturday Review*, December 27, 1969, p. 17.

glish teacher who has never made a film? The art teacher who has been trained in the visual arts? Graduate students of film schools? (Because professional filmmakers do not have the time to teach on a regular daily or weekly basis, graduate students could be trained to teach high school students. This is a suggestion the American Film Institute could explore. If those who have no training in film decide they are capable of teaching filmmaking, a Fad of the Sixties will pass into oblivion during the Seventies.)

Is there, then, no reason to teach high school students to make films? Yes, there is, but it does not pertain to any of the dramatic, fashionable, grandiose reasons cited and questioned previously. Indeed, the reasons for teaching filmmaking are so basic, they might seem blatantly obvious. Still, it might refresh teachers to analyze the obvious before they announce the grandiose. A giant of early documentary cinema can help us.

At the summary session of the 1969 Robert Flaherty Film Seminar, Mrs. Frances Flaherty, a woman dedicated to preserving her husband's memory and passing on to a younger generation the heritage of her husband's art, reminded 75 filmmakers, teachers, librarians, and students of Pudovkin's charge, "The basic aim of cinema is to teach people to see all things new."[11] Later, she quoted the French philosopher de Chardin, "To see more is to become more. Deeper seeing is closer union . . . to see or to perish is man's condition."[12]

In the remarkable study film for *Louisiana Story*, Mrs. Flaherty reminisces, "Bob always used to say that the camera is a seeing machine. And the job of the director is to help the viewer discover and explore for himself." Robert Flaherty's idea is striking. Yet, the documentarian's point raises some complex questions. If the camera is a seeing machine, whose sight is more crucial—the operator's or the viewer's? If it is the camera's operator who is seeing, then how can we be certain that his seeing machine will work if he does not have Flaherty's confidence in an audience astute and willing enough to want to discover and explore? If the camera is a seeing machine, should the photographer and director record every reality they feel the audience should see? And what about the camera and the functions we have expected art to fulfill—namely, to communicate ideas and emotions? To organize life into meaningful patterns? To make order out of chaos? To reveal universal truths through the self-imposed individuality of the artist? What becomes the function of the seeing machine when one renounces these traditional beliefs about art's functions? Suppose one accepts, instead, composer John Cage's argument that art is meaningful only when it is born of chance and indeterminancy? Cage believes the artist must work to make discoveries

11 Robert Flaherty Film Seminar, August 26–September 2, 1969, The Hotchkiss School, Lakeville, Connecticut. Remarks made September 2, 1969.
12 Op. cit.

in his daily life. Only chance will open to us possibilities we could never realize if we accepted only another person's notions of life and art.[13]

But what about students and the seeing machine? In too many of our high schools, students will graduate without ever having been taught how to see. That is deplorable. Rightfully, we train our students how to read, write, think, listen, and speak. Although our more aware schools encourage students to use reading machines, tape recorders, slide, over-head and movie projectors, too many neglect to cultivate their student's visual perception. By the time they have been graduated from high schools, too many students are visually illiterate. Many of our students look, yet do not see. Work with high school seniors who have just begun film projects and you will understand why the old saying, "They have eyes, yet see not," is a cliché. It's a cliché because it's true for so many people in so many places. Unless students have been made aware of the process of visual perception, how can they help their audiences to see the phenomena they have arranged to have projected on the screen?

We have seen how today's magazines report the development of high school filmmaking activities throughout the country. Some educators claim that, when students have convincingly demonstrated throughout their high school years that the book and pens they have been using are purposeless, a camera might help unsatisfied students to develop images of themselves that will increase their self respect. Or, to state it another way, because film is supposed to "turn kids on," it is instant panacea. This justification for filmmaking should be questioned by all who deplore the use of any art form as a device to "save" people. Rodger Larson, Jr., with his students in New York City's ghettoes, would be the first to admit that his students do not make films for therapy. They make films because they are so committed to the art that they are willing to work ten hours for each minute of film that is eventually projected on the screen. The students, whose films project unbelievably vital reactions to life, are fiercely dedicated. They want their films screened not because they reflect people whose lives have been saved by film. They want their films screened because they are valid, important works which have become so because of the talent, intelligence, and stamina necessary for their creation.

Others believe that the camera provides us with a machine that can cultivate, sharpen, and deepen our powers of seeing. When students have cultivated these powers, then they can help to fulfill the Flaherty ideal: helping viewers discover and explore. In addition to helping students learn how to see, a filmmaking program can help students to make patterns. The intelligent making of patterns depends upon one's intelligent manipulation of materials to express the patterns.

[13] John Cage, "45' for a Speaker," *Silence* (Cambridge, Massachusetts: The M.I.T. Press, 1967), pp. 146–193.

What about the patterns in student-made films? What assignments can students be given which will help them to cultivate visual awareness and make patterns which connect with ideas and points in the film?

After they have been taught and shown why it is important to care for and clean their cameras, as well as projectors and other pieces of equipment, students might shoot the following assignments. The assignments are basic; they're also necessary if students are going to approach their work with care, thought, and discipline. Each assignment is for one roll of film.

1. Select an area with definite boundaries (a room, a house, a street, a field). With images and lighting, capture the atmosphere of that space. Emphasize good lighting, sharp focus, and meaningful framing. Keep the camera stationary. Use a tripod. Do not pan, tilt, or zoom.

2. Return to the area used for the first assignment. In addition to shooting for the same specifications, use such camera movements as the pan, tilt, or zoom.

3. Shoot a person leaving for and arriving at his destination. Stress continuity and character motivation so the audience understands how and why the individual travels from point to point.

4. Edit the exercise in continuity.

5. Shoot two persons conversing. Do not rely on recorded sound, obvious signals, or titles. Rely, instead, on significant gestures so the audience understands the topic of the conversation.

6. Edit the conversation exercise.

7. Shoot a one minute commercial. Rely on striking images, sounds, and lighting to "sell" the product.

8. Select a composer whose last name begins with B (Bach, Beatles, Beethoven, Bernstein, Brubeck, etc.) Choreograph and edit the movement of the images to the music of the composer.

During the remaining weeks of the course, students may work on "longer" projects (about 10–20 minutes). After students have selected the ideas for their films, they may submit treatments, scripts, or storyboards before they shoot. (Incidentally, the technical crew should have no more than a director, cameraman, and editor. If too many students are assigned to a project, those who are not actively involved will lose interest.) Ask students to screen their unedited rushes so others may comment about the quality of the shooting and the possibilities for final editing.

Instant success and recognition cannot be promised to anyone who makes films; indeed, the teacher who promises and expects instant rewards contributes to one of the more generic deficiencies of the under-25 generation.

Robert Flaherty did not use his seeing machine for instant purposes. During a thirty-year career as a filmmaker, Flaherty made only four feature length films. Today, *Nanook of the North, Moana, Man of Aran,* and *Louisiana Story* still seem in advance of their day. A man committed to the ideal that a filmmaker must help the audience to discover phenomena, he knew one does not learn how to see instantly. One learns how to see after much careful and thoughtful work with his camera. The goals of a filmmaking program—to help students see and encourage them to make meaningful patterns—are modest. And yet, properly realized, these are goals one can spend a lifetime trying to fulfill.

Introducing students to an awareness of the essentials required for seeing may well be the only realistic, honest, and sensible reason for encouraging students to make films. On the high school level, all one can—and should—do is introduce students to an awareness of the essentials required for seeing. A high school filmmaking program should not become a professional filmmaking school. Why? Most public schools cannot compete with the facilities many colleges and university film departments offer their students. If a high school teacher encourages his students to think they are filmmakers on the basis of one course in filmmaking, he's as dishonest as his colleague who tells a child, "My! Only someone with your rare talent could have made this work of art," when the work of "art" was thoughtlessly conceived and artlessly completed. During the Sixties we have witnessed the damage done by such dishonest, though well intentioned, teachers who were more concerned with protecting the child's ego than with cultivating his intellect and artistic talent. Film critic Pauline Kael has questioned the results: "Did anyone guess or foresee what narcissistic confidence this generation would develop in its banal 'creativity?' Now we're surrounded, inundated by artists. And a staggering number of them wish to be or already call themselves 'filmmakers'."[14]

---

[14] Pauline Kael, "Movie Brutalities," *Kiss Kiss Bang Bang* (Boston: Little, Brown and Company, 1968), p. 17.

FILM AND THE MEDIA (R)EVOLUTION

David J. Powell

As film study has found its way into more schools at many levels, so the nature of the study has been changed, bent and sometimes wrenched into ever more complex patterns. To present any kind of coherent picture of film study or courses has become virtually impossible. Courses now range from film history to multi-sensory environmental awareness. Each variation uses film to a greater or lesser degree and most refer to the relevant nature of film as a medium—justification for offering the course.

Film has its own history for it now boasts historic individuals and movements. But it has also been a revolutionary new vehicle of expression and a vehicle for revolutionary expression. Film is caught up in revolutions. It is part of the revolution in communication and of revolutionary innovations in education.

There can be no one endorsed or approval-sealed way of teaching or learning about film. Film must find a place in education for itself and not for its relation to literature or as a substitute for social experience. Therefore, arguments that seek to assert film-as-medium-of-expression over film-as-art approaches to teaching are only examples of the desire of educators to defend territorial aspirations. Clarification lies not in choosing between rivals but in understanding the many ways film functions in the experience of the individual and within the total pattern of communication used by mankind. This task is complicated by the fact that film is still evolving as a medium and there is much that remains to be known about the nature and effects of film.

It is helpful to look at the role of film in a recently-completed project. The North Reading Screen Education Project was a two-and-a half-year project funded by the U.S. Office of Education in June 1967. The project offered a series of courses at the senior high level and a small experimental course at the sixth-grade level. Film was studied as a form of experience, as an expressive tool of communication, as a mirror of society and its concerns, and as an art form in which structural phenomena and experiences common or analogous to the other arts could be found. Most of the courses stressed production, active involvement and group work.

Films were viewed, discussed, scripted, shot, and shown. In order that the nature of the "Image Language" could be more thoroughly ex-

FROM *Audiovisual Instruction* (January 1971), pp. 29–31. Reprinted by permission of the Association for Educational Communications and Technology and the author.

perienced, understood and practiced, still photography, recording and television were also part of the courses offered. A great deal of direct and indirect feedback was obtained from the students on the nature of their experiences and their reactions to them.

Many of the results and activities that resulted were expected prior to the start of the project. Students completed the courses; the courses became both sought after and more demanding. Students who had found little success in verbal modes regained confidence in the ability to express themselves. Most students' self-knowledge increased or became a more reasonable assessment of their personality and manner of working. The traditional structures of grades proved inadequate or impossible yardsticks in the screen education classes.

Some students abused new-found liberties, and others wasted much time in fruitless pursuits. The initial structuring of the courses and use of equipment led to frustrating delays or periods of rushed work. The preponderance of non-academic students led to strategies of learning and an overall image that tended either to repel or to encourage easy dismissal of the courses by other more academic students. The majority of problems were corrected with time or required other changes within the total environment set by the school and its parent system.

There were a number of results that point toward the nature and the extent of the presently confused role that film study has in education. A number of changes were manifest in the students themselves. Many expressed strong preferences for the experiential mode of the screen education courses. There were many instances of a redefining of the student's relationship with the authority of a teacher or administrator. In most cases this was a change helpful to the student. In addition, several students professed having found a new and happier perspective on their necessary involvement with school.

The work of the project also affected the school itself. The free-wheeling nature of the student activities led to sharp criticism from some of the faculty and, at times, polarized this already divided body. Indeed, screen education became the whipping boy for those threatened by the movement toward student's rights and participation. The courses provided valuable experiences for those students who had become mental, if not physical, dropouts. The restrictions imposed by schedules and physical plant were able to change despite their immutable appearance. The school moved away from the normal running-down-to-a-halt finish to the year into a series of activities planned and run by students themselves. Much of this initiative came from the Project and its structures of student responsibility. This reflected the interdisciplinary nature of much of the work done in the Project. Boundary lines between subjects became less meaningful, and it was clear that screen education or film study could not be part of any one discipline, nor become a subject cut off from any others. The role of the teacher changed from the traditional fount-of-all-wisdom posture to that of knowledgeable facilitator. The change was not easy and made very stringent demands upon the teachers' skills and understanding of themselves.

The results of the Project suggest a number of things. First, film leads inexorably to involvement with other media, other disciplines and society as a whole. The realization of media as a social tool came later in the Project and particularly in the case of film as a way of bringing about adult awareness and understanding of youth. Second, we need to give more weight to the experience that students bring with them to schools—the nature of learning has changed from a process of gaining knowledge of facts to learning how to learn. Third, the highly-structured human and physical environments of the schools tend to work against the process of growth and development. All of these point toward changes in the role of the teacher and the knowledge and skills that are needed in the profession. Many of these conclusions are revolutionary to many educators; all are evolutionary within the changing patterns of communication experienced and used by the young, regardless of their experiences in formal education.

We have been told that "movies turn kids on," or that "filmmaking/ picture making gets the kids writing," or "the urban kid can attack his environment with a camera." All of these may or may not be true, but none of them is more than naive enthusiasm. At another level, all these statements or their elaborations do emphasize that the increased use of film has gone to the heart of the contemporary educational malaise— namely, the lack of youth involvement in the processes of our life as they sit in the school or roam its corridors. Such statements offer false hope that film will cut through the confusion of education and reach the disaffected by merely turning out the lights and turning on the projector. Unfortunately, such statements do not indicate the need for skilled, knowledgeable teachers and administrators versed in the pros and cons of film study. Film courses can rapidly become yet another journey through the acknowledged classics or a frustrating melange of hasty encounters with poorly selected equipment that fails to produce the promised new world of vision.

Film's legacy is a dual one. First there are the "experiments that failed" and the courses that stopped "when the bond issue didn't go through." Second are the thoughtful and exploratory programs that have evolved a coherent design and a clear place in the curriculum. We are entering a new phase of courses in film and in media that avoid past pitfalls and are designed with close regard for the students and what is known about the nature of media and how they may be studied. These approaches respond to the kinds of understandings that experiments like the North Reading Project have provided about the nature of teaching and learning film and other media. They reflect recent discussions of the complex relationship linking communication, technology and social structures. A brief view of some of these recent ideas is necessary to see how they emerge in current educational theory and practice found in film and media programs.

The mounting concern for the quality of our physical environment has begun to provide new ways of thinking about the information environment. The concept of the ecosystem in which total elements cohere organically and interdependently has spawned a new concept of the ecology of communication. This concept stresses that all our systems of communication—personal, public, biological, mechanical, electronic, direct and symbolic—interpenetrate and constitute a continuously experienced whole that is both rational and non-rational. The media are most closely representative of this wholeness. They embrace many modes of communication and expression—visual image, spoken and written words, gesture, facial expression, sound image. The ecological nature of communication may be most directly experienced and comprehended through such media.

Another key development is the arrival of a new generation of tools accessible to many people. These are information tools. They allow not only the recording and later presentation of experience, but also the immediate and restructured presentation of that experience. Photography, films and recordings provided records of events but had little ability to re-order or restructure those events in relation to one another. Films and sound recordings may be easily edited into unique, coherent sets of images. Videotape provides an instant visual and audio record of events. Slide tapes allow the selective juxtapositioning of visual and audio images. Prior to this development, most individuals were consumers of such media and in those cases where production was possible, it was primitive compared with the manipulative possibilities of the media industries. Thus, there was little chance to do anything more than experience the perceptions and expression of the few working in these media.

We can now obtain easy access to or possession of the new second-generation tools and use them to make our own statements, simple or complex, about our most immediate environment. The next generation of tools will make possible the re-ordering and restructuring of conceptual designs and systems. This will move us toward news ways of perceiving processes of complex events or ecosystems. Our tools of communication will increasingly allow us to structure and restructure experience in ways that will be more closely representative of the organic and seamless nature of man in his environment.

These simplified views of future developments are not offered as recommended goals for the teacher of films or media. Ideas of this kind made into goals do not of themselves provide viable guidelines for practice. The real value of these ideas lies in showing the emerging pluralism of practice in film teaching from a natural and inevitable movement toward a new balance within the total pattern of communication experienced and used by the young. The character of this movement resists absolutes or immutable standards. It must be clear to students that they must be primarily concerned with investigating and extending their own experience. The freedom to question through experiment and playing with the process must be encouraged and made possible by the kind of environment created around the students. In this way, it is possible to provide the kind of opportunity the student needs in order to learn how to learn. We must agree that the ultimate goals of the student are at the outset unknown to us and to him; and that whatever they may be, they cannot be constrained by the limits of the teacher's own knowledge and abilities.

In designing and evaluating the kinds of activities that occur, the following guidelines provide a possible framework:

1. The nature of the medium will and must influence your goals and use of time and materials.

2. The nature of student experience is different from your own and those who write about film. A current film may be an important experience to students at this point in their growth, but be a minor film in other respects.

3. Communication is an organic whole, an ecosystem. Film may reveal concepts about the nature of sound that require experiments with sound alone.

4. The use of tools of expression (the pen, the camera, the brush) is a means to an end and not an end in itself. Insisting on visuals always in focus may prevent important discoveries about other kinds of images.

5. The emphasis should be on changing or modifying not the student, but the environment.

6. The environment should be responsive and interactive at the human and physical levels. It should be possible to work outside the classroom and with other non-teaching personnel in response to a student's needs.

7. Wherever possible, active involvement in the process, or in bringing about change, should be the learning mode.

8. Many activities should seek to make the strange familiar and the familiar strange.

These guidelines are directed toward using the as yet partial knowledge of film and other media in a way that will make use of the evolutionary and revolutionary nature of such particularly when used by the students themselves.

Written Composition

FOR *a number of years the National Council of Teachers of English has recommended that the typical load for a teacher of secondary school English be four classes containing fewer than 100 students. One of the primary justifications underlying this recommendation is the awareness of NCTE that the reading of student-written papers consumes an unbelievable amount of time. If teachers have more than four classes with more than 100 students, then either they assign fewer compositions or they spend far too much of their professional time in checking comma faults and spelling errors. The former practice is the more common: Teachers require fewer written themes.*

Recently, however, teachers of English have come to realize that what precedes the writing may be as important as what follows it. The kinds of assignments given, the pre-writing discussions, and the revision prior to ultimate evaluation lead not only to improved student writing but also to a reduction in the amount of time required for evaluation. Good themes, those which students have written after extensive discussion and with considerable revision, may be gotten through more quickly than can those hastily written, uninspired, and uninspiring rough drafts created by students who are simply told "Go, thou, and write."

It is in accordance with this philosophy, that what comes before the writing is as important as what follows it, that the selections in this section were chosen. Larson advocates a nongraded composition program that includes "a continuous succession of writing tasks for which the student must carefully develop specified abilities." Bacig offers a basis for composition grounded in humanistic thought. Hartig's article explores students' attitudes and purposes in writing, two aspects of the total composition process about which teachers of English regularly operate with false assumptions. The next two selections suggest techniques of developing student competency in writing style; Gaston's with the use of literature and Demarest's with the use of slang and profanity. The final two selections discuss evaluation. Stratta, one of the leaders in English education in Great Britain, offers some solid "considerations." Maughan discusses what must be the ultimate evaluation, that by the students themselves.

TOWARD A NON-GRADED PROGRAM IN ENGLISH COMPOSITION

Richard L. Larson

UNLIKE most other elements in the English curriculum, indeed in the entire high school curriculum, the work in written composition is intended to help students achieve successful *performance*, not simply cognitive knowledge (as in the study of language) or sensitivity in the understanding of others' writing (often the goal of the study of literature).

Yet, in designing curricula, teachers of English often overlook this objective. Since other elements in the English curriculum are concerned with teaching substantive information and techniques for analyzing literary texts—information and techniques that can be divided among several grades for teaching—teachers find it convenient to divide the study of composition into separate steps and procedures that can be assigned arbitrarily to different grades, despite the fact that successful performance in composition is the writing of a complete, effective piece, not just the mastering of discrete "steps."

For the sake of convenience, teachers overlook the fact that a student's progress in composition is measured by his ability to perform increasingly complex writing tasks; to produce, that is, complete pieces of increasing complexity. Instead they determine a student's progress by whether he has covered particular concepts and can execute certain procedures (define a term, invent a metaphor, compose a three-paragraph theme) that have been assigned to be taught in his grade. If he has discussed and practiced these procedures, he advances to the next grade, irrespective of whether he can solve the problems he faces when he must address a complete statement to a specified audience on a particular subject.

When the student, having discussed the concepts and practiced the steps assigned by the curriculum to his grade, moves into the next grade, he may face rhetorical problems and writing assignments that he is not equipped to handle. Sensing his inadequacies, the teacher in that grade may consider it necessary to instruct him again in the concepts, procedures, and "principles of grammar" that were treated in earlier grades.

->>>

FROM *Bulletin of the National Association of Secondary School Principals*, Vol. 54 (September 1970), pp. 22–32. Reprinted by permission of the publisher and the author.

Repetitious, Trivial, Irrelevant

When, as is often the case, this whole process repeats itself through three or four successive grades, the student can be excused for feeling that instruction in writing is repetitious, trivial, and irrelevant to the job that a writer faces—that of producing forceful, complete pieces for his readers. These feelings, in turn, lead to indifference about writing—and this attitude may result in performance that seems to confirm the teacher's suspicion: the student did not learn what he should have learned before he reached that teacher's class.

The repetition of what was not learned in earlier grades continues, and the study of composition seems increasingly tedious. Conversely, the student who is ready to attempt fairly complex rhetorical performances before some of his fellow-students are ready for them may find the teacher in his grade unprepared to accept them or to respond intelligently to them. As a result, his progress in composition is unnecessarily slowed.

None of the more popular instructional and curricular reforms in composition today eliminates this exigency of the student's being moved along grade by grade, more on the strength of accomplishments in other parts of the curriculum than composition. The suggestion that writing be presented to students as an act of discovering one's voice, even oneself, in the expression of meaningful personal experiences or observations, is no doubt a valuable concept in the making of assignments, but it does not address the problem of how to measure the student's progress, nor does it suggest what to do with the student whose progress is slow. And composition is still seemingly the same subject, year after year.

The curriculum with an articulated sequence of writing assignments for each grade—popular today among curriculum writers—still moves the student to the next grade (and the next sequence of assignments) without considering how successful he has been in mastering the problems presented to him in the previous grade. And the "spiral" curriculum, which repeats assignments that are increasingly demanding in successive grades, is no improvement over the kind of curriculum which emphasizes separate steps and procedures (first discussed in this article), unless the individual student can get off the spiral into instructional programs that suit his own pace in learning.

Reducing Student Frustration

There may be no way to end frustration for teachers and students of composition, short of completely individualized instruction. But that is an administrative impossibility in virtually every school, and the authors of learning programs have yet to produce a program by which the student can learn composition entirely at his own pace. Yet it *is* possible to eliminate the frustration felt by a student who has been moved forward, on the basis of tests in literature and language, to a class where he cannot do the work in composition. And it is also possible to reduce or eliminate the frustrations felt by students who are making superior progress but remain in the same "grade" with unsuccessful students because assignment to a grade is based on tests passed, facts learned, and procedures practiced. Frustrations that result from administrative organization of the classes, that is, can be reduced.

The way to reduce them is to abandon organizing the composition program by grades. Instead of automatically moving the student into the next grade if his average mark on all parts of English is deemed passing, make a separate determination of his progress in composition, and then decide whether he needs further practice in the kinds of composing he has recently been attempting. If he needs this practice, assign him to a class in which he will get it. And, as a corollary, instead of demanding that the student remain a full year (or semester) in a class that is practicing activities a student has mastered or can master quickly, arrange for that student to move on to the next group of tasks, more difficult and challenging than those which other students of his age may still have to work on.

In other words, the secondary school curriculum in composition can be designed as a continuous succession of writing tasks for which the student must carefully develop specified abilities. The student must be moved along the succession only as rapidly as he can learn what is required in order to accomplish these tasks. The tasks should be complete pieces of writing, not exercises in isolated procedures.

Several objections, of course, can be made against such a proposal. Composition, one could argue, is not the only subject in the English curriculum, nor is the course in composition a separate course in the school. Most schools expect that particular works of literature, and critical concepts, will be assigned in a given grade, and some schools specify information about language and techniques of reading to be acquired in each grade.

Other Studies Pose Problems

To design the English curriculum around work in composition, and advance students on the basis of their achievements in composition, would make it possible for a student who progresses rapidly in composition to bypass other required studies in the English curriculum—a consequence many teachers of English might be unwilling to accept even as a price for a more honest, reasonable program in composition.

Furthermore, a curriculum based on composition would require students who were not progressing well in writing to repeat the literature and language curriculum of a given class while they were continuing on the same problems in composition—or so the objectors might argue.

In addition, if teachers were to specialize in teaching particular segments of the composition curriculum, a non-graded program would demand a good deal of flexibility in the assignment of students to teachers. A student might be moved at any time during the year from one teacher to another, as he completed the program taught by the first teacher and became ready for the material offered by the second. Finally, such a proposal does away with the opportunity for neat recording of semester or quarter marks; indeed, evaluation of a student in the non-graded curriculum would simply consist of determining what point in the composition program he had reached at the end of a year and, perhaps, comparing the student's rate of progress with what might be identified as a "typical" rate of progress achieved by students at that age.

These problems make the adoption of a non-graded program in composition, however attractive in theory, most difficult in practice. If the theoretical justification is sound, however, some sort of compromise program might well be sought—one that takes advantage as fully as possible of non-grading while avoiding some or all of its attendant difficulties. One such compromise is currently being tested in a high school in Hawaii that enrolls students with a variety of backgrounds, from the children of military families that have traveled widely to the children of Samoan immigrants who have hardly traveled at all and whose command of English is tenuous at best. The school also has a substantial turnover of English teachers each year. It is by no means a school advantageously situated to try out new curricular plans.

The compromise, though encouraged by the school's administration, is largely the work of teachers in the department of English. The teachers regard it as their own curriculum and want to make it succeed. Teachers report that students appear to like the new curriculum, and to find composition at least not as onerous as it had been under earlier instructional plans.

Modules of Instruction

In this school, the program in composition is divided into seven modules, each module designed to require at least one semester's work of all but a very few students. Each module stipulates its objectives—the levels of accomplishment students are expected to reach before they can be said to have completed the module. In addition to this statement of objectives, the description of each module contains a list of writing assignments that will help students attain those objectives. The assignments designated in each module are sufficiently general that teachers may use the same assignment several times, in reference to different subjects; some ask the student to write about language or semantic problems; others require him to write about literary works; still others ask him to write about personal experience, observation, or reading.

The modules are sequentially arranged, so that the objectives and associated writing assignments in module two are more demanding than those in module one, and so on. In each module, appropriate assignments are given in approximate order of difficulty, "difficulty" being defined, in the absence of firm data about the kinds of tasks that give the greatest trouble to students, by the number of logical and rhetorical steps required for completion of the assignment. For example, an assignment requiring the student to describe an object, compare it with a similar object, and evaluate the two objects on stated criteria would be more "difficult" than one that required only description of one object or one that required comparison simply for the sake of giving the reader a complete and clear understanding of both objects.

Given the varied subject matter of the suggested assignments, it is not possible to say for sure that the assignment listed tenth in one module is demonstrably more difficult for all students than the assignment listed fifth. Some assignments, indeed, are probably suitable to different modules; it is not necessary that each assignment in the upper modules be more difficult than all of those in the lower modules. Relatively uncomplex assignments can sometimes help students as much to reach the level of achievement required by a module as can more complex assignments.

Nor is all of the work in module three, for example, necessarily more difficult than the work at the end of module two. The early assignments in one module may indeed, on the definition given, be less "difficult" than those at the end of the previous module. But later modules are, on the whole, manifestly more demanding than the earlier ones, and indeed the work suggested for the seventh module is as difficult as, or more difficult than, that in most college freshman courses in composition.

Initial Testing

The program operates as follows: Students entering the school—most are ninth-graders, though children of military families may enter at any point in the high school program—take objective tests in reading and composing, and are assigned initially to a module on the basis of their test scores. (Scores on tests currently available may not be the best measures of the students' competence in writing. Placement might be more exact if students wrote a brief test theme, but the duties of teachers do not now allow them time to read such themes and establish standards in advance of registration.)

If their performance on early assignments in that module indicates the need for a different placement, students may be moved forward into a more advanced module or backward into a less advanced one. Once assigned, a student remains in his module until, in the judgment of his teacher, he has met the requirements for advancement from that module. He may remain in one module for several semesters.

If the student spends more than one semester in a module, he works with different teachers in the second and later semesters. These teachers apply the theme assignments suggested for that module to different subjects, so that the student does not simply feel that he is repeating himself. Teachers handling sections that include many students who are repeating a module meet with teachers whose sections include students new to the module, to choose literary texts and language materials for the "repeater" sections, in order to ensure that students do not repeat the same texts semester after semester.

But if the student's progress in his module is rapid, he may be moved ahead to the next module at any time up to half-way through the semester. Moving a student ahead late in a semester might send him into a class that has had considerable practice in more advanced work and would probably do the student so moved very little good; hence, the stipulation that no student may ordinarily be moved ahead after the mid-point of a semester. Thus, no student is moved ahead in the study of composition faster than his progress warrants. But the talented student, especially one who is placed at module three or four when he enters the school and moves along one module per semester, may complete the required program in composition during or before his final year in school, and may proceed to independent study or tutorial work, or may even take university courses if his schedule permits. On the other hand, modules one and two are essentially remedial, designed for students whose work in composition before high school has been minimal or whose level of accomplishment is relatively low.

Increased Emphasis on Writing

In day-to-day classroom work, the teachers in this school almost inevitably give more attention than many teachers now do to the student's work in composition. Instead of assigning exercises and drills in rhetorical techniques and the construction of sentences, the teacher assigns complete compositions that are increasingly demanding, all of which require the student to accomplish a specific purpose. Assignments are chosen from the list of suggestions, or the teacher offers a comparable assignment of his own. To assist the student in facing the problems in each assignment, to help him with the development of ideas as well as an organizational plan, the teacher must allow time for pre-writing activities, including extensive discussion of the subject to be treated.

To help students see the need for improvement in their work, and to develop in them the power to make judgments about it, the class engages in considerable discussion of student papers. Class discussion helps to guide the writer, when revision of his assignment is required. Since the curriculum for each module also includes the study of literature and language, the teacher makes writing assignments based on the work in language and literature, thereby assuring that students will study these subjects more thoroughly than they might for factual tests or even for tests involving short essays. Discussion of literary texts often culminates in a writing assignment. Thus, the work in composition supports, instead of supplants, the study of other elements of English.

Although the implication of this program is that a student's progress in English is defined by his performance in composition, authorities at this high school are prepared to accept this definition because they regard skill in composing as the most important single skill their students should acquire from the English curriculum. Even so, the program does not lead to neglect of literature and language. Some periods of English and American literature and some concepts in language are assigned for presentation to students in each module, but literary texts to be read, and anthologies to be used, vary from teacher to teacher.

The student who leaves a module at mid-semester may miss some of the work of that module, but such a student might reasonably be encouraged, and counted upon, to do some of this reading on his own. The student who remains in a module more than one semester, as previously noted, is almost sure to read different texts and be exposed to different ways of approaching these texts. Composition assignments and exercises in writing about literature within each module assure that all students practice responding to literature and engage in analysis, interpretation, and evaluation of suitable texts.

The program also responds to some of the other objections raised earlier to complete non-grading. Since most movement from module to module occurs at well-defined times, there is no need for the kind of flexibility required if each student moved at exactly his own pace and could change classes at any time during the semester. The number of sections needed in each module can be predicted with good reliability from semester to semester, and the number of students moving within a semester is not normally large enough to cause serious attrition or overload in any one section.

The Matter of Grading

Finally, marks need not be given for composition—an activity in which reliable grading is notoriously difficult to achieve. If marks on the report card are needed, they can be based mainly on the student's work in literature, language, and (where required) reading skills, as well as the overall quality of his work in composition. For students who move from one module to another within a semester, the teachers can consult with each other in determining a report card rank. Whether or not the student receives his diploma can still be based on attendance, effort, and achievement in literature and language. The school does not now require students to complete a specified number of modules in composition in order to graduate, although it could institute such a requirement if it wished.

The success of this program—its effect on the performance of students graduating from this high school—is yet to be measured, of course, since the program has been in operation only two years. But the program has already enjoyed one kind of success: it has been put to work spiritedly and enthusiastically, despite the readjustments in scheduling and teaching technique it demands, by the teachers in the school. Indeed, so committed are the teachers to the program that they may prefer it to the secondary portion of the state-wide curriculum in English for grades K-12 currently envisaged by planners (many of them university faculty and experienced secondary teachers from the mainland) at the State Department of Education's Curriculum Development Center.

In teachers' attitudes toward the program at this high school lie several lessons for administrators who would prefer, if they could get it, the honesty of a non-graded program over traditional curricula in composition. First, though the administration may take the lead—may *have* to take the lead—in moving the school toward a non-graded program in composition, the adoption of such a program, indeed of any new curriculum, must be the deliberate decision of English teachers at the school, after the implications of such a program have been thoroughly explained. The teachers described in this essay were encouraged by the principal and his deputy—who had had previous experience with non-graded English—to consider the possibility of installing a non-graded program. But the school decided to develop its program only after careful consultations involving teachers, the department chairman, all school administrators, and members of the state university faculty.

Second, even if university specialists are brought to the school to assist with development of the program, these specialists should not simply write the program and hand it to the teachers, nor should they try to implant a curriculum written for another school faculty and student body. Each school, each student body, is different from most others, and new curricula must reflect the unique features of that school. Decisions about the pace of a non-graded (or any other kind of) curriculum, about the kinds of performance to be expected of students finishing each part of the curriculum, and the kinds of assignments to be built into the program, must be fundamentally the decisions of teachers who will use that program when it is finished.

The Teachers' Role

It was the teachers in the Hawaii high school—in consultation with university specialists—who decided the content of each module and the quality of performance that will permit the student to exit from that module. It was the teachers, in particular, who recognized the need for a couple of modules of essentially remedial instruction—instruction designed for students whose elementary and intermediate programs in writing had been non-existent, sketchy, or ineffective. It was the teachers who contributed most of the assignments included in the several modules. The role of the outside advisers was limited to asking questions, clarifying and arranging assignments, and seeing to final duplication of the program materials.

Two other steps are necessary to the introduction of a new program of this sort. If, as was true in the Hawaii school, annual turnover of teachers is high, the curriculum design and instructional emphases must be complete and clear enough to be understood by new teachers coming into the school. And the administration must give what help is necessary to make new teachers familiar with the concepts underlying the program, either by asking one of the experienced teachers (for example, one of those who helped draft the program) to lead workshops explaining it, or by inviting outside specialists to lead such discussions. On-going evaluation and revision must be provided for. The curriculum, after all, is an outline and guideline, not a straitjacket that deprives professional people of the opportunity to exercise their judgment in making decisions about their classes.

Teachers using the program should be encouraged, within the spirit of the program and in conformity with the objectives of each module, to try out assignments not specified in the curriculum materials, if they feel these assignments will assist the students. Teachers should also be encouraged to evaluate continuously the success of individual assignments as well as the suitability of objectives both for the program as a whole and for individual modules. After the program has been in use for a year or so, teachers should be brought together, as the teachers in the Hawaii school were, to reexamine the program; suggest changes in objectives; add, delete, or rearrange assignments; and exchange ideas on how to prepare students to work effectively on the various assignments.

Once introduced, that is, the program should not be thought of as finished; it should be regarded as in process, in a state of continuing revision and improvement. If it is so regarded, then all teachers at the school, experienced and new, can feel that they are professional people sharing in significant professional activities, activities they will recognize that none of them could carry on as successfully alone. From such a feeling of shared professional accomplishment may come a proud commitment to the new curriculum and a determination to see it work. That determination can help make a curriculum succeed; if teachers lack it (as they may if a curriculum is imposed upon them from an outside source), the best-conceived curriculum on any subject will fail.

A HUMANE RATIONALE FOR COMPOSITION

Tom Bacig

I N my first year of teaching I told my class of high school seniors that while I would justify most of what I taught on "shaky" humanistic grounds, I could with equanimity claim that what I taught them about writing would be useful, would help them to achieve success in college, or would make them better equipped to survive in the business jungle. At this moment I can only attribute my arrogance at that moment to a view of the arena of discourse no wider than the freshman English course and the college paper, and a naive faith in the efficacy of teaching a paragraph rhetoric. That same naivete produced a three week writing unit, taught simultaneously to three sections of senior English, requiring students to write a paragraph a day and the teacher to read 75 paragraphs a day. Suffice it to say that at the end of three weeks my office was full of paragraphs that students didn't want to write and that I didn't want to read. I don't mean to imply that the students didn't learn some things, or even that the only thing they learned was to dislike writing more than they already did. But whatever

F R O M *Minnesota English Journal*, Vol. 6 (Spring 1970), pp. 5–11. Reprinted by permission of the publisher and the author.

they learned had no more to do with them as human beings than most Freshmen English programs or college papers do.

If I were teaching that class now, I might begin by asking the students why anyone, students or teachers, ought to compose. How many essays will the typical student write after he leaves the schools? How many do teachers write? If the student becomes a politician, will he write his own speeches? Will he turn out handwritten drafts of letters to his constituents? If he's in business, will he write out his correspondence? As a matter of fact, some equally pertinent questions might be asked about his experiences in the schools. In how many of his classes does he write essay exams or term papers? How often is he called on to deliver prepared speeches in his classes? When he moves from the high school to the college, does the demand for "composed" speeches and essays increase or decrease? We might press additional questions here, but I think the point is already perhaps too well made. Perhaps I could then get my students, with just wrath, to turn to the larger community and proclaim that if "they" want us to learn composition "they" had better make certain that every teacher becomes a teacher of writing and speaking, and that business men and senators stop using secretaries, dictating machines and ghost writers; perhaps the students would settle for becoming competent secretaries and ghost writers to fulfill the increasing demand for such people in our society; or they might, as I hope they would, reject the utilitarian rationale for instruction in composition altogether.

Once they have rejected the utilitarian rationale, I'm not sure that my students might not go on to reject learning to write. But if I can assume that they might press the question a bit further, I believe they might discover a new rationale, a rationale of a higher order and broader scope. Without trying to detail sources or develop the argument completely, I think my students would discover that the real rationale for writing is in its humanizing potential, its capacity to help us order our universe or discover our "selves." Perhaps they might even point out the private contemplative experience that writing makes possible, noting that privacy is hard to come by in mid-century America, or that in writing they could for a change, revel in their differences, their idiosyncrasies, their individuality, thereby coming to new understandings of themselves and others. If my hypothetical (and wonderfully perceptive) students did reach such conclusions, they would not, I think, be far from agreeing with the statements made by the CEEB's Commission on English in *Freedom and Discipline.* The commission suggests that what one learns in learning to write is to ". . . care for the truth, care for the audience, care for one's own integrity." It is also I think what John Holt had in mind when, in introducing Herbert Kohl's *Teaching the Unteachable,* he said:

. . . What we have to recognize is that it is the effort to use words well, to say what he wants to say, to people whom he trusts, and wants to reach and move, that alone will teach a young person to use words better. No doubt, given this starting point, some technical advice and help may at times be useful; but we must begin from here or we will make no progress at all.

If we were operating from a humane rationale like the one my hypothetical and incredibly cooperative students discovered, Mr. Holt's statement could at least serve as the starting point for a new approach to composing. Before taking up that new approach, I want to enter a few disclaimers. I want to avoid the too easy rejection of concern with "technical advice" that Mr. Holt mentions. One of the easiest errors to make in the pursuit of freedom is to ignore the demands of discipline. The task of helping students to express themselves must involve a concern with providing students with the conventional means that a linguistic community uses to communicate. While it is obviously foolishness to begin teaching children to compose by teaching them to spell, it is equally foolish to suppose that they can share experience fully using the written language, if they do not become minimally competent in spelling and in using a dictionary or word list. As a matter of fact, perhaps the problem here results principally from our blurring of some important distinctions between teaching our students how to deal with questions of substance and questions of form, a bugbear that is not new to us.

For the moment, reservations in hand, we might do better to consider briefly the amazing fluency of our students with the spoken language. In the light of our concern with expression we ought to note that, while our students are not necessarily brilliant at declamation or debate, they do in most informal situations succeed admirably in expressing themselves. They invent elaborate excuses for lateness or missing work, they hoodwink assistant principals and us, they speak of love, war and politics with one another, they coin new phrases and words, they swear and joke. When we note that, though to be sure they are more and less successful in these various uses of language, most of them, despite tremendous differences in IQ, reading ability, and Iowa Basic Skills scores, do manage to use the spoken language to express an incredible range of nuances and understandings, a question suggests itself. Why is their formal speaking and writing, their effort at composing so unsuccessful?

I don't think we need to look far for the answer. Let's contrast their experiences in learning to speak and write. The infant babbling in his highchair produces, accidentally, DA DA. Much to his surprise, suddenly he is the center of an almost incredible uproar. He is being patted, poked, kissed and fed. Since most of this is eminently enjoyable he soon establishes some connection between action and consequence. As he continues to make noises and receives encouragement, he begins to produce more complex utterances, imperfectly. How are these imperfect utterances treated? Imagine yourself in the living room of a friend whose small child has just entered the room and produced a stream of what appears to be complete gibberish. His mother responds, however, with complete understanding and gives him a cookie and a glass of milk. The experience is almost enough to make one doubt one's sanity. Gradually, of course, mothers and fathers, friends, relatives, and strangers force refinement of those early crude utterances, and one variety or another of English, French or Spanish arises. But the process begins in love and acceptance.

Contrast Johnny's first experiences with producing the written language. Pen in hand, he is told to reproduce a meaningless series of chicken scratches arranged in a particular order. In some cases he is praised when he finally manages to write "johnny" for the first time, but often as not he's almost immediately informed that his work isn't neat enough or small enough, or that it's backwards. Far too frequently his experiences in sophisticating his skills in composing begin and end by being judged as totally inept; and in almost all cases no one ever reads and reacts to his writing as though it really mattered to Johnny or to anyone else. By the time he is in high school or in a freshman English course his papers come back bloody rags, demonstrating his increasing weakness. We could talk just as easily about his experiences in preparing speeches, though "show and tell time" tends to qualify our picture a bit. In either case the effort to write or prepare speeches does not begin in love or understanding. It begins and ends in evaluation and judgment.

Of course all of this is an exaggeration and probably ought to be carefully hedged. But exaggerated as it is, it comes too close to the truth. When we must admit, as most of us do, that for most of our teaching lives we've never *taught* composition; we've simply graded papers and written critiques of speeches, the exaggeration doesn't miss the mark by much.

If this is the case, what do we need to do to change our practice, to make composition humane and humanizing? And, moreover, what can we do to provide our students with the skills they need to achieve higher levels of self-expression? While no one can claim that any carefully tested, surefire methods to accomplish these goals are immediately available, it does seem clear that there are some basic principles that generate particular practices that ought to inform our teaching of composition. We ought, for example, to make the simplest kind of application of Bloom's taxonomy (Benjamin Bloom, et al., *Taxonomy of Educational Objectives, Handbook I: Cognitive Domain; Handbook II: Affective Domain*, New York: David McKay Co., 1956, 1964) to our discussion of composition. In a word, we need to recognize that there are effective or attitudinal dimensions to the teaching of composition. We ought to recognize that the task of making students want to write and speak or making them like writing and speaking is a task requiring strategies different from those necessary to build habits of punctuation and spelling. In this regard the most obvious need is to convince students that they can use the written language to share experience, to shape experience, to discover things about themselves, without fear of being graded or evaluated, without fear of teacher reprisals, or adminstrative outrage. This may involve learning to hear our students speak of the failings of our schools, our colleagues, and ourselves. We may even have to admit we are not all good writers, and ask our students to help us with our own writing. But if we can find honesty and integrity in our students' compositions, if we can make our students want to write, even enjoy writing, the pain of facing our own weaknesses seems a small price to pay.

Another set of basic principles or processes that ought to inform our teaching of the "new" composition emerges from considering the "old" rhetoric. If, as many have suggested, the trivialization of the old humane rhetoric has consisted in part in dropping any real concern with the canon of invention, we might accept that one of the ways to broaden and humanize contemporary rhetoric would be to reintroduce a concern for invention. More precisely, what we need to reintroduce are the playful and creative dimensions of the composing process. For Aristotle, invention, the search for the available means of persuasion, followed dialectic, the search for truth. Using the terms in these senses, perhaps it would be more accurate to say we need to reintroduce a concern for dialectic or discovery. In other words, we need to go beyond asking our students to sort the conventional wisdom either by getting "sources" from the library or by employing updated versions of the classical canons of invention. The library research paper or Edward Corbett's *Classical Rhetoric for the Modern Student* (New York, 1965) are useful, but must be transcended. To accomplish our transcendence we will have to give up one debilitating canard. We will have to stop assuming that imagination is a gift of the gods or a genetically coded capacity. We will have to recognize that all of our students have creative potential and that we have not met our responsibility as teachers when, in starting the creative writing "unit", we say, "Be creative!"

Creative behavior can be and has been analyzed, and some exercises in creative thinking have even been suggested. William Gordon's *Synectics*, for example, while it is often mechanistic and simplistic, does suggest some technique that might be used to encourage creative prewriting. His discussion of the use of personal analogy is a case in point. Asking students to identify themselves with inanimate objects, thus giving the objects the capacity to respond to and sense the world around them, can produce interesting notes which in turn can be used to write descriptive poetry or prose. In the following example a student began by trying to describe a drinking fountain. While I can't avoid smiling at the choice of subject, I can't halp but be taken by the resulting notes. Something in them makes even water fountain descriptions worth the effort. Perhaps "making the familiar strange" is its own reward.

> Sleek and silvery
> Every angle gleaming
> Upright, proud
> Austere and haughty
> Metallic taste, frigid
> Galvanic to the touch
> Warmed infrequently
> By pulsating fingers
> And suspended exhalation
> From the yawning
> Abyss of
> Copper
> Caves
>
> Who would guess
> That through
> These steely coils
> Flows the
> Sustenance
> Of Life.
>   —GLENDA HOLT

Clearly the object of such exercises is not to produce poems or prose. Instead the object is to encourage students to play with language and perception. Out of such play discovery or poetry may emerge, or if it doesn't, we might at least hope that a tolerance for the idiosyncratic and a sense of the freedom within the constraints of language and perception will.

Having thus made a start at "taking our students where they are," at becoming a real audience for whatever it is they have to say and at helping them sense and develop their creative potentials, we can take up the task of "providing technical advice," of developing skills. Here we may have much to learn from a careful study of the language acquisition process. We might also learn from the classical rhetoricians of the Roman schools and our colleagues who teach foreign languages. We might note, for example, the way in which parents accept rough approximations initially, and then gradually demand closer compliance with accepted usage, insisting finally on near perfect performance. We might also notice the unbelievable number of repetitions that parents and foreign language teachers encourage. We might ask ourselves why the classical rhetoricians had their students spend so much time memorizing and imitating the speeches and writings of the "masters."

I want to produce some evidence that the game is worth the candle, but I find this hard. My own most recent work in teaching composition may be with students who are too far gone, too much products of what we've been doing in the name of utility. I will say, that I have had some experiences in my advanced composition course, a course designed for prospective teachers, that reinforce my present views. In that course we have had some success in getting students to want to write by avoiding grading their work. While I think the mechanics of the operations of the course are not important at this point, you might be interested in a piece of student writing that indicates one potential outcome of providing students with freedom and finding that they do wish to write.

A VERSION OF A FABLE
By James Johnson

. . . the howling moon was lost falling in a wilderness changing under a pair of Jack Frost underwear as I lay by my sunshine companion asleep in the dark cave of love. A self-made grizzly bear growled awakening my absent senses.

"Out of the cave." It was purple at first.

"Out of the cave." Again but less purple.

He lit a cigar and filled two glasses with brandy. He gave me one glass. "Skoal."

"But my companion?"

"That is another dimension of these lonely bloody woods. Skoal and I shall tell . . ."

We skoaled and he began to tell a sleepy broken tale he too had once met—a girl with golden hair . . .

It was a worried silly once upon a time wisdom but the bear was entitled to a wondered share in the universal dream of all. He was once a black-eyed kid, so he said, driving a yellow cadillac and living luxury in a dingy papered shack. His mother was a scrub kneed wide bottomed working woman who scrubbed out the bowery places and came home to cook a perfect porridge. His father was a gambling bear. What summer brought fall would fill and winter eat. Spring was sometimes honey. Sometimes not. The porridge was hot one special spring day so the three drove over the bridge and bought in Superior a jug of wine made cheaper with dirtier tracks of another tread but drank well with the perfect porridge. Anyway, they returned in wishbone time, home to drink and dine. Pa's porridge was perfect Ma's porridge was perfect. The third was gone. The kid he growled once, he said, then he drank the wine. His sorrow tapered sad to bad. He slid upstairs and there—that was where he found the girl— the storybook girl the one with the golden hair, who awoke too soon and ran down the stairs away and away.

The kid left home to find the bear and a life his own. Sometimes he flew upside down laughing in the crosswinds, soaring among the barren branches, eating flesh and bone unpealed, and falling into the pond and stream running along the hill to the top of the mountain searching for something within the bees precious tree but only finding a yellow head bouncing in love in a one way canyon breathing breathless air and wanting not the honey but the golden hair. All summer he teased the young and small without reason and jealously watched the male and female enjoying most the female—the salmon, the berry, and the other selfless dying autumn myths. He found a cave in which to dream not deep as the pool in the stream and the mirror on the pond but instead hollow and long as the canyon of breathless air where the girl with the golden hair is a dreaming silence. Tomorrow the springtime sprung memories all over. Honey trees and berry vines and new salmon running times with sunshine lightening the endless canyon rising and setting within an elusive endless canyon that was cold and nowhere—the girl running thru with raving golden hair.

Dreams that rise in youth sometimes set younger yet when summer salmon swam with summer wine while bears with valid ids were drinking and the dreaming grizzly bears were sexing still for honey forgetting tomorrow only for a sorrow as an alley as ancient as the one way canyon. Otherwise make the wine in autumn then sleep all winter sometimes hanging empty sometimes hanging together with kisses in the morning or sometimes with a thankful bleeding heart that asks only for today what is. Salmon berry wine within a grizzly bear lives. While golden hair is a multiple of zeroes in the mist.

I looked up to a dream disappearing. I was alone. My companion with the superficial raying hair was gone from the cave of love. It was no longer dark. The moon had changed; its shape was fading, dying remembering only a summer heaven while in the east fermenting was golden hair to live but for today and to die tonite and to vanish quickly with one real drink with reality . . .

While I'm not sure I can paraphrase Jim Johnson or that I know precisely what he meant, I am hesitant to say that he ought to straighten out his syntax. He has gotten beyond me; he is better than I am; I enjoy his writing, question him about it and even suggest changes, but we both recognize the ironies in our respective roles. I hope that I can find this in more situations with more students.

I would like to close with a quotation. I've been discussing a new rationale for teaching composition and some implications of such a rationale for teaching practice. If anyone asks for a rationale beyond the rationale, a reason for humanizing composition, I think he might well find it in these words of D. K. Smith which appeared in the October, 1967, issue of *Minnesota English:*

> Our students are saying, or seem to me to be saying, that they want possession of an art of discovering more honest, more meaningful, more

satisfying relationships with other human beings. They want to know how to escape from the masks of concealment, suspicion, and hostility which infect their engagements with elders and peers. They want to know how to discover what it is that lies between man and man, the truth which is not the possession of one or the other, which does not exist at all prior to an actual engagement, which is created in the act of engagement, which is experienced rather than objectified, and which underlies all sense of community among men. They want, in short, not simply the skill of managing their speaking and writing in ways which will be reputable and traditionally efficient, but a skill in discovering the symbols that mark the gulf separating them from others, or in discovering the symbols that define the way in which men separated by such gulfs can still treat each other as human beings, and not as threatening objects.

STUDENT ATTITUDES AND PURPOSES IN WRITING

Hugo Hartig

THE extensive literature on the teaching of composition tends to place great emphasis upon the importance of providing students with plenty of opportunity to practice the art of writing, on the self-evident theory that the best way to learn how to write is to write. Another strong, and no doubt proper, emphasis is placed upon the teaching of understandings about language and logic, and semantic and rhetorical principles. But a most important aspect of the writing process has received very little systematic attention, perhaps because it seems to be more psychological than linguistic in nature. That is the question of the role played in the writing process by attitude and purpose on the part of the writer.

Teachers of composition cannot safely assume that every student who is given a writing assignment, and who is taught some principles of effective writing, necessarily has much desire to write effectively. More likely, many students are in the fell clutch of apathy, and couldn't care less about becoming good writers. Therefore it would seem to be very important indeed for composition teachers to be concerned about basic attitudes and purposes that students may or may not bring to their writing tasks.

Effective theme writing depends very much upon the writer's having

→≫-→≫

F R O M *Wisconsin English Journal,* Vol. 13 (October 1970), pp. 33–36. Reprinted by permission of the publisher and the author.

a clear and complete conception of his exact purposes in writing. The first step in planning a theme, in fact, is to think carefully about specific purposes that one may have for writing. If these purposes are clear in the writer's mind, his theme will be more consistent and persuasive and the writer will have greater conscious control over the tone of his writing, which is ordinarily a most elusive aspect of style.

A writer may have several purposes at once, and therefore he needs to identify all of them and decide which of them he wishes to make most apparent to his reader. The writer should also be aware that he may have "hidden purposes," that often are not so hidden as he may think. That is, if a writer has some purpose that he does not wish the reader to be aware of, he may attempt to conceal that purpose by asserting some other one. But of course if he does this, he is engaging in propaganda, and the careful reader will see through his deception. Many student themes are essentially a kind of propaganda, because their purpose is not clearly evident. Good readers are irritated by unclear purposes or by expository writing that does not really mean what it says. Of course, artful literary irony in expository writing is another matter, although even that many readers dislike. The point is that people can see through phoniness in writing just as quickly as in speech, so honesty of purpose is essential.

Some purposes that theme writers may have can be categorized into types, since they are general purposes which frequently are present in the theme-writing situation. For example, it is possible to identify what could be called the *assignment purpose,* which is perhaps the most obvious reason for writing a theme. The writer writes because he is required to produce a theme as part of his class work in English. This purpose is taken for granted, and many students believe that it is the only "real" purpose that they have for writing. Unfortunately, it is not a sufficient purpose for a theme. Students do sometimes succeed in cranking out a kind of pseudo-theme by following all of the common rules for theme writing, but the resulting "creation" is usually notable only for its sterility and lack of creativity. The assignment purpose is actually no purpose at all, and it cannot by itself lead to good writing. It is, in fact, a major obstacle to the production of good writing by students. The students who succeed in writing genuine themes are those who are able to forget the assignment purpose, and who therefore are able to find some more genuine purposes for writing.

Writing for a Reader

A more valid purpose for writing is what might be called (for lack of a better term) the *altruistic purpose.* It is not too unrealistic to believe that most people have a desire to give of themselves for the sake of others; it would hardly be human to be consistently concerned only with oneself. At any rate, it seems very likely that one of the most powerful motives for writing is altruistic, and that successful writers virtually without exception show great concern for the reader. They have a conscious desire to please the reader, to avoid offense, to help him to understand, to respect his feelings and his intelligence, and to make his life easier.

No doubt students need to become more aware of the significance of the altruistic purpose in writing. It is the key to readability in writing. Young people are likely to be quite self-centered and even defensive in their reaction to the writing situation, and it is this very egocentricity that defeats their attempts at writing improvement. They need to realize that writing is essentially a social activity, directed toward others, for the sake of others. It requires social maturity and a sense of responsibility. One of the reasons, perhaps, that the "hippies" have produced so little writing is that they are concerned largely with themselves and their own sensations. Non-conformity is not an unmixed virtue; one can be so unconcerned about other people that he loses (or fails to develop) the ability to communicate meaningfully. One cannot write effectively if he believes, consciously or unconsciously, that the audience is "the enemy."

Closely related to the altruistic purpose in theme writing is the *persuasive purpose*. All themes, not just those that are editorials or arguments in the formal sense, are made effective to the extent that they are persuasive and convincing. The writer needs to show that he takes his work seriously, that he is a clear thinker, and that he means what he says. Exaggeration and lack of precision lead the reader to doubt the reliability of the writer. Communication research tends to back up this assertion. Studies of opinion formation show that people are most likely to be convinced by communications that appear to be credible at the source. That is, the believability of the writer himself—as it is reflected in the writing, or as it is communicated by other means—is the single most important factor determining the effectiveness of a piece of writing. Not "what you say" but "who you are" seems to be significant to your reader. A writer's style communicates his personality and his credibility, in a subtle manner, and thus determines his effectiveness as a writer. Perhaps this means that successful writers are in actuality genuine and sincere people.

A fourth purpose for theme writing would seem to be significant. This could be called the *informational purpose*. Every expository theme exists primarily to convey the writer's ideas and thought processes, and to support these by factual evidence and logical reasoning. The writer's purpose thus should be to use the utmost honesty in the support of his ideas. He should strive to tell the truth, and to be completely straightforward with the reader. Expository writing must reflect the highest intellectual integrity on the part of the writer, not only for the sake of credibility, but to carry out the altruistic purpose as well. Of course, different readers may respond differently to various styles of writing. For example, some people's response to the writing of a well-known newspaper columnist is that it reflects a depressingly low level of intellectual integrity. But many other readers consider him to be a man of unusual perceptivity and distinguished intellect. But as a general rule, an attitude of frankness and sincerity in the writer's personality will almost certainly be reflected in his writing.

The informational purpose requires not only intellectual honesty, but also a certain modesty in drawing conclusions. The writer who draws firm conclusions from insufficient factual evidence merely causes the reader to doubt his reliability and judgment. Modesty is good strategy in writing. On the other hand, the writer must make definite generalizations and conclusions, since this is central to the informational purpose. The effective writer makes generalizations that are clear, precise and significant, that are stated in such a way as to avoid giving the impression that the writer considers them to be the "last word" on the subject. The "sweeping statement" is the hallmark of propaganda, and the careful writer usually tries to avoid it, especially when his material seems controversial.

Creativity in Writing

Another purpose for writing that is worthy of mention is the *self-expressive purpose*. No doubt many writers see in their writing a means for self-expression. Perhaps the need to "win friends and influence people," or to make a favorable and powerful impression upon others is very basic to human nature. Communication, either spoken or written, is the principle means we have for satisfying this basic drive.

Writing is a particularly good method for self-expression because it provides an opportunity to plan a strategy, to correct mistakes, and to revise for effectiveness. Indeed, literary history abounds with people who were unprepossessing, or even ineffectual . . . except in their writing, where they could be gigantic. Just as some people have deliberately cultivated skill in public speaking, or in debate, in order to become personally more forceful, others have cultivated ability in writing. Perhaps every writing assignment offers some opportunity to develop powers of self-expression and self-assertion, and therefore perhaps this purpose should always enter into a writing task. But certainly some kinds of writing are more suited to the self-expressive purpose. Traditionally, self-expression has been considered a strong motivation for creative literary efforts, such as the writing of poetry. But other kinds of writing, as well, may offer great opportunity for self-expression.

So-called "creative" writing is sometimes distinguished from other kinds of writing, such as reportage or expository writing, no doubt to emphasize the "practical" or applied nature of the "non-creative" writing. But even the most practical and informational writing can be very creative. Creativity is much more an attitude on the part of the writer than it is a characteristic of certain kinds of writing.

The *creative purpose* in writing is probably closely related to the self-expressive purpose. But the "creative urge" goes beyond self-expression, and concerns itself with the desire to achieve, at an ever higher level, in terms of an artistic standard or ideal.

We usually think of self-expression as the assertion of one's individuality in a creative and fulfilling way. But because even expository writing does reflect the writer's personality, and because it has power to influence others, it too can be an effective means for self-expression and self-realization. Unquestionably many writers find a great deal of creative challenge and satisfaction in the writing process. In a way, all creative achievements represent a kind of adult "showing off," since adults, like children, take much pleasure in displaying their unique abilities and achievements. Perhaps the writing process is always difficult, but many writers have found special satisfaction in making the difficult thing seem easy. This motive should not be underestimated as a motive for student writing, and should not be limited to the writing of poetry or fiction.

Writing and Thinking

One final purpose for writing that may be cited is not primarily a communication purpose, although it may lead to better communication. That is the purpose, that many writers have, to clarify and explore their own thoughts and ideas. This is what could be called the *problem-solving purpose.* There is mystery and magic in writing, because somehow our abstract thoughts and vagrant ideas are crystallized in the process of writing; and it becomes possible for us to create logical structures and solutions to problems that are more complex and powerful than we could hope to create or even understand easily if we could not see our ideas in writing. Our writing generally reflects a level of thinking considerably above our usual stream of consciousness. Because this is true, our writing usually represents, for ourselves at least, something that has distinct value as a kind of commodity. Teachers should encourage students to respect and value their own writing, to care about it, to go back to it, and to read and revise it again and again. We can learn much about ourselves by studying our own writing. And no doubt the desire to read one's own writing, and to have it in a readable form, is a powerful motivation for writing in the first place. It is the custom in many schools for the teacher to retain all student writing, presumably to prevent plagiarism or to provide evidence of work completed. Very likely, however, this practice is a bad one, because it conditions young people to believe that writing is not to keep and cherish, but to give away, never to see again. Such an attitude toward writing is the opposite of creative.

All of these motives for theme writing are essentially attitudes and feelings that students may have about their writing. They are attitudes that precede the act of writing, but they exert a powerful influence upon the result. The question of how these attitudes are formed in the first place is perhaps not as significant as how desirable attitudes can be encouraged. It seems likely that among intelligent students there is a causal relationship between attitudes and understandings. In other words, if students understand how *important* certain attitudes are in the writing process, they may be able consciously to develop those attitudes. Instruction in composition should include a good deal of continuing thoughtful discussion of the attitudes that influence writing effectiveness, what these attitudes are, how they are influential, and how they can be cultivated.

TEACHING A CONCEPT OF STYLE FOR LITERATURE AND COMPOSITION

Thomas E. Gaston

HERE is a riddle for your students: What does a great writer have in common with a chic woman and a crowd-pleasing fighter? The answer is *style*. And when you give your students this answer, you will have already interested them in the question of what constitutes style. That the same word, *style*, is used to describe the way one man uses his dukes and another man uses his words should challenge students to discover what the cases have in common. Since the abstract is most easily taught in terms of the concrete and since youngsters already appreciate—even if they have not analyzed—the "style" of their sports heroes and movie stars, you will find this approach to literary style exciting not only

FROM *English Journal* (January 1970), pp. 65–70. Copyright © 1970 by the National Council of Teachers of English. Reprinted by permission of the publisher and Thomas E. Gaston.

to your verbally proficient students but also your intelligent skeptics. Students looking forward to careers in such "practical" fields as business, engineering, and technology are often surprised and pleased to discover that style in literature, so far from being an elusive spiritual delicacy for the effete esthete, is in fact quite analogous to what they like most about their idols of the silver screen and the sports arena.

But what are the similarities between the style of, say, a Sugar Ray Robinson and an F. Scott Fitzgerald? Our main teaching point is this: *Style in any endeavor is the product of a purposeful, patterned interaction between the predictable and the unpredictable.* To focus on this tension between the expected and the unexpected is to take an approach to style that is both accurate (as far as it goes) and teachable. For this reason, the thesis is worthy of detailed analysis.

It says first that both elements, the convention as well as the innovation, are essential for anyone to have a style, no matter what the endeavor, because the surprise must take place within a system. Neither essayist nor athlete can break the rules, though either may find it good strategy to feint and threaten to do so. A well-turned sentence surprises us with its turn but must remain a sentence nonetheless; if it does not, our labor aborts and gives birth to shock instead of surprise. Style then is spontaneity without solecism. Total conservatism is monotony, total freedom, madness. Between them lies the area of meaningful life, the area of style. To teach an appreciation for a style, therefore, it is necessary to do two things. First we must define the expectations which govern the effort. Then we must identify the extent and the nature (and thus the significance) of the deviation from those expectations. We define the expectations; then we find the surprises.

The sport of boxing, for instance, is subject to all the physics of leverage and velocity as well as to the Marquis of Queensbury rules. The chic woman becomes stylish only by keeping her clothes in perspective with the conventions of dress accepted by her culture. Likewise, the writer must not ignore the structure of his language, the tradition of his genre or the present attitude of his readers towards his subject, for these are the foundations of the reader's expectations. And these expectations constitute, after all, the center of the ring in which style must play. But ring-center is only the starting point. It is far from the whole boxing match.

All that we have said and all that we have to say here is about style— be it noted—not *stylism*. Style is that individual imprint on an activity that moved Buffon to say, "The style is the man himself." Style in this sense is the opposite of *stylism*. An activity is stylized precisely when it is so predictable that individual innovation is disallowed. Whatever is stylized is anathema to style. The excellence aimed at in stylism is an archetypal perfection of execution. The golfer practicing his swing, the boxer holding to the classic stance, and the dancer pursuing a perfect pirouette—each has subordinated his own nature to the nature of his task. Where convention is everything, we have not style but stylization.

Another distinction, one you may not want to bother your students with unless they bring it up, is also useful. To help define the role of surprise in style, let us distinguish at the outset between what is truly predetermined and what is merely expected. Let us say that it is determined that one boxer will not beat another into submission with a club or throw twelve-foot punches. The rules of boxing preclude the club, and the laws of physics preclude twelve-foot punches. Whether they originate in agreement (like the rules of boxing) or in physical necessity (like the laws of physics), predetermined constraints are arbitrary and universal. They brook no exceptions. Thus, whatever they deal with is completely predictable.

But our expectations, based on our past experiences with boxing, enable us to predict many other things with reasonable accuracy, though with less than perfect certainty. Both fighters will use both hands, for instance. Each will use one hand as a "guard." Right-handed fighters will strike more blows with their left hand, etc. We are pretty sure of these things, not because they are determined (i.e., necessary) but because they are true of most fighters and most fights. Some years ago, in Tennessee, however, a one-armed boxer gave a good account of himself in amateur boxing events. But, since he had no left arm, he struck all his blows with his right and used almost no guard. In fact, he violated almost all of our expectations at every fight, though of course he obeyed the rules. The case of the one-armed boxer nicely illustrates the differences between predetermined constraints, which must be followed by necessity or by definition, and conventional constraints, to which most participants subject themselves but which they are free to break whenever their ingenuity and virtuosity permit. We can now restate our thesis more accurately: *Style consists of purposeful and patterned violations of expectations, violations that approach but never exceed predetermined limits* (of "fairness" or "good taste").

What, then, can we say about the expectations we readers bring with us when we meet the stylist on the printed page? We can start by noting the origin of those expectations: nothing less than our *entire previous experience with language*. The great bulk of this experience, of course, has been with oral language, in casual conversation. And, of that small proportion of our linguistic life which has involved written language, most of our reading and writing has dealt with simple pedestrian prose. This fact remains true, even of literate adults. The technical reports and everyday journalism we read, the letters to friends and notes to milkmen we write, like the chats we have, all employ language in its work clothes. And language in its work clothes grudgingly earns its union wage with workmanlike competence. But it performs no extra services; it has no time for style.

We all deal regularly with language in its work clothes. It is our trusted servant, and we have long since come to anticipate its simple, unimaginative ways. So our acquaintance with work-a-day language conditions our expectations of all language. These expectations are of three types: phonological, syntactic, and semantic. The phonology of work-a-day language holds only to the predetermined rules of stress, pitch, and juncture that make English sentences English. Other sounds are scattered in accidental disarray; for the milkman would not appreciate a poem, nor does the school principal expect a well-wrought essay. Our syntactic expectations lead us to anticipate pretty much the same clause density and compounding practices we are accustomed to in work clothes language, where phrases work like gnarled muscles to carry meaning gracelessly but adequately. And, semantically, we know that language in its work clothes will strive for clarity at any cost. When it brings our news or delivers our message to the paper boy, work-a-day language carries one and only one literal meaning. Neither ambiguity nor paradox nor figurative expression belong in work clothes. We soon learn not to expect them.

All these expectations, the stylist considers and playfully thwarts. In the realm of semantics, he works to "decentralize" his words, employing them not with their central (and hence their most hackneyed) meanings but pushing each one to the very edge of its semantic range. One thinks immediately of E. E. Cummings' "there's nothing as *something* as one," in which he turns a pronoun into an adjective out of pure playful audacity. Or watch Donne bypass the common noun use of *shroud* to take the word in its less common verb countenance: "Whoever comes to *shroud* me, do not harm. . . ." Prose stylists do the same kind of thing. Remember these sentences from the third paragraph of Fitzgerald's "The Poor Boy"?

> Let me tell you about the very rich. They are different from you and me. They *possess* and *enjoy* early, and it does something to them, makes them soft where we are hard, and cynical where we are trustful, in a way that, unless you were born rich, it is very difficult to understand [italics mine].

My dictionary tells me that *possess* and *enjoy* are both transitive verbs. You can make the same point to your students by asking them, books closed, to use the two words in sentences. Without exception, they will include direct objects. "Peter enjoys novels," they will write or, "He possesses innate dignity." Having thus focused their expectations, you may want to lead the class to decide why Fitzgerald chose this particular surprise for his reader. They will quickly recognize that the omission of the object implies an almost unlimited generalization. Rich people can possess and enjoy anything, it says; therefore, why bother to enumerate? (How does this differ from the effect rendered by Caesar's famous employment of the same stylistic device: "I came, I saw, I conquered"?)

Though it takes us momentarily away from semantics into syntax, let us, before we leave the Fitzgerald passage, note that it is an excellent example of how the stylist can *manipulate* our expectations so as to increase his opportunities to surprise us. Remember how the ping-pong virtuoso lets the game settle into an established rhythm and then—Slam! One quick drive triples the tempo of the game and often scores against an off-guard opponent. An alert class will find parallels in the strategy of a smart quarterback or a good chess player. With your help, they can observe the same process in literature. Fitzgerald's first sentence has eight words, his second seven. Both are simple, straightforward sentences. They are simple in structure and simple also in their assertions. Then Wham! Fitzgerald breaks out of his own pattern in one grand thirty-nine word compound-complex sentence in which the predications in the several clauses range all the way from the vague triviality ("it is difficult to understand") to the profoundly original observation ("makes them soft where we are hard, and cynical where we are trustful. . . ."). Like Cassius Clay's dazzling footwork in the corner of the ring or Bart Starr's last-second passes with linemen crashing at him, Fitzgerald's virtuosity shows him most in command when things threaten to go awry. All thirty-nine words come to rest in a gem of a sentence that shines the more brightly because of its setting. By courting chaos, the stylist wins harmony.

But we were discussing semantic-based surprises. The most frequent of these is novel association, usually an unexpected comparison, in which the stylist juxtaposes ideas that are normally considered quite unrelated. Everyone has seen television-comedy psychiatrists give word association tests in which the patient is asked to respond to a list of cue words with the first "response" words that pop into his mind. Such tests work, of course, because "normal" associations are quite predictable. Kent and Rosanoff found, for instance, that 650 subjects out of one thousand responded "light" to the stimulus word "lamp."[1] But the stylist nudges us out of our associational ruts. He bypasses the obvious to fix on new comparisons. Who before Leacock ever linked old men and cosmetics into one concept? "A young girl studying economics," he wrote in "On the Need for a Quiet College," "is as wide of the mark as an old man studying cosmetics." In the same work he compares the English gentry to cows in an ample pasture. And, turning back to Fitzgerald, remem-

[1] George A. Miller, *Language and Communication* (New York: McGraw-Hill Book Co., Inc., 1951), pp. 176–177.

ber the wife at Gatsby's party who appeared beside her husband "like an angry diamond"?

Nothing is a better index to the power and the purpose of a writer than the ideas he chooses to yoke together and the way he does it. Thus, in this passage from *Walden,* Thoreau's sharp eye slyly selects just those points which expose the concealed contradiction:

> One farmer says to me, "You cannot live on vegetable food solely, for it furnishes nothing to make bones with"; and so he religiously devotes a part of his day to supplying his system with the raw material of bones; walking all the while he talks behind his oxen, which with vegetable-made bones, jerk him and his lumbering plough along in spite of every obstacle.

And likewise with James Baldwin in "Notes of a Native Son":

> The situation in Harlem had grown bad enough for clergymen, police-men, educators, politicians, and social workers to assert in one breath that there was no "crime wave" and to offer, in the very next breath, sug-gestions as to how to combat it.

In both cases it is the juxtaposition that supplies surprise, and the sur-prise is the style.

Another kind of semantic surprise is symbolism. Thus, in the Baldwin passage just noted, we find this sudden switch from the literal to the symbolic:

> Perhaps the most revealing news item, out of the steady parade of re-ports of muggings, stabbings, shootings, assaults, gang wars, and accusa-tions of police brutality, is the item concerning six Negro girls who set upon a white girl in the subway because, as they all too accurately put it, she was stepping on their toes. Indeed she was, all over the nation.

Frost's "Stopping by the Woods on a Snowy Evening" achieves the same metamorphosis of the literal into the symbolic by the simple repe-tition of the last line, "And miles to go before I sleep." Still another semantic surprise is paradox. Again, Leacock: "Real study, real learning must, for the individual, *be quite valueless or it loses its value*" [italics mine]. Metaphor, simile, epithet, paradox, irony, ambiguity—all these elements of style are manipulations of meaning which surprise the reader and occupy his peripheral attention through a cycle of bemuse-ment and amusement.

We have already seen that syntax may also be manipulated for this purpose. Indeed, almost every rhetoric handbook extolls the virtues of balanced, parallel, and periodic sentences, and then wisely admonishes students to vary their sentences. What should also be mentioned, how-ever, is that random variation effects little improvement. Frenetic syntax is not style. Our teaching point stated that the elements of style are *purposeful* and *patterned* surprises. The writer's intention supplies the purpose, of course, and the singleness of his personality imposes the pattern. The verbal mannerisms of a Norman Mailer are as distinctive as the physical mannerisms of an Elvin Hayes.

The practiced stylist uses hundreds of subtleties beyond precise description by the linguist or the rhetorician to set up just those expectations that he wishes to play off of. He affects syntactic habits that he knows he will break; he repeats key words and characteristic structures; he uses all kinds of links and signal words to remind us of what has gone before and to guide our guesses of what is to come. Only by patterning sentence variations against the anticipations he arouses does the writer achieve style.

Sinclair Lewis' use and sudden abandonment of incremental repetition in the first paragraph of *Elmer Gantry* shows how context-sensitive syntactic options can be.

> Elmer Gantry was drunk. He was eloquently drunk, lovingly and pugnaciously drunk. He leaned against the bar of the Old Home Sample Room, the most gilded and urbane saloon in Cato, Missouri, and requested the bartender to join him in "The Good Old Summer Time," the waltz of the day.

Each sentence takes off from, and soars above, the one before it, the three appositives playfully twisting their sentences in our mental grasp as we read.

And let us be honest enough to admit that some of the most successful syntactic surprises are achieved by a flippant disrespect for the venerable rules of thumb in our handbooks. "Don't use expletives," we warn our students. "They weaken your sentences." But the expletive beginning gives added force to the ending of this sentence in Thornton Wilder's *Bridge of San Luis Rey*:

> There was something in Lima that was wrapped up in yards of violet satin from which protruded a great dropsical head and two fat pearly hands; and that was its archbishop.

We advise our students to put only comparable ideas into parallel grammatical form, but much of the power of this James Baldwin sentence (again from "Notes of a Native Son") comes from his surprising violations of parallelism:

> Then the house was suddenly full of *relatives, friends, hysteria, and confusion* and I quietly left my mother and the children to the care of those impressive women, who, in Negro communities, at least, automatically appear at times of bereavement *armed with lotions, proverbs, and patience, and an ability to cook* [italics mine].

Baldwin's sentence makes us realize the inadequacy of a vague rule that would banish his genial freedom to exorcise the sophomoric inanities of semiliterate composition students. Legalism be hanged! This is good writing because Baldwin went just as far as he could but—the letter of the law notwithstanding—not too far.

Such are the sources of syntactic surprise. But before we go on, let us think a moment about why a well-turned parallel sentence, say, is such a pleasure to read. Isn't it because we are so used to the loose shuffling structures of work-a-day language? A carefully crafted sentence gives us more order, more structure, than we expect. The craftsmanship is a bonus that delights our esthetic sense all the more because it does with style everything a less elegant paraphrase could do. A well-executed counter-punch is only beautiful if it carries enough power to justify itself. Style gives us both efficiency and elegance; it gets the job done.

All this is true also of phonological surprises. Except in the meter and fixed rhyme schemes of poetry, phonological surprises invariably take the form of bonuses superimposed on, but never interfering with, the rest of the passage. It is so with Baldwin's alliterative use of the consonants /w/ and /hw/: "I had discovered the *w*eight *of wh*ite people in the *w*orld." It is true also of this sentence from Cardinal Newman's "Idea of a University": "Liberal edu*c*ation makes not the *Ch*ristian, not the *C*atholic, but the gentleman." Here the parallelism focuses on the alliteration of the hard /k/ sounds in *Christian* and *Catholic* and thus heightens the contrast with the soft /j/ of *gentleman,* emphasizing exactly the contrast Newman intended to stress.

If you are especially interested in the role of style in poetry you may want to read H. A. Gleason's discussion of phonological patterning in Chapter 18 of his *Linguistics and English Grammar* (Holt, 1965). Gleason's treatment fits nicely with our view of style. But we have said enough to give you the drift. Assonance, consonance, internal rhyme, and the like all come as bonuses for the reader. The trick is to place rhyme and meter into the picture as elements, the *presence* of which is predetermined. But their manifestation—how they are worked out in any particular instance—is open to stylistic play. It is predetermined that a Shakespearean sonnet will rhyme just so; everyone knows the rhyme scheme. But no man alive can anticipate which words Shakespeare will couple with which or what his pairings will enable him to do with his meaning. Yet, somehow, the very rhymes which cannot be predicted in advance seem, in retrospect, inevitable.

Probably this kind of analysis of poetic style is better reserved for your most promising students and better postponed until after they have had plenty of practice with prose selections. Meanwhile, whenever you want to help your students appreciate the style of an essay they have read or improve the style of a theme they will write, remember to start with what they already dig. Granted, it is a long way from Muhammed Ali and Steve McQueen to Norman Mailer and C. P. Snow, but let's face it. So far as your students are concerned, Muhammed and Steve are where it's at. *They* already have style.

SLANG AND PROFANITY:
THEIR USES IN ENGLISH COMPOSITION

David P. Demarest, Jr.

THERE are many reasons why English teachers do not normally encourage slang and profanity in the composition classroom: fear that discipline problems may be exacerbated, the tradition that the classroom's role is to teach standard English, a belief that slang and profanity are slovenly and clichéd. For teachers concerned—as I am—with inner city students, especially blacks, the problem of pedagogical attitude is intensified because slang and profanity are closer to normal usage for such students than for their white suburban peers. Students whose neighborhood or ethnic sense of identity reinforces the use of "he be the baddest," "scag" (for heroin), "mawfucka," "raise" (for parent), "heavy" (for good), etc., cannot be expected, one would think, to take easily to the standard English of the classroom: there always is a cuss word or a choice bit of slang that will do the job better. Well-intentioned educators have proclaimed something of a Pygmalion theory (as Henry Higgins puts it in his song: "it's the aooow and garn that keep her in her place, not her wretched clothes and dirty face"). Inner city black students especially, the argument goes, are likely to speak such deviant dialect that standard English is as big a hurdle for them as it is for foreign language students. Appropriate instruction for such students apparently is not to encourage use of dialect, slang, and profanity. Instead they must learn the language of mainstream America, of the "establishment," if they are to live and prosper in this society.

Although such arguments are reasonable—certainly one end of education is integration into a linguistic community—it is my purpose here to advocate the use of slang and profanity in composition, particularly in regard to black inner city students. The benefits of such a strategy I think are manifold. From the point of view of the English teacher, there can be the gain of writing qualities that English teachers often

REPRINTED by permission from the October 1970 issue of *The Clearing House.*

preach—simplicity, naturalness, directness, vividness (after listening to academic jargon in the college classroom, I've often announced the slogan "Four-letter words are best"). It is hard to tell a class of teen-agers—twelfth graders or college freshmen—to honor such qualities unless one permits slang and profanity. Beyond the gain in stylistic naturalness, the freedom to use their own vocabulary may encourage students to be more genuinely self-expressive in their writing. Such a gain is well worth seeking because inner city students are likely to view the classroom as a hostile environment (a prison cell) and pencil and paper as the weapons of the enemy. Allowing the use of slang and pro-fanity may be a means of showing the teacher's respect for the student's experience, a means of making the student feel more at home in the classroom. If such an atmosphere can be established, perhaps students can be brought to enjoy a classroom study of language, including stand-ard English, and to understand that pencil and paper can be used to think about problems important to them.

The classroom situation that I base my remarks on is a special pro-gram. In 1968–69 approximately 30 inner city twelfth-graders (two-thirds of them black) were invited to spend half of each school day on the university campus, to eat lunch, then to take classes in English and math taught by college instructors. As the English teacher, I felt that in this special situation I could do certain things with the students—perhaps I might say, take certain risks—that the average high school teacher might be more cautious about. If I let the students use pro-fanity in class, I would not, for instance, have to worry about being taken to task by a harried administrator, nor would I have to worry greatly about some of the disciplinary problems that conceivably might ensue: if the students became noisy and rebellious, I could console my-self that I had to spend only an hour with them a day; moreover, they would not communicate uproarious dissent to a population of their friends and peers waiting in the halls.

As one means of encouraging the students to express themselves naturally on paper, I assigned a journal to be handed in each week, an ungraded piece of work in which they could write anything they wanted to. The response ranged from poems to stories to academic essays (some-times designed to be passed in for another subject back in the home high school), physics problems, personal narratives and speculations, book reports, etc. "Anything they wanted" had to admit plagiarism, of which I got some, and it also rapidly came to include art work—politi-cal cartoons, abstractions, and just plain scribbles. The slogan "Four-letter words are best" came up in a class discussion of bureaucratic jargon, and I told the class that if they wanted to cuss in their journals they could (for his first journal one student handed in a page made up entirely of "fuck-you's"). It is not surprising that I was soon getting some journals each week that were notable for their concentrations of slang and dialectal usage.

Here is an instance.

Today more and more young people find themselves getting high. The most common is drinking. Reefer is another way of becoming high that is becoming common. Heroin is finding its place too. Out of all these I have experienced two. These are drinking and reefer or bush. I like to get high off of both. The bush high is a smooth mellow high. It takes you through plenty of changes. It makes music sound better to me. It's slower and the instruments are more distinct. When I'm high off of bush I like to listen to jazz. I could dig smoking about four "dynamite j's" and listening to *74 miles away*. It gives you an out of sight "peck jones." That means it makes you hungry. It can make a bowl of beans taste like steak and mashed potatoes. When you've layed off some bad bush you can really do some square business rapping. It gives you the power to blow any broad's mind. "Grogging" is bad too. It's not mellow as "smoke" but it gives you a good partying high. Grog some vodka or gin or rum or "bush-ead" and you got a nice partying high. Drinking just might have some slight after effects. There is also another pretty nice high. This one is from nul's. All they do is make you nod. There are some other ones that I haven't tried and don't plan to. The "bo" high is a bad thing. I heard it puts you through a lot of weird changes. "Scag" is supposedly the bad-dest. They say it feels almost as good as sex. Some of the dudes I saw that have a "jones" be in pretty bad shape when they can't "get over." Those are the only ways I'm hep to either from hearsay or actual experi-ence. I know you've been high off some drink before, but I recommend the bush to you.

From the perspective of an English teacher, a number of observations can be made about this paper. It is vivid and concrete: it does not have the prefabricated, textureless quality of a lot of undergraduate prose. Moreover—what I like best—it is a paper about language, a paper in which the student is *enjoying* looking at language. The essay begins on impersonal stilts: perhaps the author was trying academese. It then quickly shifts into slang and dialect for a virtuoso in-quotes display. In going to slang, the author is trying to appeal to his teacher (the final advice indicates that), but in the process he's used a vocabulary that he knows and enjoys, and he has thought about language.

This kind of conscious display of language, encouraged I believe by the idea of the journal, began to show up before long in what were presumably more formal writing situations. At one point in the first semester, for example, the students were asked to write a personal state-ment that could be used on their college applications.

Here is one result of that assignment:

I know this "brother" named Al. Talkin' 'bout class, man he stays clean!
He had a sixty-seven hog last year, bought a '68 Mark III this year and
now he's planning on getting a '69 Mark III. And his flat, man his "crib"
is "laid" like no other crib you've seen before.

There aren't too many ways you can run into enough "dust" to acquire
these luxuries. He made his by running his game down on the "sisters"
including the blue-eyed ones. He's also risking a jail sentence. I would like
to make mine legally. I think that is what college is all about. Going to
college and graduating will prepare you for a better job than if you had
not gone. And I hope everyone knows, in the phrase "better job" better
means "more money." That is why I would like to go to college.

brother: black person (male)	laid: nice, sharp
clean: dresses nice	dust: money, lines
hog: Cadillac	running his game: pimping
flat: house	sisters: black person (female)
crib: house	blue-eyed sisters: white girls

This paper employs a more self-conscious manipulation of language
than the first paper: it not only flourishes the student's special linguistic
knowledge, but more than the first paper it teases and satirizes the
ignorance of the white establishment (this, after all, is addressed to a
college admissions office). Slang has become a conscious literary device,
a means by which the student can defend his own dignity by twitting
university officials for their ignorance. The paper is not subtle, but from
an English teacher's view it is a good performance.

These two papers suggest certain broad hypotheses about the relation of inner city students to language, hypotheses that challenge any
middle-class assumption that inner city students are linguistically unsophisticated, either in their use of slang or their knowledge of standard
English. First, in response to their shared sense of ethnic identity, inner
city blacks especially have a feeling for, indeed a love of, language—
their language—that may have no clear counterpart among the attitudes
of suburban white students. When black kids get together and begin
to talk in ways no white can follow, weaving their voices through
rhythmic and tonal changes as well as slang vocabulary, when they slap
their knees and "woo-ee" with the pleasure of listening to each other,
they are enjoying language—to a degree that few of their white peers
do or that few of their teachers realize. And pedagogically the question
(if not the answer) is simple: what can be done in the classroom with
this love of language?

These papers suggest another important hypothesis: at least by the
time inner city students are in high school, they know more of standard
language than teachers know of theirs. Their use of the "establishment's"
language may be imperfect, but such students' enjoyment of slang—

clearly black students' pleasure in dialect—is partly an awareness that they are violating an "official" standard. (It is a truism that in our society blacks know more about whites than whites know about blacks: the same principle seems applicable to language.) Certainly the second paper follows the official conventions of syntax. The writer is showing simultaneous mastery of two conventions—that of the white college and that of black, inner city slang.

The two papers I have cited so far are perhaps relatively unsophisticated, even though they show the students' enjoyment of slang and dialect and their awareness of different language levels. From time to time, however, a number of students in the class were able to do quite sophisticatd things with their language skill. One way in which this occurred was the attempt to set down as accurately as possible the pronunciation and intonation of slang and dialect.

DONOUGHTS   DOUGHNUTS
DOUGHNOUGHTS

One day I was eatin' some doughnuts,
They were good. wooo! Lawd they wuz
good!
They wuz like dynamite!
OH, WOW, they were heavy, heavy,
goooood!
It wuz like drinkin' six bottles of Robitusin
they were so good!
I started screamin' "They're good! Augh
they're good!"

BROWNIES   BROUGHNIEGHS
BEROUNYS

Then I got a hold of a brownies,
WOOOOOOOOOOOOOOOOOOOOOOOOO OO!
It shot my mind out!
Lawd, it was nasteeeee!
If nasty was ever, it was that brownie!
An old, dried-up, *nasty,* gagg-you, stick-in-
your-throat, choke-you, kill you, funeral-
ize-you, bury-you, run-you-down-when-your
dead,

BROWNIE

This paper is a celebration for its own sake of the joy of slang and dialect. The author's typography communicated to the other students almost like musical notation.

The student's freedom to use dialect, slang and profanity was sometimes applied vividly and emphatically in themes on rather typical

English-class topics—as, for instance, in this response to why Fitzgerald begins Chapter Two of *The Great Gatsby* with the ashheaps.

> The ash heaps in Chapter II remind me of the way the people in Chapter I acted. The people in Chapter I are conceited, wealthy and they think they are God's gift to the human race. To me they are stinking and obnoxious. The people in Chapter I seem to consider people other than the aristocratic class, as dirt or ashes. You see they thought the outside world was unnecessary and they thought (literally) to hell with it. Ashes are very insignificant and those obnoxious clods in Chapter I considered people insignificant. Ashes could also symbolize the form people turn to after death, and the creepy dummies in Chapter I thought the other or the poor people should be dead. Ashes can also imply how useless the outside world really is. Who needs ashes thought the fools in Chapter I. I say who needs bastards like those snobbish, punkity people in Chapter I.

This paper, written in class in about half-an-hour, may not be long on evidence, but its assertions are insightful and, most important, well emphasized by the special vividness of the well chosen slang or cuss word.

I will confess that the class *was* a noisy one, and some of the students, in good conservative teen-age fashion, were perplexed that I allowed slang and profanity: they saw a great symbol of discipline threatened, and they worried also about "proper" language for the English classroom (one of these conservatives described me in his journal as a "weird dude"). But perplexity may be an inevitable learning step, and the anxiety of the conservatives did not stop the class, even the conservatives themselves, from continuing their use of slang and profanity in the journals. The best students continued to ponder language, their own place in the linguistic scheme of things.

> *Sometimes I amaze myself with my amount of Bladder Control.*
> I might as well own up to the fact that I'm fairly well hung up on cars. I don't know when or how this happened but now its starting to get damn ridiculous.
> The fact that I spend the greater portion of my time with my face stuck in a car magazine is part of this. I would estimate that since 1964 I've had over 200 various car magazines. I started with: Hot Rod. Then I moved on to Motor Trend. From there I went to Road & Track. Now I'm on Car & Driver which is the damn best of any of them.
> Now comes the funny part. If I love cars so much, why the hell am I so bashful about it? I've found out that people through the years who don't know a damn thing about cars can really put you on the spot. A couple of weeks ago the subject came up between me and a certain person who is hooked on Dodge Chargers. According to this person, a Charger was "bad" because "iss a baad mawfuckin' chine!" period. When I said something about a Road Runner, I got, "a mawfuckin' Sheveyll could beat

a mawfuckin' Rowwed Runnuh!" Nothing I could say about power-to-weight ratios, frontal-area, choce (sic) of engines, rear axle ratios etc. could budge this individual from his chauvinistic stand. ("get duh hayull outuh mah fayse mawfuckuh!")

Why didn't I tell him about the Chargers 375 hp. engine against the Road Runners 425 h.p. Hemi engine? Why didn't I tell him about the Road Runners lighter curb weight?, or a dozen other things that I could have rattled off like that (clic)? I'll retaliate now in this individuals language: "Ain' no mawfuckin' Chawjuh gon' beet no gawdamm Himmi Rowwed Runnah no muwfuckin' taym!"

This paper consummately represents the kind of linguistic awareness one hopes to stimulate in a composition course. The author has created with language—pedantic, technical jargon—a persona for himself, the portrait of a fall guy who is mocked by another language he also knows —the earthy slur of slang. But the paper is not only about language: it is about two worlds, two qualities of response. A chance to use slang and profanity has perhaps helped this student to work out on paper a truth that his background has already taught him—that language is a choice of allegiance, and that as a bright black teen-ager, an inner city student prepping for a place in the "system," he will always be measuring the special gains and losses of knowledge of two worlds.

SOME CONSIDERATIONS WHEN MARKING

Leslie Stratta

Introduction

FOR many teachers of English, especially young and inexperienced teachers, the marking of written work can be a problem. There are several, but different, reasons for this. Teachers are sceptical about the value of marking, especially its ability to improve written competence; they are uncertain what to look for, and consequently are uncertain about criteria; some are unhappy about marking 'creative' writing, arguing that by doing so violence is done to the pupils' 'creativity.' Because there is this uncertainty, it might be profitable to explore the

FROM *English in Education* (Autumn 1969), pp. 45–46. Reprinted by permission.

subject in an article of this kind, considering some of the attitudes, values and standards teachers of English might bring to their pupils' written work, in the hope that some of their uncertainties can be resolved. The article will, therefore, confine itself to the day to day on-going writing of the classroom rather than writing for examination purposes,[1] and it will be slanted more towards secondary than primary writing, although it is hoped that some of the exploration will also be of benefit to teachers in the top end of the primary school.

The Writing Experience

Before considering marking in any detail, it might be profitable to consider first, albeit briefly, some aspects of the writing experience itself, in the hope that these will throw into sharper perspective the role of marking.

Vigotsky, discussing writing in *Thought & Language,* suggests that 'the development of writing does not repeat the developmental history of speaking. Written speech is a separate linguistic function, differing from oral speech in both structure and mode of functioning. Even its minimal development requires a high level of abstraction. It is speech in thought and image only, lacking the musical, expressive, intonational qualities of oral speech. In learning to write, the child must disengage himself from the sensory aspect of speech and replace words by images of words. Speech that is merely imagined and that requires symbolisation of the sound image in written signs (i.e., a second degree of symbolisation) naturally must be as much harder than oral speech for the child as algebra is harder than arithmetic. Our studies show that it is the abstract quality of written language that is the main stumbling block, not the underdevelopment of small muscles or any other mechanical obstacles.

'Writing is also speech without an interlocutor, addressed to an absent or imaginary person or to no one in particular—a situation new and strange to the child. Our studies show that he has little motivation to learn writing when we begin to teach it. He feels no need for it and has only a vague idea of its usefulness. In conversation, every sentence is prompted by a motive. Desire or need lead to request, question to answer, bewilderment to explanation. The changing motives of the interlocutors determine at every moment the turn oral speech will take. It does not have to be consciously directed—the dynamic situation takes

[1] Britton, J. N., Martin, N. C. and Rosen, H., *Multiple Marking of English Composition,* The Schools Council Examinations Bulletin No. 12 (H.M.S.O. 1966). This is one of the most recent discussions of marking English composition for examination purposes.

care of that. The motives for writing are more abstract, more intellectualised, further removed from immediate needs. In written speech, we
are obliged to create the situation, to represent it to ourselves. This demands detachment from the actual situation'.[2]

If Vigotsky is correct in arguing that 'In learning to write, the child
must disengage himself from the sensory aspect of speech and replace
words by images of words', that 'writing is also speech without an interlocutor, addressed to an absent or imaginary person or to no one in
particular' and that unlike speech 'The motives for writing are more
abstract, more intellectualised, further removed from immediate needs',
then it is small wonder that many pupils find writing difficult to master.
The problem is shown even more clearly in a further point made by
Vigotsky when he argues that 'the physiological functions in which
written speech is based have not begun to be developed in the proper
sense when instruction in writing starts. It must build on barely emerging, rudimentary processes'.[3] Although Vigotsky is talking about pupils
at the infant and early junior stage, some of the points he is making
have relevance for older pupils, for, as we all know, although many
pupils manage eventually to overcome these difficulties and write with
ease and confidence, many do not, and leave school only partially or
barely literate. Part of the reason for this may be poor and haphazard
teaching, but part may be that many pupils continue for quite some
time to find it difficult to write to 'an absent or imaginary person or
to no one in particular', and consequently continue to find it difficult
'to create the situation (and) to represent it to (themselves)'.

Before discussing further the implications of Vigotsky's argument, it
might be profitable, at this juncture, to consider, again briefly, why it
is important for pupils to write with competence. One obvious reason
is that in a literate society people need to be literate, and writing is
one aspect of literacy. However, another reason, not quite so obvious,
is that in the act of writing we are encountering experience in a different
manner from when we talk, which is the mode of language we operate
in most of the time. Whereas talk is, on the whole, a spontaneous, public mode of language which we are continually using to organise, order,
and make sense of the flux of experience we are encountering hourly in
our lives, writing is a more reflective and private mode of language, when
we have more time to think over our experiences and ideas and explore
them anew, perhaps seeing them afresh and gaining new insights into
them. Presumably, as teachers of English, we want to encourage a reflective attitude in our pupils, and a preparedness to explore anew.
Writing would seem appropriate in developing these abilities.

2 Vigotsky, L. S., *Thought and Language* (M.I.T. & Wiley, 1962), pp. 98–9.
3 Vigotsky, L. S., *Thought and Language* (M.I.T. & Wiley, 1962), p. 100.

The Classroom Context

If writing is a more reflective and private mode of language than talk in which to operate upon experience, and if Vigotsky is right when he says that 'it is the abstract quality of written language that is the main stumbling block', then the implications of both for the teacher of English are far reaching. It is obviously important that the English classroom must be a place where reflective work can go on, but equally important it must be a place where pupils, whether junior or secondary, are helped through the difficulties of operating in a mode of language more abstract than speech. And the difficulties may, at times, be as great for the pupil with good syntactical control who is trying to explore new or difficult experiences, as they are probably all the time for the pupil with poor syntactical control who is exploring more familiar experience. In order then to help pupils, especially those who have poor control of writing, to move with less difficulty to the more abstract activity of writing, it would seem sensible if initially some attempt were made to explore experience in more concrete terms, where pupils would be more likely to be at ease, and consequently succeed. One obvious starting point is through talk, another is drama. Through talk pupils begin to probe and explore their experiences in a very concrete manner. And by initially interchanging impressions and ideas in this concrete manner, they can begin to get at least a partial control over the subject eventually to be written about.

But for talk to be successful during this initial probing, there must be a climate of mutual respect between pupil and pupil, and pupil and teacher; the classroom must become a place in which it is natural to talk over things, to put forward very personal or tentative, even sometimes silly thoughts, without fear of ridicule or scorn. It must be a place where talking over ideas and exchanging impressions can take place in small groups, as well as in the larger class group. And it must be a place where, during these initial probings, the teacher sees his role changing as the situation demands. The delicacy and complexity of his role is hinted at in this passage from *Growth through English*. The 'teacher can help by noticing and reinforcing a potential change in the level or direction of the discussion, summing up an attitude perhaps, making an issue quite explicit, or calling for an instance when generalizing seems to have lost touch with reality'.[4]

It is in the context of this kind of classroom atmosphere, together with the awareness of the difficulties that pupils face when trying to write, that we teachers of English need to ask the question—what then is the function of our marking?

4 Dixon, J., *Growth through English* (N.A.T.E. Reading, 1967), pp. 34–5.

Some Criteria

Many of the important issues can probably be quickly, and dramatically, raised by looking at the following piece of writing[5] from a boy aged 16 years.

SAYING GOODBYE

Only an hour to ago befor I leves to cattes the train which will take me to portmorth with a thurnded other fellows, Going to the same place. for all your nown they mike be on the sane boat. I wounder whats its like in the R.N. Mike be good, seeing atlacing all day. And new port each week. half an hour to before the train. I wonder that mums thinkin I pett his evy her eyes out right now. Shes all. right, she won be seeing men lie every day and night. she got dads pensiver and the ransen bock. finteen mins heft peter get redy for the startion's Come on mum where's dad, 'In the car'. 'right'. We araidy at the startions the train just aggraidy. every kissing their muns dads wives childs good bye. We good-bye mums good-bye I write to you evert day and I see you every time I am, on leve. Bye mun, bye dad bye they must be take it bad. her only son going to war for the first time. Bye.

HOWARD.

Because there is a problem of deciphering, this ill-spelt, poorly punctuated piece may, at first sight, cause irritation, difficulty, indifference and even hostility. However, if one takes the trouble to get below its surface appearance and endeavours to read the piece as the pupil might have wanted it to be read, the transformation can be both dramatic and rewarding.

SAYING GOODBYE

Only an hour to go before I leave to catch the train, which will take me to Portsmouth with a hundred other fellows going to the same place. For all you know, they might be on the same boat. I wonder what it's like in the R.N. It might be good seeing the Atlantic all day, and a new port each week.

Half an hour to go before the train. I wonder what mum's thinking. I bet she's crying her eyes out right now. She's all right. She won't be seeing men die every day and night. She's got dad's pension and the ration book.

Fifteen minutes left. Better get ready for the station.

"Come on mum, where's dad?"

---

[5] London Association for the Teaching of English, *Assessing Compositions* (Blackie, 1965), p. 19. This pamphlet is a valuable discussion of the problems of assessing composition.

"In the car."

"Right."

We're all ready at the station. The train is just ready. Every one is kissing their mums, dads, wives and children goodbye.

"Well goodbye mum. Goodbye. I'll write to you every day, and I'll see you every time I'm on leave. Bye mum. Bye dad. Bye."

They must be taking it badly. Her only son going to the war for the first time.

"Bye".

HOWARD.

Once deciphered, we see immediately that the piece, at several levels, is very competent indeed. For example, there is a skillful suggestion of time passing, with the tempo increasing as the minutes ebb away; there is a sensitive awareness of the situation, shown exceptionally cleverly from one angle; the writer is able to move easily from the inner world of the young man's thoughts to the outer world of action and decision making.

By approaching pieces of writing of this kind then in a positive rather than negative frame of mind, we are more likely to discover where, and in what manner, the pupil has succeeded. And by taking the trouble to dig below the surface appearance, the teacher demonstrates that he is genuinely interested in what the pupil is trying to say. (Of course, to be able to do this, the teacher has to be a sensitive and practised reader).

Once one approaches marking in this way, however, looking first for achievement, the question of standards is immediately raised, for despite this pupil's sensitivity and skill, the fact still remains that his control is poor at the very important levels of syntax and spelling, both crucial aids to the reader. It is at moments like this that one is brought sharply up against the question—how is one to respond to the writing of one's pupil's? Could it not be argued by demonstrating to the pupil that one is genuinely interested in what he has to say, despite his obviously poor control of syntax and spelling, that this is tantamount to accepting slovenliness and sloppiness? If, of course, the teacher sees his rôle as assessor, marking each piece of writing against a fixed standard, this standard being concerned in the main with syntactical and spelling accuracy, then any response which is sympathetic to the writing despite these deficiencies could be construed in this way. If, however, the teacher believes that it is essential for his pupils to learn to handle the written mode of language flexibly, sensitively, exactly and fluently, so that the language used, across the spectrum of personal to impersonal styles, conveys the experience into words in as faithful a manner as each pupil is individually capable of at that moment; and if he wants his pupils to become increasingly aware of the possibilities of language, its subtleties, power and limitations, then he will know that response is more complex than being concerned mainly with syntax and spelling; just as each piece of writing is concerned with more than only this. Consequently, he will know that marking is a more complex activity than merely spotting syntactical and spelling errors. In recognising a pupil's strengths the teacher is not automatically endorsing his present limitations, being sympathetic need not mean an acceptance of inferior work from a sentimental attitude to the pupil. A sympathetic approach will accept the pupil's present standard as a starting point, but will always desire to raise it in the best possible way. But how to raise it is, of course, what teachers of English, in the main, find very difficult.

Some Practice

If the teacher accepts each pupil's present standard as a starting point, it soon becomes obvious that these will differ between pupils even in the same class, let alone the same year. Consequently, responding and marking, if they are to be most helpful to each individual, will have to be concerned with individual needs, and must be thought of as means of helping each pupil in his personal growth to maturity. Howard's needs, for example, are very different from this 14 year old's, who says little but with greater control of syntax and spelling.

FACES

A person's face gives you your first impression of them, yet you must be careful of the long thin-lipped criminal's face which conceals a loving heart. Or equally careful of the jolly, round-faced murderer, whom you would not associate in any way with crime. Yet some are easier to decide about; the butler's quiet dignity, the porter's honest boredom, the schoolboy's happy smile during games, his bored look over the evening's prep. Quiet concentration is often evident in the face of someone reading.

Faces are to a certain extent a person's individual badge. They come in all shapes, sizes, and expressions. Long faces, round faces, craggy faces, thin lips, thick lips, blue eyes, grey eyes, moustaches, beards, clean-shaven faces, hooked noses, straight noses. Faces show many of the person's thoughts and reactions, through the eyes, but mainly through the shape of the mouth, or what it says. Faces can have many expressions, sad, happy, laughing, crying, contented, painted, smiling, surprised, shocked, angry. Indeed a face is what gives you your first impression of somebody.

Probably the most effective way of helping each pupil is to discuss his work with him individually. If, as has been suggested, the classroom is a place where things are talked over in an atmosphere of mutual trust and respect, then the talking over of individual work on completion will give the teacher the opportunity to show in some detail where the work succeeds and where it might be improved or reshaped. It also reaffirms the teacher's interest in his pupils as individuals. This, however, is perhaps a counsel of perfection at least for the secondary school teacher, for with classes of thirty or more pupils and perhaps only five or six periods of English per week, he cannot see each pupil individually after each piece of writing. He can, though, see some, perhaps four or five. And if he is systematic, he can perhaps see all his class individually two or three times per term, which is better than not at all. There is also something to be gained from talking over the work with individuals, or groups of pupils, while they are in the process of writing. By doing this, the teacher can advise and suggest in a manner which has immediate personal relevance, something not easily done if the work is taken away on completion. Similarly, correcting can be explained in an individual manner. Points of syntax, for example, have a better chance of being understood because of his individual attention. Again with classes of thirty or more, individual attention is difficult; but if the teacher works systematically with different pupils each time writing takes place, he can, with luck, see each pupil individually approximately once every three weeks or so.

Most marking, however, takes place away from the classroom on completion of the writing. And this can have its advantages, in that the teacher can consider coolly each piece of work free from the immediate pressures of the classroom situation. The suggestions which follow may be more appropriate for this kind of practice.

Marking for individual needs may frequently mean marking selectively. And this can take different forms. For example, were Howard's work to be marked comprehensively at the level of syntax and spelling, one could have the teacher write as much as the pupil, which would be ineffective for two reasons. Firstly, there would almost certainly be far too many different kinds of corrections for him to understand and begin to come to terms with, and secondly, more importantly, he would almost certainly be demoralised. However, if one were to mark the syntax and spelling selectively, concentrating perhaps at the level of syntax on full stops for sentence endings and capital letters for sentence beginnings, and at the level of spelling on some of the most frequently used words, such as 'go' and 'before',[6] the pupil might have a better chance of understanding his weaknesses, which might subsequently result in his gaining a more sure control of the written mode.

Another form of selective marking, at the level of syntax or spelling,

[6] McNally, J. and Murray, W., *Key Words to Literacy*, (Schoolmaster Publishing Co. Ltd., London, 1962). This publication has a useful list of the most frequently used words.

is to mark in some detail perhaps only the first or final side of a piece of written work. In marking only the first side, one is probably concentrating on the most controlled part of the work, and in marking only the final side, one is concentrating on probably the least controlled, when one's pupils may well have been flagging. Individual needs will determine where the teacher chooses to concentrate his attention.

Selective marking need not, of course, be concentrated exclusively on syntax or spelling. One could, for example, inform the pupils beforehand that the piece of writing will be marked for ability to describe a person's external appearance realistically, or to organise the points in an argument, or for an exciting adventure, and so on. In this way, the pupil's attention can be focussed on an aspect of writing the teacher feels it important for him, at that moment, to try to gain more control of, without there being undue distraction from other aspects. As has already been argued, one is, of course, working towards mastery of many aspects, not least syntax and spelling, but for many pupils this is a slow and difficult task, which may be helped, at least in the early stages of their attempting something new, by being invited to concentrate only on this new aspect and being assured that the writing will be marked selectively.

One important consideration when marking is to recognise that writing is not an undifferentiated task, but that there are several different kinds of writing tasks, and many pupils will find not all of them easy to control. The kinds of linguistic resources and strategies that a person needs in order to handle these different writing tasks are as yet unknown, but what some teachers are slowly beginning to realise is that many pupils seem to find narrative easier to handle than argument, and it may be this sequence which pupils need to move through in order to gain a flexible and fluent control of different writing styles, from the personal to impersonal.[7] In the light of this, undifferentiated judgments on a pupil's ability to write must be seen as crude assessments indeed of his ability, As we mark, we must have some awareness of the different demands each writing task makes, and consequently mark accordingly. A breakdown in syntax need not necessarily be due to carelessness, but could equally be caused by the pupil attempting to grapple with a complex or painful experience which is just eluding him at that moment, either because he cannot quite control the style of language which the experience demands, or because he cannot quite focus up the experience sharply enough.

Yet another consideration the teacher must be aware of is his prejudices regarding subject matter, and pupils. To be objective is, of course, difficult, but the teacher, when marking, must be concerned

[7] Britton, J. N., Martin, N. C. and Rosen, H., *Abilities to Write*, (*New Education*, October, 1966).

not to let his prejudices cloud his judgment. A pupil he likes, writing about a subject he likes, is in grave danger of not being marked or advised for his needs, if the teacher is blind to his own prejudices.

I should like now to consider the comments one makes about the written work of pupils, and the giving of numerical marks for each piece. If, as I have tried to argue, responding and marking is a positive activity, aimed to help pupils gain better control of the written mode, and to help them in their personal growth to maturity, then the comments the teacher makes, both orally and written, are of vital importance. It is, therefore, essential that they are personally meaningful to the pupil, showing him where he personally has succeeded and where he personally needs to concentrate more attention. Thus, comments such as 'poor' or 'good' tell the pupil little or nothing, and suggest that the teacher is either uncertain about how to respond, or is unwilling to do so. To tell Howard, for example, that he must 'try harder with punctuation' or that his work is 'fair' would almost certainly be meaningless. It might be more profitable to comment that he has 'sensitively caught the young man's thoughts and skillfully suggested the passing of the final hour before departure'. Positive personal comment such as this can help him to accept more readily the further comments one would want to make on some aspect of the uncertain control of syntax.

With regard to numerical marking, it can be argued that if marking is for the pupil's benefit, it is essentially the teacher's remarks, and not numerical marks, which are important. Consequently there is no need to mark numercially and pupils begin to accept this. While I personally am sympathetic to this point of view, the fact remains that many teachers will not be convinced of this, arguing that pupils prefer to receive marks in addition to comment. This being the case, how then is one to mark Howard's piece? At the level of imaginative insight, and control of time passing, his work would score high, perhaps eight or nine out of ten; but at the level of syntax and spelling, his work is poor and would score low, perhaps only one or two out of ten. How does one resolve this conflict? If one averages out the two marks and gives five out of ten, this again would tell Howard nothing. It certainly would not tell him in what respects the writing has succeeded or failed. One partial resolution, and it is only a partial resolution, is to give two marks, one for technical control, the other for imaginative insight, good argument, or whatever it is that one has required of the pupils. At least, by doing this, one is telling the pupil something more meaningful about his work, than any crude global mark will tell, for he does realise, to some degree, where he has succeeded and where more effort needs to be concentrated.

At this juncture, it might be worth considering those pupils who are never really poor, but who never really produce exciting work. If marks are being given, does one continually give these pupils an average mark? If one is convinced that the pupil is trying, it would seem to me that a never varying average mark hardly encourages him. If marking is for personal needs, then it would seem to me that there is a pressing need, in order to encourage him, for the averagely competent pupil to be told every so often that his work is very good, whether or not it really is. Nothing can be more depressing than to try hard yet never have one's work enthused over.

Preventing Errors

So far, this article has been discussing the kinds of responses we, as teachers of English, might make to the work after it has been written. I should like now to consider what we might do, prior to receiving the finished work, in order to help pupils gain more sure control of the written mode, especially at the level of syntax and spelling.

An important consideration, frequently lost sight of in the secondary school especially, is that a pupil needs to be given sufficient time to write. If, as has been argued, writing is a more reflective, personal way of encountering experience than the more spontaneous public way of talk, and we think it essential that our pupils be encouraged to develop a more reflective attitude to experience than some, at least, have already, then they must be given time to reflect. The secondary school timetable, chopped up daily, as it is, into small chunks, too often militates against this. Where possible writing ought to take place within a double rather than a single period, or if this is not convenient and writing is started during a single period, time should be allowed, either at home or in a subsequent period, for the work to be completed. The quality of the writing will almost certainly be that much poorer if pupils are constantly racing against the clock; and this will be especially so if they are encountering a new style, or exploring a new facet of experience, for the first time.

If pupils then are to be given time to reflect, they must also be encouraged to do so. Too often, with students in training at least, one sees interesting preparatory work have less effect, because pupils are not restrained from writing immediately about almost the first thing which appeals to them, or enters their heads. Had they been encouraged to make notes before writing, in order to try to sort out and crystallise their ideas more sharply, the quality of their work would, almost certainly, have been that much better. Obviously, with pupils struggling to gain a rudimentary control of writing, one would not, at first, insist on note making, for the prior aim with them is to facilitate ease and desire to write. But once a measure of control has been gained, it is important to encourage a more reflective attitude.

In addition, it is also important to encourage pupils to work more carefully and meticulously. Many errors of syntax and spelling, for example, are caused through carelessness, not ignorance, and can be eradicated, in time, when pupils are encouraged to check over their work carefully before handing it in. It is important, however, that they are systematically reminded to do this, for unless this is done with each piece of work, meticulous habits may never be formed, at least with some pupils. This is especially so with work done at home, for here there may be distractions which help to reinforce, or even cause, careless attitudes. Consequently, work done at home will often need to be read through more carefully before it is handed in, and it would seem sensible, therefore, if the teacher himself collected it in the English lesson, but before doing so, allowed some minutes for it to be checked through.

Despite all that one does in helping pupils, there are some who seem always to find aspects of writing, especially syntax, difficult to control. It may be, as Vigotsky argues, that writing is 'speech in thought and image only, lacking the musical, expressive, intonational qualities of oral speech', and that for this reason these pupils are unable to hold written sentence rhythms and tunes in their heads. This problem can, at times, be overcome if the pupil is asked to read aloud his work, either to the teacher working with him individually, or on completion and prior to handing in. On reading aloud, many pupils seem to hear more clearly the sentence rhythms and tunes, and often discover the errors themselves.

Handing Back

Equally important as writing is the manner in which the written work is handed back for unless this is done thoughtfully and tactfully, the time spent on reading and commenting on the work can be largely time wasted. If all the pupil does, after his writing has been returned, is to glance cursorily at the comments, note a mark if one has been given, and finally confine the work to the limbo of his desk, to be taken out again only when called upon to write a further piece, then most of the teacher's effort will have been wasted. And as importantly, an opportunity will have been lost to extend each pupil's horizons, through discussing and savouring the work of the whole class. Time spent handing back writing can be time well invested, and if most is to be gained from this activity, it cannot be hurried.

Perhaps its most valuable aspect is that the pupils are considering language in operation, trying to understand more about words and experience. Also valuable is that in discussing their work they are being helped to build up both confidence in ability to control the written mode, and pride in achievement. But in order for this to happen, it is again essential that response starts positively. The following piece, written by a 13 year old, might be well worth discussing positively before one draws attention to its shortcomings.

A Building Site

The strong muscular men swing their mullets, sweat with the saw at the toughest wood, laying and cementing the bricks in their rows, and controlling the various machinery. The powerfull cranes move to and fro carrying their heavy loads from one place to another, the loaded lorries bring continuously the various materials required, and the sound of sturdy drills burying themselves deep into the stuborn gravel.

The sound of noisey hammering, of tractors, and drills echoes around the site as men set about their work. The foreman shouting his orders destinct and clear as he inspects the work, and men talking as they give each other an helping hand.

If one were to choose this piece to discuss with a class, one might focus on its rhythm, for this, I would suggest, is one of its strengths. The discussion might, for example, explore the muscularity of the rhythm, and ask what, if anything, this adds to the experience, echoing, as it does, the muscularity and toughness of the men and their work. And if it were thought to be appropriate, one might, in addition, introduce another piece for consideration, perhaps from an adult writer, where rhythm again echoes sense. By looking at an example of writing from the pupil where the experience is probably more familiar, and juxtaposing it against one from an adult where the experience may be less familiar, one can extend individual experience.

Or one might choose to explore the interesting, if occasional, use of vocabulary such as 'sturdy drills' and 'stubborn gravel,' by asking the class to consider in what way the meaning would alter, and whether this would be important, if the writer had written 'hard gravel' instead of 'stubborn gravel,' and 'strong drills' instead of 'sturdy drills.'

Group discussion of this kind, sympathetically exploring how a pupil has tried to order experience and put it into words, can open new horizons into experience for the whole class, and, as importantly, illustrate something of the possibilities of choices in language, and how these modify experience.

In addition to discussion of this kind, one can discuss points of syntax with the class, especially those which might be creating difficulties. This might be done by writing on the board an example from the work, where perhaps the control has broken down, and then inviting the class to discuss how it might be improved. In this manner the pupils are examining an example of living language (as distinct from many 'exercises', the language of which is usually sterile and divorced from experience), where a pupil has tried to organise experience for a purpose. In addition, one is hoping that the pupils are beginning to understand why mistakes are being made.

If the comments written by the teacher at the end of a piece of work are to be read and understood, pupils will need time for this. An appropriate moment might be after a selection of their work has been discussed, and all of it returned. Pupils can then settle down to read the comments, ask for further elucidation where needed, and then perhaps write some corrections, for example reshaping a sentence or two where control has broken down, or where the meaning has faltered.

Displaying Work

For a pupil's written work to have its fullest impact, it needs to be read, not only by the teacher, but by other pupils in the school. Nothing can convince him more that his work has little or no significance, if after writing it, it is remorselessly confined to the darkness of his desk. If work then is to be read by a wide audience, it needs to be displayed in classroom, corridor or hall, where other pupils can see it, and subsequently talk about it. Interest will be quickened by these displays, not only in the writing itself, but also in presentation. Once it is recognised that writing which is to be displayed should be presented in a pleasing manner, aspects of writing, such as handwriting and general layout of the page, will be seen to play an important part both in inviting the reader to read, and helping him to do so. Discussion of layout of presentation can show clearly that neatness in writing has relevance, and can help to improve general standards of care. The importance of presentation can be taken further if pupils are invited to mount displays. Discussion of layout, considering, for example, juxtaposition of pictures, photographs, newspaper cuttings, and so on, can open awareness of the significance of aesthetic statements, in addition to written statements.

Conclusion

It might be appropriate to end an article of this kind by posing the question—are there some pieces of writing which are better not commented on, and some which perhaps defy, even transcend comment? The following short poem,[8] written by a 14 year old girl in a Secondary Modern School, is perhaps in this last category. How do you respond to it, and how would you comment upon it?

---

8 I am indebted to Mr. Michael Hughes for this poem, which was written by a pupil in a Sussex school.

HE DIED FOR HIS COUNTRY

A letter came telling me
"He died for his country"
What will I say
When my fatherless child asks why and how?
"He died for his country"
The boy won't understand—
The suffering and pain he went through,
And me—the heartache and longing.

SELF-EVALUATION OF WRITTEN EFFORT —THE MOMENT FOR LEARNING

Reese P. Maughan

THE customary way the classroom teacher goes about the business of evaluating the written work of her pupils in today's classrooms can be seriously questioned. No sensible reason is there for holding so doggedly to the persistent practice she employs in marking and scoring the innumerable papers which come across her desk—a practice which lags far behind the sweeping changes which have taken place in the mode of the written expression itself. Her appraisal of the paper work of her pupils, after they have left for home or after they have gone to other classrooms, contributes little or nothing to their learning. Actually, her "pupil writes-teacher marks" way of appraisal works against learning. Instead of building correct habits and skills and bringing about meaningful understandings and deeper appreciations, her pencil-checking intrusions are more apt to work at crosspurposes with what she is attempting to teach. Most reprehensible of all, the taciturn effect this common procedure of appraisal has upon learning English usage and language skills, where growth in the skills of expression falls far short of favorable acceptance, bespeaks little in its favor. Indeed, of all learning experiences resulting from written effort, those associated directly with the acquirement of the skills of expression suffer greatest loss from this standard method of paper-appraisal. Such charges may sound untenable, but they deserve thoughtful consideration, viewed in the light of what is known about how learners learn. This, notwithstanding the fact that since our

->>> ->>>

FROM *Education*, Vol. 91 (November–December 1970), pp. 169–174. Reprinted by permission of the publisher and the author.

public schools began, the conventional way for managing the pencil-and-paper work of pupils is for the teacher to do the evaluating herself.

Conditions of Learning Are Violated

True and effectual learning conditions do not run counter to human nature and human needs. Our biologically-fixed patterns of behavior, inherent and immutable as they are, prescribe the ways the learner learns; any devised artifices, no matter how skillfully contrived and executed, are of little avail if they work in opposition to human constitutional bent. The teacher's sole appraisal, carried out in seclusion, is a practice which in no way agrees with the inherent qualities of human nature. This contention is based upon a well-known but oft-forgotten principle of learning prescribed in particular by the constitutional qualities of the learner, namely: the learner learns best if he has a clear knowledge of how well he is doing in his attempt to learn (12:13). A corollary to this primary condition of learning follows: *immediate* knowledge of the nature of performance gives the learner a decided edge over those who are not so informed—over those who encounter delayed knowledge of results (12, 7:234–236), particularly when he has the opportunity to inform himself by actually seeing the results of his efforts (7:236). The factor of immediacy in knowing the results seems to be equally as important as the knowledge of the results itself. The teacher's appraisal of the written accomplishment at the end of the day, or more often later, takes knowledge of performance away from the learner's grasp until long after the effective moment for learning has lost its impulse. Unless the learner knows how well he achieves in his attempts to learn, and unless such knowledge comes at the propitious time, learning is nil.

Written accomplishment must be honestly evaluated in order that the learner's scholastic achievements and relative progress can be determined. Furthermore, appraisal of the written performance is essential in order to ascertain, not only what has been learned of what has been taught, but also how productive has been the instruction—whether it has been superior or inferior, effective or not so effective. The weakness of the prevailing method lies, however, not in what is done in the way of appraisal, but what is not done. Better still, *how* the written product is appraised is more to the point. That the teacher assesses the paper work of the classroom most efficiently cannot be disputed; that she, herself, should mark and score the pupil's written performance can be openly challenged.

The "Teacher Marks" Manner of Appraisal Is Total

The conventional method of evaluating the written work of the class-room is so indiscriminate and all-embracing that any other approach appears to be nonexistent. A deeply imbedded conviction holds that the teacher's own unremitting efforts in marking countless papers pays off—that in some inexplicable way, such constant application to the assessment of all paper effort contributes immeasureably to the teaching-learning process. For some reason not clearly understood, training institutions for teachers seem to ignore or fail to implement ways and means for making practical use of these known truths about learning, and the beginning teacher enters the classroom with a false confidence that, by persevering unfalterably in the line of duty by appraising written endeavor as did her predecessors, all will be well and good. Checks and marks on papers are the reins to which the teacher holds firmly; the teacher makes all decisions and passes sole judgment on the paper performance, all in secrecy and seclusion. Instances in which the pupil has any part in the initial assessment of his own performances are rare indeed; he writes and having written, he meekly relinquishes his offering and then moves on to some new task to write again and again.

Each school day, teachers become enmeshed in the process of "correcting papers" at odd moments and in situations which would be startling if they were not so common. The teacher who secludes herself in a corner of the lunchroom to eat her lunch with one hand, while the other is hard-pressed in the business of checking papers, is no rare exception. The typical thinking regarding the proper way the paper work of the classroom should be managed is probably reflected by one who recently remarked, "Correcting papers is just a part of the job of being a teacher."

The Learner Has a Vested Right

Almost all the written work of the school day has one common feature of its own—a pattern characterized by short, abbreviated responses signified by a word or phrase, a stroke of the pencil or a number, or by some other symbol intended to designate skill and understanding. Hardly any part of the pencil-and-paper effort can be regarded as writing in its broader sense because the rhetorical or compositional factors are missing; few sentences are written in full, and the paragraph is even less common. There are exceptions, of course, to this usual pattern of performance, but the occasions when the pupil expresses himself in writing in an original and creative form are quite fragmentary. For the most part, the rhetorics of expression are already done for him, and only a slight imprint on his paper is needed to denote his reasoning and understanding. This kind of written endeavor, impressive in scope and often considered erroneously as tests and test-exercises, covers all phases of the curriculum and is by no means related narrowly to a few limited subjects. It is an integral part of nearly every written task of the school day.

Written effort, indicated primarily by objective, short-answer responses with which education is so highly infested in today's classrooms, hardly warrants the need for the teacher to become so picayune in the *modus operandi* of assessment with such telling effects. Fortunate or unfortunate as this may be, short-answer responses are inevitably with us in all classroom climates, and the learner quickly adapts to this way of expressing his acquired skills and achievements. If he learns to adjust so easily to this way of responding in written activity, by the time he reaches fourth grade (2:63) and even earlier, he can as readily take over the attendant chore of marking and scoring his own written performance under the capable leadership of his teacher. If immediate knowledge of accomplishment is essential as a basic condition for learning, and if nearly all the written activities of the classroom are as readily assessable by the learner as by his teacher, to deprive him of the opportunity to bring the results into broad daylight hardly makes sense, particularly when they can be assessed in an atmosphere of communication where language and the spoken word can flourish. The learner's awareness of the nature of his performance must come without delay and surely before his paper starts on the assembly line toward his teacher's desk. In all fairness to the learner, self-evaluation (evaluation of accomplishment by the learner himself) is his right and responsibility.

> The basic dichotomy between teaching and learning in our schools arises because we teach children by external authoritarian methods which are the reverse of their internal biological growth and learning process. So the basic problem is one of how to change abnormal teaching methods into a normal learning process (5:26).

According to Findley and Scates,

> . . . we do not want such external authority to pass continually upon the quality of our performance. We recognize that to a reasonable extent, self-appraisal is our right and our responsibility. Acceptance of these views imposes upon the school the responsibility of developing in children both the habits and the abilities of self-appraisal (2:67).

Written Effort Makes for Learning

That the pencil-and-paper work of the classroom characterized by short-answer responses is of vital value as a learning experience by itself is well recognized and fully supported in our educational thinking. Its purpose has much more substance than the simple intent to measure what has been learned of what has been taught, although measurement of accomplishment is an appurtenant part of the process. The actual act of putting one's skills, knowledge, and reasonings on paper, even though expressed only by a word or symbol to denote understanding, helps to bring vague thoughts and disconnected ideas into focus which would otherwise tend to remain evanescent and in default of clear meaning. The act of writing helps to bring the learner to a decision-making moment when, although what he writes may not always be free from error, his pencil imprints bring to a head many facets of past learning increments; thus, actual and existent conclusions take over what may have been fantasy and imaginative thinking. Except for the ply of the pencil in this business of learning, the life in the classroom would indeed lack substance, and learnings would often resolve themselves into half-learnings.

Making the Appraisal the Basic Part of the Learning

So far, so good. The pencil-and-paper effort induces learning significantly. However, to bring the written experience at this point to an abrupt end by releasing the written performance to the teacher for her appraisal is most unfortunate. The learner should become immediately aware of his errors, his misconceptions and false understandings as shown on his paper; such blind incomprehension cannot be left hanging in the balance. Sole appraisal by the teacher would mean that, to the learner, the crucial part of what he is attempting to learn—that which manifests false reasoning and misunderstanding—would indeed tend to remain unlearned and dormant. Thus, such erroneous habits and incorrect understandings must needs be first unlearned, then relearned later at a more inopportune time and with the expenditure of greater effort.

What the learner puts on paper is manifestly part of himself, distinctly palpable to him and usually assessable by him with his teacher's help. His own appraisal centers attention upon learning, per se, and not upon sheer measurement. Discriminating knowledge about the quality of his performance comes to him forthwith and without delay; he is learning in complete agreement with proved laws of learning which cunning and adroitness cannot change. His own appraisal affords him every opportunity to weigh all aspects of the problem at the very moment of assessment—this in a carefully guided and controlled climate of oral communication. He not only listens to what others have to say, but also he will have the urge to ask questions himself when expedient, and he will be impelled to offer his own interpretations and understandings in order to strengthen his position and to bring about logical solutions. All of these deliberations, carefully guided and brought to intelligent conclusions, occur in an atmosphere in which outside authority is removed sufficiently, so that the decision-making responsibilities rest with the pupil, and not with his teacher. When the teacher does the evaluating, the locus of the evaluation is in the teacher, and not in the learner. But when the learner evaluates [his own written effort], the locus of the evaluation is in the learner, and not in his teacher (9:213). To the teacher, self-evaluation of written performance is a way of teaching pregnant with consequential possibilities; to the learner, it is a true way of learning.

It is more than a way for learning the skills, the simple facts, and the elementary understandings which are planned and usually intended as the work of the day. In the process of self-appraisal, mastery of such "lower order habits" (10:302) serve as the bases for advancement toward the acquisition of the "higher order habits" (10:302) where, during the deliberative talk, the isolated facts and simple learnings grow into highly integrated relations and understandings with broad meanings and practical applications. And most significant of all, manifest improvements and telling effects begin to show in the learner's growth in ability to talk his way through to clarity and with ease.

The Unique Place of Language in Self-Evaluation

Language occupies a key place in all learning of whatever kind—a place of import which cannot be equalled. Its significance in the learning process lies in the fact that it is basically a part of all thinking and writing and speaking; it cannot be regarded as an academic subject in the same sense as science or mathematics or social studies. The language skills are learned at all times of the day, more out of the classroom than within. In this era of the spoken word, where "At least ninety per cent of all communication is spoken (8:164)," the individual's ability to use language skillfully and with ease circumscribes largely the quality of living and the "life-space" (4:157–177) in which he lives. This kinship of language to all classroom living and learning points the way to the more effective approaches for teaching the language skills, and the path leads directly toward the learner's own appraisal of his written performances whenever possible. Numerous research studies and investigations have shown that English usage and the skills of expression are best learned when less direct approaches than the formal learning-of-rigid-rules-of-grammar are employed.

> Whatever the value of formal grammar may be to adult specialists in comparative linguistics, . . . the fact remains that no scientific study of the many available in English and foreign languages has shown that sentence analysis, diagraming, parsing, or nomenclature-drill is of the slightest benefit in improving a person's personal use of language (6:171).

The opportunity to enter into conversation when there is a felt need for talking in a face-to-face relationship is the *open-sesame* to the acquirement of a practical and versatile working-kit in English. The skills of expression develop gradually through listening and practice in speaking—through gain of confidence in actually saying what is on one's lips. Where the emphasis is on the thought (3:525) or the meaning (1:294) of what is to be said, the effect on learning language skills is highly significant. So conclusive is the evidence pointing to the more informal approaches, all of which is undocumented by any evidence to the contrary (11:646), that leading authorities in the field admonish against organizing separately-scheduled classes for teaching English and the arts of expression to young people. Instead, the skills of expression are best learned throughout the entire school day in learning situations associated with each and every subject.

Self-Appraisal of Written Performance Becomes a Language Adventure

If English usage and the language skills are best learned when the learner becomes the oral participant, this moment of critical appraisal of what he writes affords the ideal medium for sharing thoughts and knowledge which serves to ameliorate differences. The basic problem is to set up favorable opportunities which will assure desire and need for the pupil to talk, and this kind of appraisal, promoted under carefully-laid guide lines and capable leadership, offers this ingenuous need. Once the process gets under way, speaking out at the right time is natural and normal behavior for any pupil who has something to say. This, especially when he has the attendant responsibility to determine and put a tag upon the quality of his performance. No matter what the subject at issue may be, he is learning in full agreement with his optimal growth potential, and learning English usage through the spoken word becomes an integrant part of the process. The appraisal item may concern itself with the spelling of a word or a mathematics problem, our trade relations with Soviet Russia, present flood-control measures in Central California, a detail about the laws of heat exchange, the effect of a change of altitude on the barometer, or whatever, but even though attention is focused mainly upon the subject matter in progress, learning English usage and the arts of expression waxes strong. The informal environment of self-appraisal, where each pupil has an entrusted obligation which he cannot ignore, makes talk-togetherness inevitable. Far too many pupils go from day to day without speaking a single word of relevance in our classrooms. The self-evaluative procedure, however, makes certain the non-speaker is brought out of his oral lethargy on his own volition, especially if the detail in question calls for thinking and reasoning on the level of the higher mental processes.

If intensive training in comprehensive specifics were needed as a prerequisite to the preferment of self-evaluation of written endeavor, continuance of the present "teacher marks" method of appraisal as standard procedure might be justified. But further professional training is quite unnecessary; the plight in which the teacher finds herself cannot be attributed to lack of know-how. After the details for marking and scoring have been carefully defined by mutual effort, the process can move smoothly forward with no superfluous innovations or impedimenta which need cause any disruptive changes. The inevitable questions and comments which lend aid to the common purpose are bound to crop up about particular items as they are being presented and, when they arise, the time is ripe for deliberative talk, guided and open to all. The diverse interpretations and discriminative explanations coming from pupils (and teacher) bring to light new insights and meanings which help to close the wide gap between teaching and learning. And when the pupil gives voice to an urge which stirs him to speak, his growth in ability to express himself ably manifests itself strongly. Such is the way to learning and to language power. As soon as every pupil is satisfied and can come to a conclusion about the accuracy of his response, then, and only then, is attention turned to the next detail to be assessed.

The Role of the Teacher in the Evaluative Process Emerges

The role of the teacher takes on a new look and finesse. Release from her former pedantic chore frees her so that she may exercise her true function in the classroom—a function which is more akin to the professional image of a highly trained person, skilled and fully capable of affecting the true purpose of evaluation in the teaching-learning process. Though she does not handle the pupil's written work during the appraisal procedure itself, she is by no means insensitive about the way it is being appraised by its owners. It is she who guides the discursive action to logical and culminating conclusions in a talk-together environment, so that intelligent understandings and deep appreciations are attained. Final judgments and decisions are still hers to control, some of which may frequently warrant acceptance of unforeseen and unanticipated answers on occasion. Her role in the process, and that of the pupils, complement each other.

If a teacher has a firm conviction that he who truly learns must also appraise, and if she is willing to discipline herself to a line of action in which she accepts the role of leader and mediator, but a role not less important, the major step in the right direction will have been achieved. To release to the pupil the ply-of-the-pencil in what has been considered the teacher's exclusive domain is not always easy unless there is a sincere belief that, by doing so, learning is greatly enhanced. Its worthiness can be seen if only there is not such a hurry to get through with what is under way and on to a nebulous something else. Once the theory is accepted as a way of teaching and learning, the matter of implementing and putting it into effect is simple and direct.

REFERENCES

1. Dawson, Mildred. *Teaching Language in the Grades,* Yonkers, New York, 1951.

2. Findley, Warren J. and Scates, Douglas E. "Obtaining Evidence of Understanding," *National Society for the Study of Education, Forty-fifth Yearbook,* Part I, Chapter 4. Used by permission.

3. Frogner, Ellen. "Grammar Approach Versus Thought Approach in Teaching Sentence Structure," *English Journal,* XXVIII (September 1939), 518–556.

4. Havighurst, Robert J. and Neugarten, Bernice L. *Society and Education,* Boston: Allyn and Bacon, Inc., Chapter 7, pp. 158–178.

5. Hopkins, L. Thomas. "Guiding Learning," *Childhood Education,* XXIX (September 1952), 26–29. Used by permission.

6. Kaulfers, Walter V. "Common Sense in the Teaching of Grammar," Elementary English, (May 1944) 168–174. Used by permission.

7. Kingsley, Howard L. and Garry, Ralph. *The Nature and Condition of Learning,* Second Edition, Englewood Cliffs, New Jersey: Prentice-Hall, 1957. Used by permission.

8. Los Angeles County Superintendent of Schools Office, California, *Guiding Today's Youth, A Guidance Book for Teachers and Administrators of Secondary Schools,* 1961. Used by permission.

9. Rogers, Carl R. "Divergent Trends in Methods of Improving Adjustment," *Harvard Educational Review,* XVIII (Fall 1948), 209–219. Used by permission.

10. Sims, Verner M. "Objective Tests and Teachers' Measurements," *School and Society,* XXXVI (1932), 300–302. Used by permission.

11. Smith, Dora V. "English Grammar Again!" *English Journal,* XXVII (October 1938), 643–649.

12. Thorndike, Edward L. *Human Learning,* New York: Appleton-Century-Crofts, 1932. Used by permission of Robert L. Thorndike.

Language Study
in the Schools

FEW *aspects of secondary school English programs are so puzzling as their attention to language. Traditional grammar has long been a subject of obloquy among research specialists in English. Their findings indicate that it is of very limited effectiveness no matter what the conventional purposes teachers use to justify its inclusion in their classwork.[1] Yet this research has had relatively little impact in many schools if one may judge from the chalkboards still covered with verb conjugations and sentence diagrams. Beginning in the late 1950s and continuing throughout the decade of the 1960s structural linguistics and transformational/generative grammar came on strong, offering what appeared to be panaceas for all the ills created by traditional grammar. But they promised more than they could deliver and teachers soon discovered that a student who could not diagram a sentence in the manner of traditional grammar did not do much better when confronted with constituent analysis or transformational trees.*

The net result in schoolroom use of these three grammars is difficult to gauge with accuracy. In some schools teachers turned from grammar entirely, arguing that since none of them work, why should they waste their and their students' time? In other schools, teachers, well schooled from their years of classroom study of traditional grammar and resentful of some of the calumny heaped upon such study by the new grammarians, became defensive and taught traditional grammar with a heightened passion, even if not with demonstrably better results. And, in still other schools, "linguistics based" study of language assumed center stage. Which of these patterns is currently dominant is anyone's guess, but it does seem safe to argue that in few schools today is grammar study of any kind receiving the emphasis it received only a decade or so ago.

1 Walter S. Monroe, ed., *Encyclopedia of Educational Research,* rev. ed. (New York: The Macmillan Company, 1950), p. 393. See also Sherwin's article in the opening section of this volume.

In part, this lessened attention to some system of formal grammar stems from the competition among the grammars. But also in part it reflects an awareness among teachers that other aspects of language study merit classroom time. Semantics, dialect study, language history, and usage have all emerged as legitimate elements of language instruction in the secondary schools. It seems likely that these trends toward a language study that is not exclusively grammar will continue in the years ahead.

The articles in this section are indicative of these shifts in philosophy and pedagogy of language instruction. Bushman, in the opening selection, offers compelling arguments for broad-based language instruction. In the next two articles, Laird and Franks urge caution in what teachers do with grammar, any grammar. Weingartner discusses semantics and registers his dissatisfaction that the dominance of grammar study has had the effect of making the study of semantics a second-class citizen in the schools, an element of language all but ignored in most classrooms. Bruner stresses the provocative issue of the relationship between language and thought, a subject about which there needs to be considerable experimentation.

The final three articles treat a major concern of English teachers today: What, if anything, should they try to do about the language of their culturally impoverished students, especially their ghetto-based black students? Sledd, Fasold, and Baratz are all language scholars of the first rank and their thoughts on this vital, practical issue deserve careful consideration.

THE POWER OF LANGUAGE: CAN THE STUDENT SURVIVE WITHOUT IT?

John H. Bushman

> Bright is the ring of words
> When the right man rings them.
>
> ROBERT LOUIS STEVENSON

> Give me the right word and the right accent, and I will move the world.
>
> JOSEPH CONRAD

> Whenever we come upon one of those intensely right words in a book or a newspaper, the resulting effect is physical as well as spiritual, and electrically prompt.
>
> MARK TWAIN

THAT mastery of the linguistic process aids the individual in fulfilling his role as an individual is one of my most firm convictions. I further believe that this power of language will enable the individual to participate in greater depth in the functions of the community through his actions as a social being. Man's ability to understand himself and others, and thus to effect change in himself and others, is deeply dependent on his ability to use his language effectively.

How then can the teacher of English help the student to acquire this power of language? I believe that the English curriculum as it now exists must be changed at the secondary level and in the elementary schools as well. It is quite evident that the typical English language component of the curriculum is not adequate and certainly not effective.[1] John Algeo[2] suggests a possible reason for this dilemma. He states that the English teacher has not clearly understood the difference between the "teaching about" and the "teaching how to," and thus has not separated them in the classroom; and as a result, the classroom is a hodgepodge

---

[1] There have been many studies that substantiate this claim; a more recent one is James R. Squire and Roger K. Applebee, *The National Study of High School English Programs—High School English Instruction Today* (New York: Appleton-Century-Crofts, 1968).

[2] John Algeo, "Linguistic Marys, Linguistic Marthas: The Scope of Language Study," *College English* 31 (December 1969).

FROM *English Journal* (November 1970). Copyright © 1970 by the National Council of Teachers of English. Reprinted by permission of the publisher and John H. Bushman.

of material and method. Most of the content in today's English classes
fits into the "teaching how to" classification, and the material that
doesn't fit that pattern is usually not presented at all. I would be the
first to agree that proficiency in communication skills is needed; but I
do not believe that the same skills need to be taught year after year.
We must revise the curriculum, and we can do this by strengthening the
language component. There is an abundance of material available for
"teaching about" the English language, and it seems to me that at the
same time we are "teaching about," we are also improving the "how to"
as we add to the student's linguistic resources, increasing his awareness
of the range of choice. I most wholeheartedly agree with Algeo when he
says: ". . . English teachers should stop fretting and fussing about so
many things. They should abandon the role of Martha and choose
instead the part of Mary by concentrating on the one thing that is
necessary—teaching about English."

For the student to learn about English and as a result to acquire the
power of language, I suggest that he investigate three general areas:
(1) the evolution of English, (2) the operation of contemporary English,
and (3) the operation of the "student's English." I see these three general areas structured into seven categories. Of course, in this paper there
is not enough space to develop each fully, but I would offer a partial
list of topics which might be included.

I. Exploring the Nature of Language

Certainly one of the most important topics for discussion in any classroom is the nature of language itself, if for no other reason than that
language is a purely human phenomenon. What is language? Some of
the suggested definitions may be carefully examined. How do animals
communicate? Is it through language? Just how does a child acquire
language? Does the child have the "innate" capacity to learn language,
as recent theories of Chomsky and Lenneberg would suggest? What
about the relationship between language and culture? Certainly works by
Sapir, Boas, Whorf, Carroll, and others are appropriate resources for the
older student who is interested in the cultural influence on language and
the influence of language on culture. As a specific example, euphemisms
and taboos in language provoke stimulating discussions not only as they
relate to the English language but to other languages of the world.
Students on all academic levels enjoy working with euphemisms in their
dialects. They find it interesting to note that no longer is one buried in
a "graveyard" but in a "cemetery" or a "memorial park"; that the man
who picks up the trash or garbage is no longer the "trashman" or "gar-
bageman" but the "sanitary engineer"; and that one is no longer "poor"
but either "needy," "culturally deprived," "underprivileged," or "disad-

vantaged." There are many other examples which the students thoroughly enjoy investigating. The nature of language includes many other topics as well: language and symbols, the relationship of language to speech, and the concept of linguistic change.

II. Exploring the Structure of Language

The process of how meaningful units of English are combined into a system called language is an exciting study for the elementary school student as well as those students in the secondary school. The phonology, morphology, and syntax of English provide interesting topics for students who wish to study the grammar of their language for its own sake. However, if one accepts the premise, which I do, that a child knows the basic structure of his language by the time that he enters school, I see very little sense in forcing him to confront the grammar of English in pure form from Grade 3 to Grade 12 with the claim that it will increase the student's ability to speak and write better. I would rather emphasize the communication process through oral and written composition. Only when there are definite "trouble spots" in the communication within the child's dialect or within the "standard dialect," if you will, should there be any direct teaching of grammar, and, in this case, only if the teacher truly believes that what he is about to teach will effect change in the student's ability to effectively communicate. At this time, the best of all grammar systems should be used to help the student through this particular "crisis." Recent studies by Bateman, Zidonis, and Mellon indicate that transformational grammar may be helpful in alleviating problems in sentence construction.

A second area within the structure of English framework is the spelling system. Among the many questions for the student to investigate are: What is the relationship of the English alphabet to the sound system? Is the spelling system chaotic or does it follow a regular pattern most of the time? Study of these and other related questions provides the student with an understanding of the English sound system and how it operates in its relation to graphemes.

III. Exploring Usage in Language

Students should investigate the concept of language usage from its early beginnings; through the "authoritarian" influence of the eighteenth century; and through the "usage doctrine" advocated by the linguists of the nineteenth and twentieth centuries. How do the doctrine of "right vs wrong" and the "myth of absolute correctness" fit in with how usage is taught, or perhaps not taught, in the classroom? Is the student "wrong" when he says: "It is me"; "I am going to get my allowance, ain't I"; or

"Who are you going to the movie with?" Who sets the criteria for appropriateness? Another topic for study in the usage category is the dictionary. When did dictionaries first appear? Have the purposes of the dictionary changed? What makes *Webster's III* so acceptable? Or unacceptable? Certainly, a study of slang and the "levels of usage" and "functional varieties" of English is most beneficial. Materials from John Kenyon, James Sledd, Robert Pooley, Robert Hall, Wilson Follett, Bergen Evans, and Martin Joos, to mention only a few, and the curriculum materials available through the Oregon and Minnesota Curriculum Centers provide great resources for a study of this kind.

IV. Exploring Language Heritage

The heritage of American English is an interesting topic to begin a study of the history of the English language. Students have greater interest in studying a language which has obvious relevance to them. In many instances a study of this nature could easily parallel a literary and /or historical survey of America. Alternatively, American English and its development can be related to American literature, and British English and its development to English literature. Topics of general interest include the external history of British English as well as the internal characteristics of the language as it passed through the three major periods—Old English, Middle English, and Early Modern English. One basic area that must be included in any study of language development is linguistic change. What are the influences that effect change in language? What influences on English can be attributed to the Romans, the French, and the Scandinavians? How much linguistic borrowing has occurred and what effect has it had on the grammar and lexicon of the English language? These are just a few of the many questions that seem appropriate for this category.

V. Exploring Geographical and Social Dialects

Of the seven categories perhaps this one arouses greatest enthusiasm in the student as he has the opportunity to investigate his own dialect. His idiolect offers contrast to that of his neighbor's; and soon the student begins to see how his dialect is different from those of others in his school, community, state, and nation. He soon realizes that his language is unique, that no one else speaks exactly the same as he does. Material from the Linguistic Atlases along with other studies in this area provide an enormous wealth of information. Moreover, we should not overlook the opportunity that the students have for original field work. All this material makes the list of possible topics for inquiry practically endless. A few that I believe stimulate interest at all levels include characteristics of specific dialect areas, the major differences between American and British English, use of dialects in literature, immigration and dialect areas, dialects of "inner city" vs "suburbia," and dialect differences vs "standard" English.

VI. Exploring Semantics

The student has ample opportunity through his conversations, his reading of the press, and his listening to radio and television to learn of the symbolic function of language. Just why do words mean what they mean? What relationship does psychology have to the communicative process? What relationship does semantics have to the culture in which we live? How is the meaning of a word affected by its etymology? In finding answers to these questions students find an exciting topic of language study. Certainly, the study of the language used in politics and advertising is most beneficial to the student as he investigates the "power of language."

VII. Exploring the "Silent Language"

The non-linguistic features that accompany language use are extremely important in the communicative process, as Edward Hall indicates in his book *The Silent Language.* The student need only analyze the gestures, tone of voice, facial expressions, proxemics, and the language of time to realize how one communicates nonverbally. If students are to appreciate these non-linguistic features and to use them effectively, what better place to learn about them and to practice them than in the classroom?

The question that many will ask is, will this approach to the language component work? Or will it simply fall into the same rut in which we find the present system? I suggest that it will not follow the "well known path" simply because of the enormous wealth of material that exists for study from the early grades through high school. This material just doesn't exist if we continue to follow the present emphasis on "teaching how to" in the English classroom.

I would emphasize too that the English curriculum cannot be effective if all that it offers is the language component. We still need to include literature and composition in the curriculum, and if we carefully integrate these three components, the effort will be successful.

Perhaps it is a bit too early to make final judgments. However, curriculums similar to what I have partially described here have been in operation for some time in the Project English programs in Nebraska, Minnesota, and Oregon. Reports from these centers indicate that their curriculums are successful. We can only hope that they continue to be successful and that a similar emphasis spreads to other school districts throughout the country.

Most of this paper has been concerned with the content of the language component; little has been said about the organization of the curriculum or the methods used in the classroom.

I do not feel as some do that this material be organized in a "sequential curriculum"; i.e., that the curriculum materials are pre-organized and packaged for each grade level. Instead of "sequential" I see the curriculum more as a "spiral curriculum" starting early in the elementary years, third grade perhaps. For example, the "spiral curriculum" might include in the third grade parts of category number five—Dialect Study —by exploring superficially the various kinds of dialects that the students find in the classroom, in the home, or among relatives. This study then becomes a building process, adding new information from year to year. The student might climax his study in the high school by investigating specific phonological, lexical, and syntactical characteristics of the Northern, Midland, and Southern dialects. He might also do field work projects within his community. The "spiral curriculum," for example, allows for the material presented in this paper at least to be introduced in the early grades. I emphasize the importance of starting in the early grades to get students involved in a study of their language with all its component parts, so that the youngsters may see that language study is more than just a study of grammar. If I might include a personal note here: I know that interest abounds in the elementary schools, for I have on various occasions visited these classrooms and discussed with the children the whole spectrum of the English language. The minds of these children were filled with questions, and throughout all of the discussions, the students were constantly probing to find out more about the history of the language they speak.

Throughout most of the school experiences, I would hope that much of the language study would be realized through the "question-probing" technique. Students as well as the teacher should flood the classroom with questions concerning language—questions to which they may or may not know the answers and questions for which there may not be answers. In the early years, the process tends to be more heuristic; as the student becomes more mature and sophisticated, the process is more research oriented. The art of problem solving is important as it fosters within the student the opportunity for critical thinking; and thus, he learns, among other things, the vital process of abstraction. The teacher along with the students has moved away from the pre-organized material to open inquiry.

Thus, the seven categories of the language component of the English curriculum offer a vast number of resources for study; but more than that, they offer a way for the student to gain the "power of language" and, thus, the ability to sustain control over his world in the community in which he lives.

LANGUAGE: WHAT TO DO ABOUT A DROP-IN

Charlton Laird

ROUGHLY a quarter century ago, Modern Language Study dropped in on us, and was made more or less welcome among our admittedly legitimate charges, literature and composition. The drop-in was received with a degree of coolness in many quarters, not to say fury. Obviously he was a relative, but many teachers of English would have preferred that he stay where he belonged, wherever that was. Teachers knew about language study, of course; there was Philology, a sort of academic uncle, highly respectable, but he lived a long way off and had never had much to do with the family of composition and literature teachers. As a sibling, he was an asset and very little bother. But this modern chip off the old block—if, indeed, he was a chip off the old block and not just a chip on somebody's shoulder—was by no means reticent. He arrived, he stayed, and he had obvious beatnik qualities. He seemed to have no use, he paraded the marketplace, he was curiously attractive to the young, and the older folks could make little sense of his jargon.

That, as I indicated, was roughly a quarter century ago. The Second World War was over, or about to be over. English teachers, during the 1930s, had been made aware, *ad nauseum,* that they had been doing their job rather badly. They were teaching little literary appreciation and not much competence in the oral or written use of the language. True, they had received some help; the New Criticism had arrived, and if he looked at the onset rather too much like the scape-grace son of the Lost Generation, and if he was later to resemble a Berkeley beatnik, a use was found for him. The New Criticism, somewhat tamed and disciplined, stimulated a new approach to the teaching of literature that was soon so nearly standard that the teaching of literary history as literature called almost for an apology. Obviously, the teaching of literature had greatly improved. Nothing comparable had happened in

->>>

FROM *English Journal* (November 1969), pp. 1199–1205. Copyright © 1969 by the National Council of Teachers of English. Reprinted by permission of the publisher and Charlton Laird.

composition, however; teachers were still teaching grammar as it was enshrined in the parts of speech, although hundreds of experiments had confirmed what most sensitive teachers knew already, that teaching the parts of speech had almost no perceptible impact on writing or speaking. Meanwhile, some good teaching was being done; some teachers knew how to write, and using such solid volumes as the Thomas, Manchester, and Scott and Rankin, Thorpe, and Solve, they were teaching young people to write. Such teachers were few, however, and there had been no revolution. The public wanted a revolution, and obviously it had reason.

During the war nothing could be done. Many of the more mentally receptive teachers were in the armed forces, most of the courses were directed toward producing officers, and even if new textbooks could have been conceived, paper and type metal were not available to print them. Meanwhile, structural linguistics had proven itself as a military adjunct; with it, prospective interpreters had learned unfamiliar languages with a speed that no such body of students had attained before. Clearly, when the Second World War was over, something had to be done, and to some of the willing reformers what should be done was obvious—the curriculum should be turned over to the linguists, especially to the structural linguists.

I need not survey what happened. All sorts of people everywhere began to see that the study of language, pure or applied, can be exciting, that it can revitalize the teaching of English both for the teacher and the taught, that it can be used to pull a scattered curriculum together, and the like. Thousands of individuals and dozens of organizations, especially the National Council of Teachers of English and the federal government, promoted so vigorously the study of language and the re-training of teachers that a new day in English teaching has dawned much sooner than most of us could have imagined. Teachers now have much better materials than they ever had; more well-qualified teachers are available than ever before, and more have good reasons for what they do. We have centers for the pursuit and dissemination of knowledge; many school systems are alert to new trends and are assiduously making something of them, and if some systems have not as yet profited greatly from the new light, many are seriously trying, and most of the remainder are aware that they should be trying. A few years ago, almost anyone who addressed a general audience, or even an audience of school teachers, on the new thought and action in language, was asked if this was not a passing fad. That question is now asked less frequently, and it is obviously anachronistic; the serious study of language, and the application of this study to the teaching of English at all levels are here to stay. Thus the question today is not whether we shall continue to make use of language in the classroom; the question is, have we been making the best use of it?

We have not done badly, although the movement toward the application of modern linguistics has been fought, often in high and powerful places. That the study of language and of applied linguistics in the teaching of the native language has prospered is proof positive that the movement has been winning friends, and it could not have won that many friends that fast unless it was producing tangible, obvious results. That is might have produced different results or better results is a proposition we have not had much opportunity or occasion to consider. Perhaps the whole movement has now gone far enough so that we may appropriately ponder it more deliberately than we usually have in the past. What should we now emphasize? What should we now be doing that we have as yet not much done?

On the whole, I should say we have done rather better with grammar than with other aspects of language. Perhaps we need not have. The world's experience generally seems to suggest that the deliberate learning of grammar provides one good approach to the learning of a second language, but that it is less useful, if useful at all, in teaching the use of the native language to the natives. However that may be, we seem to have evidence that learning a first language naturally and learning a second or third language artificially are sufficiently different mental processes so that a teacher should not hop nonchalantly from one to the other assuming that they are the same. For better or for worse, however, we have the tradition of the Little Red School House still with us, the so-called "grammar school." The public expects grammar; school administrations equate English with grammar and usage, and many teachers are unhappy unless they can teach grammar. All this is changing, but it has not changed rapidly, and it will not. Thus with new linguistic material available, the school systems, the textbook publishers, and the teachers themselves have moved more rapidly toward a new grammar than toward anything else that they have been offered.

Within a few years after structural approaches appeared in this country, structural textbooks were being published, curriculums were being revised along structural lines, and teachers were frantically preparing themselves to teach the new grammar. Some of us remained moderately unreconstructed; others were bewildered. I recall many conversations with teachers who said in effect, "I know we can't go on teaching the old grammar, but I don't like structural linguistics, and there isn't anything else, is there?" I assured them there was something else, that in the near future we would have many somethings else, that we were going in a good direction and that the serious teacher had only to be alert and keep her perspective. I never dreamed how right I was, because I could not imagine that generative grammar would develop so rapidly as it has. So far as I have observed, structural linguistics is now in effect dead as an elementary and secondary classroom device in this country, except as it has been incorporated into transformational grammar.

This fact may be worth noting, since I believe it embodies a principle still operative. When structural grammar ballooned fifteen or twenty years ago, I was worried that one inadequate grammar would be replaced by another grammar, perhaps not equally inadequate but far from being the panacea for all our ills, and that we would shift from one fad to another fad without the fundamental changes in direction that were needed. Since I wish not to repeat myself without making it clear that I know I am doing so, I trust you will forgive me for mentioning an article I published at the time, in which I suggested that even though structural linguistics has great virtues, as it surely has, it may not have all virtues.[1] If it should provide eventually the most scientific grammar of English, the most scientific grammar need not be the most teachable grammar; that even though it has been useful in teaching a foreign language it may not be equally useful in teaching a native language; if it is useful for some sorts of minds and for certain age groups we do not know thereby that it will be ideal for all persons and ages; and that if it has its uses we have no assurance that it cannot be overused. I went on to suggest that structural linguistics does not very well reflect the normal mental processes, at least not the mental processes of native speakers of English, and that I entertained a stubborn suspicion that the grammatical statement which most nearly reflects the mental processes of native speakers will likely be the most useful in the classroom.

These observations still seem to me valid; one has only to substitute the words *transformational grammar* for *structural linguistics*. Generative grammar seems to be highly successful in the elementary school, probably because the generative principle is sound and does reflect the way minds work, and because generative grammar relies more on meaning and on what used to be called function than did structural approaches. On the other hand, transformational grammar has as yet been of relatively little use in more advanced teaching, possibly because the present generative statement, simple in its elements, rapidly becomes complex, or possibly because the transform does not represent the normal working of the human mind. The concept of the transform may simplify the grammatical statement; apparently it does, and if so, it is a valid grammatical device, but it may or may not provide the clearest

[1] "Structural Linguistics: Notes for a Devil's Advocate," *College English*, 24 (1962) 93–97.

explanation of the way the language is working or the handiest means of teaching the use of the language.

Furthermore, even though transformational grammar has its use, it may be overused; I believe that in some current textbooks it is over-emphasized, and that the best curriculums of the future will make more use of other linguistic and rhetorical devices and less of grammar, of any grammar. Meanwhile, one should observe that we already have other generative approaches that are in some ways more promising than transformational grammar; I refer to tagmemics, and at the moment especially to stratificational grammar. These approaches have the very great advantages of proposing to deal with all aspects of language use, including elements both larger and smaller than the sentence, and they seem to approach the basic mental processes. These approaches have not as yet been much refined even on the scholarly level, but one might add that some of these systems, perhaps at the moment particularly stratificational grammar, seem not farther from the textbook stage than was transformational grammar ten years ago.

What can one say in general as to the impact of recent grammatical study? Obviously, the net affect is greatly to the good. We have outgrown the notion that English grammar is one eternal, unalterable thing. We have come to realize that no grammatical statement, however impeccable, can accurately reflect the grammar itself, that we can have as many valid grammatical statements as there are valid assumptions, and that all grammatical statements may have their uses. Practically, in the classroom we are now teaching grammar better than we used to; both structural linguistics and transformational grammar have their uses, and even those teachers who are still professing the unadulterated parts of speech have profited from the grammatical ferment of our day and have tended to liberalize their approaches. If we are not headed in the best of all possible directions, we are going in good directions; the conscientious teacher need only take advantage of the best that is offered and remember that we have not heard the last word about new grammars: as there is no one grammar of English there is no one New Grammar either.

If, as teachers, planners of curriculums, and writers of textbooks we have done our most nearly adequate work in adapting grammatical thinking to classroom use, I fear we have done our least inspired promotion in the general field of language understanding. This was to have been expected. Teachers are practical people; we have to be. Students sit before us and they must be taught today; any conscientious teacher likes to measure results tomorrow. Furthermore, we are all human; we prefer describable methods and quick, measurable results. The unfortunate fact is that when one deals with human minds and anything as complicated as human language, the most desirable ends are likely not to be very tangible; they cannot be immediately attained, and they cannot be unerringly pursued by simple, direct methods. They require time and they require teachers who have broad backgrounds and philosophic grasp as well as practical methods. Learning to inscribe on the board, "A sentence can be rewritten as noun phrase plus verb phrase" is much easier than asking oneself what happens when a child learns a word and what this learning process implies.

Here, however, I surmise is the major advantage of teaching language in the classroom. Language is complex beyond belief; learning processes are still more complex, and the learning of language is a project for the years, not for the lesson unit. Any study long continued becomes boring, as many a student who has been subjected to what has been called English will assure you. But students need not be bored; neither need teachers. We have learned to teach the native language better because we have learned to make literature more exciting than it used to be, and we are learning to make language exciting, although not so exciting as it could be if more teachers know more about it. When a youngster studies language he studies himself, the mind, society, mankind, and the revelation of these in his daily life. True, this statement will be no news to many of you, perhaps no news to any of you. The very fact that you are interested in this topic suggests that you know at least something of the possibilities of language teaching, of making teaching better by making it more fun. Usually, the more a teacher needs a session like this one, the less likely he is to come. In that case you are likely to agree with me that we have only begun to realize the potentialities of language as an excitant.

Other uses of the study of language there are, of course, too many to be surveyed here, but I might mention a few that seem to me rather too much neglected. I have lately become convinced that the improvement of both writing and reading require better vocabularies and more familiarity with complex sentence structures than most of our students command. Not enough is being done along these lines, perhaps because a good direct method is not very obvious. Teaching vocabulary, for example, is a little like teaching virtue; one does not much improve morality by saying, "Now, be good," and one does not teach much vocabulary by saying, "Go ahead, learn some words." We have made progress; the old device of learning prefixes and suffixes has its uses, but they are less adequate than have sometimes been supposed. The General Semanticists who have had the virtue of having made themselves heard, have alerted us to some aspects of meaning, and thus subjects like the language ladder of specificity and the dangers of weasel words in advertising are often taught. In my own view, however, we shall get farther in the end with broader approaches to vocabulary, and fortunately we have other approaches that have not, as yet, been much employed, for example, etymology. Probing into the origin and growth of words is so much fun that even the newspapers have taken it up, but curiously the schools have not as yet done much with it. Youngsters get excited about the growth of words; they can have fun discovering word origins and pursuing semantic change, and whenever students have fun with language they are learning, perhaps learning faster and more lastingly than in any other way we can hope to promote. Perhaps the difficulty here stems from the fact that, to teach etymology, a teacher must know something about it and many do not. They need not remain in ignorance; for a time almost all good etymology was enshrined in dictionaries the layman could not use; discussions of the subject tended to be shrouded in scholarly prose. Now, however, all that is over; desk dictionaries, at least some of them, include Indo-European bases and clear, factual statements about etymology; etymological dictionaries are available at modest prices and in non-technical terminology; all aspects of modern language study, including etymology, are surveyed in books written for the layman. No longer need teachers fail to take advantage of etymology as a classroom tool; learning to use the tool takes a little time, but really not much.

Another procedure too little practiced by students of language and even less applied by teachers is what is sometimes called psycholinguistics. How does the mind work with language, and how does language structure the mind? How is language learned? Here, again, we have essentially exciting material for the classroom, partly because, being human beings, students like to study themselves. And each of them is a walking, chattering laboratory of language learning. Probably their most important jobs are learning to control their physical bodies, learning to school their minds and their emotions, and learning language. In the latter two, the study of language learning helps. Students can be intrigued, for example, by the simple fact that most language grows out of human use, by the use of people like themselves, and fundamental here are principles with which they think constantly, with specialization, generalization, onomatopoeia, naming, and the like. Language grows by figures of speech, such as those that lie beneath much slang, a fact which fascinates youngsters, but most of those students who come to me have never heard of these matters. Obviously, a good many elementary and secondary teachers have been missing an opportunity to excite their students.

Vocabulary grows by psychological means, and thus psycholinguistics and etymology inevitably work together, and this combination, also, can be intriguing. Furthermore, such background can be put to practical, immediate use. Students can be led to see that if they know a little about the growth of words, the relationships of words through etymology and through mental processes, they can almost always relate an unknown to a known word. If students know about cognates, they can see that the middle syllable of *confluence* is merely another form of the word *flow,* and thus *confluence* means flowing together. With this background they will understand the word at once, and with a bit of this sort of thing they can learn dozens of related words more easily than they can learn one isolated word, and they are likely to develop deeper feelings and clearer understandings of the words they do control. Along these lines, also, more use can be made of the dictionary, not only as a tool in writing and reading, but as an approach to the problem of meaning. If students themselves will endeavor to make a dictionary, and face seriously the problem of what one does when he tries to formulate a statement about the use of a word, they are likely to gain insights into language and the workings of the human mind that are rare without such an experience.

The problem of sentence structure is much more complicated, and here modern linguistic study has not given the teacher as much help and direction as I could wish. In fact, some of the new insights have been unintentionally misleading. Grammatically, "John was spanked by me," may be a transform of "I spanked Johnny," but as bits of a language in use they are quite different. A study of the nature of an analytic language, of the impact of such a grammar upon the choice of subjects, for example, has not been much exploited. The fact is, of course, that the supposed five kernel sentences do not well reflect basic English structures, and the working language does not become readily apparent from them, any more than it became apparent through the older talk about compound and complex sentences. For example, consider the following sentence, which a former candidate for the Presidency recently addressed to a large audience: "It is now clear the voting public has gotten up on its homework and knows different." I am not sure I can identify the kernel sentences here—I am especially intrigued by the sequence "knows different"—and if I could I fear I should not thereby teach students much about improving sentence structure. Our language now works so much with complex predicates in which supposed verbs, particles, modifiers, and complements became intertwined that trying to identify kernel sentences may seem a rather futile business. However that may be, I find teachers not much aware of this problem. Furthermore, if I do not know how best to teach complex sentence structures, I do know that some awareness of the working of analytic grammar can help to teach the strengths of the active voice along with the uses and the nature of the misuses of the passive and the expletive, as can study of the intricacies of subordination and modification. I know, also, that extensive and close reading of adult writing will help, but this whole problem is extremely complex, not very well worked out in a teachable way, and it verges into rhetoric, which is presumably not our business today.

One more suggestion and I am done. We are becoming aware of dialects, how to study them and what their import is. Here we have excellent information, but the schools are using it less than they might. The study of dialects, particularly as it is being revealed by such techniques as linguistic geography, can be downright fascinating. Dialect interests people, and most users of language have only an inkling of its spread, of its growth, and the way it lives. Thus dialect study, too, can be used to make the study of English exciting, but it has also a very practical use. One of our most difficult problems, surely, is the teaching of something approaching standard English in the ghettos, and here among the impediments are the lack of understanding of and sympathy for ghetto speech, and the need of self respect among the ghetto speakers. Making moral pronouncements about dialect and telling people that everyone speaks dialects does not help much, but getting people excited about the study of dialects does help. Youngsters thrown into the welter of dialects, regional and social, that swarm upon the earth will be brought to an understanding of usage and usage problems that is likely to be impossible in any other way. Similarly, onomastics, the study of naming, can help; all children have names and live surrounded by names; they are intrigued by names, but they know little about them, and here, again, teachers are failing to take advantage of widespread interest and exciting, fresh material.

In recent decades we have gone far in the study of language, and in the application of this study to teaching. We may well go farther.

THE LINGUISTIC GOSPEL: A DISSENT

Jesse Gibson Franks

MODERN linguists who concern themselves with the problem of teaching English generally agree that the linguistic approach to the study of this subject is markedly superior to what is referred to, with no little condescension, as the "school grammar" or "prescriptive" or "authoritarian" method, and that the new method, or "new gram-

≫≫≫≫≫≫≫≫≫≫≫≫≫≫≫≫≫≫≫≫≫≫≫≫≫≫≫≫≫≫≫≫

FROM *School and Society*, Vol. 99 (February 1971), pp. 98–101. Reprinted by permission of the publisher and the author.

mar," will produce wide-eyed, enthusiastic, deeply conversant students of a kind never before seen in the history of language pedagogy. This paper suggests that such claims may be exaggerated. What follows is not an attack upon the science of linguistics. The work of modern linguistic scholars who have made the study of language the absolutely fascinating thing it has become under their aegis deserves the highest respect.

But the champions of the new method of language teaching, among whom Prof. Charles C. Fries has no doubt been the most influential, have overlooked, among other things, a very important characteristic of our American mass-education system: most of its students—not to mention teachers—are not scholars and never will be; the linguistic approach is, for them, simply overwhelming. And those who do have any scholarly talent or aspiration too often develop, in a linguistically-oriented program, a feeling very like contempt for the written as opposed to the spoken language, a handicap of some seriousness for a scholar, and, whether intended by the leaders and supporters of such a program or not, a necessary consequence of their influence and stated position. There is, too, the added difficulty and an inevitable one, that the programs of eminent linguists who have been most active in this work have been implemented wrongly by their lesser disciples. But the leaders must share the blame, nevertheless, for they have made general, law-giving statements of questionable validity and have promised rewards not within their giving. And these things they need not have done in order to accomplish or pursue their aims.

Let us look at some of these statements and promises, which may be grouped under three major pronouncements: "The spoken language *is* the language;" "Authoritarianism (prescriptiveness) in the language-teaching and language-usage is not to be tolerated—*heard* usage is the only arbiter;" and "The 'school grammar' approach to English teaching is a waste of time."

1. "The spoken language *is* the language." I am in holy dread of touching this sacred precept with my profane hands. But it must be dealt with; in fact, a dealing with is long overdue for this piece of dogma, for it lies at the very life's heart of the whole linguistic canon. Thus Prof. Fries: "The speech *is* the language. The written record is but a secondary representation of the language. To 'master' a language it is not necessary to read it, but it is extremely doubtful whether one can really *read* the language without first mastering it orally."[1]

And thus Edward Sapir: ". . . phonetic language takes precedence

---

[1] *Teaching and Learning English as a Foreign Language* (Ann Arbor: University of Michigan Press, 1966), p. 6. All subsequent references to Prof. Fries are from this source.

over all other kinds of communicative symbolism. . . ."[2] And thus many others of no less distinction in the field of linguistics. But what Sapir means by "precedence" or what Fries intends by "secondary" is hard to appreciate unless we suppose that they both simply are stressing the fact that speech occurred in human history before writing, which no one, I fancy, cares to dispute. But that the written language thereby does become "secondary" or merely "substitutive," or in any sense less real or significant than the spoken, is a palpable falsehood, and its propagation has done rather widespread damage.

For primitive peoples, the spoken language is indeed *the* language, even those in which ancillary forms of communication, including perhaps a kind of writing, may be employed: their whole culture is speech-oriented and would disintegrate without oral language. But in practically all of the English-speaking world, even in rude America, the written word, compared in relative significance with the spoken, *is* the language, if we must make a choice. Our culture would collapse without it and our technology become impotent. But this would not be the consequence if the spoken language were dispensed with; indeed, our cultural and scientific progress (if it may be termed that) quite conceivably might be accelerated were we all to stop talking entirely and begin to read and write exclusively instead.

Seymour Chatman once remarked on the "monolithic monolingualism" of American college undergraduates, suggesting that for many of them the reading of Shakespeare, Pope, Johnson, even Matthew Arnold, was in a very real sense an attempt to read a foreign language.[3] And the reason for this is clear: the reading of such students has been very close to the colloquial, or speech, level. But the usual speech of most of us, and that of other civilized users of language as well, lacks the complexity, concentration, order, and range of a scientific or literary discourse; and the typical American student in his reading often does find himself confronted with a form of communication every way as baffling as a foreign tongue, which in fact, for him, it is. And unless he can accommodate himself to the intricacies of this new medium, which lacks the rhythms, pitches, stresses, and intonations of the one he is more at home in, but which contains a great many other things peculiar only to the written language, he may as well go back to talking all the time or reading the funnies. For, despite Prof. Fries's maxim that writing is a kind of "secondary repetition of the language," we do not write, as a rule, at all as we speak. And we do not read in the way we listen. Such a means of communicating can not properly be called a "repeti-

2 "Language," *Encyclopaedia of the Social Sciences*, vol. 9 (New York: Macmillan, 1933), p. 155.

3 "Linguistics and Teaching Introductory Literature," *Language Learning*, 9: 3–10, iii–iv, 1956–57.

tion" of speech, for there is little in ordinary speech which answers to it or it to speech.

Moreover, when linguistic sages insist on the preeminence of the spoken language, they are assuming a static condition of human expression and communication which in other, but quite analogous, circumstances they repudiate. Fries, *e.g.*, notes the absurdity of those "authorities" who insist on a former, perhaps etymologically more apparent, meaning of a term while ignoring the later stages, and very often the earlier, of meaning evolution which the word may have passed through. Such persons want to fix the "true" meaning of a word at an arbitrary point in its development with no better justification than their own prejudice or ignorance or both. But it appears to have escaped Prof. Fries's and others' notice that they are applying precisely the same kind of reasoning when they insist that speech *is* the language. For speech is only one stage in language development. Before speech there was gesture (let us assume) and after speech, writing; there may have been earlier means of communication than gesture; it seems to me very likely that there will be a successor to writing. In any event, it is just as unfair to postulate that writing is "secondary" or "subsidiary" to speech as it would be to maintain that speech is a kind of repetition of gesture and is, therefore, "secondary" to or "substitutive" for the real thing, gesture.

Then too, the etymological meaning of the word *language* and the prevalence of the term *tongue* as a synonym for it are adduced as evidence that language must mean speech: in other words, an attempt to fix the meaning of a word at a certain point in its development—in this instance because of the "true" meaning—a reprehensible act unless performed by a linguist.

In fine, whatever historical importance speech may have for us and no matter how awkward we should find getting on without it to be, it is by no means any longer an absolute necessity. But linguists like Prof. Fries have written and read so much about the spoken language that it seems to them to have more significance than it has.

2. "Authoritarianism (prescriptiveness) in language-teaching and language-usage is not to be tolerated—*heard* usage is the only arbiter." Fries puts it this way: "The practical standard of pronunciation must thus be the speech of those we hear" (p. 7). And again: "The only *true* and *correct* meaning of a word, therefore, must be the particular content put into it by actual present usage" (p. 89).

This is discouraging. Prof. Fries probably does not intend fully all that is implied by these utterances, but they are just the sort of dicta which students—and teachers—fix on as lodestars and allow to mislead them. The undue emphasis upon *present, heard* usage makes it unduly difficult for some students to pass from the colloquial to the literary level of discourse, however easy Prof. Fries himself may find it. For example, *awful,* as Fries accurately observes, scarcely ever is used, at least in American parlance, in its etymological sense. And a student inured to the linguistic approach and convinced of the trustworthiness of the Fries touchstone may be unwilling or unable to accept it in that sense. But suppose, from whatever motive, he is reading, say, Kipling's "Recessional." Without a strong feeling for the more primitive implications of that word, he will miss the solemnity and fatality of that poem, depending as it does so much upon an earlier meaning of *awful.*

Moreover, "usage" is a more comprehensive and complicated matter than the new grammarians suppose. The "authorities"—the "protectors" of the language—whom they condemn may be comparatively ignorant men; certainly their acquaintance with language is not that of a Sapir, a Fries, or a Whorf. But that is not the point; what is the point is that many persons do need such lesser men—or are convinced that they need them, which is the same thing—do seek after them, and to a large extent do follow them. And the linguistic habits of these followers are just as authentically a part of usage as is that resulting from any so-called "natural" form of language development. In a word, the linguist's concept of usage overlooks some important facts, the fact of human nature being one of them.

And as for "correctness" or what constitutes "educated speech," the attitude of the new grammarians is, effectively, that "anything goes"— although as a rule they do not say so explicitly. Fries comes very close to saying it in the passage quoted above, and perhaps even closer in the following: "The only basis for correctness in grammar must be usage, for the schools the usage of those who are carrying on the affairs of the English-speaking people" (p. 43).

But all speakers of English carry on the affairs of the English-speaking people in some sort. To determine who is carrying on an affair and who is not is perhaps no easier than deciding immediately what "educated speech" is, and we have not come very far. But all speech is not really acceptable, despite Prof. Fries's assurances. Now this is not to say that there is anything intrinsically "wrong" about one's native dialect or one's peculiar language mannerisms of whatever origin. If one's speech or writing is wrong, it is because it gets the user into trouble; if one wants to use provincial or dialectical speech (and he may have excellent reasons for wishing to do so), that is his affair. But he ought to be prepared to show that if he does not know better, he does at least know different.

One suspects that the linguistic scientists are asking us to give up one kind of authoritarianism in language for another, namely their own. Some of us are not perfectly convinced that it is a good exchange.

"Only by using to the full the results of scientific linguistic study will our efforts avoid the futile practices based upon our traditional beliefs concerning language and make possible unmistakable progress toward *good* English" (p. 120).

Those practices based upon traditional beliefs were not infallibly futile; a fair-sized group of writers and speakers made some sort of reputation for themselves before the results of scientific linguistic study began to save the rest of us and set us on the road toward good English.

Meanwhile, there seems to be no reason, moral or otherwise, why we, as teachers, should not teach toward a standard, the best that we can come by, according to our lights. To the extent that we are ignorant of the language and how and by whom it is used, to that extent our students will receive bad instruction. But that can not be helped. However, to suggest to a student that one pronunciation or one grammatical usage is as good as another (though both may be "acceptable"), provided only that he has heard it used somewhere or sometime, is to do him an injustice and to ignore the facts: "despícable" may be considered correct; "between she and I" may be considered acceptable. Or they may not be, depending upon the place and circumstances. It might be well to say to our students (and I do say it to my own): "You are here to learn the best usage I can acquaint you with; if you do not wish to practice such speech and writing habits as are here encouraged, that is your concern. But you are not, at least in this class, expected to make any signal contributions to the evolution of the language. As educated persons, your attitude should, in my view, be tolerantly conservative. The language will change and grow without your conscious effort; you need only see to it that you do not resist the change or look with contempt upon the language habits of others."

3. "The 'school grammar' approach to English teaching is a waste of time." We need not be so much interested here in denying this accusation as in comparing the effectiveness of "school grammar" with that of the "new grammar." Leonard Bloomfield once observed that "Our schools are conducted by persons who, from professors of education down to teachers in the classroom, know nothing of the results of linguistic science, not even the relation of writing to speech, or of standard language to dialect. In short, they do not know what language is, and yet must teach it, and in consequence waste years of every child's life and reach a poor result."[4]

But the failure of school grammar (so far as it failed) was not and is not owing completely to the inherent weakness of the approach— of which it has many (whereas the linguistic approach has none)—but to the fact that it was not taught. The study of grammar, even school

4 "Why a Linguistic Society?" *Language,* 1: 5, 1925.

grammar, demands a certain amount of painstaking effort; it often must be pursued with determination when more pleasant activities are available. One high school senior recently declared to me proudly that she did not know the difference between a noun and a verb, that she and her teacher regarded the study of grammar, including sentence diagramming, as silly. One learned, her teacher had said, what one needed to know of such matters by listening to and imitating others (a favorite, though out-of-context, principle of Fries's).

Actually, many school grammars have served their limited purposes well. They never were meant to make linguistic scholars of those who studied them—though it may be doubted they ever prevented anyone from achieving that distinction—and did not require deep learning of those who taught from them. And this was as it should be. Or had to be, if you will, in an educational system like ours. Certain other charges against pre- or extra-linguistic approaches to grammar are likewise a bit gratuitous and give one the feeling that the priests of the new faith need a whipping-boy. Robert Lado complains, for instance, of school-grammar "definitions that do not account for the facts of language"[5]— which indeed they do not. But neither do Mr. Lado's. Or anybody else's. In fact, no definition of whatever kind ever was known to account fully for anything. But the nomenclature of school and traditional grammar is a durable base from which even the most innovating of modern linguists do not and can not depart too radically.

The non-linguistic (a term of convenience, not necessarily of complete accuracy) approach or approaches also are condemned as disjointed, piecemeal, fragmentary. But does the new grammar present a complete picture? It would be rash of its sponsors to claim this, though rashness is not a quality unknown in them. But it is a question anyhow whether "fragmentary" knowledge is a bad thing. We might reconcile ourselves, perhaps, without being overmodest, to the notion that human knowledge of any subject is fragmentary. But it is not rendered thereby of no account.

Moreover, to censure the heritage from which the school grammars sprang is supercilious and unjust. If English grammars originally were written, as Fries observes, to serve as introductions and helps to the study of a second language, they surely had a noble beginning. And the fact that such textbooks imposed the grammar of a foreign tongue upon English, so far from being a shortcoming, is a tribute to the comprehension and resourcefulness of their makers. In their turn, the 18th-century grammarians, the deepest-dyed villains of all, fulfilled a real need and did it pretty well; they did the best they could with what

5 *Linguistics Across Cultures: Applied Linguistics for Language Teachers* (Ann Arbor: University of Michigan Press, 1957), p. 51.

they had, and if they accommodated English grammar to Latin and Greek forms, it just may have been because they saw (perhaps as a result of an awareness of what Noam Chomsky calls "deep structure") that English and Latin and Greek were amenable to this treatment to an extent that some of our modern linguists are unwilling to admit or perhaps have overlooked for the moment.

In any case, something by way of a guide had to be created; some codifying and systematizing urgently were needed, and the 18-century grammarians provided these—although, of course, they did it very badly from the enlightened point of view of our modern linguists. But we ought to reflect that in those days there were no Frieses or Bloomfields. And since before their time the English language was in such inept hands for so long, one marvels that it is usable at all today. One muses pityingly how men like Chaucer, Shakespeare, Milton, and Dr. Johnson ever created anything worth reading; for they could not, in their pristine ignorance, have had any real sense of the wonder and complexity of their language, which they slopped about in a most superficial and pre-scientific manner.

Is it too fanciful to suggest that perhaps the tension between the authoritarians and standardizers (including, by the way, men like Dryden, Swift, and Johnson) on the one hand, and the freewheeling masses, among other influences, on the other, actually might have been a good thing for the English language? Of course, we can not say with complete assurance that in the absence of, for example, Dr. Johnson's *Dictionary*, we would have suffered an irreparable loss. But probably even the most liberal of modern linguists would hesitate to affirm that English would have been better off without it. There appears, in other words, to be a kind of inevitability about standardizing and attempts at standardizing language, just as there is an irrepressible tendency toward unregulated growth. And this would seem to be not only a necessary condition but a happy one.

In sum: First, the spoken language, at least for most civilized persons, is decidedly not *the* language; we are in no wise critically dependent upon it as we are, in the present at any rate, upon the written. This heresy must be rooted out, even if we have to try Charles Fries before a tribunal of bookworms and *auto-da-fé* him with a sentence of being talked to death by his own followers. Second, usage alone no more can determine correctness than the 18th-century grammarians and standardizers were able to do it. Indeed, the latter have the better of it. Dr. Johnson's influence alone upon correct forms of English has been greater than that of all the modern linguists combined, and we may forgive them some of their resentment. But there is no particular reason to regret that this is so. Finally, "school grammar" has been productive of no more ignorance of the language than has the "new grammar." When

we had school grammar, our teachers at least felt guilty that they were
not teaching their students anything about language. Now, in the hey-
day of the linguistic approach, they still may not teach them anything
about language, but the new method has made it unnecessary for them
to feel guilty about it.

SEMANTICS: WHAT AND WHY

Charles Weingartner

THE definition of semantics offered here is intended to be appropriate
to the purposes of teachers of English in the schools. This may make
it unique. Since one of the larger purposes of the teaching of English
is that of increasing the ability of students to use language effectively,
semantics can be defined as the study of language operations in real
human contexts, with emphasis on the human consequences of these
"operations." The focus of such language study is on the dynamics of
human meaning-making processes.

This definition places *meaning* (or, more precisely, the processes of
meaning-making) at the center of language study, with meaning being
determined on the basis of the human behavior (and its consequences)
that a specific language situation produces. Beauty lies in the eye of the
beholder, which is to say that meaning lies in the behavior of the language user. We begin speaking as we think, and end up thinking as we
speak. And, in turn, we behave as we think.

Semantics, operationally defined, is based on the fact that the meaning
of language lies in the human consequences it produces. Any language
use that produces no human consequence in a given situation is meaningless.

This definition distinguishes semantics from other more conventional
modes of language study, such as "grammar," by examining language as
a process in actual human contexts, rather than as an abstract taxonomy
of signs and symbols to be ritualized into a series of prescriptions and
proscriptions intended to preserve some arbitrary notion of "correctness."
From the point of view defined here, any deliberate use of language that
produced an intended response would be "correct." Operational definitions generally are vulnerable to the charge that they are "merely prag-

FROM *English Journal* (November 1969), pp. 1214–1219. Copyright © 1969 by the
National Council of Teachers of English. Reprinted by permission of the publisher and
Charles Weingartner.

matic." It should be noted, however, that the business of daily life is "merely pragmatic."

Semantics, with the study of human meaning-making processes as its primary concern, can comprise the most relevant dimension of the study of English for all students, whatever roles they play, immediately in their daily lives, which brings us to a rationale for including semantics in the teaching of English.

In an interview published in *Horizon,* Ernest Hemingway is quoted as saying that the one characteristic a person must have to be a great writer is "a built-in, shock-proof crap-detector." The burden of this rationale is: (1) that to survive in an environment increasingly characterized by misinformation and even anti-information (cf. the "pseudo-event" as described by David Boorstin in *The Image,* Atheneum, 1962) the most important piece of "equipment" that education can provide a student with is a "built-in, shock-proof crap-detector," and (2) that the study of semantics provides a viable manner for students to acquire this "equipment."

As research amply and dismayingly reveals, students do not acquire such equipment in the usual English curriculum.

Considering the fact that language using is the one kind of behavior that distinguishes human beings from all other forms of life, and that language comprises the basic vehicle for meaning-making and the communication of meaning among humans, the omission of substantive attention to meaning-making processes in the teaching of English seems nothing less than incredible. It is not as if attention has not been called to the importance of such study long since. For example, in 1923, C. K. Ogden and I. A. Richards pointed the direction in *The Meaning of Meaning* (Harcourt—A Harvest Book):

> The practical importance of a science of Symbolism even in its present undeveloped form needs little emphasis. All the more elaborate forms of social and intellectual life are affected by change in our attitudes toward, and our use of words (p. ix).

As is well known, Richards went on to illuminate the inability of honors students in literature at Cambridge to make viable meanings from untitled and anonymously presented poems in his study *Practical Criticism* (Harcourt, 1929).

The fact that even honors students are left cognitive paraplegics after years of conventional courses in "language and literature" would seem to provide a reasonable basis for questioning the common simple-minded assumptions upon which most English teaching is still based.

James R. Squire's study, *The Responses of Adolescents While Reading Four Short Stories* (NCTE Research Report No. 2, 1966), replicated the sense of Richards' study, and found students suffering from the same kind of illiteracy in meaning-making. While Squire did not use Richards' terminology for identifying various kinds of learned obstacles to cognitive strategies that prevented students from dealing with the language in the "literary" items they confronted so as to permit communication (with the author) to occur, he summarized the inability of these adolescents in Chapter VII of the study, titled "Sources of Difficulty in Literary Interpretation," as follows:

> A study of the transcripts [of student responses] reveals six sources of difficulty to be particularly widespread among these 52 adolescent readers: the reader fails to grasp the most obvious meanings of the author; the reader relies on stock responses when faced with a seemingly familiar situation; the reader is "happiness bound"; the reader approaches literature with certain critical predispositions; the reader is sidetracked by irrelevant associations; and the reader is determined to achieve certainty in interpretation and is unwilling to hold judgment in abeyance. Other causes of difficulty occur, but these are the most common. Because the four stories were selected as representative of much fiction that is included in anthologies for ninth- and tenth-graders, the six sources of difficulty in interpretation may well represent fairly widespread reading problems of adolescents in this age group (p. 37).

A knowledge of semantics would improve the ability of students to "interpret" (make viable meanings of) these stories because they would learn, as Squire's language reveals that he has yet to, that we do not "get" (cf. Squire's "grasp") meaning from words (or anything else), we can only *ascribe* meanings; they would also learn to identify specious analogies and inferences; and they would learn to delay judgment.

Richards' study, forty years earlier, and based upon the responses of students one might expect to be much more sophisticated and proficient in viable meaning-making than those in Squire's study, makes it clear that "reading problems" are not confined to American adolescents, nor to any particular group of students, irrespective of the "track" they may be placed in. Indeed, one can predict that if a study of this type were conducted among a random sample of NCTE members the results would be about the same as Richards' and Squire's.

As is suggested above, the study of semantics can do more to help students become more perceptive and sophisticated users of language than any other form of language study. Language, after all, is the medium through which all human sensory input is filtered and organized, and in which most meanings are codified. Language comprises the essential currency in the transactions called cognitive activity.

The term "meaning-making" is used here to stand for the language-centered cognitive processes otherwise vaguely referred to by such terms as "critical thinking."

"Critical thinking" has long been claimed as one of the major objectives of the teaching of English, but research has so far failed to verify the accomplishment of it via the usual English curriculum, for reasons similar to those identified by Richards and Squire.

Semantics is one operational dimension of language study that consists of learning (through direct and immediate student analysis of the real language used in their personal environments) a system for making distinctions among various kinds of language functions and forms that in turn constitutes an identifiable process that can be called "critical thinking."

There is increasing documentation to support this contention. Two representative research reports are: (1) "An Investigation of the Effects of Instruction in General Semantics on Critical Reading Ability," by Howard Livingston (*California Journal of Educational Research,* 16 [March 1965] 93–96) and (2) "Communicating Sense and Nonsense: Effects of General Semantics Training Upon Some Fifth-Grade Children," by Rachel Lauer (*Pathways in Child Guidance,* 7 [March 1965] 13–15).

Livingston, a professor of English at Pace College (New York), found that, following two periods a week for five weeks of instruction in selected principles and techniques of general semantics, tenth-grade students made statistically significant greater gains in scores on the *Watson-Glazer Critical Thinking Appraisal* than did a comparable group that did not have such instruction.

Lauer, chief psychologist for the New York City Schools, gave fifth-graders twenty-six lessons in semantics over a period of five months. Using various measures of language-thought performance, including tests of inferential thinking, and expository writing, she reported: "Results of this research give substantial evidence that general semantics can be effectively taught to young children and that it can result in significant changes in their thinking quality which do not ordinarily accrue to the same degree from the regular curriculum."

While *The English Language Arts* (the first of the NCTE Commission on the Curriculum Series, 1952) makes reference to "critical thinking as a goal of the language arts program," and to "semantics" (largely in the sense in which the term is defined here), a later title in that series, *The English Language Arts in the Secondary School,* includes no reference either to "critical thinking" or "semantics." It does include, however, a good deal of attention to "grammar."

More recent publications, apparently regarded as substantive "position papers," at least among the most voluble members of the English teaching establishment, including the *NASSP* (National Association of secondary School Principals) *Bulletin* on "The English Curriculum" (April 1967); and the report of the College Entrance Examination Board's Commission on English, *Freedom and Discipline in the Teaching of*

English; and, most recently, Herbert Muller's report on the Dartmouth Conference, *The Uses of English*, reveal little or no interest in "critical thinking" or "semantics."

Perhaps the most accurate indication of the interests and concerns of those in leadership positions who are asked (or who volunteer) to speak for the teaching of English and to define its mission in the stormy present can be found in *Freedom and Discipline* which is the source of the "tripod" metaphor now most commonly used to structure the English curriculum. In the paperback version of this report of the Commission on English, the section titled "Language" runs just over twenty-three pages. This section, it turns out, deals almost exclusively with "grammar," and essentially advocates transformational grammar as the best of all possible grammars. On the twenty-first page of this section on "language," the first sentence of the third paragraph reads: "Some consideration must also be given to the problem of meaning." And that is the only mention of meaning in the whole section on language! Clearly, grammarians, despite all of the research revealing the sterility of grammar study, are dominant in determining the parameters of "language study." To emphasize the tragedy of this circumstance it might be suggested that the least significant observation to make about the State and Defense Departments' use of language about Vietnam is that it is grammatically correct.

The fatuousness of grammarians and literary dilettantes would be deplorable enough if what was taught in the name of English in the schools was, despite them, relevant and viable, but such is not commonly the case.

This rationale subscribes to Aldous Huxley's observation ("Education on the Non-verbal Level," *Daedalus* [Spring, 1962]) that:

> . . . even on the verbal level, where they are most at home, educators have done a good deal less than they might reasonably have been expected to do in explaining to young people the nature, the limitations, the huge potentialities for evil as well as for good, of that greatest of all human inventions language. Children should be taught that words are indispensable but also can be fatal—the only begetters of all civilization, all science, all consistency of high purpose, all angelic goodness, and the only begetters at the same time of all superstition, all collective madness and stupidity, all worse-than-bestial diabolism, all the dismal historical succession of crimes in the name of God, King, Nation, Party, Dogma. . . . Generals, clergymen, advertisers, and the rulers of totalitarian states—all have good reasons for disliking the idea of universal education in the rational use of language. To the military, clerical, propagandist, and authoritarian mind such training seems (and rightly seems) profoundly subversive. To those who think that liberty is a good thing, and who hope that it may some day become possible for more people to realize more of their

desirable potentialities in a society fit for free, fully human individuals to live in, a thorough education in the nature of language, in its uses and abuses, seems indispensable. Whether in fact mounting pressures . . . will permit this kind of subversive linguistic education to be adopted . . . remains to be seen.

One of the obvious pressures against the inclusion of this kind of linguistic education (semantics) is the existing English curriculum.

The teaching of English, as a matter of fact, turns out to be a pedestrian exercise in "covering" the content of some textbook that publishers in their wisdom (with the assistance of grammarians and literary dilettantes) have seen fit to peddle. The "English curriculum," then, is determined not by educational philosophers, nor by thoughtful members of the community, nor, even, by teachers of English. It is determined by publishers of textbooks. And publishers of textbooks, it should be noted, are not in business to *educate* anyone (that is, to equip them with built-in, shock-proof crap-detectors). They are in business to make money. The reasons publishers give for publishing bowdlerized, emasculated, irrelevant pap designed to elicit benign approval from the conservatives who purchase their products are essentially those given by other purveyors of crap for profit. The TV ad agencies and networks, for example, say, as we all know, "We are giving the public what it wants." Now this "reason" is despicable enough for a nationwide flea market to give to justify what it does, but for an enterprise that is ostensibly "educational" it is outrageous. A dope pusher can justify his activities on the basis of the same reason.

As all peddlers, including the most ubiquitous ones in our times, those on TV, know—you can't afford to antagonize someone you want to sell something to. Publishers, obviously, share this "ethic." Education, however, as contrasted with training or indoctrination, is a process that has as its purpose the "liberation of the spirit." This liberation occurs largely through having those to be educated confront questions about themselves and their tribe, and its attitudes, beliefs, values, assumptions, and rituals, that they probably would not confront if left to their own devices. This process makes *education* a subversive activity. Expert crap-detectors (including just about all artists, and especially writers) are commonly regarded as subversives or heretics. The fable of the snake and the apple is still an accurate commentary on this point. Students of semantics learn how to ask questions rather than merely memorize answers.

New questions lead to new answers, and the custodians of the old answers are outraged by them. Anyone who wants to keep a system fixed at a certain point is, of course, a conservative. He simply wants to conserve a pattern that he believes to be right and good and true and beautiful. He will defend it to the death. If not his own, then someone else's. The conservative is the textbook publisher's audience, because he comprises the bulk of the population concerned with textbook publishing.

What has this got to do with semantics in the schools? Almost everything. The "study of language," in English, now means the study of grammar. The textbooks, the old courses of study, and even most of the "new" materials from the curriculum centers are full of it. Semantics, to be included as part of English, will probably have to displace grammar, and such a development seems most improbable. Grammar is not subversive. Semantics, as Huxley points out, most certainly is. The irony in this is intensified by considering the fact that the one task all human beings pursue during most of the time they are awake (and, if recent research into sleep is any indication, during much of the time they are not awake, too) is that of making meanings—of making some kind of "sense" of sensory intake. Some people have to make meanings of "higher orders" than others, and from denser and more complex "data," but the basic task remains for all of us. Most contemporary literature, especially dramatic literature, illustrates the problems that beset us because of the difficulty of this task in a rapidly changing environment. The most crucial ability for all of us to develop, then, is that of making accurate and adequate—"viable"—meanings out of the deluge of data that engulfs us from moment to moment all through the day. This task is tricky business, even in a relatively stable environment where the data coming in are patterned, redundant, and, so, predictable. We learn, in such an environment, a sequence of meanings and ritualize them, and they "work" in an environment which replicates itself day by day— meaning-making here is largely the memorization of fixed, routine responses. But, in a changing environment, especially a rapidly and constantly changing environment, the new (non-routine, and frequently unexpected) data that assault us demanding that we make meaning of them can be almost literally endless. Our first inclination (reaching for our Linus-blanket) is to assign old meanings to the new data (looking into the rear-view mirror), in a wistful gesture intended to dispel, or at least to minimize, the anxiety we suffer as a result of uncertainty and unpredictability. And here a curious paradox develops: to the degree to which we succeed in forcing new data into old meanings we fail to discover what the new data can and do mean. It seems as if the ultimate function of all human symbols is to exorcise the demon of uncertainty. And if we are illiterate in how these symbols (language) work, we are in the same position with respect to our total environment that the adolescents Squire studied were in relation to the four short stories. By which we intend to indicate that this rationale for including semantics in the teaching of English holds that no dimension of English can be more relevant to the demands of the stormy present than semantics, and that we must disenthrall ourselves by shifting it to the center of the English program.

It has been the occasion of much dismay on NCTE executive levels that federal appropriations for the study of the "humanities" (the purpose of which used to be "the liberation of the spirit") have been dwindling. Surely, if the relevance of such study, including "English," to the stormy present were more generally apparent, support for it could be expected to increase rather than diminish. Indeed, there is a precedent for this in the experience of World War II, when a concern for communication and semantics emerged as a large part of the teaching of English. Grammar and literary trivia seem not to be high priority items in a time of crisis. And we are now in an era of chronic crises. And many of these crises we talk ourselves into via rhetoric that fondles old, irrelevant meanings and blocks us from generating new, viable ones. We still talk, for example, of "winning" wars.

In 1952, Lee Deighton presented a paper at the Sixtieth Annual Meeting of the West Virginia State Teachers Association titled, "The Survival of the English Teacher." The burden of this paper was that teachers of English had lost touch with reality, and that they could best establish the relevance and importance of the teaching of English to our national and personal purposes by emphasizing the study of language in a manner virtually identical with what we are calling *semantics* here. He asked, for example, "Will anyone seriously defend the position that grammar is more important in our daily lives than straight thinking or a knowledge of how to control the effects of our language on others?"

It is not encouraging that seventeen years later the same question still needs to be asked.

TEACHING A NATIVE LANGUAGE

Jerome Bruner

I HAVE OFTEN thought that I would do more for my students by teaching them to write and think in English than teaching them my own subject. It is not so much that I value discourse to others that is right and clear and graceful—be it spoken or written—as that practice

REPRINTED by permission of the publishers from Jerome S. Bruner, *Toward a Theory of Instruction,* Cambridge, Mass.: The Belknap Press of Harvard University Press, Copyright, 1966, by the President and Fellows of Harvard College.

in such discourse is the only way of assuring that one says things right and courteously and powerfully *to oneself*. For it is extraordinarily difficult to say foolishness clearly without exposing it for what it is— whether you recognize it yourself or have the favor done you. So let me explore, then, what is involved in the relation between language and thinking, or better, between writing and thinking. Or perhaps it would be even better to speak of how the use of language affects the use of mind.

Consider this. As between reading, listening, and speaking, one falls asleep most easily reading, next most easily listening, and only with the greatest difficulty while writing or speaking—although I have seen both the latter happen among those deprived of sleep for long periods. There is an important difference between deciphering (as in listening or reading), and enciphering (as in speaking or writing). In listening or reading our span of attention typically lags behind the furthermost point where our eye or ear has traveled. We hold words and phrases in mind until we can tie the utterance together. A colleague of mine has been studying the retrospective integrating mechanisms involved in listening, and he finds his subjects holding decisions in abeyance until they see what is coming, which then permits them to go back over what has been said in order to give it a final syntactical rendering. Of course, we aid our auditors and readers by reducing the amount of memorial baggage they carry to the end of a sentence. And so we write:

This is the dog that chased the cat that killed the rat,

and avoid:

This is the rat that the cat that the dog chased killed.

In speaking or writing, the pattern is quite different: the arrow points forward. The speaker or writer rides ahead of rather than behind the edge of his utterance. He is organizing ahead, marshaling thoughts and words and transforming them into utterances, anticipating what requires saying. If the listener is trafficking back and forth between the present and the immediate past, the speaker is principally shuttling between the present and the future. The plight of the listener is to "fall behind"; of the speaker, to "get ahead of himself." Falling behind is a state in which the listener has insufficient processing time for decoding; getting ahead of oneself is a failure to anticipate properly. Pressed for time, the listener falls further and further behind, the speaker gets further and further ahead of himself. It is not surprising, then, that listening is soporific in the sense of blurring the present with the past. The tonic effect of speaking is that one thrusts the edge of the present toward the future. In one case anticipation is forced into abeyance. In the other, it dominates the activity.

You will quite properly have guessed that I am about to urge that reading be rescued from its passivity and turned into a more active enterprise. Indeed, I do believe just that. But it is not a new theme. We have all discovered it (with delight) on our own. As a student, I took a course with I. A. Richards, a beautiful man and a great necromancer. It began with that extraordinary teacher turning his back to the class and writing on the blackboard in his sharply angular hand the lines:

> Green grows the golden tree of life.
> Gray is all theory;

For three weeks we stayed with the lines, with the imagery of the classic and romantic views, with the critics who had sought to explore the two ways of life; we became involved in reading a related but bad play of Goethe's, *Torquato Tasso,* always in a state of dialogue though Richards alone spoke. The reading time for eleven words was three weeks. It was the antithesis of just reading, and the reward in the end was that I owned outright, free and clear, eleven words. A good bargain. Never before had I read with such a lively sense of conjecture, like a speaker and not a listener, or like a writer and not a reader.

I need not argue the virtues of reading oneself awake. Rather, I mean to pose a somewhat different problem, though a closely related one. Let me begin by stating rather baldly—though there is indeed ample evidence to support my point—that language is a major instrument of thought. When we are thinking at the far reach of our capacities, we are engaged with words, even led forward by them. Take the first appearance of syntax in the life of the child. During his second year, he develops that curious but powerful construction, the one-word utterance or holophrase: *Mummy, sticky, allgone, no, daddah.* If you study the course of growth, you will discover that on a certain day, and it should be celebrated with an anniversary party each year, the child mysteriously constructs a syntactical utterance. Mother washes jam from his hands. He says, *Allgone sticky.* If you keep observing you will discover further that during the next weeks he drives the new construction to its limit: a syntactic structure composed of a closed pivot class, *allgone,* and an open class that contains practically every other word in his vocabulary. *Allgone* what have you. Soon new pivot words emerge, always in this same kind of privileged position with regard to the other words in his vocabulary. In the first month after their appearance, there will be a few dozen utterances containing a pivot construction. A few months later they will number well over a thousand.

What has this to do with our subject? It has precisely this to do with it: the child has acquired not only a way of saying something but a powerful instrument for combining experiences, an instrument that can now be used as a tool for organizing thoughts about things. It has been remarked that words are invitations to form concepts. It can equally be said that the combinatorial or productive property of language is an invitation to take experience apart and put it together again in new ways. Consider the new-found power and grace of the child we considered a moment ago. He returns from a trip in his stroller: *allgone byebye.* I am urging, in effect, that in some unknown but considerable measure, the power of words is the power of thought. There has been the teaching of English, as it has come to be called in the past half century. But it may well be teaching the calculus of thought as well. Indeed, I should like to urge that the closest kin to the teacher of English composition is the teacher of mathematics. The latter is teaching a somewhat artificial-ized calculus of thought that applies principally to what are called well-formed problems. The ill-formed problems for which the calculus of grammar is most useful are incalculably more interesting and strenuous. That is what the teacher of composition has in his charge.

How conceive of language as a calculus of thought for ill-formed problems—problems, that is, without unique solutions? I should prefer to look at it from the point of view of the functions that language serves the speaker outwardly, and then to consider which of these functions also serve internally to help us organize our thoughts about things. My distinguished colleague and friend Roman Jakobson has some penetrating comments to make on this subject.[1] He suggests that there are six discernible functions of language: emotive, conative, referential, meta-lingual, poetic, and phatic. It is a formidable list. He derives it from the nature of discourse, and if we assume that much of thought is internalized discourse or dialogue, it seems reasonable to suppose, does it not, that these functions should be represented in thinking. Discourse consists, in its essentials, of an *addresser*, an *addressee*, a *contact* that joins them, a *message* passing between them, a *context* to which the message refers and a linguistic *code* that governs the way in which messages are put together and things referred to. The referential func-tion of language has to do with the manner in which things are pointed to by utterances. "That is a man." "What happened to the team spirit?" The emotive function expresses the internal feelings of the addresser through words or intonation. "How nice to be here" is a banal example. "Damn" is better. The conative function seeks to produce behavior in the addressee. "Get thee to a nunnery," or "Please hold my hat." The phatic function has as its aim the maintenance of contact, and is best illustrated by the "uh-huh" uttered over the telephone when we wish to make it clear to the other that we are still there. Opening sentences between old friends long separated and newly met provide a treasury

1 In T. A. Sebeok, ed., *Style in Language* (New York: John Wiley & Sons, 1960), pp. 350–374.

of phatic utterances. The poetic function has to do solely with the message for its own sake. "A girl used to talk about 'the horrible Harry.' 'Why horrible?' 'Because I hate him.' 'But why not *dreadful, terrible, frightful, disgusting?*' 'I don't know why, but *horrible* fits him better.' " Jakobson proclaims triumphantly, and quite correctly, "Without realizing it, she clung to the poetic device of paramasia." In the jargon of linguistics, the poetic function shifts the emphasis from rules of word selection to rules of word combination, the pure concern with the structure of the message, the delight of all who care about words. And finally the metalingual. It is jurisprudence applied to language: does this or that utterance fit the code—is or is not "mare" the feminine of "horse," and what is its contrast class? Or simply, "Do you know what I mean?"

I hope I have not bored you with the technicalities of making a single point. The point is, simply, that language serves many functions, pursues many aims, employs many voices. What is most extraordinary of all is that it commands as it refers, describes as it makes poetry, adjudicates as it expresses, creates beauty as it gets things clear, serves all other needs as it maintains contact. It does all these things at once, and does them with a due regard to rules and canons such that a native speaker very early in life is usually able to tell whether they were well done or botched. I would like to suggest that a man of intellectual discipline is one who is master of the various functions of speech, one who has a sense of how to vary them, how to say what he wishes to say—to himself and to others. Too much contact maintenance and too little reference is a bore. Too much expression and too little anything else is a muddle. What is true of external discourse may also be true of internal discourse with oneself. But consider now the relation of external and internal language. Can one be clear to oneself and turbid in saying it?

The shape or style of a mind is, in some measure, the outcome of internalizing the functions inherent in the language we use. Let me illustrate what is meant by internalization by citing two experiments, both by Russian psycholinguists.[2] Each experimenter set a task that was straightforward enough. When one kind of display appeared, the young subjects were to press a bulb in their right hand; when the other appeared, the left-handed bulb was to be pressed. In the first experiment, conducted by Martsinovskaya, children between the ages of three and eight were the subjects. Their first task was to press one bulb when a red circle appeared, the other when a green appeared. The circles were presented on either gray or yellow backgrounds. It is an easy task responding to a figure on a ground, and three-year-olds do it as well as

---

[2] For details, see A. R. Luria, *The Role of Speech in the Regulation of Normal and Abnormal Behavior* (New York: Liveright, 1961).

the older children. Now, when the task was mastered, the children were told to ignore the red and green figures and respond instead to the backgrounds, one bulb for yellow and the other for gray, regardless of what color figure appeared on them. Under these circumstances, the younger children had great difficulty. They seemed unable to inhibit reactions to the figures, were somehow unable to instruct themselves properly. The older children took it in stride. And now the second experiment, this one carried out by Abramyan, again with children of the same age range. He argued that the difficulty experienced by the younger children in Martsinovskaya's experiment was that they were unable to encode the instructions in internal language in a fashion that would permit them to regulate their own behavior. Their internalized language went no further than concrete declaration. If the instructions could be converted into such a declarative form, then they would succeed. So he repeated the earlier experiment with only one variation: he substituted airplane silhouettes for the circles in the original experiment. Now when the child had to shift from figure to ground they were able to say, "Airplanes can fly on sunny days—yellow background; but they cannot fly on cloudy days—gray background. Press with one hand when the airplanes can fly, with the other when they cannot." With this small change, the three-year-olds could perform quite as well as the eights. Language, in short, provides an internal technique for programming our discriminations, our behavior, our forms of awareness. If there is suitable internal language, the task can be done.

This is a very simple, perhaps too simple, experiment. It does, however, raise a deep question about the relation between being able to do or think something on the one hand and being able to say it to oneself on the other. That there is some intimate relationship is quite plain, though it is equally plain that we are only beginning to understand the nature of that relationship. The Chinese proverb can sometimes be reversed, and there are instances in which a single word is worth a thousand pictures—the word "implosion" was classified top secret by the Manhattan Project during the war. But words have limits. When we follow Mr. MacLeish in admitting that a poem is mute, what we are saying, I suspect, is that words do not fully exhaust the knowledge and sensibility contained in our acts and our images.

I am not urging that the word is the summit of all intellectual discipline and cultivation. Rather, I would suggest that the way of language in knowing is the most powerful means we have for performing transformations on the world, for transmuting its shape by recombination in the interest of possibility. I commented earlier that there should be a special birthday to celebrate the entrance of the child into the human race, dated from the moment when he first uses combinatorial grammar. Each of the functions of language has its combinatorial necromancy, its enormous productiveness. It is with the cultivation of these combinatorial powers that I am concerned.

Now let me return to instruction in one's native language and the degree to which it may also be instruction in the use of the implements of thought. Let me exaggerate. If there is not a developed awareness of the different functions that language serves, the resulting affliction will be not only lopsided speaking and writing, but a lopsided mind. Like the children in the two experiments, the afflicted person will be restricted in his coping to events for which his stunted language provides suitable equipment. And one day he may be forced to fight a forest fire with a water pistol.

But how does one achieve awareness, mastery, and finesse in the various functions to which language is devoted? How indeed does one become masterfully adept at the rules for forming functionally appropriate utterances for the consumption of others or for one's own consumption, *save by exercise?* Many of us have delighted over the years in the weekend competitions of the *New Statesman*. "Write the Declaration of Independence in the style of the Old Testament." Or, "Do a prose rendering of the 'Charge of the Light Brigade' in the style of Henry James." There is a comparable delight in Max Beerbohm's *Christmas Garland* or Raymond Queneau's *Exercises in Style.* To write in different styles and in different voices—a beseeching account of evolution, an expressive account of Newton's Law of Moments, whatever —surely this is one right path.

I confess to having achieved one minor success in the teaching of English. The pupil was one of my own children. Several years ago she was applying for entry to a college that requires applicants to write an autobiographical sketch. She wrote one and brought the piece to me for comment. It was very much her—full of her warm enthusiasm—and yet the written document was almost a caricature of a warm-hearted girl. It is difficult to be graceful in one's comments about another's writing, and the more so when there is a close bond between critic and his charge. You cannot say to a seventeen-year-old girl, however gay your tone of voice, "My dear, this is gushy." The diagnosis of gushiness carries no remedial prescription with it. I stumbled on the happy formula. Could she rewrite the piece without a single adjective, not a one? Two hours later she returned with the news that her first draft had been disgustingly effusive, that I should have told her so, and that in spite of my failure in candor the sketch was being rescued from its original state. I suspect something more happened than just a change in writing.

It is the case that the skills of speaking and listening precede those of reading and writing. Why does writing come so hard to the schoolchild? There is often a lag of from six to eight years between his "linguistic age" in writing and in speaking. Written speech is obviously a quite different enterprise from oral speech. The brilliant Russian psychologist Vygotsky suggested that writing and reading are second-order abstractions. In spoken speech there is more likely to be not only a referent present, but a great amount of steering provided by the social demands of the dialogue. Written speech may bear the same relation to spoken speech that algebra bears to arithmetic. A written word stands for a spoken word used in any context whatever. A spoken word "stands for" a thing or state or thought—not another word in a different medium. In written language, moreover, no interlocutor is presupposed and none is there. Spoken utterances are normally determined in large part by the demands of a dialogue, with the interlocutor helping frame our decisions about what requires saying. Whoever uses written speech must detach himself from immediate social interaction altogether and conjure up in his own mind a situation appropriate to the written words with which he is dealing.

Let me suggest, then, that by virtue of its very separation from immediate dialogue, the act of writing creates a new awareness about the nature and powers of language. But if this is so, why is it that a man through his entire life as *Homo scribens* will continue to write with no improvement in his sense of craft and little improvement in his use of mind? It may well be that to become aware of what one has written requires that one hear it, listen to it, compare the spoken with the written version. Perhaps the paraphernalia of the "language laboratory" should be used, if only to have students read their compositions to a tape and then suffer the tape to read back aloud what they have written. There should be a tutor nearby, doubtless, to correct and encourage. But I am hard put to know what he would say to his charge. I would rather have the tutor play another role—not at the student's elbow but speaking from the tape. Let him take the student's composition and rewrite it in various styles, each capitalizing on different functions of language and on different techniques of saying or organizing what the student said. Then let the student write some more and listen, listen, listen.

It was Dante, I believe, who commented that the poor workman hated his tools. It is more than a little troubling to me that so many of our students dislike two of the major tools of thought—mathematics and the conscious deployment of their native language in its written form, both of them devices for ordering thoughts about things and thoughts about thoughts. I should hope that in the new era that lies ahead we will give a proper consideration to making these tools more lovable. Perhaps the best way to make them so is to make them more powerful in the hands of their users.

BI-DIALECTALISM: THE LINGUISTICS OF WHITE SUPREMACY

James Sledd

BECAUSE people who rarely talk together will talk differently, differences in speech tell what groups a man belongs to. He uses them to claim and proclaim his identity, and society uses them to keep him under control. The person who talks right, as we do, is one of us. The person who talks wrong is an outsider, strange and suspicious, and we must make him feel inferior if we can. That is one purpose of education. In a school system run like ours by white businessmen, instruction in the mother tongue includes formal initiation into the linguistic prejudices of the middle class.

Making children who talk wrong get right with the world has traditionally been the work of English teachers, and more recently of teachers of that strange conglomerate subject which we call speech. The English teacher in the role of linguistic censor was once a kind of folk heroine (or anti-heroine), the Miss Fidditch of the linguists' diatribes. Miss Fidditch believed in taking a strong stand. It never occurred to her that her main job was making the lower classes feel so low that they would try to climb higher. Instead, Miss Fidditch taught generations of schoolchildren, including future linguists, to avoid *ain't* and double negatives and *used to could* and *hadn't ought,* not because *ain't* would keep them from getting ahead in the world, but because *ain't* was wrong, no matter who used it, and deserved no encouragement from decent people who valued the English language. She did her job all the better for thinking that she was doing something else.

Miss Fidditch is not popular any longer among educators. Though the world at large is still inclined to agree with her, the vulgarizers of linguistics drove her out of the academic fashion years ago, when they replaced her misguided idealism with open-eyed hypocrisy. To the popular linguists, one kind of English is as good as another, and judgments to the contrary are only folklore; but since the object of life in the U.S.A. is for everybody to get ahead of everybody else, and since linguistic prejudice can keep a man from moving up to Schlitz, the linguists still teach that people who want to be decision-makers had better talk and write like the people who make decisions. The schools

➤➤➤-➤➤➤

FROM *English Journal* (December 1969), pp. 1307–1329. Copyright © 1969 by the National Council of Teachers of English. Reprinted by permission of the publisher and James Sledd.

must therefore continue to cultivate the linguistic insecurity which is already a national characteristic but must teach the youngsters to manipulate everything else; for neither Miss Fidditch's dream of a language intrinsically good, nor a humbler ideal of realizing the various potentialities of the existing language in its responsible use, can get in the way of the citizenry in its upward anguish through the pecking order. The linguists think that people who do knowingly what Miss Fidditch did in her innocence, will do it more efficiently, as if eating the apple made a skilled worker out of Eve.

As long as most people agreed that up is toward Schlitz and another TV set, and as long as they could pretend that every American eaglet can soar to those great heights, Fidditch McFidditch the dialectologist could enforce the speech-taboos of the great white middle class without complaint: either the child learned the taboos and observed them, or he was systematically penalized. But the damage done to the Wasps' nest by World War II made difficulties. People who talked all wrong, and especially black people, began to ask for their share of the loot in a world that had given them an argument by calling itself free, while a minority of the people who talked right began to bad-mouth respectability and joined the blacks in arguing that it was time for a real change. Some black people burned up the black parts of town, and some students made study impossible at the universities, and in general there was a Crisis. Optimists even talked of a revolution.

The predictable response of the frightened white businessman's society was to go right on doing what it had done before—which had caused the crisis—but to do it harder and to spend more money at it. Education was no exception. Government and the foundations began to spray money over the academic landscape like liquid fertilizer, and the professional societies began to bray and paw at the rich new grass. In that proud hour, any teacher who could dream up an expensive scheme for keeping things as they were while pretending to make a change was sure of becoming the director of a project or a center and of flying first-class to Washington twice a month. The white businessman strengthened his control of the educational system while giving the impression of vast humanitarian activity.

Black English provided the most lucrative new industry for white linguists, who found the mother lode when they discovered the interesting locutions which the less protected employ to the detriment of their chances for upward mobility. In the annals of free enterprise, the early sixties will be memorable for the invention of functional bi-dialectalism, a scheme best described by an elderly and unregenerate Southern dame as "turning black trash into white trash." Despite some signs of wear, this cloak for white supremacy has kept its shape for almost a decade now, and it is best described in the inimitable words of those who made it. Otherwise the description might be dismissed as a malicious caricature.

The basic assumption of bi-dialectalism is that the prejudices of middle-class whites cannot be changed but must be accepted and indeed enforced on lesser breeds. Upward mobility, it is assumed, is the end of education, but white power will deny upward mobility to speakers of black English, who must therefore be made to talk white English in their contacts with the white world.

An adequate florilegium may be assembled from a volume entitled *Social Dialects and Language Learning* (NCTE, 1964), the proceedings of a conference of bi-dialectalists which was held in 1964. William A. Stewart of the Center for Applied Linguistics begins the chorus (p. 13) by observing among our educators "a commendable desire to emphasize the potential of the Negro to be identical to white Americans"—a desire which is apparently not overwhelming, however, among the Black Muslims or among the young men who have enjoyed pot-shooting policemen for the past few summers. Editor Roger W. Shuy next speaks up (p. 53) for social climbing by our American Indians, who have been notably reluctant, throughout their unfortunate association with their conquerors, to adopt our conquering ways. Our linguistic studies, Shuy remarks in the purest accents of fidditchery, "should reveal those elements, both in speech and writing, which prevent Indians from attaining the social status which, with socially acceptable language, they might otherwise attain." A similar desire to be at peace with status-holders is suggested (p. 66) by Ruth I. Golden, who opines that "a human being wants most of all to be recognized as an individual, to be accepted, and to be approved." Since Southern speech brings "negative reactions when heard by employers in Detroit," where Dr. Golden labors in the schools, she devotes herself to stamping out /i/ for /e/ in *penny* and to restoring /l/ in *help* (pp. 63 f.).

An admirable scholar from New York, William Labov, then agrees (p. 88) that "recognition of an external standard of correctness is an inevitable accompaniment of upward social aspirations and upward social mobility," and advises that people who (like Jesus) prefer not to take excessive thought for the morrow can probably be made to. In Labov's own words, "since the homes of many lower class and working people do not provide the pressures toward upward social mobility that middle-class homes provide," and since adults in those lower reaches are sometimes resistant to middle-class values, we must "build into the community a tolerance for style shifting which is helpful in educational and occupational advancement," and we must build into the children, "starting from a level not much above the nursery school and going on through high school, a tolerance for practice in second role playing" (pp. 94–97, 104).

Presumably Labov sees nothing wrong in thus initiating children into the world of hypercorrection, insecurity, and "linguistic self-hatred" which marks, as he has said elsewhere, "the average New Yorker" (*The Social Stratification of English in New York City*, Center for Applied Linguistics, 1966, Chapter XIII); and Charles Ferguson, the eminent ex-director of the Center for Applied Linguistics, is equally confident of *his* right and duty to remake his fellow men in his directorial image. Talking about the Negroes in our Northern cities, Ferguson says that "we have to face a rather difficult decision as to whether we want to make these people bi-dialectal . . . [please to remark Ferguson's choice of verbs] or whether we want . . . to impose some kind of standard English on these people and to eradicate the kind of substandard English they speak" (p. 116). To cite another NCTE volume (*Language Programs for the Disadvantaged* [NCTE, 1965], p. 222), if the black children of the ghetto "do not learn a second kind of dialect, they will be forever prevented from access to economic opportunity and social acceptance." Middle-class white prejudice will rule eternally.

The bi-dialectalists, of course, would not be so popular with government and the foundations if they spoke openly of the supremacy of white prejudice; but they make it perfectly clear that what they are dealing with deserves no better name. No dialect, they keep repeating, is better than any other—yet poor and ignorant children must change theirs unless they want to stay poor and ignorant. When an NCTE "Task Force" set out to devise *Language Programs for the Disadvantaged* (NCTE, 1965), it laid down a perfect smoke screen of such hypocrisy, as one would expect from persons who felt called upon to inform the world that "without the experience of literature, the individual is denied the very dignity that makes him human" (p. v) but that not "all disadvantaged children are apathetic or dull" (pp. 24 f.).

"In this report" (p. 117), "teachers are asked to begin by accepting the dialect of their students for what it is, one form of oral communication. . . ." Teachers are warned particularly that they "need to accept the language which Negro children bring to school, to recognize that it is a perfectly appropriate vehicle for communicating ideas in the Negro home and subculture" (p. 215), that it is "essentially respectable and good" (p. 227). But though teachers must not attack "the dialect which children associate with their homes and their identity as Negroes" (p. 215), they must still use all the adult authority of the school to "teach standard informal English as a second dialect" (p. 137), because the youngster who cannot speak standard informal English "will not be able to get certain kinds of jobs" (p. 228).

The most common result of such teaching will be that white middle-class Midwestern speech will be imposed as mandatory for all those situations which middle-class white businessmen think it worth their while to regulate. In the words of Chicago's Professors Austin and Mc-David (p. 245), "future educational programs should be developed in terms of substituting for the grammatical system of lower-class Southern speech [read: black Chicago speech] that of middle-class Chicago white speech—at least for those economic and social situations where grammatical norms are important." Labov goes so far as to ask (*Social Dialects and Language Learning*, p. 102) whether Northern schools should tolerate Southern speech at all—whether they should not also correct the "cultivated Southern speech" of privileged children who move North.

The description of compulsory bi-dialectalism may be completed by examining the methods which its proponents advocate for perpetuating the supremacy of white prejudice. Essentially, those methods are derived by analogy from structuralist methods of teaching foreign languages—methods whose superiority has been claimed but never demonstrated and whose intellectual foundations vanished with the demise of structuralist ideas. As an eminent grammarian privately observed after a recent conference, "The achievements of the operators will continue to lie in the field of getting and spending government money. . . . They seem to have an unerring instinct for finding ways of spending it unprofitably—on conferences at which they listen to each other, for example. Now they're out to teach standard English as a second dialect through techniques that have served very poorly in teaching second languages."

High on the list of those techniques is incessant drill on inessentials. In theory, the drills are the end-product of a long process of systematic comparison of the children's nonstandard dialects with the standard dialect which they are to be taught; but since the systematic comparisons have never been made, the bi-dialectalists fall back on a simple enumeration of a few dozen "features of pronunciation, grammar, and vocabulary which can be considered indices of social stratification" (Roger Shuy, "Detroit Speech," in A. L. Davis, ed., *On the Dialects of Children*, p. 13). Professor Rudolph Troike of the University of Texas was thus simply platitudinizing piously when he told the TESOL convention in 1968 that "any instructional program . . . must begin with as full an *objective* knowledge as possible" of both or all the dialects involved. The escape hatch in Troike's statement is the phrase *as full as possible*. What is usually possible is an unsystematic list of shibboleths—the simplification of consonant clusters, the Southern pronunciations of *walk* and *right*, *ax* for *ask*, the dropping of post-vocalic /r/, *ain't* and *fixin' to*, *bofe* and *mouf* for *both* and *mouth*, and the like. These innocent usages, which are as familiar as the sun in the late Confederacy, are apparently the terror of Northern employers, who the bi-dialectalists assume are almost suicidally unconcerned with such details as character, intelligence, and training for the job. The fact is, of course, that Northern employers and labor leaders dislike black faces but use black English as an excuse.

Having established, however, that a child of darkness under her tutelage says *mouf*, the pretty white lady sets out to rescue his soul. First she plays tapes of Southern speech to convince her victims, who understand Southern speech far better than they understand hers, that Southern speech often makes "complete understanding of content . . . difficult," "not readily comprehensible"—as is demonstrated by the fact that the pretty white lady would never have detected her victim's four-letter word just by listening and without watching his lips (New York Board of Education, *Nonstandard Dialect*, pp. 1, 14, 17). The difficulty of detecting him is all the more reason for fearing the iniquitous *mouf*-sayer: it proves he is a cunning devil who probably says *dentissoffice* too and who perpetrates such subversive "malapropisms" as "The food in the lunch room is not fitting to eat" (*On the Dialects of Children*, p. 23). How else *would* he spell *fitten?* But for such a hardened rogue, a good many "motivational activities" are likely to be necessary before the pretty white lady can really start twisting the thumbscrew with her drills.

Yet the drills are available, and the pretty white lady will use them when she sees her time. She has drills of all kinds—repetition drills, substitution drills, replacement drills, conversion drills, cued answer drills, the reading in unison of long lists of words like *teeth / reef, toothbrush / waffle, bathtub / alphabet, weather / weaver*. To get rid of *dentissoffice*, she may have students debate such propositions as "Ghosts do exist" or "Formal school tests should be eliminated"; and before a really "culminating activity" like playing "Pack the Trunk" she may "divide the class into consonant-cluster committees to seek out words containing" clusters like *sks, sps,* or *kt* (*Nonstandard Dialect, passim*). At this point the class might be invited to suggest a context for a replacement drill—maybe something like "Teacher! teacher! Billy Joe say that Tommy ——— Bessy!" This last suggestion, it must be confessed, has not yet been made in the literature, but it seems considerably more stimulating than choral recitation of Poe's "Bells" (Ibid., p. 35).

Perhaps it need not be added that existing tests and evaluations of such "instructional materials" are something of a farce. If bi-dialectalism is really harder to acquire than bilingualism (Einar Haugen in *Social Dialects and Language Learning*, p. 125), teachers and texts ought surely to be superb, and judgments on them ought to be severe; but New York City's curriculum developers can give "highest priority" to making the children change *a* to *an* before nouns beginning with a vowel (*Nonstandard Dialect*, p. 14), and Texas' Professor Troike can argue the success of his methods by showing that after six months of drills a little black girl could repeat *his hat* after her teacher, instead of translating automatically to *he hat*. Unfortunately, tapes do not record psychological damage, or compare the effectiveness of other ways of teaching, or show what might better have been learned in the same time instead of learning to repeat *his hat*.

So much for a description of mandatory bi-dialectalism, a bit enlivened (since the subject is dreary) by irreverent comment, but not distorted in any essential way. In the U. S. A., we are being told, everybody wants approval—not approval for doing anything worth approving, but approval for doing whatever happens to be approved. Because approval goes to upward mobility, everybody should be upwardly mobile; and because upward mobility is impossible for underdogs who have not learned middle-dog barking, we must teach it to them for use in their excursions into the middle-dog world. There is no possibility either that the present middle class can be brought to tolerate lower-class English or that upward mobility, as a national aspiration, will be questioned. Those are the pillars on which the state is built, and the compassionate teacher, knowing the ways of his society, will change the color of his students' vowels although he cannot change the color of their skins.

It is not at all certain that the bi-dialectalists, for all their absurdities, can be dislodged from their well-carpeted offices. They are supported by the National Council of Teachers of English, the Modern Language Association of America, the Center for Applied Linguistics, the federal government, the foundations, the governments of a number of major cities, and by black people who have made it into the middle class and so despise their origins and their less efficient fellows. In the best of times our top dogs are pleased by docility, if not mobility, among the beasts below; and in 1969 a new ice age is beginning. Newspaper headlines tell us that the Department of Health, Education, and Welfare has been urged to relax its requirements for desegregation of schools immediately but quietly, and President Nixon loses his Miami tan at the thought that militant students will "politicize" our universities—as if government grants to upwardly mobile faculty had not politicized them long ago. In Lyndon Johnson's Texas the citizens of Austin vote down an open housing law, their board of education then justifies segregated schooling by the established pattern of segregated housing, and the governor of the state praises the state university as the source of brain-power to assist the businessman in the lucrative exploitation of what the governor proudly calls the "insatiable appetite" of Texans. The only revolution we are likely to see is the continued subversion, by the dominant white businessman, of the political and religious principles on which the nation was founded.

Yet though the times are bad, they are not hopeless, at least not in the small, undramatic world of English education; and the bi-dialectalists are so gorgeously absurd that the breath of laughter may collapse their card-house if only enough people can be brought to see it as it is. It is not simply quixotic, then, to add to a laughing description of imposed bi-dialectalism a more serious statement of reasons why it cannot succeed and should not be tolerated even if it could—a statement which can lead, in conclusion, to the proposing of an alternative policy.

The argument that bi-dialectalism cannot be forced is easy to make out, even, in part, from the reluctant admissions of some of its proponents. Two principal reasons have already been suggested, the ignorance and unproved methods of the bi-dialectalists. The term *ignorance* is used literally, and in all fairness. Whatever one thinks of teaching standard English by methods like those for teaching foreign languages, contrastive analyses of our different dialects are a prerequisite—but a prerequisite which has not yet been supplied. Until very recently, the principal sources of information were the collections for the *Linguistic Atlas;* but they are unsystematic, partially out-of-date, and in some respects inaccurate and superficial. Where, for example, should one go for descriptions of intonation and its dialectal variants, for accurate accounts of the system or systems of verbal auxiliaries, for analyses of the speech of ghetto children instead of rustic ancients? Such minimal essentials are simply lacking. In fact, it might be said that for all the talk about revolutionary advances in linguistics, neither the structural nor the generative grammarians have yet produced a satisfactory basic description of even standard English.

The best descriptions of all our kinds of English would still not be enough to make coercive bi-dialectalism a success. The English teacher's forty-five minutes a day for five days in the week will never counteract the influence, and sometimes the hostility, of playmates and friends and family during much the larger part of the student's time. Formal education could produce real bi-dialectals only in a vast system of state nurseries and boarding schools to which the children of the poor and ignorant would be consigned at an early age; but such establishments would be prohibitively expensive, intolerable to the people, and still not absolutely certain of success, because the most essential of all conditions might not be met—namely, the desire of the children to talk like the white middle class.

When one thinks about it in these realistic terms, the whole argument about bi-dialectalism begins to look schizophrenic, as out-of-this-world as an argument whether Lee should surrender at Appomattox or fight back. There is no evidence that the bi-dialectalists, if they actually had good textbooks, better teachers, and as much money as the country is spending to devastate Vietnam, would really know what to do with those fictional resources. Instead of clear ideas, they offer clichés, like the familiar attacks on "traditional methods and approaches" or the protected pedagogue's arrogant assurance that illiterates can have no human dignity. They fly off quickly into high-sounding vaguenesses, talking (for example) about "differences in social dialect and associated versions of reality" (*Social Dialects and Language Learning*, p. 68), as if metaphysics rested on a preconsonantal /r/. At their most precise, they suggest the prudential avoidance of Southern pronunciations of *walk* and *cough* in Washington because Negroes there look down on new arrivals from Georgia and the Carolinas. They happily assume what they should prove—that intensive training in "standard informal English as a second dialect" has produced or can produce large numbers of psychologically undamaged bi-dialectals, whose new accomplishment has won them or will win them jobs that otherwise would have been impossible for them to get. When their guard is down, the bi-dialectalists actually confess that they *have* no concrete program, since "no one program at any level yet seems applicable to a significant number of other classes at the respective level" (*Language Programs for the Disadvantaged*, pp. 30 ff.).

Some awareness of their difficulties, and some uncertainty about priorities, seem indeed to be spreading among the bi-dialectalists (though it would be too much to hope that if their present bandwagon falls apart they will consider themselves discredited and resign their membership in the Society of Mandarin). For one thing, they have become aware of the significance of reading, which William A. Stewart, as late as 1964, could reduce to the level of "socially desirable embellishments" (*Social Dialects and Language Learning*, p. 10). In his latest book, however, *Teaching Black Children To Read*, Editor Shuy announces "the simple truth that speaking standard English, however desirable it may be, is not as important as learning to read" (p. 118). His colleagues Walter A. Wolfram and Ralph W. Fasold are even closer to enlightenment. In the same new volume (p. 143), they hesitantly admit that "there is some question about the degree to which Standard English can be taught to the ghetto child in the classroom at all"; and Fasold meant what he said, for he had said it before at the Milwaukee convention of the NCTE. Though that august body was still congratulating itself on its concern with "a language component for the so-called culturally divergent," it had to bear with Fasold's embarrassing confession: "Because of the operation of social forces in the use of language," he said, "forces which are only poorly understood, it may not be possible to teach Standard English as a second language to Black English speaking children unless they are interacting with Standard English speakers in a meaningful way outside the classroom" (*Convention Concerns—1968*, p. 10). The Center's linguistician came as close as standard English would allow to saying that it is segregation which makes black people talk different and that there would be no slum children if there were no slums.

No doubt the most important of Fasold's poorly understood social forces is one which everybody but white linguists has understood for a long time: black people may just not want to talk white English. Several years ago, Labov observed that some of his more rebellious New York subjects were deliberately turning away from social-climbing New York speech toward a black Southern model (*Social Dialects and Language Learning*, pp. 96 f.), and today comment on "the new feeling of racial pride among black Americans" (*Teaching Black Children To Read*, p. 142) is a platitude. Wolfram and Fasold go on to the quite unsurprising speculation that that pride may even extend to the Negro's speech. "If a realization develops that this dialect, an important part of black culture, is as distinctively Afro-American as anything in the culture, the result may well be a new respect for Black English within the community" (p. 143). More plainly, condescending middle-class white charity is not wanted any more, if it ever was, in language-teaching or anywhere else. We should learn from the example of the British: the social cataclysm of the Second World War, and the achievement of political power by labor, did more to give the "disadvantaged" English youngster an equal chance than charitable bi-dialectalism ever did. We are past the stage when white teachers, whether Africans or Caucasians, can think well of themselves for trying to turn black people into uneasy imitations of the whites.

The immorality of that effort is the chief reason why enforced bi-dialectalism should not be tolerated even if it were possible. Predators can and do use dialect differences to exploit and oppress, because ordinary people can be made to doubt their own value and to accept subservience if they can be made to despise the speech of their fathers. Obligatory bi-dialectalism for minorities is only another mode of exploitation, another way of making blacks behave as whites would like them to. It is unnecessary for communication, since the ability to understand other dialects is easily attained, as the black child shows when she translates her teacher's prissy white model "*his* hat" into "*he* hat." Its psychological consequences are likely to be nervous affectation, self-distrust, dislike for everyone not equally afflicted with the itch to get ahead, and eventual frustration by the discovery that the reward for so much suffering is intolerably small. At best the altered student will get a somewhat better job and will move up a few places in the rat-race of the underlings. At worst he will be cut off from other blacks, still not accepted among whites, and economically no better off than he was before.

White teachers should hope, then, that their black students will be recalcitrant, so that bi-dialectalism as a unilateral condition for employment can be forgotten. It would make better sense, if pedagogues insist on living in a fantasy world, to require whites to speak black English in their dealings with blacks, since the whites have more advantages than the blacks and consider themselves more intelligent; or perhaps we should be hard-headedly consistent in our brutalities and try to eradicate the vices which really do enrage employers—like intellectual questioning, or the suspicion that ours is not the best of possible worlds.

Indeed, the educationists' faith in education would be touching if it were not their way of keeping up their wages. Nothing the schools can do about black English or white English either will do much for racial peace and social justice as long as the black and white worlds are separate and hostile. The measure of our educational absurdity is the necessity of saying once again that regimented bi-dialectalism is no substitute for sweeping social change—*necessity* being defined by the alternative of dropping out and waiting quietly for destruction if the white businessman continues to have his way.

The reply that the educational system should not be politicized is impossible for bi-dialectalists, since bi-dialectalism is itself a political instrument. They may purge themselves of inconsistency, and do what little good is possible for English teachers as political reformers, if instead of teaching standard English as a second dialect they teach getting out of Vietnam, getting out of the missile race, and stopping the deadly pollution of the one world we have, as horribly exemplified by the current vandalism in Alaska.

One use for a small fraction of the resources that would thus be saved would be to improve the teaching of the English language. Bi-dialectalism would never have been invented if our society were not divided into the dominant white majority and the exploited minorities. Children should be taught that. They should be taught the relations between group differences and speech differences, and the good and bad uses of speech differences by groups and by individuals. The teaching would require a more serious study of grammar, lexicography, dialectology, and linguistic history than our educational system now provides—require it at least of prospective English teachers.

In the immediate present, the time and money now wasted on bi-dialectalism should be spent on teaching the children of the minorities to read. Already some of the universal experts among the linguists have boarded this new bandwagon, and the next round of government grants may very well be for programs in reading and writing in black English. That might be a good thing, particularly if we could somehow get rid of the tired little clique of operators who have run the professional societies of English teachers for so long. Anyway, the direct attack on minority language, the attempt to compel bi-dialectalism, should be abandoned for an attempt to open the minds and enhance the lives of the poor and ignorant. At the same time, every attempt should be made to teach the majority to understand the life and language of the oppressed. Linguistic change is the effect and not the cause of social change. If the majority can rid itself of its prejudices, and if the minorities can get or be given an education, differences between dialects are unlikely to hurt anybody much.

(The phoniest objections to this proposal will be those that talk about social realism, about the necessity for doing something even—or should one say particularly?—if it's wrong. That kind of talk makes real change impossible, but makes money for bi-dialectalists.)

WHAT CAN AN ENGLISH TEACHER DO ABOUT NONSTANDARD DIALECT?

Ralph W. Fasold

IN order to get the problem of what an English teacher can do about nonstandard dialects[1] into perspective, we should ask what English teachers hope to accomplish in the classroom. It may be that there are as many objectives as there are teachers, but I have little doubt that almost every teacher wants all of her pupils to be able to read well and to use correct English in both speech and writing. It will be my contention that reaching the objective in reading and writing may well involve some highly unorthodox procedures for children who speak nonstandard English. I am further going to suggest that trying to teach all students to speak correct English may not even be a reasonable objective.

What it means to read well is relatively clear. We expect every educated person to be able to read and understand any written material he is likely to use. But it is a good deal less clear just what it means to "use correct English in speech and writing." The whole issue hangs on the no-

---

1 There are numerous notions of the term "dialect" within and outside of the linguistics profession. The concept used in this paper is that a dialect is to a language as a piece of pie is to the whole pie. Just as one cannot bite into a pie which has been cut into pieces without biting into one of its pieces, so one cannot speak a language without speaking one of its dialects. Some of these dialects are accepted as standard, others are not so accepted and are considered nonstandard.

⇶⇶⇶⇶⇶⇶⇶⇶⇶⇶⇶⇶⇶⇶⇶⇶⇶⇶⇶⇶⇶⇶⇶⇶⇶⇶⇶

F R O M *The English Record* (April 1971), pp. 82–91. Reprinted by permission of the publisher and the author.

tion of "correct English." Contrary to the opinion of some teachers, there is no single set of rules which defines what is correct in language at every time and in every place. What is correct English for one person might be very incorrect for another, and vice-versa. This assertion is not new; linguists have been making statements of this kind for years. An analogy from mathematics is sometimes used as a counterargument. Just because a child has always thought that $2 + 2 = 5$ does not mean that his arithmetic teacher should allow him to continue to think so. Similarly, the argument runs, just because a child has always said "I ain't got none" does not mean his English teacher should allow him to continue to use this construction. But the analogy is a mistaken one. Relations in arithmetic have inherent truth value. The sum of 2 and 2 must be 4; it could not conceivably be anything else. Grammar rules do not determine something which is *inherently* correct. If grammar rules are properly formulated and understood, they are descriptions of how people happen to use language to communicate with each other. A grammar rule is correct only so long as it accurately predicts how sentences are actually used in a certain speech community. The same grammar rule becomes incorrect if the members of the speech community cease using the kind of sentences it predicts. A rule which is correct for one speech community becomes incorrect if it is applied to the speech of a different community in which the sentences it predicts are not used. A grammar rule which says that present-day English speakers use sentences like "Thou goest well" would be incorrect since it predicts sentences that are no longer used. In the same way, rules which disallow the use of "ain't" and the use of two negatives in the same sentence are incorrect for communities of speakers of nonstandard English. These rules would predict that a sentence like "I ain't got none" do not occur, but the simple fact is that they do occur. From another angle, the correct grammar for the same nonstandard English speaking community would not allow the sentence "I haven't any" since this kind of sentence does not occur. The useful notion of "correct English grammar" is that a correct English grammar accurately describes how English is used by a community of its speakers. This implies that there are as many correct grammars as there are communities of speakers.

Many teachers, even if they come to accept the linguist's notion of correct, will still object that nonstandard dialect should be eliminated because it keeps its speakers from thinking logically. But linguists have found that logical thinking can be expressed in *any* grammatical system which has so far been investigated. Many linguistic scientists would agree that the ability to express logic is a property of *all* human language. If we examine what is objectionable in nonstandard English, we find from the point of view of logic, that much of it is very trivial. "He go to school" expresses the same concept as "He goes to school." The absence of the suffix spelled *es* does not obscure the meaning of the sentence; nor does it make it illogical in any sense. Most standard English speakers prefer the second version of the sentence simply because it is customary for educated people to use "goes" with subjects like "he."

Other sentences which follow nonstandard grammar rules instead of standard English rules strike some observers as defective. Sentences with double negatives, for example, are said to be illogical since "two negatives make a positive." But if we return to our concept of language as a communicative tool, we see the problem disappear. When a speaker of nonstandard English utters a sentence like "He didn't do nothing" he means "He didn't do anything" and his meaning is perfectly well understood by other nonstandard English speakers and—let us be honest—by standard English speakers as well. If a child who uses nonstandard English intends a negative sentence and his intention is understood, then there is no problem of logic, no matter how many negative words he puts into the sentence to emphasize its meaning. We cannot claim that there is something inherently illogical about sentences with double negatives unless we are prepared to claim that all French speakers, for example, think illogically. French is one of several languages which *require* two negative words in common kinds of negative sentences.

A similar kind of reasoning applies to the use of nonstandard sentences in which the speaker "leaves out the verb," as in "They bad kids." It would be serious indeed if there were speakers who left out any verb indiscriminately, but it turns out that the verb "left out" by nonstandard English speakers is always "is" or "are." As in the case of double negatives, we find here that the predication relationship, which must be expressed by a form of "to be" in standard English, is perfectly well understood by anyone who speaks the dialect and by most standard English speakers. A look at the languages of the world reveals that there are several in which words for "to be" can be omitted without misunderstanding: Hebrew, Russian and Siamese being only three examples. There are also other points in which nonstandard grammar might be said to inhibit logical reasoning, but these examples are sufficient to indicate the futility of his line of inquiry.

Some distinctions seem to be made somewhat more readily in standard dialects of English than in some nonstandard ones. The distinction between "can" and "could" is one which some black nonstandard speaking children do not seem to control, at least in the same way the distinction is made in standard English. These youngsters tend to use "could" in sentences like "I could ride a bicycle" where "can" would be expected in standard English. On the other hand, there are other subtle distinctions which are easy to make in nonstandard dialect which can only be made periphrastically in standard English. When a speaker of one black nonstandard variety of English says "I been done learned that," far from simply torturing English grammar, he is making an emphatic statement which cannot be made by using "I've learned that" or the like. The meaning here is that the speaker has learned the item in question thoroughly some time ago and it is superfluous to suggest he learn it again. The nearest equivalent in standard English would be something like "I learned that a lo-o-ng time ago" where a time adverb and intonation must be used to cover an area which is handily covered by the resources of the nonstandard grammar. On balance, there are probably about the same number of subtle distinctions which are possible in each dialect of English; they are just different distinctions.

The problem of language *use* is another issue which should be kept separate from questions of inherent language ability. It is quite likely that there are syntactic constructions present in a child's grammar which he is not accustomed to use in ways necessary for functioning in school. Carl Bereiter provides a classic example of this (Bereiter 1965: 200) although he mistakenly gives it as an example of language disability. Bereiter observed that some disadvantaged four-year-old black children cannot perform "simple 'if-then' deductions." He gives the following example:

> The child is presented a diagram containing big squares and little squares. All the big squares are red, but the little squares are of various other colors. "If the square is big, what do you know about it?" "It's red."

The child cannot make the correct response, therefore he is incompetent in using if-then constructions. But Bereiter himself goes on to admit:

> This use of *if* should not be confused with the antecedent-consequent use that appears in such expressions as, "If you do that again, I'm going to hit you," and which the child may already be able to understand.

In other words, even Bereiter would not deny that the child has the grammatical skill to at least interpret if-then constructions. One could even go further and show that a child who doesn't even use the word "if" still has mastered the if-then logic. A sentence like "You don't stop messin' wif me, I'ma hit you upside you head" demonstrates mastery of if-then logic just as surely as "If you should continue to annoy me, then I shall beat you about the head." What Bereiter is calling a language disability is a question of use. The children he is referring to may be perfectly well able to use if-then logic. Their difficulty comes in applying it to Bereiter's problem concerning the colored squares. Incidentally, his problem strikes me as a formidable test of *any* four-year-old's ability.

In the light of these considerations, we can return to our consideration of what might be reasonable objectives for English teachers in dealing with nonstandard dialect. There are four areas of language skill traditionally discussed by applied linguists: hearing, speaking, reading and writing. We will consider possible objectives in terms of each of these four areas.

Although any teacher could probably relate isolated anecdotes about children who do understand spoken standard English, it is likely that hearing is the area in which there are the fewest problems related to dialect differences. Even children who are most severely restricted to ghettoes come into contact with standard English from earliest childhood through television and radio. As a result, they gain considerable competence in understanding standard dialects, which are, after all, closely related to their nonstandard variety of English.

Dr. Joan Baratz (1969) has performed an interesting experiment which serves to illustrate this very point. In part of the experiment, she asked black children who spoke nonstandard English to repeat sentences in standard English. Many of these children did not repeat the sentences exactly but gave the nonstandard equivalent. What does this mean? It does not mean that the youngsters were so linguistically handicapped that they could not even repeat a simple sentence; in fact, a similar group of middle-class white youngsters were equally incapable of repeating sentences given them in nonstandard English. What these children had done was to decode the standard English sentence correctly and recode it in more familiar patterns. These results demonstrate clearly the fact that children who do not speak standard English still may be able to understand it.

Research which indicates that some children are poor at "auditory discrimination" (Wepman 1960) is received by linguists with some uneasiness for two reasons. First, it is a well-known fact that people are good at discriminating only those phonetic contrasts which are used to differentiate words in their own language. An English speaker for this reason would have considerable difficulty distinguishing the Siamese word *pit* 'to close' from the word *bit* 'twist' because of the special phonetic qualities of the Siamese *p*. In his turn, the Siamese speaker will have trouble distinguishing the English word *rip* and *lip* since *r* and *l* do not differentiate Siamese words. Similarly, there are certain sounds which distinguish words in standard English which do not have this function in some nonstandard dialects. Giving youngsters who speak such dialects an "auditory discrimination test" based on standard English is rather like giving an English speaker a test based on Siamese phonetic distinctions. A poor showing would not necessarily indicate difficulty in auditory discrimination in either case.

Another reason for poor performance on such tests is difficulty with the instructions, as pointed out by Marion Black (1968). She sees these difficulties as indicating deficiencies in cognitive development, but they are better understood as the result of culture conflict. Unlike the middle class child, the lower class child does not come to school expecting to play this kind of game with words, although as Thomas Kochman points out (1969) black ghetto youngsters are, or come to be, proficient in other kinds of verbal skills the middle class child knows nothing about. In general there is nothing the English teacher need worry about with regard to hearing in most cases.

The second major area has to do with speech. It is perfectly clear that proficiency in understanding standard dialects of English does not imply proficiency in speaking standard English. Proficiency in speaking standard English, then, could be proposed as a goal for an English teacher to set for her nonstandard English speaking pupils. We have already indicated that there are two poor reasons for setting this goal. The desire to teach absolutely correct English is a poor reason because no variety of any language is ultimately and inherently "correct" in the sense that mathematical relationships are. Teaching standard English for the purpose of giving the children a basis for cognitive development is a poor reason because nonstandard syntax is equally capable of providing such a base. Nevertheless, another reason might be advanced for teaching standard English linguistic forms. Even if the contention that nonstandard English is correct for a child in some situations is accepted; even if there is agreement on the adequacy of nonstandard English for cognitive development, there is still the question of social acceptability. The use of a socially unacceptable dialect may well place a person at a social and economic disadvantage. No one would hire a young woman as a receptionist and switchboard operator if her grammar is nonstandard; and no one would hire a young man as an automobile salesman if his English is not acceptable to potential customers. This argument has considerably more merit than the other two, and is, in fact, the position taken by myself and Roger Shuy in the introduction to *Teaching Standard English in the Inner City* (Fasold and Shuy 1970). Nevertheless, I have more recently come to the conclusion that even this argument has a very serious flaw. To a large degree, what the English teacher does in the classroom with regard to spoken standard English is irrelevant. Speakers who start out speaking nonstandard English but find that they need to learn standard English will learn it, and those who do not will not, almost independently of what their English teachers do. The reason is that learning spoken language is unlike any other kind of learning. Spoken language cannot be taught only with the methods, materials and motivational strategies used to teach other subjects. I have serious doubts that one very necessary factor in learning new spoken skills, whether a new dialect or a whole new language, even *can* be supplied in the classroom. It is crucial that there be a viable expectation and desire on the part of the learner to become a member of the group represented by the speakers of the new language, dialect or style. If this factor is present, other methods and motivations may also contribute to successful learning of new spoken language skills. But if it is missing, nothing that goes on in the classroom can make up for its absence.

Psychologists and others interested in second language acquisition—which is different in degree but not in kind from second dialect acquisition—have realized the crucial importance of group reference to successful language learning. Discussing the learning of Hebrew by immigrants to Israel, Professor Simon Herman (1961: 162–163) states:

> If, as our analysis would indicate, group references play an important part in the choice of a language, it would follow that the readiness of a person to learn and use a second language may depend in part on the measure of his willingness to identify with the group with which the language is associated—or, at any rate, on his desire to reduce the social distances between himself and that group.

Whyte and Homberg (1956:13) found that this factor sometimes outweighed even inborn language-learning ability in predicting the success of U.S. businessmen in learning a second language in Latin America:

> A strong psychological identification with the other people and culture may more than make up for below average learning ability whereas a man of superior language ability may fail to make the necessary psychological identification and make poor progress.

John Gumperz (1966) gives an example which illustrates that absence of this group reference factor can nullify the tendency for people to learn the speech habits of those who have superior social status. There are three tribes in South India who have lived together for hundreds of years. Two of these tribes occupy a socially inferior position to the third. Yet members of these tribes do not learn the prestige language of the third tribe because the caste-like social system precludes the possibility that they will ever be accepted as members of the higher group.

If similar studies of second dialect learning were available, I am sure the same observations would be made. Without an expectation of acceptance on the part of the learner, there is small hope of success in language or dialect teaching. If this expectation is present, the new language or dialect is likely to be learned, even in the absence of formal teaching. Some nonstandard English speakers have such an expectation with respect to the standard English speaking community; others do not. I know of no really effective way that it can be provided in the classroom for those who do not.

I suspect that almost any English speaker can provide himself with a feel for the sort of rejection of prestige speech which is involved here. There are certain points of grammar which are taught as correct, and most standard English speakers will admit that they "should" use them, yet they don't. Some examples of these appear in the table below.

Rule	One "should" say	One often says
Use nominative forms of pronouns when they are the subjects of understood verbs.	He is human, just like you or I.	He is human, just like you or me.
Never end a clause with a preposition.	The slot in which it goes.	The slot it goes in.
Use "may" to request permission.	May I have another piece of pie?	Can I have another piece of pie?
Use "whom" as direct object.	Whom did you meet?	Who did you meet?
Make the *t* sound distinct from the *d* sound between vowels.	bet-ter	bedder

Most English speakers who have been through elementary school will recognize these rules as some of those which govern correct English. Yet I am sure that honest reflection will reveal that some or all of these rules are usually ignored in ordinary conversation. This poses an interesting dilemma. Why do so many educated speakers fail to use what they would admit is correct English? Many people would say that they are just not as careful with their speech as they should be. But the reason most people are not more "careful" is that to follow these rules would actually render their speech socially unacceptable. Not unacceptable because it is "sloppy" but unacceptable because it would be considered "snobbish." In essence, what this behavior means is that we do not really aspire to membership in the kinds of social circles where such rules are really followed. If we were to base our speech on this kind of rules, we know we would soon gain a negative reputation among our friends and acquaintances for "putting on airs." In spite of this eminently good reason for not using this variety of English, most Americans still have the vague feeling that speech is basically careless and that we really should follow the rules. A very similar situation exists for some nonstandard English speaking youngsters. They may well have the feeling that their speech is not as good as it should be; they may even be able to cite the rules they are violating. But the cost in terms of damaged reputation among their peers is so high that the assumption of standard English forms is not likely to take place unless they begin associating with youngsters who use standard English. The average schoolteacher probably will not find himself in the position to join the "upper crust" of society, but if this opportunity were to arise, I have no doubt that the teacher would fairly quickly and largely unconsciously adopt the speech appropriate to that social class. Similarly, a nonstandard English speaking individual, if he feels that he has a viable chance to become a member of a social group which uses standard English, and if he desires to do so, will also fairly quickly and largely unconsciously adopt standard English—and probably not before.

In summary then, language or dialect learning is a unique kind of learning which depends very heavily on a psychological factor of group reference. If this is not present, the best efforts of the English teacher is in grave danger of being completely nullified. If it is present, nonstandard dialect speakers can be expected to learn standard English, with or without formal teaching.

By continually correcting the children in her class, the teacher is capable of having an effect. She can succeed in giving the children a profound sense of linguistic insecurity and doubt about their language and even their personal worth. The teacher can easily have a negative effect but has a slight chance of actually teaching spoken standard English.

The third area of language with which an English teacher might be concerned is reading. The goal of teaching every student to read is a legitimate one. The best suggestion that linguists have been able to make with regard to reading has to do with the match between the language of the learner and the language of the reading materials. The hypothesis is that learning to read is easier if the language in the reading materials matches the language of the learner as closely as possible. For speakers of nonstandard English, this means that the materials used in beginning reading be constructed in accordance with the rules of nonstandard grammar. This hypothesis is currently being tested for children who speak black nonstandard English by the Chicago Board of Education and independently by the Education Study Center in Washington, D.C. To my knowledge, neither organization has published the results of their experiments, but the procedure seems reasonable. I will say no more here about reading, but further discussion of teaching reading to nonstandard dialect speakers is to be found in Wolfram 1970, Stewart 1969 and Wolfram and Fasold 1969.

With regard to writing, it may be important to take a hard look at just what kinds of writing are likely to be needed by a given group of nonstandard dialect children. Perhaps it would be more realistic to focus on writing personal and business letters and on answering questions on various forms than on developing the ability to write a literary critique of a short story, novel or poem. In some of these styles, personal letters for example, it may be unnecessary to insist that every detail of standard English grammar be observed. If a personal letter is to be written to a peer, there would seem to be little point in writing it in a "foreign" standard dialect. However in business letters, in filling in forms and in other official kinds of writing, only standard English grammar is accepted as correct and the ability to use it is a justifiable goal for an English teacher to set for all her students. In the process, it would be useful for the teacher to be able to distinguish three categories of errors. (1) There are errors of organization and logical development of arguments and similar difficulties. This kind of problem will be shared by all students regardless of dialect and linguistics has nothing to say about how such problems should be dealt with. (2) Then there are spelling and grammatical errors based on interference from a nonstandard dialect. In a study of written compositions by black inner city students admitted to a major university, over 40% of the errors found were due to dialect interference. (3) Finally, there are errors in spelling, punctuation and grammar which are not traceable to dialect interference.

A variety of apparent errors in the written work of nonstandard English speaking people are not errors in the strictest sense at all. They are simply the reflection in writing of the differences in grammar, pronunciation and verbal expression between the nonstandard dialect and the standard one by which the writing is being judged. In the area of grammar, when one of the university freshmen mentioned above wrote "Keith attitude" when standard English would call for "Keith's attitude" he was merely reflecting the rules of his nonstandard grammar. In standard English, this kind of possessive construction requires 's. According to the rules of the nonstandard dialect in question, 's may be used, but does not have to be. When another of these students spelled "closest" as "closes," he revealed that his pronunciation rules allow the elision of the *t* sound after *s* at the end of a word. Other cases arise when a writer uses an expression current in his speech community but perhaps unknown to the teacher. When one of the university freshmen wrote "Keith had negative changes about De Vries," he was using a common expression among black people. In this context, it means that Keith went through a change of opinion about De Vries. A teacher unfamiliar with the expression "to have changes" or "to go through changes" might well treat this expression as an error.

Other spelling, grammar and style errors occur which cannot be traced to dialect interference and should be considered genuine errors. In the same set of compositions discussed above, the misspellings "laied" for "laid" and "tring" for "trying" were observed. There is no pronunciation feature of the nonstandard dialect involved which would account for these spellings. In grammar, the use of the clause "in which you live in" is not called for by the grammar of any nonstandard dialect. An example of what might be called a style problem is the expression "in results of this," presumably for "as a result of this." All of these usages, along with mistakes in capitalization and punctuation, are appropriately treated as errors unrelated to dialect conflict.

This division into dialect and general errors has at least two implications for teaching writing. In a real sense, the dialect related "errors" are not errors at all, they are correct usages based on a different grammar rule system. Since this is the case, their correction is perhaps not as urgent as the corrections of mistakes which are not founded on *any* rule system. This may mean that several writing exercises would be allowed to go by with no mention being made of the dialect related errors. In some styles of writing, personal letters perhaps, elimination of dialect interference errors might not ever be appropriate.

In order to carry out such a teaching strategy, of course, it would be necessary for the teacher to be able to identify which mistakes are which. This same ability carries over into the areas of reading and speech as well. If a teacher were to follow the suggestion of some scholars (Goodman 1965, Wolfram 1970) that nonstandard English speaking children be allowed to read aloud in their own dialect, the teacher would have to know what is correct in the dialect so that she could distinguish dialect readings from misreadings. In the area of speech, the teacher needs this ability to distinguish dialect pronunciations from genuine speech impediments.

A case can be made for requiring teachers of youngsters with nonstandard dialects to be trained in the grammatical and pronunciation rules of nonstandard dialects of English. In the past, of course, very little of this has been done. There are a few sources to which an interested teacher could go to find partial descriptions of some nonstandard speech. McDavid (1967) provides a list of common nonstandard features from a number of dialects. Fasold and Wolfram (1970) give a semitechnical description of most of the features of the kind of nonstandard English used by urban black people. The Board of Education of the City of New York (1967) has prepared a booklet, distributed through the National Council of Teachers of English, which deals with the nonstandard kinds of English found in that city. None of these descriptions, however, is completely adequate.

There is much an observant teacher can do on his own to distinguish dialect features from more basic difficulties. To do this, he must accept a basic linguistic rule-of-thumb: everyone speaks his language correctly. If several youngsters use the same "bad grammar" feature consistently, it is safe to assume that their dialect rules call for that very construction. Sometimes, one child may seem to have speech problems different from his agemates. His difficulties are likely to be due to some other cause than dialect interference. All speakers of any language occasionally make mistakes because of "slips of the tongue" and nonstandard dialect speakers are no exception. But no speakers make the same slips all the time; if it seems that a speaker constantly makes the same "mistakes" he is no doubt following the grammar of another dialect. If a teacher accepts this rule-of-thumb and applies it carefully in observing his students, he will soon find himself able to make the necessary distinctions.

The answer to the question posed in the title of this article is first, that an English teacher probably cannot do very much about his pupils' spoken language habits and very likely would not want to if he could. What the teacher should do about nonstandard dialect in the teaching of reading may well turn out to be "use it." Finally, in teaching writing skills, a teacher should learn that there are more crucial aspects of writing than dialect related areas and that some writing styles may allow for continued use of dialect constructions.

BIBLIOGRAPHY

Baratz, Joan C. 1969. "Linguistic and Cultural Factors in Teaching Reading in an Urban Negro School System." *Elementary English* 46:199–203.

Blank, Marion. 1968. "Cognitive Processes in Auditory Discrimination in Normal and Retarded Readers." *Child Development* 39:1091–1101.

Bereiter, Carl. 1965. "Academic Instruction and Preschool Children," in Richard Corbin and Muriel Crosby (eds.), *Language Programs for the Disadvantaged*, 195–215. Champaign, Illinois: National Council of Teachers of English.

Board of Education of the City of New York, 1967. *Nonstandard Dialect.* Champaign, Illinois: National Council of Teachers of English.

Fasold, Ralph W. and Walt Wolfram. 1969. "Some Linguistic Features of Negro Dialect," in Ralph W. Fasold and Roger W. Shuy (eds.) *Teaching Standard English in the Inner City*, 41–86. Washington, D.C.: Center for Applied Linguistics.

Goodman, Kenneth S. 1965. "Dialect Barriers to Reading Comprehension." *Elementary English* 42:853–860. Reprinted in Joan C. Baratz and Roger W. Shuy (eds.) *Teaching Black Children to Read*, 14–28. Washington, D.C.: Center for Applied Linguistics, 1969.

Gumperz, John J. 1966. "On the Ethnology of Lingustic Change," in William Bright (ed.), *Sociolinguistics*, 27–49. The Hague: Mounton & Co.

Herman, Simon R. 1961. "Explorations in the Social Psychology of Language Choice." *Human Relations* 14:149–164.

Kochman, Thomas. 1969. " 'Rapping' in the Black Ghetto." *Trans-Action* 6 (February 1969):26–34.

McDavid, Raven I., Jr. 1967. "A Checklist of Significant Features for Discriminating Social Dialects," in Eldonna Everetts (ed.) *Dimension of Dialect*, 7–10. Champaign, Illinois: National Council of Teachers of English.

Stewart, William A. 1969. "On the Use of Negro Dialect in the Teaching of Reading," in Joan C. Baratz and Roger W. Shuy (eds.) *Teaching Black Children to Read*, 156–219. Washington, D.C.: Center for Applied Linguistics.

Wepman, J. M. 1960. "Auditory Discrimination, Speech, and Reading." *Elementary School Journal* 60:325–333.

Whyte, W. F. and A. R. Homberg. 1956. "Human Problems of U.S. Enterprise in Latin America." *Human Organization* 15:11–15.

Wolfram, Walt. 1970. "Sociolinguistic Alternatives in Teaching Reading to Nonstandard English Speakers." *Reading Research Quarterly* 6:9–33.

Wolfram, Walter A. and Ralph W. Fasold. 1969. "Toward Reading Materials for Black English Speaking Children: Three Linguistically Appropriate Passages," in Joan C. Baratz and Roger W. Shuy (eds.) *Teaching Black Children to Read*, 138–155. Washington, D.C.: Center for Applied Linguistics.

EDUCATIONAL CONSIDERATIONS FOR TEACHING STANDARD ENGLISH TO NEGRO CHILDREN

Joan C. Baratz

I T is commonplace to observe that lower class Negro school children do not speak like white children—lower or middle class. Although there is considerable agreement on this empirical observation, there is a great deal of discussion and debate concerning its source, significance and consequence.

The Difference-Deficit Question

The systematic research on the language of lower class Negro children has produced two general conceptual vantages concerning their verbal abilities—one camp, composed generally of psychologists and educators, has tended to view the language of black children as defective—i.e. the language of Negro children is underdeveloped or restricted in some way. These experimenters attribute the deficit to environmental factors, frequently observing that the mother doesn't interact with the child enough, doesn't read books to him, etc. The other camp, composed mainly of linguists, has viewed the language of lower class Negro children as a different yet highly structured, highly developed system.

For several years these two "camps" operated quite independently— psychologists went along describing deficiencies while linguists went about detailing differences. Recently, however, with the advent of interdisciplinary programs, each group has developed an increased awareness of the other's position.

➤➤➤➤➤➤➤➤➤➤➤➤➤➤➤➤➤➤➤➤➤➤➤➤➤➤➤➤➤➤➤➤➤➤➤

REPRINTED by permission from *Teaching Standard English in the Inner City*, ed. by Ralph Fasold and Roger Shuy (Washington, D.C.: Center for Applied Linguistics).

The question then arises as to whether a *deficit model* and a *difference model* can co-exist. Can a language be a fully developed, complex system (according to the linguists) and yet still be deficient—insofar as it produces speakers with language and cognitive deficits (according to certain psychologists)? Or to put it another way, can these children have speech and language problems that affect inter- and intra-personal communication that are not related to the dialect? Aside from about 5% of lower class Negro children who along with 5% of the other populations of children, have speech and language deficits due to neuro-physiological or psychological difficulties, it is not possible to generally characterize the speech of lower class children as deficient.

Those psychologists who wish to believe that there is such a thing as a fully developed different system that produces cognitive deficiency rely heavily on the writings of Basil Bernstein, while not always showing that they clearly understand his work. Bernstein speaks of the language of lower class speakers as a "restricted code" as opposed to the "elaborated code" available to the middle class. For Bernstein, this distinction seems to refer to language use, with no clear indication that speakers limited to restricted code suffer any cognitive deficit; only that their orientation toward the verbal channel will be different from that of elaborated code speakers.[1] Many followers of Bernstein, however, have confused superficial forms with specific processes. If a form is missing in Negro non-standard, it is assumed that the process is absent as well. To show the fallacy of this, one need only point out that in Negro non-standard the conceptual scheme "if" is, under certain conditions, used without any overt representation of the form "if." Thus while in standard English one might say "I don't know *if Robert can* come over tonight," in Negro non-standard the equivalent would be "I don't know *can*

---

[1] Bernstein, B. "Social Class, Linguistic Codes and Grammatical Elements," *Language and Speech,* 5, 1962, 221–240. Studies have proliferated from Bernstein's writings that take his assumptions and hypotheses concerning language and categorically turn them into a taxonomy of lower class speech. For example, studies that show greater use of pronouns in lower class than in middle class speech have been erroneously interpreted to indicate greater abstraction on the part of middle class speakers. On the contrary, there is no research to indicate saying "The big red fire engine drove through the street," is any more abstract than saying "It drove through the street." Speech style is being confused with (and substituted for) language abstraction. Bereiter perhaps is most glaring in his "bastardization" of Bernstein when he suggests that if the child "does not know the word *not* . . . he is deprived of one of the most powerful tools of our language." (Bereiter, C. E., "Academic Instruction and Pre-school Children," in Corbin, R. and Crosby, M., (eds.) *Language Programs for the Disadvantaged,* National Council of Teachers of English, Champaign, Ill., 1965). Although the Negro child does not use *not*—i.e. "this is not a book," he does use "ain't no"—i.e. "that ain't no book" which is no less powerfully logical!

Robert come over tonight." In the standard English version a vocabulary item is used to fulfill the interrogative function; in Negro non-standard a structural shift is used. Nevertheless, both sentences (standard English and Negro non-standard) are equally capable of conveying the question-ableness of Robert's availability in the evening.

The researchers who concerned themselves with applying the restricted and elaborated code thesis to explanations of cognitive impairment in young black children not only relied heavily on superficial structural differences in language production (whose relationship to cognition is not clear), but also these same researchers failed to deal with the socio-cultural variable and the role it might play in speech elicitation. For example, the task, "describe this picture," may be perceived differently by different groups in different settings. Mexican peasants, when given a picture of people engaged in an activity, are likely to "describe the picture" by detailing personality factors "she's sad," whereas lower class English boys may be more likely to describe the action that the individuals are engaged in—"he's throwing him the ball." Middle class white Americans may feel that "to describe a picture" is to elaborate on all the details of a picture—i.e. setting, action and feelings. This does not mean, of course, that Mexican peasants are incapable of responding to pictures by detailing the setting or the actions that are taking place. One need only define the task as such, i.e. "tell me what is happening in this picture," rather than "describe the picture."

Erickson[2] has illustrated that black children use both restricted and elaborated codes—the frequency of either code being determined by the subject matter, the setting, and to whom the individual is speaking. He has demonstrated the futility of presuming that black children do not use elaborated codes.

Perhaps of more importance than the demonstration that black children use both elaborated and restricted codes is the evidence most clearly demonstrated by Labov that one can produce highly abstract concepts while using extremely "restricted" codes.

A black teenager was asked, "Just suppose there is a God; would he be white or black?" When he responded "He'd be white" the interviewer asked "Why?" "Why? I'll tell you why. Cause the average whitey out here got everything, you dig? And the nigger ain't got shit, y'know y'unerstan?' So-um-for-in order for that to happen, you know it ain't no black God that's doin' that bullshit." The code the teenager has used is clearly non-standard and, in terms of the Bernstein classification system, can be viewed as "restricted." Nonetheless in terms of logic and com-

2 Erickson, Fredrick, "F' Get You Honky!": A new look at black dialect in school, *Elementary English,* 46, No. 4, 1969, 495–499.

plexity it is no less restricted than the elaborated standard English equivalent "I know that God isn't black, because if he were, he wouldn't have arranged the world the way it is."[3]

Those researchers who would feel that language styles can be hierarchically distributed with more elaborated codes indicating more complex thought will first have to deal with the matter of equivalences across codes. The absence of such discussions in the literature, along with the fact that there has been little demonstration that the presence of certain linguistic forms and usages impair cognitive ability makes it quite clear that the deficit model cannot be applied in relation to cognitive ability and language style.

Indeed, the fact that the language structure and style is different in the black community from that of the white mainstream serves only to indicate that the tests that black children are given initially cannot be used as measurements of potential so much as evidence of what black children know about the mainstream culture. Their poor performance by white mainstream standards merely indicates that they must be taught how to negotiate in a cultural setting that is different from their own.

Nonetheless, the differences in language structure and usage can be handicapping to the non-standard speaker when he is expected to operate in a system that demands the use of standard English structure and style. This language difference will create a problem in terms of oral communication in standard English settings. But the scope is even broader. His success in school programs may be hindered because interference from his different linguistic system can cause difficulties in his learning to read and write standard English, the *lingua franca* of the public schools.

Is It Necessary for Black Children to Learn Standard English?

Given the fact that many black children do not speak standard English upon entering school (and quite frequently still do not speak it when leaving school), the question is raised: what should the school system do about this situation? Should the school system require that these children learn standard English?

There are those voices in the academic community who say no, standard English need not be taught to these children.[4] These critics rightly

---

3 Taken from Labov, W., "The Logic of Non-standard," *The Florida FL Reporter*, Spring, 1969, 60–74, 169. Also printed in Alatis, J. (ed.), *Monograph Series on Languages and Linguistics* (*20th Annual Round Table Meeting*), Georgetown University Press, Washington, D.C., 1969, 1–45. For a discussion of the problems of employing a deficit model see Baratz and Baratz, Early childhood intervention: The social science basis of institutional racism, *Harvard Educational Review*, Winter, 1970.

4 Wayne O'Neil ("Paul Roberts' Rules of Order: The Misuse of Linguistics in the

feel that the child's language system is a fully developed, totally adequate linguistic system which is no better or worse than standard English and therefore, they think, it should be accepted as a perfectly adequate substitute for standard English.

Nevertheless, there are several discrepancies, overt and implied, in the argument against teaching standard English to black children. First, although it is true from a linguistic viewpoint that all dialects (Negro non-standard, Standard American English, Oxford English, etc.) are equal, it is also true from a social viewpoint that some dialects are considered more valuable than others in certain contexts. The linguistic relativity, then, does not take into account the social reality. Middle class individuals still rate Standard American English as more desirable than Negro speech. Pejorative ratings are associated with Negro non-standard speech despite its viability, complexity and communicativeness as a linguistic system.[5]

Indeed, despite the fact that various dialects may be used orally, the exigencies of reading and writing call for standard English and there are virtually no voices in the black community calling for newspapers and textbooks, to say nothing of carpenters' manuals, written in Black English.

The existence of standard English is not the result of a political conspiracy "to keep the black man down." But rather standardization is a socio-linguistic fact of life. Societies are socially stratified—whether the organization is a clan, a tribe or a nation-state. It would be nice to think that there are complex, socially stratified societies where the spectrum of standard language is so broad as to include all the different grammars and usages of persons speaking the many varieties of that language under the label of "standard." Sad to say, human behavior just doesn't operate like that. To date, wherever research has been done—in Europe, Asia and Africa—this has not been the case. One variety of the language

---

Classroom," *The Urban Review*, 2, No. 7, 1968, pp. 12, 17) insists that "instead of 'enriching' the lives of urban children by plugging them into a 'second' dialect . . . we should be working to eradicate the language prejudice, the language mythology, that people grew into holding and believing." Although I agree with Mr. O'Neil that something should be done concerning misconceptions about language in the educational establishment, I do not feel that this should be done *instead* of second dialect teaching but rather in addition to the second dialect training for Negro ghetto children. Learning the mainstream tongue is as important for the black child as is eradicating the misconceptions in *both* the white and black community concerning this original dialect.

5 The pejorative ratings of Negro non-standard English by most blacks is a factor which must be taken into account here. Negro self hate is perhaps a more potent force today than white oppression, in the denial of the worth of Negro dialect. For more information on attitudes toward Negro non-standard speech see Shuy, Roger W., Baratz, Joan C., and Wolfram, Walter A., Sociolinguistic factors in speech identification—Final report, MH15048-01, NIMH, 1969.

invariably becomes the standard—the variety that has grammar books written in it, the one for which an orthography is established, the one that is studied by the populace in school. Language standardization appears to be a universal aspect of language variation in a national context—particularly one involving literacy. There is standard English, standard Arabic, standard Yoruba and standard Hausa, just to note a few. Standardization is not a political invention of racist whites to exploit the Negro, rob him of his heritage, and denigrate his language.

The second fallacy of the "don't teach standard English" argument is the implication that in the process of learning standard English, the black child will necessarily be taught to devalue his "native tongue"— non-standard vernacular. There is no reason to assume that a child cannot learn several dialects of English, and where it is appropriate to use them, without weakening his self-confidence, self-identity and racial pride.

Another problem with such an argument is that it overlooks the point that in refusing to teach standard English to these children we cut off even further their possibility of entering the mainstream of American life.[6]

And finally, not teaching the black inner-city child standard English not only further hinders his ability to ultimately compete in the mainstream of society in terms of oral skills, but also makes the child's task of learning to read considerably more difficult.[7]

It seems clear from the discussion above that it is necessary to teach standard English to non-standard speakers. They must know the language of the country if they are to become a part of the mainstream of that society. The need for teaching standard English to these children, however, does not rule out the use of non-standard English within the classroom. It does not contradict the call for new, more meaningful curricula for these children, nor does it exonerate past failures on the part of the school system. It simply reaffirms the goal of the school system to turn out literate citizens who can compete in and contribute

[6] I do not wish to suggest that the use of standard English by black children will insure their success in middle class white America or that it will erase prejudice against Negroes; nevertheless, since standard English is the language of the mainstream it seems clear that knowledge of the mainstream system increases the likelihood of success in the mainstream culture.

[7] Study after study has demonstrated that children with a different language system from that of the national language have a great deal of difficulty learning to read when taught to read in the national tongue (UNESCO Conference on World Literacy, 1953). The Negro non-standard speaker trying to learn to read with a standard English text is in much the same position as children learning to read a language other than the one they speak. For further discussion of this issue see, Baratz, J. and Shuy, R. *Teaching Black Children to Read,* Center for Applied Linguistics, Washington, D.C., 1969.

to the mainstream culture. In order to do this the school must teach all children the language of the mainstream.

Who Should Teach Standard English to Black Children?

Once it is determined that it is necessary to teach black children standard English, the question arises as to who should do this. Who in the school system is prepared to deal with this problem? At the present time there is no individual department in the school system than can deal with it.

Some English teachers, despite their previous training towards conceptualizing standard English as right and "God given" and all other dialects as wrong and bad, have begun to take an interest in the issue of training Negro non-standard speakers. Some speech teachers, despite their previous tradition of looking at deviance from standard language as pathology, have begun to express concern over helping black children learn to speak standard English. Some foreign language teachers with their background in comparative linguistics have also become interested in dealing with the problem of "second language learning" as it applies to black children learning to speak standard English. It is my feeling that from this cadre of interested individuals with their varied backgrounds a specialist can emerge who will be effective in coping with the language problems of ghetto youngsters. Such an interested person, however, must be well-trained. High motivation and a dedicated soul are not substitutes for competence when it comes to teaching children.

One of the first issues to be dealt with concerning the teacher is the question: Should the teacher who wishes to teach black children be black?

Many black nationalists have been insisting that the teachers of black children be black. What these same nationalists have scrupulously avoided discussing is the fact that many middle class Negroes (from which, of course, the majority of black teachers continue to be drawn) are as anti-ghetto black as the white teachers. They share the white teachers' ignorance and prejudice toward the black child and his language.[8] They are careful to proclaim that they never spoke dialect.[9]

---

[8] It was a Negro, Charles Hurst, Jr., who coined the now disreputable term "dialectolalia" which he defined as an abnormal speech pattern characterized by "oral aberrations such as phonemic and sub-phonemic replacements, segmental phonemes, phonemic distortions, defective syntax, misarticulations, limited and poor vocabulary, and faulty phonology. These variables exist commonly in unsystematic multifarious combinations." (Hurst, Charles, *Psychological Correlates in Dialectolalia*, Cooperative Research Project #2610, Communication Sciences and Research Center, Howard University, 1965.

[9] At a recent talk on Negro non-standard, I noticed two Negro teachers who stood

They, too, believe all the current dogma and mythology concerning the child's homelife and its consequent effect on his learning. A black teacher may surely be helpful to these children in terms of the teacher's own experience as a black person, but that in itself does not provide any assurance that the child will learn simply because the teacher is the same color as he (surely the failure of the black school system is a testament in part to that fact). Just as high motivation and good intent are not enough, black skin per se does not insure effective teaching of black children—competence, which is colorless, is a necessary ingredient for success.

Developing an Urban Language Specialist

1. *The need for a specialist.* What does the teacher of black children have to know? How is she to be trained?

First, a teacher who wishes to work with language and speech programs for black children must receive training concerning language. What is language? What are dialects? How do social factors influence language and language learning? What are the functions of a language? What is the relationship of spoken language to written language and reading? What is linguistic interference?

Second, she needs specific training in learning the child's vernacular. What is his language like? More specifically she should learn the dialect.[10] In the process of learning the dialect, I believe that the teacher will develop a greater respect for what it is she is asking of her children and what the difficulties are in learning another system, especially one which in many ways is superficially comparable to standard English. In addition, in learning the non-standard dialect, the teacher will understand that one can learn another dialect of English without "changing" or "improving" the dialect that one already speaks.

Those teachers who already know the dialect will also need some of this training so that they can reorient their notion about Negro dialect, and can specify the areas where interference from the dialect will affect performance in standard English. Thus they will be able to anticipate problems as well as prepare lessons for teaching standard English.

Teachers will also have to learn something of foreign language teaching techniques to aid them in preparing materials for presentation to children, and some of the evaluation procedures of speech therapy (with

---

in the doorway and assured all departing whites that "they always spoke this way" (in standard English).

10 Learning a foreign language is not the same as learning a second dialect. The literature in verbal learning has indicated again and again that it is harder to learn material that is quite familiar than it is to learn two sets of distinct material.

specific adaptations in reference to dialect speakers) to help them in assessing their effectiveness and the children's progress. Training of these teachers must also include discussions of the language arts curriculum so that their new knowledge can be applied to making changes in materials and presentations that will aid in teaching reading and writing skills.

Lastly, these inner-city teachers must be familiar with the ghetto culture in addition to its distinctive language patterns. In talking about familiarity with ghetto culture one must be careful not to confuse psychological and socio-logical data with its emphasis on normative behavior for ethnological fact. For example, the sociological fact that there is quite often no "man in the house" does not give us much information concerning what a ghetto family really is like. Perhaps the best example of confusing psychological data (interpreted on the basis of a false premise-deficit thesis) for reality is the history of the professional conceptualization of the ghetto child's linguistic competence.[11] Since most people take the psychological data on face value they presume that ghetto black children are verbally destitute and are truly amazed when they discover that verbal ability is highly regarded in the ghetto; ability to "sound" is important and that the man of words is given considerable status by his compatriots.[12] Black children in elementary school are busy becoming proficient in the various toasts and in playing the dozens[13] even if they are all but mute when it comes to dealing with standard English situations in the classroom. The teacher must be aware of the different learning styles of ghetto youth and how they may affect the way material should be presented.[14]

Obviously the teacher who is to work in the black inner-city schools, and who is to institute new curricula with teaching styles suited for black children will have to be provided with a training program which

[11] See Baratz, J., "The Language of the Economically Disadvantaged Child: A Perspective," *ASHA*, 1968; and Language and Cognitive Assessment of Negro Children: Assumptions and Research Needs, ASHA, 1969.

[12] See for example, Ulf Hannerz, "Walking My Walk and Talking My Talk," in Hannerz, U., *Soulside: Inquiries into Ghetto Culture and Community*, Columbia University Press, New York, 1969.

[13] Playing the dozens, joining, sounding, rapping are terms for distinct verbal styles in the ghetto. For more information see Abrahams, R., *Deep Down in the Jungle*, Hatboro, Pa. Folklore Associates, 1964; Kochman, T., "Rapping" in the Black Ghetto, *Transaction*, 1969, pp. 26–34; Labov, W. et al., "A Study of the Non-standard English of Negro and Puerto Rican Speakers in New York City," Cooperative Research Project No. 3288, Volume II, *The Use of Language in the Speech Community*, Columbia University, 1968.

[14] Some excellent beginning work on differences in cognitive styles in different ethnic groups can be found in Lesser, G. and Stodolsky, S., "Learning Patterns in the Disadvantaged," *Harvard Educational Review*, 37, No. 4, 1967.

incorporates the content described above. Such a specialist with this kind of training is sorely needed.

2. *Programs and materials available.* Granting that it is necessary for a specialist to teach standard English to non-standard speakers, and given the fact that from various disciplines an individual can be trained to work with these children what kind of program should be instituted? What does the trained specialist do? First let us look generally at what has been done in the past and then discuss what needs to be done, and what the problems are that must be overcome in order to do the job well.

Speech and language programs have been devised that focused on the language abilities of preschoolers, elementary and secondary students, drop-outs and adult "new careers" people.

The preschool programs are best represented by the intervention programs known generally as "head start." The programs were developed on a deficit model, and most program directors believed that they were teaching these children language (not a second language). These programs were generally of two types:

a. Enrichment—here it was presumed that the language of the black child was underdeveloped due to lack of stimulation, poor mothering, etc., and the program was designed to compensate for this. The children learned about neighborhood workers, the friendly policeman, colors, nursery rhymes, etc. The best of the middle class nursery school was presented to these children.

b. Academic—the now famous Bereiter and Englemann[15] approach. These intervention programs were not based on under-development of skills but rather on a presumed absence of the skills. These programs attempted to teach the children language arts[16] and mathematic skills through formalized instruction.

Since one of the avowed purposes of these early childhood intervention programs was to "improve language skills" (tacitly defined in these programs as teaching the child to speak standard English) one would have to say the programs were a failure in that there are no data to indicate that following a preschool intervention program, these children were more proficient speakers of standard English.[17]

Despite the failure of these preschool programs to improve the black

[15] Bereiter, C. and Engelmann, S., *Teaching Disadvantaged Children in the Preschool,* Prentice-Hall, Englewood Cliffs, N.J., 1967.

[16] Language arts involved formal instruction in the authors' concept of oral standard English and in beginning reading.

[17] Almost all of the data presented to date (see for example, Klaus and Gray, The early training project for disadvantaged children: A report after five years, *Monograph of the Society for Research in Child Development,* 33, 1968) involve shifts (and transitory at that since they do not appear to be sustained once the child enters school) in IQ scores.

child's command of standard English, due largely to a lack of knowledge of what language is and how children learn language, the question still remains as to whether a child can be taught standard English as a "quasi foreign language" at the preschool level. With adequately trained teachers and special materials perhaps the question of the optimal period for teaching these children standard English can be discerned. However, the optimal period for teaching children a second dialect still remains to be determined.

The junior high and high school programs have generally been zeroed in on as "prime-times" to teach standard English as a second language to black children. The problem with many of these programs is that they use the jargon of second language teaching but actually have as their goal the replacement of what they consider a substandard system (Negro non-standard English which they give credence to as a legitimate system but to which they assign secondary status) with standard English.[18]

A prototype of such a program is Ruth Golden's "Improving Patterns of Language Usage." Although Mrs. Golden asserts that Negroes in low socioeconomic classes use non-standard language patterns, she goes on to say that these patterns are "antiquated and awkward in structure." Further, she indicates that Negro non-standard English is inferior since the "level of language (Negro non-standard English) which has served very well for their parents is inadequate for them (Negro students)."[19] Despite the fact that she says the language patterns of Negro students ought not be solely those of the Negro community (implying more than one system) she actually feels that they should be solely standard English speakers as evidence by her disappointment that ". . . many students who can speak well in class are not sufficiently motivated to continue in an acceptable (to her) informal pattern, but often revert to substandard as soon as they leave the classroom." Her misinterpretation of the students' appropriate use of two language systems (standard English for the classroom and Negro non-standard English for the peer group) as "insufficient motivation for using standard English" clearly indicates that her program is one of eradication of old patterns and replacement with acceptable patterns.

Mrs. Golden's program, as with most of the teaching English as a

18 See for example Ruth Golden's *Improving Patterns of Language Usage,* Wayne State University Press, Detroit, 1960 or Virginia French Allen, "Learning a Second Dialect Is not Learning Another Language," *Monograph Series on Languages and Linguistics, 20th Annual Roundtable Meeting,* Georgetown University Press, Washington, D.C., 1969, 189–202, where despite using second language learning analogy Mrs. Allen concludes with an anecdote concerning the fact that the child is "worth revising."

19 Golden, R., *Improving Patterns of Language Usage,* Wayne State University Press, Detroit, 1960.

second language to Negro non-standard English speakers programs, relies on pattern practice as the *modus operandi* for acquiring standard
English. The programs generally do not use contrastive techniques but
rather rely simply on repetition of standard English patterns.

Nevertheless, programs have been initiated that genuinely respect the
language of the student and that attempt to teach standard English
using contrastive techniques.[20] The materials developed at the Center
for Applied Linguistics provide one example of such a program.[21] This
program not only implicitly recognizes the legitimacy of the students'
system but also uses both standard and non-standard constructions in
instruction and drill techniques. With such a teaching system, the student learns not only what standard English is but also how and where
it differs from non-standard English.

This technique is extremely important when dealing with teaching
English as a "quasi-foreign language" and serves to underline one of the
main differences between second language teaching and second dialect
teaching. In second language teaching the language to be learned is
distinct enough from the students' own system so that he knows, for
example, he is speaking French, whether well or poorly, and not English.
In second dialect learning this is not always so and in many instances
the student does not know where non-standard English leaves off and
standard English begins. Therefore he quite often may not be sure, unless he is specifically instructed, when he is using standard English and
when he is using forms that appear to be standard English. For example,
in Negro non-standard English *he working* would mean that he is working right now, whereas *he be working* means he is working repeatedly
over a period of time. In standard English *he is working* can be used for
cases both of immediacy and of duration. If the Negro non-standard
English speaker is instructed to use *he is working* without explicitly discussing the different uses in standard English and Negro non-standard
English, he may use *he is working* for immediate situations only (therefore really not speaking standard English though using standard English
forms) and may hypercorrect *he be working* to *he bees working* to denote
a kind of duration.

Unfortunately the Center for Applied Linguistics' materials, although
based on a more sophisticated understanding of language and a quite
thorough knowledge of both standard English and Negro non-standard

[20] See for example Gladney, M. and Leaverton, L., "A Model for Teaching Standard English to Nonstandard English Speakers," *AERA* paper, 1968, for contrastive
approach with young children or Johnson, K., "An Evaluation of Second Language
Techniques for Teaching Standard English to Negro Students," *NCTE* paper, 1968,
for use with older students.

[21] The materials, *English Now,* developed by Irwin Feigenbaum are currently
being published by New Century.

English (like many of the "second language learning" programs for Negro inner-city children), have not been evaluated in a teaching context. However, the Center materials have the distinct advantage of having been developed in the field situation and used in the classroom, and thus the course developers were able to get initial impressions concerning the efficiency and effectiveness of their lessons.

If we presume that materials to teach standard English as a second dialect can be developed and that specialists can be trained to teach with them and to generate more material, the question still remains how shall such a specialist be incorporated into the school system. It seems that the answer to such a question depends upon the level at which the new material is introduced.

Teaching the details of standard English in junior high and high school might well be treated as a separate course. Kenneth Johnson has indicated that teaching standard English as a separate subject as opposed to incorporating it within the existing language arts curriculum may well be the most effective approach.[22] Giving the specialist the role of standard English teacher with emphasis on oral language proficiency clearly denotes a function in the same way that the French teacher's role is identifiable. In the same way that the French teacher must be trained in second language techniques, French language, French culture and history, the standard English teacher must be trained in second language techniques, Negro non-standard English and Afro-American culture and history. The standard English teacher, unlike the English teacher who wishes to teach the formal aspects of a language as well as stylistic conventions—i.e. the business letter, the essay, etc.—to students who already know the language, understands her job as teaching standard English to non-standard English speakers. She does not assume they know the language she is teaching.

3. *The role of the specialist.* What the role of the specialist in the preschool and elementary school should be is less clear. If we had a distinct bilingual situation here, one might suggest that the specialist actually teach the primary grades in Negro non-standard English while incorporating procedures for teaching standard English into the curriculum. However, one of the distinctions between a school which must deal with children who speak a different language as opposed to a school where a different dialect is taught involves mutual intelligibility. A class full of non-English speaking children with a teacher who speaks only English will no doubt have to resort to gestures and pictures in order to function at all. This is not true in the case of Negro non-standard English speaking children and a standard English speaking teacher. With

22 Johnson, K. "An Evaluation of Second Language Techniques for Teaching Standard English to Negro Students," *NCTE* paper, 1968.

a little bit of tuning in on both the teacher and the children's part and with a shared vocabulary the classroom is able to "function" from the very beginning although they speak differently. However, continued failure of many black inner-city schools indicates that this kind of functioning is not adequate.

The most effective use of the specialist at the primary level might be as classroom teacher. In this role she could use her knowledge of Negro non-standard English to teach the child standard English and to aid the child in his initial attempts to read.[23] Although she would use standard English as the medium of instruction (except when she is contrasting standard English and Negro non-standard English) she would allow the children to use Negro non-standard English in responding (except of course when she was teaching standard English) thereby not confusing knowledge of standard English with knowledge of the subject matter— science, math, etc. to be learned.[24] As the child progressed through the primary grades and became more proficient in standard English, use of more standard English could be demanded within the classroom. Such an approach would allow the child to learn the expected language response system before he was required to use it. Of course, a program such as the one discussed above is promulgated on the assumption that it is both possible and efficient to teach young children standard English using a "quasi foreign language" approach. This assumption should be tested.

Conclusion

This paper has attempted to deal with some of the issues involved in educating black children who do not speak standard English. Questions have been raised concerning whether these children should learn standard English, who should teach them, how a specialist should be trained and what such specialists should do. This author firmly believes that the success of black children in our public school system is very much dependent upon the teacher's recognition of the fact that these children may not speak standard English, and that if they do not speak standard English, formal instruction in the language arts cannot continue to be predicated on the assumption that all the children know standard English. The dialect of black non-standard speaking children

[23] The Education Study Center is currently involved in a reading project in the District of Columbia using dialect texts as initial readers.

[24] I remember being in a third grade class that was discussing the Revolutionary War. The teacher asked "Who crossed the Delaware River with troops? A young Negro boy responded "Dat George Washington" to which the teacher replied "No, that was George Washington." With such a correction the class, I am sure, was confused as to the right answer and the boy learned not to volunteer information again!

must be incorporated into the curriculum as part of the process of teaching these children standard English skills. Only then can such a child learn a second dialect (standard English) without experiencing shame and humiliation towards his native dialect.

Oral Activities in the English Class

THE English classroom has traditionally been a place where a considerable amount of talking went on, most of it by the teacher. Students were expected to listen. There were, in truth, some oral activities, some recitations or discussions or panel presentations, but, typically, these served ends other than those of increased facility in oral communication. The students recited on the novel they were reading or discussed the meaning of a poem or held a panel discussion to provide background data for their upcoming composition assignment. Talk for the sake of talk, talk that had socialization or oracy as its goal, was taboo.

Happily, today's English class differs from these earlier examples. Students in many English classes do talk—and talk a lot. They give speeches, meet in small groups, carry on debates, and play roles. Oral work has assumed an important dimension in English.

The articles in this section are intended to reinforce those teachers who are striving to increase the amount of oral work in their English classes. Wilkinson begins with an overview of oral activities and provides a compelling term—"oracy"—to identify the objective he hopes teachers will strive for. Lindman addresses directly the problem of improving oral work with students whose past schooling has trained them to be silent. Wood advocates brainstorming as "a creative way to learn" and provides some valuable tactics for the teacher anxious to try this exciting method. Post links the teaching of literature with oral work. The last two articles move in more specifically on certain kinds of oral work: Miller discusses theatre and urges, teachers to make their teaching of drama more dramatic. Clark and Nelson present some guidelines for the development and evaluation of high school speech programs.

THE CONCEPT OF ORACY

Andrew Wilkinson

I⊤ would be inappropriate for a visitor such as myself to make prescriptions as to what should be going on in English teaching in North America. The most I can do is to describe what seems to me to be liberal, suitable, good British practice, and where it has relevance to the American situation you will obviously be able to make your own comparisons; where it hasn't relevance you will be able to make your own rejections. First of all then I would like to talk about the fundamental processes going on in English teaching because it is impossible for me to talk about the aspect indicated in my title without going a little deeper. If I were asked to write a book on the teaching of English in a time of great shortage, and the publisher allowed me three words only, this would present me with something of a problem. Eventually I would produce three words which would seem to me to describe the essential process that we are concerned with in the teaching of English. These words would be the *verbalization of experience.* In other words, it's encouraging people to put what they have experienced into words— when I'm writing I'm putting something that happened to me into words, when I'm speaking I'm putting something that happened to me into words. But the conventional English teaching is more than this— literature for instance. So obviously my definition is incomplete. My publisher, however, is adamant; I can only have three words. This is an even greater problem, but at last I have an inspiration. I switch them around. The other part of the process encouraging English teaching is the *experience of verbalization.* "Verbalization" is what other people write and what other people say. And we as readers read what they write and we as listeners listen to what they are speaking. The definition seems to include something essential, expressed fairly simply. It seems to me that one cannot subtract any more words from it. But if I had to, at this publisher's command, I'd have to leave out anything but the word "experience." I'd have to say that this is where we start from, this is the first thing in the teaching of English.

We would have to consider what one meant by experience, what sort of experiences must one build into the English class teaching. We might think first of the students. What sort of experiences would be meaning-

F R O M *English Journal* (January 1970), pp. 71–77. Copyright © 1970 by the National Council of Teachers of English. Reprinted by permission of the publisher and Andrew M. Wilkinson.

ful to them. For instance, what has happened to them; what has happened to their brothers and sisters; what when they were lost; what when their father or mother went away; what happened to a girl when she fell down? And what happens to the child in the classroom when we bring in a pipe of soap bubbles and we begin to blow it and we say —now look at that bubble; describe it in words; now can you describe that infinitesimally tiny noise it makes when it bursts? And we bring other experiences into the classroom; the sound of a bell, just a single stroke of a bell and what it evokes in their minds; or we circulate a bottle with a strange scent in—what does this evoke? These are experiences. Or we circulate a piece of rusty iron, or driftwood. How evocative this can be, like Henry Moore's statues. And there are the experiences when the students go out and visit places, or when they read things; when they read *Huck Finn;* or when they read *The Old Man and the Sea,* and they suddenly become old, and they suddenly become courageous and noble. And when they see a film of, for instance, a bullfight and the beauty and the cruelty cause them to really assess what's been happening to them during this film. Or when they see pictures of children or old people or young people or happiness. And when they see a sparrow peck about in the gravel as Keats saw a sparrow peck about in the gravel. The point about mentioning Keats here or any other writer, is that we are realizing the same process of creation goes on within a child as in a great creative artist—an excited response to and an organization of experience. I think it is summed up by what Coleridge said: "I cannot write without a body of thought." And by thought he means more than thought in the limited sense. He means the interreactions of the whole sensibility—of thought, of feeling.

Now, if one makes this basic assumption, one can proceed to look at the implications this kind of statement has for our varied approaches to the teaching of English.

In the past, we in England certainly, have tended to start with a group of skills, we've made goals or objectives of a variety of skills. And these skills tend to be those we can define pretty clearly; skills of grammar, for instance, and spelling and paragraphing and topic sentences. We tend to spend so much time with these things that it's easy to forget the central activity. Now the switch in emphasis in English teaching is a switch to the centrality of experience so that the skills emerge in the *process* of verbalizing the experience, and they don't have the status of immediate goals. The experience is the thing one starts with. This I think is a shift of emphasis. Now, again, we tend conventionally, and I think this is useful, to think of English as having three facets. We tend to think of it as having the facets of language, literature, and composition. Now this may be an example of the way that words determine our thought processes rather than our thought processes choose words in which to express themselves. Language, literature, and composition, we tend to think of as either reading skills or writing skills. This certainly has been the tendency in the past, and this has made our thinking about English teaching very *literary*, i.e., based on reading and writing. Supposing however we don't start with those three headings, but with the verbalization of experience; and the experience of verbalization. One starts with the verbalization of experience, that is one starts with producing language, and of course we call this *production*. Now the way we produce language is twofold—by speaking it and by writing it. And then we come to consider the other aspect—the *reception* of language. We receive it by reading and we receive it by listening. Reading and writing are the skills of literacy. When you look at speaking and listening, however, we find that we have hitherto had no word in which to make a description of those two skills. And to come back to a point I made earlier in a slightly different connection, our thinking is often determined by the words we have, and not to have a word for a concept may be not to think at all about that concept.

	production	reception
	speaking	listening
LITERACY	writing	reading

When we came to carry out research into the spoken language in the University of Birmingham, England, we found that there were no words for a large number of features of the spoken language. For instance, what sort of word, what grammatical term, can you apply to a word which is the most common in the English language, the word *er?* It is a language feature, not just a mistake. The more we look at language we realize that to *er* is human, may even be divine. For words like *er*, and pauses and hesitations, and groups like *you know, you mean, know what I mean*, which have been called faults in the past, have really definite virtues (we have called them stabilizers). And they are just one more indication of the way we tended to look at the spoken language in the way that we look at the written language and yet these two are not the same at all. The examples here are fairly lighthearted, but the serious point is that for the central concept of speaking and listening there was no term and so we offered in all deference the term "oracy," to describe these skills as a parallel to literacy (Wilkinson and others, University of Birmingham School of Education, 1965). Thus our model is completed.

	production	reception
ORACY	speaking	listening
LITERACY	writing	reading

Now in England this seems to fulfill a need. One can't foist off a word onto an unwilling public: either a word fulfills a need and it's used and it lives, or it doesn't and it dies. It seems in this case, at the moment, it is fulfilling a certain need, the point being that it is a word which enables one to think about the importance of these skills of speaking and listening; and these skills are, of course, not only important but fundamental. Our communication is most of the time through speaking and listening, and very little of the time through reading and writing, and the less able our children are, the more this is true and will ever be true. Psychologists have led us to see how fundamental the spoken language is to the development, not only of the human ability to speak, not only of the human ability to communicate, but the human ability to develop fully a personality, and to develop cognitively. An English document, called the Newsom Report (1963), I would just like to read you a little bit of because it seems to me that this does sum up some of the importance that we now attach to the spoken language. "There is no gift like the gift of speech, and the level at which people have learned to use it determines the level of their companionship and the level at which their life is lived." Speech determines the level of our companionship, the level at which our lives are lived. This is very different from the old attitude towards speech and listening which was a kind of frill subject, perhaps taught by someone coming in from outside. The report goes on:

This matter of communication affects all aspects of social and intellectual growth. There is a gulf between those who have, and the many who have not, sufficient command of words to be able to listen and discuss rationally; to express ideas and feelings clearly; and even to have any ideas at all. We simply do not know how many people are frustrated in their lives by inability ever to express themselves adequately; or how many never develop intellectually because they lack the words with which to think and reason. This is a matter as important to economic life as it is to personal living; industrial relations as well as marriages come to grief on failures in communication.

There we have it. Speech (including listening) is a central factor in the development of the personality and closely related to human happiness and well being. And so, with those fairly preliminary but important remarks, I want to turn in a little more detail to these two aspects of oracy—speaking and listening.

I am now concerned with speaking or talking. We should teach speech in the way that we learn speech, and this is not by having speech lessons separated from English lessons, it's not by having drama lessons separated from English lessons, it's not by having elocution lessons separated from English lessons. What we mean by speech is not interpretative language, it's not reciting a poem, or even giving a public speech (very few people ever have to give public speeches). What we are concerned with is a certain quality of language which consists, not in interpreting other people's words, but in putting one word of our own, next to another word of our own, next to another word of our own, and so on in the creative utterance which we are all using all the time while we are speaking. So it follows that we must start with situation. The task of any teacher of English, and this applies to literacy as well as oracy, is the creation of situations in which language is the natural outcome. When I speak to you, you must answer; when you speak to me I must answer, unless I contract out (by for instance being rude or embarrassed). Ninety-nine times out of a hundred the speech situation is compulsory; we must communicate when we are in the situation. If I am in an elevator and there is only one other person in it, perhaps a person of the opposite sex, the elements in the compulsory speech situation are all there but something is lacking. Englishmen certainly would probably avoid eye contact with English women in this lift because that is almost the equivalent of assault (I have yet to find out what the American custom is on this!). But the lift stops between floors and the elements in the compulsory speech situation are all present and in addition that little bit of tension which compels speech. There's a speaker, there's a listener, there's a context, and there's a subject, a desperate need to talk. The illustration is silly but the point is serious. We do find words, we do talk, in conversations when we have to answer, in discussions when we are confronted with points, in lifts when there are some things that must be said. There's that little bit of compulsion about it.

Now this, it seems to me, is the basic device for speech training, a *compulsory situation*. I am not meaning compulsory in any authoritarian sense. I think I have defined sufficiently the kind of thing I mean. Now the normal classroom school situation does not provide these compulsory situations in profusion. In fact, it scarcely provides them at all in many cases, because in the conventional classroom we often get to have a gigantic prestige figure, to use the language of the social-psychologists, and you have a series of low prestige figures, and they're seated in rows, so that the communication tends to go one way only. There may be a question-and-answer session, but the whole purpose of much fast questioning is to preclude anything but a single response. The teacher knows the answer, and there's only one possible answer he will accept. The others can only say one thing. We can't develop speech under those circumstances. Now the whole richness of conversation is that you can say absolutely anything to anybody in answer to anything. Remember King Henry IV, Part I, when Prince Hal is teasing Falstaff and he keeps reminding him of the gallows. Falstaff replies, "By the Lord, thou sayest true, Lad . . . And is not my hostess of the tavern a most sweet wench?" (I.ii.34). This is certainly a creative response, a creative strategy for moving away. It comes out from that situation.

The basic conversational situation, the basic discussion situation, is one in which two or three or half-a-dozen are sitting around, and ideas get discussed and pushed around. So the basic situation for development of oracy, for oral production, is the group situation; and the practice in the English classrooms that I am thinking of is to have a large amount of splitting children up into groups and working in that way. There's a point in the California State film on English teaching— that children should have an opportunity sometimes to take the equal or even the superior role. I think that's a very wise statement. But it is not of course appropriate all the time. The teacher's function is crucial. It's the teacher who directs the students' language. Adults stretch children's language. The basic device is to split the grade into small groups, sometimes only of two. Very withdrawn children may be helped by only having one other to talk to, and by not being overwhelmed by very loquacious students. It is a big undertaking to discuss the sort of work that one would think is appropriate in groups, and obviously I can't go into it in detail. I would just like to take one or two examples. One I'm going to take from my limited experience of America. I saw recently some very interesting work in inter-age teaching whereby older children, after a training session, are given the responsibility for teaching younger children certain things. In their training session they discuss tapes and interviews of these younger children, and they discuss these in a certain type of language. They discuss this in the sort of language which you do discuss things objectively in. Then they go and teach these young children and they adopt a slightly different language, an expository language that we would adopt in simplifying your language for younger children. We don't talk to everybody like it. And these are genuine situations. The fourteen-year-old students have to communicate with one another, with their group leaders; they have to communicate with young children, they have to explain. And the situations are compulsory.

We may mention briefly other examples, more conventional for the English classroom. For instance children come in to a new grade, perhaps a new school as they do in England at eleven. The teacher splits them up into groups and announces the topic is "schools." One group discusses schools their parents went to, another the difficulties of getting to school, the third schools they went to before, the fourth their impressions of the new school. They discuss these things and then one of their number in each group reports back to the whole class and then, perhaps as a further exercise, they write something about their ideal school. Their responses then are both oral and written because oracy and literacy move in and out of one another. Again, younger students may be split into groups to discuss a picnic. Perhaps they are given certain guidance. In the United Kingdom in both the elementary schools in the higher grades and in our secondary schools, some teachers give little sheets with discussion hints on. Discussion hints are very simple; about the picnic for instance—where shall we go; who shall we invite; what food shall we take with us; what shall we do when we get there. Such headings give that little bit of necessary guidance. Meanwhile the teacher is going around to these groups, and giving that little bit of lift; saying, "Yes, but haven't you forgotten so and so?" and, to a higher group of students, "What exactly do you mean by that?" or "Shouldn't you consider this?"

This group situation can be extended in the field of literacy. Some of our children write group novels for instance. They discuss the plot and characters first and then write, section by section. Some of our children discuss poems in groups and then read them back to the rest of the form or discuss them. In each case different types of language will be used because we all have, as I have tried to imply, varieties of language for different situations. We do not speak to everybody in the same way, and sometimes we are unaware that we make all kinds of subtle changes. A man doesn't speak to his employer in the terms he uses for his wife or somebody else's wife.

I have been hinting that there is guidance implicit in the learning situation. Of course, it's terribly important to get children to talk, especially younger children. They need to build confidence, but when all is said and done, it is not just one gigantic village pub gossip we are aiming at. Children are being gradually moved in the directions of *relevance*, of *objectivity*, of *depth*, and of *reciprocity*. I needn't perhaps go into this, but if you have suffered like I have, attending numerous meetings in which every single further point raised seems to be off the issue, and the chairman follows it up off the issue, it does seem to me that the sense of relevance is one of the most serious drawbacks in our speech skills. Depth of course is obvious; objectivity is obvious. This is what educated human beings ought to be able to attain to. Reciprocity is of course the sense of the other person, that delicate sense of somebody else with rights, the way that you get the emanations coming from them, and the way you get on their wavelength, and *listen* to them. These are very important things. The kind of discussion I am thinking of should gradually encourage these things.

May I now turn to listening, because if speaking is neglected, listening is unheard of in common educational practice. The new linguistics, I think, has contributed a great deal to our knowledge of the spoken language, and has modified our attitudes towards it. It has much to contribute to our teaching but not the sort of contribution that some people are suggesting it should make in English schools. I would be very suspicious of formal grammatical training derived from the new linguistics, or anything resembling it, but the spoken language I think is a field in which we can interest children in language. There's a magnificent passage in the preface to that great 1765 dictionary of Samuel Johnson. He's talking about the words he has put in and the words he has left out and, quite clearly, he's not very enthusiastic about certain words. These are the words which he dubs in his dictionary *low* or *mean* or *barbarous* or *bad*. It is very interesting that many of them are spoken and not written words. Here is the passage.

> That many terms of art and manufacture are omitted, must be frankly acknowledged; but for this defect I may boldly allege that it was unavoidable; I could not visit caverns to learn the miner's language, nor take a voyage to perfect my skill in the dialect of navigation, nor visit the warehouses of merchants, and shops of artificers to gain the name of wares, tools, and operations, of which no mention is found in books; what favorable accident or easy enquiry brought within my reach, has not been neglected, but it had been a hopeless labor to glean up words by courting living information, and contesting with the sullenness of one, and the roughness of another.

What does Johnson mean by courting living information? He means that he is not going to listen to words as they are on the tongues of men, nor to have words which are not found in books, nor to listen to living speech. Johnson was deaf, and he hadn't time. What he did do was a monument, and he was anyway within the assumptions of his age. But we are not any longer bound by those assumptions. What I am saying is that listening in schools could be made fascinating by providing what Johnson called "living information," by providing tapes and records and perhaps videotapes of the spoken language. In England there are radio plays, in both countries there are records available; but more there are tape recorders. We have the ability to get conversations down on tape or to make conversations, to put specially on tape, to record different dialects, different idiolects, to ask questions about the difference between the spoken and the written language, to ask questions about the sorts of relationships which are going on as expressed through language. The conventional training in listening, both in England and America, and particularly in America, has been skill training, and the conventional listening tests have been skills. The American teachers have started off, not with the linguistic material, not with this rich, living information, but with psychological skills, the ability to separate the main from the subordinate point, the ability to recognize signposts in information. There is nothing wrong with this, of course, but it's all the time a question of emphasis, what the priorities are. The material has been testing material, not teaching material. Listening tests so far have taken a piece of written English which has then been read aloud. Scholars have then been surprised that the correlations with reading skills are pretty high. It was Lindquist in 1959 in the *Yearbook of Mental Measurements* (Gryphon Press, 1959) who made this point, though he probably didn't realize that what was wrong was that they were testing the same material. What we want in the listening field is "living information," and I think the time is right, both in the United Kingdom and in America, for the construction of a new spoken literature (the word *literature* is question begging), a new body of "living information" which will motivate our children, including the less able children who are not terribly interested in books but who are listening and speaking all the time.

To summarize, I have been arguing that we cannot separate oracy from literacy; in describing the concept of oracy I am not advocating something off track. It is part and parcel of the verbalization of experience. I would like also to add that not only can we not separate it from literacy, but also that we cannot separate English from other subjects in the timetable, because the verbalization of experience is going on the whole time in these areas, using different sorts of language. My suggestions as far as the spoken language are concerned have been that we could profitably (certainly in the United Kingdom) pay much more attention to the kinds of situations which are not so prestige ridden, more group situations which produce natural speaking, that we could pay more attention to the living language, and that we could, in Johnson's words, "court living information."

IMPROVING ORAL RESPONSE

Margaret Rohner Lindman

ONE of the most common difficulties in high school teaching is the handling of question-answer classroom situations. Perhaps students of today really are more passive; perhaps they are less interested; perhaps they are so conditioned by television that they don't know how to make an oral response. Whatever the reasons, many of them fail to give an honest response to the query of the teacher. Too often their only reaction is a mute, blank stare or at least a denial of previous instruction. Sometimes the response is a mere parroting back of the words uttered by the teacher or printed in the textbook. The teacher's basic problem remains, "When a sincere question is asked, why doesn't the student give a thoughtful answer?"

The Lesson in Passivity

Why do students seem to be so passive? Because they have adopted a do-nothing philosophy? That seems unlikely. More students than ever before are anxious to EXCEL IN TODAY'S SCIENTIFIC WORLD and to GO TO COLLEGE TO HELP SAVE THE WORLD. This increase of anxiety increases individual measures of self-protection. Students consider question-answer sessions as evaluative situations (and quite often they are) and therefore cloak themselves in the safety of silence. Teacher attitudes often lead students to believe that total ignorance is more easily forgiven than an erroneous answer.

The student has no way of knowing what effect an original or thoughtful answer will have on a teacher. The struggle to communicate as well as to handle unfamiliar facts or concepts places the student in a very awkward position. His response may sound vague, incoherent, disorganized, and even sharply critical.

The response may expose unflattering attitudes (based on values inharmonious with the teacher's values), opinions (areas of genuine disagreement) and behavior (not having listened carefully). The teacher may engage in a battle of wits with the student, a battle the student cannot win.

Recently, a teacher asked his class if warfare was good. To his dis-

FROM *The High School Journal*, Vol. 54 (December 1970), pp. 211–214. Reprinted by permission of the publisher and the author.

appointed surprise, he discovered a number of students were in favor of it. He immediately gave an emotional and intellectual tirade on the evils of warfare. The speech was brilliant and devastating. Though it failed to change the students' views it did silence them. The students had learned. They learned not to challenge the values of the teacher. Had he taken time to hear their points, he might have been able to influence their thinking and at least encouraged them to examine both sides of the question.

The degree of student interest in a topic of discussion can be misjudged by the teacher. Many times students have been arbitrarily assigned complicated, time-consuming tasks because the teacher confused superficial response with depth of interest. Undesired extra assignments are sometimes the penalty paid for oral response.

Loss of status in the group may also be a penalty for oral response. Though somewhat diminishing (due, perhaps, to N.M.S., P.S.A.T., A.C.T., etc. recognition) the labels of "brain," "radical," "stuffed-shirt," "loud mouth" and "know-it-all" are quite common weapons used by weaker students. Powerful social stigma is attached to these terms of derision. Few peer-group-conscious students are secure enough and sufficiently motivated to risk rejection. The teacher should seek ways of reinforcing desirable behavior and be aware of factors that penalize it.

The Responsibility for Change

Obviously something must be done or question-answer situations will continue to be ineffective. It is unrealistic to believe that, by some miracle, students suddenly will change. The first persons to make the change must be the teacher and the administrator. The responsibility for change initially rests on the shoulders of the administrators and teachers, not on the shoulders of the students.

We know that with sufficient motivation students do become actively involved, and participate in discussion. Thousands of words have been written on the subject. Yet many high school teachers are still too dependent on the vague, long range goals of students (going to college, winning a scholarship) to engender interest in daily classroom activities. Many are too dependent on the compulsory aspects of education for student motivation. Teachers and administrators must focus their attention on the very vital and basic educational problem of day-to-day motivation of the high school student. Teachers need workshops, inservice training sessions, consultants, etc., to study effective methods of motivating students, ways to communicate with students effectively, and ways in which students can communicate with them. This is an ever-present problem that demands continuous study and effort.

What a Teacher Can Do

The best laid plans can go awry. Consider the case of the teacher who had presented superior content to her class in a lively manner. She had concerned herself with the types of questions she asked. They required more than a one-word answer and were thought-provoking. In spite of this the response of her students was weak.

Analyzing her problem, she realized that just as it took time and study for her to change, students too need time to adjust. She gave direct instruction as to types of questions, their function, and possible appropriate answers.

Sample questions helped the students distinguish between rhetorical questions and oral-response questions. Students were asked to identify questions of fact, opinion, and value.

The teacher pointed out appropriate language clues to watch for in identification of questions. For example, the phrase "think about," "consider," "reflect on," etc. are terms often appearing in the rhetorical question when no oral response is necessary. Phrases such as "take a guess," "let's hear ideas about," "what is your opinion," "who knows about," etc. indicate that an oral response is desired.

The following ground rules were established by one class regarding the conduct of discussions:

1. The teacher will allow thinking time when a student is asked a question.

2. If the student is getting off the track, or if the answer seems too involved, the teacher only reserves the option of polite interruption.

3. All students are expected to participate in the discussion.

4. Students may challenge or disagree with one another and with the teacher as long as they are courteous and are able to support their positions.

5. The students may ask for clarification of the question if it is not clear.

6. The teacher may request clarification if the response is unclear.

7. A prearranged signal will be used to indicate inaudibility.

8. Discussion participants may feel free to modify their views if other positions seem more reasonable, more feasible, or better, in the light of further information. The modification is permissible, not mandatory.

9. The teacher will evaluate pupil response on the basis of quality and quantity.

10. If other limitations are to be placed, such as textbook-only answers, time limit, brief answers only, the teacher will indicate this before beginning the discussion.

Ground rules have a way of binding the teacher as well as the students to a consistent mode of behavior. They are effective only if both parties respect them.

Students get a feeling of worth when they know that their opinions as well as their memories are respected. They admire a well-phrased question. Clarity is equally important. No matter how brilliant a student may be, he cannot respond effectively unless he understands the question. Some teachers are guilty of ambiguity, or of couching a question in obscure or advanced vocabulary to impress students with their profundity. The answer of the student depends on the clarity of the question as well as on the listening ability of the teacher.

Too often teachers accept ridiculous, vague, or even erroneous statements of students without challenge. When the teacher fails to listen and/or fails to pursue the discussion, students are tempted to engage in the double-talk game. They never really answer the question at hand but they employ appropriate vocabulary, receiving the absent-minded nod of approval from the teacher. Some of the more adroit students seem able to time their answers to suit the teacher's interest span or the time set aside for discussion.

Only the most insensitive student fails to perceive rushing and preoccupation on the teacher's part. At those times only the foolish would volunteer more than a one-word answer—and seldom does anyone offer opposition. One of the most effective methods to discourage student oral response is to appear impatient or hurried.

The attitude of the teacher can be a primary factor in encouraging the two-way communication so essential in the classroom. Teachers who are truly concerned about improving student performance can initiate procedures specifically designed to sharpen and evaluate oral response. Jerome Bruner reminds us that "If the teacher is learning, teaching takes on a new quality." Nowhere is this statement more pertinent than in the improvement of question-answer techniques in the classroom.

BRAINSTORMING: A CREATIVE WAY TO LEARN

Robert W. Wood

M AN is a highly creative creature who prefers to learn by doing, exploring, testing, questioning, and modifying ideas. However, the traditional elementary school has not usually found it "economical" to foster learning by a process that is so natural to children.

Education for today and the future must be relevant and meaningful. It must equip each student with a process by which he may solve the many complex problems that will eventually evolve. It is the purpose of this article to discuss one problem solving technique that has proven to be highly successful on all levels of learning.

Brainstorming is a creative problem solving technique that has been used successfully in business, government, industry, and to a limited degree in the field of education. In the classroom, brainstorming can provide a student the means by which early contact with peers becomes a stimulating and challenging experience. Children might be asked to solve practical problems that arise during the day or to solve problems that might be proposed by the teacher or students during a social studies lesson. One noted researcher has found that even first grade children can profitably use the brainstorming technique.

Small group interaction has long been cited as an effective teaching technique. This interaction is of importance because the pupil has the opportunity to become actively involved in the process of learning. Developing a positive self-concept by active participation would be one of the major benefits derived from group brainstorming.

There are many who claim that in a search for ideas there can be no implicit techniques—and rightly so, if the technique means a rigid set of rules. Any attempt to lay down hard-and-fast methods would be nothing but terminology masquerading as technology, but, there can be—and are—certain principles in the form of guides to procedure.

Brainstorming Principles

Alex F. Osborn, the father of modern day brainstorming outlined four basic principles for effective brainstorming:

1. Critical judgment is ruled out, criticism of ideas must be with-

F R O M *Education*, Vol. 91 (November–December 1970), pp. 160–162. Reprinted by permission of the publisher and the author.

held until later. Many creative thoughts have been lost simply because a person thought others would think his ideas insignificant and of no value. Many students start out their question with—"This may be a stupid question, but . . ." Education and experience have trained most children and adults to think critically rather than creatively, and this preface to a question is an example.

As a result, they tend to impede their fluency of ideas by applying their critical power too soon. By deferring judgment during a brain-storming session, children will be able to conceive a large number of creative ideas.

2. "Free-wheeling" is welcomed. The wilder the idea, the better; it is easier to tame down than to think up.

3. Quantity is wanted. The greater number of ideas the more likeli-hood of potential solutions. Practically all the experiences with group brainstorming confirms the principle that quantity helps breed quality.

4. Combination and improvement are sought. In addition to contrib-uting ideas of their own, participants should suggest how ideas of others can be turned into better ideas; or how two or more ideas can be com-bined to make one.

Steps to Successful Brainstorming in the Elementary Classroom

1. Description of brainstorming and statement of instructions. Explain to the children that brainstorming is a way of stating the greatest number of ideas in a limited amount of time. Emphasize the idea of spilling out ideas as quickly as possible while applying the deferred judgment principle. A short practice session could be attempted by asking the children to write a list of as many items as possible under the heading, "the things we do at school." After several minutes, stop the listing and compile the number of different ideas on the chalkboard. You may wish to discuss with the children the following questions: Did each of you contribute some ideas? Were you able to avoid being crit-ical of each other's contributions? This deferred judgment principle must be accomplished before effective brainstorming can take place.

2. Divide the class into brainstorming groups. Beginning groups seem to function well with 3 to 11 members. The groups can be all boy, all girl, or mixed. An odd number in the group might assure the availa-bility of a majority, and thus avoid the danger of a split between two cliques of equal number. It will help if the teacher selects a few indi-viduals who serve as selfstarters for each group. With proper planning and guidance the whole room can brainstorm a problem or just one individual can use this technique. Several groups can be brainstorming at one time within the classroom.

3. Selection of a group leader and secretary. Each group should

have a leader who would present the problem and keep the group actively engaged in the brainstorming process. The function of the secretary would be to write in brief form all ideas as they are presented. At times the ideas may tumble out so fast that even a shorthand expert would have difficulty recording them verbatim. It may be necessary to have two secretaries, each one jotting down every other idea. A tape recorder can also be utilized with transcription of the tape to be made later.

4. Selection of the problem. The problem to be brainstormed should be one that will arouse student interest. This may not be easy to do, but a way usually can be found to make the problem relevant to many interests. Many times a functional problem, like what to do during the upcoming party, could be used as a starting point. After the technique is refined, problems dealing with academic topics could be brainstormed. Students should assist in the selection process.

5. Statement of the problem. Problems can be presented that will encompass several areas of study. Social studies is a particularly good area in which children can brainstorm. The major objective in selecting a problem and stating the problem properly, is to make sure that it is specific, not general.

The guiding principle is that a problem should be simple rather than complex. Failure to narrow the problem to a single target can seriously mar the success of any brainstorming session. Sometimes a session can be conducted to break down broad problems into their specific components. But in the normal course of events, make sure the problem is simple and specific.

Another principal to be considered is that the problem must be one that lends itself to many possible answers. If there are just a few possible solutions to the present one, then it would be wise to select another problem.

6. The brainstorming session begins. The problem should be explained, and the group leader should then discuss the four basic principles (as spelled out earlier in this article). Placards stating these principles could be displayed to act as a constant reminder to the children.

After these preliminaries are completed, the leader then calls for suggestions on how the problem could be solved. What happens if all of the children's hands go up? If this occurs the group leader could simply go around the table and let each person present one idea in turn. A brainstormer should present only one idea at a time. The fun is just beginning! If a child has some idea that is directly related to the previous statement, he can snap his fingers to be recognized by the leader. The leader should give priority to the finger snappers and thus make the most of the power of association. The students will find this exciting and challenging! Throughout this entire procedure the secretary should be taking brief notes. However, a tape recorder works very well with elementary school children.

Past experiences indicated the optimum time for beginners using brainstorming is about ten minutes. As their experience in this activity increases so can the time period. A typical sixth grade class can handle thirty to forty-five minutes.

As the children's brainstorming skills become more sophisticated with time, new variations can be tried. After a brief amount of time on a problem, the leader can stop the session and ask the group members to keep the problem on their minds until the next day when they will be asked for their afterthoughts. Maybe you could come up with some new variations.

7. Evaluation of the presented ideas. After the brainstorming session has been completed, the secretary of the group should prepare a list of all ideas suggested during the session. At this point the teacher has to make a decision. Should the ideas be evaluated by the group of students who thought up the ideas or by an entirely different group? It is usually wise to have the final evaluation done by those directly responsible for the problem. This may or may not be the group that did the brainstorming. The teacher has a great deal of latitude when choosing the method of evaluation. To facilitate this evaluation, it is often advisable to prepare a check-list of criteria by which students and teachers can evaluate the ideas. The following criteria could be used to evaluate each idea:

1. Is it feasible?
2. Is the idea simple enough?
3. Is it timely?
4. Is is appropriate?
5. Is it efficient?
6. Is it an improvement?

It is important that the criteria are appropriate for the problem being brainstormed. With each new problem you may need to create a new check-list. If desired, the entire class can work together to determine the relative worth of the presented ideas. This evaluation process usually develops into a most effective and meaningful type of group interaction. During the final evaluation, the students should attempt to apply the final ideas to the problem to determine whether or not the ideas are applicable.

If application is not feasible, the children could conduct a debate or continue with class discussion on the relative worth of the ideas.

At this point a very important concept must be noted. In many areas of instruction, particularly in the social studies, there is not a "right" or "wrong" answer. From this type of learning experience the children will have the opportunity to discover the dichotomies in our society. It is important that children find out how the real world operates and how to evaluate real problems. The teacher should integrate the final evaluated ideas into his teaching lesson.

Comments

After teaching on the elementary and the university level it is the author's opinion that this technique of problem solving has much merit. It is becoming more apparent every day that people have inhibitory factors that tend to cut down the creative flow of ideas. If the idea of deferred judgment could be instilled in children and adults, many more ideas would come forth in a discussion. Brainstorming will make learning an active process. The children will have fun with this technique and soon will become very skilled and perceptive in the art. Brainstorming provides a setting that gives the child a feeling of security. The participants who have something to contribute may now do so without fear of being squelched.

In summary, the elementary school must provide experiences and equip the student with effective techniques to adequately solve the complex problems he will face in the future. Let's put group brainstorming in its place. It is only one of the phases of idea finding which, in turn, is only one of the phases of the creative problem solving process.

REFERENCES

1. Gowan, J. C., Demos, G. D., and Torrance, E. P. eds., *Creativity: Its Educational Implications.* New York: John Wiley and Sons, 1967.

2. Osborn, Alex F., *Applied Imagination.* New York: Charles Scribner's Sons, 1963.

3. Smith, J. A., *Creative Teaching of the Social Studies in the Elementary School.* Allyn and Bacon, Inc., 1967.

THE ORAL APPROACH TO THE TEACHING OF HIGH SCHOOL LITERATURE

Robert M. Post

JUNIOR and senior high school literature instructors seek to instill in their students an appreciation and understanding of worthwhile literature. They are in essence attempting to teach their pupils *to read,* and, more specifically, to read perceptively. Reading sensitively is not merely recognition of symbols or of their obvious meanings, nor is it the ability to "sound them out." True reading entails awareness of the multiple tensions of the dramatic situation, knowledge of the prosodic elements, and many other intricate insights.

Teaching which depends solely or to a great extent upon silent reading overlooks the long oral tradition in the sharing and enjoyment of literature. Silent reading also fails to reveal the *whole* piece, especially in lyric verse and dramas which were written essentially to be spoken and heard.

Experts in the field of oral interpretation consider their art an excellent approach to the world of literature. In the preface to *The Oral Study of Literature,* Thomas O. Sloan stated the central principle of the book as follows: "the proper application of oral interpretation is as a discipline through which the student engages in the study of literature."[1] Charlotte I. Lee based her textbook on "the twofold conviction that the study of literature is a rewarding and challenging experience, and that sharing the results of such study with an audience gives motivation and focus to analysis, and pleasure and satisfaction in performance."[2] Don Geiger believed that "oral interpretation is one more means by which the 'art of reading,' including critical understanding and sensibility, is advanced."[3] Paul N. Campbell stated a primary tenet as follows:

> One of the basic premises of this book is that, in its printed form, a piece of literature exists as a bunch of squiggles on a page, and in order to

[1] Thomas O. Sloan, ed., *The Oral Study of Literature* (New York: Random House, 1966), p. viii.

[2] Charlotte I. Lee, *Oral Interpretation,* Third ed. (Boston: Houghton Mifflin, 1965), p. v.

[3] Don Geiger, *The Sound, Sense, and Performance of Literature* (Chicago: Scott, Foresman, 1963), p. 11.

FROM *The Speech Teacher,* Vol. 17 (March 1968), pp. 156–159. Reprinted by permission of the publisher and the author.

turn those squiggles into laughter, or anger, or throat-clutching regret (and without this sort of "translation" literature is of interest only to the typographer) the reader must, in a very real sense, interpret that piece of literature. He must *always* interpret it for himself, and he *may* interpret it for an actual audience. Further, an important part of that interpretation must be *oral*.[4]

Robert Beloof called interpretation "a technique of criticism and pedagogy."[5]

It is with the pedagogical aspect of oral reading that this article is concerned. More specifically, its purpose is to suggest ways in which the high school teacher may utilize oral interpretation to enhance his students' insights into literature. The emphasis here is upon teaching, not training in performance. However, the literature and its performance cannot be arbitrarily separated. If the oral approach is to succeed, the performance must realize the literature as completely as possible. A poor reading will not do this.

As a first step the teacher must clarify what good oral reading entails. Some attention should be given to the proper application of vocal and physical techniques. There are many books in oral interpretation to which the teacher may turn for guidance.[6] The teacher or an invited guest may read to the class to serve as a model of good oral interpretation. Recordings by professional actors and oral readers are also helpful. Harcourt, Brace and World and Houghton Mifflin are two publishers who have related recordings available for use with their high school literature textbooks. Team teaching, in which the English and the speech instructors work together, is an excellent way to insure that both the oral and the literary components are justly conveyed.

Students will learn from the oral approach to literature not only through what they interpret themselves, but also from hearing others read selections. In literary pieces with multiple voices, such as narratives and plays, added learning will accrue from group or ensemble readings.

Assignments for the oral approach may be made in various ways, but they should begin with a thorough silent reading of the selection, followed by a discussion analyzing the selection. John Ciardi wrote that "The only reason for taking a poem apart is that it may then be put back together again more richly."[7] After a thorough analysis, the selection may be "put back together again" by reading it aloud. A slightly different approach is to follow the silent reading with an initial discus-

---

4 Paul N. Campbell, *Oral Interpretation* (New York: Macmillan, 1966), p. ix.

5 Robert Beloof, *The Performing Voice in Literature* (Boston: Little, Brown, 1966), p. vii.

6 See, for instance, Beloof; Wilma H. Grimes and Alethea Smith Mattingly, *Interpretation: Writer, Reader, Audience* (San Francisco: Wadsworth, 1961); and Lee.

7 John Ciardi, *How Does a Poem Mean?* (Boston: Houghton Mifflin, 1959), p. 664.

sion followed by the oral reading which is in turn followed by a more intensive discussion. The latter approach has the advantage of integrating the oral interpretation more completely with the assignment and thus increasing the understanding.

The teacher may designate selections or parts of them to specific students for oral reading when the assignment is originally made. Students should have time to practice for their oral presentations. Impromptu reading seldom does justice to the literature and will defeat the purpose of the assignment.

Any Shakespearean play, Goldsmith's "She Stoops to Conquer," Thornton Wilder's "Our Town," Tennessee Williams' "The Glass Menagerie," George Bernard Shaw's "Pygmalion," J. M. Barrie's "The Old Lady Shows Her Medals," John Millington Synge's "Riders to the Sea," or any other plays in the course syllabus *demand* reading aloud. While drama lends itself perfectly to oral recreation, stories or portions of novels with considerable dialogue can be handled in much the same way, parts may be assigned with a narrator to read the exposition.

An example of a story which would benefit from the oral approach is Ernest Hemingway's "Old Man at the Bridge," from the eleventh grade volume of the Adventures in Literature Series.[8] As the dialogue of the story is read aloud, the two main characters—an old man and a young man—will emerge more vividly for the students than they have from a silent reading. When the old man is vocally interpreted with a higher pitch, lower volume, slower rate, choppier and more hesitant rhythm, and a "thinner" quality than the younger man, his basic character becomes clearer. The picture becomes even clearer when the old man is interpreted with "drooping" posture as opposed to the more rigid posture of the younger man.

Shirley Jackson's "The Lottery" from the same text is another story with which the oral approach is effective. The theme of tradition and the attitude toward it comes to life as the speeches of Old Man Warner are read aloud, while the irony of Tessie Hutchinson's situation is emphasized when a breezy, casual rendering of her first speeches is heard contrasted with her frustrated and terrified cries as the scapegoat at the conclusion of the story.

The oral approach can be especially helpful in instilling an appreciation of verse. If each student prepares a different poem to read to the class, the group has time to become acquainted with more poets and poems than if all the students study the same selections for silent reading. The assignment, including many poems suggested by the instructor,

---

[8] Edmund Fuller and B. Jo Kinnick, eds., *Adventures in American Literature* (New York: Harcourt, Brace and World, 1963).

can be centered around broad themes.[9] A unit of poetry on "Famous Men" may include Ben Jonson's "To the Memory of My Beloved Master, William Shakespeare," Paul Engle's "To Praise a Poet: Robert Frost," W. H. Auden's "In Memory of W. B. Yeats," and Stephen Spender's "I Think Continually of Those Who Were Truly Great." An assignment on "Human Nature" may incorporate Edwin Arlington Robinson's "Richard Cory," Robert Browning's "My Last Duchess," W. H. Auden's "Museé des Beaux Arts," and Robert Frost's "Mending Wall." A series on "Immortality" may embrace John Donne's "Death Be Not Proud," Rupert Brooke's "The Soldier," William Cullen Bryant's "Thanatopsis," and Emily Dickinson's "Because I Could Not Stop for Death." A final example of this type of assignment is "Beauties of Nature," including Sidney Lanier's "The Marshes of Glenn," Edna St. Vincent Millay's "God's World," e.e. cummings' "chanson innocente," and Gerard Manley Hopkins' "Pied Beauty."

Divisions of the anthology may suggest themes around which to develop a project. If *Exploring Life* for the ninth grade is used, the areas may include "People Like You," "Search for Adventure," "Fair Play and Foul," "Facing Life," "The Family," "Sidelights on America," "People Who Dared," "On the Lighter Side," and "The Things That Count."[10]

Verse selections may also be organized chronologically, or they may be organized according to types of poetry. Three types of poetry with sample selections are ballads ("Get Up and Bar the Door," "Sir Patrick Spens," Stephen Vincent Benét's "The Ballad of William Sycamore," and Rudyard Kipling's "The Ballad of East and West"), odes (Percy Bysshe Shelley's "To a Skylark" and "Ode to the West Wind" and John Keats's "Ode on a Grecian Urn" and "Ode to a Nightingale"), and sonnets (by Spenser, Shakespeare, Milton, and others).

Choral or unison reading might be introduced to make the class work more interesting and to add variety. For unison work care must be taken to choose the selections that lend themselves well to this form. Some selections which may be adapted for choral reading from *Adventures in American Literature* for the eleventh grade are Vachel Lindsay's "General William Booth Enters into Heaven," Stephen Vincent Benét's "The Mountain Whippoorwill," the Indian folk literature, and the Western songs and ballads.[11]

Assignments utilizing the oral approach to literature may sometimes

9 Unless indicated, the examples which follow are not taken from a single text nor are they recommended for any one grade, but all are selections which have appeared in one or more high school literature anthologies.

10 Harold H. Wagenheim, Elizabeth Voris Lathrop, and Matthew Dolkey, eds., *Exploring Life* (New York: Holt, Rinehart and Winston, 1963).

11 Fuller and Kinnick, op. cit.

be focused upon special occasions. If a patriotic holiday is the unifying motif, several selections from *Adventures for Readers* for grade eight may be used[12]; the possibilities include William Bradford and Edward Winslow's "So Goodly a Land," Rosemary and Stephen Vincent Benét's "George Washington," Henry Wadsworth Longfellow's "Paul Revere's Ride," Arthur Guiterman's "I Sing the Pioneer: Daniel Boone," Bernard De Voto's "Lewis and Clark," and others. Paul Engle's "An Old-Fashioned Iowa Christmas" from the same text makes a good Christmas assignment for which worthwhile selections are difficult to find.

The oral approach to the teaching of high school literature is a pleasant and helpful adjunct to the education of both those who perform and those who listen. Orally interpreting literature is certainly not the only way to teach the appreciation and understanding of worthy pieces of writing, nor is it a panacea which will remedy the problems of the English teacher. It is simply one rewarding way to study literature. Regardless of how the oral approach is used in the junior or senior high school class, literature presented in this manner will be re-created as living experience for the student.

[12] Egbert W. Nieman and Elizabeth C. O'Daly, eds., *Adventures for Readers* (New York: Harcourt, Brace and World, 1963).

YOU'RE KILLING THEATRE

Victor B. Miller

I am going to suggest that most English teachers today do not really know what dramatic action is. Or even what are the real and essential differences between narrative and dramatic. Or how a playwright builds characters for actors to work in. How *could* teachers know these things? Teachers are people and American people go through two (at least) processes that guarantee the death of a vital theatre. First, the mimetic impulse is throttled by "growing up" and all the people who "help" people grow up; second, plays are taught as if they were novels with interior descriptions left out. (The teacher finishes the novel-play by supplying these descriptions.) Thus the teacher teaching English today has been himself the victim of an awful state of affairs, and contributes to the death of drama every time he and his classes hit a "Dramatic

FROM *Connecticut English Journal*, Vol. 2 (Spring 1970), pp. 3–10. Reprinted by permission of the publisher and the author.

Literature" unit. *Dramatic Literature* is truly a term to conjure with. You have to admit, as a term, it's pretty honest: it promises that the plays will be examined with the same tools used on the novel, the poem, and the short story. It doesn't seem to bother anyone.

Don't be angry with me; I'm a playwright as well as whatever else I am, and I know that dramatic literature doesn't exist. Not until someone (director, producer, actors, designers) makes some choices and tries them in front of someone else does something exist: theatre. My play (or if you will allow the comparison, Shakespeare's play) is to the production what a sheet of notes is to a concert: the design of a certain dynamic. No matter how good the poetry, the play isn't finished whether it's between two paper Bantam covers or Morocco leather, Which is why it's so hard to dig up true copies of Shakespeare's plays: the man was concerned with finishing the play on stage—which is the only place you can finish plays. The script itself was treated with no more consideration than a lot of the props. But we don't revere props, so instead of leather-bound boxes of stage rocks, we collect leather-bound copies of words, hoping like mad the words are really the ones Shakespeare "had his actors say" and not one dreamed up by a printer and several friends. And that brings me back to my first sentence, for most Americans think of a play as a playwright "having actors say" his lines. We just don't know what dramatic action is. And neither do your students no matter how "dramatic" a reader you or they are.

I get the feeling you've heard all this before in various guises by various members of the rash of "new" romantic educators. Already you are saying that you can't be expected to take kids to every play you read, or stage every play you read, or that your kids just can't act or read for that matter. You don't have enough time. Your desks are bolted to the floor. The principal won't let you move the desks. If the kids get out of their seats to "do" a drama, you'll lose classroom discipline. Your ex-students always remember your reading of Mark Antony (it gets better every year.) Oddly enough, in an article like this, in a magazine like this, full of as many indictments as these, I do have some answers to the problems I have delineated.

By I, I mean CENTER FOR THE DEVELOPMENT OF THEATRE TECHNIQUES IN EDUCATION, a department, headed by Mrs. Mary Hunter Wolf, of the American Shakespeare Festival Theatre in Stratford, Connecticut. As Project Director of A Dramatic Arts Program for Technical Students for the State Department of Education, I have been working for the past three years with Mrs. Wolf and her staff to solve the problems of teaching drama within the English curriculum. What the Center has developed to solve my program's needs has been a series of workshops and an approach to teaching that can begin to make classrooms incredibly creative places to live in. More specifically the

Center has developed ways in which teachers and students can really get into what theater (and "Dramatic Literature") is.

In an article I can only indicate a few of the kinds of things that can go on in a Drama Unit. It is absolutely necessary that a teacher who wants to learn the techniques experience them, and there is precious little experiential learning in an article. That is the point. Dramatic action cannot be described into anyone. Where drama happens is between the lines on the page. Via theatre games and improvisional techniques you can provide your students with the essential experience of dramatic action.

The origins of theatre games and improvisation are many; there is no catechism, although by far the most influential creator of theatre exercises has been Viola Spolin (*Improvisation For the Theater*, Northwestern University Press). She has collected and invented as complete a group of activities as anyone in the field, although her prime concern is with theatre groups and courses with production as the ultimate goal. Originally these exercises were devised, with the advent of a more realistic, more personal kind of drama, to assist directors to help actors find the inner life of a character, scene, or incident in a play, as well as to help young actors in training develop their imaginative, creative instruments. If you substitute the word teacher for director and student for actor, you have made the leap of thought which got Mrs. Wolf and a few other theatre people like her into the field of educational research and development. Actors have trouble understanding and feeling the dynamic of a scene and so do students. Believe me, you cannot lecture or talk an actor into the right impulse or mood or whatever; nor will his performance be one whit better for knowing that "some critics aver Hamlet is Oedipally involved with Gertrude." Granted the student does not need to perform the role for posterity, nor does he need to perform the role at all, but wouldn't it be worthwhile for him to try to experience some of the impulses, some of the relationships, some of the doubts, within a "controlled" situation? We think so. And we think so without asking that teachers take theatre courses (heaven forbid) or students become actors. By adapting theatre games to classroom use, we are succeeding. And what's more, the techniques work in social studies, science, math, "senior problems" or anything else you and your curriculum committee can dream up.

Take the game of "Airport" for instance. Developed by Paul Sills, the son of Viola Spolin and director of Chicago's "Second City Troupe," Airport is a metaphor both for the basic elements of theatre and for a way in which teachers and students can work together more creatively. A "landing strip" is made by placing two lines of chairs back to back about four feet apart. A good length for the runway is twelve feet. The space between the chairs is then strewn with obstacles, books, shoes, etc. One student is blindfolded: he is the pilot who is trying to land his plane on a foggy night on a runway which is covered with wrecks, potholes, etc. His radio transmitter is dead; he can hear the control tower, but he cannot speak. Another student becomes the control tower, and chooses one location from which to give directions during the landing. The pilot is placed at the end of the runway; his object is to get through the twelve feet of littered runway without touching any of the objects along the way. Any touch is a crash, and a new pilot and new control tower try their hand at it. Each student should get a chance to try both flying and controlling. You will find that students begin to develop all kinds of theories about how to direct one another, how to slide, move their feet, judge distances, etc. After a while they begin to get very tricky and very successful. The game works whatever the ages. We have done it with elementary, secondary and college groups. Why? Because Airport contains within it every element of theatre, including the rehearsal process in a symbolic form. You have lights (of a sort), a set, two actors, given circumstances, and a drama that is played out in front of an audience. Moreover, if you want to know what empathy is, watch the faces of the audience, listen to the oohs and ahs, look at the body English they use . . . and all because someone with a blindfold is about to step on a book. That's theatre, and any professional company working would give its box office to get responses as vivid and alive as those. It's a metaphor for the rehearsal process in that you have an actor and a director and a "play" that must derived from the actor-training of the Moscow Art Theatre, is made be worked out. More important, the process of approaching a drama, quite clear. Every character in a play has an objective, an obstacle, and an action in every scene. If you want to call the pilot Hamlet, and the runway the play, Hamlet's objective is to get to the end safely, which might mean Hamlet wants to avenge the death of his father, or he wants to bring dignity back to his country, or any other concept the director and actor agree upon. But Hamlet confronts obstacles (shoes, books) which can be labeled Rosencrantz, Laertes, his love for his mother, his own dilemma. To get to his super-objective, he must confront his obstacles and deal with them: action. This is the beginning of what dramatic action is: what you do to get around an obstacle. It doesn't take a giant step to get over a slipper, and it doesn't take a giant step to get around Polonius. To get over a wastebasket makes you do something specific, to get over Ophelia does too. Objective, obstacle, action. A good formula for beginning to deal with what is dynamic about a play.

What about not being able to ask a question back? The broken transmitter? (Obviously the game is not perfect, and yes, actors do talk back to their directors, fortunately.) The broken transmitter adds an element to the game besides making it more exciting. It demonstrates a kind of relationship, an aspect of the director-actor relationship, which can best be termed trust. You will discover that the successful "pilots" are usually blessed with a trustworthy control tower. There's something about the controller's voice, his assurance, his specificity that makes the pilot shake less, stand better, move freer. It says a lot about relationships where one person yields control to another—like schoolrooms. The pilot does not lose his dignity, he doesn't "hack around" when the tower is quiet, for he and the tower are engaged in a task. The tower must take the pilot's peculiar problems into consideration, and the pilot must trust the tower, giving up his control willingly. Finally, the game will tell more about being specific than all the lectures about clarity. (It was beautifully pointed out to me when I played Airport with a group of teachers at North Haven High School, that there are all kinds of clarity which teachers and students don't necessarily agree on. Two ladies breezed through the runway using unspecific words like "smidgeon," "teeny-tiny" and "glumph." The point is they knew exactly what they meant and they accomplished the task as a team. And yet how many teachers give full credit to the kind of communication that goes beyond the actual word spoken or written?)

Airport is, of course, a very basic game. From there you can move forward, depending upon the group, the individuals, the play, the day, and a number of other variables. Step by step the students are offered an atmosphere where they can make a mistake, where their creative contributions have value, where they can take a chance on an interpretation just to see how it goes, where they can experiment with situations parallel to aspects of the play, where they can know what are and live with the results of a decision they have made. A game like "Building Characters" lets even the most withdrawn student know the freedom of a creative act and share with his peers what may appear to be a pretty crazy English period.

In Building a Character, the students (seated in a circle if possible) each choose a made-up name and made-up occupation. The leader/ teacher asks each to tell who he is until all have been introduced. The leader then begins asking each one about his life, his job, his likes and dislikes, and encourages the other students to ask questions if they feel like it. (The only right and wrong in this game is not paying attention; how can you be wrong about somebody you created?) By the end of the second phase everyone has begun to build something of a biography of his new character, and they can be outrageously funny if the kids feel free to work. Now, the leader chooses one person to sit at a table at the front of the room. It's a big restaurant and he or she is eating lunch. There's only one seat left in the place and it's across from student #1. The leader chooses a second person to go up and ask if he may sit down. Somewhere during the course of the meal the two "actors" *must* get across to each other and the audience what they do for a living, without being really blatant about it. It should come out of their conversation, their action, the way they walk or hum or something before they talk about it. In other words, a less successful go would be "May I sit down? I'm Joshua Perkins and I grind walnuts for a living." The leader stops each scene after the objectives have been reached—or not—and tries different pairs of eaters. Then he tells them it is the next day. Same restaurant, only now he mixes up the pairs, and each must somehow get across something about the person he met the day before. You can keep building to a third, fourth and fifth day, mixing pairs ad infinitum until our friend Joshua Perkins has amassed an incredible biography as a result of hearing about himself from others on stage and playing himself on stage, always adding what happens to his file. The scenes themselves are worth a year's work on dramatic literature. Conflicts happen, characters are born, and points are made clear about a playwright and actors not "indicating" things to an audience: i.e. what you know about Hamlet comes from what he does in dealing with life's activities, not from what Shakespeare *tells* you via signals and sentences. ("I'm Joshua Perkins and I grind walnuts for a living.") What now? Since I don't know why you chose to do this exercise, I can't tell you. Perhaps you may want the kids to write their "autobiographies." What did happen to Joshua that made him get into walnuts? With videotape, you might want to do the most successful scenes in the cafeteria. If you don't know which were the most successful, the students will be only too happy to tell you *and why.* Perhaps you might want them to play the game, using characters from the play you are studying. What did happen to Laertes when he was ten that contributed to the finished product? The scenes between Laertes and Ophelia in the automat may not be in iambic pentameter, but if the students have been led along according to their needs, you'll learn more about how much is transmitted to students from a script than you ever knew before, and the kids will find the parallels between the characters in the play and themselves far better than if you had said "Laertes is a lot like you, isn't he?"

To be sure, some students will do better than others—you can't escape that, but if the atmosphere is free, most everyone will find his own brand of success. And notice at no time did you say "we're going to do some acting." Everything comes about as a result of another step. Concentration is focused on a task to be accomplished, a problem to be solved, not on how to make the biggest hit, read the best, or disguise those inane truisms out of *Cliff's Notes.*

By now, many of you must have begun to like what seems to be a new educational wrinkle, a gimmick for getting plays across to kids who don't always care as much as we'd like. Please, no. Improvisational techniques can be gimmicks; they certainly seem to be gimmicks: they're flashy and fun and painless, and the kids might even learn something. Improvisation is not the overhead projector of the '70's, a panacea which is rolled in and out of classrooms, misused, and finally unused. Nor is it sensitivity training or role playing. It is a way in which teacher and student can work deeply together; it is a way of individualizing instruction without breaking up into thirty one-student classrooms; it is a way by which a student can be freed to create on a richer level, to make personal statements about who and what he is. You have now passed through the gimmick and into an area where education and life are not all that far apart. Simply, this means the training of teachers in improvisation so that they can recognize needs and supply new problems. And it means taking a few chances, moving a few desks around, making a little more noise than the guidance counselor is used to, having other teachers think you're losing your marbles. In return the students will challenge you more than ever and touch you deeper than ever.

STANDARDS FOR APPRAISING AND BUILDING HIGH SCHOOL SPEECH PROGRAMS

Richard W. Clark and Oliver W. Nelson

FOR many years leaders in both speech education and secondary education in general have placed considerable faith in the efficacy of a required course in speech fundamentals for providing youth with the opportunity and the means for developing essential speech competence. An article[1] recently published in this journal directed attention to the potential importance of the speech fundamentals course in the high school curriculum and offered criteria for evaluating such courses. We commend the authors of the article for their careful and constructive treatment of the subject. However, important as a basic course in speech fundamentals is to secondary school speech education, we would

[1] Henrietta H. Cortright, Doris S. Niles and Dorothy Q. Weirich, "Criteria to Evaluate Speech I in the Senior High School," *The Speech Teacher*, XVII (September 1968), 217–224.

$\ggg\text{-}\ggg$

FROM *The Speech Teacher*, Vol. 18 (September 1969), pp. 181–186. Reprinted by permission of the publisher and the authors.

remind speech educators and secondary school leaders that the speech communication needs of youth will generally require much more attention and continued guidance than can be provided in one or two semesters of work in speech fundamentals. We wish to emphasize that many educators who see speech education as an integral and essential part of the secondary school curriculum conceive it not merely as a course in speech, but as a comprehensive and well defined *program* comparable in purpose, content, and quality to any other legitimate segment of the curriculum. And although we are limiting our discussion to the secondary program, we heartily concur with those educators who recognize the necessity of developing a well structured program which begins when a child enters school and continues in a well articulated pattern into his advanced education.

Therefore, while we applaud efforts to set standards for a basic course in speech, we submit that in the interest of sound speech education, it is paramount that we view speech education in a somewhat broader sense, with the fundamentals course forming the nucleus of the speech program. Accordingly in this paper we shall first outline what we regard as the essential features of and standards for a sound secondary school speech program. We shall then provide a set of procedural guidelines which can be used as a checklist for evaluating speech instruction in secondary schools.

I

If speech education is to attain the status it deserves in secondary schools, *it must distinguish itself*—prove its indispensability in the education of youth. Just as one must earn the right to speak, so must speech education earn its right to a place in the high school curriculum. The overriding problem then is one of a continuing search for foci, curricular designs, and instructional methods which will help speech achieve this distinction.

School leaders, believing firmly in the *potentials* of well planned speech education, must help establish the conditions in secondary schools that will afford speech education the opportunity to prove its worth. Given this opportunity, speech education will earn a respected place in the family of high school subjects, provided its objectives are wisely conceived, and it is carefully designed and competently taught.

The first test then of worthy speech education can be found in the character of its general objectives. The following statements are intended to provide speech education with an appropriate focus:

The general objectives of speech education, must, first of all, be linked realistically to comprehensive goals of secondary education. Although during this century such goals have been variously defined, nearly all of them have stressed the importance of the development of discriminating values, critical thinking, and effective communication.

Speech education serves such general objectives when it

1. Concerns itself with the "source and substance of ideas," together with the creative processes of communicating these ideas effectively and honestly.

2. Teaches an understanding and appreciation of speaking and listening as vital forms of personal and social behavior and the primary means by which we educate ourselves.

3. Furthers an understanding of the meaning of "Freedom of Speech" and helps pupils to develop the willingness and the abilities to exercise this freedom with appropriate responsibility.

4. Maintains standards of excellence which require that "a speaker shall earn the right to speak."

5. Assists pupils to adapt effectively and comfortably to the demands of the common speaking activities of today's world.

6. Teaches that the primary purpose of speaking is to communicate— to secure a desired response in a listener, not merely to exhibit or display one's self.

7. Helps pupils gain speaking facility through appropriate attention to the basic elements which comprise a unified act of speaking, namely: thought processes, attitudes, use of language, voice and articulation, and bodily action.

8. Helps pupils develop the skills and attitudes essential to effective, discriminate, and appreciative listening required in today's complex world of sound.

First and foremost, then, speech education that is to prove its worth must be based on a sound and meaningful theory of speech as embodied in the foregoing objectives. However, if it is to earn and maintain its rightful place in the high school community, *speech education, moreover, must be well designed*—indeed, *designed as a program,* not merely a course, a special service, or an extra-curricular activity, but a program, delineated in writing with appropriate goals, plans for achieving the goals, and attention to division of responsibility for implementing the program. Whether such a program is conceived as a distinct speech education program, or viewed as an integral part of the English Language Arts Program need not become a crucial issue. What really matters is that there be a program in which speech education is recognized as a necessary and integral object and function of secondary education.

A speech program worthy of recognition should meet four primary requirements: First, the speech program should be *comprehensive*. It must include speech training for *all* children throughout their high school careers, in *all* basic types of speech activities, with appropriate levels of achievement set for each grade. Moreover, it should enlist the services of *all* high school personnel for it will be understood that good speaking and listening are aids to good learning.

Second, the speech program must also be *flexible* and *prescriptive.* It must be designed to meet individual speech needs of pupils: it will make provision for children with speech defects and for the gifted, as well as for the great majority who need guided instruction in the normal development of speech.

The following design is suggested as one possibility for meeting the foregoing program criteria:

A. Curriculum Instruction

    1. In designated course(s) in speech:

        a. A required course in the fundamentals of speech for *all* high school pupils.

        b. Follow-up elective course(s) in public speaking, oral interpretation, dramatics and/or debate for the talented or interested pupils.

        c. Taught by personnel broadly trained with a major or its equivalent in speech.

    2. In English or language arts classes:

        a. As an integral part of a coordinated program of speaking, listening, reading and writing.

        b. As a means of providing for the *continuous* guidance and training necessary for establishing good habits of speaking and listening begun in the required speech class.

        c. Taught by personnel trained in both English and speech with at least a minor or its equivalent in speech.

    3. In classes other than those designated as speech or English:

        a. As an effective implement for communicating and integrating the learnings incident to all subject matter fields.

        b. As a means of habitizing speech and listening learnings gained in provisions 1 and 2 above.

        c. Guided by teachers who have a functional command of the basic speech forms (public speaking, discussion, etc.) and possess good personal speech habits.

B. Co-curricular experiences in speech activities:

    1. Dramatics   ⎫ Directed by
    2. Discussion and debate   ⎪ speech
    3. Assembly programs   ⎬ trained
    4. Student council, class or club organizations ⎭ personnel

C. Special Services for the handicapped in speech and hearing:

    Provided by personnel whose special training meets requirements for Clinical Membership in American Speech and Hearing Association.

Third, if speech education is to attain and maintain a place of distinction in the high school program, *it must be judged in terms of its results.*

This will require the further refinement of the aforementioned objectives in terms of measurable *behavioral* objectives. Speech education must make a difference—must produce positive improvements in children's attitudes toward speaking and listening and in their abilities to communicate effectively and responsibly. These results must be observable wherever the individual engages in speaking and listening—in daily classes, club meetings, assemblies, community activities. The goal: most children in high schools should be able to prove by the time they are graduated that "speech education makes a difference."

Finally, if speech education is to be judged *in terms of its product,* then obviously *what is taught and how it is taught become all important.* It is *instructional quality* which determines the ultimate effectiveness and worth of speech education. This principle, we believe, must be applied initially and wholeheartedly to planning and teaching the fundamentals course—the vital center of the Speech Program. It is from this crucial center that all other strands of the program emanate and receive their orientation and vitality.

II

The preceding account outlines what we believe to be essential components of and standards for a sound high school speech program. But regardless of whether high school educators choose the foregoing specifications or some other design for meeting the speech education needs of youth, they may find it profitable to apply the following procedural criteria[2] for evaluating on-going provisions for speech education or for guiding the development of new speech programs in their schools.

A. Procedures in planning the speech program.

    1. Is there a definitely planned, *written* curriculum which provides guidelines for instruction but allows for individuality in the teacher's classroom approach?

    2. Have the general and specific objectives of speaking and listening instruction been based on an analysis of the following:

       a. The distinctive nature of speaking and listening as forms of human communicative behavior?

       b. The communication needs of a literate democratic society?

       c. Special community needs and interests?

---

[2] The National Council of Teachers of English developed a similar set of criteria for evaluating the English program, including speaking and listening, in 1962. (See "A Check List for Evaluating the English Program in the Junior and Senior High School," *The English Journal,* LV [April 1962], 273–282.) The present list was developed by one of the authors after a committee of teachers evaluating the speech program in the Bellevue Public Schools, Bellevue, Washington, found the original NCTE list too limited in scope.

    d. The immediate and potential needs and interests of the students?

3. Does the program of instruction in speaking and listening represent a carefully and realistically planned sequence?
   a. Are average expectancies defined for each grade level?
   b. Does the program provide for individual pupil differences within grade levels?
   c. Is there provision for communication between personnel responsible for speech instruction at various grade levels?

4. Is there a consistent effort on the part of the faculty to keep informed on and to evaluate innovations in curriculum?
   a. Has consideration been given to such items as team-teaching, programmed learning, advanced placement, and use of lay assistants for teachers?
   b. Is there a regular program for evaluating such new developments?

B. Instruction Program.
   1. Is specific instruction in speech included in both the Junior and Senior High School program?
      a. Does the program include instruction in how to improve speak- and listening as well as practice in using these skills?
      b. Is this instruction required of all students?
   2. Does the program avail itself of vital information associated with communication theory, general semantics, and group dynamics?
   3. Does the instructional program stress the communication of ideas?
      a. Is an effort made to assure that the purpose of each assignment is clearly defined in the minds of the speakers and listeners?
      b. Are students provided with tools for logical evaluation of the ideas with which they work?
      c. Are students held to high standards of accuracy in their reporting of information obtained from listening, reading, and viewing?
      d. Are there specific provisions for developing in students respect for the ideas of others and a commitment to the values of free exchange of ideas?
   4. Does the instructional program provide a balanced emphasis on the elements of speech—attitudes, thinking, voice and articulation, bodily action, and language?
      a. Are students encouraged to develop positive attitudes toward themselves, their audience, and their subject when they speak?
         (1) Are students given instruction in the analysis of self regarding attitudes and the attitudes of their listeners?
         (2) Are attempts made to improve detrimental attitudes, such as

fear, indifference, and self-centeredness, often evident in speaking situations?

b. Are students given instruction in logical-creative thinking essential to the preparation, delivery, and evaluation of a speech?

   (1) Are students instructed in basic patterns of organization of expository and persuasive speeches?

   (2) Are students given training in reflective thinking?

   (3) Are standards for evaluation of speeches developed with the students in such a way that they can apply them to the speaking they listen to outside of class?

c. Are students given instruction in voice and articulation which allows them to speak with a maximum of effectiveness?

   (1) Are there adequate provisions for dealing with extreme devations from normal speech patterns?

   (2) Are students given instruction which allows them to develop a maximum of pleasantness, variety, and clarity in their voices?

d. Are students given instruction which allows them to use bodily action as an aid to their speaking and listening?

   (1) Are distracting mannerisms corrected?

   (2) Are students instructed in how to use their bodily actions to clarify and emphasize their ideas?

   (3) Are students given instruction in how to gain greater interaction between speaker and listener through appropriate bodily action?

e. Are students given instruction in the use of oral English which enables them to choose and combine words with an effective style?

   (1) Are the basic elements of appropriate English usage stressed in all speaking exercises?

   (2) Are students encouraged to speak with appropriateness, vividness and forcefulness as characteristics of their style?

5. Is instruction in the important forms of public and private speech included in the program: e.g., interviews, expository and persuasive extemporaneous speeches, group discussions, oral interpretation of literature, debate, and parliamentary procedure?

6. Is specific instruction given in listening to understand, to evaluate, and to appreciate?

7. Does the program provide for the development of appreciation of the legitimate theater and for instruction in dramatic performance?

8. Is specific instruction in speech supplemented by applied speech instruction in English, social studies and other classes? Is this supplementary instruction coordinated with the basic instruction in speech?

9. Does the program allow for and encourage participation by students in extra-curricular speech activities, such as student government, service organizations, dramatic productions, debates, and community speaking?

C. Personnel policies and procedures.

1. Is the basic speech instruction given by teachers who have been especially trained in speech and related fields of study?
2. Is the academic freedom of the individual teacher adequately protected?
3. Are adequate instructional materials available for use by speech teachers?
4. Are the teaching loads of speech teachers maintained at a level which makes possible effective teaching?
   a. Are individual classes held to a number which allows students to speak frequently enough—approximately twenty students per class?
   b. Are total class loads held to a number which allows the teacher adequate time for careful correction of written work associated with speaking and listening assignments?
5. Do the teachers have adequate secretarial service and supplies?
6. Are non-teaching duties held to an absolute minimum?
7. Are teachers given adequate time for participation in activities which lead to professional growth?

III

Wise and progressive educators believe firmly in the practice of continuously and systematically evaluating the design, procedures, and products of their educational programs. No branch of the high school curriculum can afford to seek immunity from careful inspection and possible subsequent overhauling of its content and methods. Obviously speech education is no exception. Indeed, in our opinion, no field of learning and instruction in the high school curriculum is presently more in need of critical attention and more deserving of constructive development than Speech. This monograph attempts to offer some useful bases for critically examining secondary school speech education and laying the foundation for sound speech programs.

REFERENCES

Balcer, Charles L., and Hugh F. Seabury, *Teaching Speech in Today's Secondary Schools,* New York: Holt, Rinehart and Winston, Inc., 1965. Chapter I, "Speech Education: Its Contribution to Education and Society."

Braden, Waldo W. (ed.), *Speech Methods and Resources,* New York:

Harper and Brothers, 1961. Chapter I, "The Scope of Speech Education: An Overview"; Chapter II, "Speech as an Academic Discipline"; Chapter III. "Attitudes and the Teaching of Attitudes."

Buys, William E., Charles V. Carlson, Hite Compton, and Allan D. Frank, "Speech Communication in the High School Curriculum," *The Speech Teacher*, XVII (November 1968), 297–317. (Contains an excellent bibliography.)

Communication in the High School Curriculum—Speaking and Listening. Subject Field Series/Bulletin D-1. Superintendent of Public Instruction, State of Illinois, Springfield. Chapter I, "Speech Education in a Democracy."

Cortright, Henrietta H., Doris S. Niles and Dorothy Q. Weirich, "Criteria to Evaluate Speech I in the Senior High School," *The Speech Teacher*, XVII (September 1968), 217–224.

Reid, Loren, *Teaching Speech*, Third ed. (Columbia, Mo.: Artcraft Press, 1960). Chapter II, "The Aims of Speech Education."

Robinson, Karl and E. J. Kerikas, *Teaching Speech* (New York: David McKay Company, Inc., 1963). Chapter I, "Speech in Contemporary Education."

Weaver, Andrew T., Gladys Borchers and D. K. Smith, *The Teaching of Speech* (New York: Prentice Hall, Inc., 1952). Chapter I, "Speech Education and the Needs of School Children"; Chapter III, "The Scope and Purpose of the High School Curriculum."